NEW AGE INTERNATIONAL

WEBSTER'S QUICK REFERENCE DICTIONARY NOTEBOOK

NEW AGE INTERNATIONAL PUBLISHERS

Printed in India at Ajit Printers, Delhi.

C-09-06-3708
ISBN(10): 81-224-2208-X
ISBN (13) : 978-81-224-2208-5
Indian Edition Price: Rs. 75.00

PUBLISHING FOR ONE WORLD

NEW AGE INTERNATIONAL (P) LIMITED, PUBLISHERS
4835/24, Ansari Road, Daryaganj, New Delhi - 110002
Visit us at **www.newagepublishers.com**

a, A *indefinite article* used before a word beginning with a consonant; —*adj.* for each; first in order

aard´vark *n.* an African mammal that feeds on ants and temites

aard´wolf *n.* a mammal of the hyena family that feeds on termites

a·ba´ *n.* a sleeveless Arab robe

a·back´ *adv.* pressed backward; to the rear —**taken aback** caught by surprise, disconcerted

ab´a·cus *n.* an ancient device for performing calculations by the use of rows of beads on rods

a·baft´ *adv.* toward the stern of a ship —*prep.* further back than

ab·a·lo´ne *n.* an edible shellfish lined with mother–of–pearl

a·ban´don *n.* spontaneity; unrestrained enthusiasm —*vt.* to give up; forsake; to give in to emotion —**a·ban´don·ment** *n.*

a·ban´doned *adj.* forsaken; unrestrained; lacking modesty; shameless

a·base´ *vt.* degrade; dishonor

a·base´ment *n.* humiliation, shame

a·bash´ *vt.* to make confused; to embarrass —**a·bash´ed·ly** *adv.*

a·bash´ment *n.* confusion, disorientation, embarrassment

a·bate´ *vi., vt.* to lessen; to reduce —**a·bat´a·ble** *adj.*

a·bate´ment *n.* a lessening; mitigation —**a·bat´or** *n.*

ab´a·tis *n.* a defensive barricade

a·bat·jour´ *n.* a device for deflecting sunlight; a skylight

ab´at·toir *n.* a slaughterhouse

ab·ax´i·al *adj.* facing away from the axis

ab´ba·cy *n.* the office or jurisdiction of an abbot

ab´bess *n.* director of a nunnery

ab´bey *n.* a monastery or nunnery

ab´bot *n.* the director of a monestary

ab´bot·cy, ab´bot·ship *n.* the office and trappings of an abbot

ab·bre´vi·ate *vt.* to shorten

ab·bre´vi·a´tion *n.* a shortened form

ABC´s *n.* the basics; rudimentary elements; beginning knowledge

ab´di·cate *vi., vt.* to formally renounce a responsibility; to give up a throne —**ab´di·ca´tion** *n.*

ab·do´men *n.* the lower portion of the human trunk, from the diaphragm to the pelvic girdle

ab·dom´i·nal *adj.* pertaining to the abdomen —**ab·dom´i·nal·ly** *adv.*

ab·du´cent *adj.* of a muscle that pulls away from the the body

ab·duct´ *vt.* to kidnap; to carry away

ab·duc´tion *n.* a kidnapping; the abducting of a person by force

ab·duc´tor *n.* a muscle that pulls away from the axis of the body

a·beam´ *adj., adv.* at right angles to the keel of a ship

a·be·ce·dar´i·an *adj.* primary, rudimentry —*n.* a beginning student

a·bed´ *adj.* in bed

ab·er´rance, ab·er´ran·cy *n.* deviation from the right or usual course

ab·er´rant *adj.* abnormal —*n.* a strange or abnormal person —**ab·er´rant·ly** *adv.*

ab´er·ra´tion *n.* an abnormality; a deviation; delusion, derangement —**ab·er·ra´tion·al** *adj.*

a·bet´ *vt.* assist or support in wrongdoing —**a·bet´ment** *n.*

a·bet´tor, a·bet´ter *n.* one who assists; an accessory or collaborator

a·bey´ance *n.* a temporary state of suspension; a hiatus

a·bey´ant *adj.* in a dormant state

ab·hor´ *vt.* to loathe

ab·hor´rence *n.* a strong aversion.

ab·hor´rent *adj.* detestable; causing disgust —**ab·hor·rent·ly** *adv.*

a·bid´ance *n.* continuance

a·bide´ *vi.* to stay in a place; to remain unchanging —*vt.* to wait for; endure; submit to

a·bid´ing *adj.* continuing, steadfast —**a·bid´ing·ly** *adv.*

a·bil´i·ty *n.* power, faculty; competence; endowed with skill

a·bi·o·gen´e·sis *n.* the theory that life may be created from inorganic matter —**a·bi·o·ge·net´ic** *adj.*

a·bi·og´e·nist *n.* one who believes in the spontaneous generation of life

a·bi·ot´ic *adj.* regarding inorganic matter; not organic; not living

ab·ject´, ab´ject *adj.* wretched; beyond all hope; without self esteem —**ab·ject´ly** *adv.*

ab·jec´tion *n.* a degrading condition.

ab·jure´ *vt.* renounce under oath; recant or retract; abstain from —**ab·ju·ra´tion** *n.*

ab·la´tion *n.* a wearing away; surgical excision of tissue —**ab·late** *vt., vi.*

ab´la·tive *adj.* in grammar, expressing separation or removal from source, as *freedom from fear*

a·blaze´ *adj., adv.* on fire; aroused to passion or excitement; fervent

a´ble *adj.* possessing adequate ability; qualified —**a´bly** *adv.*

a´ble·bod´ied *adj.* sound of body; physically capable

a·bloom´ *adj.* in bloom; flowering.

ab´lu·ent *adj.* used for cleaning —*n.* a cleansing agent

ab·lu´tion *n.* the act of washing; a bath; a ceremonial washing during a religious ceremony

a´bly *adv.* in a competent manner; proficiently

ab´ne·gate *vt.* to give up, as a privilege or desire —**ab´ne·ga·tor** *n.*

ab·ne·ga´tion *n.* rejection or renunciation; self–denial; disavowal

ab·nor´mal *adj.* unnatural; differing from the normal or average

ab·nor·mal´i·ty *n.* an aberration; an oddity or anomaly; a malforma-tion or peculiarity

ab·nor´mal·ly *adv.* to an unusual degree; exceedingly, exceptionally.

ab·nor´mi·ty *n.* a monstrosity or perversion.

a·board´ *adv.* onto a conveyance; in agreement, as to support for a common cause —**all aboard** a warning to passengers that the vehicle is about to depart

a·bode´ *n.* a dwelling; a place of habitation or residence

a·bol´ish *vt.* to put an end to; to invalidate —**a·bol´ish·ment** *n.*

ab´o·li´tion *n.* the act of terminating or eliminating

ab·o·li´tion·ist *n.* one who wishes to abolish something

a·bom´i·na·ble *adj.* hateful; horrible; offensive —**a·bom´in·a·bly** *adv.*

a·bom·i·na´tion *n.* extreme disgust or abhorrence; that arousing feelings of disgust

ab´o·rig´i·nal *adj.* native or indigenous —*n.* a native inhabitant

ab·o·rig´i·ne *n.* a native or earliest known inhabitant of a region

ab´o·rig´i·nes *pl. n.* first inhabitants; the flora and fauna of an area

a·bort´ *vi.* to bring forth young before full development; to terminate prematurely —*vt.* to cause an early, unsuccessful conclusion

a·bor´tion *n.* a miscarriage; a failure to evolve normally; the product of failure, a monstrosity; a failed attempt —**a·bor´tion·ist** *n.*

a·bor´tive *adj.* useless; vain or futile

a·bound´ *vi.* to be plentiful

a·bout´ *adv.* almost or approximately; in another direction —*prep.* in or around an area; particular to or associated with: *an air about her*; approximating: *departing about noon*; in regard to: *a book about money management*

a·bout´·face *n.* a turn to the rear; an abrupt reversal

a·bove *adv.* over; overhead; higher in rank —*adj.* foregoing or preceding —*n.* something before or over —*prep.* rising over or higher: *the moon above the lake* —**above all** having precedence; most important

a·bove´board *adj., adv.* candid, forthright; with nothing concealed

a·brade´ *vt.* to scrape or wear away

a·bra´sion *n.* the act or result of a wearing away; an injury from contact with a rough surface

a·bra´sive *adj.* wearing; capable of eroding; disagreeable or offensive —*n.* a material which abrades, as sandpaper or emery —**a·bra´sive·ly** *adv.* —**a·bra´sive·ness** *n.*

a·breast´ *adv.* side by side

a·bridge´ *vt.* to shorten; to condense, by reducing to fewer words; to lessen or deprive, as of civil rights

a·bridg´ment *n.* that which has been shortened; an abstract

a·broad´ *adv.* away; in a foreign land; widely circulated

ab´ro·gate´ *vt.* to repeal or annul; to abolish —**ab´ro·ga´tion** *n.*

a·brupt´ *adj.* sudden; unexpected —**ab·rupt´ly** *adv.*

ab´scess *n.* a collection of pus in a body cavity

ab·scis´sa *n.* in a graph, the distance of a reference point from the Y–axis, parallel to the X–axis

ab·scis´sion *n.* severance or removal; in speaking, an abrupt pause for dramatic effect

ab·scond´ *vi.* to leave quickly and secretly

ab´sence *n.* a deficiency or inadequacy; truancy; lack or want

ab´sent *adj.* not present; lacking; inattentive —**ab·sent´** *vt.* to remain away —**ab´sent·ly** *adv.*

ab·sen·tee´ *n.* one who is absent —*adj.* of one not present: *absentee landlord*; of action by one absent: *an absentee vote*

ab´sen·tee´ism *n.* the state of being absent; the frequency of absence

ab´sent–mind´ed *adj.* preoccupied; unmindful of immediate demands; forgetful —**ab´sent·mind´ed·ly** *adv.* —**ab´sent·mind´ed·ness** *n.*

ab´sinthe *n.* wormwood; an anise flavored liqueur

ab´so·lute *adj.* complete; perfect; without reservation; unadulterated; not dependent on an arbitrary standard —*n.* that which is perfect

absolute zero *n.* 459.6° F. below zero; the temperature at which a substance would be wholly deprived of heat

ab´so·lu·tion *n.* exoneration; vindication; forgiveness; the ceremonial remission of sin

ab´so·lut·ism *n.* despotism; a principle that grants a ruler unlimited powers —**ab·so·lu·tis´tic** *adj.*

ab·solve´ *vt.* to acquit of guilt or complicity; to free from an obligation; to pardon or remit from sin —**ab·solv´a·ble** *adj.* —**ab·solv´er** *n.*

ab·sorb´ *vt.* to engross completely; to assimilate; to occupy entirely —**ab·sorb´a·ble** *adj.*

ab·sor´bent *adj.* disposed to absorb —*n.* a substance that absorbs —**ab·sorb´en·cy** n.

ab·sorb´ing *adj.* stimulating or enticing —**ab·sorb´ing·ly** *adv.*

ab·sorp´tion *n.* the process of absorbing; concentration or preoccupation —**ab·sorp´tive** *adj.*

ab·stain´ *vi.* to forbear; to avoid or shun voluntarily

ab·ste´mi·ous *adj.* avoiding excess; temperate —**ab·ste´mi·ous·ly** *adv.*

ab·sten·tion *n.* temperance; foregoing —**ab·sten´tious** *adj.*

ab´sti·nence *n.* the practice of avoiding something, such as intoxicating drink —**ab´sti·nent** *adj.*

ab´stract *adj.* apart from the absolute or concrete; theoretical; difficult to understand; impersonal; of a style of art —*n.* an abridgment; a summary; a non–specific idea or term —**ab·stract´** *vt.* take from; to condense; to form a notion of: *an* *abstract concept* —*adj.* general; theoretical; considered apart from the specific —**ab·strac´tion·al** *adj.*

abstract art a school of art that makes use of designs based on relationships rather than representation of objects

ab·stract´ed *adj.* disassociated or apart; obscure; preoccupied —**ab·stract´ed·ly** *adv.*

ab·strac´tion *n.* preoccupation; an ideal —**ab·strac´tive** *adj.*

ab·struse´ *adj.* difficult to comprehend —**ab·struse´ly** *adv.*

ab·surd´ *adj.* irrational; preposterous; ridiculous

ab·surd´i·ty *n.* that which is preposterous or ridiculous

a·bun´dance *n.* a quantity in excess of need; plenty

a·bun´dant *adj.* bountiful; more than enough —**a·bun´dant·ly** *adv.*

a·buse´ *n.* improper use; misapplication; cruel treatment —*vt.* to use incorrectly; to harm by improper use; to injure by mistreating

a·bu´sive *adj.* characterized by abuse; serving to abuse — **a·bu´sive·ly** *adv.*

a·but *vi.* to touch; border; form a line of contact —*vt.* border on

a·but´ment *n.* a supporting element of a structure; a buttress

a·bys´mal *adj.* bottomless; extreme —**a·bys´mal·ly** *adv.*

a·byss´ *n.* a bottomless gulf; a chasm; a tremendous depth

ac·a·deme´, ac´a·deme *n.* a place of learning; an academy; a scholarly environment

ac´a·dem´ia *n.* the academic world; institutions of learning collectively

ac´a·dem´ic *adj.* scholarly; of traditional learning; theoretical or hypothetical —*n.* a scholar; member of a learned society — **ac·a·dem´i·cal·ly** *adv.*

a·cad´e·my *n.* a preparatory school; a society of scholars

a cap·pel´la *adj.* vocal music without instrumental accompaniment

ac·cede´ *vi.* to come into an office; agree to —**ac·ced´ence** *n.*

ac·cel´er·ate *vi.* to move more rapidly; to hurry —*vt.* to increase the speed of; to hasten the natural course of: *to accelerate growth*

ac·cel´er·a´tion *n.* a hastening, the rate of increase in speed

ac·cel´er·a´tor *n.* a device that controls speed; that which increases speed, flow, etc.

ac´cent *n.* voice stress in the pronunciation of a word; a mark (´)to indicate vocal stress; a manner of speaking which differs from place to place —*vt.* to stress; to speak or produce with an accent

ac·cen´tu·ate *vt.* stress; emphasize —**ac·cen´tu·a·tion** *n.*

ac·cept´ *vt.* to take what is offered; to agree to; to embrace as true; to take in as a member —**ac·cept´ance** *n.*

ac·cept´a·ble *adj.* satisfactory; worthy of acceptance; adequate, although not entirely pleasing: *an acceptable level of error* —**ac·cept´a·bly** *adv.*

ac·cept´ed *adj.* generally believed

ac´cess *n.* an approach or passage; permission to enter; a means of obtaining —*vt.* to gain the use of, as a computer program or data

ac·ces´si·ble *adj.* easily reached; easily influenced; allowing access; attainable —**ac·ces´si·bil´i·ty** *n.*

ac·ces´so·ry, ac·ces´sa·ry *adj.* added; aiding, contributing; supplemental —*n.* an accomplice; a thing added —**ac·ces´so·rize** *vt.*

ac´ci·dent *n.* an unexpected occurrence; a misadventure; an unintentional act

ac·ci·den´tal *adj.* happening by chance; fortuitous; incidental —**ac·ci·den´tal·ly** *adv.*

ac·claim´ *vt.* to applaud; to receive with approval; to approve by proclamation —*vi.* to applaud or shout —*n.* enthusiastic applause

ac´cla·ma´tion *n.* applause; general approval

ac·cli´mate, ac·cli´ma·tize´ *vi., vt.* to grow accustomed

ac·clam´a·to·ry *adj.* expressing joy and adulation

ac·cliv´i·ty *n.* an upward slope

ac´co·lade´ *n.* any honor or award; words of praise

ac·com´mo·date´ *vi.* to become adjusted —*vt.* to supply food or lodging; adapt; be suitable for

ac·com´mo·da´tion *n.* an adaptation; a reconciliation; a convenience; board or lodging; assistance; a willingness to provide assistance

ac·com´pa·nist *n.* one who plays or sings to enhance a performance of another —**ac·com´pa·ni·ment** *n.*

ac·com´pa·ny *vt.* to go with; to escort; to play or sing with another; to supplement; to occur at the same time: *cold accompanied by fever*

ac·com´plice *n.* an associate in crime; a knowing confederate

ac·com´plish *vt.* to perform; to fulfill, as an obligation; to complete

ac·com´plished *adj.* completed; fulfilled; proficient; refined

ac·com´plish·ment *n.* something completed; a worthly attainment

ac·cord´ *n.* agreement; spontaneous desire —*vi.* be in agreement; harmonize —*vt.* to grant; bring into harmony —**of one´s own accord** freely done, without urging —**according to** as per direction or plan; as reported

ac·cord´ance *n.* conformity; accord; harmony

ac·cord´ing·ly *adv.* as a result

ac·cost´ *vt.* to confront

ac·count´ *n.* a computation; a report; a record of transactions —*vi.* to provide a reason; to be responsible —*vt.* to impute

ac·count´a·ble adj. having liability; responsible; able to be explained —ac·count·a·bil´i·ty n.

ac·count´an·cy *n.* the office and duties of an accountant

ac·count'ant *n.* one experienced in keeping accounts; one records or audits financial records

ac·count´ing *n.* a settlement; a statement of the finances of an organization; the profession of recording financial transactions

ac·cred´it *vt.* to certify; to send with credentials

ac·cre´tion *n.* a growth; an accumulation or addition, as of a sedimentary deposit

ac·cru´al *n.* an increase or accumulation; something that increases

ac·crue´ *vi.* to increase; to be added to, as interest

ac·cu´mulate *vt.* to pile up; to gather —*vi.* to increase — **ac·cu´mu·la·tor** *n.*

ac·cu´mu·la´tion *n.* a collection; a growth or increase

ac·cu´mu·la·tive *adj.* tending to increase

ac´cu·ra·cy *n.* a measure of precision; correctness; exactness

ac´cu·rate *adj.* very exact; precise; capable of precise measurement; within set limits — **ac´cu·rate·ly** *adv.*

ac·curs´ed, ac·curst´ *adj.* under a curse; deserving a curse

ac·cu·sa´tion, ac·cu´sal *n.* act of accusing or being accused

ac·cuse´ *vi.* to verbalize charges —*vt.* bring a charge against — **ac·cus´ing·ly** *adv.*

ac·cused´ *n.* a person or persons charged with a crime

ac·cus´tom *vt.* to make or become familiar through use; to adapt to

ac·cus´tomed *adj.* habitual or usual; customary; characteristic

ace *n.* a single spot on a playing card or die; one who excels, an expert; in tennis, a point won on the serve —*vt.* score an ace

ac´er·bate *vt.* to make harsh or bitter; intensify; to annoy

a·cer´bic, a·cerb´ *adj.* sour tasting; harsh in manner or language —**a·cer´bi·ty** *n.*

ac´e·tate´ *n.* a fiber used in the making of textiles

a·ce´tic *adj.* sour; having the sourness of vinegar; containing acetic acid or vinegar —**a·ce´ti·fy** *vi., vt.*

acetic acid *n.* a colorless sour acid; the chief component of vinegar

ac´e·tone *n.* a colorless, flammable liquid ketone used as a solvent

a·cet´y·lene *n.* a colorless, flammable gas used as a fuel in welding

a·ce´tyl·sal´i·cyl´ic acid *n.* aspirin

ache *vi.* to hurt; to suffer throbbing pain; to suffer loss; to feel sympathy —*n.* a dull protracted pain —**ach´i·ness** *n.* —**ach·y** *adj.*

a·chieve´ *vi.* reach an objective —*vt.* to accomplish; to complete successfully —**a·chiev´a·ble** *adj.*

a·chieve´ment *n.* the act of accomplishing; a notable act; an accomplishment

ac´id *adj.* sour and sharp; caustic or sarcastic —*n.* a sour substance

a·cid´ic *adj.* having the properties of acid

a·cid´i·fy *vi.* to turn acid —*vt.* to transform into acid

a·cid´i·ty *n.* sourness and tartness; degree of acid strength

acid test a test of quality, veracity, etc.; a severe test

ac·knowl´edge *vt.* to admit or confess; to certify; show appreciation; confirm receipt of — **ac·knowl´edge·a·ble** *adj.*

ac·knowl´edge·ment, ac·knowl´edg·ment *n.* recognition of responsibility; a response; appreciation; confirmation of receipt

ac´me *n.* the highest point; zenith

ac´ne *n.* a skin affliction

a´corn *n.* fruit of the oak tree

a·cous´tic, a·cous´ti·cal *adj.* pertaining to sound or the sense of hearing —**a·cous´ti·cal·ly** *adv.*

a·cous´tics *pl. n.* the study of sound; the sound quality in a place

ac·quaint´ *vt.* to make aware of; to inform; to introduce —**be acquainted with** familiar, but not well known

ac·quaint´ance *n.* knowledge; familiarity; an associate; one known to another

ac´qui·esce´ *vi.* to comply without enthusiasm; to accept as inevitable —**ac´qui·es´cence** *n.* —**ac´qui·es´cent** *adj.*

ac·quire´ *vt.* to obtain or gain

ac´qui·si´tion *n.* a thing gained; an appropriation

ac·quis´i·tive *adj.* prone to acquire —**ac·quis´i·tive·ly** *adv.* —**ac·quis´i·tive·ness** *n.*

ac·quit´ *vt.* to pronounce innocent; to discharge a trust; to behave or act: *he acquitted himself well*

ac·quit´tal *n.* a discharge of duty; in law, a finding of not guilty, or being set free by judgment of a court

ac·quit´tance *n.* a settlement of liability; proof of settlement

a´cre *n.* a land measure equal to 4,840 square yards

a´cre·age *n.* property; a single parcel of land

ac´rid *adj.* sharp in taste or smell; pungent —**ac´rid·ly** *adv.* —**ac´rid·ness** *n.*

ac·ri·mo´ni·ous *adj.* sarcastic; caustic; acerbic

ac´ri·mo·ny *n.* sharp or bitter speech or temperament

ac´ro·bat *n.* a trapeze artist, gymnast, or tumbler — **ac´ro·bat´ic** *adj.*

ac´ro·bat´ics *n.* gymnastics

ac´ro·nym *n.* a word formed from the initial letters of a name such as *NASA* for *National Aeronautics and Space Administration*

ac·ro·pho´bi·a *n.* a fear of heights —**ac·ro·pho´bic** *adj.*

a·cross´ *adv.* from one side to the other; on the opposite side —*prep.* at the other side; from one side to the other; upon: *I came across the papers yesterday*

a·cros´tic *n.* a written message whose initial letters form a word or another message

a·cryl´ic *adj.* of or made from acrylic resin —*n.* a transparent resin; an acrylic substance such as paint or fiber

act *vi.* to behave oneself; to perform a function or produce an effect: *acid acts on metal* —*vt.* to play on the stage; to behave in a certain way —**act as** to serve temporarily —**act up** be troublesome

act´ing *adj.* standing in for another; operating —*n.* a stage performance; an affectation

ac´tion *n.* putting forth energy; decisiveness: *a man of action*: the result of activity; a manner of movement; moving parts; a thing done; a law suit —**ac´tions** *pl. n.* one's behavior or conduct

ac´tion·a·ble *adj.* forming the basis for a lawsuit

ac´ti·vate *vt.* to make active; to purify by aeration —**ac´ti·va´tion** *n.*

ac´tive *adj.* energetic, lively; operative: *an active volcano*; taking part: *an active member*, —**ac´tive·ly** *adv.*

ac·tiv´i·ty *n.* lively movement; a planned undertaking; a transaction

ac´tiv·ism *n.* involvement in social issues —**ac´tiv·ist** *n.*

ac´tu·al *adj.* existing in fact —*n.* a thing that is real —**ac´tu·al´i·ty** *n.*

ac´tu·al·ise (*Brit.*), **ac´tu·al·ize** (*US*) *vt.* to make real; portray realistically

ac´tu·al·ly *adv.* truly; as a matter of fact

ac´tu·ar·y *n.* one who calculates risk as for insurers —**ac·tu·ar´i·al** *adj.*

ac´tu·ate *vt.* to impel; put in motion; cause to act —**ac´tu·a·tion** *n.*

a·cu·i·ty *n.* insight; discernment in reasoning or perception

a·cu´men *n.* insight; quick to understand; intelligence; sagacity

ac·u·punc·ture *n.* an Oriental treatment for pain or illness using fine needles —**ac´u·punc·tur·ist** *n.*

a·cute´ *adj.* pointed, sharp; keen of mind; serious, as an acute illness; intense, as pain —**a·cute´ly** *adv.*

ad *n.* an advertisement

ad´age *n.* a proverb or maxim

ad´a·mant *adj.* unyielding; resolute in belief —**ad´a·mant·ly** *adv.*

a·dapt´ *vi.* to grow adjusted to —*vt.* to make suitable; to accommodate —**a·dapt´a·ble** *adj.* —**a·dapt·a·bil´i·ty** *n.*

ad·ap·ta´tion *n.* something modified; the process(or a thing) By which something is modified

a·dapt´er, a·dap´tor *n.* a device for modifying for a different use; a connecting device

a·dap´tive *adj.* capable of being modified —**a·dap´tive**·ly *adv.*

add *vi.* to increase; to perform addition; —*vt.* to increase; to total numbers; to speak or write more —**add up** to total; seem reasonable

ad´dend *n., pl.* **ad·den´da** a number added to an existing number, called the *augend*

ad·den´dum *n.* an addition; a thing to be added, such as an appendix

ad´dict *n.* one given to illegal drugs or alcohol —**ad·dict´** *vt.* to be devoted to: *addicted to work*; to be dependent on: *addicted to drugs*

ad·dic´tion *n.* psychological or physiological dependence; a compulsion

ad·dict´ed *adj.* predisposed to

ad·dic´tive *adj.* habit–forming

ad·di´tion *n.* the process of summing numbers; something added; an increase —**ad·di´tion·al** *adj., n.*

ad´di·tive *n.* an ingredient that alters flavor, performance, etc. —*adj.* tending to increase

ad´dle *vi.* to become confused —*vt.* to cause to be; to muddle: *addled by strong drink* —*adj.* confused, incoherent

ad´dle·brained´ *adj.* confused; flustered; also **ad´dle·pat´ed**

ad·dress´ *vt.* to speak or write to; to direct to: *address a letter*, to attend to: *address a problem* —*n.* a speech; one's bearing or manner; a specific location

ad·dress´a·ble *adj.* approachable; able to locate, as computer data

ad·dress·ee´ *n.* one addressed

ad·duce´ *vt.* to cite as an example or proof —**ad·duc´i·ble** *adj.*

ad·duct´ *vt.* to pull toward the body —**ad·duc´tion** *n.*

ad·duc´tor *n.* of a muscle that pulls toward the median axis of the body

ad´e·noid *n.* glandular tissue at the upper part of the throat —*adj.* glandular

a·dept´ *adj.* extremely skilled; proficient —**ad´ept** *n.* a person who is highly skilled; an expert —**a·dept´ly** *adv.*

ad´e·quate *adj.* barely sufficient; suitable for immediate need —**ad´e·qua·cy** *n.* —**ad´e·quate·ly** *adv.*

ad·here´ *vi.* to stick; to follow closely; to follow faithfully —**ad·her´ence** *n.*

ad·he´sion *n.* sticking or being stuck; a close attachment

ad·he´sive *adj.* tending to stick; gummed —*n.* that causing adhesion —**ad·he´sive·ness** *n.*

adhesive tape material coated with adhesive, for securing or binding

ad hoc´ relating to a particular thing

ad hoc committee a committee formed for a particular purpose

ad in´fi·ni´tum to infinity; forever; unlimited

ad´i·pose *adj.* pertaining to fat

ad·ja´cence ad·ja´cen·cy *n.* the state of being near or neighboring

ad·ja´cent *adj.* near or joining; neighboring

ad·jec·ti´val, ad´jec·ti·va´ *adj.* like an adjective

ad´jec·tive *n.* a word that modifies a noun; a phrase used as an adjective —*adj.* pertaining to or functioning as an adjective

ad·join´ *vt.* to be close; to touch; to unite —*vi.* to be close or in contact

ad·journ´ *vi., vt.* to end; postpone; to move to another place —**ad·journ´ment** *n.*

ad·judge´ *vt.* to order by law; to decide judicially

ad·ju´di·cate *vi.* to perform the function of a judge —*vt.* to decide judicially —**ad·ju´di·ca´tion** *n.* —**ad·ju´di·ca·tive** *adj.*

ad´junct *adj.* supplementary; additional —*n.* something added; one assigned as a subordinate; a nonessential quality

ad·jure´ *vt.* to charge under oath; to appeal intently —**ad·jur´a·to·ry** *adj.*

ad·just´ *vi.* to adapt or conform —*vt.* to arrange so as to fit; to reconcile differences —**ad·just´a·ble** *adj.*

ad·just´ment *n.* the process of adjusting; amount of settlement: *an insurance adjustment*; an allowance for wear

ad´ju·tant *n.* an assistant who carries out the directives of a superior

ad lib´ *adj.* created spontaneously: *ad lib remarks* —*adv.* spontaneously —*vi., vt.* to improvise —*n.*

ad·min´is·ter *vi.* to perform managerial duties; to assist —*vt.* to manage; to dispense, as justice; to conduct, as a swearing in or test; to provide assistance

ad·min´is·trate *vt.* to administer

ad·min´is·tra´tion *n.* the act of administering; power or party in office; term of office; settlement of an estate —**ad·min´is·tra´tive** *adj.*

ad´mi·ra·ble *adj.* deserving admiration —**ad´mi·ra·bly** *adv.*

ad·mi·ral·ty *n.* the jurisdiction of an admiral; the branch of the juiciary responsible for maritime affairs

ad·mi·ra´tion *n.* appreciation, as of something rare or beautiful; that which causes appreciation, approval, etc.

ad·mire´ *vt.* to regard with wonder; to esteem; to respect —*vi.* to express admiration —**ad´mi·ra·bly** *adv.*

ad·mis´si·ble *adj.* worthy of consideration; allowable —**ad·mis´si·bil´i·ty** *n.*

ad·mis´sion *n.* the act of admitting; the price paid for entrance; the right to enter; confession

ad·mit´ *vt.* to allow to enter; to be the means to enter; to allow membership, as to a club or society; to accede to or acknowledge —*vi.* to afford entrance

ad·mit´tance *n.* right or permission to enter; the act of admitting; admission or entrance

ad·mit´ted *adj.* accepted as valid; confessed; acclaimed; acknowledged

ad·mit´ted·ly *adv.* confessedly

ad·mix·ture *n.* a combination; a blending of ingredients; an additional ingredient

ad·mon´ish *vt.* to counsel; offer a mild rebuke; instruct —**ad·mon´ish·ment** *n.*

ad´mo·ni´tion *n.* a mild rebuke; a warning —**ad·mon´i·to´ry** *adj.*

a·do´ *n.* unnecessary activity; bustle; commotion

a·do´be *adj.* made from sun–dried brick —*n.* a sun–dried brick; a building made from such bricks; the earth or clay of which the bricks are made

ad·o·les´cence *n.* the period of growth from childhood to maturity

ad·o·les´cent *adj.* characteristic of youth; youthful; lacking maturity —*n.* a youth

a·dopt´ *vt.* to raise as one's own; to take up and follow: adopt a change; to enact, as a law —**a·dop´tion** *n.* —**a·dop´tive** *adj.*

a·dor´a·ble *adj.* delightful; enchanting —**a·dor´a·bly** *adv.*

ad´o·ra´tion *n.* worship or reverence; deep affection or esteem

a·dore´ *vi., vt.* to cherish; to be especially fond of —**a·dor´ing·ly** *adv.*

a·dorn´ *vt.* decorate or embellish; to beautify —**a·dorn´ment** *n.*

ad·re´nal *adj.* near the kidneys; of the adrenal glands —*n.* an adrenal gland

adrenal gland either of two small glands located above the kidneys

ad·ren´al·in, ad·ren´al·ine *n.* a stimulant secreted by the adrenal glands

a·drift´ *adj., adv.* wandering; lacking direction or purpose

a·droit´ *adj.* clever or resourceful; expert —**a·droit´ly** *adv.*

ad·sorb´ *vt.* to retain gas or liquid on a surface —**ad·sorp´tion** *n.*

ad´u·la´tion *n.* base flattery; extravagant praise —**ad´u·late** *vt.* —**ad´u·la·to·ry** *adj.*

a·dult´ *adj.* fully developed; full–grown; mature in manner; of or for a mature person —*n.* a fully grown person or animal; one who has attained legal majority

a·dul´ter·ant *n.* a substance that tends to contaminate

a·dul´ter·ate´ *adj.* impure; contaminated —*vt.* to make impure; to lessen the value of —**a·dul´ter·a´tion** *n.*

a·dul´ter·ous *adj.* characterized by or relating to adultery

a·dul´ter·y *n.* sexual unfaithfulness by one who is married

ad va·lo·rem in proportion to value

ad·vance´ *adj.* before due: *an advance payment*; before the rest: *an advance party* —*n.* progress; an improvement; a prepayment —*vi.* to make progress; to rise —*vt.* to move forward; to offer or promote; to pay before due

ad·vanced´ *adj.* ahead of: *an advanced student*; late in time: *the advanced stage of a project*

ad·vance·ment *n.* furtherance: *the advancement of science*

ad·van´tage *n.* a favorable circumstance; superiority; a gain or benefit —*vt.* to benefit; to be of service to —**take advantage of** put to good use; to exploit

ad´van·ta´geous *adj.* providing advantage; beneficial —**ad´van·ta´geous·ly** *adv.*

ad´vent *n.* a coming, as of an important event
ad·ven´ture *n.* an exciting undertaking; a speculative venture —*vi.* to venture; to take risks —*vt.* to place at risk — **ad·ven´tur·er** *n.*
ad·ven´ture·some *adj.* inclined to risky or hazardous activities
ad·ven´tur·ous *adj.* inclined to take risks; characterized by risk; hazardous —**ad·ven´tur·ous·ly** *adv.*
ad´verb´ *n.* a word that qualifies a verb, adjective, or other adverb, as to define time, place, manner, degree, etc. —**ad·verb´i·al** *adj.*
ad´ver·sar´y *n.* an opponent; one openly antagonistic —**ad´ver·sar´i·al** *adj.*
ad´verse, **ad·verse´** *adj.* acting against; unfavorable; moving in opposition —**ad·verse´ly** *adv.*
ad·ver´si·ty *n.* a state of hardship; difficult circumstances; misfortune
ad´ver·tise´ *vi.* to proclaim publicly; to request publicly such as for employment —*vt.* to give public notice of; to proclaim the advantage of —**ad´ver·tis·er** *n.*
ad·ver·tise´ment *n.* public notice in the media to sell, announce an event, etc.
ad´ver·tis·ing *n.* any method of publicizing; the business of publicizing
ad·vice´ *n.* counsel or guidance
ad·vis´a·ble *adj.* deserving of recommendation; opportune — **ad·vis´a·bil´i·ty** *n.*
ad·vise´ *vi.* offer advice —*vt.* give advice; recommend; to inform —**ad·vis´er**, **ad·vi·sor** *n.*
ad·vised´ *adj.* deliberately considered; informed
ad·vis´ed·ly *adv.* with forethought; carefully; prudently
ad·vi´so·ry *adj.* having power to advise; offered as advice —*n.* a recommendation; information
ad´vo·ca·cy *n.* pleading of a cause; support for a cause
ad´vo·cate *n.* one who pleads or argues a cause; a supporter; a lawyer —*vt.* to support or defend; to promote a cause; to argue in favor
adze, adz *n.* a cutting tool similar to an axe
ae´gis *n.* protective power; sponsorship or patronage
aer´ate *vt.* oxygenate; charge with gas; to purify by exposure to air —**aer·a´tion** *n.*
aer´i·al *adj.* of or like air; performed in the air or by aircraft; growing in the air; insubstantial or spiritual —*n.* (*Brit.*) a device for receiving radio or television signals
aer´i·al·ist *n.* an aerial acrobat
aer·ie *n.* the nest of a bird; any dwelling at a high elevation
aer´o·dy·nam´ics *n.* the study of bodies moving in the air
aer´o·nau´tics *pl. n.* the study of the design and operation of aircraft —**aer·o·nau´tic**, **aer·o·nau´ti·cal** *adj.*
aer´o·plane (*Brit.*) *n.* a fixed–wing aircraft
aer´o·sol *adj.* pertaining to a substance dispensed as a fine spray —*n.* a suspension of fine particles; a substance under pressure released as a fine spray
aerosol bomb container holding a liquid released as spray or foam
aer´o·space *adj.* of the near outer space; of the science of space flight —*n.*
aerospace industry the business of designing and manufacturing space craft
aes´thete *n.* a connoisseur of beauty, fine art, etc.; one devoted to refinement and pretentious in appreciation of art and culture
aes·thet´ic, **aes·thet´i·cal** *adj.* prizing the artistic; characterized by taste —**aes·thet´i·cal·ly** *adv.*
aes·thet´ics *n.* the study of beauty and art, and the feelings they evoke
a·far´ *adv.* remotely; from a distance
af´fa·ble *adj.* pleasant; friendly — **af´fa·bil´i·ty** *n.* —**af´fa·bly** *adv.*
af·fair´ *n.* a bit of business; a social gathering; a minor dispute; a small matter; a romantic liaison
af·fect´ *vt.* to influence; to arouse emotion; be partial to; make a pretense of —*n.* an emotion
af´fec·ta´tion *n.* an elaborate pretense; an artificial manner
af·fect´ed *adj.* acted upon, as by a drug; influenced emotionally; feigned to impress others; acting in an unnatural manner
af·fec´tion *n.* kind feelings for another; a fondness; love
af·fec´tion·ate *adj.* expressing fondness; loving —**af·fec´tion·ate·ly** *adv.*
af´fi·da´vit *n.* a written statement made under oath and notarized
af·fil´i·ate *vt.* to take in as a member; to join or associate with —*vi.* to become allied —*n.* one allied with another as a member, partner, etc. —**af·fil´i·a´tion** *n.*
af·fin´i·ty *n.* any natural attraction; a close relationship; a spiritual attraction between persons; the force by which chemical elements form compounds; a resemblance that suggests common origin
af·firm´ *vt.* to declare to be true; to ratify, as a statute —*vi.* to make a formal declaration — **af´fir·ma´tion** *n.*
af·firm´a·tive *adj.* positive; supportive —*n.* expressing confirmation
affirmative action a program for correcting past discrimination
af·fix´ *vt.* to attach or fasten; to add, as a signature; to attribute blame or responsibility —**af´fix** *n.* something added
af·fla´tus *n.* articulation of divine knowledge; any creative impulse
af·flict´ *vt.* to oppress; to cause distress —**af·flic´tive** *adj.* — **af·flic´tive·ly** *adv.*
af·flic´tion *n.* a state of distress; that which causes suffering; a misfortune; a calamity
af´flu·ence *n.* wealth; abundance; a rich supply
af´flu·ent *adj.* prosperous; generously supplied —*n.* a wealthy person; a stream or river that flows into another — **af´flu·ent·ly** *adv.*
af·ford´ *vt.* be able to meet expenses; undergo without inconvenience; to confer or grant: *afford one pleasure* — **af·ford´a·ble** *adj.*
af·front´ *n.* an intentional insult —*vt.* to insult; treat with arrogance
a·fi·cio·na´do *n.* an enthusiastic fan
a·field´ *adv.* off the usual path: of endeavors which have gone astray
a·fire´ *adj., adv.* on fire; of one who exhibits great enthusiasm
a·float´ *adj., adv.* resting on the surface; drifting; of a financial state: *they barely remain afloat*
a·foot´ *adj., adv.* on foot; walking; progressing: *something is afoot*
a·fore´men·tioned *adj.* stated earlier; referred to previously
a·fore´said *adj.* said before
a·fore´thought *adj.* premeditated
a·foul´ *adj., adv.* entangled —**run afoul of** get into difficulty with
a·fraid´ *adj.* filled with fear or apprehension; anxious; regretful: *I'm afraid there's been a mistake*
a·fresh´ *adv.* once again; anew
aft *adj.* of the stern of a vessel —*adv.* toward the rear; astern
af´ter *adj.* subsequent; succeeding in time or place —*adv.* at a later time —*prep.* later than; in succession: *time after time*; in pursuit of: *searching after knowledge*; concerning: *inquire after* —*conj.* following: *after dinner we talked*
aft´er·burn´er *n.* a device in a jet engine that ignites unburned gas
af´ter·ef·fect *n.* a symptom which follows the initial effects
af´ter·glow *n.* the glow after a light source has disappeared; a pleasant feeling after an enjoyable experience
af´ter–hours´ *adj.* following the business day; of an establishment open past the legal closing time
af´ter·im·age *n.* the impression remaining after stimulus is gone
af´ter·life *n.* life after death
af´ter·math *n.* the consequence or result of an action
af´ter·noon *n.* part of the day between noon and sunset
af´ter·shock *n.* tremors following in the wake of an earthquake
af´ter·taste *n.* a taste remaining in the mouth after eating
af´ter·thought *n.* a notion occurring after a decision or action
af´ter·ward, **af´ter·wards** *adv.* subsequently; in the time following
a·gain´ *adv.* one more; at another time; repeated; furthermore
a·gainst´ *prep.* pressing upon; in comparison to; in opposition to
a·gape´ *adj., adv.* open–mouthed; anything left open, as a door
a´gar *n.* a substance obtained from seaweed and used as a culture medium or a food product
ag´ate *n.* a type of quartz; a child's marble; in printing, 5? point type
age *n.* a stage of life; a time in history; the condition of being old —*vi.* to ripen or mature —*vt.* to cause to grow old —**of age** legally responsible
a´ged *adj.* advanced in years; characteristic of old age —*n.* elderly persons —**aged´** *adj.* at the age of; brought to a desired state by time, as *an aged steak*
age´ism *n.* discrimination based on age; undue preoccupation with age
age´less *adj.* not changed by age; not limited by time; eternal — **age´less·ness** *n.*
a´gen·cy *n.* an active force; the means for doing something; the business of acting for others; the office of an agent; a division of a governmental department
a·gen´da *n., pl.* **a·gen´da** or **a·gen´dum** a catalogue of aims; a schedule of duties, events, etc.
a´gent *n.* person or thing that serves to change; one who acts for another; an authorized representative
ag·glom´er·ate´ *adj.* densely clustered; gathered into a mass —*n.* things thrown together; fused volcanic rock —*vi., vt.* form into a mass —**ag·glom·er·a´tion** *n.*
ag·glu´ti·nate *adj.* joined together —*vi., vt.* to join; to form a term by combining words; to mass together by adhesion
ag·glu·ti·na´tion *n.* a mass; a combination which forms a new word
ag·gran´dize *vt.* make great; to make seem greater — **ag·gran´dize·ment** *n.* — **ag·gran´diz·er** *n.*
ag´gra·vate´ *vt.* to make worse; to exasperate or annoy — **ag´gra·va´tion** *n.*
ag´gre·gate´ *adj.* gathered together; forming a cluster; of mineral fragments —*n.* a collection; an entire amount; a mixture of mineral fragments —*vt.* to collect into a mass; to amount to —**ag´gre·ga´tion** *n.*
ag·gres´sion *n.* an act of hostility; the instinct to act forcefully; assertiveness
ag·gres´sive *adj.* disposed to hostile or belligerent action; bold and assertive —**ag·gres´sive·ly** *adv.* —**ag·gres´sive·ness** *n.* —**ag·gres´sor** *n.*
ag·grieve´ *vt.* to cause sorrow; to distress
a·ghast´ *adj.* horrified; astonished
ag´ile *adj.* exhibiting quickness and dexterity; mentally alert — **ag´ile·ly** *adv.* —**ag´ile·ness**, **a·gil´i·ty** *n.*
ag´i·tate´ *vi.* to stir interest by incessant discussion —*vt.* to stir up; to perturb; to move sharply and irregularly — **ag´i·ta´tion** *n.*
a·glow´ *adj., adv.* glowing

ag·nos´tic *adj.* claiming inability to prove the existence of God; skeptical —*n.* one who embraces agnosticism; a doubter or questioner

ag·nos´ti·cism *n.* the doctrine that man lacks any valid knowledge; the theory that origins must remain unknown; the belief that the existence of God cannot be proved

a·gog´ *adj., adv.* excited; agitated; in a state of impatient curiosity

à·gon´ic *adj.* forming no angle —**agonic line** an imaginary line where magnetic north and true north coincide

ag´o·nize *vi.* sustain extreme distress; struggle over —*vt.* to torture; to cause torment —**ag´o·niz·ing** *adj.* —**ag´o·niz·ing·ly** *adv.*

ag´o·ny *n.* suffering caused by pain; an intense emotion; a violent effort

ag·o·ra·pho´bi·a *n.* fear of open spaces

a·grar´i·an *adj.* pertaining to distribution of lands; relating to agricultural interests —*n.* an advocate for equitable distribution of farm land or income

a·gree´ *vi.* to be like minded; to consent; to correspond; to come to terms —*vt.* to acknowledge

a·gree´a·ble *adj.* pleasurable; amiable; in accord with —**a·gree´a·bly** *adv.*

a·greed´ *adj.* brought into harmony; resolved by consent

a·gree´ment *n.* an understanding between parties; a contract

ag´ri·bus´i·ness *n.* an enterprise associated with agriculture, such as food processing or farm machinery

ag´ri·cul´ture *n.* the business that deals with land and livestock cultivation —**ag·ri·cul´tur·al** *adj.*

ag·ri·cul´tur·al·ist, ag·ri·cul´tur·ist *n.* one who studies or engages in agriculture

a·gron´o·my, ag·ro·nom´ics *n.* the applying of science to raising crops —**a·gron´o·mist** *n.*

a·ground´ *adj., adv.* on the shore; stranded —**run aground** of a vessel which beaches in shallow water

a´gue *n.* chills and fever

ah *interj.* an exclamation of surprise

a·ha´ *interj.* an exclamation of triumph, derision, etc.

a·head´ *adv.* in advance; at the front; before due —**get ahead** to improve one's lot

a·hem´ *interj.* a sound made in the throat to gain attention

aid *n.* assistance; one who assists —*vi., vt.* to provide assistance to

aide *n.* a confidential assistant

AIDS *Acquired Immune Deficiency Syndrome* *n.* a viral disease that attacks the body's immune system

ail *vi.* be in poor health —*vt.* to affect with pain or distress —**ail´ing** *adj.*

ail´ment *n.* a slight illness

aim *vi.* have a purpose; to point, as a firearm —*vt.* direct toward: *aim your remarks to me* —*n.* an act of pointing; an intention

aim´less *adj.* without purpose —**aim´less·ly** *adv.*

air *n.* the atmosphere; a light breeze; a tune; a characteristic manner; an affectation —*vt.* to ventilate; to announce abroad

air bag a device to protect the occupants of an automobile

air´borne´ *adj.* carried by air; flying

air´ brake´ *n.* a brake operated by compressed air

air´ con·di´tion·ing regulation of the temperature and humidity of inside air —**air´–con·di´tioned** *adj.*

air´craft´ *n.* a flying machine

aircraft carrier a ship that functions as a base for airplanes

air´drop *n.* supplies delivered by parachute from an aircraft —*vt.* to discharge by parachute from an aircraft

air ex·press´ *n.* shipment by air

air´freight´ *n.* freight shipped by airplane

air gun *n.* a weapon or tool operating on compressed air

air´hole, air´ hole *n.* a hole made by air or by which air is allowed to escape; a breathing hole

air´ing *n.* exposure to air as to freshen; a stroll outdoors; a public debate; a broadcast

air´lift´ *n.* the movement of supplies by air —*vt., vi.*

air line *n.* a tube, hose, etc. for supplying air

air´line *n.* an organization operating aircraft for passengers and cargo; the routes which aircraft travel

air´lock *n.* a chamber with controlled air pressure, providing a link between a vessel and it's surrounding environment

air´mail´ *n.* mail carried by airplane —*vt.*

air´plane´ (*US*) *n.* a fixed–wing aircraft

air pocket *n.* a vertical air current

air´port´ *n.* a base for aircraft

air pres´sure *n.* pressure of the atmosphere

air pump *n.* a device for compressing or moving air

air´speed *n.* speed measured in relation to the surrounding air

air´space´ *n.* area above a nation, subject to its jurisdiction

air´strip *n.* an airport; a stretch of ground used to land aircraft

air´tight *adj.* not allowing air in or out; complete, with no weakness: *an airtight alibi*

air´waves *n. pl.* the medium traveled by radio and television signals

air´worthy *adj.* of an aircraft conditioned for flight

air´y *adj.* open to the atmosphere; breezy; porous

aisle *n.* a narrow passageway between seats, people, etc.

a·jar´ *adj., adv.* partly open

a·kin´ *adj., adv.* related by blood; similar in some fashion

à la after the manner of

al´a·bas´ter *n.* a variety of gypsum used for statuary, vases, etc. —*adj.* smooth and white

à la carte according to the menu; items priced individually

a·lac´ri·ty *n.* willingness; readiness; liveliness —**a·lac´ri·tous** *adj.*

à la mode´ according to fashion; in food service, often a dish served with ice cream

a·larm´ *n.* a warning; a device which alerts; a sudden fright —*vt.* warn of danger; to frighten

a·larm´ing *adj.* causing fright or apprehension —**a·larm´ing·ly** *adv.*

a·larm´ist *n.* one easily alarmed; one who excites without cause

a·las´ *interj.* an expression of disappointment or sorrow

al´ba·core *n.* a tunny; a salt water food fish of the tuna family

al´ba·tross´ *n.* sea bird of the South Seas; symbol of affliction

al·be´it *conj.* although; even though; notwithstanding

al·bi´no *n.* anything lacking natural pigmentation

al´bum *n.* a blank book, as for photographs or stamps; a sound recording

al·bu´men *n.* a type of protein such as found in eggs and milk —**al·bu´mi·nous** *adj.*

al´che·my *n.* an ancient art dedicated to unlocking mysteries such as universal healing or eternal youth

al´co·hol *n.* a clear liquid used as a solvent or intoxicant; a beverage containing alcohol

al·co·hol´ic *adj.* containing alcohol; caused by alcohol or alcoholism —*n.* one suffering from alcoholism

al´co·hol·ism *n.* habitual excessive consumption of alcohol

al´cove *n.* a recess connected to a large room; a secluded retreat

ale *n.* a type of beer

ale´house *n.* a place where beer is sold for consumption on premises

a·lert´ *adj.* ready for action; bright; lively —*n.* a warning signal; preparedness —*vt.* to prepare; to warn

al·fres´co, al fres´co *adj.* occuring out of doors —*adv.* in the open air

al´gae *pl. n., sing.* **al´ga** a simple organism that lives in water

al´ge·bra *n.* a mathematical system of highly formalized rules and symbols —**al·ge·bra´ic** *adj.* —**al·ge·bra´i·cal·ly** *adv.*

al´go·rithm *n.* a systematic method of problem solving; a set of computer instructions

a´li·as *n.* an assumed name

al´i·bi *n.* defensive plea; excuse

a´li·en *adj.* foreign; owing allegiance to another country; unfamiliar; inconsistent: *alien to his nature* —*n.* one not a citizen of the country; a stranger

al´ien·a·ble *adj.* that can be legally transferred, as property

al´ien·ate´ *vt.* to antagonize; to transfer property or title

al´ien·a´tion *n.* a feeling of not belonging; indifference

a·light´ *adj., adv.* lighted, as a fire —*vi.* dismount; to land or perch

a·lign´ *vt.* arrange into a line; to adjust; to identify with —*vi.* to come into line —**a·lign´ment** *n.*

a·like´ *adj.* matching in some way; equivalent —*adv.* in like manner

al´i·ment *n.* food; something that provides nourishment —**al·i·men´tal** *adj.*

al·i·men´ta·ry *adj.* pertaining to food or nutrition; supplying nutrition

alimentary canal the path traveled by food through the body

al´i·mo·ny *n.* an allowance paid after a dissolved marriage

a·line´ *vi.* to come into line —*vt.* arrange in a line; come into agreement —**a·line´ment** *n.*

a·live´ *adj.* functioning; alert; in existence; animated —**alive with** abounding

al´ka·li´ *n.* a soluble substance that neutralizes acids —**al´ka·line** *adj.* —**al·ka·lin´i·ty** *n.*

al´ka·loid´ *n.* an alkaline substance

all *adj.* entire; greatest possible: *in all respects*; primarily; *all neck and legs* —*n.* entirety —*pron.* everyone or each one; everything —*adv.* entirely; exclusively —**after all** nevertheless —**all but** almost —**all in** tired —**all in all** all things considered —**all out** without constraint —**at all** under any condition; in any way

al·lay´ *vt.* to calm; reduce in intensity, alleviate

al´le·ga´tion *n.* an assertion made without proof

al·lege´ *vt.* to attest; to assert; to plead in support or denial

al·leg´ed *adj.* asserted; not proven —**al·leg´ed·ly** *adv.*

al·le´giance *n.* loyalty; an obligation of loyalty

al·le·gor´ic, al·le·gor´i·cal *adj.* pertaining to allegory —**al·le·gor´i·cal·ly** *adv.*

al´le·go´ry *n.* use of people or animals to represent abstract concepts; symbols employed in literature; any symbolic representation

al´ler·gen *n.* a substance that produces an allergic reaction

al·ler´gic *adj.* caused by allergy; susceptible to; having aversion

al´ler·gist *n.* one who diagnoses and treats allergies

al´ler·gy *n.* unusual sensitivity to a substances

al·le´vi·ate´ *vt.* to relieve; to lessen —**al·le´vi·a´tion** *n.*

al·le´vi·a´tive, al·le´vi·a´to·ry *adj.* tending to relieve, as in severity

al´ley *n.* a narrow street or passageway —**al´ley·way** *n.*

al·li´ance *n.* a formal agreement between countries or persons; a union by treaty, marriage, etc.

al·lied´ *adj.* closely related; affiliated, as by treaty

al´li·ga´tor *n.* an American or Chinese reptile, similar to the crocodile with a shorter, wider snout

al·lit´er·a´tion *n.* a series of words beginning with the same consonant sound: *"Peter Piper picked a peck..."* —**al·lit´er·ate** *vi., vt.* —**al·lit´er·a·tive** *adj.*

al´lo·cate *vt.* to allot or assign a share; to designate for a particular purpose

al´lo·ca·tion *n.* a thing or amount set aside

al·lot´ *vt.* to apportion to; to distribute by lot —**al·lot´ment** *n.*

all´–out´ *adj.* wholehearted, concentrated

al·low´ *vt.* permit to have, happen, do, etc.; to acknowledge as true; provide for: *allow for contingencies* —**al·low´a·ble** *adj.*

al·low´ance *n.* that allowed; amount budgeted; a discount; a variance to be reckoned

al´loy *n.* a mixture of metals; anything that lessens value or purity —*vt.* to combine metals; make metal less pure by mixing

all´·time´ *adj.* unparalleled

al·lude´ *vi.* to refer to casually or indirectly

al·lure´ *vt.* tempt; attract —*vi.* be subtly attractive —*n.* appeal; the ability to attract; a quality that attracts

al·lur´ing *adj.* appealing; attractive; seductive —**al·lur´ing·ly** *adv.*

al·lu´sion *n.* a casual or indirect reference —**al·lu´sive** *adj.*

al·lu´vi·um *n.* soil deposited by moving water —**al·lu´vi·al** *adj.*

al´ly *n.* those unified for a common purpose —*vt.* to unite —*vi.* to form an alliance; to become united

al´ma·nac *n.* a yearly publication with facts about weather, astronomical data, etc.

al´mond *adj.* of the taste, color, etc. of an almond —*n.* fruit of the almond tree; the tree itself

al´most, al·most´ *adj., adv.* close to; very nearly

alms *n., sing. & pl.* a donation

a·lone´ *adj., adv.* unaccompanied; detached; excluding all others; unique, without equal

a·long´ *adv.* tracing the length of; progressing beside; advanced in distance or time —*prep.* following the path of —**all along** the entire time; from the beginning —**get along** to persevere; to live in harmony

a·loof´ *adj.* distant; reserved —*adv.* apart —**a·loof´ness** *n.*

a·loud´ *adv.* audibly; out loud

al´pha·bet´ *n.* the symbols of a written language

al´pha·bet´i·cal *adj.* of a written language; arranged in order —**al´pha·bet·ize** *vt.*

al´pha·nu·mer´ic *adj.* data comprising letters and numbers

al·read´y *adv.* by this time or a time referred to

al´tar *n.* a place for sacred offerings; the focus of a place of worship

al´ter *vt.* to modify; adjust fit; to spay —*vi.* to undergo change —**al´ter·a·ble** *adj.* —**al·ter·a´tion** *n.*

al´ter·cate´ *vi.* quarrel; to argue bitterly —**al´ter·ca´tion** *n.*

al´ter·nate *adj.* every other; following by turns —*vt.* use in turn —*vi* occur by turns —*n.* a substitute —**al´ter·nate·ly** *adv.*

al´ter·na´tion *n.* a changing back and forth

al·ter´na·tive *adj.* providing a choice —*n.* a choice; an option; something that must be decided —**al·ter´na·tive·ly** *adv.*

al·though´ *conj.* even though

al·tim´e·ter *n.* an instrument for measuring altitude

al´ti·tude´ *n.* elevation; the angle of a celestial body in relation to the horizon

al´to´ *n.* musical range between tenor and mezzo–soprano

al´to·geth´er *adv.* in all; all things being considered

al´tru·ism *n.* unselfish regard for others —**al·tru·is´tic** *adj.* —**al·tru·is´ti·cal·ly** *adv.*

a·lum´na *n., pl.* **a·lum´nae** a female graduate

a·lum´nus *n., pl.* **a·lum´ni** a person who has graduated

al´ways *adv.* for all time; every time

a·mal´gam *n.* a mixture

a·mal´ga·mate *vt.* combine with mercury; to unite or integrate —*vi.* to become combined; to mix with another metal

a·man´u·en´sis *n., pl.* **a·man´u·en´ses** one employed to copy manuscripts; a secretary

a·mass´ *vt.* to accumulate

am´a·teur *adj.* done by a non–professional —*n.* one participating for pleasure only, not profit; one who lacks skill

am·a·teur´ish *adj.* lacking professional skill —**am·a·teur´ish·ly** *adv.*

a·maze´ *vt.* to fill with wonder; to astonish —**a·maze´ment** *n.*

am·bas´sa·dor *n.* a diplomat —**am·bas·sa·do´ri·al** *adj.*

am´bi·ance, am´bi·ence *n.* character of a place; atmosphere

am´bi·dex´trous *adj.* able to use either hand well; dexterous

am´bi·ent *adj.* encompassing; of the surrounding area

am·big´u·ous *adj.* not clear; vague; open to misinterpretation —**am´bi·gu´i·ty** *n.*

am·bi´tion *n.* a firm aspiration; a desired goal; passion or energy

am·bi´tious *adj.* marked by aspiration; eager; appearing difficult —**am·bi´tious·ly** *adv.*

am·biv´a·lent *adj.* of contradictory emotions; unsure —**am·biv´a·lence** *n.*

am´bu·lance *n.* a vehicle for transporting the sick or injured

am´bu·lant *adj.* moving about

am´bu·la·to´ry *adj.* able to walk; able to move about

am´bus·cade´ *n.* an ambush; a hiding place —*vt.* to attack suddenly from hiding

am´bush *n.* a surprise attack; those hiding in wait; a deception or trap —*vt.* to lie in wait; to attack

a·mel´io·rate´ *vi., vt.* to make or become better; to improve —**a·mel´io·ra·tive** *adj.*

a·men´a·ble *adj.* agreeable; responsive to authority; open to criticism —**a·me´na·bly** *adv.*

a·mend´ *vt.* to improve; to change; to free of error —*vi.* to improve —**a·mend´a·ble** *adj.*

a·mend´a·to·ry *adj.* serving to correct or improve

a·mend´ment *n.* a correction; a removal of error; an addition which alters

a·mends´ *pl. n.* compensation for a wrong; an apology

a·men´i·ty *n.* a pleasant quality

A·mer·i·ca´na *n.* things typically American or associated with American history

A·mer´i·can·ism *n.* a manner or custom peculiar to the US; a fondness for or loyalty to the US and its institutions

am´e·thyst *n.* bluish–violet type of quartz; a bluish–violet color

a´mi·a·ble *adj.* friendly; good–natured —**a·mi·a·bil´i·ty** *n.*

am´i·ca·ble *adj.* agreeable; congenial —**am´i·ca·bly** *adv.*

a·mid´, a·midst´ *prep.* among; in the middle of

a·mi´no ac´id anorganic acid; part of the protein molecule

a·miss´ *adj.* out of order; improper, faulty —*adv.* wrongly; in an improper way —**take amiss** to be offended

am´i·ty *n.* friendly relations; good will

am´me·ter *n.* an instrument for measuring an electric current

am´mu·ni´tion *n.* a projectile; an explosive used as a weapon; information to attack or defend

am·ne´si·a *n.* loss of memory —**am·ne´si·ac** *n., adj.*

am´nes·ty *n.* an official pardon —*vt.* grant a pardon to

am´ni·on *n.* the membranous sac surrounding a fetus

a·moe´ba *n.* a one–celled protozoan —**a·moe´bic** *adj.*

a·mong´, a·mongst´ *prep.* in the midst of; included within an array

a·mor´al *adj.* without concern of ethical distinction; lacking a sense of right or wrong —**a·mo·ral´i·ty** *n.*

am´o·rous *adj.* loving; passionate; of desire; connected with love —**am´o·rous·ly** *adv.*

a·mor´phous *adj.* lacking form; unorganized —**a·mor´phism** *n.*

am´or·tise (*Brit.*), **am´or·tize** (US) *vt.* to discharge a debt by regular payments —**am´or·tis·a·ble, am´or·tiz·a·ble** *adj.* —**am·or·ti·sa´tion, am·or·ti·za´tion** *n.*

a·mount´ *n.* total; a quantity; the entire value or effect —*vi.* add up to; be equal to

am·per´age, am´per·age *n.* the strength of an electrical current

am´pere *n.* standard unit for measuring an electric current

am´per·sand *n.* a symbol (&) representing the word *and*

am·phet´a·mine *n.* a stimulant used as a medication

am·phib´i·an *n.* an animal or craft that functions in water or on land

am·phib´i·ous *adj.* living or operating in water and on land

am´phi·the´a·ter *n.* a structure with seats rising from a central arena

am´ple *adj.* large in capacity or size; more than enough; sufficient —**am´ply** *adv.*

am´pli·fi´er *n.* a device that reinforces electrical impulses

am´pli·fy *vt.* increase or expand —**am´pli·fi·ca´tion** *n.*

am´pli·tude´ *n.* extent, largeness, fullness

am´pul, am´pule *n.* a vial of medication, often for injection

am´pu·tate´ *vt.* to surgically remove —**am´pu·ta´tion** *n.*

a·muck´ *adj.* in a frenzy; crazed —*adv.* in a barbarous manner

am´u·let *n.* a magical charm

a·muse´ *vt.* to occupy pleasantly; to induce a smile or laughter

a·mus´ing *adj.* entertaining; causing laughter

a·muse´ment *n.* a diversion; that which brings pleasure; a feeling of enjoyment

amusement park a recreational area

an *adj., indef. art.* each or any; an article before words beginning with a vowel sound

a·nach´ro·nism *n.* something out of its proper order —**a·nach·ro·nis´tic** *adj.*

an·aer´obe *n.* a microorganism that exists without oxygen —**an·aer·o´bic** *adj.*

an´aes·the´si·a (*Brit.*) *n.* loss of sensation or sensitivity

an´aes·the´si·ol·o·gy (*Brit.*) *n.* the study of anaesthesia and its effects —**an·aes·the·si·ol´o·gist** (*Brit.*) *n.*

an´aes·thet´ic (*Brit.*) *adj.* of or producing anaesthesia: making insensitive —*n.* an agent that produces a loss of feeling —**an´aes·thet´i·cal·ly** *adv.*

an·aes´the·tise (*Brit.*) *vt.* to render insensitive to pain

an´a·gram´ *n.* a word or phrase made by rearranging the letters of another word or phrase

an·al·ge´si·a *n.* deadening of pain without loss of consciousness

an·al·ge´sic *n.* medicine that relieves pain —*adj.* causing analgesia

an´a·log (*US*) *adj.* of data depicted by a continuous variable

an´a·logue (*Brit.*) *adj.* of data depicted by a continuous variable

a·nal´o·gous *adj.* similar in certain ways

a·nal´o·gy *n.* partial similarity; comparison based on similarity

a·nal´y·sis *n.* division of a thing into parts for examination

an´a·lyst *n.* one skilled in examination or study; a psychoanalyst

an´a·lyt´ic, an·a·lyt´i·cal *adj.* pertaining to analysis; expert in analysis —**an·a·lyt´i·cal·ly** *adv.*

an´a·lyse (*Brit.*), **an´a·lyze** (*US*) *vt.* break down for study; make analysis; to psychoanalyze

an·a·phy·lac´tic *adj.* of a severe reaction to a usually harmless substance

an·a·phy·lax´is *n.* abnormal sensitivity; anaphylactic shock

anaphylactic shock severe reaction caused by exposure to a usually harmless substance

an·ar´chic, an·ar´chi·cal *adj.* promoting anarchy; lacking order —**an·ar´chi·cal·ly** *adv.*

an´arch·y *n.* absence of governmental authority —**an´arch·ist** *n.* —**an·ar·chis´tic** *adj.*

a·nath´e·ma *n.* an ecclesiastical ban; denunciation; anything greatly disliked

a·nat´o·mist *n.* a specialist in or student of anatomy

a·nat´o·mise (*Brit.*), **a·nat´o·mize** (*US*) *vt.* dissect for study; study in great detail

a·nat´o·my *n.* the structure of an organism; dissection for study **—an·a·tom´i·cal** *adj.* **—an·a·tom´i·cal·ly** *adv.*

an´ces·tor *n.* a forefather; one from whom descended; a forerunner **—an·ces´tral** *adj.* **—an´ces·try** *n.*

an´chor *n.* a device that secures in place *—vt.* to hold in place; to fix firmly *—vi.* to lie at anchor; be fixed in place

an´chor·age *n.* a place where ships lie at anchor; a fee for anchoring

an´cho·rite *n.* a religious recluse

an´chor·per´son *n.* the primary reporter for a newscast

an´cient *adj.* very old; antiquated *—n.* one from the distant past; a very old person

an´cil·lar·y *adj.* secondary

and *conj.* as well as; added to

and´i·ron *n.* a metal support for wood in a fireplace

an·drog´y·nous *adj.* bearing both male and female characteristics; of a style not distinctly male or female **—an·drog´y·nous·ly** *adv.* **—an·drog´y·ny** *n.*

an´droid *n.* an automaton that resembles a human

an´ec·dot·al *adj.* consisting of anecdotes **—an´ec·dot·al·ly** *adv.*

an´ec·dote *n.* a short amusing story

a·ne´mi·a *n.* a deficiency of red blood corpuscles or hemoglobin

a·ne´mic *adj.* afflicted with anemia; listless; lacking vitality **—a·ne´mi·cal·ly** *adv.*

an·e·mom´e·ter *n.* a device for measuring the force of wind

an·er·oid *adj.* not using fluid, as *an aneroid barometer*

an´es·the´si·a (*US*) *n.* loss of sensation or sensitivity to pain

an´es·the´si·ol·o·gy (*US*) *n.* the study of anesthesia and its effects **—an·es·the·si·ol´o·gist** (*US*) *n.*

an´es·thet´ic (*US*) *adj.* of or producing anesthesia: making insensitive to pain *—n.* an agent that produces loss of feeling **—an·es´the·tist** (*US*) *n.*

an·es´the·tize (*US*) *vt.* to render insensitive to pain

an´eu·rysm, an´eu·rism *n.* swelling of an artery

a·new´ *adv.* again; freshly

an´gel *n.* a supernatural being; a guiding influence; a backer

an´ger *n.* strong displeasure; ire; wrath *—vt.* to make irate; to provoke *—vi.* to become angry

an·gi´na pec´to·ris heart condition marked by severe pain

an´gle *n.* ulterior motive; stratagem; viewpoint; fishing tackle; intersection of two lines or planes *—vi.* obtain by cunning; fish with hook and line **—an´gu·lar** *adj.* **—an·gu·lar´i·ty** *n.*

an´gler *n.* a fisherman; one who schemes to achieve an end

An´gli·cise (Brit.), **An´gli·cize** (US) *vi.* to become like the English *—vt.* to appropriate an English style

an´gling *n.* the skill of fishing with special hooked lures

An·glo´phile *n.* a devotee of England and its institutions

an´gry *adj.* showing displeasure; threatening; indicating anger **—an´gri·ly** *adv.* **—an´gri·ness** *n.*

angst *n.* feeling of apprehension

ang´strom, ang´strom u´nit measure of wavelength; a hundred millionth of a centimeter

an´guish *n.* severe misery *—vi., vt.* experience or cause distress

an´gu·lar *adj.* like an angle; gaunt; lacking grace

an·hy´drous *adj.* of a chemical compound which contains no water

an´i·mal *n.* a living creature; creatures of the earth, separate from man; a brutal person *—adj.* pertaining to animals; like an animal

an´i·mate *adj.* living; lively *—vt.* make lifelike; stimulate

an´i·mated *adj.* spirited; lively; vivacious

an´i·ma´tion *n.* the process of imparting life or spirit; being alive; the making of cartoons

an´i·mism *n.* belief in a soul; the belief that inanimate objects possess a spirit **—an´i·mis´tic** *adj.*

an´i·mos´i·ty *n.* a strong feeling of hostility; hatred

an´i·mus *n.* animosity; an animating energy or purpose

an´ise *n.* aromatic seeds used for flavoring and medicine

an´i·seed *n.* anise seed; the seed of the anise plant

an´kle *n.* the joint connecting the foot and the leg

an´nals *pl. n.* a chronological record; any historical account

an·neal´ *vt.* to make less brittle; to strengthen by trial

an´ne·lid *adj.* of a group of segmented invertebrates, as earthworms, leeches, etc. *—n.*

an´nex *n.* something added; an auxiliary building **—an·nex´** *vt.* to add; to incorporate into **—an´nex·a´tion** *n.*

an·ni´hi·late *vt.* to destroy; to defeat **—an·ni´hi·la·tor** *n.*

an·ni´hi·la´tion *n.* total destruction

an´ni·ver´sa·ry *n.* a date occurring at the same time each year; celebration of a past event

an´no·tate´ *vt.* to provide a commentary **—an·no·ta´tion** *n.* **—an´no·ta·tive** *adj.*

an·nounce´ *vt.* to proclaim; to make known; to report the appearance of **—an·nounce´ment** *n.* **—an·nounc´er** *n.*

an·noy´ *vt.* bother; irritate *—vi.* be bothersome **—an·noy´ance** *n.* **—an·noy´ing** *adj.*

an´nu·al *adj.* occuring every year *—n.* a publication issued once a year; a plant that lives only one season **—an´nu·al·ize** *vt.* **—an´nu·al·ly** *adv.*

an·nu´i·ty *n.* annual allowance; receipt or payment of a stipend

an·nul´ *vt.* make or declare invalid; to revoke **—an·nul´ment** *n.*

an´nu·lar *adj.* formed like a ring; marked by rings

an·nun´ci·ate *vt* to announce **—an·nun´ci·a·tor** *n.*

an·nun·ci·a´tion *n.* a proclamation; the act of announcing

an´o·dyne´ *adj.* soothing; able to eliminate pain *—n.* medication that eases pain or soothes

a·noint´ *vt.* sprinkle or rub with oil or ointment; to consecrate

a·nom´a·ly *n.* deviation from a norm; a peculiarity **—a·nom´a·lous** *adj.*

an·o´mic *adj.* socially unstable *—n.* one alienated from society

a·non´y·mous *adj.* lacking attribution; lacking distinctive characteristics **—an·o·nym´i·ty** *n.* **—a·non´y·mous·ly** *adv.*

an·oth´er *adj., pron.* one other; different

an´ser·ine *adj.* of or like a goose; foolish or silly

an´swer *n.* response; an action in kind: retaliation; a solution *—vi.* to respond; prove sufficient; be accountable; correspond *—vt.* to act in response; to be sufficient; to correspond

an´swer·a·ble *adj.* accountable; able to be responded to

ant *n.* a small communal insect

ant·ac´id *adj.* correcting acidity *—n.* an alkali; a remedy for acidity

an·tag´o·nism *n.* animosity; mutual hostility or opposition

an·tag´o·nist *n.* an adversary; one who or that which opposes **—an·tag·o·nis´tic** *adj.* **—an·tag·o·nis´ti·cal·ly** *adv.*

an·tag´o·nize´ *vt.* to oppose

an´te *n.* initial stake in poker; a reward; an inducement *—vt.* to bet before a hand is dealt; to pay one's share *—vi.* to pay up

an´te·ce´dent *adj.* going before, preceding *—n.* that which logically precedes; noun or pronoun to which a relative pronoun refers

an´te·cham·ber *n.* a room which serves as an entranceway

an´te·date *vt.* to backdate; to occur earlier than

an·te·di·lu´vi·an *adj.* before the Biblical flood; antiquated *—n.* anything that lived before the Biblical flood; anything very old

an´te·lope´ *n.* a graceful quadruped allied to the deer

an´te·me·rid´i·an *adj.* before noon

an·ten´na *n., pl.* **an·ten´nae, an·ten´nas** sensory organs of an insect; device for transmission of radio or television signals

an·te·pe´nult *n.* third syllable from the end of a word

an·te·pe·nul´ti·mate *adj.* the third from the end

an·te´ri·or *adj.* toward or at the front; earlier in time

an´te·room *n.* a waiting room; an antechamber

an´them *n.* a hymn; triumphal music **—national anthem** the official song of a nation

an´ther *n.* part of the stamen in a flower that holds pollen

an·thol´o·gise (*Brit.*), **an·thol´o·gize** (*US*) *vi.* compile or publish an anthology *—vt.* include in an anthology

an·thol´o·gy *n.* a collection of literary selections; an assortment or catalog of comments

an·tho·zo´an *n.* a class of marine creatures including corals and sea anemones **—an·tho·zo´ic** *adj.*

an´thra·cite´ *n.* a hard coal

an´thrax *n.* an infectious disease

an´thro·poid *adj.* similar to a human; of man, apes, and monkeys *—n.* any of the larger apes **—an´thro·poid´al** *adj.*

an´thro·pol´o·gy *n.* study of the customs and culture of man **—an·thro·po·log´ic, an·thro·po·log´i·cal** *adj.* **—an·thro·pol´o·gist** *n.*

an·thro·po·mor´phic *adj.* having human form or characteristics

an·thro·po·mor´phism *n.* endowing a spirit or natural phenomena with human attributes

an·thro·po·mor´phise (*Brit.*), **an·thro·po·mor´phize** (*US*) *—vt., vi.* to attribute human qualities to things not human

an´ti- *prefix* against or opposed

an´ti·bi·ot´ic *adj.* preventing bacterial growth *—n.* substance that destroys microorganisms

an´ti·bod´y *n.* protein in the body that neutralizes harmful matter

an´tic *adj.* bizarre; incongruous *—n.* a caper or prank; a ridiculous act

an·tic´i·pate´ *vt.* to foresee; be prepared for; act so as to forestall; take too hastily *—vi.* consider prematurely **—an·tic´i·pa´tion** *n.* **—an·tic´i·pa·to·ry** *adj.*

an´ti·cli´max *n.* a reduction in effectiveness **—an´ti·cli·mac´tic** *adj.* **—an´ti·cli·mac´ti·cal·ly** *adv.*

an·ti·cli´nal, an·ti·clin´ic *adj.* a downward incline on two sides, as an arch of rock stratum

an·ti·cline *n.* rock stratum forming an upward bend

an´ti·dote´ *n.* substance used to counteract a poison **—an·ti·dot´al** *adj.*

an´ti·freeze *n.* a cooling agent

an´ti·gen, an·ti·gene´ *n.* a substance that provokes development of antibodies **—an·ti·gen´ic** *adj.*

an´ti·he·ro *n.* an unlikely champion; one without the usual qualities attributed to a hero

an´ti·his´ta·mine´ *n.* drug to treat cold and allergy syptoms

an·ti·ma·cas´sar *n.* a covering for the backs and arms of chairs

an·ti·mag·net´ic *adj.* resistant to the influence of a magnetic field

an´ti·mat´ter *n.* charged particles in opposition to matter

an´ti·mo·ny *n.* a metallic element used in alloys and pigments

an·ti·pas´to *n.* an appetizer of delicacies

an·tip´a·thy *n.* a strong or deep-seated aversion **—an·tip·a·thet´ic** *adj.*

an´ti·phon *n.* a verse chanted in response; passages arranged for alternate chanting **—an´ti·phon´ic, an´ti·phon´i·cal** *adj.*

an´ti·pode *n.* exact opposite

an·tip´o·des *pl. n.* anything at the opposite extreme

an·ti·py·ret´ic *adj.* relief of fever *—n.* medicine to relieve fever

an·ti·quar´i·an *adj.* of antiquity or the collection of antiquities *—n.* a dealer in antiquities

an´ti·quate *vt.* to make old or obsolete; to make appear old

an´ti·quat·ed *adj.* old–fashioned; out of date; no longer useful

an·tique´ *adj.* old; made much earlier; of an ancient style —*n.* a relic; an object valued for age; an ancient style —*vt.* make to resemble an antique
an·tiq´ui·ty *n.* ancient history; an ancient relic
an·ti·sep´sis *n.* the destruction of harmful bacteria
an´ti·sep´tic *adj.* thoroughly clean; able to destroy harmful bacteria —*n.* a substance that destroys harmful bacteria
an·ti·so´cial *adj.* adverse to social contact; opposed to social order; disruptive
an·tith´e·sis *n., pl.* **an·tith´e·ses** opposing thoughts or expressions; the direct opposite
an·ti·thet´ic, an·ti·thet´i·cal *adj.* being in opposition — **an·ti·thet´i·cal·ly** *adv.*
an´ti·tox´in *n.* an antibody; a drug that acts against disease
an·ti·trust´ *adj.* opposition to practices in restraint of trade; pertaining to the regulation of trusts, monopolies, etc.
an·ti·ven´in *n.* antitoxin which protects against venom
an´to·nym *n.* a word opposite in meaning to another —**an·to·nym´ic, an·ton´y·mous** *adj.*
an´trum *n., pl.* **an´tra** a cavity, esp. in a bone; a sinus cavity
a´nus *n.* the opening at the lower end of the alimentary canal
an´vil *n.* heavy metal block used as a base for forming metals; a fixed base
anx·i´e·ty *n.* a feeling of uneasiness; a cause for anxiety; eagerness; tension or dread
anx´ious *adj.* apprehensive over an uncertainty; impatient for fulfillment —**anx´ious·ly** *adv.*
an´y *adj.* one or some —*pron.* one or more of several —*adv.* at all
an´y·bod·y *pron.* any person —*n.* a person of importance
an´y·how *adv.* in any way whatever; in any case
an´y·more *adv.* at this time
an´y·one *pron.* any person
an´y·thing *adv.* at all; in any way —*n., pron.* a thing of any kind
an´y·way *adv.* in any event; nevertheless
an´y·where *adv.* in any place
a·or´ta *n.* large artery from the heart that carries blood to all of the body except the lungs
a·part´ *adj.* separated; disassociated —*adv.* separately; independently —**apart from** with the exception of
a·part´heid *n.* the policy of racial discrimination in South Africa
a·part´ment (*US*) *n.* rooms serving as living quarters
ap´a·thy *n.* lack of emotion; unconcern; lacking interest —**ap´a·thet´c, ap´a·thet´i·cal** *adj.*
ape *n.* a large tailless primate, as a gorilla; one who imitates; one who is rude or clumsy —*vt.* to imitate —**ape´like** *adj.*
a·per·ri·tif *n.* a beverage, often wine, served before a meal
ap´er·ture´ *n.* an opening; a hole or slit
a´pex *n.* climax; the highest point
a·pha´sia *n.* loss of ability to speak or understand — **a·pha´si·ac, a·pha´sic** *adj., n.*
a·phe´li·on *n.* the point in an orbit farthest from the sun
aph´o·rism *n.* a wise saying; an adage —**aph·o·ris´tic** *adj.*
aph·ro·dis´i·ac *adj.* intensifying sexual desire —*n.* a substance to intensify sexual desire
a·pi´an *adj.* pertaining to bees
a´pi·ar´y *n.* a place where bees are kept
a·piece *adv.* for each; to each
a·plomb *n.* self–confidence
a·poc´a·lypse´ *n.* symbolic destruction of evil; prophetic revelation; total destruction — **a·poc·a·lyp´tic, a·poc·a·lyp´ti·cal** *adj.*
a·poc´ry·pha *pl. n.* writings of questionable authenticity
a·poc´ry·phal *adj.* not genuine; of dubious origin; fictitious
ap´o·gee *n.* the highest point in an orbit
a·po·lit´i·cal *adj.* of no political importance
a·pol´o·gist *n.* one speaking in defense of a person or cause
a·pol´o·gy *n.* a formal argument or defense; an expression of regret —**a·pol·o·get´ic** *adj.* — **a·pol´o·gise, a·pol´o·gize** *vi.*
ap·o·plec´tic *n.* one subject to attacks of apoplexy —**ap·o·plec´tic, ap·o·plec´ti·cal** *adj.* showing symptoms of apoplexy
ap´o·plex·y *n.* a fit of anger; sudden disorder of the nervous system: a stroke
a·pos´ta·sy *n.* abandonment of one´s beliefs or principles — **a·pos´ta·tize** *vi.*
a·pos´tate *n.* one guilty of apostasy —*adj.*
a·pos´tle *n.* one sent by Christ to preach; a missionary; an adherent —**a·pos´tle·ship** *n.*
a·pos´to·late *n.* the office, duties, etc. of an apostle
ap·os·tol´ic, ap·os·tol´i·cal *adj.* of an apostle; of the succession from the Apostles; papal
a·pos´tro·phe´ *n.* a mark (') to show omission, form a possessive, and certain plurals
a·poth´e·car·y *n.* one who prepares medications
ap´o·thegm *n.* a terse saying; a maxim
a·poth´e·o·sis *n.* the exaltation of a person to divine honors; deification —**a·po·the´o·size** *vt.*
ap·pal´, ap·pall´ *vt.* to horrify; stun —**ap·pal´ling, ap·pall´ing** *adj.* —**ap·pal´ling·ly, ap·pall´ing·ly** *adv.*
ap´pa·ra´tus *n.* a device designed for a particular use
ap·par´el *n.* clothing
ap·par´ent *adj.* evident; seeming to be —**ap·par´ent·ly** *adv.*
ap·pa·ri´tion *n.* a strange manifestation
ap·peal´ *vi.* request aid; be looked on favorably; plead for rehearing —*vt.* request hearing in a higher court —*n.* a request for aid; a favorable quality; petition to a higher power — **ap·peal´ing·ly** *adv.*
ap·pear´ *vi.* come into view; seem to be; to be published; to present oneself as ordered by law
ap·pear´ance *n.* a semblance; one's demeanor; publication; attendance, as in court
ap·pease´ *vt.* to calm; to satisfy —**ap·pease´ment** *n.* —**ap·peas´a·ble** *adj.*
ap·pel´lant *adj.* regarding appeals —*n.* one who appeals
ap´pel·la´tion *n.* a name or title —**ap·pel´la·tive** *adj., n.*
ap·pend´ *vt.* to add; to attach
ap·pen´dage *n.* an addition; subsidiary part —**ap·pen·dic´u·lar** *adj.*
ap·pend´ant *adj.* attached; allied in a subordinate position
ap·pen·dec´to·my *n.* removal of the appendix
ap·pen´di·ci´tis *n.* inflammation of the vermiform appendix
ap·pen´dix *n., pl.* **ap·pen´dix·es, ap·pen´di·ces** supplementary material; an outgrowth
ap´per·tain´ *vi.* be relevant; to relate
ap´pe·tite´ *n.* a desire for food or drink; any compelling desire
ap´pe·tiz´er *n.* a small amount of food served before a meal; a sample that stimulates — **ap´pe·tiz´ing** *adj.*
ap·plaud´ *vi., vt.* express approval; commend or praise — **ap·plaud´a·ble** *adj.* —**ap·plaud´a·bly, ap·plaud´ing·ly** *adv.*
ap·plause´ *n.* approval shown by clapping of hands
ap´ple *n.* fruit of the apple tree; various exotic fruits or trees
ap´ple·jack *n.* brandy distilled from apple cider
ap´ple·sauce *n.* cooked, spiced and puréed apples; that which is nonsense or not believed
ap·pli´ance *n.* a device designed for a special purpose
ap´pli·ca·ble *adj.* pertinent; appropriate —**ap´pli·ca·bil´i·ty** *n.* —**ap´pli·ca·bly** *adv.*
ap´pli·cant *n.* candidate for a job
ap·pli·ca´tion *n.* something applied; a formal request; close and consistent attention
ap·pli´ca·to·ry *adj.* that can be used; practical
ap´pli·ca·tor *n.* a device for applying a substance to a surface
ap·plied´ *adj.* put into practice; of something practical
ap·pli·qué´ *n.* an ornament —*vt.* to decorate by applying
ap·ply´ *vi.* request; be relevant — *vt.* spread on; use; devote to a particular use
ap·point´ *vt.* to name or select
ap·point·ee´ *n.* one selected
ap·point´ment *n.* a scheduled meeting; a position
ap·por´tion *vt.* to distribute — **ap·por´tion·ment** *n.*
ap·pose´ *vt.* arrange side by side or opposite —**ap·pos´i·tive** *adj.*
ap´po·site *adj.* pertinent; fit
ap·po·si´tion *n.* in immediate connection —**ap·po·si´tion·al** *adj.* —**ap·po·si´tion·al·ly** *adv.*
ap·praise´ *vt.* set a value for; to estimate worth
ap·pre´ci·a·ble *adj.* sufficient to be noticed; apparent
ap·pre´ci·ate *vt.* show gratitude; recognize and understand; increase in value —**ap·pre´ci·a´tion** *n.* —**ap·pre´ci·a·tive** *adj.*
ap´pre·hend´ *vt.* to capture; grasp mentally; await with dread —*vi.* to comprehend — **ap´pre·hen´sion** *n.*
ap·pre·hen´si·ble *adj.* able to be understood
ap·pre·hen´sive *adj.* troubled; possessing understanding — **ap·pre·hen´sive·ly** *adv.*
ap·pren´tice *n.* one learning; a beginner —*vt.* accept as an apprentice —**ap·pren´tice·ship** *n.*
ap·prise´, ap·prize´ *vt.* to notify or make aware
ap·proach´ *vi.* draw near —*vt.* come near; be similar —*n.* means of access; a technique — **ap·proach´a·ble** *adj.*
ap´pro·ba´tion *n.* approval; high regard —**ap·pro´ba·tive, ap·pro´ba·to·ry** *adj.*
ap·pro´pri·ate´ *adj.* suitable; proper —*vt.* to take; set apart — **ap·pro´pri·ate·ly** *adv.*
ap·prov´al *n.* consent; official sanction; a favorable opinion
ap·prove´ *vi.* express approval — *vt.* give consent; to view favorably —**ap·prov´ing·ly** *adv.*
ap·prox´i·mate *adj.* similar; close —*vt.* come near —**ap·prox´i·mate·ly** *adv.* —**ap·prox·i·ma´tion** *n.*
ap·pur´te·nance´ *n.* an adjunct —**ap·pur´te·nant** *adj.*
a´pron *n.* a protective covering; the front of a stage
ap´ro·pos´ *adj.* appropriate — *adv.* with respect to; regarding
apse *n.* a building projection
apt *adj.* appropriate; likely, probable; competent, talented — **apt´ly** *adv.* —**apt´ness** *n.*
ap´ti·tude *n.* a natural gift; quickness of understanding
aq´ua *adj.* light blue–green —*n.* a blue–green color
aq´ua·cul´ture *n.* cultivation of fish or plants in water
a·quar´i·um *n.* a fish tank; a building for exhibiting sea life
aq´ua·tint *n.* an etching for tints or washes; the copper plate used; a wash print
aq´ua vi´tae *n.* alcohol; distilled spirits
aq´ue·duct´ *n.* conduit for water
a´que·ous *adj.* watery; formed by or containing water
aq´ui·line *adj.* like an eagle; curved, like an eagle's beak
ar·a·besque´ *n.* intricate scroll-work design; a ballet position
Ar´a·bic *adj.* of the language and culture of Arabia —*n.* any of the Middle Eastern languages
Arabic numerals the figures 0, 1, 2, 3, 4, 5, 6, 7, 8, 9
ar´a·ble *adj.* suitable for farming
a·rach´nid *n.* class of insects that includes spiders and scorpions
Ar´a·ma´ic *n.* an ancient Semitic language
ar´bi·ter *n.* one qualified to judge
ar´bi·trar·y *adj.* discretionary; capricious; autocratic —**ar·bi·trar´i·ly** *adv.* —**ar´bi·trar·i·ness** *n.*
ar´bi·trate *vi., vt.* to settle by submitting to a third party
ar´bi·tra´tion *n.* referral of dispute to a disinterested party
ar´bi·tra´tor *n.* a judge
ar´bor *n.* a place shaded by low trees or vines
ar·bo´re·al *adj.* pertaining to trees
ar·bo·res´cent *adj.* branching — **ar·bo·res´cence** *n.*

ar·bo·re´tum *n.* botanical garden
ar´bor·vi´tae *n.* evergreen shrub
arc *n.* a section of a curve
ar·cade´ *n.* a row of shops
ar·cane´ *adj.* secret; mysterious
arch *adj.* most distinguished; crafty —*n.* a curved supporting structure —*vi.* be curved like an arch —*vt.* to form into a curve
ar´chae·ol´o·gy (*Brit.*) *n.* the study of places and artifacts of the past —**ar·chae·o·log´i·cal** *adj.* —**ar·chae·ol´o·gist** *n.*
ar·cha´ic *adj.* ancient; old–fashioned
arch´an·gel *n.* a high ranking angel
ar´cha·ism *n.* an obsolete expression; an antiquated style
arch´bish´op *n.* a church official
arch·bish´op·ric *n.* the office of an archbishop
arch·dea´con *n.* a lay church official —**arch·dea´con·ate** *n.*
arch´di´o·cese *n.* the jurisdiction of an archbishop
arch·en´e·my *n.* chief adversary
ar´che·ol´o·gy (*US*) *n. var. of archaeology* —**ar·che·o·log´i·cal** *adj.* —**ar·che·ol´o·gist** *n.*
ar´cher·y *n.* the art of shooting with bow and arrow
ar´che·type *n.* a standard pattern; model —**ar´che·typ·al** *adj.* —**ar·che·typ´i·cal·ly** *adv.*
arch´fiend´ *n.* a principal demon
ar´chi·pel´a·go *n.* a chain of islands
ar´chi·tect´ *n.* a designer; a planner —**ar·chi·tec´tur·al** *adj.* —**ar´chi·tec´ture** *n.*
ar´chive, ar´chives *n.* place where records are collected and stored —**ar·chi´val** *adj.*
arch´way *n.* passage under an arch
arc lamp, arc light a high intensity light
arc´tic *adj.* of the polar regions
ar´dent *adj.* passionate; enthusiastic; zealous —**ar´dent·ly** *adv.*
ar´dor *n.* passion; enthusiasm
ar´du·ous *adj.* laborious; strenuous —**ar´du·ous·ly** *adv.*
a´re·a *n.* a section of land; the extent or scope of anything
area code (*US*) a three digit telephone prefix by locality
a´re·a·way´ *n.* open space in or around a building
a·re´na *n.* an area for sporting events; a sphere of conflict
ar´gent *adj.* like silver; gray–white —*n.* silver; a silvery quality or color
ar´gen·tine *adj.* silvery —*n.* a silver–white metal of tin and zinc
ar´gil *n.* white clay; potter's earth
ar´gon *n.* an inert gas
ar´got *n.* words peculiar to a group, trade, etc.
ar´gue *vi.* to dispute —*vt.* attempt to prove —**ar´gu·a·ble** *adj.* —**ar´gu·a·bly** *adv.*
ar´gu·ment *n.* reason offered as proof; the art of reasoning; a discussion or debate —**ar·gu·men·ta´tion** *n.*
ar·gu·men´ta·tive *adj.* disposed to argue; characterized by argument; open to question
ar´gyle, ar´gyll *n.* a design of diamonds overlaid with a contrasting design
a´ri·a *n.* a melody; an elegant solo
ar´id *adj.* dry, parched; desolate, barren; dull, uninteresting
a·rise´ *vi.* ascend upward; to emanate from something
ar´is·toc´ra·cy *n.* government by the privileged; nobility; the upper class
a·ris´to·crat´ *n.* member of the aristocracy —**a·ris·to·crat´ic** *adj.* —**a·ris·to·crat´i·cal·ly** *adv.*
a·rith´me·tic´ *n.* calculating by numbers —**ar·ith·met´ic, ar·ith·met´i·cal** *adj.*
arithmetic mean the middle value of a group of numbers
arithmetic progression a sequence of values which differ by a constant quantity
ark *n.* a flat–bottomed boat
arm *n.* an upper limb; part of a garment; part of a chair; thing that functions like an arm; a weapon —*vi.* prepare for conflict —*vt.* provide with weapons
ar·ma´da *n.* a fleet of warships
Ar´ma·ged´don *n.* a decisive battle
ar´ma·ment *n.* forces equipped for battle; equipping for war
ar´ma·ture *n.* a core which revolves through a magnetic field; arms or armor; protective devises, as an animal's shell
arm´chair *n.* a chair with sides
ar´mis·tice *n.* a truce; a temporary cessation of hostilities
ar·moire´ a large storage cabinet
ar´mor *n.* protective covering; the vehicles of war —*vt.* to don armor —**ar´mored** *adj.*
ar´mor·er *n.* a manufacturer of arms; custodian of small arms
ar´mor·y *n.* place where arms are manufactured or stored
ar´my *n.* body of soldiers; a large number
a·ro´ma *n.* an agreeable odor; a distinctive quality —**ar´o·mat´ic, ar´o·mat´i·cal** *adj.*
a·round´ *adv.* so as to surround; in the opposite direction; from place to place; in proximity —*prep.* encircling; on the other side of; in proximity
a·rouse´ *vt.* to awaken; to stir up, excite —**a·rous´al** *n.*
ar·peg´gi·o *n.* sounding of notes of a chord in rapid succession
ar·raign´ *vt.* to accuse; summon to face charges —**ar·raign´ment** *n.*
ar·range´ *vt.* put in order; come to terms; orchestrate music
ar·range´ment *n.* that arranged; the way in which something is ordered; a musical adaptation
ar´rant *adj.* notoriously wicked
ar·ray´ *n.* orderly display; fine garments; impressive gathering —*vt.* gather in order; adorn
ar·rear´, ar·rears´ *n.* behind; that which is behind —**in arrears** behind in payment
ar·rest´ *n.* capture —*vt.* to slow or stop; to capture and detain
ar·rest´ing *adj.* attracting attention; noteworthy
ar·rive´ *vi.* to reach a destination; attain success —**ar·riv´al** *n.*
ar´ro·gant *adj.* overbearing; marked by vanity —**ar´ro·gance** *n.* —**ar´ro·gant·ly** *adv.*
ar´row *n.* a pointed shaft
ar´row·root *n.* a nutritious starch used in food preparation
ar·roy´o *n.* a steep–sided dry gulch; a stream
ar´se·nal *n.* place where arms are made or stored
ar´son *n.* setting of fire with criminal intent —**ar´son·ist** *n.*
art *n.* skill; any craft requiring skill; creative work —**arts** *pl. n.* the humanities
ar·te´ri·al *adj.* of vessels that carry blood from the heart; like an artery: *an arterial highway*
ar´ter·y *n.* vessel that carries blood from the heart; any main channel, as of communication
art´ful *adj.* crafty or cunning; ingenious or resourceful —**art´ful·ly** *adv.* —**art´ful·ness** *n.*
ar·thri´tis *n.* painful inflammation of a joint —**ar·thrit´ic** *adj.*
ar´thro·pod *n.* invertebrate with a segmented body, such as an insect, spider, or crab
ar´ti·choke´ *n.* an edible plant resembling the thistle
ar´ti·cle *n.* written piece; clause in a document; a distinct item
ar·tic´u·lar *adj.* pertaining to the joints —**ar·tic´u·lar·ly** *adv.*
ar·tic´u·late *adj.* clearly spoken —*vi.* speak clearly; to be jointed —*vt.* to speak clearly; to form with joints —**ar·tic´u·la´tion** *n.*
ar´ti·fact´ *n.* an article fashioned by humans, especially a relic
ar´ti·fice *n.* a clever scheme
ar´ti·fi´cial *adj.* not natural; imitation; affected —**ar·ti·fi·ci·al´i·ty** *n.* —**ar·ti·fi´cial·ly** *adv.*
ar·til´ler·y *n.* ordnance, cannon; a branch of the military
ar´ti·san *n.* a craftsman; one skilled
art´ist *n.* one skilled, esp. with a sense of style —**ar´tist·ry** *n.*
ar·tiste´ *n.* a skillful performer
ar·tis´tic, ar·tis´ti·cal *adj.* pertaining to arts; pleasing; receptive to art —**ar·tis´ti·cal·ly** *adv.*
art´less *adj.* without deception; natural; innocent; unskilled; lacking taste —**art´less·ly** *adv.* —**art´less·ness** *n.*
art´y *adj.* affected; ostentatious —**art´i·ness** *n.*
as·cend´ *vi.* move or slope upward —*vt.* move upward; succeed, as to a throne —**as·cend´a·ble, as·cend´i·ble** *adj.* —**as·cent´** *n.*
as·cend´ant, as·cend´ent *adj.* rising; commanding —*n.* position of prominence —**as·cend´an·cy, as·cend´en·cy** *n.*
as´cer·tain´ *vt.* make certain —**as·cer·tain´a·ble** *adj.* —**as·cer·tain´a·bly** *adv.*
as·cet´ic *adj.* austere; *n.* one who leads a life of austerity —**as·cet´i·cism** *n.*
as·cribe´ *vt.* to impute; attribute as coming from or caused by
a·scor´bic ac´id *n.* vitamin C
as´cot *n.* a type of necktie
a·sex´u·al *adj.* having no distinct sexual organs —**a·sex·u·al´i·ty** *n.* —**a·sex´u·al·ly** *adv.*
ash *n.* residue left from burning; a tough, elastic tree or its wood
a·shamed´ *adj.* shame caused by a failing; impeded by embarrassment —**a·sham´ed·ly** *adj.*
ash´en *adj.* pale in color; pertaining to ash wood
a·shore´ *adv.* on the shore; aground
ash´y *adj.* like ashes; ash colored; covered with ashes
a·side´ *adv.* to one side; apart
as´i·nine *adj.* silly —**as´i·nine·ly** *adv.* —**as·i·nin´i·ty** *n.*
ask *vi.* make inquiries —*vt.* to question; inquire about; make a request; state a price
a·skance´ *adv.* with suspicion; with a sideways glance
a·skew´ *adj., adv.* out of line; to one side
a·slant´ *adj.* slanting; tilted —*adv.* in a slanting position
a·sleep´ *adj.* dormant; sleeping; dead —*adv.* into a state of rest
a·so´cial *adj.* avoiding social contact; self–centered
asp *n.* the European viper
as·par´a·gus *n.* a plant with tender, edible shoots
as´pect *n.* appearance; a particular viewpoint
as·per´i·ty *n.* roughness; harshness
as·perse´ *vt.* to accuse falsely; to slander —**as·per´sion** *n.*
as´phalt´ *n.* a material used for paving —**as·phal´tum** *n.*
as·phyx´i·ate *vt.* to suffocate —**as·phyx´i·a´tion** *n.*
as´pic *n.* gelatin garnish or mold
as´pir·ant *adj.* aspiring —*n.* one who tries; a candidate
as´pi·ra´tion *n.* extreme desire; a thing desired
as·pire´ *vi.* long for or seek after
as´pi·rin *n.* acetylsalicylic acid; a remedy for headache or fever
ass *n.* a beast of burden; a stubborn or foolish person
as·sail´ *vt.* attack violently —**as·sail´a·ble** *adj.* —**as·sail´ant** *n.*
as·sas´si·nate *vt.* to murder; to attack by slander or inuendo —**as·sas´sin, as·sas·si·na´tion** *n.*
as·sault´ *n.* an attack —*vi., vt.* make an attack upon
as·say´ *n.* a testing —*vt.* analyze
as·sem´blage *n.* a gathering
as·sem´ble *vi., vt.* gather; put together —**as·sem´bly** *n.*
assembly line an arrangement for efficient manufacturing
as·sent´ *n.* agreement; consent —*vi.* agree —**as·sent´er, as·sen·tor** *n.* —**as·sent´ing·ly** *adv.*
as·sert´ *vt.* declare; state —**as·sert´a·ble, as·sert´i·ble** *adj.* —**as·ser´tion** *n.*
as·ser´tive *adj.* authoritative; insistent —**as·ser´tive·ly** *adv.* —**as·ser´tive·ness** *n.*
as·sess´ *vt.* set a value; impose, as a tax; to evaluate —**as·sess´a·ble** *adj.* —**as·sess´ment** *n.*
as´set *n.* property of value
as·sev´er·ate *vt.* declare firmly
as·sid´u·ous *adj.* painstaking; diligent —**as·sid´u·ous·ly** *adv.*
as·sign´ *vt.* to designate; appoint; to ascribe —**as·signment** *n.*
as·sig·na´tion *n.* an appointment; an illicit meeting
as·sim´i·late *vi.* be absorbed —*vt.* absorb; adapt or conform —**as·sim·i·la´tion** *n.*
as·sist´ *n.* act of helping —*vi.* aid —*vt.* help; work as a helper —**as·sis´tance** *n.* —**as·sis´tant** *n.*
as·so´ci·ate´ *adj.* joined with others; linked —*n.* a co–worker;

thing linked —*vt.* unite; bring into relationship —*vi.* be in league with —**as·so´ci·a´tion** *n.*
as´so·nance *n.* resemblance in sound; an approximation
as·sort´ *vi.* fall into like groups —*vt.* classify; divide into groups
as·sor´ted *adj.* consisting of variety; diverse; sorted or classified
as·sort´ment *n.* a collection
as·suage´ *vt.* alleviate; calm
as·sume´ *vt.* undertake; take for granted —**as·sum´a·ble** *adj.*
as·sump´tion *n.* supposition —**as·sump´tive** *adj.*
as·sur´ance *n.* confidence; conviction; encouraging statement
as·sure´ *vt.* to convey confidence; to guarantee —**as·sur´ance** *n.*
as·sured´ *adj.* undoubted; sure
as´ter·isk *n.* a star–like character (*) used to mark references
asth´ma *n.* a respiratory ailment
asth·mat´ic *n.* one suffering from asthma —**asth·mat´ic, asth·mat´i·cal** *adj.* affected with asthma
a·stig´ma·tism´ *n.* a visual defect —**as·tig·mat´ic** *adj.*
a·stir´ *adj., adv.* moving about
as·ton´ish *vt.* to stun, amaze —**as·ton´ish·ing** *adj.*
as·ton´ish·ment *n.* surprise; wonder; thing causing surprise
a·stound´ *vt.* astonish; startle —**as·tound´ing** *adj.* —**as·tound´ing·ly** *adv.*
as´tral *adj.* of the stars
a·stray´ *adj., adv.* off the correct path; erring
a·stride´ *adj., adv* with one leg on each side
as·trin´gent *adj.* stern; severe —**as·trin´gen·cy** *n.* —**as·trin´gent·ly** *adv.*
as´tro·dome *n.* enclosed field for sporting events; a structure for making celestial observations
as´tro·labe *n.* an old navigational instrument
as·trol´o·gy *n.* belief that stars can influence human affairs —**as·trol´o·ger** *n.* —**as·tro·log´i·cal** *adj.*
as´tro·naut´ *n.* a space traveler
as·tro·nau´tics *pl. n.* the science of space travel
as·tro·nom´ic, as·tro·nom´i·cal *adj.* of astronomy; numerous —**as·tro·nom´i·cal·ly** *adv.*
as·tron´o·my *n.* study of stars, planets, etc. —**as·tron´o·mer** *n.*
as´tro·phys´ics *n.* study of the physical properties of stars, planets, etc. —**as·tro·phys´i·cist** *n.*
as·tute´ *adj.* exhibiting a keen mind; shrewd —**as·tute´ly** *adv.*
a·sun´der *adj.* disconnected —*adv.* in pieces
a·sy´lum *n.* sanctuary; home for the sick
a·sym´me·try *n.* lack of proportion
a·sym·met´ric, a·sym·met´ri·cal *adj.* disproportionate
at´a·vism *n.* retrogression —**at´a·vist** *n.* —**at·a·vis´tic** *adj.*
a·tax´i·a *n.* failure to control muscular movement —**a·tax´ic** *adj., n.*
at´el·ier *n.* an artist's studio
a´the·ism *n.* denial that gods exist —**a´the·ist** *n.* —**a·the·is´tic** *adj.* —**a·the·is´ti·cal·ly** *adv.*
ath´lete *n.* one trained in athletics —**ath·let´ic** *adj.* —**ath·let´i·cal·ly** *adv.*
ath·let´ics *pl. n.* sporting contests, gymnastics, etc.
a·thwart´ *adv.* from side to side —*prep.* across; in opposition to
a·tilt´ *adj., adv.* tilted upward
at´las *n.* a book of maps
at´mos·phere´ *n.* air encircling earth; mood of an environment; decor —**at·mos·pher´ic** *adj.* —**at·mos·pher´i·cal·ly** *adv.*
at·mos·pher´ics *n.* broadcast interference
a´toll *n.* a coral island and its reef, enclosing a lagoon
at´om *n.* a tiny particle; smallest combinable particle —**a·tom´ic** *adj.* —**a·tom´i·cal·ly** *adv.*
atomic clock a precise instrument for measuring time
atomic energy energy liberated by fission or fusion of atoms
atomic number number which serves to identify an element
atomic weight the weight of an atom of an element relative to that of an atom of carbon
at´om·ize´ *vt.* to separate into atoms; to make liquid into a fine spray —**at´om·iz·er** *n.*
a·to·nal´i·ty *n.* lack of tonal quality —**a·ton´al, a·ton·al·is´tic** *adj.* —**a·ton´al·ly** *adv.*
a·tone´ *vi.* to make amends —**a·ton´a·ble, a·tone´a·ble** *adj.*
a·tone´ment *n.* reparation for wrong
a·top´ *adj., adv.* on or at the top
a´tri·um *n.* entrance hall; open area in a building; one of the chambers of the heart
a·tro´cious *adj.* cruel, wicked; offensive, tasteless —**a·tro´cious·ly** *adv.* —**a·troc´i·ty** *n.*
at´ro·phy *n.* a wasting away of body tissue —*vi., vt.* to waste away —**a·troph´ic** *adj.*
at·tach´ *vi.* to adhere —*vt.* to fasten on; to take by legal means —**at·tach´a·ble** *adj* **at·tach´ment** *n.*
at·ta·ché *n.* a person assigned to a diplomatic mission
attaché case *n.* a briefcase; a flat case with a hinged lid
at·tack´ *n.* hostile action —*vt.* strike out against; assault; take up vigorously —**at·tack´er** *n.*
at·tain´ *vi.* to arrive —*vt.* to gain; to achieve —**at·tain´a·ble** *adj.* —**at·tain´ment** *n.*
at·tain´der *n.* loss of civil rights by one sentenced for a crime
at´tar *n.* a fragrant oil extracted from flower petals
at·tempt´ *n.* a try —*vt.* to try; make an effort —**at·tempt´a·ble** *adj.* —**at·tempt´er** *n.*
at·tend´ *vi.* to heed; give care —*vt.* minister to; to accompany; be present
at·tend´ance *n.* one's presence; the record of one's presence over time; collectively, those who attend
at·tend´ant *adj.* present; waiting upon; following as a consequence —*n.* one who waits upon; a servant; an accompaniment
at·ten´tion *n.* concentration; alertness; notice; attentiveness
at·ten´tive *adj.* thoughtful, considerate —**at·ten´tive·ly** *adv.*
at·ten´u·ate *vt., vi.* make or become thin or fine; reduce or become lessened —**at·ten´u·a·ble** *adj.* —**at·ten·u·a´tion** *n.*
at·test´ *vt.* to testify; to certify under oath
at´tic *n.* an area directly beneath the roof and above the last full floor of a building
at·tire´ *n.* clothing —*vt.* to dress
at´ti·tude´ *n.* bearing of a person; position in relation to a surface; disposition
at·tor´ney (*US*) *n.* a lawyer
at·tract´ *vt.* be drawn towards; entice —**at·trac´tion** *n.*
at·tract´ive *adj.* having power to entice —**at·tract´ive·ly** *adv.* —**at·tract´ive·ness** *n.*
at´tri·bute´ *n.* a quality or characteristic —**at·tri´bute** *vt.* to impute —**at·trib´ut·a·ble** *adj.*
at·tri´tion *n.* wearing away; loss of workers, as by retirement
at·tune´ *vt.* to adjust; to bring into conformity with
a·typ´i·c, a·typ´i·cal *adj.* not characteristic; inconsistent with the norm
au´burn *adj., n.* reddish–brown color
auc´tion *n.* a sale by bid —*vt.* to sell by bid —**auc·tion·eer´** *n.*
au cou·rant´ *adj.* up to date; fashionable
au·da´cious *adj.* bold, daring —**au·da´cious·ly** *adv.* —**au·da´cious·ness, au·dac´i·ty** *n.*
au´di·ble *adj.* able to be heard —**au´di·bly** *adv.*
au´di·ence *n.* a formal interview; those who attend a show, etc.
au´di·o *adj.* involving sound waves —*n.* sound
audio frequency sound waves within the range of human hearing
au´di·o·phile´ *n.* one interested in high–fidelity sound
au´di·o·vis´u·al *adj.* embracing both sound and sight —*n.* material that incorporates sound and sight
au´dit *n.* a verification of finances —*vt.* to examine; to attend college classes as a listener
au·di´tion *n.* a tryout —*vi., vt.* to try out, as for a job
au´dit·or *n.* one who examines accounts; one who attends a class without credit
au´di·to´ri·um *n.* a meeting room
au´di·to·ry *adj.* pertaining to hearing
au´ger *n.* a boring tool
aug·ment´ *vi., vt.* to increase; supplement —**aug·men·ta´tion** *n.* —**aug·men´tive** *adj.*
au grat´in *adj.* cooked with cheese or bread crumbs
au´gur *vi., vt.* to predict; be an omen
au´gu·ry *n.* the art of divination; an omen
au·gust´ *adj.* inspiring reverence; imposing
au na·tu·rel´ *adj.* of ungarnished food; nude
aunt *n.* the sister of one's parent or the wife of one's uncle; a title of affection
au´ra *n.* an invisible field or quality; a gentle breeze
au´ral *adj.* pertaining to the hearing
au´re·ate *adj.* the color of gold
au´ri·cle *n.* one of two atriums of the heart; the outer ear
au·ric´u·lar *adj.* relating to hearing
au·rif´er·ous *adj.* containing gold
au·ro´ra *n.* the dawn; a luminous display in the polar night sky
aus´cul·tate *vt.* to examine by listening —**aus·cul·ta´tion** *n.*
aus´pice *n.* an omen; patronage
aus·pi´cious *adj.* favorable; fortunate —**aus·pi´cious·ly** *adv.* —**aus·pi´cious·ness** *n.*
aus·tere´ *adj.* stern; plain in decor —**aus·ter´i·ty** *n.*
au·then´tic *adj.* genuine; official —**au·then´ti·cal·ly** *adv.* —**au´then·tic´i·ty** *n.*
au·then´ti·cate´ *vt.* verify; prove genuine —**au·then´ti·ca´tion** *n.* —**au·then´ti·ca·tor** *n.*
au´thor *n.* one who originates —**au´thor·ship** *n.*
au´thor·ise´ (*Brit.*), **au´thor·ize´** (*US*) *vt.* to approve; to permit —**au´thor·ised, au´thor·ized** *adj.*
au·thor·i·tar´i·an *adj.* autocratic; strict —*n.* an advocate of authority
au·thor´i·ta·tive *adj.* with authority —**au·thor´i·ta·tive·ly** *adv.*
au·thor´i·ty *n.* power to command; one invested with power
au´to·bi·og´ra·phy *n.* one's life story —**au´to·bi´o·graph´i·cal** *adj.* —**au´to·bi´o·graph´i·cal·ly** *adv.*
au·toc´ra·cy *n.* absolute rule; a dictatorship; a state governed by an absolute ruler
au´to·crat´ *n.* an absolute ruler —**au·to·crat´ic** *adj.* —**au·to·crat´i·cal·ly** *adv.*
au´to·graph´ *n.* signature —*vt.* to sign
au´to·mate *vt.* to operate by automation
au´to·mat´ic *adj.* involuntary; self–operating —**au·to·mat´i·cal·ly** *adv.*
au´to·ma´tion *n.* automatic operation
au·tom´a·ton *n.* a robot; a machine controlled by a computer; one who moves mechanically
au´to·mo·bile (*US*) *n.* a passenger vehicle; a car
au·to·nom´ic *adj.* involuntary; acting unconsciously —**au·to·nom´i·cal·ly** *adv.*
autonomic nervous system that which controls involuntary actions of the body
au·ton´o·mous *adj.* independent; acting without supervision —**au·ton´o·mous·ly** *adv.*
au·ton´o·my *n.* self government; functioning of a group apart from its parent organization
au´to·pi´lot *n.* a device to maintain an aircraft's course and attitude
au´top·sy *n.* medical examination of a dead body
au´tumn *n.* the season between summer and winter; (*US*) fall —**au·tum´nal** *adj.*
aux·il´ia·ry *adj.* helping; supplementary
a·vail´ *vi.* to assist or aid —*vt.* to be of value —*n.* benefit

a·vail´a·ble *adj.* at one´s disposal; obtainable **—a·vail´a·bil´i·ty** *n.*

av´a·lanche´ *n.* a mass of snow or earth falling from a height; anything in an abnormal quantity

a·vant–garde´ *adj.* reflecting recent trends *—n.* those who promote new or unconventional techniques

av´a·rice *n.* greed; a passion for wealth **—av·a·ri´cious** *adj.* **—av·a·ri´cious·ly** *adv.*

av´a·tar *n.* the incarnation of a Hindu god; physical phenomenon

a·venge´ *vt.* to exact punishment for a wrong

av´e·nue *n.* a wide street; an approach; a means of access

a·ver´ *vt.* to declare to be true

av´er·age *adj.* of a median value; not exceptional *—n.* the value of several elements divided by the number of elements *—vt.* to find or fix an average value

a·verse´ *adj.* opposed; reluctant **—a·verse´ly** *adv.*

a·ver´sion *n.* a dislike; profound distaste; that which is distasteful **—a·ver´sive** *adj.*

a·vert´ *vt.* to turn away; ward off **—a·vert´a·ble, a·vert´i·ble** *adj.*

a´vi·ar´y *n.* a place for keeping birds

a´vi·a´tion *n.* the development and operation of aircraft **—a´vi·a·tor** *n.*

av´id *adj.* eager; enthusiastic **—av´id·ly** *adv.*

av·o·ca´tion *n.* a hobby; a sideline **—av·o·ca´tion·al** *adj.*

a·void´ *vt.* shun; keep from happening **—a·void´a·ble** *adj.* **—a·void´a·bly** *adv.* **—a·void´ance** *n.*

av´oir·du·pois´ *n.* the system of weights of the United States

a·vow´ *vt.* declare openly; confess **—a·vow´a·ble** *adj.*

a·vow´al *n.* acknowledgment; open admission

a·vowed´ *adj.* readily acknowledged; openly declared **—a·vow´ed·ly** *adv.*

a·vun´cu·lar *adj.* of an uncle

a·wait´ *vt.* watch for; be ready for

a·wake´ *adj.* not sleeping; alert *—vi.* to wake; become aware *—vt.* arouse; to make aware

a·wak´en *vi., vt.* to awake

a·wak´en·ing *adj.* stimulating; exciting *—n.* a rekindling

a·ward´ *n.* a judgment; a prize *—vt.* to grant by judgement

a·ware´ *adj.* familiar with; conscious **—a·ware´ness** *n.*

a·wash´ *adj., adv.* at water level; overflowing; inundated: *awash in job applications*

a·way´ *adj.* at a distance *—adv.* distant; to the side; diligently: *working away*; removed from one´s keeping; immediately: *fire away —interj.* begone

awe *n.* wonder or fear *—vt.* to fill with wonder

awe´some *adj.* overwhelming; inciting awe

awe´struck *adj.* stunned; impressed

aw´ful *adj.* inspiring fear; dreadful; formidable

aw´ful·ly *adv.* in a dreadful manner; exceedingly: *awfully bright*

a·while´ *adv.* for a time

awk´ward *adj.* clumsy; embarrassing **—awk´ward·ly** *adv.* **—awk´ward·ness** *n.*

awl *n.* a pointed tool

awn *n.* bristlelike part of grasses

awn´ing *n.* a structural projection to ward off sun and rain

awry´ *adj., adv.* not straight

ax, axe *n.* a tool for chopping wood

ax´i·al *adj.* along an axis

ax´i·ol´o·gy *n.* study of values

ax´i·om *n.* an adage **—ax´i·o·mat´ic** *adj.* **—ax·i·o·mat´i·cal·ly** *adv.*

ax´is *n., pl.* **ax´es** a line around which an object rotates

ax´le *n.* a shaft for a wheel

az´i·muth *n.* the arc between the horizon and a star

a·zo´ic *adj.* referring to the time on earth before the appearance of life

az´ure *adj.* sky–blue *—n.*

b, B *n.* second letter of the alphabet; second–rate, as *a B–movie*

bab´ble *n.* rippling sound; incoherent noises *—vi.* prattle foolishly *—vt.* disclose carelessly

babe *n.* an infant; one lacking in experience or knowledge

ba´bel *n.* a bedlam of sounds

ba´by *adj.* childish; small *—n.* an infant; youngest or smallest; one who acts like a child *—vt.* to handle gingerly **—ba´by·ish** *adj.*

baby doll a short woman´s nightgown

baby food puréed food for an infant

baby grand a small grand piano

baby´s–breath a plant having small white or pink flowers

ba´by·sit´ *vi., vt.* to care for children **—ba´by–sit·ter** *n.*

bac´ca·lau´re·ate *n.* a bachelor´s degree; a farewell address

bac·cha·nal´ *adj.* drunken revelry *—n.* a reveler; a riotous feast **—bac·cha·na´lia** *n.* **—bac·cha·na´lian** *adj.*

back *adj.* in the rear; isolated; of an earlier time *—adv.* toward the rear; to a bygone place or condition *—n.* hindmost part; spine of a body; far side; part of an object not normally used: *back of a knife*; spine of a book *—vi., vt.* move or cause to move backward; support or assist

back´bit´er *vt.* one who speaks ill of another

back´bone *n.* the spinal column; the main support: *backbone of the country*; courage; spunk

back burner place of low priority

back´drop *n.* a background

back´er *n.* a supporter; one who provides financial help or encouragement; an apologist

back´fire *n.* a fire set to halt a forest fire; premature explosion in an engine; backward explosion in a gun *—vi.* set a backfire; explosive sound of a backfire; achieve an opposite result

back´gam´mon *n.* a board game for two players, often involving wagers

back´ground *n.* that in the rear; part of a picture or scene behind the main object; peripheral; one´s experience; sound to enhance a performance; a description of prior events

back´hand *adj.* not straightforward or sincere *—adv.* with a backhand stroke *—n.* a movement made with the hand turned backward

back´hand·ed *adj.* with the hand turned backward; insincere; ironic; turned in an opposite direction

back´ing *n.* support; a group of supporters; the act of moving backward; material added for strength

back´lash´ *n.* a sharp recoil; a reaction

back´log´ *n.* a reserve; orders to be filled or processed

back´–ped·al *vi* to retreat

back seat *n.* a seat in the rear; a position of secondary importance

back´side *n.* the back part; the posterior or rump

back´slap *vi.* insincere friendliness *—vt.* to be overly friendly

back´slide *vi.* return to old ways

back´spin *n.* reverse rotation; a rebounded effect or result

back´stage´ *adj.* situated off–stage *—adv.* behind or to the side of the stage *—n.* the rear or sides of a stage, as wings or dressing rooms

back´stairs´ *n.* stairs at the back of a dwelling *—adj.* underhanded; indirect

back´stop *n.* a screen on a playing field to confine the game projectile *—vi.* to sustain or reinforce

back´stretch *n.* the part of a racecourse farthest from the spectators

back talk *n.* an insolent or argumentative response

back´track *vi.* to retrace steps; retreat from an earlier opinion

back´up *n.* support; an accumulation: something held in readiness

back´ward *adj.* reversed; bashful; retarded *—adv.* in the direction of the back; toward time past; in reverse order **—back´wards** *adv.* **—back´ward·ness** *n.*

back´wa·ter *n.* a place judged to be backward or undeveloped

back´woods *adj.* undeveloped; culturally deprived *—n.* a sparsely settled area; an area not culturally advanced

ba´con *n.* cured meat from the back or side of a hog

bac·te´ri·a *n. pl., sing.* **bac·te´ri·um** microorganisms that cause disease, fermentation, etc. **—bac·te´ri·al** *adj.*

bac·te´ri·cide *n.* a substance which destroys bacteria

bad *adj.* not satisfactory; unacceptable; evil; naughty; offensive; incorrect; detrimental; unfortunate; improper; concerned: *feel bad about* **—not bad, not half bad, not so bad** rather good *—n.* that which is bad; those who are bad

badge *n.* a symbol of authority

badg´er *n.* a burrowing mammal *—vt.* to tease or pester

bad´i·nage *n.* playful banter

bad´ly *adv.* incorrectly; offensively; detrimentally; with intense desire

baf´fle *vt.* to confound; to obstruct or impede **—baf´fle·ment** *n.* **—baf´fling** *adj.*

bag *n.* a sack, purse, suitcase, etc.; amount a bag contains *—vi.* to bulge or hang loosely *—vt.* place in a bag; to attain, as by hunting **—in the bag** certain **—left holding the bag** charged with responsibility or blame **—bag and baggage** completely; with all one´s possessions

bag´a·telle´ *n.* a trifle

ba´gel *n.* a hard roll shaped like a doughnut

bag´gage *n.* luggage; a lascivious woman; useless idea or practice

bag´gy *adj.* loose; ill–fitting

bag´man *n.* one who collects or distributes illegal money

ba·guet´, ba·guette´ *n.* crystal of a narrow, rectangular shape

bail *n.* security to insure appearance in court *—vt.* to free one on security; to remove water **—bail´ment** *n.* **—bail´or** *n.*

bail´iff *n.* an officer of the court

bail´i·wick *n.* the office of a bailiff; one´s place or sphere of influence

bail out parachute from an airplane; post bond; distance oneself from unpleasantness

bails´man *n.* one who posts bail

bait *n.* an enticement *—vt.* to lure or entice; to tease or provoke

bake *vi.* to become firm and dry from heat *—vt.* to cook or harden with dry heat

bak´er *n.* one who makes and sells baked products **—baker´s dozen** thirteen, giving extra to avoid penalty for short count

bak´er·y *n.* a place for making or selling baked goods

baking powder a baking soda mixture used as a leavening agent

baking soda (*US*) sodium bicarbonate; a compound used in cooking, cleaning, as an antacid, etc.

bak´sheesh, bak´shish *n.* a gratuity; a bribe

bal·a·lai´ka *n.* a three–stringed musical instrument of Russian origin

bal´ance *n.* a device for weighing; amount owed; a state of equilibrium; amount left; a state of harmony *—vi.* to be equal *—vt.* to compare; to compensate; to reconcile, as financial records

balance of payments difference between payments and receipts for trade between nations

balance of power comparison of the relative strength of nations

balance of trade a comparison of the value of imports and exports

balance sheet a statement of financial condition

bal´co·ny *n.* a platform outside an upper window; an upper level of seats in a theater

bald *adj.* without hair or natural covering; unadorned

bal´der·dash *n.* nonsense

bald´faced *adj.* audacious, brazen; obvious, as *a baldfaced lie*

bale *n.* a large bundle —*vt.* to tie or wrap —**bal´er** *n.*
ba·leen´ *n.* whalebone
bale´ful *adj.* noxious; harmful
balk *vi.* refuse to proceed or take part
balk´y *adj.* prone to stop suddenly; reluctant to participate
ball *n.* a sphere; game that uses a round object for throwing, hitting, etc.; a formal dance
bal´lad *n.* a sentimental song; a song or poem that tells a story —**bal·lad·eer´** *n.*
bal·lis´tics *n.* the study of the motion of projectiles —**bal·lis´tic** *adj.*
bal·loon´ *n.* a bag inflated so as to float; a small inflated toy or decoration; final payment on an installment loan
bal´lot *n.* paper vote; a vote cast; a list of those running for office
ball´point pen´ a writing instrument that distributes ink by use of a ball bearing
ball´room *n.* a large room for parties and dancing
bal´ly·hoo *n.* boisterous patter; an overblown promotion
balm *n.* an ointment for healing or soothing; anything soothing
balm´y *adj.* aromatic; soothing; slightly mad; very foolish —**balm´i·ness** *n.*
ba·lo´ney, **bo·lo´gna** *n.* a large, mild sausage; idle or nonsensical talk
bal´sa *n.* a tree of tropical America; the light wood from the balsa tree
bal´sam *n.* a fragrance; a tree which exudes balsam; an aromatic ointment; a soothing or healing agent
bal´us·ter *n.* one of the pillars which support a hand rail
bal´us·trade *n.* a hand rail and its supporting balusters
bam·boo´ *n.* a hollow–stemmed grass
bam·boo´zle *vi.* to practice trickery —*vt.* to deceive
ban *n.* a prohibition; an ecclesiastical sentence of interdiction —*vt.* to forbid or prohibit; to impose a ban
ba´nal *adj.* commonplace; trite —**ba·nal´i·ty** *n.* —**ba·nal´ly** *adv.*
band *n.* a flat strip of material; a broad contrasting stripe; a range of frequencies: *a broadcast band*; a group of persons —*vi.* to associate —*vt.* to encircle or join with a strip of material; to unite
band´age *n.* cloth to bind a wound —*vt.* to bind or cover with a cloth
ban·dan´a, **ban·dan´na** *n.* a large, brightly colored handkerchief
ban´dit *n.* a robber, thief; one who steals or defrauds
band´lead·er, **band´mas·ter** *n.* leader of a group of musicians
ban·do·leer´, **ban·do·lier´** a broad belt with loops for cartidges
band saw a motor driven saw
band shell (*US*) a bandstand for outdoor concerts
band´stand *n.* an outdoor stage for musicians or other entertainers
band´wag·on *n.* a decorated wagon that carries a band in a parade —**climb on the bandwagon** change to an apparently winning position
ban´dy *adj.* curved or bowed —*vt.* exchange quips; to pass along
ban´dy·leg´ged *adj.* bowlegged
bane *n.* a cause of distress or destruction; a deadly poison
bang *n.* a sudden loud noise; enthusiasm —*vt.* to strike loudly —*vi.* to make a loud noise; to strike noisily
ban´ish *vt.* to exile; to dismiss or drive away —**ban´ish·ment** *n.*
ban´is·ter, **ban´nis·ter** *n.* a handrail along a staircase
ban´jo *n.* a stringed instrument with a long narrow neck and circular sound box
bank *n.* a mound or heap; edge of a body of water; sloping of a curve or turn; financial institution; supply held in reserve; like elements stored together —*vi.* incline an airplane; trade at a bank —*vt.* form a slope; rebound at an angle; to deposit in a bank —**bank on** have faith in —**bank´a·ble** *adj.*
bank account an account with a bank; funds available to the holder of such an account
bank book a record of the transactions of a bank account
bank´er *n.* the owner or manager of a bank; a bank executive; one who holds stakes in a game of chance
bank note a promissary note issued by a bank
bank´roll (*US*) *n.* money which one possesses —*vt.* to back financially —**bank´roll·er** *n.*
bank´rupt *adj.* insolvent; unable to pay debts; wanting: *morally bankrupt* —*n.* one unable to pay debts —*vt.* cause to default
ban´ner *n.* a flag; a large display of greeting, advertisement, etc.; a newspaper headline
ban´quet *n.* a feast; a formal dinner
ban·quette´ *n.* a bench for seating along a wall, as in a restaurant
ban´shee *n.* in Gaelic folklore, a spirit whose wailing predicts death
ban´tam *n.* a small domestic fowl
ban´tam·weight *n.* a boxer who weighs from 113 to 118 pounds
ban´ter *n.* light–hearted jesting —*vi.* to exchange jibes —*vt.* to tease —**ban´ter·ing·ly** *adv.*
bap´tism *n.* purification rite of the Christian Church; an initiatory rite or experience —**bap´tis·mal** *adj.*
bap´tise (*Brit.*), **bap´tize** (*US*) *vt.* to consecrate by a ceremony
bar[1] *n.* an oblong piece of rigid material; anything that blocks access; the legal profession; a stripe to denote rank; a division in a musical score —*vt.* to close off; to exclude
bar[2] *n.* (*Brit.*) a room in a public house or club where drink is sold
bar[3] *n.* (*US*) establishment where beverages and food are sold
barb *n.* a sharp spine; a sharp retort
bar·bar´i·an *adj.* uncivilized —*n.* an uncultured person —**bar·bar´ic** *adj.* —**bar·bar´i·cal·ly** *adv.*
bar´bar·ism *n.* a savage state
bar·bar´i·ty *n.* brutal or crude conduct; vulgarity
bar´ba·rous *adj.* lacking in culture; crude; brutal —**bar´ba·rous·ly** *adv.* —**bar´ba·rous·ness** *n.*
bar´be·cue´ *n.* an outdoor celebration; food cooked over an open fire —*vt.* to roast over a charcoal fire; to baste with a tangy sauce
barbed *adj.* having pointed ends; sharp or piercing
barbed wire fencing wire with sharp pieces at regular intervals
bar´ber *n.* one who trims the hair, beard, etc. —*vt.* to trim the hair
bard *n.* a poet
bare *adj.* lacking clothing or covering; stark, plain; meager —*vt.* uncover, expose —**bare´ness** *n.*
bare´back *adj.* animal without a saddle —*adv.* without a saddle
bare´faced *adj.* with nothing concealed; impudent; obvious: *a barefaced lie*
bare´hand´ed *adj.* without benefit of a tool or weapon other than hands
bare´ly *adv.* only just; scarcely
bar´gain *n.* an understanding; a good price —*vi.* to negotiate
barge *n.* boat carrying freight on inland waters —*vi.* act clumsily
bar´i·tone´ *n.* musical range between bass and tenor
bark *n.* the covering of a tree; sound made by a dog —*vt.* to make the sound of a dog
bar´keep *n.* one who operates a bar; a bartender
bark´er *n.* one whose patter is intended to attract patrons
barn *n.* a farm building
bar´na·cle *n.* a type of marine crustacean
barn´storm *vi.* to tour rural areas, as for politicking
ba·rom´e·ter *n.* instrument that measures atmospheric pressure; anything that predicts change —**bar·o·met´ric** *adj.*
bar´on *n.* in British peerage, rank above a baronet and below a viscount; one having great power
bar´on·age, **bar´o·ny** *n.* the sphere of influence of a baron
ba·roque´ *adj.* characteristic of the style of 16th and 17th century Europe; pertaining to that period —*n.* the baroque form; anything characteristic of the baroque style
bar´racks *pl. n.* buildings for housing soldiers, workers, etc.
bar·ra·cu´da *n.* a large, voracious fish found in tropical seas
bar·rage´ *n.* heavy artillary fire; anything overwhelming
barred *adj.* blocked or decorated with bars; banned; not allowed
bar´rel *n.* a cylindrical storage container; any cylinder
bar´ren *adj.* incapable of reproducing; unproductive; desolate —**bar´ren·ly** *adv.* —**bar´ren·ness** *n.*
bar·rette´ (*US*) *n.* a small appliance for keeping hair in place
bar´ri·cade´ *n.* barrier or blockade —*vt.* to create a barrier
bar´ri·er *n.* an obstruction
bar´ris·ter *n.* an attorney
bar´tend´er *n.* one who mixes and serves beverages
bar´ter *n.* the exchange of goods or services —*vi., vt.* to trade
ba´sal *adj.* fundamental
ba·salt´ *n.* a dark volcanic rock
base *adj.* humble; cowardly; corrupt —*n.* a foundation; a starting place —*vt.* to form or place on a foundation; to establish a basis for
base´born *adj.* illegitimate; born of lower class parents; common
base´less *adj.* with no foundation; groundless; gratuitous
base´line *n.* a point of reference
base´ment *n.* a foundation or floor below the main floor of a building
bash *n.* a shattering blow —*vt.* to strike with a heavy blow
bash´ful *adj.* timid; shy —**bash´ful·ly** *adv.* —**bash´ful·ness** *n.*
ba´sic *adj.* fundamental; forming a basis —**ba´si·cal·ly** *adv.*
ba´sil *n.* an aromatic plant of the mint family or its leaves
ba·sil´i·ca *n.* an ancient Roman building; a church built after the Roman style
ba´sin *n.* a wide, shallow container; an area drained by a body of water
ba´sis *n.* fundament principle; an essential quality or ingredient
bask *vi.* to relax in warmth; to revel in the glow of a pleasant situation
bas´ket *n.* a container made of woven material
bas–re·lief´ *n.* a sculpture of raised subjects from a flat background
bass[1] *adj.* of the lowest musical range —*n.* the lowest voice in music; an instrument in that range
bass[2] *n.* a food or game fish
bas´si·net´ *n.* basket for a baby; container for baby clothes, etc.
bas·soon´ *n.* a double–reed bass wind instrument —**bas·soon´ist** *n.*
bass´wood *n.* the linden tree; the wood of the linden tree
bas´tard *adj.* born out of wedlock; unusual or irregular; of inferior quality —*n.* an illegitimate child; a hybrid plant or animal; that which deviates from the usual —**bas´tard·ize** *vt.* —**bas·tard·i·za´tion** *n.*
baste *vt.* to sew with loose stitches; to moisten food while cooking
bas´ti·on *n.* a strongly defended position
bat *n.* a cudgel; a stick for striking a ball; a nocturnal flying mammal —*vi.* to take a turn at bat —*vt.* to strike with a bat
batch *n.* a quantity processed at one time; a number of things
bath *n.* the act of cleansing; liquid for bathing; a room set aside for bathing; natural springs claimed to have healing power —**take a bath** suffer a financial loss

bathe *vi.* wash; take a bath; go into water; be covered with liquid *—vt.* to immerse in liquid; to wash; cover, as though with liquid: *bathed in moonlight*
bath´robe (*US*) *n.* a loose, casual garment, usually closed at the front with a belt
ba·tik´, bat·tik´ *n.* a process for dying fabric in a complex, multicolored design; the fabric
ba·tiste´ *n.* a fine, sheer fabric
bat·on´ *n.* a short staff
bat·tal´ion *n.* a large group
bat´ten *n.* a narrow strip of wood; a strip used to stiffen a theater flat or hold a strip of lights *—vt.* to strengthen or secure with battens
bat´ter *n.* a mixture used to coat food *—vt.* subject to blows; to damage by beating or use
bat´ter·y *n.* a number of things used together; the illegal touching of a person; a device for storing an electrical charge
bat´ting *n.* material for stuffing pillows, comforters, etc.
bat´ty *adj.* a little crazy; odd
bau´ble *n.* a worthless trinket
bawd *n.* the operator of a brothel
bawd´y *adj.* racy; indecent; vulgar **—bawd´i·ly** *adv.* **—bawd´i·ness** *n.*
bawl *n.* a loud outcry *—vi.* sob noisily; bellow **—bawl out** berate
bay *adj.* reddish–brown *—n.* reddish–brown horse; wide inlet of the sea; compartment for storage; the laurel which provides bay leaf for seasoning food; the cry of a dog in pursuit *—vi.* to cry out as a hound in pursuit **—at bay** cornered; held off
bay´ou *n.* a marshy inlet; a creek flowing through a delta
bay window a set of windows that project outside a building
ba·zaar´ *n.* a market or fair
beach *n.* a sandy shore; a place for sunbathing or swimming *— vi., vt.* to strand a boat
bea´con *n.* a warning signal
bead *n.* small decorative ornament; drop of liquid; front sight of a rifle *—vi.* to gather in drops *—vt.* to decorate with beads **— draw a bead** take careful aim
beak *n.* a bird's bill
beak´er *n.* a container with a lip for pouring
beam *n.* large section of wood or metal; part of a balance; a shaft of light *—vi., vt.* shine, radiate
bean *n.* a leguminous plant, it's pod, or seeds; the head *—vt.* to hit on the head, as by something thrown
bear *vi.* suffer a burden; be productive; have reference to *—vt.* to possess; endure; produce offspring; assume a burden **— bear down** exert pressure **— bear in mind** remain conscious of **—bear out/bear witness** confirm or support **—bear up** maintain strength or attitude **—bear´a·ble** *adj.* **—bear´a·bly** *adv.*
bear *n.* large animal with shaggy hair; ill–tempered person; one who expects a decline in price
beard *n.* facial hair *—vt.* to defy boldly **—beard´ed** *adj.*
bear´ing *n.* manner; a machine part; a compass heading; relevance
bear´ish *adj.* rough; surly; inclined to sell in anticipation of a decline **—bear´ish·ly** *adv.*
beast *n.* an animal other than a human; animal qualities; one who is savage or brutal **— beast´li·ness** *n.* **—beast´ly** *adj.*
beat *adj.* exhausted *—n.* a blow; repeated fluctuation; area covered by a policeman or watchman *—vt.* strike repeatedly; to sound by striking; shape by hammering; to mix by stirring; to best another *—vi.* to pulsate
be·a·tif´ic *adj.* making happy; showing pleasure **—be·a·tif´i·cal·ly** *adv.*
be·at´i·fi·ca´tion *n.* a condition of blessedness **—be·at´i·fy** *vt.*
be·at´i·tude´ *n.* perfect happiness
beau *n.* an escort; a sweetheart
beau·ti´cian *n.* one skilled in hairdressing, manicure, etc.
beau´ti·ful *adj.* pleasing to the senses
beau´ti·fy´ *vt.* to make beautiful **—beau´ti·fi·ca´tion** *n.*
beau´ty *n.* anything that by its quality pleases the senses **— beau´te·ous** *adj.*
beaux–arts´ *n.* fine arts
bea´ver *n.* a large aquatic rodent; high hat made from beaver fur
be´bop *n.* improvisational jazz
be·calm *vt.* to induce tranquility; to cease moving
be·cause´ *conj.* for the reason that
beck´on *vi., vt.* to summon *—n.* a summoning gesture
be·cloud´ *vt.* to obscure
be·come´ *vi.* to come to be; to change into *—vt.* to suit
be·com´ing *adj.* attractive; suitable
bed *n.* a place where one sleeps; a base or foundation; a specially prepared area: *flower bed, road bed* **—marriage bed** lying together for the purpose of procreation
be·daz´zle *vt.* to blind; to impress
bed´ding *n.* linens for a bed; litter for an animal's bed; a foundation
be·deck´ *vt.* to adorn; to decorate
be·dev´il *vt.* harass or torment; to bewitch **—be·dev´il·ment** *n.*
bed´lam *n.* great confusion
be·drag´gle *vi., vt.* to soil or soak
bed´rid·den *adj.* confined to bed
bed´rock *n.* solid rock beneath the surface material
bed´room *n.* a room for sleeping
bedroom community a residential area for those who work elsewhere
bed´sore *n.* an ulcer on the body
bed´spread *n.* a bed covering
bed´stead *n.* the framework which supports springs, mattress, etc.
bed´time *n.* time for going to bed
bee *n.* an insect that produces honey; a social gathering
bee´bread *n.* food for bees
beech *n.* a tree with smooth, ash–gray bark that produces an edible nut; the wood of the beech tree
beef *n.* an adult ox, cow, steer, etc. or its flesh; muscle; a complaint
beef´y *adj.* large or muscular **— beef´i·ness** *n.*
bee´hive *n.* a nesting place for a colony of honey bees; a busy place
bee´line *n.* the shortest distance **—make a beeline for** go directly and quickly
beer *n.* an alcoholic beverage fermented from malts and hops; beverage made from roots
bees´wax *n.* a substance secreted by honey bees
beet *n.* a fleshy root vegetable
be·fall´ *vi.* to come about; to occur *—vt.* to happen to
be·fore´ *adj.* preceding in time or place *—conj.* sooner than; rather than *—prep.* ahead of; in front of; in advance of
be·foul´ *vt.* contaminate, pollute
be·friend´ *vt.* accept as a friend; to assist
be·fud´dle *vt.* to confuse
beg *vi., vt.* ask for alms; to plead
beg´gar *n.* one who begs; one impoverished *—vt.* to seem inadequate: *beggar the question*; to impoverish
beg´gar·ly *adj.* like a beggar; poverty–stricken; squalid
be·gin´ *vi., vt.* start; come into being
be·gin´ner *n.* a novice; one starting
be·gin´ning *n.* onset; a starting time or place; the first part
be·grudge´ *vt.* to envy another; give reluctantly **—be·grudg´ing·ly** *adv.*
be·guile´ *vt.* deceive; defraud; to charm **—be·guil´ing·ly** *adv.*
be·have´ *vi., vt.* to conduct oneself well **—be·hav´ior** (*US*), **be·hav´iour** (*Brit.*) *n.* **—be·hav´ior·al, be·hav´iour·al** *adj.*
be·he´moth *n.* a huge beast
be·hest´ *n.* a decree; a command
be·hind´ *adv.* toward the rear; in the past; in arrears *—prep.* at the far side of; following; not revealed
be·hold´ *vt.* to view
beige *adj.* light brownish–gray *— n.* the color of natural wool; a fabric of undyed, unbleached wool
be´ing *n.* that exists; conscious existence; essential nature of a thing
be·la´bor *vt.* denounce at length; needlessly prolong an argument
be·lat´ed *adj.* past the proper time **—be·lat´ed·ly** *adv.*
belch *vi.* to expel gas through the mouth; to expel violently
be·lea´guer *vt.* to harrass or annoy; to besiege
bel´fry *n.* a bell tower
be·lie´ *vt.* misrepresent; prove false
be·lief´ *n.* faith; trust; an expectation
be·lieve´ *vi.* have trust *—vt.* accept as true; expect **—be·liev´a·ble** *adj.* **—be·liev´a·bly** *adv.*
be·lit´tle *vt.* to disparage
bell *n.* a metallic instrument, struck to emit a tone; anything bell–shaped; a flared end
bel´la·don´na *n.* deadly nightshade; a poisonous herb
bell´boy *n.* a hotel porter
belle *n.* a pretty female
bel´li·cose´ *adj.* hostile; aggressive **—bel´li·cose·ly** *adv.*
bel·lig´er·ent *adj.* warlike; at war *—n.* one engaged in war **— bel·lig´er·ence, bel·lig´er·en·cy** *n.*; **bel·lig´er·ent·ly** *adv.*
bel´low *vi., vt.* to cry out *—n.* a loud cry
bel´lows *pl. n.* a device for producing a stream of air
bel´ly *n.* the abdomen; the stomach; any similar protrusion
bel´ly·ache *n.* a pain in the stomach; *vi.* to complain
bel´ly·but·ton *n.* the navel
belly dance a dance marked by gyrations of the hips and abdomen
bel´ly·ful *n.* all that the stomach can hold; all that one can endure
belly laugh boisterous laughter
be·long´ *vi.* to be part of
be·long´ings *pl. n.* all that one owns
be·lov´ed *adj.* cherished *—n.* one who is loved
be·low´ *adv.* in a lower place *— prep.* farther down; inferior
belt *n.* a band worn around the waist; band connecting wheels in a machine; a moving line that transports from one place to another; a geographic zone; a blow *—vt.* to encircle or secure with a belt; to strike **—below the belt** unfair
belt´way (*US*) *n.* roadway around a city
be·moan´ *vi., vt.* to express sorrow; mourn
be·muse´ *vt.* to absorb or preoccupy **—be·mus´ed·ly** *adv.*
bench *n.* a long hard seat; a work table; the office of a judge; judges collectively
bench mark, bench´mark *n.* a surveyor's marker; a reference point
bend *vi.* to turn; to yield; bow *— vt.* to curve or incline; to subdue *—n.* a curved part **— bend´a·ble** *adj.*
be·neath´ *adj., adv.* below; in a lower position *—prep.* below or under; subordinate; unbefitting: *beneath her dignity*
ben´e·dic´tion *n.* invocation of blessing **—ben·e·dic´to·ry** *adj.*
ben´e·fac´tion *n.* the act of helping; the help given **—ben´e·fac´tor** *n.*
be·nef´i·cence *n.* active goodness; a charitable act **—be·nef´i·cent** *adj.* **—be·nef´i·cent·ly** *adv.*
ben´e·fi´cial *adj.* advantageous; profitable **—ben·e·fi´cial·ly** *adv.*
ben´e·fi´ci·ar·y *n.* one who holds or receives a benefit or inheritance
ben´e·fit *n.* a thing that helps; an activity to aid a cause; payments received for retirement, illness, etc. *—vi.* to help *—vt.* to aid
be·nev´o·lence *n.* a bent to do good; a charitable act **— be·nev´o·lent** *adj.* **—be·nev´o·lent·ly** *adv.*
be·nign´ *adj.* kindly; medically harmless **—be·nign´ly** *adv.*

bent *adj.* curved or warped; deformed; resolved —*n.* tendency; an inclination; an innate talent

be·numb *vt.* to daze or stun; to deaden or paralyze

be·queath´ *vt.* to pass on, especially after death —**be·queath´al** *n.*

be·quest´ *n.* a thing passed on

be·rate´ *vt.* to reprimand or scold

be·reave´ *vt.* to deprive of by death —**be·reave´ment** *n.*

be·ret´ *n.* a flat soft cap

ber´ry *n.* a small juicy fruit

ber·serk´ *adj., adv.* violent, rampaging; out of control

ber·serk´er *n.* an early Norse warrior notable for savagery in battle

berth *n.* a sleeping place; a position in a ship's crew; room for ships to clear at sea; space to anchor

be·seech´ *vt.* to implore; to beg —**be·seech´ing·ly** *adv.*

be·set´ *adj.* troubled; beleaguered —*vt.* torment; decorate

be·side´ *prep.* adjacent to; alongside

be·sides´ *adv.* furthermore; else; in addition —*prep.*

be·siege´ *vt.* to lay siege to; to overwhelm, as with information

be·smirch´ *vt.* to defame; bring dishonor upon

best *adj.* finest —*adv.* to the highest degree —*vt.* to defeat

bes´tial *adj.* of a beast; savage; brutal —**bes·ti·al´i·ty** *n.*

be·stir´ *vt.* to stir to action

be·stow´ *vt.* give —**be·stow´al** *n.*

best´sell´er *n.* that which outsells all others; that selling extremely well —**best´-sell´ing** *adj.*

bet *vi., vt.* to wager —*n.* the stake in a wager —**bet´tor, bet´ter** *n.*

be´ta·tron´ *n.* an electron accelerator

be·tray´ *vt.* to be disloyal; to lead astray —**be·tray´al** *n.*

be·troth´ *vt.* to commit to marry —**be·troth´al** *n.*

be·throthed´ *adj.* engaged to be married —*n.* person to whom one is engaged

bet´ter *adj.* more suitable; improved; recovering —*adv.* in a more suitable fashion —*n.* one in a superior position —*vt.* improve; outdo —**bet´ter·ment** *n.*

be·tween´ *adv.* in an intermediate position —*prep.* of that which separates or connects

bev´el *adj.* biased; sloping —*n.* a sloping surface; an angle; a tool for measuring angles —*vi.* to slant —*vt.* to cut at an angle

bev´er·age *n.* liquid for drinking

bev´y *n.* a group

be·wail´ *vt.* to lament

be·ware´ *vi., vt.* be on one's guard

be·wil´der *vt.* confound; astonish —**be·wil´der·ing·ly** *adv.* —**be·wil´der·ment** *n.*

be·witch´ *vt.* enchant or charm; to captivate —**be·witch´ing** *adj.* —**be·witch´ing·ly** *adv.*

be·yond´ *adv.* farther away —*prep.* surpassing

bi·an´nu·al *adj.* twice each year

bi´as *n.* prejudice; partiality —*vt.* to influence

bible *n.* a writing sanctioned or approved —**bib´li·cal** *adj.*

bib·li·og´ra·phy *n.* a list of information sources —**bib·li·og´ra·pher** *n.*

bib´li·o·phile *n.* a collector of books

bi·cam´er·al *adj.* having two legislative bodies

bicarbonate of soda (*Brit.*) sodium bicarbonate; a compound used in cooking, cleaning, etc.

bi·cen·ten´ni·al *adj.* occurring once in two hundred years —*n.* a two hundred year anniversary —**bi·cen·ten´a·ry** *adj., n.*

bi´ceps *n.* a muscle having two points of connection

bick´er *n.* a petty quarrel —*vi.* to quarrel

bi·cus´pid *n.* a tooth with a two–pointed crown

bi´cy·cle *n.* two–wheeled vehicle propelled by the rider —*vi., vt.* to ride a bicycle —**bi´cy·clist** *n.*

bid *n.* amount offered; attempt —*vt.* to request; make an offer; to declare openly —**bid´der** *n.*

bid´dy *n.* a hen; a gossip

bi·en´ni·al *adj.* lasting two years; every two years —*n.* a plant that lives two years

bi´fo·cals *pl. n.* corrective lenses for both near and distant vision

bi´fur·cate *vi., vt.* to split in two —**bi´fur·cate, bi´fur·cat·ed** *adj.* forked; having two branches —**bi·fur·ca´tion** *n.*

big *adj.* large; important; massive; substantial; generous

big´a·mist *n.* one having two or more spouses —**big´a·mous** *adj.* —**big´a·my** *n.*

big´heart·ed *adj.* generous —**big´heart·ed·ly** *adv.*

big´ot *n.* intolerant person —**big´ot·ed** *adj.* —**big´ot·ry** *n.*

bi´jou *n.* an ornament or bauble; a piece of jewelry; a trinket

bike *n.* a bicycle; a motorcycle

bi·ki´ni *n.* a brief bathing suit

bi·lat´er·al *adj.* reciprocal; involving two parties —**bi·lat´er·al·ly** *adv.*

bile *n.* a digestive fluid secreted in the liver; bitterness or hostility

bi·lin´gual *adj.* able to converse in two languages

bil´ious *adj.* of bile or ailments of the liver; ill–tempered —**bil´ious·ly** *adv.* —**bil´ious·ness** *n.*

bilk *vt.* to cheat or swindle; to defraud —**bilk´er** *n.*

bill *n.* an invoice; (*US*) paper money; a draft of a law; a bird's jaw; a beak —*vt.* to tender an invoice

bill´board *n.* a large outdoor sign

bil´lion (US) *n.* one thousand million

bill of fare a restaurant menu

bill of lading a shipping document

bill of sale a document attesting to the transfer of property

bil´low *n.* a large wave; a surging mass —*vi., vt.* to surge —**bil´low·y** *adj.*

bi·month·ly *adj., adv.* every two months

bin *n.* a receptacle for storage

bi´na·ry *adj.* comprised of two parts; of a numbering system in base two

binary star a double star

bind —*vt.* to make fast; to fasten together; to obligate —*vi.* to tie; to be obligatory —*n.* a difficult situation

bind´er *n.* one who binds books; something that joins; a temporary agreement

bind´ing *adj.* obligatory, required —*n.* something used to join

bi·no´mi·al *adj.* of a two part equation —*n.* a mathematical equation

bi´o·as·tro·nau´tics *n.* study of life in a weightless environment

bi´o·chem´is·try *n.* biological or physiological chemistry

bi´o·de·grad´a·ble *adj.* readily decomposed through bacterial action

bi·o·e·col´o·gy *n.* the study of the interrelationship of animals and plants to their environment

bi·og´ra·phy *n.* the story of a person's life —**bi·og´ra·pher** *n.* —**bi·o·graph´ic, bi·o·graph´i·cal** *adj.*

biological clock the natural cycles in the life of an organism

biological warfare use of microorganisms as a weapon of war

bi·ol´o·gy *n.* the science that deals with life forms —**bi·ol´o·gist** *n.* —**bi·o·log´i·cal** *adj.* —**bi·o·log´i·cal·ly** *adv.*

bi´op·sy *n.* the removal of tissue for laboratory analysis

bi´o·sphere *n.* all life on earth; earth area which supports life

bi´o·tin *n.* a B vitamin

bi·par´ti·san *adj.* consisting of two parties —**bi·par´ti·san·ship** *n.*

bi·par´tite *adj.* having two parts

bi´ped´ *n.* any creature with two feet

bi·po´lar *adj.* having two poles; of opposing doctrines, natures, etc.

birch´bark *n.* the bark of the birch tree; a canoe made from the bark —*adj.* resembling the birch

birch beer a beverage flavored with oil of birch

bird *n.* a feathered animal

bird of prey a bird that hunts

birth *n.* the act of coming into life; background or lineage

birth´mark *n.* an impression on the skin evident at birth; a blemish

birth´right *n.* rights by virtue of being born into a family or country

birth´stone *n.* a gem associated with a particular birth month

bi´sect *vt.* divide into two parts —**bi·sec´tion** *n.*

bi·sex´u·al *adj.* of both sexes

bish´op *n.* a ranking member of the clergy; a chess piece

bish´op·ric *n.* office of a bishop

bisque *n.* a thick, creamed soup

bit *n.* small scrap; a boring tool; a minor part; a mouthpiece

bitch *n.* a female dog —*vi.* complain

bite *n.* taking by the teeth; the amount taken; damage made by teeth; a stinging —*vi.* to grip; to hurt; have a sharp taste; to take bait —*vt.* seize with the teeth; sting

bit´ter *adj.* acrid tasting; cruel or harsh; resentful —**bit´ter·ly** *adv.* —**bit´ter·ness** *n.*

bit´ters *n.* a flavoring or tonic made from bitter herbs

bit´ter·sweet *adj.* a flavor both bitter and sweet; pleasure accompanied by pain or sadness

bi·week´ly *adj., adv.* occurring once every two weeks

bi·year´ly *adj., adv.* occurring once every two years

bi·zarre´ *adj.* extremely unusual

blab *vi., vt.* to chatter; to reveal —**blab´ber** *n., vi.*

black *n.* the absence of color; the opposite of white —**black´en** *vi., vt.*

black–and–blue *adj.* bruised

black and white written; not in full color; clearly expressed

black art sorcery; witchcraft

black´ball´ *vt.* to ostracize

black´board´ *n.* a surface for drawing or writing with chalk

black eye discoloration around the eye; a blemish to one's reputation

black´guard *n.* a villain, scoundrel

black´–heart´ed *adj.* wicked, sinister

black hole a collapsed star

black light ultraviolet light

black´list *n.* those excluded —*vt.* to deliberately exclude

black magic sorcery, witchcraft

black´mail´ *n.* extortion —*vt.* to extort payment by threat

black market illegal trade

black´–mar´ket *vt.* to trade on the black market —*adj.*

black´out´ *n.* loss of electrical power; a temporary loss of consciousness

black sheep one who is different; an outcast

black´smith *n.* a worker in iron

black tie formal; a formal affair

black´top (*US*) *n.* a road surface —*vt.* to surface with asphalt

bladder *n.* an internal body pouch; anything resembling such a pouch

blade *n.* a plant leaf; a broad, flat surface; a cutting part

blame *n.* condemnation; accountability —*vt.* charge with responsibility; condemn or rebuke —**blam´a·ble** *adj.* —**blame´ful** *adj.*

blame´less *adj.* innocent; irreproachable —**blame´less·ly** *adv.* —**blame´less·ness** *n.*

blanch *vi.* to whiten —*vt.* make white; bleach; immerse food briefly in boiling water

bland *adj.* soothing, mild; insipid

blan´dish *vt.* persuade by flattery

blank *adj.* empty, vacant —*n.* a void; emptiness; a form —**draw a blank** unable to remember or accomplish

blan´ket *adj.* encompassing —*n.* a bed covering; a thing that covers —*vt.* to cover; to canvass

blank verse unrhymed poetry

blare *n.* a harsh noise —*vi., vt.* to sound loudly

blar´ney *n.* flattering speech

bla·sé´ *adj.* indifferent, unconcerned

blas´pheme´ *vt.* to speak or act irreverently —*vi.* to utter blasphemy

blas´phe·my *n.* profane or irreverent expression —**blas´phe·mous** *adj.*

blast *n.* sudden rush; a harsh sound; an explosion —*vi.* make a harsh sound; to set off an explosive —*vt.* explode; denounce
blast furnace a furnace for separating impurities from metallic ore
bla´tant *adj.* offensively noisy; obvious —**bla´tant·ly** *adv.*
blaze *n.* burst of light —*vi.* burn
bla´zer *n.* a sports jacket
bleach *n.* a cleaner —*vi.* to grow white —*vt.* to remove color; to make white
bleach´ers *pl. n.* bench seating
bleak *adj.* desolate; dreary; gloomy
blear´y *adj.* blurred or indistinct —**blear´i·ly** *adv.*
bleat *n.* the cry of an animal —*vi., vt.*
bleed *vi.* lose vital fluid; run together, as dye —*vt.* draw fluid or gas; to impoverish
blem´ish *n.* a defect —*vt.* deface
blend *n.* amixture —*vi., vt.* to mix; make a gradual transition
bless *vt.* to consecrate; to favor —**bless´ed·ness** *n.*
bless´ed *adj.* consecrated; blissful; rewarded
bless´ing *n.* an invocation; grace; divine sanction; good fortune
blight *n.* plant disease; anything that damages —*vt.* destroy
blimp *n.* an airship
blind *adj.* sightless; unseen —*n.* that obscures or conceals —*vt.* to deprive of sight; to dazzle
blind´fold *n.* that restricting sight —*vt.* to cover the eyes of; to mislead
blind´ing *adj.* swift; faster than the eye —**blind´ing·ly** *adv.*
blind spot an area of restricted vision; a prejudice
blink *vi., vt.* to flicker the eyelids; flash on and off, as a light
blink´er *n.* a flashing light; (*US*) an automobile turn signal
blintz, blintze *n.* a filled pancake
bliss *n.* happiness; ecstasy, rapture —**bliss´ful** *adj.* —**bliss´ful·ly** *adv.*
blis´ter *n.* a bulging sac; a transparent covering for merchandise —*vi., vt.* to form a blister
blithe *adj.* gay; lighthearted; vivacious —**blithe´ly** *adv.*
bliz´zard *n.* a violent snowstorm
bloat *vi., vt.* to swell
blob *n.* clump of indefinite shape
bloc *n.* a political alliance
block *n.* large chunk; a system of pulleys; a related group; a barrier —*vt.* hinder or restrict; form a plan —**block´age** *n.*
block´ade´ *n.* a barrier —*vt.* to set up a barrier
block´bust·er *adj.* extravagant —*n.* an extravagant work; an investor who uses deception to buy property at reduced prices
block´head *n.* a stupid person —**block´head·ed·ness** *n.*
block letter a plain character, without serifs or embellishment
blond *adj.* of fair skin; light finish
blonde *n.* a blond female
blood *n.* a vital body fluid; heritage; kinship
blood bank a reserve of blood
blood bath a massacre; wholesale replacement of executives
blood brother a male sibling; one bound by an oath or ceremony
blood count analysis of blood
blood´curd·ling *adj.* frightening; ghastly
blood´ed *adj.* pedigreed; of known stock
blood´hound *n.* a dog used to track; one relentless in pursuit
blood´less *adj.* lacking blood; without bloodshed, peacful; indifferent
blood´let·ting *n.* bloodshed; a replacement of many employees
blood money payment for an illegal deed; gain from suffering
blood pressure a measure of the force of blood in the arteries
blood relation, blood relative one related by birth
blood´shed *n.* carnage; slaughter
blood´stained *adj.* soiled by blood; guilty of shedding blood
blood´suck·er *n.* a parasite; one who takes —**blood´suck·ing** *adj.*
blood´thirst·y *adj.* barbarous; inclined to murder; ruthless —**blood´thirst·i·ly** *adv.*
blood vessel any of the arteries, veins, or capillaries
blood´y *adj.* bleeding or containing blood; bloodstained; murderous —**blood´i·ly** *adv.* —**blood´i·ness** *n.*
bloom *n.* a flower; a healthy glow —*vi.* to flower; to glow
bloop´er *n.* a mistake; a silly blunder
blos´som *n.* a flower —*vi.* develop
blot *n.* a flaw; dishonor; a spot —*vt.* stain; dishonor; to get rid of
blotch *n.* a stain —*vt.* to blemish
blotch´y *adj.* discolored; blemished
blouse *n.* a loose shirt
blow *n.* a sharp rap; a setback; a blast of air; a windstorm —*vi.* move air; be carried on air; be stormy —*vt.* expel air; propel by air; to waste; fail; to leave —**blow up** explode; to form by blowing; enlarge a photograph
blow´out *n.* the bursting of a tire; a large party or celebration
blow´torch *n.* a tool that produces an intense flame
blow·up *n.* an explosion; an enlarged photograph
blub´ber *n.* whale fat; excess fat —*vi.* to weep
bludg´eon *n.* a heavy club —*vt.* to strike with a club; to bully
blue *adj.* blu in color; despondent —*n.* the color of a clear sky —*vt.* to make blue in color
blue baby a child born with a heart or respiratory defect
blue´bell *n.* any of a variety of plants with blue bell–shaped flowers
blue blood, blue´blood *n.* an aristocrat; high society —**blue´–blood·ed** *adj.*
blue chip, blue´chip *adj.* of a stable company; of anything preceived as stable —**blue´–chip** *adj.*
blue collar an industrial worker
blue´grass *adj.* of a type of mountain music —*n.*
blue jeans, blue·jeans *n.* a type of trouser made from blue denim
blue laws laws prohibiting transaction of business on Sunday
blue´nose *n.* one who imposes a moral code on others
blue–pen´cil *vt.* to edit or correct
blue´print *n.* engineer's drawing; any detailed plan of action
blue ribbon first prize
blue–sky´ *adj.* of no intrinsic value; a wish or dream
blue streak fast, lively or animated
bluff *adj.* abrupt in manner —*n.* a steep bank; a deception —*vt.* mislead by feigning; to deceive
blun´der *n.* a mistake —*vi.* make a foolish error; move clumsily
blunt *adj.* not sharp; plain–spoken; slow–witted —*vt.* to dull; reduce effectiveness —**blunt´ness** *n.*
blur *n.* anything hazy —*vt., vi.* make or become indistinct —**blur´ry** *adj.*
blurb *n.* a brief announcement; a comment on a book cover or jacket
blurt *vt.* say without thinking
blush *n.* a sudden reddening; a reddish color —*vi., vt.* become red —**blush´er** *n.* —**blush´ing·ly** *adv.*
blus´ter *n.* arrogant speech —*vi.* blow in gusts; act arrogant or bullying —**blus´ter·ing·ly** *adv.* —**blus´ter·ous, blus´ter·y** *adj.*
bo´a *n.* a large snake; a long scarf
boar *n.* a mature male pig
board *n.* a plank; a panel; meals provided; group that regulates —*vt.* supply with meals; get on
board´er *n.* lodger; paying guest
board foot a measure of lumber
boarding house an establishment that provides rooms and meals
boarding school a school that provides a residence and meals
board´walk *n.* a wooden walkway
boast *vi., vt.* to brag —**boast´ful** *adj.* —**boast´ful·ly** *adv.*
boat *n.* a vessel of inland seas —**boat´ing** *adj., n.*
bob´bin *n.* a spool for thread or yarn
bobby pin (*US*) a metal hair pin
bob´sled *n.* a long sled
bock beer a dark German beer
bod´ice *n.* upper part of a dress
bod´i·ly *adj.* physical; of the body —*adv.* totally, entirely
bod´y *n.* physical structure; a main part; a person; a group; density
body politic society; those united
bog *n.* a small swamp or marsh
bo´gus *adj.* of doubtful authenticity
bo·he´mi·an *n.* one who is unconventional, as an artist or writer
boil *vi.* to bubble; to cook in boiling liquid; to churn; seethe with rage —*vt.* heat to boiling; to process in boiling liquid
boil´er *n.* a tank producing steam; a tank for heating and storing water
boiling point the temperature at which a liquid boils; conditions which cause one to lose control
bois´ter·ous *adj.* noisy; rowdy —**bois´ter·ous·ly** *adv.*
bold *adj.* daring; forceful; impudent —**bold´ly** *adv.* —**bold´ness** *n.*
bold´–faced, bold´faced *adj.* impudent; brazen
bo·le´ro *n.* a Spanish dance; a short jacket
bol´lix *vt.* bungle; mismanage
bol´ster *n.* a long pillow —*vt.* to prop up; to reinforce
bolt *n.* a bar for securing; a threaded fastener; a roll of cloth; a sudden start —*vi.* to spring; to break away —*vt.* to secure with a bar; to eat hurriedly; to break away
bomb *n.* a casing filled with explosives; a failure —*vi.* to fail utterly —*vt.* to attack with bombs
bom·bas´tic *adj.* high–sounding but meaningless —**bom´bast´** *n.* —**bom·bas´ti·cal·ly** *adv.*
bomb´shell *n.* a bomb; a sudden shock; a rude awakening
bo´na fide *adj.* genuine; sincere; in good faith
bo·nan´za *n.* a rich source; a profitable venture
bon´bon *n.* a small candy
bond *n.* a formal obligation; that which binds —*vt.* protect by bond; place in bonded storage; tie or join
bond´age *n.* servitude, enslavement
bond´ed *adj.* secured by a bond; in bonded storage; bound by fetters
bonds´man *n.* one who furnishes a bond for a fee
bone *n.* hard tissue forming the skeleton —*vt.* to remove bones
bon´er *n.* silly mistake; a blooper
bon´fire´ *n.* a large outdoor fire
bon´net *n.* a females hat
bo´nus *n.* an extra payment; any extra benefit
bon´y *adj.* of bones; skinny, emaciated; with many bones, as a fish —**bon´i·ness** *n.*
boob *n.* one who is foolish; an oaf
booby trap a device designed to be set off by an unsuspecting victim
book *n.* pages bound together with a cover; part of a lengthly work; a body of information
book´case *n.* a freestanding set of shelves for books or artifacts
book´end *n.* a device to keep a row of books in place
book´ie *n.* a bookmaker
book´ish *adj.* scholarly; given to studying —**book´ish·ly** *adv.* —**book´ish·ness** *n.*
book´keep·ing *n.* recording of financial dealings —**book´keep·er** *n.*
book´let *n.* a small book
book´mak·er *n.* one who accepts wagers —**book´mak·ing** *n.*
book´mark *n.* a device to keep the reader's place in a book
book´mo·bile´ *n.* a mobile library
book´plate *n.* a label in a book
book review a verbal or written commentary about a book
book´worm *n.* one who spends considerable time reading or studying
boom *n.* a deep sound; an upturn —*vi.* make a deep sound
boo´me·rang *n.* a bent stick that returns when thrown; a thing that acts differently than planned
boon *n.* good fortune

boon´dog·gle *n.* a pointless project; a no–win situation
boor *n.* one who is vulgar or unrefined —**boor´ish** *adj.* —**boor´ish·ly** *adv.* —**boor´ish·ness** *n.*
boost *n.* assistance; an increase —*vt.* push upward; to increase; promote
boot *n.* a covering for the foot —*vt.* to kick; dismiss from a job
booth *n.* a stall for displaying goods; partially isolated seating
boot´leg´ *adj.* illegal —*vi., vt.* to sell illegally —**boot´leg·ger** *n.*
boo´ty *n.* loot; spoils of war
booze *n.* an alcholic beverage —**booz´er** *n.* —**booz´y** *adj.*
bor´der *n.* a boundary; margin —*vt.* extend along the boundary
bor´der·line *adj.* marginal; of questionable value —*n.* an edge or line
bore *n.* a round hole; dull person —*vt.* make a hole; make weary
bore´dom *n.* lack of interest; listlessness
bor´ing *adj.* uninteresting, tiresome —**bor´ing·ly** *adv.*
bor´ough *n.* in Britain and some US states, an incorporated town
bor´row *vi., vt.* take with agreement to return; adopt an idea
bos´om *n.* the breast; closeness
boss *n.* supervisor; one in charge —*vi., vt.* to supervise
boss´y *adj.* like a boss; domineering —**boss´i·ness** *n.*
boss´ism *n.* control of a political district by an autocratic leader
bot´a·ny *n.* the study of plants —**bo·tan´i·cal** *adj.* —**bot´a·nist** *n.*
botch *n.* shoddy work —*vt.* bungle; do a shoddy job —**botched** *adj.* —**botch´y** *adj.*
both´er *n.* a cause of irritation; vexation —*vi.* concerned with; fuss over —*vt.* trouble; inconvenience —**both´er·some** *adj.*
bot´tle *n.* a glass container; the amount a bottle holds —*vt.* to put into bottles —**bot´tler** *n.*
bot´tle·neck´ *n.* an obstruction
bot´tom *adj.* of the lowest pcint —*n.* lowest part; seat of a chair
bouf·fant´ *adj.* puffed out
bough *n.* the branch of a tree
boul´der *n.* a large rock or stone
bou´le·vard´ *n.* a broad paved street
bounce *n.* a rebound; capacity to rebound; zest, spirit —*vi.* rebound; spring; return a check for lack of funds —*vt.* to throw and cause to rebound; to eject an undesirable; to dismiss —**bounc´er** *n.*
bound *adj.* obligated; determined; tied or restricted —*n.* a leap —*vi.* to leap; to border on —*vt.* to cause a leap or bounce; to mark a border
bound´a·ry *n.* a border or limit
bound´less *adj.* without end; unlimited —**bound´less·ly** *adv.* —**bound´less·ness** *n.*
boun´te·ous *adj.* plentiful —**boun´ti·ful** *adj.* —**boun´ti·ful·ly** *adv.*
boun´ty *n.* a profusion; a reward
bou·quet´ *n.* cut flowers; fragrance
bour´bon *n.* a whiskey —*adj.* made from or with bourbon
bour·geois *adj.* of the middle class; conventional —*n.*
bour·geoi·sie´ *n.* the middle class
bout *n.* a struggle; an occurrence
bou·tique´ *n.* a small specialty shop
bou·ton·niere´ *n.* a lapel flower
bo´vine *adj.* of oxen or cows
bow *n.* a bending; the front of a ship; a curve; a device for shooting arrows; a decorative knot —*vi., vt.* to bend the body in greeting; to yield
bow´el *n.* an intestine —*pl.* **bow´els** the intestines; the inside of anything perceived as deep and dark
bowl *n.* a deep dish for food; anything similar —*vt.* play at bowling
bowl´er *n.* one who bowls; a derby
bowl´ing *n.* a game of tenpins
box *n.* a squarish container
box´car (*US*) *n.* a rail freight car
box´er *n.* a prizefighter
box office location where tickets are sold, as for a sporting event
box score detailed statistics
box seat premium seats
boy *n.* a male youth —**boy´hood** *n.* —**boy´ish** *adj.* —**boy´ish·ly** *adv.*
boy´cott´ *n.* a refusal to deal with —*vt.* to avoid dealings with
bra *n.* a brassière; swimsuit top
brace *n.* a support or fastener; a pair of marks { } to connect elements; a pair —*vt.* support; fit with braces; steady oneself
brace´let *n.* jewelry for the wrist
brack´et *n.* an angled support; a pair of marks [ ] to enclose words; a group of associated elements —*vt.* to support or enclose; to group associated elements
brack´ish *adj.* slightly salty; disagreeable in taste
brad *n.* a small finishing nail
brag *vi., vt.* to boast —*n.* a boast; thing boasted about; a boaster
brag·ga·do´ci·o *n.* bravado; a swaggering manner
brag´gart, **brag´ger** *n.* one who boasts; a blowhard
braid (*US*) *n.* interwoven hair; a band of woven material —*vt.* to interweave; to trim with braid
braille *n.* writing for the blind
brain *n.* the center of thought; mental ability; a bright person
brain´child *n.* that produced by one's own creative powers
brain´less *adj.* lacking common sense; mindless
brain´pow·er *n.* the ability to think; intellect
brain´storm *n.* inspiration —*vi.* take part in a session designed to generate ideas —**brain´storm·er** *n.*
brain´wash´ *vt.* to indoctrinate
brain´y *adj.* extremely intelligent; quick–witted —**brain´i·ness** *n.*
braise *vt.* to simmer in liquid
brake *n.* a device for slowing or stopping —*vi., vt.* slow or stop
bran *n.* the outer husk of grain
branch *n.* an extension —*vi.* to extend from the main part
brand *n.* a burning stick; a mark of ownership, stigma, etc.; a trademark —*vt.* to mark with a brand
bran´dish *vt.* to wave menacingly
brand´–new *adj.* recently introduced or acquired; not used
bran´dy *n.* an alcoholic beverage
brash *adj.* impetuous; insolent —**brash´ly** *adv.* —**brash´ness** *n.*
brass *n.* an alloy of copper; things made from the alloy; boldness, impudence; high–ranking persons —*adj.* of or made from brass
brass´y *adj.* brazen; impudent —**brass´i·ly** *adv.* —**brass´i·ness** *n.*
brat *n.* a badly behaved child —**brat´ty** *adj.*
bra·va´do *n.* false courage; bluster
brave *adj.* courageous; bold —*vt.* to face courageously —**brave´ly** *adv.*
brav´er·y *n.* courage
bra·vu´ra *n.* a showy display; ostentation
brawl *n.* a noisy quarrel —*vi.* to quarrel noisily
brawn *n.* muscle; muscular strength —**brawn´i·ness** *n.* —**brawn´y** *adj.*
bray *n.* the harsh cry of a donkey; any similar noise
bra´zen *adj.* like brass; bold, impudent —**bra´zen·ly** *adv.* —**bra´zen·ness** *n.*
bra´zier *n.* a coal heater or cooker; a worker in brass
breach *n.* break; violation of a contract; disagreement —*vt.* to break through; violate agreement
bread *n.* a baked or fried food made from grain; food in general; money
bread and butter essentials; primary, as a product line
bread line a distribution of free food; those waiting for free food
breadth *n.* width
bread´win·ner *n.* the one who works to support others
break *n.* a breach; an interval of rest; luck or opportunity; a sudden move —*vi.* come apart; become inoperable; sever; to happen suddenly; run away —*vt.* part by force; to ruin; cause to fail; to violate a contract —**break´a·ble** *adj.*
break´age *n.* things broken; an allowance for things broken
break´down *n.* failure to work; a separation for analysis
break´er *n.* a wave that strikes the shore
breakfast *n.* the first meal of the day —*vi.* to eat breakfast
break´–in *adj.* of a period of trial —*n.* unauthorized entry
breaking point maximum stress that can be tolerated
break´neck *adj.* of travel at high speed; dangerous
break´through´ *n.* notable finding
break´up *n.* a tearing down or disintegration; a separation
break´wa·ter *n.* a harbor barrier to shield against the impact of waves
breast *n.* the front of the chest
breast´plate *n.* a piece of armor to protect the chest
breath *n.* air taken into the lungs; the act of breathing; a light breeze; a whisper
breathe *vi., vt.* to take air into the lungs; to whisper —**not breathe a word** promise to keep a secret
breath´er *n.* a break; a brief rest
breath´tak·ing *adj.* exciting; awe–inspiring
breeches *pl. n.* tapered trousers ending just below the knee
breed *n.* a group of common ancestry; a particular type —*vi.* to originate; to reproduce —*vt.* to bring forth young; to rear —**breed´er** *n.*
breed´ing *n.* production of offspring; good manners, courtesy
breeze *n.* a gentle wind; easily done —*vi.* move quickly —**breez´i·ly** *adv.* —**breez´y** *adj.*
breeze´way *n.* an enclosed passageway between buildings
breth´ren *pl. n.* brothers
brev´i·ty *n.* quality of being brief
brew *vi., vt.* make beer, coffee, etc; formulate a plan
bribe *n.* payment to influence —*vi.* to pay illegally —**brib´er·y** *n.*
brick *n.* a building block; a reliable person —*vt.* to build with brick
brick´bat *n.* a harsh comment; an aspersion
brid´al *adj.* of a bride or wedding
bride *n.* a married woman
bride´groom *n.* a married man
brides´maid *n.* bride's attendant
bridge *n.* span over an obstacle; any similar structure or link
bridge´work *n.* dentures
bri´dle *n.* a harness; a restraint —*vi.* take offense —*vt.* control
brief *adj.* momentary; concise —*n.* a summary —**brief´ly** *adv.*
brief´case *n.* hand luggage
brief´ing *n.* a short summary of a situation; a set of instructions
brig *n.* a brigantine; a ship's jail
bri·gade´ *n.* an organized group
brig´an·tine *n.* two–masted ship
bright *adj.* full of color; quick–witted; lively; auspicious, encouraging —**bright´ly** *adv.* —**bright´ness** *n.*
bright´en *vi., vt.* to make bright, as by polishing
bril´liant *adj.* full of light; dazzling; ingenious; talented —*n.* a fine gem —**bril´liance** *n.* —**bril´liant·ly** *adv.*
brim *n.* the lip of a container; a projection, as on a hat —*vt., vi.* to fill or be full —**brim´ful** *adj.*
brim´stone *n.* sulphur
brine *n.* a salt solution; the sea —**brin´i·ness** *n.* —**brin´y** *adj.*
bring *vt.* to convey, to influence —**bring about** cause to happen
brink *n.* an edge or limit
bri´oche *n.* a light, rich bread
brisk *adj.* quick; active; stimulating —**brisk´ly** *adv.* —**brisk´ness** *n.*
bris´tle *n.* short, stiff hair —*vi.* become tense; take offense —**bris´tly** *adj.* —**bris´tli·ness** *n.*
brittle *adj.* easily broken; fragile; unbending —**brit´tle·ness** *n.*
broach *vt.* to bring up for discussion
broad *adj.* wide in scope; open, obvious; general —**broad´en** *vi., vt.* —**broad´ly** *adv.* —**broad´ness** *n.*
broad´cast´ *adj.* of radio or television —*vi., vt.* make known

broad´cloth´ *n.* a fine, smooth cloth
broad´–mind´ed *adj.* open to the unconventional —**broad´–mind·ed·ly** *adv.* —**broad´–mind·ed·ness** *n.*
bro·cade´ *n.* a heavy fabric covered with a raised design
bro·chure´ *n.* a booklet or folder
brogue *n.* a type of accent
broil *vt.* cook by direct exposure to intense heat —**broil´er** *n.*
bro´ken *adj.* in pieces; out of order; imperfect; ill or dispirited
bro´ker *n.* one who trades for others
bro´ker·age *n.* office of a broker; fees charged by a broker
bron´co *n.* a horse of the west
bronze *n.* alloy of copper and tin
brooch *n.* a large decorative pin
brood *adj.* of a breeding animal —*n.* offspring hatched at one time; all the children in a family —*vi., vt.* to sit eggs; meditate morbidly; to pine or grieve
brook *n.* a small stream
broom *n.* a bundle of stiff fibers
broth *n.* a clear, thin soup
broth´el *n.* a place of prostitution
broth´er *n.* a male sibling; a close friend; a fellow member —**broth´er·hood** *n.*
broth´er–in–law *n.* brother by marriage
brow *n.* the forehead; the projecting top of a steep bank
brow´beat *vt.* to intimidate; to harangue —**brow´beat·er** *n.*
brown´–bag (*US*) *vi., vt.* to carry lunch; to bring liquor to a restaurant —**brown–bag´ger** *n.*
brown´out *n.* a dimming of lights
brown´stone *n.* a row house fronted with brown stone
browse *vi., vt.* to feed on shoots or leaves; to examine casually
bruise *n.* a slight injury —*vt.* to wound without breaking the skin; to damage one's ego, etc.
bruis´er *n.* a large, strong man
brunch *n.* a late breakfast
brunet, **bru·nette´** *adj.* having dark hair or eyes —*n.*
brunt *n.* main shock or impact
brush *n.* bristles attached to a handle; a dense growth; a light touch; a brief encounter —*vi., vt.* use a brush; to touch lightly
brusque *adj.* abrupt; discourteous; curt —**brusque´ly** *adv.*
bru´tal *adj.* extremely cruel —**bru·tal´i·ty** *n.*
bru´tal·ise (*Brit.*), **bru´tal·ize** (*US*) *vt.* degrade or demean —**bru·tal·i·sa´tion**, **bru·tal·i·za´tion** *n.*
brute *adj.* unreasoning; savage —*n.* beast; barbarian; monster
brut´ish *adj.* bestial; savage —**brut´ish·ly** *adv.* —**brut´ish·ness** *n.*
bub´ble *n.* a tiny ball of trapped gas —*vi., vt.* to make or form bubbles —**bub´bly** *adj.*
buc·ca·neer´ *n.* a pirate
buck *n.* a male animal —*vi., vt.* to move in an effort to throw a rider
buck´et *n.* a container for carrying water, coal, etc.
buck´le *n.* device for joining ends; a decoration like a buckle —*vi., vt.* join with a buckle; bend under heat or pressure
buck´ram *n.* a coarse cloth
buck´shot *n.* heavy shot
buck up encourage or cheer
bu·col´ic *adj.* of a country setting —**bu·col´i·cal·ly** *adv.*
bud *n.* a small growth preceding a leaf or flower —**nip in the bud** end in the early stages —**bud´like** *adj.*
bud´dy *n.* close friend; a comrade
buddy system pairing for protection
budge *vi.* to move a little
budg´et *n.* a projection of need —*vi., vt.* to plan for future needs —**bud´get·ar·y** *adj.* —**bud´get·er** *n.*
buff *vt.* to shine, polish; to burnish —**in the buff** naked
buf´fet *n.* a blow —*vt.* to strike
buf·fet´ a sideboard for storage and serving food; informal meal
buff´er *n.* something that polishes; padding
buf·foon´ *n.* a clown or jester; a fool —**buf·foon´ish** *adj.*
bug *n.* an insect; disease–causing microorganism; annoying defect; a device for eavesdropping —*vt.* to eavesdrop; to annoy
bug´a·boo *n.* a gremlin; something causing difficulty, fear, or anxiety
bug´–eyed *adj.* amazed; astonished
bug´gy *adj.* infested with bugs; eccentric, crazy —*n.* a light carriage
bu´gle *n.* a hunting or military horn —*vi., vt.* to signal with a bugle
build *n.* one's physical form —*vi.* put up a building; to increase —*vt.* construct; cause to grow
build´ing *n.* a structure with sidewalls and a roof
build´up *n.* promotion; puffery; a gradual increase
built´–in *adj.* installed as a part of a structure
built´–up *adj.* covered by buildings
bulb *n.* a tuberous root; anything similar
bul´bous *adj.* round; shaped like a bulb; rotund, corpulent
bulge *n.* a swelling; a projection —*vi., vt.* to swell; project
bulk *adj.* of the aggregate; not broken down —*n.* the main part —*vi., vt.* to enlarge, expand
bulk´head *n.* a wall of a ship
bulk´y *adj.* of significant size; awkward or difficult —**bulk·i·ness** *n.*
bull *n.* the adult male of some animals; a speculator
bull´doz·er *n.* an earth–moving machine; one who aggresively promotes —**bull´doze** *vt.*
bul´le·tin *n.* a brief statement; a timely report; a newsletter
bul´let·proof *adj.* safe from bullets; of an unbreakable agreement
bull´frog´ *n.* a large North American frog
bull´head´ed *adj.* stubborn; obstinate —**bull´head·ed·ly** *adv.* —**bull´head·ed·ness** *n.*
bull´horn *n.* a hand–held amplifier
bul´lion *n.* bulk gold or silver
bull´ock *n.* a steer; a castrated bull
bull´pen *n.* waiting area for a baseball team; any waiting or holding area; those available to be used
bull's´eye *n.* the center of a target; the achievement of a goal
bul´ly *n.* one who intimidates the weak —*vi., vt.* to intimidate
bul´wark *n.* a fortification; the side of a ship above the deck
bum *adj.* of inferior quality; worthless —*n.* tramp; a loafer; one addicted to a pursuit —*vi.* live by begging —*vt.* to get by freeloading
bum´mer *n.* a bad experience; a washout
bump *n.* a blow; a bulge or swelling —*vi., vt.* hit or collide with
bump´er *adj.* remarkably large —*n.* a guard to protect against contact
bump´kin *n.* an unrefined person
bump´tious *adj.* arrogantly conceited —**bump´tious·ly** *adv.*
bump´y *adj.* marked by bulges; rough; irregular —**travel a bumpy road** undertake a difficult task
bun *n.* a small bread roll
bunch *n.* a cluster of like things —*vi., vt.* to gather together
bun´dle *n.* things bound together —*vt.* make in bundles; dress warmly
bung *n.* a stopper in a barrel or cask
bun´ga·low´ *n.* a small house
bun´gee, bungee cord *n.* elastic cord used to secure cargo
bun´gle *vi., vt.* make or work clumsily —*n.* an imperfect deed —**bun´gling·ly** *adv.*
bun´ion *n.* inflammation on a toe
bunk *n.* a bed attached to a wall; any sleeping place; meaningless information —*vi.* rest or stay
bunk´er *n.* a fortified position
bunk´house *n.* sleeping quarters
bunk mate, **bunk´mate** *n.* one who shares living and sleeping space
bun´ny *n.* a rabbit
bunt *vi., vt.* hit a baseball lightly —*n.* —**bunt´er** *n.*
bun´ting *n.* cloth for flags; a decorative banner; baby's wrap
buoy *n.* a channel marker —*vt.* keep afloat; encourage —**buoy´ant** *adj.*
bur´den *n.* a heavy load; a responsibility —*vt.* to weigh down —**bur´den·some** *adj.*
bu´reau (*US*) *n.* chest of drawers; office, department, or agency
bu·reauc´ra·cy *n.* governing through departments with limited jurisdiction or authority —**bu´reau·crat** *n.*
bu·reau·crat´ic *adj.* to act strictly according to rules —**bu·reau·crat´i·cal·ly** *adv.*
bu·reau´cra·tise (*Brit.*), **bu·reau´cra·tize** (*US*) *vi., vt.* make into a bureaucracy —**bu·reau·cra·ti·sa´tion**, **bu·reau·cra·ti·za´tion** *n.*
burg *n.* a small town or village
bur´geon *vi.* to grow rapidly or profusely; to flourish
burg´er *n.* a ground food patty; a sandwich made with a patty
bur´gla·ry *n.* a breaking in to rob —**bur´glar** *n.* —**bur´glar·ize** *vi.*
bur´i·al *n.* the act of burying
bur´lap (*US*) *n.* a coarse cloth for sacks and upholstry backing
bur·lesque´ *n.* broad comedy; satire; theatrical entertainment —*vt.* to imitate with mockery or satire
bur´ly *adj.* strong and muscular —**bur´li·ness** *n.*
burn *n.* an injury by fire —*vi.* be on fire; emit light or heat; injured by fire; heated by emotion —*vt.* set on fire; consume by fire —**burnt** *adj.*
bur´nish *n.* a smooth luster —*vt.* to polish —**bur´nish·er** *n.*
bur·noose´, **bur·nous´** *n.* a long hooded cloak
burp *n.* belch
bur´ro *n.* a donkey
bur´row *n.* a hole that shelters —*vi., vt.* to dig or hide —**bur´row·er** *n.*
bur´sar *n.* the comptroller of a college or university
bur´sa·ry *n.* a treasury
burst *n.* a sudden action —*vi. vt.* break suddenly
bur´y *vt.* place in the ground; to cover; to remove from mind; to completely absorb oneself
burying ground an ancient cemetary
bus *n.* a vehicle for a large number of passengers; an omnibus; (*Brit.*) a large, double–decker vehicle
bus´boy *n.* a restaurant worker
bush *n.* a low woody plant; a low wooded area —**beat around the bush** to talk without commitment —**bush´i·ness** *n.* —**bush´y** *adj.*
bushed *adj.* tired; fatigued
bush´el *n.* a dry measure of 4 pecks
bush´ing *n.* a sleeve for reducing friction between machine parts
bush´whack *vi., vt.* to ambush
busi´ness *n.* commerce; buying and selling; one's occupation; any matter for concern
busi´ness·like *adj.* professional
buss *n.* a kiss —*vi., vt.* kiss playfully
bust *n.* a sculpture of the upper body; the chest; a failure; a severe downturn —*vi., vt.* break; make or become bankrupt
bus´tle *n.* brisk activity —*vi.* to move briskly —**bus´tling·ly** *adv.*
bus´y *adj.* active; occupied —**bus´i·ly** *adv.*
bus´y·bod·y *n.* a meddler
bus´y·work *n.* useless activity
butch´er *n.* one who sells meat; a murderer —*vt.* process meat; massacre; do sloppy work —**butch´er·y** *n.*
but´ler *n.* a manservant
butler's pantry a station between kitchen and dining room
but´ter *n.* an edible fat; a spread like butter —**but´ter·y** *adj.*
but´ter·ball *n.* a chubby person
but´ter·fat *n.* fat from milk
but´ter·fin·gered *adj.* clumsy
but´ter·fly´ *adj.* of or like a butterfly —*n.* an insect with colorful wings
but´ter·milk´ *n.* the liquid remains from churning butter
but´ter·scotch *n.* a flavoring of brown sugar and butter —*adj.*

but´ton *n.* a small fastener; a thing resembling a button —*vi., vt.* fasten with buttons

but´ton–down *adj.* of a collar with buttoned tips; conservative

but´ton·hole *n.* a slit to receive a button —*vt.* compel one to listen

but´tress *n.* a structure that reinforces; reinforcement —*vt.* reinforce —**flying buttress** an arched buttress bracing a wall

bux´om *adj.* full–figured —**bux´om·ly** *adv.* —**bux´om·ness** *n.*

buy *n.* a purchase; a bargain —*vt.* obtain for money; accept as valid

buy off to bribe

buy time to stall

buzz *n.* a droning; a low murmur; a telephone call —*vi.* make a droning sound; talk excitedly —*vt.* speak rapidly; make a telephone call; signal with a buzzer

by *prep.* proximity in space or time; at the hand of; through the medium of —*adv.* near

by´–and–by´ *n.* sometime in the future

bye law (*Brit.*) the rules governing an association or organization

by´gone *adj.* past —**let bygones be bygones** forgive a past indiscretion

by´law (*US*) *n.* rules governing an association or organization

by´–line *n.* an attribution; a naming of the author

by´pass´ *n.* an alternative route —*vt.* to detour; to circumvent

by´–path *n.* a route seldom taken

by´–play *n.* peripheral events

by´–prod´uct *n.* material accumulated during processing; a secondary product

by´stand·er *n.* one who is present, but not involved

byte *n.* a set of binary digits; a computer word

by´way *n.* a side road

c, C *n.* third letter of the alphabet; third–rate; symbol for 100

cab *n.* a taxicab; an area for the operator of heavy equipment

ca·bal´ *n.* plotters; a secret plot

cab´a·la, cab·ba´la *n.* mystical teachings; mystical or esoteric doctrine —**cab·a·lis´tic** *adj.*

ca·ba´na *n.* a bathhouse

cab·a·ret´ *n.* a nightclub

cab´in *n.* a small house; a room on a boat or plane

cabin boy an apprentice seaman

cab´i·net *n.* an article of furniture; a body of advisors

cab´i·net·mak·er *n.* a craftsman in wood —**cab´i·net·ry** *n.*

cabin fever anxiety or boredom from living in a confined space

ca´ble *n.* heavy rope; a bundle of insulated conductors; a cablegram; cable television —*vt.* connect with cable; send a cablegram

cable car vehicle drawn by cable

ca´ble·gram *n.* a message carried by undersea cable

cable television transmission of television signals by cable

ca´ble·vi·sion *n.* cable television

ca·boo´dle *n.* a batch or group

ca·boose´ (*US*) *n.* last car on a train

cab·ri·o·let´ *n.* a small carriage

cab´stand *n.* place where taxicabs or carriages wait for fares

ca·ca´o *n.* a tropical tree or its seeds, used to make chocolate products

cache *n.* a place for storing; material stored; computer memory that stores data for quick retrieval

ca·chet´ *n.* mark of authenticity

ca·coph´o·ny *n.* dissonance; a harsh noise —**ca·coph´o·nous** *adj.* —**ca·coph´o·nous·ly** *adv.*

cac´tus *n., pl.* **cac´ti, cac´tus·es** desert plant with spiney leaves

cad *n.* a nasty person; a rogue

ca·dav´er (*US*) *n.* a dead body

ca·dav´er·ous *adj.* pale, gaunt

ca´dence, ca´den·cy *n.* a rhythmic sound; a measured beat —**ca´denced, ca´dent** *adj.*

ca·den´za *n.* a musical flourish

ca·det´ *n.* a military student

cadge *vi., vt.* to beg; acquire by begging; freeload —**cadg´er** *n.*

ca´dre *n.* staff; key personnel

ca·du´ce·us *n.* emblem of the medical profession —**ca·du´ce·an** *adj.*

cae·sar´e·an, caesarean section *n.* delivering a baby by surgery

ca·fe´, ca·fé´ *n.* a coffeehouse

café au lait a beverage of equal parts dark coffee and scalded milk

caf´e·te´ri·a *n.* a limited service restaurant; (*US*) a facility where employee meals are served

caf·feine´ *n.* a stimulant in tea and coffee —**caf´fein·at·ed** *adj.*

caf´tan *n.* a long, loose robe or dress

cage *n.* a place of confinement —*vt.* put in confinement

ca´gey *adj.* cunning; shrewd, clever —**ca´gi·ly** *adv.* —**cag´i·ness** *n.*

cai´man, cay´man *n.* a Central or South American crocodile

cais´son *n.* ammunition chest; a wagon for carrying ammunition

caisson disease a condition suffered by divers who surface too quickly

ca·jole´ *vi., vt.* appeal repeatedly; wheedle by flattery —**ca·jol´er·y** *n.* —**ca·jol´er** *n.* —**ca·jol´ing·ly** *adv.*

cake *n.* a sweet pastry; something formed into a patty or block —*vi., vt.* to harden; form a crust

cake´walk *n.* a strutting dance; a thing easily accomplished

ca·lam´i·ty *n.* extreme misfortune; tragedy —**ca·lam´i·tous** *adj.* —**ca·lam´i·tous·ly** *adv.*

cal´ci·fy *vi., vt.* turn to stone or stone–like —**cal·ci·fi·ca´tion** *n.*

cal´ci·mine *n.* a white liquid used to cover plastered walls

cal´ci·um *n.* a mineral essential to growth of bones, teeth, etc.

cal´cu·late´ *vt.* use mathematics; estimate —**cal·cu·la´tion** *n.* —**cal´cu·la·tor** *n.*

cal´cu·lat·ed *adj.* computed or reckoned; deliberate

cal´cu·lat·ing *adj.* scheming; shrewd or crafty —**cal´cu·lat·ing·ly** *adv.*

cal´cu·lous *adj.* relating to or having a stony deposit

cal´cu·lus *n., pl.* **cal´cu·li, cal´cu·lus·es** a stone–like deposit; a system of computation

cal´dron, caul´dron *n.* a large kettle

cal´en·dar *n.* a system of recording a year; a list of appointments

calf *n., pl.* **calves** the young of certain animals; a cured hide; back of the leg below the knee

cal´i·ber *n.* the diameter of a cylinder; the quality of a person

cal´i·brate *vt.* to regulate or adjust —**cal·i·bra´tion** *n.*

cal´i·co´ *n.* a printed cotton cloth

cal´i·per *n.* a device for measuring thickness or diameter

ca´liph, ca´lif *n.* Islamic leader

ca´liph·ate *n.* land ruled by a caliph

cal´is·then´ics *pl. n.* exercises

cal·lig´ra·phy *n.* artistic writing; embellished writing —**cal·li·graph´ic** *adj.*

call´ing *n.* one's profession

calling card a card that identifies a caller; a business card

cal·li´o·pe´ *n.* a steam–powered instrument like a pipe organ

cal´lous *adj.* heartless; indifferent —**cal´lous·ly** *adv.* —**cal´lous·ness** *n.*

cal´low *adj.* young and inexperienced; immature —**cal´low·ness** *n.*

cal´lus *n.* thickened skin

calm *adj.* still; tranquil; composed —*n.* stillness; tranquility —*vi., vt.* to soothe or pacify —**calm´ly** *adv.*

calm´a·tive *n.* a sedative

cal´o·rie *n.* a measure of heat; large calorie, used to measure energy produced by food —**ca·lor´ic** *adj.* —**ca·lor´i·cal·ly** *adv.*

cal·o·rif´ic *adj.* producing heat; high in calories —**cal·o·rif´i·cal·ly** *adv.*

ca·lum´ni·ate *vi., vt.;* to spread rumors —**ca·lum·ni·a´tion** *n.*

ca·lum´ni·ous *adj.* slanderous —**ca·lum´ni·ous·ly** *adv.*

cal´um·ny *n.* slander; defamation

calve *vi., vt.* to give birth to a calf

ca·lyp´so *n.* music of Trinidad

ca·ma·ra´de·rie *n.* good fellowship

cam´ber *n.* arching; curvature

cam´bric *n.* a fine linen fabric

cam´cord·er *n.* a video camera

cam´el *n.* common beast of burden in the deserts of Asia and Africa

cam´e·o´ *n.* a shell or gem carved in relief; a brief appearance

cam´er·a *n.* a device for recording visual images —**cam´er·a·man** *n.*

cam´er·a lu´ci·da *n.* an optical device for projecting an image

cam´ou·flage´ *n.* protection through deceptive use of color and form; a device to conceal

camp *n.* a temporary living area; something flamboyant or outdated —*vi., vt.* to live outdoors —**camp´er** *n.* —**camp´site** *n.*

cam·paign´ *n.* undertaking to achieve an objective —*vi.* participate in such an undertaking

cam·pa·ni´le *n.* a bell tower

cam·pa·nol´o·gy *n.* the art of designing and making bells —**cam·pa·nol´o·gist** *n.*

camp´fire *n.* an outdoor fire

cam´pus *adj.* of a school or its surroundings —*n.* the grounds or buildings of a complex

ca·nal´ *n.* an artificial waterway; waterway made navigable; duct or channel —*vt.* build a canal

can´a·pé *n.* an appetizer of bread spread with meat, cheese, etc.

ca·nard´ *n.* misleading tale; hoax

can´cel *vt.* to invalidate; rescind; delete —**can·cel·la´tion** *n.*

can´cer *n.* a malignant growth; any infectious evil —**can´cer·ous** *adj.*

can·de·la´brum *n., pl.* **can·de·la´bra** a large, branching candle holder

can´did *adj.* straightforward, honest; impartial —**can´did·ly** *adv.*

can´di·date *n.* a nominee

can´died *adj.* coated with sugar

can´dle *n.* a wax cylinder with a wick burned for light —*vt.* to examine in front of a bright light

can´dle·light *adj.* lighted by candles; of soft light —*n.* subdued light

can´dle·pow·er *n.* a measure of intensity of light

can´dle·stick *n.* a candle; a candle holder; a candelabrum

can´dor *n.* frankness or honesty

can´dy (US) *n.* a confection of sugar and flavoring —*vt.* glaze with sugar

candy striper hospital volunteer

cane *n.* the stem of a woody plant; the plant; rattan used in weaving; walking stick; rod for flogging —*vt.* beat with a cane

cane´brake *n.* a stand of sugar cane

cane sugar sugar from cane

ca´nine´ *adj.* of or like a dog —*n.* a dog; a sharp–pointed tooth

can´is·ter *n.* a small container

can´ker *n.* an ulcerous sore; something that corrupts —*vi., vt.* to infect or corrupt —**can´ker·ous** *adj.*

canned *adj.* (*US*) of processed food in metal containers; recorded; prepared ahead; contrived

can´ner *n.* one involved in processing and packaging of food

can´ner·y *n.* an industrial plant where raw food is processed

can´ni·bal *n.* any creature that eats its own kind

can´ni·bal·ise (*Brit.*), **can´ni·bal·ize** (*US*) *vi., vt.* devour one's kind, remove parts for use elsewhere

can´ny *adj.* cautious, watchful; shrewd —**can´ni·ly** *adv.*

ca·noe´ *n.* a light, narrow boat —*vi., vt.* travel or carry by canoe

can´on *n.* church law; an established principle, a standard

ca·non´ic, ca·non´i·cal *adj.* about church law; accepted —**ca·non´i·cal·ly** *adv.*

can´on·ist *n.* an authority in canon law —**can·on·is´tic** *adj.*

can´on·ize *vt.* to sanctify or consecrate; to glorify, venerate

canon law rules governing a church

can´o·py *n.* a protective covering; anything similar —*vt.* to create an overhead covering

cant *n.* a sloping surface; terminology of a particular group; insincere speech —*vi., vt.* slope or cause to slope; speak in a jargon
can·ta·loupe´ *n.* variety of melon
can·tan´ker·ous *adj.* quarrelsome, disagreeable
caf´e·te´ri·a *n.* a limited service restaurant; (*US*) a facility where employee meals are served
can·teen´ *n.* a container for drinking water; a place serving food; (*Brit.*) a cutlery collection
can´ti·cle *n.* a hymn
can´ti·lev·er *n.* a projection anchored by a wall
can´tor *n.* a choir leader; a leader in prayer or scripture reading
can´vas *n.* a heavy cloth for sails, tents, etc.; an oil painting
can´vass *vi., vt.* to seek out opinions, votes, etc. —**can´vass·er** *n.*
can´yon *n.* a narrow gorge
cap *n.* covering for the head; any cover —*vt.* place a top on; to cover
ca´pa·ble *adj.* having skill —**ca·pa·bil´i·ty** *n.* —**ca´pa·bly** *adv.*
ca·pa´cious *adj.* spacious; massive; having much space —**ca·pa´cious·ly** *adv.* —**ca·pa´cious·ness** *n.*
ca·pac´i·ty *n.* The ability to hold; having aptitude; proper qualifications
cape *n.* a sleeveless outer garment, a cloak; a point of land
caper *n.* a playful leap; a silly action —*vi.* leap playfully; frolic
cap´il·lar´y *adj.* like a hair; of hair–like blood vessels —*n.* tiny blood vessels
cap·il·lar´i·ty *n.* action of a liquid and a solid that encloses it
cap´i·tal *adj.* punishable by death; most significant; first–rate —*n.* a seat of government; assets; an uppercase letter; the top of a column
cap´i·tal·ise (*Brit.*), **cap´i·tal·ize** (*US*) *vt.* to write in uppercase letters; to finance; exploit for profit —**cap·i·tal·i·sa´tion, cap·i·tal·i·za´tion** *n.*
cap´i·tal·ism *n.* a system of private ownership —**cap´i·tal·ist** *n.* —**cap·i·tal·is´tic** *adj.*
capital punishment death penalty
Capitol home of the US Congress —**capitol** home of a state legislature
ca·pit´u·late´ *vi.* to surrender —**ca·pit·u·la´tion** *n.*
ca·pote´ *n.* a long, hooded cloak
ca·price´ *n.* an impetuous action; tending to be unpredictable —**ca·pri´cious** *adj.* —**ca·pri´cious·ly** *adv.* —**ca·pri´cious·ness** *n.*
cap´size *vt.* to upend —**cap´siz·a·ble** *adj.*
cap´stan *n.* a device for hoisting anchor; a spindle for magnetic tape
cap´sule´ *n.* a small container, such as for a seed or for medicine; a closed compartment in a spacecraft —**cap´su·lar** *adj.*
cap´sul·ize *vt.* to summarize; to furnish in abbreviated form
cap´tain *n.* a military officer; a group leader
cap´tion *n.* a heading; descriptive matter
cap´tious *adj.* critical; fond of finding fault —**cap´tious·ly** *adv.* —**cap´tious·ness** *n.*
cap´ti·vate´ *vt.* to attract; to fascinate or bewitch
cap´tive *adj.* held prisoner; restricted; fascinated —*n.* a prisoner —**cap´tiv´i·ty** *n.* —**cap´tor** *n.*
captive audience listeners held by charisma; those who cannot leave, as at a business meeting
cap´ture *n.* taking or being taken; that taken —*vt.* take and hold; to captivate —**cap´tor, cap´tur·er** *n.*
car *n.* an automobile; an area for passengers, as of an elevator; (*US*) a railway passenger vehicle
ca·rafe´ *n.* a beverage container
car´a·mel *n.* burnt sugar flavoring; a candy; the color of burnt sugar —**car´a·mel·ize** *vi., vt.*
car´at *n.* unit of weight for gems
car´a·van *n.* a company of travelers; a file of vehicles or pack animals; (*Brit.*) a mobile home
car·a·van´sa·ry *n.* an inn; a haven for caravans
car´a·vel *n.* a small, 15th century sailing ship
car´a·way *n.* a flavoring seed; the herb that produces such seeds
car´bine *n.* a light rifle
car´bo·hy´drate *n.* an organic compound; the main source of energy in food
car´bon *n.* a nonmetallic element present in all organic compounds
car´bo·nate *vt.* to infuse with carbon dioxide —**car·bon·a´tion** *n.*
carbon dating determining age by measuring carbon 14 —**car´bon–date** *vt.*
car·bon di·ox·ide *n.* gas released by respiration and absorbed by plants
carbon 14 a radioactive isotope of carbon used to date relics
car´bon·ize *vt.* convert to carbon; to coat or combine with carbon
car·bon mon·ox·ide *n.* a colorless, odorless, poisonous gas
carbon copy an exact duplicate
car·bon tet·ra·chlo·ride *n.* a colorless solvent used as cleaning fluid
car´bun·cle *n.* red gemstone; a skin eruption similar to a boil
car´bu·re·tor *n.* device for mixing air and gas for an engine
car´cass *n.* a dead animal; the human body
car·cin´o·gen *n.* a cancer–causing substance —**car·cin·o·gen´ic** *adj.*
car·ci·no´ma *n.* a cancerous growth
car·ci·no·ma·to´sis *n.* spread of carcinoma throughout the body
card *n.* a stiff paper; a witty or amusing person —**credit card** an authorization to purchase on credit —**trading card** cards depicting persons, events, etc.
car´da·mom *n.* a spice
card´board *n.* a stiff paper —*adj.* of or like cardboard
card–carrying *adj.* of a member; one espousing a cause
car´di·ac´ *adj.* of the heart
car´di·gan a buttoned sweater
car´di·nal *adj.* primary; foremost
cardinal number a number that designates quantity
car·di·ol´o·gy *n.* the study of the heart, its function, and diseases
car·di·ol´o·gist *n.* one who specializes in diseases of the heart
card shark an expert at cards
card table a table designed for playing cards or other games; a table with folding legs
care *n.* concern; acting with caution —*vi., vt.* feel concern
ca·reen´ *vi., vt.* to lean; to swerve
ca·reer´ *n.* one's progress; a line of work —**ca·reer´ist** *n.*
care´free *adj.* without concern or worry; lighthearted
care´ful *adj.* cautious; attentive to detail; frugal —**care´ful·ly** *adv.* —**care´ful·ness** *n.*
care´giv·er *n.* one charged with the health and well–being of another
care´less *adj.* reckless, lacking caution; inattentive —**care´less·ly** *adv.* —**care´less·ness** *n.*
ca·ress´ *vt.* touch lightly; stroke lovingly —*n.* expression of affection; gentle touching —**ca·ress´ing·ly** *adv.* —**ca·ress´ive** *adj.*
car´et *n.* a proofreader's mark (^)
care´tak·er *n.* one who maintains or preserves
care´worn *adj.* weary; showing the effects of a burden
car´fare *n.* the price of a ride
car´go *n.* freight
car´i·ca·ture *n.* exaggerated likeness; something inferior —*vt.* ridicule; create a distorted likeness
car´ies *n.* the decay of teeth
car´il·lon *n.* a set of musical bells —**car·il·lon·neur´** *n.*
car´load *n.* the amount that can be carried by a vehicle
car´mine *n.* deep red
car´nage *n.* a massacre; the remains of a slaughter
car´nal *adj.* of the flesh; of worldly pleasures; temporal
car´ni·val *n.* merrymaking; local festival; (US) a traveling show
car´ni·vore *n.* any creature that consumes the flesh of another
car·niv´o·rous *adj.* flesh–eating
car´ol *n.* song of joy —*vi.* to sing
car´o·tene, car´o·tin *n.* a substance that converts to vitamin A
ca·rot´e·noid *adj.* of a pigment in the yellow to red range —*n.*
ca·rot´id *adj.* of the two main arteries of the neck —*n.*
ca·rouse´ *n.* drunken revelry —*vi.* engage in drunken revelry
car·ou·sel´, car·rou·sel´ *n.* a merry–go–round; a revolving device that feeds a continuous stream
carp *vi.* to find fault; to complain
car´pen·ter *n.* worker in wood —*vi.* to work with wood —**car´pen·try** *n.*
car´pet *n.* thick covering for a floor
car´pet·bag *n.* a type of luggage made from carpeting
carpetbagger one who moves to an area to profit from local conditions
car pool a group who share rides —**car´pool** *vi.*
car´port *n.* an open structure for protecting an automobile
car´riage *n.* one's bearing; a horse–drawn vehicle
car´riage *n.* (*Brit.*) a railway passenger vehicle
car´ri·er *n.* anything that transports; one infected by disease without symptoms —**common carrier** a company that transfers goods
car´ri·on *n.* decaying flesh
car´ry *vt.* convey from one place to another; support or sustian
carried away caught up in events
carry on operate or manage; remain firm in adversity; behave childishly
car´ry·o·ver *n.* something left from a previous time
car´ry–out, car´ry·out *adj.* of food eaten off the premises
cart *n.* a small wheeled conveyance that is pulled or pushed —*vt.* to transport by cart —**cart´er** *n.*
cart off to take away
cart´age *n.* the act of transporting; a charge for transporting
carte blanche full authority
car´tel´ *n.* business alliance; any coalition for a common cause
car·tog´ra·phy *n.* the art of making maps
car´ton *n.* a cardboard box
car´toon´ *n.* a caricature; a line drawing —*vi., vt.* to make or draw cartoons
car´tridge´ *n.* a small carrier for material such as film or tape
cart´wheel *n.* an acrobatic maneuver that involves turning the body perpendicular to the ground
carve *vt.* to fashion or divide by cutting —**carve up** to divide; to share
carv´ing *n.* a figure made by cutting
cas·cade´ *n.* a succession of steep waterfalls; a number of devices connected in series —*vi., vt.*
case *n.* an instance: *in any case*; a legal action; a container —**just in case** for contingency —**on his/her case** critical, fault-finding
case study an analysis
case´work·er *n.* a social worker
cash *n.* money at hand; currency; liquid assets —*vt.* convert to cash —**petty cash** money kept on hand for incidentals —**cash´a·ble** *adj.*
cash–and–carry terms of a sale: no credit and no delivery
cash´book *n.* a record of cash transactions; a cash journal
cash box storage for cash receipts, petty cash, etc.
cash crop produce grown to sell
cash discount a rebate for cash
cash´ew *n.* an edible nut or its tree
cash·ier´ *n.* one responsible for the receipt and disbursement of cash
cash´mere *n.* a type of fine wool
cash reg·is·ter *n.* a machine for recording sales and storing cash

cas´ing *n.* framework; the outer covering of sausage

cask *n.* a barrel

cas´ket *n.* a small chest; a coffin

cas´se·role *n.* an earthenware pot; the slow baking of food; food cooked and served in a single dish

cas·sette *n.* a small case for film, magnetic tape, etc.

cas´sock *n.* a clergyman's robe

cast *n.* the act of throwing or projecting, as an object or a glance; a thing formed in a mold; the actors in a theatrical production; the appearance of a thing —*vi., vt.* throw; to select performers

cast´a·way *n.* a person or thing abandoned

caste *n.* social position or status

cas´ti·gate´ *vt.* to criticize severely —**cas´ti·ga´tion** *n.* —**cas´ti·ga·tor** *n.*

cast´ing *n.* that formed in a mold

cast iron an alloy of iron

cas´tle *n.* a fortification

cast´off *adj.* discarded —*n.* discarded material, a remnant

castor oil oil of the castor bean, a lubricant and medication

cas´trate *vt.* to remove testicles; to spay; to make ineffectual

cas´u·al *adj.* without plan; haphazard; careless —**cas´u·al·ly** *adv.*

cas´u·al·ty *n.* a serious accident; one harmed

cat·a·bol´ic *adj.* of conversion of tissue to energy —**ca·tab´o·lism** *n.*

cat´a·clysm *n.* major disturbance —**cat·a·clys´mal** *adj.*

cat´a·comb´ *n.* an underground cemetery

cat´a·lep·sy *n.* a condition marked by rigidity and a trancelike state —**cat·a·lep´tic** *adj.*

cat´a·log´, cat´a·logue´ *n.* a book of merchandise; any listing of related material —*vi., vt.* to list or classify

ca·tal´y·sis *n.* a change in the rate of a chemical reaction with use of an additive

cat´a·lyst *n.* substance that alters a chemical reaction; anything that brings conclusion or resolution —**cat·a·lyt´ic** *adj.*

cat´a·ma·ran´ *n.* a sailboat with twin hulls

cat´a·mount *n.* a wildcat

cat´a·pult *n.* a seige weapon; a device for launching aircraft —*vi., vt.*

cat´a·ract´ *n.* a large waterfall; a disease of the eye

ca·tarrh´ *n.* inflammation of a mucous membrane

ca·tas´tro·phe *n.* great disaster; complete failure —**cat·a·stroph´ic** *adj.* —**cat·a·stroph´i·cal·ly** *adv.*

cat burglar a stealthy thief

cat´call *n.* a sound of disapproval —*vi., vt.* to jeer

catch *n.* a prize; that captured; a drawback; fastener —*vt.* take hold; take unawares; overtake

catch´all *n.* a place where things are kept or left; a useless item

catch´ing *adj.* contagious

catch on understand, comprehend; to become popular

catch phrase a slogan or motto

catch´y *adj.* attention–getting; easily remembered

cat´e·chise (*Brit.*), **cat´e·chize** (*US*) *vt.* to teach by questioning —**cat·e·chi·sa´tion, cat·e·chi·za´tion** *n.*

cat´e·chism *n.* questions for teaching fundamentals —**cat´e·chist** *n.*

cat·e·chu´men *n.* one being instructed in fundamentals

cat´e·gor´i·cal *adj.* without qualification; absolute —**cat·e·gor´i·cal·ly** *adv.*

cat´e·go·rize *vt.* classify or type; arrange —**cat·e·go·ri·za´tion** *n.*

cat´e·go´ry *n.* a classification

cat·e·na´tion *n.* formed in succession; a continuity —**cat´e·nate** *vt.*

ca´ter *vi.* to provide food; to indulge —**ca´ter·er** *n.*

cat´er·waul *n.* wail, as of a rutting cat; discordant screeching —*vi.*

cat´gut *n.* tough line, as used for stringing musical instruments

ca·thar´sis *n.* a cleansing or purgation —**ca·thar´tic** *adj.*

ca·the´dral *n.* a large church

cathedral ceiling a vaulted dome

cath´e·ter *n.* a slender tube for internal examination, passing fluid, etc. —**cath´e·ter·ize** *vt.*

cath´ode–ray tube a vacuum tube that displays images

cath´o·lic *adj.* broad in scope or taste —**ca·thol´i·cise** (*Brit.*), **ca·thol´i·cize** (*US*) *vi., vt.*

cat´nap *n.* a light sleep —*vi.* doze

cat´nip *n.* a type of mint

cat–o´–nine´tails *n.* a whip

cat´tle *n.* livestock

cat´ty *adj.* catlike, cunning; malicious, vindictive, spiteful

catty–corner, catty–cornered *adj.* diagonal —*adv.* at a diagonal

cat´walk *n.* a narrow walkway

cau´cus *n.* a closed conference; a faction within a political party

cau´dal *adj.* of or like a tail; near the tail —**cau´dal·ly** *adv.*

cau´date *adj.* having a tail

caul *n.* membrane over a fetus

caul´dron *n.* a large kettle

caulk *n.* a malleable sealer —*vt.* to apply a sealer

caus´al *adj.* of cause and effect —**caus´al·ly** *adv.* —**cau·sal´i·ty** *n.*

cau·sa´tion *n.* the act of causing

cause *n.* an agent of change; an objective —*vt.* to make happen

cause´way *n.* an elevated road

caus´tic *adj.* corrosive; biting or sarcastic —**caus´ti·cal·ly** *adv.*

cau´ter·ise (*Brit.*), **cau´ter·ize** (*US*) *vt.* destroy or seal by heat

cau´tion *n.* discretion; prudence; a warning —*vt.* to warn; to admonish —**cau´tion·ar·y** *adj.* —**cau´tious** *adj.* —**cau´tious·ly** *adv.*

cav´al·cade´ *n.* procession; series

cav´a·lier´ *adj.* casual; nonchalant; hauty —*n.* armed horseman; a gentleman —**cav·a·lier´ly** *adv.*

cav´al·ry *n.* mounted soldiers

cave *n.* a hollow under the earth

ca´ve·at *n.* a formal notice

cave´–in a place where the surface gives way

cave man prehistoric man; a rough or crude individual

cav´ern *n.* a hollow in the earth, a large cave —**cav´ern·ous** *adj.*

cav´i·ar *n.* the eggs of a fish: roe

cav´il *n.* a trivial objection —*vi.* to quibble —**cav´il·er** *n.*

cav´i·ty *n.* a hole or hollow place

ca·vort´ *vi.* to frolic; to prance

caw *n.* the call of a crow —*vi.*

cay *n.* an offshore island or reef

cay·enne´ *n.* a hot red pepper

CD *n.* a compact disc

cease *vi., vt.* to stop —**ces·sa´tion** *n.*

cease–fire a temporary cessation

cease´less *adj.* without end; never stopping —**cease´less·ly** *adv.*

cede *vt.* to surrender

ce·dil´la *n.* mark under the letter c (ç) to indicate an *s* sound

ceil´ing *n.* the top of a room; an upper limit —**hit the ceiling** grow excited; lose one's temper

cel´e·brant *n.* one who celebrates

cel´e·brate´ *vt.* to commemorate; to praise publicly; make known —**cel·e·bra´tion** *n.* —**cel´e·bra·tive** *adj.* —**cel´e·bra·to·ry** *adj.*

cel´e·brat·ed *adj.* widely praised

ce·leb´ri·ty *n.* one who is famous

ce´ler´i·ty *n.* quickness; dispatch

ce·les´tial *adj.* of the sky or heavenly bodies —**ce·les´tial·ly** *adv.*

celestial navigation laying a course by sighting on the stars

cel´i·ba·cy *n.* sexual abstinence; being unmarried

cel´i·bate *adj.* practicing celibacy —*n.* one who practices celibacy

cell *n.* a small plain room; the fundamental component of organisms; basic unit of a storage battery

cel´lar *n.* an underground area

cell division the means by which cells reproduce

cel´lo *n.* a stringed instrument of the violin family —**cel´list** *n.*

cel´lo·phane´ *n.* thin, transparent material from cellulose

cell phone, cellular phone (*US*) a mobile telephone

cel´lu·lar *adj.* like a cell; consisting of cells

cel´lule *n.* a small cell

cel´lu·lite *n.* fatty deposits

cel´lu·lose *n.* a complex carbohydrate from cell walls of plants, used in many products

Cel´si·us *adj.* of a thermometer on which the freezing point of water is 0° and the boiling point is 100°.

ce·ment´ *n.* a building material; an adhesive —*vt.* to join with cement; to unite firmly

cem´e·ter´y *n.* a place of burial

ce´no·bite *n.* a member of a religious order living communally

cen´o·taph *n.* a monument; an empty tomb

cen´ser *n.* an incense holder

cen´sor *n.* one authorized to examine for objectionable material —*vt.* to judge what is suitable —**cen´sor·a·ble** *adj.* —**cen´sor·ship** *n.*

cen·so´ri·ous *adj.* expressing censure; faultfinding —**cen·so´ri·ous·ly** *adv.* —**cen·so´ri·ous·ness** *n.*

cen´sur·a·ble *adj.* open to reproach; at fault

cen´sure *n.* disapproval; an official rebuke —*vt.* express disapproval

cen´sus *n.* a count of population

cen´taur *n.* a mythical creature, half man and half horse

cen·te·nar´i·an *n.* one who has lived to the age of 100 years

cen·ten´ni·al *adj.* of 100 years —*n.* one–hundredth anniversary

cen´ter (*US*) *n.* middle point or part; a hub —*vi.* to focus —*vt.* place on or at a point of focus

cen´ter·board *n.* a panel that descends below the keel of a sailing vessel

centered (*US*) *adj.* focused; concentrated; self–confident; at the center

center of gravity (*US*) the point at which weight is concentrated

cen´ter·piece *n.* a dominating decoration or display

cen·tes´i·mal *adj.* of a hundredth part

cen´ti·grade´ *adj.* divided into one hundred degrees; of the Celsius thermometer

cen´ti·gram *n.* one hundredth part of a gram

cen´ti·me´ter *n.* one hundredth part of a meter

cen´tral *adj.* at or near the center; significant; of a single origin —**cen·tral´i·ty** *n.* —**cen´tral·ly** *adv.*

central heating a heating plant that serves an entire building

cen´tral·ism *n.* concentration of power at one place —**cen´tral·ise** (*Brit.*), **cen´tral·ize** (*US*) *vi., vt.*

central nervous system brain and spinal cord of the body

cen´tre (*Brit.*) *n.* the middle point; a hub —*vi.* to concentrate —*vt.* to place on or at a point of focus

centred (*Brit.*) *adj.* focused; self–confident; at the centre

centre of gravity (*Brit.*) the point at which weight is concentrated

cen´trif´u·gal *adj.* moving away from a center —**cen·trif´u·gal·ly** *adv.*

centrifugal force tendency of anything revolving to move outward

cen´tri·fuge *n.* a device that forces matter outward

cen·trip´e·tal *adj.* moving toward a center

cen·tu´ri·on *n.* in ancient Rome, a commander of one hundred men

cen´tu·ry *n.* one hundred years; a group of one hundred

ce·phal´ic *adj.* of the head

ce·ram´ic *adj.* made from baked clay —**ce·ram´ist** *n.* —**ce·ram´ics** *n.*

ce´re·al *n.* a grain used as food; food prepared from grain —*adj.*

cer´e·bral *adj.* of brain or intellect

cerebral palsy a disorder from damage to the central nervous system

cer´e·brum *n.* the front of the brain

cer´e·ment *n.* a shroud; a burial garment

cer·e·mo´ni·al *adj.* of a ritual; stately —*n.* a formal system of ritual —**cer·e·mo´ni·al·ly** *adv.*

cer·e·mo´ni·ous *adj.* with great formality; devoted to ritual or ceremony —**cer·e·mo´ni·ous·ly** *adv.*
cer´e·mo´ny *n.* a formal rite or ritual; a formality
ce·rise´ *adj.* bright red
cer´tain *adj.* definite; reliable; inevitable; of an indefinite quality —**cer´tain·ly** *adv.* — **cer·tain·ty** *n.*
cer·tif´i·cate *n.* an official document
certificate of deposit document confirming the deposit of funds
cer´ti·fi·ca´tion *n.* affirmation
cer´ti·fied *adj.* authorized; approved; vouched for
certified public accountant an accountant recognized as having knowledge of his trade
cer´ti·fy *vt.* make known; to declare in writing — **cer´ti·fi·a·ble** *adj.* — **cer´ti·fi·a·bly** *adv.*
cer´ti·tude *n.* conviction; confidence
ce·ru´le·an *adj.* of an azure blue color
cer´vi·cal *adj.* of the cervix
cer´vix *n.* neck; a neck–like part
ces·sa´tion *n.* ending or stopping
ces´sion *n.* a surrender or renunciation; a waiver
cess´pool *n.* a large receptical for effluence; a place that is corrupted
chad *n.* bits of paper from tape or cards used in computer processing
chafe *n.* irritation or wear from friction —*vi.* rub; become irritated —*vt.* irritate; annoy —**chafe at the bit** show impatience
chaff *n.* the waste from threshing; anything worthless
chaf´ing dish´ *n.* a warming dish
cha·grin´ *n.* embarrassment —*vt.* to embarrass
chain *n.* set of links; set of connected elements; a thing that binds —*vt.* to bind or restrain
chain gang a prison work party
chain letter a letter containing information to be passed on
chain lightning lightning having many branches; a person seen to move quickly
chain reaction a series of events
chain saw a portable power saw
chain store a group of retail outlets
chair *n.* place for sitting; position of authority —*vt.* preside over
chair´lift *n.* a conveyance for transporting skiers up a hill
chair´man, chair´person *n.* one who officiates
chaise longue, chaise lounge *n.* a chair with support for the legs and back
cha·let´ *n.* a style of Swiss house
chal´ice *n.* a goblet
chalk *n.* type of limestone; a marker for a blackboard —*vt.* write with chalk —**chalk´y** *adj.*
chalk´board *n.* a slate; a surface for writing with chalk
chal´lenge *n.* a difficult task; invitation to compete; a questioning —*vt.* invite to compete; call into question —**chal´lenge·a·ble** *adj.*
chal´leng·ing *adj.* difficult, formidable; intriguing, fascinating
cham´ber *n.* bedroom; meeting room; an enclosed space
cham´ber·maid *n.* one who cleans
chamber music light music for performance by a small musical group
chamber of commerce organization that promotes business
champ *n.* a champion —*vt.* to chew
cham·pagne´ *n.* sparkling wine; the yellowish color of the wine
cham´pi·on *n.* supporter of a cause; one with attributes of a winner —*vt.* fight for; support
chance *adj.* fortuitous; unplanned —*n.* random or unexpected occurrence; a wager; an opportunity —*vi.* occur accidentally —*vt.* risk —**chanc´i·ness** *n.* —**chanc´y** *adj.*
chan´cel·ler·y *n.* office of chancellor
chan´cel·lor *n.* president of a university; a prime minister
chan´de·lier´ *n.* an elaborate hanging light fixture
change *n.* alteration; a substitution; transformation; coins — *vt.* make different; exchange; transform
change´a·ble *adj.* adaptable; temporary; unstable, flighty — **change·a·bil´i·ty, change´a·ble·ness** *n.* —**change´a·bly** *adv.*
change´less *adj.* constant; permanent
change of heart shift in thinking
change of pace something dissimilar; respite from the usual
change´o·ver *n.* passing to another; a transformation; an altering
chang´er *n.* one who changes; that which changes records, disks, etc.
chan´nel *n.* a bed for naturally flowing water; a passageway for liquid; a band or route for communications —*vt.* wear into ruts; send through a conduit; to direct
chan´nel·ing *n.* the concept of being a conduit for a spiritual force
chant *n.* a primitive musical form; a rhythmic recitation — *vi., vt.*
cha´os *n.* extreme confusion — **cha·ot´ic** *adj.* —**cha·ot´i·cal·ly** *adv.*
chap *n.* a man or boy —*vi., vt.* to roughen the skin
chap·ar·ral *n.* a thicket
cha·pa´ti *n.* Indian skillet bread
cha·peau´ *n., pl.* **cha·peaus´, cha·peaux´** a hat
chap´el *n.* a small room set aside for worship; a small church
chap´er·on´ *n.* one who oversees —*vt.* to overseer or supervise
chap´lain *n.* a clergyman
chap´let *n.* prayer beads
chaps *n.* leg protectors
chap´ter *n.* part of a book; distinct period; branch of a lodge
char *vi., vt.* scorch; to charcoal
char´ac·ter *n.* a written or printed symbol; a distinctive quality; moral strength; a person in a story; an odd or strange person —**character assassination** slander
char·ac·ter·is´tic *adj.* typical; distinguishing —*n.* a distinctive style —**char·ac·ter·is´ti·cal·ly** *adv.*
char´ac·ter·ize *vt.* to depict, typify
cha·rade´ *n.* a game of acting out; a thinly disguised deception; a sham
char´broil *vt.* broil over charcoal; barbecue —**char´broiled** *adj.*
char´coal´ *n.* charred wood used as fuel; a stick for sketching — *vt.* to charbroil; to sketch with charcoal
charge *n.* asking price; a financial obligation; an assigned duty; one under another's care; a call to attack; mild excitement —*vt.* set a price; incur financial obligation; command; hold liable; accuse; attack — **charge´a·ble** *adj.* —**charge account** permission to purchase on credit
char·gé d'af·faires´ *n.* a diplomat
char´i·ot *n.* two–wheeled, horse–drawn vehicle; the family car —*vi., vt.* to ride in a chariot
cha·ris´ma *n.* leadership quality; charm, appeal
char´is·mat´ic *adj.* having charisma; of a religious group —*n.* one reputed to have divine powers
char´i·ta·ble *adj.* generous; forgiving —**char´i·ta·bly** *adv.*
char´i·ty *n.* almsgiving; institution for aiding those in need
char´la·tan *n.* a fake; one who claims falsely
charley horse a muscle cramp
charm *n.* something having magical power; that attracts or pleases —*vt.* to please
charmed fortunate, lucky —**live a charmed life** experience good fortune
charm´ing *adj.* captivating; appealing —**charm´ing·ly** *adv.*
chart *n.* a map; a graphic representation —*vt.* make a map or graph
char´ter *n.* permit that grants right or authority —*vt.* establish by charter; lease
charter member one who joins at the beginning
char·treuse´ *n.* a pale green color; a liqueur —*adj*
char´y *adj.* cautious
chase *n.* pursuit —*vt.* pursue; drive away —*vi.* follow in pursuit
chasm *n.* a narrow gorge or ravine; any sharp division — **chas´mal** *adj.*
chaste *adj.* virtuous, pure in thought or conduct —**chaste´ly** *adv.* —**chaste´ness, chas´ti·ty** *n.*
chas´ten *n.* correct by punishing
chas´tise´ *vt.* punish; scold sharply —**chas´tise´ment** *n.*
chas´ti·ty *n.* purity; innocence
chat *n.* casual conversation —*vi.* to converse —**chat´ty** *adj.*
cha·teau´ *n.* a country house
chat´tel *n.* personal property
chat´ter *n.* foolish talk —*vi.* to speak foolishly; to click rapidly
chat´ter·box *n.* a constant talker
chauf´feur *n.* a hired driver; one who drives —*vt.* to drive for another
chau´vin·ism *n.* fanatical patriotism; irrational belief in one's superiority —**chau´vin·ist** *n.* — **chau·vin·is´tic** *adj.*
cheap *adj.* inexpensive; of little value
cheap´en *vt.* depreciate; debase
cheap shot an underhanded remark
cheap·skate *n.* tightwad; a miser
cheat *n.* a swindle; a fraud —*vi., vt.* to defraud; be dishonest
check *n.* a slowing; examination; an invoice; negotiable instrument; pattern of squares —*vt.* slow forward progress; examine
check´er·board *adj.* of a pattern of squares —*n.* a game board of squares used to play checkers and chess
checking account (*US*) money that can be transferred by check
check´list *n.* a reference list
check´mate *n.* a winning move in chess; an action that thwarts
check´–out, check´out *n.* a tally of purchases; the time a place must be vacated; verification
check´point *n.* a location for inspection or verification
check´room *n.* a place for temporary storage of coats
check´up *n.* an examination
ched´dar *n.* a type of cheese
cheek *n.* the side of the face; impertinence, rudeness
cheek´bone *n.* a bone at the side of the face near the top of the cheek
cheek´y *adj.* brazen, bold; impertinent
cheer *n.* a good mood; a source of pleasure; encouragement —*vi., vt.* to gladden; to sound approval —**cheer´ful** *adj.* — **cheer´ful·ly** *adv.* —**cheer´ful·ness** *n.*
cheer´lead·er *n.* one who leads cheering for a team; one seen as overzealous in promoting cause
cheer´less *adj.* dreary; dismal; barren —**cheer´less·ly** *adv.*
cheer´y *adj.* happy; light–hearted; jaunty —**cheer´i·ness** *n.*
cheese *n.* a food made from milk
cheese´cake *n.* a pie–like dessert; picture of a scantily clad person
cheese´cloth *n.* a loosely woven cotton cloth
chees´y *adj.* of or like cheese; lacking quality
chef *n.* a cook; the director of a kitchen staff
chem´i·cal *adj.* of chemistry —*n.* substance involved in a chemical process —**chem´i·cal·ly** *adv.*
chemical warfare the use of chemicals an enemy
che·mise´ *n.* a type of dress or an undergarment for women
chem´is·try *n.* study of the properties of matter —**chem´ist** *n.*
chem·o·ther´a·py *n.* treatment of illness by the use of chemicals
cheque *n.* (*Brit.*) an invoice; a negotiable paper; a design of squares
cher´ish *vt.* hold dear; protect
che·root´ *n.* a type of cigar
cher·vil *n.* an herb used for flavoring

chess *n.* a board game for two
chest *n.* the upper part of the front of a body; a box; a cabinet
chest´nut *n.* an edible nut or its tree; a reddish–brown horse —*adj.* a brownish color
chest of drawers furniture with drawers for storage
chest´y *adj.* having a large chest; buxom
chev´ron *n.* uniform insignia
chew *vt., vi.* grind with the teeth; to consider —**chew out** to scold; upbraid —**chew the fat, chew the rag** to talk; converse
chew´y *adj.* of food that is tough or difficult to chew —**chew´i·ness** *n.*
chic *adj.* stylish; smartly dressed —*n.* refinement in style or manner
chi·can´er·y *n.* deception; trickery
chi´chi *adj.* elegant; of an overdone style; of a haughty manner
chick *n.* a young bird
chick´en *n.* a domestic fowl; a coward —*adj.* fearful, timid; overly strict —**chicken out** back down
chicken feed an inconsequential amount; insignificant
chicken pox a childhood disease
chicken wire a light fencing
chic´le *n.* substance in chewing gum
chic´o·ry *n.* a flowering plant, its edible leaves, or its root
chide *vi., vt.* to scold quietly —**chid´ing·ly** *adv.*
chief *adj.* significant; most important —*n.* a leader
chief executive, chief executive officer highest ranking administrator of an organization
chief justice head of a judicial body
chief´ly *adj.* of or like a chief —*adv.* especially, mainly, primarily
chief of staff the leading director of an organization
chief of state a head of government
chief´tain *n.* a chief
chif·fon´ *n.* a lightweight cloth
chif·fo·nier´ *n.* chest of drawers
child *n., pl.* **chil´dren** an infant; offspring —**child's play** easy
child´bear·ing *n.* carrying an unborn child; giving birth —*adj.*
child´birth *n.* bringing forth a baby
child´hood *n.* infancy to puberty; a time of growth and development
child´ish *adj.* acting like a child; immature; silly —**child´ish·ly** *adv.* —**child´ish·ness** *n.*
child´less *adj.* having no offspring
child´like *adj.* exhibiting attributes of a child; innocent; adolescent
chil´i *n.* a type of pepper
chill *adj.* slight cold —*n.* coldness; shivering caused by illness —*vt.* to make cold
chill´er *n.* that shocks or frightens
chill´y *adj.* of a cold, uncomfortable environment; discourteous or unfriendly —**chill´i·ness** *n.*
chill´ing *adj.* frightening; causing concern —**chill´ing·ly** *adv.*
chime *n.* a bell; the sound of bells —*vi., vt.* sound in harmony
chi·me´ra *n.* imaginary monster; a wild fancy —**chi·mer´i·cal** *adj.*
chim´ney *n.* a vent for smoke
chimney sweep one who cleans chimneys
chin *n.* the front of the lower jaw —*vi.* to idly chat or gossip
chi´na *n.* procelain; fine dinnerware
china cabinet, china closet a cupboard
chine *n.* a backbone or spine
chink *n.* a crack or slit —*vt.* to fill in a crack —**a chink in one's armor** a weakness
chi´no *n.* a cotton cloth —**chinos** casual slacks made from the cloth
chi·noi·se·rie´ *n.* oriental style
chintz´y *adj.* cheap; gawdy, vulgar; of poor quality
chip *n.* a small piece; a thin slice; game piece —*vi., vt.* to break off —**chip in** contribute —**have a chip on one's shoulder** be testy —**in the chips** wealthy
chipped beef thinly sliced, dried beef
chip´per *adj.* light–hearted; cheerful
chi·rop´o·dist *n.* a podiatrist; a specialist in disorders of the foot —**chi·rop´o·dy** *n.*
chi´ro·prac´tor *n.* one who treats disorders by manipulation
chis´el *n.* a tool for shaping wood —*vt.* cut with a chisel; cheat; obtain by deception —**chis´el·er** *n.*
chit *n.* a bill; a marker or IOU
chit´chat *n.* idle, meaningless, talk
chiv´al·ry *n.* qualities attributed to a knight —**chiv´al·rous** *adj.* —**chiv´al·rous·ly** *adv.*
chive *n.* a flavoring herb
chlo´ri·nate *vt.* purify with chlorine —**chlo·rin·a´tion** *n.*
chlo´rine *n.* a chemical for water purification, cleaning, etc.
chock *n.* stopper or wedge; guide for lines on the deck of a ship
chock–full *adj.* filled to the brim
choc´o·late *n.* flavoring from cacao beans —*adj.* flavored with cacao
choice *adj.* preferred; superior —*n* right of choosing; thing chosen; alternative; a favored part
choir *n.* group of singers; part of a church set aside for singers
choir´boy *n.* a choir member; one perceived as being pious
choke *n.* sounds of one choking; a device that alters air flow —*vi.* have difficulty breathing; have difficulty performing —*vt.* throttle or strangle; obstruct or restrict —**choke back** suppress, as tears
choke´ber·ry *n.* bitter fruit reputed to cause choking
choke´bore *n.* shotgun bore that maintains a tight pattern
choke´cher·ry *n.* a chokeberry
choke collar a dog collar that tightens as strain is put on the leash; a leather collar with metal studs
choke chain leash for a choke collar
choke down to eat with difficulty
chok´er *n.* one who throttles; a closely fitting necklace
choke up to block or clog; overcome by emotion
chol´er *n.* a state of irritation; anger or rage —**chol´er·ic** *adj.*
cho´line *n.* a B vitamin
choose *vi., vt.* to select; to prefer
choos´y *adj.* selective; fastidious
chop *n.* a cut of meat; a sharp blow —*vt.* cut into small pieces
chop´per *n.* a helicopter
chop´py *adj.* marked by quick starts and stops or moves; discordant
chop´sticks *n.* rods used in the orient to manipulate food
chop su´ey a quasi–oriental dish
cho´ral *adj.* of a performance by a choir or chorus, or the music
cho·rale´ *n.* a choir or chorus; musical work for a choir or chorus
chord *n.* a set of musical tones; anything harmonious; straight line joining points on an arc
chore *n.* small task; difficult job
cho·re´a *n.* a nervous disorder
cho´re·o·graph *vi., vt.* to create and direct a dance; to carefully plan and direct any activity
cho´re·og´ra·phy *n.* creation and direction of dancers —**cho·re·og´ra·pher** *n.*
chor´tle *n.* quiet laugh; a chuckle —*vi., vt.* to chuckle or snicker
chorus *n.* a group of singers or dancers; a group acting in accord; a refrain —*vi., vt.* to perform in unison
chos´en *adj.* selected; favored
chow *n.* a breed of dog; food —**chow time** meal time
chow´der *n.* soup; a hodge–podge —**chowderhead** addled thinker
chow mein´ a quasi–oriental stew
chris´ten *vt.* name; bring into service —**chris´ten·ing** *n.*
chris´ten·dom *n.* the time of Christianity; area populated by Christians; the known world
Christian *adj.* of the followers of Christ —*n.* a follower of Jesus —**Christian name** one's given name
Chris·ti·an´i·ty *n.* the Christian religion; Christians generally
chro·mat´ic *adj.* of colors; of a musical progression
chro´ma·tin *n.* the substance in cells that forms chromosomes
chrome *n.* chromium for plating —*vt.* to plate with chromium
chro´mi·um *n.* a metallic element
chro´mo·some´ *n.* a strand of DNA
chron´ic *adj.* recurring; habitual
chron´i·cle *n.* an ordered record; a detailed report —*vt.* record or narrate —**chron´i·cler** *n.*
chro·nol´o·gy *n.* an ordered record of events —**chron·o·log´ic** *adj.* —**chron·o·log´i·cal·ly** *adv.*
chro·nom´e·ter *n.* a device for measuring time with great accuracy
chro·nom´e·try *n.* the study of accurate measure of time
chub´by *adj.* round and plump
chuck *n.* device for securing a tool; shim —*vt.* throw; discard
chuck´le *n.* a quiet laugh —*vi.* to laugh quietly
chuck´le·head *n.* foolish person
chum *n.* a friend or associate; bits of fish used as bait —*vi.* hang about together; to attract game fish with bait —**chum´mi·ness** *n.*
chump *n.* one who is gullible; a victim; stupid or foolish person
chunk *n.* a lump; a substantial amount —*vt.* cut or form lumps
chunk´y *adj.* stocky; containing solid bits —**chunk´i·ness** *n.*
church *n.* a place of worship; group of worshippers —**church´go·er** *n.*
church´ly *adj.* pious; worshipful; of a church or its offices
church´war·den *n.* a long clay pipe
church´y *adj.* of one preoccupied with religion or affairs of a church
church´yard *n.* the grounds about a church; a burial ground
churl *n.* a bumpkin; a curmudgeon
churl´ish *adj.* crude, vulgar; grouchy, surly —**churl´ish·ly** *adv.*
churn *n.* a device for making cream into butter —*vi., vt.* to make butter; to agitate —**churn´er** *n.*
chute *n.* an inclined trough
chut´ney *n.* spicy fruit relish
chutz´pah, chutz´pa *n.* brazenness; audacity; insolence
cic´a·trix *n., pl.* **cic´a·tri·ces, cic´a·trix·es** a scar
cic´a·trise (*Brit.*), **cic´a·trize** (*US*) *vi., vt.* to heal by forming a scar
ci´der *n.* juice from apples
ci·gar´ *n.* roll of smoking tobacco
cig´a·ret´, cig´a·rette´ *n.* finely cut cured tobacco rolled in paper
cil´i·a *n. pl., sing.* **cil´i·um** small hair–like projections
cinch *n.* a wide belt; an easy task —*vt.* to secure with a cinch
cinc´ture *n.* a belt or sash; that encircles —*vt.* bind or encircle
cin´der *n.* rock–like material formed by great heat; material burned that has not turned to ash
cinder block a concrete block
cin´e·ma *n.* a movie theater; making of films; motion–picture industry
cin·e·ma·tog´ra·pher *n.* operator of a motion–picture camera; one who produces or directs films
cin·e·ma·tog´ra·phy *n.* the art of motion picture photography
cin·e·rar´i·um *n.* a place where the ashes of cremated bodies are kept
cin´na·bar *n.* mercuric sulphide, source of mercury; bright red
ci´pher *n.* zero; a thing of no value; a secret code; an encoded message
cir´ca *prep.* about, approximate
cir·ca·di´an *adj.* of twenty–four hour biological rhythms
cir´cle *n.* a round figure; a group of people; extent of influence; a cycle —*vi.* to revolve; move in a circle —*vt.* to move around; to surround

cir´clet *n.* a small circle
cir´cuit *n.* a continuous route; journey in exercise of a calling; course of electricity —**cir´cuit·ry** *n.*
circuit board an insulated board containing elements of a circuit
circuit breaker a device that interrupts an electrical circuit
circuit court traveling judiciary
cir·cu´i·tous *adj.* roundabout or devious —**cir·cu´i·tous·ly** *adv.*
cir´cu·lar *adj.* round; of that moving in a circle; circuitous — *n.* a widely distributed advertisement
cir´cu·late´ *vi., vt.* to move freely; move on a predetermined course —**cir´cu·la·to·ry** *adv.*
cir·cum´fer·ence *n.* boundary of a circle —**cir·cum·fer·en´tial** *adj.*
cir´cum·lo·cu´tion *n.* an evasive, lengthly means of expression
cir´cum·nav´i·gate *vt.* travel around —**cir·cum·nav·i·ga´tion** *n.*
cir´cum·scribe *vt.* circle; define limits of —**cir·cum·scrip·tion** *n.*
cir´cum·spect´ *adj.* cautious; prudent —**cir·cum·spec´tion** *n.*
cir´cum·stance *n.* happening
cir´cum·stan´tial *adj.* of little importance; inconclusive
cir´cum·vent *vt.* to bypass; avoid by craft —**cir·cum·ven´tion** *n.*
cir´cus *n.* a traveling show; frantic activity or disorder
cis´tern *n.* storage tank; a container for rain water; a reservoir
cit´a·del *n.* a stronghold; a refuge
ci·ta´tion *n.* quotation; summons to appear; a commendation
cite *vt.* to quote; summon before a court of law —**cit´a·ble** *adj.*
cit´ied *adj.* of or like a city
cit´i·fy *vt.* to build up; become like a city or city person — **cit´i·fied** *adj.*
cit´i·zen *n.* one entitled to protection of the state; an inhabitant
cit´i·zen·ry *n.* citizens collectively
cit´ric *adj.* pertaining to citrus fruit or the acid of the fruit
cit·ron·el´la *n.* a pungent oil
cit´rus *n.* oranges, lemons, limes, etc. or their trees —*adj.*
cit´y (*US*) *n.* an incorporated area
cit´y (*Brit.*) *n.* urban area with a cathedral or named by royal warrant
city council governing body of a city
city hall the seat of city government —**can't fight city hall** the futility of opposing established authority
city manager administrator of a city
city planning the process of regulating growth and change in a city
cit´y·scape *n.* view of a city skyline
city slicker one suave or urbane
civ´ic *adj.* of a city or its citizens
civ´ic–mind´ed *adj.* in the best interests of a city or its citizens
civics *n.* the study of the rights and duties of citizenship
civ´il *adj.* of citizens; civilized; formally polite; pertaining to rights of individuals —**civ´il·ly** *adv.*
civil defense a program for training volunteers to protect and aid in the event of attack or disaster
civil disobedience opposition to government by noncompliance
civil engineer one who specializes in community services, such as roads and bridges
ci·vil´ian *n.* one not associated with the military, law enforcement, etc. —*adj.* of civilians or civil life
ci·vil´i·ty *n.* courteous behavior
civ·i·li·sa´tion (*Brit.*), **civ·i·li·za´tion** (*US*) *n.* culture of a people; protection of a civilized state
civ´i·lise (*Brit.*), **civ´i·lize** (*US*) *vi., vt.* to convert from a savage state —**civ´i·lised**, **civ´i·lized** *adj.*
civil law the rights of individuals
civil liberty the right to act without undo interference by government
civil war war within a nation
clab´ber *n.* thick sour milk —*vi., vt.* to curdle
clad *adj.* clothed; covered by metal
clad´ding *n.* a layer of metal; the process for covering with metal
claim *vt.* demand as a right; state as fact —*n.* a demand; basis for a demand; thing demanded; an assertion —**claim´ant, claim´er** *n.*
clair·voy´ant *adj.* of ability to sense that not apparent —*n.* — **clair·voy´ance** *n.*
cla´mant *adj.* crying out noisily; insistent —**cla´mant·ly** *adv.*
clam´ber *vi.* to climb
clam´my *adj.* unpleasantly cold and damp —**clam´mi·ness** *n.*
clam´or *n.* loud outcry —*vi.* demand insistantly —**clam´or·ous** *adj.*
clamp *n.* a device used to join or hold —*vt.* to join with a clamp
clamp´down *n.* enforcement of restrictions —**clamp down** grow restrictive; forbid or prohibit
clan *n.* a family; a tribe; a group with common interests —**clan´nish** *adj.*
clan·des´tine *adj.* secret, hidden —**clan·des´tine·ly** *adv.*
clang *n.* a metallic sound —*vi.*
clang´or *n.* persistent clanging — *vi.* to make noise —**clang´or·ous** *adj.*
clap *n.* a sharp sound; a blow — *vi., vt.* make a sharp sound; applaud
clap´board *n.* wood siding —*vt.* to apply wood siding
clap´trap *n.* idle words
clar´et *n.* a dry red wine
clar´i·fy *vi., vt.* to make or become clear —**clar·i·fi·ca´tion** *n.*
clar´i·net´ *n.* a woodwind instrument —**clar·i·net´ist** *n.*
clar´i·on *adj.* clear, distinct —*n.* a medieval trumpet; the sound made —*vt.* proclaim distinctly
clar´i·ty *n.* quality of being clear
clash *n.* a harsh noise; a conflict —*vi.* to come into conflict
clasp *n.* a fastener; an embrace —*vt.* to fasten; to embrace
class *n.* distinct type; social rank; quality —*vt.* grade or rank
class action suit legal action on behalf of a group of people
clas´sic *adj.* of the highest order; famous; traditional; uncomplicated —*n.* a work that is famous or traditional —**clas´si·cal** *adj.*
clas´si·cism *n.* qualities associated with ancient Greece or Rome; classical scholarship — **clas´si·cist** *n.*
clas´si·fied *adj.* arranged in suitable categories; secret
clas´si·fy *vt.* arrange according to a system; restrict use or distribution —**clas´si·fi·ca´tion** *n.*
class´ism *n.* awareness of difference in station; discrimination
class´mate *n.* one in the same class in school; a contemporary
class´room *n.* room for teaching
class´y *adj.* of fine manners or style; elegant; splendid
clat´ter *n.* noise; a hubbub —*vi.* rattle or reverberate
clause *n.* part of a sentence; a section of a document —**claus´al** *adj.*
claus·tro·pho´bi·a *n.* fear of confined spaces —**claus·tro·pho´bic** *adj.*
cla´vier, cla·vier´ *n.* a stringed instrument with a keyboard
claw *n.* a curved appendage for grasping; anything like a claw
clay *n.* earth that is malleable when moistened; a material used for pottery, modeling, etc.
clay´more *n.* a broadsword
clay pigeon a target for shooting; one open to attack
clean *adj.* free of contamination; pure, undefiled; distinct, readable; smooth or well proportioned; flawless —*adv.* neatly; entirely —*vi.* be cleansed —*vt.* wash or scrub; disinfect; prepare for eating
clean´–cut *adj.* clear, precise; of a pleasing appearance
clean´ly *adj.* kept clean —*adv.* in a clean manner —**clean´li·ness** *n.*
cleanse *vt.* make clean; free from sin
clean–shaven without facial hair
clean´up *n.* the process of cleaning; the ridding of corruption, vice, etc.
clear *adj.* bright, unclouded; distinct, unmistakable; calm, untroubled; unencumbered by debt —*adv.* obviously, completely —*vt.* set or make free; wipe clean; absolve; jump over —**clear the air** discuss freely — **clear up** explain —**in the clear** absolved of guilt
clear´ance *n.* exoneration; official sanction; the space between
clear´–cut *adj.* without ambiguity; denuded of trees —*vt.*
clear headed *adj.* discerning; reasonable, sensible
clear´ing *n.* area devoid of trees
clear´ing·house *n.* a facility for processing information or negotiable instruments
clear´–sight·ed *adj.* shrewd; keenly perceptive
cleat *n.* a small projection on furniture or footware; a device for securing lines
cleave *vi., vt.* to split; to separate
clem´en·cy *n.* leniency, mercy
clench *n.* a rigid hold —*vt.* make a fist; grit one's teeth
cler´gy *n.* those ordained for religious service
cler´i·cal *adj.* of a clerk or member of the clergy
clerk *n.* office worker; a counter person, as in a hotel or store
clev´er *adj.* skillful; intelligent; witty —**clev´er·ly** *adv.* —**clev´er·ness** *n.*
cli·ché´ *n.* a trite phrase
cli´ent *n.* a customer; one dependent on another
cli·en·tele´ *n.* clients as a group
cliff *n.* a high, steep face of rock
cliff´–hang·er, cliff´hang·er *n.* a story full of suspense
cli´mate *n.* prevailing weather; any condition that influences
cli·ma·tol´o·gy *n.* the study of climate —**cli·ma·tol´o·gist** *n.*
cli´max´ *n.* a final or significant element; turning point or crisis
climb *n.* scaling; advancement or improvement —*vi., vt.* mount by using hands and feet; an ascension —**climb´a·ble** *adj.*
clinch *n.* a fastening; a hug —*vt.* fasten; conclude —**clinch´er** *n.*
cling *vi.* hold fast, adhere; remain near, be emotionally attached —**cling´y** *adj.*
clinging vine one inclined to dependence on others
cling´stone *adj.* of a fruit with pulp firmly attached to the pit —*n.*
clin´ic *n.* a place for medical treatment; an infirmary or dispensary; an intensive learning session
clin´i·cal *adj.* of a clinic; sterile; scientific or objective
clinical thermometer a thermometer to measure body temperature
clip *n.* a thing cut; a fast pace; a sharp blow; a fastener —*vi.* cut off; move rapidly —*vt.* cut or cut off; shorten, as of speech; strike with a sharp blow; to cheat; to fasten
clip joint concern that overcharges
clip´per *n.* one who cuts or trims; a tool for cutting; a 19th century sailing ship
clip´ping *n.* act of cutting; that cut
clique *n.* a small exclusive group —**cli´quey, cli´quish** *adj.*
cloak *n.* a long cape; that which covers or conceals —*vt.* to cover or conceal; to camouflage
cloak´–and–dag´ger *adj.* of secret activities
cloak´room *n.* a place for coats
clob´ber *vt.* hit forcefully; to win
clock *n.* a device for marking time —*vt.* to measure time, output, distance, etc.
clock´work *n.* workings of a clock
clod *n.* a lump of earth; a dull or stupid person —**clod´dish** *adj.*
clod´hop·per *n.* a country bumpkin; a heavy shoe
clog *vi.* become obstructed —*vt.* obstruct or impede —*n.* an obstruction; a shoe with a wooden sole

clois´ter *n.* a covered walk; a place of seclusion —*vt.* seclude or protect —**clois´tered** *adj.*
close *adj.* nearby; similar; confining; restrictive; limited —**close´ly** *adv.*
close *n.* an ending, conclusion —*vi., vt.* to conclude; to shut; to connect
close by near; beside
close call, **close shave** a near miss; a narrow escape
closed shop a company that hires only union members
close´fist·ed *adj.* stingy, miserly
close´out *n.* selling discontinued items or to liquidate a business —*vi., vt.* to sell out a business
close quarters a crowded space
clos´et (*US*) *n.* a storage area —*vt.* to store; to consult privately
close´up an intimate or near view
clos´ing *adj.* of a final stage —*n.* the ending or finalization
closing costs expense of finalizing a contract
clo´sure *n.* a conclusion; that used to close
clot *n.* soft mass —*vi.* coagulate
cloth *n.* a fabric
clothe *vt.* cover; furnish with clothing —**clothes** *n.* wearing apparel
clothes´horse *n.* one who is inordinately fond of clothes
clothes peg (*Brit.*), **clothes´pin** (*US*) *n.* a device for securing clothing to a line for drying
clothes tree an upright post with hooks for hanging hats and coats
cloth´ier *n.* one who manufactures or sells clothes
cloth´ing *n.* wearing apparel
clo´ture *n.* a parliamentary maneuver for closing debate
cloud *n.* a mist of water; a mass of smoke, dust, etc.; anything resembling a cloud; shade or gloom —*vi., vt.* to obscure —**cloud´y** *adj.*
cloud´burst a sudden heavy rain
cloud´less *adj.* clear, sunny
cloud nine a state of bliss
clout *n.* a blow; power or influence —*vt.* to strike
clove *n.* a fragrant spice; segment of a bulb, as garlic
clo´ven *adj.* split; cleft
clo´ver·leaf *n.* a complex highway interchange
clown *n.* one who uses broad humor, acts like a fool, or is clumsy or incompetent —*vi.* to perform or act like a fool —**clown´ish** *adj.*
cloy *vi., vt.* make unpleasant by excess, as very rich or sweet —**cloy´ing·ly** *adv.*
club *n.* a heavy stick; a group organized for common purpose —*vt.* to strike with a club
club´foot´ *n.* a congenital deformity
club´house *n.* meeting place or facilities used by members
cluck *n.* the sound of a hen; a foolish person
clue *n.* information
clum´sy *adj.* awkward; poorly fashioned —**clum´si·ness** *n.*
clus´ter *n.* a bunch —*vi., vt.* to come together —**clus´ter·y** *adj.*
clutch *n.* a device that grabs and holds —*vt.* hold closely
clut´ter *n.* disarray
coach (*US*) *n.* passenger compartment; trainer —*vt.* to teach
coach (*Brit.*) *n.* a large vehicle for passengers —*vt.* teach or train
co·ag´u·late *vi., vt.* change to a thick soft mass —**co·ag·u·la´tion** *n.*
coal *n.* a combustible; an ember
co´a·lesce´ *vi.* unite or merge
co·a·li´tion *n.* a temporary union
coarse *adj.* rough; vulgar or obscene —**coarse´ly** *adv.* —**coarse´ness** *n.*
coars´en *vi., vt.* to make rough
coast *n.* land by the sea —*vi.* move by force of gravity; slack off
coast´er *n.* a sled; a mat
coast guard a naval force
coast´line *n.* land along shore
coat *n.* an outer garment; protective covering; a layer: *a coat of paint*
coat´dress *n.* long buttoned frock
coat´ing *n.* a cover or layer; material for making coats
coat of arms a family emblem; armorial bearings
coat´rack *n.* a post or row of hooks for hanging hats and coats
coat´room *n.* a place for coats
coat´tail *n.* the bottom of a coat
co–au´thor *n.* one who writes or creates in collaboration with another
coax *vi.* to cajole —*vt.* persuade by wheedling —**coax´ing·ly** *adv.*
co·ax´i·al *adj.* having common axis
coaxial cable cable used to transmit telephone, television, etc. signals
cob *n.* the core on which kernels of corn grow; a male swan
co´balt *n.* a metallic element
cobalt blue dark blue
cob´ble *vt.* to repair shoes
cob´bler *n.* one who makes or repairs shoes; a fruit pie
cob´ble–stone *n.* paving stone
COBOL *n.* acronym for *COmmon Business Oriented Language*; a computer programming language
cob´web´ *n.* a spider web
co´ca *n.* a tropical plant; the source for cocaine
co´caine´ *n.* a narcotic
coc´cyx *n.* the end of the spine
co·chair´ *n.* one who shares the duties of a chairperson —*vi*
cock *n.* a male bird; a device for regulating flow; striking part of a gun; pile of hay; jaunty angle —*vt.* set; set at a jaunty angle
cock–a–leek´ie *n.* Scottish soup
cock´a·ma·mie *adj.* fictional; fabricated; ridiculous
cock–and–bull story fabrication
cocked hat a three–cornered hat **knock into a cocked hat** to spoil; reveal as false
cock´eyed *adj.* out of alignment; ridiculous; faulty reasoning
cock´ney *n.* a rhyming dialect; speaker of the dialect —*adj.*
cock´sure *adj.* self–confident
cock´tail´ *n.* beverage or food served before or at the start of a meal
cock´y *adj.* overconfident; flamboyant
co´coa´ *n.* a powder from cacao beans; a beverage; brown color
cocoa butter fat from cacao seeds
co´co·nut *n.* fruit of a coconut palm
coconut milk the thin liquid from the center of the coconut
coconut oil oil from coconut meat
coconut palm a tropical tree that produces coconuts
co·coon´ *n.* a protective cover
cod *n.* a type of food fish
co´da *n.* a musical phrase
cod´dle *vt.* to overindulge; pamper or treat gently; cook by poaching
code *n.* arrangement of a body of law; a system of symbols or signs —*vt.* translate into symbols
co´deine *n.* a derivative of opium
codg´er *n.* an old man
cod´i·cil *n.* an addendum
cod´i·fy *vt.* to arrange —**cod´i·fi·ca´tion** *n.*
cod´–liv·er oil *n.* oil from the liver of codfish, rich in vitamins A and D
co´ed´ *adj.* coeducational —*n.* a female student
co·ed´it *vt.* jointly prepare for publication —**co·ed´i·tor** *n.*
co·ed·u·ca´tion·al *adj.* of an institution for male and female students
co·erce´ *vt.* to force; to compel
co·er´cion *n.* use of threats or force to compel —**co·er´cive** *adj.*
co·ex·ist´ *vi.* exist at the same time; live in harmony —**co·ex·is´tence** *n.* —**co·ex·is´tent** *adj.*
cof´fee *n.* a beverage from seeds of a tropical plant; the plant; informal gathering; light brown color
coffee beans seeds of a coffee plant
coffee break a brief rest period
cof´fee·cake *n.* bread–like pastry
cof´fee·house *n.* a café
cof´fee·pot *n.* a utensil for making and serving coffee
coffee shop a coffeehouse; a shop that sells exotic coffee and utensils
coffee table a low table
cof´fer *n.* a strongbox; a reinforced shelter; a cofferdam
cof´fer·dam *n.* a barrier to hold back water for construction taking place below water level
cof´fin *n.* a box for burial
cog *n.* gear tooth; minor functionary
co´gent *adj.* forceful or compelling
cog´i·tate´ *vi.* consider carefully
cog´nac *n.* a brandy
cog´nate´ *adj.* of common ancestry
cog·ni´tion *n.* mental processes —**cog´ni·tive** *adj.*
cog´ni·zance *n.* knowledge; awareness —**cog´ni·zant** *adj.*
cog´no´men *n.* a family name
cog´wheel *n.* a toothed wheel
co·hab´it *vi.* live together —**co·hab´i·tant** *n.* —**co·hab·i·ta´tion** *n.*
co´here´ *vi.* hold together —**co´her´ence** *n.*
co·her´ent *adj.* congruous; logically connected —**co·her´ent·ly** *adv.*
co·he´sive *adj.* sticking —**co·he´sion** *n.* —**co·he´sive·ness** *n.*
co´hort *n.* a colleague or friend; a contemporary
coif *vt.* to style hair —*n.* coiffure
coif·fure´ *n.* hair style
coin *n.* metal piece with monetary value —*vt.* to mint coins; make or invent —**coin´er** *n.*
coin´age *n.* the process of minting; money system of a country
co´in·cide´ *vi.* correspond exactly; be in accord
co·in´ci·dence *n.* a coinciding; a chance event —**co·in´ci·dent** *adj.*
co·in·ci·den´tal *adj.* characterized by chance; accidental
co·i´tus, **co·i´tion** *n.* sexual intercourse —**co´i·tal** *adj.*
col´an·der *n.* a perforated drain
cold *adj.* lacking heat or warmth; unfeeling or unfriendly —*n.* absence of heat; a viral infection —**go in cold** without preparation —**have cold feet** be reticent —**have down cold** know thoroughly —**in the cold** left out —**turn a cold shoulder** scorn or ignore
cold´blood´ed *adj.* unfeeling, callous —**cold´blood´ed·ly** *adv.*
cold chisel steel tool for cutting
cold cream a cosmetic skin cleanser
cold cuts processed meats
cold front a cold air mass
cold´heart´ed *adj.* unresponsive; lacking compassion —**cold´heart´ed·ly** *adv.* —**cold´heart´ed·ness** *n.*
cold pack a cool, wet compress; a chemical ice pack
cold snap sudden cold weather
cold sore a viral infection about the mouth following a cold, fever, etc.
cold storage a refrigerated area
cold turkey suddenly, without preparation
cold war unfriendly relations between countries without fighting
cole´slaw *n.* shredded cabbage salad
col´ic *n.* persistent discomfort experienced by an infant
col´i·se´um *n.* an arena
co·li´tis *n.* infection of the intestine
col·lab´o·rate´ *vi.* work together; cooperate —**col·lab´o·ra·tive** *adj.*
col·lage´ *n.* an artistic composition constructed of odd bits of material
col·lapse´ *vi.* to break down suddenly; fold into a compact unit —**col·laps´i·ble** *adj.*
col´lar *n.* the neck of a garment; a band worn around the neck
col´lards, **col´lard greens** *n.* a green leafy vegetable
col´late *vt.* gather together in order
col·lat´er·al *adj.* similar; pledged as a guarantee —*n.* that pledged as a guarantee —**col·lat´er·al·ly** *adv.*
col·lat´er·al·ize *vt.* pledge as security; to guarantee
col´league´ *n.* an associate

col·lect´ *vi., vt.* gather together; secure payment **—col·lec´tion** *n.*
col·lect´ed *adj.* gathered, accumulated; calm and composed
col·lect´ive *adj.* consolidated; of a venture in which people work for common good *—n.* a group; a cooperative organization
collective bargaining negotiations
col´lege *n.* an institution of learning; an association
col·le´gi·an *n.* a student at a college **—col·le´gi·ate** *adj.*
col·lide´ *vi.* come together violently
col·li´sion *n.* a coming together; a clash of opinions
col´lo·cate *vt.* arrange; categorize
col·lo´qui·al *adj.* used informally **—col·lo´qui·al·ly** *adv.*
col·lo´qui·al·ism *n.* a word or phrase used informally
col´lo·quy *n.* a formal discussion
col·lu´sion *n.* a conspiracy; a plot **—col·lu´sive** *adj.*
co´lon *n.* a puncutation mark (:); the large intestine
colo´nel *n.* a military officer
co·lo´ni·al *adj.* of an outpost
co·lo´ni·al·ism *n.* policy of settling new lands **—co·lo´ni·al·ist** *adj., n.*
col´o·nist *n.* one who founds or lives in a colony **—col´o·nise´** (*Brit.*), **col´o·nize´** (US) *vt.*
col·on·nade´ *n.* series of columns
col´o·phon *n.* a printed emblem
col´or (*US*) *n.* sensation created by varying light waves; any substance used to dye or tint *— vi., vt.* give or change color
col·or·a´tion *n.* shades and tones
col´or·blind (*US*) *adj.* incapable of distinguishing colors; without racial prejudice
col´ored (*US*) *adj.* having color; of a non–caucasian; biased
col´or·fast (*US*) *adj.* of a cloth that will not bleed or fade when washed
col´or·ful (*US*) *adj.* bright; picturesque; quaint or unusual **— col´or·ful·ly** *adv.*
col´or·ing (*US*) *n.* applying color
col´or·ize (*US*) *vt.* add color
col´or·less (*US*) *adj.* bland; uninteresting
col´ors (*US*) *n.* a banner or flag
co·los´sal *adj.* amazingly large
co·los´sus *n.* an extremely large structure or statue
co·los´to·my *n.* creation of an opening for disposal of body waste
col´our (*Brit.*) *n.* sensation created by varying light waves; substance used to dye or tint *—vi., vt.* to give or change color
col´our·blind (*Brit.*) *adj.* incapable of distinguishing colors; without racial prejudice
col´oured *adj.* (*Brit.*) having color; of a non–caucasian race; biased
col´our·ful *adj.* (*Brit.*) bright; picturesque; quaint or unusual **— col´our·ful·ly** *adv.*
col´our·ing *n.* (*Brit.*) applying color
col´our·ise *vt.* (*Brit.*) add color
col´our·less *adj.* (*Brit.*) bland; uninteresting
col´ours (*Brit.*) *n.* a banner or flag
colt *n.* young horse, donkey, etc.
col´umn *n.* a support; a vertical section of a printed page
col´um·nist *n.* a writer of commentary
co´ma *n.* a state of deep sleep
com´bat *n.* armed conflict, a battle; a struggle **—com·bat´** *vt.* fight against; contend
com·ba´tive *adj.* inclined to fight
com´bi·na·tion *n.* a blending or merging **—com·bi·na´tion·al** *adj.*
com´bine *n.* a machine for harvesting; an association **—com·bine´** *vi., vt.* join forces; unite
com´bo *n.* an instrumental ensemble
com·bus´ti·ble *adj.* easily ignited; excitable *—n.* material easily ignited **—com·bus·ti·bil´i·ty** *n.*
com·bus´tion *n.* burning
come´back *n.* return to a previous state, as in politics; a sharp retort
co·me´di·an *n.* one who writes or performs comedy
co·me´dic *adj.* pertaining to comedy
come´down *n.* a reversal of fortune
com´e·dy *n.* an attempt to amuse
comedy of errors mistakes more humorous than tragic
come´ly *adj.* attractive; pleasing in appearance **—come´li·ness** *n.*
come´on *n.* an enticement
co·mes´ti·ble *n.* food
come·up´pance *n.* a deserved humbling; retaliation
com´fort *n.* contentment; relief *—vt.* relieve; aid or assist
com´fort·a·ble *adj.* at ease; free of pain **—com´fort·a·bly** *adv.*
com´fort·er *n.* one who consoles; (*US*) a heavy bed covering
com´ic *adj.* funny *—n.* comedian
com´i·cal *adj.* amusing, humorous; facetious **—com´i·cal·ly** *adv.*
comic book illustrated stories
comic opera a humorous work in the style of grand opera
comic relief humorous incident
comic strip a series of cartoons
com´ing *adj.* drawing near; promising **—have it coming** deserve
com´ing-out´ *n.* a debut
com´ma *n.* a punctuation mark (,)
com·mand´ *n.* authority to lead; an order; ability to use well *— vt.* to order
com·man·deer´ *vt.* to take
com·mand´er *n.* one in charge
commander in chief senior officer
com·mand´ing *adj.* compelling: having authority; impressive
commanding officer one in charge of a military unit or post
com·mand´ment *n.* a regulation
com·man´do *n.* a warrior
command post temporary headquarters
com·mem´o·rate´ *vt.* to honor **— com·mem·o·ra´tion** *n.* **— com·mem´o·ra·tive** *adj., n.*
com·mence´ *vi., vt.* to begin
com·mence´ment *n.* beginning; a school graduation ceremony
com·mend´ *vt.* praise; entrust
com·mend´a·ble *adj.* worthy of praise; admirable
com·men·da´tion *n.* a medal
com·men´su·ra·ble *adj.* to the same degree; proportionate
com·men´su·rate *adj.* equivalent or comparable; corresponding
com´ment *n.* a remark *—vi.* speak or write about **—com´men·tar´y** *n.*
com´men·ta·tor *n.* one who reports
com´merce *n.* the buying and selling of goods and services
com·mer´cial *adj.* of commerce; undertaken for profit *—n.* paid advertising; (*Brit.*) a traveling salesman **—com·mer´cial·ly** *adv.*
commercial art advertising art and design
com·mer´cial·ize *vt.* operate for profit **—com·mer·cial·i·za´tion** *n.*
com·min´gle *vi., vt.* to mix together; combine
com·mis´er·ate *vi., vt.* express sorrow or pity **—com·mis·er·a´tion** *n.*
com´mis·sar·y *n.* a store or cafeteria
com·mis´sion *n.* a group given authority; duties authorized; a fee *—vt.* to grant authority
com·mis´sion·er *n.* an authority; head of a government department
com·mit´ *vt.* to do; to give for safekeeping; to bind or obligate
com·mit´ment *n.* a pledge or promise; dedication
com·mit´tee *n.* a group appointed for a special purpose
com·mo´di·ous *adj.* spacious **— com·mo´di·ous·ness** *n.*
com·mod´i·ty *n.* anything traded
com´mon *adj.* ordinary; widespread; shared *—n.* a public square **—com·mon·al´i·ty** *n.*
common carrier a company that transports passengers or freight
common denominator a multiple shared by a set of fractions; shared feature or trait
common ground agreement
common law tradition or usage
com´mon·place *adj.* ordinary *— n.* anything ordinary or trite
com´mon·sense *adj.* sound, rational
common sense reasonable judgement
common touch empathy for the average citizen
com´mon·weal *n.* public welfare
com´mon·wealth *n.* people of a state, nation, etc.; government
com·mo´tion *n.* a disturbance
com·mu´nal·ize *vt.* to form a commune; transfer property to a commune
com´mune *n.* a group formed to share labor and its rewards; a cooperative **—com·mu´nal** *adj.*
com·mune´ *vi.* to converse; be in harmony with
com·mu´ni·ca·ble *adj.* infectious or contagious
com·mu´ni·cate´ *vi.* share information; be understood *—vt.* convey information; to transmit illness
com·mun´ion *n.* close fellowship; a group comprising a fellowship
com´mu·nism *n.* a theoretical classless society marked by common ownership of property **—com´mu·nist** *n.* **—com´mu·nis´tic** *adj.*
com·mu´ni·ty *n.* society; members of a political unit; those who share a common interest
community college an educational institution
community property property held in common
community service voluntary work; work assigned as punishment
com´mu·nize *vt.* place in control of the community at large
com·mu·ta´tion *n.* a substitution; traveling to and from work
com·mute´ *vi.* travel to and from work; make an exchange *—vt.* substitute **—com·mut´er** *n.*
com´pact´ *adj.* taking little space; light *—n.* a covenant; a small car
com·pact´ *adj.* dense *—vt.* pack tightly **—com·pact´ness** *n.*
compact disk *n.* a digital storage device
com·pan´ion *n.* one who accompanies; a friend; an attendant
com·pan´ion·a·ble *adj.* cordial, congenial
companion piece part of a set
com·pan´ion·way *n.* a hall or stairway aboard ship
com´pa·ny *n.* assembly or association; guest; companionship
company store retail establishment operated for employees
company union a bargaining unit that is unaffiliated or controlled by an employer
com´pa·ra·ble *adj.* similar
com·par´a·tive *adj.* relative to others; corresponding
com·pare´ *vt.* to contrast; to resemble **—com·par´i·son** *n.*
com·pas´sion *n.* concern for another; pity; sympathy **— com·pas´sion·ate** *adj.*
com·pat´i·ble *adj.* able to exist or work together **—com·pat·i·bil´i·ty** *n.*
com·pa´tri·ot *n.* a colleague
com·peer´ *n.* comrade or friend; a peer; one's equal
com·pel´ *vt.* bring about by force
com·pel´ling *adj.* forceful; impressive
com·pen´di·ous *adj.* summarized
com·pen´di·um *n.* abridgment
com´pen·sate´ *vt.* to offset; to pay **—com´pen·sa´tion** *n.* **— com·pen´sa·to·ry** *adj.*
com·pete´ *vi.* to work against
com´pe·tence, com´pe·ten·cy *n.* adequate qualification; fitness
com´pe·tent *adj.* qualified; suitable; adequate **—com´pe·tent·ly** *adv.*
com´pe·ti´tion *n.* rivalry; a rival
com·pet´i·tive *adj.* disposed to rivalry **—com·pet´i·tive·ness** *n.*
com·pet´i·tor *n.* one who competes
com·pile´ *vt.* to arrange in order **—com´pi·la´tion** *n.*
com·pla´cence, com·pla´cen·cy *n.* contentment; self–satisfaction; apathy **—com·pla´cent** *adj.*
com·plain´ *vi.* express dissatisfaction **—com·plain´er** *n.*

com·plaint´ *n.* an expression of dissatisfaction
com·plai´sant *adj.* accommodating; obliging —**com·plai´sance** *n.*
com·plect´ed *adj.* of skin color
com´ple·ment *n.* that which completes —*vt.* make complete
com·ple·men´ta·ry *adj.* of a part that completes; corresponding
com´plete´ *adj.* lacking nothing —*vt.* conclude; accomplish successfully —**com·ple´tion** *n.*
com·plex´ *adj.* complicated —**com´plex** *n.* a group of related elements —**com·plex´i·ty** *n.*
com·plex´ion *n.* appearance of the skin; the general nature of a thing
com·pli´ance *n.* a tendency to yield; conformity —**com·pli´ant** *adj.*
com´pli·cate´ *vt., vi.* make difficult
com´pli·cat·ed *adj.* intricate, tangled; difficult to understand —**com·pli·ca´tion** *n.*
com·plic´i·ty *n.* involvement
com´pli·ment *n.* praise; courtesy —*vt.* to praise
com·ply´ *vi.* to act on a request
com·po´nent *n.* an integral part
com·port´ment *n.* conduct
com·pose´ *vt.* to form; put in order; create; to calm oneself; arrange elements for printing
com·posed´ *adj.* calm, deliberate
com·pos´er *n.* one who creates
com·pos´ite *adj.* made up of several —*n.* a material made by combining
com´po·si´tion *n.* forming or combining; placement; a thing formed
com·pos´i·tor *n.* one who sets type
com´post *n.* decomposed matter; potting soil —*vt.* make compost
com·po´sure *n.* tranquillity, self–control
com´pote *n.* marinated fruit; a stemmed serving dish
com´pound´ *adj.* made up of two or more elements —*n.* a mixture —**com·pound´** *vt.* to combine; to increase by adding to
com´pre·hend´ *vt.* understand; include —**com´pre·hen´sion** *n.*
com´pre·hen´sive *adj.* broad in scope —*n.* a graphic layout —**com´pre·hen´sive·ly** *adv.*
com´press *n.* a pad applied to a wound —**com·press´** *vt.* press together; squeeze; make compact —**com·press´i·ble** *adj.*
com·prise´ *vt.* include; consist of
com´pro·mise *n.* a settlement —*vt.* settle by concession; expose to difficulty or danger
comp·trol´ler *n.* the overseeer of financial affairs of an organization
com·pul´sion *n.* driving force; irrational impulse —**com·pul´sive** *adj.*
com·pul´so·ry *adj.* obligatory
com·punc´tion *n.* doubt from fear of wrongdoing
com·pute´ *vt.* calculate —**com·put´a·ble** *adj.* —**com´pu·ta´tion** *n.*
com·put´er *n.* an electronic device for processing data
com·put·er·ese´ *n.* terminology used by those using computers
computer graphics artwork produced with the aid of a computer
com·put´er·ise (*Brit.*), **com·put´er·ize** (*US*) *vt.* operate with the aid of a computer —**com·put·er·i·sa´tion**, **com·put·er·i·za´tion** *n.*
com´rade´ *n.* a friend or companion —**com´rade·ship** *n.*
con *adv.* against; of an opposing view —*n.* opposing; a swindle; a convict —*vt.* to swindle; to trick
con·cat´e·nate *vt.* to join; to link together —**con·cat·e·na´tion** *n.*
con´cave´ *adj.* curved like the inner surface of a sphere
con·ceal´ *vt.* to cover; keep secret —**con·ceal´ment** *n.*
con·cede´ *vt.* acknowledge; grant
con·ceit´ *n.* overly high opinion of oneself —**con·ceit´ed** *adj.*
con·ceiv·a·ble *adj.* able to be believed or understood
con·ceive´ *vt.* to understand
con´cen·trate´ *n.* a substance made dense or intense —*vi., vt.* increase density or intensity; focus one's attention
con·cen´tric *adj.* having a common center
con´cept *n.* a theory; a broad understanding
con·cep´tion *n.* a beginning
con·cep´tu·al *adj.* theoretical or abstract
con·cep´tu·al·ize *vt.* form a theory —**con·cep·tu·al·i·za´tion** *n.*
con·cern´ *n.* a matter of interest; a feeling of anxiety; a business firm —*vt.* to show interest; to cause anxiety —**con·cerned´** *adj.*
con´cert *n.* mutual agreement; a program of music —**con·cert´** *vt.* resolve by mutual agreement
con·cert´ed *adj.* harmoniously; unified —**con·cert´ed·ly** *adv.*
con·cer´to *n.* a music arranged for orchestra and a solo instrument
con·ces´sion *n.* a conceding; a thing conceded; a business venture
con·ces´sion·aire´ *n.* one who operates a business
conch *n.* a large marine mollusk
con·cil´i·ate´ *vt.* to appease, placate —**con·cil´i·a·to·ry** *adj.*
con·cise´ *adj.* succinct; brief and to the point —**con·cise´ly** *adv.*
con´clave *n.* a large gathering; a secret meeting
con·clude´ *vt.* end; deduce by reasoning —**con·clu´sion** *n.*
con·clu´sive *adj.* final; convincing —**con·clu´sive·ly** *adv.*
con·coct´ *vt.* make or devise —**con·coc´tion** *n.*
con·com´i·tant *adj.* associated with; connected —**con·com´i·tance** *n.*
con´cord *n.* harmony or agreement; a treaty
con·cord´ance *n.* an agreement; index of leading words in a text
con·cor´dant *adj.* harmonious
con´course´ *n.* a broad walkway
con´crete´ *adj.* solid; precise —*n.* a building material —*vi., vt.* to solidify —**con·crete´ly** *adv.*
con·cre´tion *n.* a hardened mass
con·cu´pis·cence *n.* intense desire —**con·cu´pis·cent** *adj.*
con·cur´ *vi.* correspond or coincide; to agree —**con·cur´rence**, **con·cur´ren·cy** *n.*
con·cur´rent *adj.* in agreement; occurring together; convergent
con·cus´sion *n.* a shock; injury caused by an impact
con·demn´ *vt.* to disapprove; find guilty; punish; declare unfit for use —**con´dem·na´tion** *n.*
con´den·sa´tion *n.* compaction; collected moisture; abridgement
con·dense´ *vt.* make dense; compress; abridge or summarize
condensed milk thick, sweet milk
con´de·scend´ *vi.* to lower oneself; be patronizing —**con´de·scen´sion** *n.*
con·de·scend´ing *adj.* patronizing
con·dign´ *adj.* suitable
con´di·ment *n.* a seasoning or relish
con·di´tion *n.* a requirement; a circumstance; a thing that modifies —*vt.* to modify or influence
con·di´tion·al *adj.* contingent
con·di´tioned *adj.* in a proper state
con·dole´ *vi.* to sympathize; to console; to comfort
con·do´lence *n.* sympathy
con´do·min´i·um[1] (*Brit.*) *n.* territory governed by two or more nations
con´do·min´i·um[2] (*US*) *n.* apartment individually owned; a building which houses such an apartment
con·done´ *vt.* foregive; disregard without protest
con´dor *n.* a large vulture
con·du´cive *adj.* contributing or leading to —**con·du´cive·ness** *n.*
con´duct *n.* the way one acts —**con·duct´** *vt.* to lead; to behave in a certain manner; to convey
con·duc´tor *n.* a leader; a guide; one in charge; material which transmits heat or electricity
con·duct´ance *n.* the ability to transmit electricity —**con·duc´tive** *adj.*
con·duc´tion *n.* conveyance
con´duit *n.* a channel
cone *n.* a geometric solid with a circular base that rises to a point
con´fab *n.* a discussion —*vi.*
con·fab·u·la´tion *n.* a conversation or informal discussion
con·fec´tion *n.* a sweet edible
con·fec´tion·er·y *n.* shop where confections are made or sold
con·fed´er·a·cy *n.* an alliance —**con·fed´er·a´tion** *n.*
con·fed´er·ate *n.* an associate or accomplice —*vt.* to unite
con·fer´ *vi.* to meet for discussion —*vt.* to grant, as an honorary degree
con´fer·ence *n.* a formal meeting
conference call a telephone connection for more than two persons
con·fess´ *vt.* to acknowlege
con·fes´sion *n.* an admission of guilt
con·fes´sor *n.* one who confesses; a priest who hears confessions
con·fet´ti *n.* bits of colored paper scattered during festivities
con´fi·dant *n.* a trusted friend
con·fide´ *vi., vt.* to share a secret
con´fi·dence *n.* trust or faith; self–assurance; something confided
confidence game a swindle
con´fi·dent *adj.* self–assured
con´fi·den´tial *adj.* secret —**con·fi·den·ti·al´i·ty** *n.*
con·fid´ing *adj.* trusting
con·fig´ure *vt.* set up or arrange
con·fig´u·ra´tion *n.* arrangement; structure
con´fine *n.* an enclosure —**con·fine´** *vt.* restrict; shut in
con·firm´ *vt.* prove; validate —**con´fir·ma´tion** *n.*
con·firmed´ *adj.* resolved; proved
con´fis·cate *vt.* seize by authority —**con·fis´ca·to·ry** *adj.*
con´fla·gra´tion *n.* a large fire
con´flict *n.* a clash of ideas or interests; open warfare —**con·flict´** *vi.*
conflict of interest moral obligation at variance with personal interest
con´flu·ence *n.* flowing together
con·form´ *vi.* adapt; follow custom or tradition —**con·form´i·ty** *n.*
con·found´ *vt.* confuse, bewilder
con·fra·ter´ni·ty *n.* brotherhood
con·front´ *vt.* come face to face —**con·fron·ta´tion** *n.*
con·fuse´ *vt.* bewilder; to mistake; to mingle indiscrimately
con·fu´sion *n.* bewilderment; a state of chaos or disorder
con·fute´ *vt.* to prove in error
con·geal´ *vi., vt.* thicken or solidify
con·gen´ial *adj.* friendly; compatible —**con·ge·ni·al´i·ty** *n.*
con·gen´i·tal *adj.* existing at birth; hereditary —**con·gen´i·tal·ly** *adv.*
con·gest´ *vt.* clog or obstruct; to overcrowd —**con·ges´tive** *adj.*
con·ges´ted *adj.* overcrowded
con·glom´er·ate *adj.* gatherered in a mass —*n.* agglomeration; diversified corporation —*vi., vt.*
con·grat´u·late *vt.* to express joy
con·grat·u·la´tions *n.* an expression of pleasure at good fortune
con´gre·gate *vi.* to assemble —**con´gre·ga´tion** *n.*
con´gress *n.* a coming together; a formal assembly
con·gru´ence *n.* state of agreement; harmony —**con´gru·ent** *adj.*
con´gru·ous *adj.* appropriate; suitable or fitting
con´i·cal *adj.* shaped like a cone
co´ni·fer *n.* evergreen tree or shrub —**co·nif´er·ous** *adj.*
con·jec´tur·al *adj.* based on speculation
con·jec´ture *n.* speculation; judgement based on scant information —*vt.* to speculate
con·join´ *vi., vt.* unite or connect
con´ju·gal *adj.* of or pertaining to marriage —**con·ju·gal´i·ty** *n.*
con´ju·gate *adj.* joined together —*vt.* to join —**con´ju·ga´tion** *n.*
con·junc´tion *n.* a joining; a word that connects
con·junc´tive *adj.* connective
con·junc·ti·vi´tis *n.* inflammation of the eyelid

con´jure *vi., vt.* summon a spirit
conk *n.* a blow —*vt.* to strike — **conk out** suddenly fail or quit
con man a confidence man; swindler
con·nect´ *vi.* become linked —*vt.* link together —**con·nec´tor** *n.*
con·nect´ed *adj.* linked; joined in order; having important contacts
con·nec´tive *adj.* serving to link —*n.* a bond; that joins or links
con·nec´tion *n.* a joining; a part that joins; a relationship
con·nip´tion *n.* a fit; a frenzy; excitement or rage
con·niv´ance *n.* secret involvement
con·nive´ *vi.* cooperate secretly in wrongdoing —**con·niv´er** *n.*
con´nois·seur´ *n.* an expert; a person of discriminating taste
con·no·ta´tion *n.* an implied meaning; an insinuation
con·note´ *vt.* to suggest or imply
con·nu´bi·al *adj.* of marriage
con´quer *vi., vt.* to overcome — **con´quer·or** *n.* —**con´quest** *n.*
con·san´guine, con·san·guin´e·ous *adj.* of common ancestry
con´science *n.* sense of right and wrong
con´sci·en´tious *adj.* guided by conscience; thorough —**con·sci·en´tious·ness** *n.*
con´scious *adj.* awake; aware — **con´scious·ly** *adv.*
con´script *n.* one drafted —**con·script´** *vt.* draft into the military
con´se·crate´ *vt.* set apart as sacred; dedicate to a worthy cause —**con´se·cra´tion** *n.*
con·sec´u·tive *adj.* in logical order —**con·sec´u·tive·ly** *adv.*
con·sen´su·al *adj.* mutually consenting —**con·sen´su·al·ly** *adv.*
con·sen´sus *n.* general agreement
con·sent´ *n.* permission —*vi.* grant
con´se·quence *n.* that logically follows; relative significance
con´se·quent *adj.* following as a result —*n.* anything that follows
con·se·quen´tial *adj.* having significance; that creates or is an effect
con´se·quent·ly *adv.* as a result
con·serv´an·cy *n.* group devoted to preservation of natural resources
con·ser·va´tion *n.* the protection of natural resources
conservation of energy the principal that energy may be converted, but is never diminished
con·serv´a·tism *n.* moderation; opposition to change
con·serv´a·tive *adj.* cautious; reserved or moderate —*n.* one reserved or moderate
con·serv´a·to·ry *n.* greenhouse; a school of music or drama
con·serve´ *n.* fruit preserve —*vt.* to guard against damage or waste
con·sid´er *vt.* carefully contemplate; bear in mind; be respectful; to deem, believe
con·sid´er·a·ble *adj.* large, extensive; substantial
con·sid´er·ate *adj.* having regard
con·sid´er·a´tion *n.* careful contemplation; payment for services
con·sid´ered *adj.* given careful thought; deliberate
con·sign´ *vt.* to give over to another
con·sign´ment *n.* goods transferred to another for sale or safekeeping
con·sist´ *vi.* to be made up of
con·sist´ence, con·sist´en·cy *n.* uniformity; texture
con·sist´ent *adj.* constant; unwavering; harmonious
con·sis´to·ry *n.* a church council
con·sole´ *vt.* comfort —**con·sol´a·ble** *adj.* —**con´so·la´tion** *n.*
con·sol´i·date´ *vi., vt.* to combine
con·som·mé´ *n.* a clear broth
con´so·nance *n.* harmony; a pleasant blending of sound
con´sort *n.* a spouse or associate —**con·sort´** *vi., vt.* to associate with
con·sor´ti·um *n.* an alliance
con·spic´u·ous *adj.* obvious, apparent; notable
con·spir´a·cy *n.* a secret plan
con·spir´a·to´ri·al *adj.* inclined to scheming or collusion; conspiring
con·spire´ *vi.* to plot secretly; to work together, as of circumstances
con´sta·ble *n.* officer of the law
con·stab´u·lar·y *n.* the jurisdiction of a peace officer; law officers collectively
con´stant *adj.* unchanging; continual; steadfast —**con´stan·cy** *n.*
con·ster·na´tion *n.* a state of confusion and distress
con·stit´u·en·cy *n.* a district; a body of supporters —**con·stit´u·ent** *adj.*
con´sti·tute´ *vt.* found, establish; to make up, be the parts of
con´sti·tu´tion *n.* basic structure —**con·sti·tu·tion·al´i·ty** *n.*
con·strain´ *vt.* confine; restrain; to compel —**con·straint´** *n.*
con·strict´ *vt.* make smaller
con·struct´ *vt.* to build; piece together —**con·struc´tion** *n.*
con·struc´tive *adj.* helpful or useful
con·strue´ *vt.* interpret or deduce; to understand
con´sul *n.* a member of the diplomatic corps —**con´su·lar** *adj.*
con´su·late *n.* the offices of a consul
con·sult´ *vi.* to exchange views — *vt.* to refer for advice or information
con·sult´ant *n.* one hired to analyze and advise
con·sul·ta´tion *n.* a meeting to inform and plan
con·sult´ing *adj.* advisory
con·sum´a·ble *adj.* subject to being expended or dissipated — *n.* material used up or spent by use
con·sume´ *vt.* to make use of; deplete, devour, or destroy
consumer goods possessions that satisfy the needs of individuals
con·sum´er·ism *n.* a passion for acquisition; advocacy of protection from false advertising or shoddy merchandise
con´sum·mate *adj.* perfect; skillful —*vt.* to complete or perfect
con·sump´tion *n.* use; amount used; a wasting by disease — **con·sump´tive** *adj.*
con´tact *n.* touch; interaction; one connected —*vt.* to touch; speak to
con·ta´gion *n.* the spread of disease
con·ta´gious *adj.* spread by contact
con·tain´ *vt.* to hold; have capacity; keep within limits — **con·tain´er** *n.*
con·tain´er·ize *vt.* place in standardized containers for shipment
con·tain´ment *n.* confinement
con·tam´i·nate´ *vt.* to pollute; make impure —**con·tam´i·nant** *n.*
con·temn´ *vt.* view with contempt
con´tem·plate *vt.* study or ponder; to consider —**con´tem·pla´tion** *n.*
con·tem´pla·tive *adj.* thoughtful; reflective
con·tem´po·rar´y *adj.* current — *n.* a peer —**con·tem´po·ra´ne·ous** *adj.*
con·tempt´ *n.* disdain; disrespect —**con·tempt´i·ble** *adj.*
con·temp´tu·ous *adj.* disdainful
con·tend´ *vi.* compete; dispute — *vt.* claim to be true — **con·tend´er** *n.*
con·tent´ *adj.* satisfied —*n.* satisfaction —**con´tent** *n.* all within
con·tent´ed *adj.* satisfied — **con·tent´ed·ly** *adv.*
con·ten´tion *n.* an argument or dispute; an assertion
con·ten´tious *adj.* quarrelsome
con·ter´mi·nous *adj.* neighboring; adjoining
con´test *n.* competition —**con·test´** *vt.* to dispute; compete
con·tes´tant *n.* one who disputes; one who competes
con´text *n.* setting; background
con·tig´u·ous *adj.* touching; adjacent —**con·tig´u·ous·ly** *adv.*
con´ti·nence *n.* moderation; self–restraint —**con´ti·nent** *adj.*
con´ti·nent *n.* a major land mass
continental drift the gradual shifting of land mass
con·tin´gence *n.* contact; adjacency
con·tin´gen·cy *n.* possibility or liklihood; that happens by chance
con·tin´gent *adj.* by chance; unpredictable —*n.* a contingency; a representative group
con·tin´u·al *adj.* repeated
con·tin´u·a´tion *n.* restarting after a pause; a thing added, an extension
con·tin´ue *vi.* to endure, remain —*vt.* persist; remain; to resume after interruption —**con·tin´u·ance** *n.*
con´tin·u´i·ty *n.* being continuous
con·tin´u·ous *adj.* unbroken; connected; without interruption
con·tort´ *vt.* to twist; distort
con·tort´ed *adj.* twisted; misshapen; deformed
con·tor´tion *n.* abnormal twisting
con´tra·band´ *adj.* of prohibited goods —*n.* illegal merchandise
con´tract *n.* an agreement —*vi., vt.* enter into agreement — **con·tract´** *vt.* acquire; shorten
con·trac´tu·al *adj.* pertaining to or implying agreement
con·trac´tor *n.* party to a contract
con·tra·dict´ *vt.* to oppose; be inconsistent —**con·tra·dic´tion** *n.*
con´trail *n.* a condensed vapor trail
con·trap´tion *n.* a contrivance; a makeshift device
con·tra·ri´e·ty *n.*; dissension or opposition; inconsistency
con´trar·y *adj.* opposing; disagreeable —**con´trar·i·ness** *n.*
con´trast *n.* difference —**con·trast´** *vi.* show difference —*vt.* to set off
con·tra·vene´ *vt.* to oppose; to contradict; to interfere or infringe upon
con·tri´bute *vi., vt.* give; submit for publication —**con´tri·bu´tion** *n.*
con·trite´ *adj.* feeling regret — **con·trite´ness, con·tri´tion** *n.*
con·triv´ance *n.* a thing created
con·trive´ *vt.* to devise or scheme
con·trol´ *n.* power or authority; a device that regulates —*vt.* regulate or restrain —**con·trol´la·ble** *adj.*
con·trol´ler *n.* an executive responsible for financial control; a device that regulates
con·tro·ver´sial *adj.* subject to debate or disagreement
con´tro·ver·sy *n.* a dispute
con´tro·vert *vt.* to dispute; to contradict —**con·tro·vert´i·ble** *adj.*
con´tu·ma´cious *adj.* disobedient
con´tu·me·ly *n.* rudeness; insolence
con·tuse´ *vt.* to injure; to bruise
con·tu´sion *n.* a bruise
co·nun´drum *n.* enigma; a puzzle
con·va·lesce´ *vi.* to recover; to regain health —**con·va·les´cence** *n.*
con·va·les´cent *adj.* regaining health —*n.* one recovering
con·vene´ *vi., vt.* to assemble
con·ven´ient *adj.* accessible; suited —**con·ven´ience** *n.*
con´vent *n.* a religious community
con·ven´tion *n.* a gathering; that generally accepted
con·ven´tion·al *adj.* customary; adhering to tradition; not unusual
con·verge´ *vi.* to approach a common point; to grow closer —**con·ver´gence** *n.* —**con·ver´gent** *adj.*
con·ver´sant *adj.* familiar or knowledgeable —**con·ver´sance** *n.*
con·ver·sa´tion *n.* verbal exchange
con·verse´ *vi.* to speak familiarly —**con´verse** *adj.* reversed; transposed —*n.* interchanged; opposite
con·ver´sion *n.* a change —**con·vert´** *vt.*

con·vert´i·ble *adj.* fitted for change —*n.* a thing designed for change
con·vey´ *vt.* transport; make known
con·vey´ance *n.* a means for moving passengers or freight; transfer of property; a deed
conveyor belt a band that moves goods, as in a manufacturing plant
con´vict´ *n.* one found guilty of a crime; one serving a sentence —**con·vict´** *vt.* find guilty; condemn
con·vince´ *vt.* to persuade
con·viv´i·al *adj.* congenial; gregarious —**con·viv·i·al´i·ty** *n.*
con·vo·ca´tion *n.* a congregation; a formal gathering
con·voke´ *vt.* call a meeting
con·vo·lute´ *vt.* form in a spiral; to twist or intertwine
con´vo·lut´ed *adj.* complicated; intricate or twisted
con´voy *n.* (*Brit.*) a company of travelers; a file of vehicles
con·vulse´ *vt.* to shake violently
con·vul´sion *n.* uncontollable muscle spasms; a severe disturbance —**con·vul´sive** *adj.*
cook *n.* one who prepares food —*vi.* act as cook; be changed by exposure to heat —*vt.* to prepare food for eating —**cook the books** to prepare false financial records —**cook up** to devise or concoct
cook´book *n.* a book of instructions for the preparation of food
cook´er *n.* a device designed for a particular type of cooking —**pressure cooker** a pot that cooks using steam pressure; a job where one works under extreme pressure
cook´e·ry *n.* art of food preparation
cook´ie (*US*) *n.* a small cake–like confection
cookie cutter a device for shaping cookies —**cookie–cutter** a project that has been precisely planned
cook´ware *n.* containers and implements for processing food
cool *adj.* more cold than hot; calm, collected; indifferent; discourteous —**cool´ly** *adv.* —**cool´ness** *n.*
cool box (*Brit.*) a cold storage unit
cool´er[1] (*Brit.*) *n.* a detention cell
cool´er[2] (*US*) *n.* a cold storage unit; a wine cocktail
cool–head´ed *adj.* disposed to remain calm or composed
coop *n.* a small cage —*vt.* to confine —**flew the coop** escaped
coop´er *n.* one who makes barrels
coop´er·age *n.* making of barrels; barrels and casks collectively; the charge for making barrels
co·op´er·ate´ *vi.* to work together; to comply —**co·op´er·a´tion** *n.*
co·op´er·a·tive *adj.* working with others; of a communal organization —*n.* association operated for the benefit of its members
cop *n.* a law officer —*vt.* to seize; to steal —**cop out** to give up
co·pa·cet´ic *adj.* fine, acceptable; peaceful
cope *vi.* to face and deal with
cop´i·er *n.* one who imitates; a duplicating machine
coping saw a hand saw with a very thin blade to cut decorative pieces
co´pi·ous *adj.* abundant; abounding in thoughts or words
cop´y *n.* reproduction; a manuscript; text —*vt.* to imitate; reproduce
cop´y·cat *n.* one who imitates
cord *n.* a light rope; (*US*) thing like a rope, as *an electrical cord;* a measure of cut firewood
cord´age *n.* rope; an amount of wood
cor´date´ *adj.* heart–shaped
cor´dial *adj.* friendly —**cor·dial´i·ty** *n.* —**cor´dial·ly** *adv.*
cord´ite *n.* an explosive
cord´less *adj.* battery–operated; requiring no cord
core *n.* the innermost part —*vt.* to remove the inner part from fruit
cork *n.* bark of the cork tree; anything made of or like cork —*vt.* to stop a bottle
cork´age *n.* a charge for serving
cork´board *n.* a wall panel
corn *n.* (*Brit.*) wheat or oats; (*US*) the edible seed of the corn plant; a hard seed, as *a peppercorn;* trite humor; a painful growth on the foot —*vt.* to preserve with salt
corn bread bread made of cornmeal
cor´ner *n.* an angle formed by two lines or surfaces —*adj.* at or near a corner —*vt.* to trap —**around the corner** in the near future —**cut corners** compromise quality, etc. —**turn the corner** survive a crisis
cor´ner·stone *n.* a basic element; a foundation stone
cor·net´ *n.* a brass wind instrument; paper or pastry formed into a cone and filled with a confection
corn flour (*Brit.*) *n.* a starch extracted from corn, used in cooking
cor´nice *n.* projected molding at the top of a building or a window
corn meal ground corn
corn´row *n.* a hairstyle pattern
corn´starch (*US*) *n.* a starch extracted from corn, used in cooking
cor´nu·co´pi·a *n.* a horn filled with fruits, etc.; a conical container
corn´y *adj.* trite; hackneyed
cor´o·nar·y *adj.* regarding arteries for blood feeding the heart muscle; pertaining to the heart —*n.* coronary artery; coronary thrombosis
coronary bypass shunting of blood around a damaged artery
coronary occlusion coronary thrombosis
coronary thrombosis obstruction of a coronary artery
cor´o·na´tion *n.* a ceremony for the crowning of a monarch
cor´o·ner *n.* a public official who inquires into any unnatural death
cor·o·net´ *n.* a small crown
cor´po·ral *adj.* of the body —*n.* a non–commissioned officer
cor´po·rate *adj.* of a corporation
corporate raider one who seeks to gain control of a corporation
cor´po·ra´tion *n.* a legal entity authorized to act as one individual
cor·po´re·al *adj.* material; tangible
corps *pl. n.* people acting together
corpse (*Brit.*) *n.* a dead body
cor´pu·lent *adj.* excessively fat —**cor´pu·lence** *n.*
cor´pus *n.*, *pl.* **cor´por·a** the main part of a fleshly structure; a comprehensive collection of writing
cor´pus de·lic´ti substantial proof of a crime; body of a murder victim
cor·ral´ *n.* enclosure for livestock —*vt.* to surround and capture
cor·rect´ *adj.* accurate; proper, suitable —*vt.* to make right; to adjust
cor·rec´tion *n.* process of making right; an amount adjusted
cor´re·late´ *vt.* establish a relationship —**cor´re·la´tion** *n.*
cor·rel´a·tive *adj.* related, corresponding
cor´re·spond´ *vi.* to be similar; conform; communicate by letter —**cor·re·spon´dence** *n.*
correspondence school instruction by mail
cor´ri·dor *n.* a long passageway
cor´ri·gi·ble *adj.* able to be reformed
cor·rob´o·rate´ *vt.* to support or strengthen —**cor·rob´o·ra·tive** *adj.*
cor·rode´ *vt.* destroy gradually —**cor·ro´sion** *n.* —**cor·ro´sive** *adj.*
cor·rupt´ *adj.* immoral; altered —*vt.* pervert, debase; alter, contaminate —**cor·rupt´i·ble** *adj.* —**cor·rup´tion**, **cor·rupt´ness** *n.*
cor·rup´tive *adj.* tending to corrupt
cor·sage´ *n.* a small flower arrangement worn on a dress or the wrist
cor´sair *n.* a buccaneer, a pirate
cor·tege´, **cor·tège´** *n.* attendants
cor´tex *n.* outer layer of an organ
cor´us·cate´ *vi.* give off flashes; to sparkle, glitter —**cor·us·ca´tion** *n.*
co´sign *vi.*, *vt.* share responsibility —**co·sig´na·to·ry** *adj.*
cos·met´ic *adj.* improving appearance; superficial improvement —*n.* a preparation to improve one's appearance —**cos·met´i·cal·ly** *adv.*
cos·me·tol´o·gy *n.* art of selecting and applying cosmetics
cos´mic *adj.* of the universe; of immense proportions
cosmic dust minute space particles
cos·mog´o·ny *n.* theories of creation
cos·mog´ra·phy *n.* study of the configuration of the universe —**cos·mog´ra·pher** *n.*
cos·mol´o·gy *n.* study of the nature of the universe —**cos·mol´o·ger** *n.*
cos´mo·naut *n.* an astronaut
cos´mo·pol´i·tan *adj.* common to the entire world; worldly —*n.* urbane or sophisticated person
cos´mos *n.* universal order
cost *n.* price; value of a thing; expense of producing or obtaining
cost´–ef·fec´tive *adj.* worth the expenditure
cost´ly *adj.* expensive; splendid —**cost´li·ness** *n.*
cost of living expense of necessities
cos´tume *n.* typical mode of dress; appropriate clothing
costume jewelry fake jewelry
cot *n.* a small, folding bed
co´te·rie *n.* a close circle of friends
co·til´lion *n.* a formal dance
cot´tage *n.* a simple house
cottage industry a small business
cot´ton *n.* soft hairs from a tropical plant, used for thread or cloth
cotton candy (*US*), **cotton floss** (*Brit.*) confection of spun suger
cot´ton·seed *n.* seed from the cotton plant, a source of cooking oil
cot´ton·tail *n.* a rabbit
couch *n.* (*US*) a sofa —*vt.* recline; to express in a particular way
cough *n.* clearing of the lungs —*vi.* to expel air suddenly and noisily
coun´cil *n.* officially appointed or elected group —**coun´ci·lor** *n.*
coun´sel *n.* advice; guidance; a legal adviser —*vi., vt.* to give advice
count *vi., vt.* number in order
count´down *n.* the final check or preparation before an event
coun´te·nance *n.* appearance —*vt.* express approval
coun´ter *adj.* opposing —*adv.* —*vi., vt.* to react or respond
count´er *n.* a device for counting; a flat working surface
coun´ter·act *vt.* to mitigate —**coun·ter·ac´tive** *adj.*
coun´ter·at·tack *n.* a move to blunt an attack —*vi., vt.* retaliation
coun·ter·bal´ance *n.* an element that counteracts another
coun´ter·claim *n.* an opposing assertion
coun´ter–cul·ture *n.* a lifestyle that opposes traditional values
coun´ter·feit *adj.* fraudulent; forged —*n.* an imitation —*vt,* copy with intent to defraud; to fake —*vi.* to practice deception
coun´ter·mand *vt.* to cancel or reverse a previous order
coun´ter·meas·ure *n.* an action in opposition to another
coun´ter·pane *n.* a bedspread
coun´ter·part *n.* an opposite member; a complement
coun´ter·point *n.* a thing that interacts with another; a musical form
coun·ter·pro·duc´tive *adj.* opposite of that intended; detrimental
coun´ter·rev·o·lu´tion *n.* opposition to reform
coun´ter·sign´ *n.* authentication; a secret sign or signal —*vt.* authenticate by signing

coun´ter·weight *n.* a balance
coun´tess *n.* a woman of noble birth
count´less *adj.* innumerable
coun´tri·fied *adj.* characteristic of a farmer or small–town dweller
coun´try *n.* area of a nation or state; a rural area —*adj.* of a rural area
country club a facility for socializing, sports, etc.
coun´try·man *n.* another citizen
country music a musical style indigenous to southern U.S.
country rock blending of country music with rock and roll
coun´try·side *n.* view of a rural area
coun´ty *n.* an administrative subdivision
county fair a festival featuring products from a county
county seat location of the government of a county
coup *n.* a splendid achievement
coup d´etat overthrow of a government
cou·pé´ *n.* (*Brit.*) a half compartment at the end of a railway car
coupe *n.* a two–door automobile
cou´ple *n.* a pair; two united socially; something that links —*vt.* to link —**coup´ler** *n.* —**coup´ling** *n.*
cou´pon *n.* entitlement to a benefit; a form of transmittal
cour´age *n.* ability to face danger or adversity with confidence
cou·ra´geous *adj.* brave; fearless —**cou·ra´geous·ly** *adv.*
cour´i·er *n.* a messenger
course *n.* direction or route; method of action; a program of study —*vi., vt.* to race; move swiftly; dash
court *n.* an open area; play area for certain games; a forum of justice; royal households —*vt.* supplicate or flatter for benefit
cour´te·ous *adj.* considerate; well–mannered —**cour´te·ous·ly** *adv.*
cour´te·san *n.* a prostitute; mistress
cour´te·sy *n.* politeness; an act of consideration
court´house *n.* home of a court
court´ly *adj.* dignified; elegant —**court´li·ness** *n.*
court of appeals a court for review of the decisions of a lower court
court of law a judicial forum
court´room *n.* room in which legal proceedings are conducted
court´ship *n.* process to gain the approval of another; a wooing
court´yard *n.* an open space in the center of a large building
cous´in *n.* a relative of the same generation who is not a sibling
cou·ture´ *n.* the designing of women's clothing; high–fashion clothing —**cou·tu´rier** *n.*
cove *n.* a small sheltered bay; a recess in a wall
cov´en *n.* an assembly of witches
cov´e·nant *n.* a binding agreement; a formal contract
cov´er *n.* thing that shields or shelters —*vt.* to place over
cov´er·all *n.* loose outer garment that covers the entire body
cover charge fixed charge at a restaurant or night club
cov´er·ing *n.* a thing used to protect or shield
cov´er·let *n.* a light bed covering
cov´ert *adj.* hidden; disguised
cov´er–up *n.* action designed to hide
cov´et *vi., vt.* desire longingly —**cov´et·ous** *adj.* —**cov´e·tous·ly** *adv.*
cov´ey *n.* a small flock of birds
cow *n.* an adult female mammal
cow´ard *n.* one who lacks courage
cow´boy *n.* worker on a cattle ranch
cow´catch·er *n.* a bumper on a locomotive to fend off obstacles
cow college a college of agriculture
cow´er *vi.* to shrink back
cow´hand *n.* a cowboy
cow´hide´ *n.* leather from a cow
cowl *n.* a hood or hooded garment; a similar covering
cow´lick *n.* an unruly shock of hair
cowl´ing *n.* covering for an engine
cow´punch·er *n.* a cowboy
co·work´er, co–work´er *n.* an associate at work
cox´swain *n.* the helmsman of a small boat or racing shell
coy *adj.* shy, demur; affecting shyness; evasive —**coy´ly** *adv.*
coz´en *vi., vt.* to deceive
coz´y *adj.* comfortable —*n.* cover for a teapot —**cozy up** attempt to get in good graces —**play it cozy** act cautiously or secretively
crab *n.* an edible crustacean; an ill-tempered person —*vi.* to fish for crabs; complain
crab´by *adj.* grouchy; ill–humored
crack *adj.* first–rate —*n.* a sharp sound; a fracture; a sharp blow; a type of cocaine —*vi., vt.* produce a sharp sound; strike; split; to break down mentally —**crack the whip** press for greater output; demand strict adherence to rules
crack´down *n.* strict enforcement or punishment —*vi.* enforce strictly or punish severely
crack´er *n.* a thin crisp wafer; (*US*) a country boy —**crack´ers** (*Brit.*) mentally deranged
crack´er·jack *adj.* outstanding
crack´head *n.* user of crack cocaine
crack´house *n.* a place where crack cocaine is processed
crack´le *n.* the finely cracked surface of some pottery —*vi.* a series of snapping or cracking noises —*vt.* produce fine cracks on pottery
crack´pot *adj.* insane; eccentric —*n.* one who is strange or eccentric
crack´–up *n.* a vehicular accident; a mental breakdown
cra´dle *n.* a baby's bed; place of early development; a device for supporting a heavy object
craft *n.* art or trade; skill in deception; ships —*vt.* to form with skill
crafts´man *n.* skilled worker; an artisan —**crafts´man·ship** *n.*
craft´y *adj.* clever; scheming —**craft´i·ly** *adv.* —**craft´i·ness** *n.*
crag *n.* a rough projecting rock
crag´gy *adj.* rough and steep; irregular —**crag´gi·ness** *n.*
cram *vt.* compress or compact
cramp *n.* sudden involuntary muscular contraction —*vt.* to restrict
cramped *adj.* confined; restraining
crane *n.* a large wading bird; a machine for raising heavy objects
cra´ni·al *adj.* of the cranium
cranial nerve *n.* nerve at the stem of the brain
cra´ni·um *n.* the skull
crank *n.* an arm for transferring motion; an eccentric or complaining person —*vi., vt.* turn a handle
crank´case *n.* an oil reservoir
crank´shaft *n.* a rod that drives a crank for transferring movement
crank´y *adj.* irritable; ill–tempered; testy —**crank´i·ness** *n.*
cran´ny *n.* a small opening
crap *n.* excrement; junk, trash; foolishness; anything useless
crap out lose at craps; drop out due to exhaustion, fear, etc.
crap´py *adj.* of inferior quality
craps *pl. n.* a game of dice
crap´shoot *n.* a risky venture
crap´u·lence *n.* excessive eating or drinking —**crap´u·lent** *adj.*
crap´u·lous *adj.* inclined to excessive eating or drinking; suffering from such excess —**crap´u·lous·ly** *adv.*
crash *n.* a sudden loud noise; a collision; sudden financial collapse —*vi.* make a loud noise; collide; fail suddenly; bed down temporarily —*vt.* to cause a noise or collision; to attend without invitation
crash helmet *n.* protective headgear
crash´–land *vi., vt.* end or set down in an unconventional manner
crash pad temporary living quarters
crass *adj.* crude; vulgar; tasteless
crate *n.* a box made of wood —*vt.* to pack
cra´ter *n.* a bowl–shaped depression
cra·vat´ *n.* a scarf worn at the neck
crave *vi., vt.* long for —**crav´ing** *n.*
cra´ven *adj.* cowardly
craw *n.* the crop of a bird; an animal's stomach —**stick in one's craw** to displease; irritate
craw´dad, craw´fish *n.* crayfish
crawl *n.* slow movement; swimming stroke —*vi.* to move on hands and knees; move slowly or feebly
crawl space (*US*) space under a house for access to wiring, plumbing, etc.
cray´fish *n.* a small fresh–water crustacean similar to a shrimp
cray´on *n.* colored wax for drawing
craze *n.* a fad —*vi., vt.* anger; enrage
cra´zy *adj.* insane; foolish; overly enthusiastic —*n.* one crazed
creak´y *adj.* squeaky —**creak´i·ly** *adv.* —**creak´i·ness** *n.*
cream *n.* a rich component of milk; that made from cream; the color of cream; the consistency of whipped cream; the best part —*adj.* containing or like cream —*vt.* remove cream from milk; to blend
cream cheese a soft cheese
cream´er *n.* a pitcher for serving cream; a nondairy product used to lighten and flavor coffee
cream puff a light filled pastry
cream sauce smooth light sauce
cream soda a vanilla flavored drink
cream´y *adj.* containing cream; of the consistency of heavy cream
crease *n.* a mark made by folding —*vt.* to make or form creases in
cre·ate´ *vt.* to originate; produce through artistic endeavor
cre·a´tion *n.* the act of creating; that created —**cre·a´tor** *n.*
cre·a´tion·ism *n.* belief in the Biblical account of the creation
cre·a´tive *adj.* displaying or rousing imagination or inventiveness
cre·a·tiv´i·ty *n.* inventiveness
crea´ture *n.* a living being
creature comforts those things that provide contentment for the body
cre´dence *n.* acceptance as true
cre·den´tial *n.* that attesting to one's knowledge or authority
cre·den´za *n.* a sideboard
credibility gap incongruity between what is said and what is done
cred´i·ble *adj.* plausible; believable
cred´it *n.* trust; approval or praise —*vt.* believe in; assign an attribute
credit card a line of credit for the purchase of goods or services
credit line the credit one is allowed
credit rating assessment ability and prospect for repaying obligations
cre´do *n.* a creed
cre·du´li·ty *n.* tendency to believe
cred´u·lous *adj.* inclined to believe
creed *n.* a statement of beliefs
creek *n.* (*US*) a stream; (*Brit.*) a small inlet of the sea —**up the creek** in a difficult predicament
creel *n.* a fisherman's bag
creep *vi.* move along the ground; move slowly with great stealth
creep´y *adj.* apprehensive; uneasy —**creep´i·ly** *adv.* —**creep´i·ness** *n.*
cre´mate´ *vt.* to incinerate
cre·ma·to´ri·um, cre´ma·to·ry *n.* a place where the dead are cremated
cre´o·sote *n.* a wood preservative
crêpe *n.* a thin crinkled cloth; a thin pancake
crepe paper a thin crinkled paper
cres·cen´do *adj., adv.* gradually increasing —*n.* a gradual increase
crest *n.* a decorative plume; a device over a coat of arms; the highest point —**crest´ed** *adj.*

crest´fall·en *adj.* saddened; shamed; disheartened
cre·ta´ceous *adj.* of chalk or a chalk–like substance
cre´tin *n.* a buffoon; one suffering from cretinism
cre´tin·ism *n.* a disease marked by deformity and retardation
cre·vasse´ *n.* deep fissure; chasm
crev´ice *n.* a narrow crack
crew *n.* a group working together
crew cut close–cropped hair style
crew´el *n.* a type of embroidery
crib *n.* a bed for a small child; a small building or bin for storage —*vi., vt.* to cheat or steal
crib´bage *n.* a card game
crick *n.* stiffness of the back or neck
crime *n.* an act in violation of the law; a disgraceful act
crim´i·nal *adj.* in the nature of a crime —*n.* one convicted of crime —**crim·i·nal´i·ty** *n.*
criminal code body of law that deals with criminal offenses
criminal court a court that tries criminal cases
criminal law law that deals with crime and punishment for crime
crim·i·nol´o·gy *n.* study or methodical investigation of crime —**crim·i·nol´o·gist** *n.*
crimp *n.* a pleat or fold —*vt.* crumple or crinkle; form into wrinkles
crim´son *adj., n.* deep red
cringe *vi.* to cower or shrink
crin´kle *vi., vt.* form in wrinkles; rustle, as paper —**crin´kly** *adj.*
crin´o·line *n.* petticoat; stiff cloth
crip´ple *n.* one deprived —*vt.* lose use of a limb; impair —**crip´pler** *n.*
cri´sis *n., pl.* **cri´ses** a decisive or turning point; traumatic event
crisp *adj.* brittle; clean and fresh; invigorating —*vi., vt.* to make crisp —**burned to a crisp** blackened so as to be inedible; severly sunburned —**crisp´ness** *n.*
crisp´y *adj.* brittle —**crisp´i·ness** *n.*
cri·te´ri·on *n.* a basis for judging
crit´ic *n.* a reviewer of movies, art, etc.; one who tends to faultfinding
crit´i·cal *adj.* tending to find fault; marked by careful analysis; dangerous; decisive —**crit´i·cal·ly** *adv.*
crit´i·cise´ (*Brit.*)**, crit´i·cize´** (US) *vi., vt.* to evaluate; to find fault —**crit´i·cism** *n.*
cri·tique´ *n.* a careful analysis
crit´ter *n.* a creature; a small animal
croak *n.* a deep, rough voice —*vi., vt.* utter a deep, rough sound; to die
crock *n.* an earthenware pot; misleading or incorrect information
crock´er·y *n.* pottery
croc´o·dile *n.* a large amphibious reptile
crocodile tears insincerity
crois·sant *n.* a light rich, breakfast roll
crone *n.* an old woman; a hag
cro´ny *n.* a close friend
cro´ny·ism *n.* favoring friends or supporters
crook *n.* a device with a curved end; one living by dishonest means —*vi., vt.* to bend
crook´ed *adj.* bent; dishonest
croon *vi., vt.* sing in a low, soft tone
crop *n.* agricultural products; amount harvested; a thing cut short —*vt.* to trim; to cut or clip
crop duster a small airplane that sprays insecticide or fungicide
crop´per *n.* one who farms on shares, a sharecropper; a bad experience; a failed venture
crop rotation changing crops each year to avoid depleting the soil
cro·quet´ *n.* a lawn game
cro·quette´ *n.* a deep–fried cake of chopped meat or seafood
cross *adj.* angry; cranky —*n.* an intersecting horizontal and vertical line; a burden, affliction; a hybrid —*vt.* intersect; travel or reach over; oppose —**cross a palm** pay a bribe
cross´beam *n.* a structural member
cross´bow *n.* a medieval weapon
cross´breed *n.* a hybrid —*vi., vt.* to produce a hybrid —**cross´bred** *adj.*
cross´check *vi., vt.* to verify
cross´–coun·try *adj., adv.* across a land; through rugged country
cross´cur·rent *n.* a flow of water across the main current; influence contrary to the main thrust
cross–ex·am·i·na´tion *n.* careful questioning, especially to refute
cross´–eyed *adj.* marked by uncoordinated eye movements
cross´–fer·ti·li·za´tion *n.* breeding with a different line
cross´hatch·ing *n.* a pattern of crossing parallel lines
cross´ing *n.* a place for moving from one side to the other; place where two ways cross: an intersection
cross´ly *adv.* in a grouchy manner
cross´–pol´li·nate *vi., vt.* to transfer pollen from one species to another
cross´–ref´er·ence *n.* tribute to another source —*vt.* refer to another mention; prepare a reference to other sources
cross´road *n.* intersection of roads; an important time or incident
crotch *n.* an intersection; the area where the legs meet at the trunk
crotch´et *n.* odd or whimsical notion
crouch *vi.* to bend low with limbs drawn close; to cower in fear
crou´pi·er *n.* one who operates a casino gambling table
crou´ton *n.* a small piece of crisp bread garnish for soup or salad
crow´bar *n.* a metal prying tool
crowd *n.* a group gathered in one place; people with something in common —*vi., vt.* squeeze or push
crown *n.* a symbol of sovereignty; power or office of a monarch; symbol of distinction —*vt.* confer with a crown; be the highest part; bring to successful completion
crow's´–feet *n.* a pattern of lines around the corner of the eyes
crow's´–nest *n.* a high platform
cru´cial *adj.* extremely significant; decisive —**cru´cial·ly** *adv.*
cru´ci·fy´ *vt.* put to death on a cross; to treat cruelly
crud *n.* gunk; a worthless or nasty thing
crude *adj.* unrefined or raw; lacking manners or tact —**crude´ly** *adv.*
cru´el *adj.* inclined to inflict; barbarous; pleasure taken in suffering; heartless —**cru´el·ly** *adv.*
cru´et *n.* a narrow mouth jar
cruise *n.* a pleasure voyage —*vi.* travel about for pleasure
crul´ler *n.* a cake fried in melted fat
crumb *n.* a piece or fragment
crum´ble *vi., vt.* break into fragments; collapse or disintegrate
crum´bly *adj.* easily broken to small pieces; consisting of fragments; dilapidated, fallen in
crum´my *adj.* cheap; shoddy; shabby
crum´pet *n.* a small batter cake baked on a griddle
crum´ple *vi., vt.* crush; collapse
crunch *n.* a difficult situation —*vi., vt.* to grind with a crackling sound
cru·sade´ *n.* a broad campaign —*vi.* participate in a campaign
crush *n.* a crowding; passing infatuation; fruit drink —*vt.* to press so as to bruise or break; to crowd; to subdue
crust *n.* a hard surface; insolence —*vi., vt.* cover with a crisp surface
crust´y *adj.* brusque, uncivil —**crust´i·ness** *n.*
crutch *n.* an aid or support
crux *n.* a decisive factor; the heart of a matter
cry *n.* a scream or shout; weeping —*vi.* scream or shout; weep —*vt.* to plead or beg —**a far cry** very different than expected
cry´ba·by *n.* one who complains
cry·o·gen´ics *pl. n.* the science of creation and effects of low temperature —**cry·o·gen´ic** *adj.*
crypt *n.* underground chamber
crypt·a·nal´y·sis *n.* the science of deciphering codes
cryp´tic *adj.* enigmatic; having hidden meaning
cryp´to·gram *n.* a coded message
cryp´to·graph *n.* a means for writing or deciphering coded messages —**cryp·tog´ra·pher** *n.*
crys´tal *adj.* of glass or certain minerals; tranparent —*n.* a high–quality glass; geometric particles of a mineral; glass covering a watch
crystal–clear easily understood
crys´tal·line *adj.* similar to or about crystal
crys´tal·lize *vi., vt.* form or cause to form a crystal; bring to permanent form —**crys·tal·li·za´tion** *n.*
cub´by·hole *n.* a small compartment
cube *n.* a solid form with six square faces; the third power of a number —*vt.* to raise to the third power —**cu´bic** *adj.*
cube steak beef tenderized by a pattern of cross cuts
cu´bi·cle *n.* a small enclosure
cub´ism *n.* an abstract art syle using geometric patterns —**cub´ist** *n.*
cuck´old *n.* a man whose wife has been unfaithful —**cuck´old·ry** *n.*
cud *n.* food regurgitated from the stomach of a ruminating animal
cud´dle *n.* an embrace —*vi., vt.* to embrace
cud´dly *adj.* affectionate; lovable; appealing —**cud´dle·some** *adj.*
cudg´el *n.* a heavy stick; a club
cue *n.* a signal or hint —*vt.* to signal
cue ball an unmarked ball struck with the cue in a game of pool or billiards
cuff *n.* a slap; the end of a sleeve; (*US*) turned up material at the end of a trouser leg —*vt.* to slap
cui·sine´ *n.* a particular style of food
cul´–de–sac´ *n.* a street with a single outlet and a turnabout at the end
cu´li·nar´y *adj.* of cooking
cull *n.* something selected for removal —*vt.* to select
cul´mi·nate´ *vi., vt.* to come or bring to completion —**cul·mi·na´tion** *n.*
cul´pa·ble *adj.* deserving blame —**cul·pa·bil´i·ty** *n.* —**cul´pa·bly** *adv.*
cul´prit *n.* one accused or guilty
cult *n.* an extremist group considered to be obsessive in their beliefs
cul´ti·vate´ *vt.* to tend crops; to promote or nurture
cul´tur·al *adj.* of a particular culture
cul´ture *n.* the characteristics of a society; enlightenment, refinement
cultured pearl a pearl grown from an implanted irritant
culture shock disorientation from exposure to the unfamiliar
cul´vert *n.* a conduit or drain passing under a road, path, etc.
cum´ber·some *adj.* unwieldy; difficult to maneuver; bulky; awkward
cu´mu·late *vi., vt.* to collect; to accumulate —**cu´mu·la·tive** *adj.*
cu·mu·lo·nim´bus *n.* a cloud structure associated with storms
cu´mu·lus *n.* a tall cloud structure with a dark, flat, moisture–laden base —**cu´mu·lous** *adj.*
cu·ne´i·form *adj.* wedge–shaped, as of certain ancient writing —*n.*
cun´ning *adj.* sly; crafty —*n.* skillful at deceiving
cup *n.* an open container for beverages; measure of 8 ounces
cup´board *n.* storage for dinnerware
cup´cake (*US*) *n.* a small cake
cup´ful *adj.* amount a cup can hold
cu·pid´i·ty *n.* avarice; greed
cu´po·la *n.* domed ceiling; a small domed structure

cur *n.* a dog; a vile person

cu´rate *n.* clergyman who assists

cu´ra·tor *n.* a custodian

curb *n.* a checking; hindrance; (*US*) a curbstone —*vt.* to subdue; check

curd *n.* coagulated milk

cur´dle *vi., vt.* to turn into curd; to coagulate

cu´ra·tor *n.* an overseer

cure *n.* agent that restores health —*vt.* effect recovery; preserve food —**cur´a·tive** *adj., n.*

cure´–all *n.* universal remedy

cur´few *n.* a time limit

cu´ri·os´i·ty *n.* a desire to learn; a rare or unusual artifact

cu´ri·ous *adj.* eager to learn; inquisitive; unusual

cur´li·cue *n.* an ornate curve

curl´y *adj.* having waves or ringlets; inclined to curl —**curl´i·ness** *n.*

cur´mudg´eon *n.* an ill–tempered or disparaging person

cur´ren·cy *n.* paper money

cur´rent *adj.* of the present —*n.* a general tendency or movement

current account (*Brit.*) deposit of funds for transfer by cheque

cur·ric´u·lum *n.* a course of study; studies offered by a school

cur´ry *n.* a piquant blend of spices; dish or sauce prepared with curry —*vt.* groom a horse

cur´sive *adj.* connected handwriting

cur´so·ry *adj.* hastily done; casual

curt *adj.* short, concise; brusque

cur´tail´ *vt.* cut short; reduce; to lessen —**cur·tail´ment** *n.*

cur´tain *n.* hanging material; something that covers or obscures —*vt.* to cover, as with a curtain

curtain call a performer's return to the stage to acknowledge applause

curtain raiser a brief entertainment before the main show

curt´sy *n.* a bow —*vi.* to make a bow

cur·va´ceous *adj.* of an attractive figure

cur´va·ture´ *n.* a curved part

curve *n.* a smooth deviation —*vi., vt.* to deviate from the straight

cush´y *adj.* easy, as *a cushy job*

cusp *n.* a projection; intersection of two lines —**cus´pi·date** *adj.*

cus´pid *n.* a tooth with a single point

cuss *n.* a person or animal —*vi., vt.* to curse

cus´tard *n.* a thick, creamy dessert

cus·to´di·an *n.* a caretaker —**cus·to´di·al** *adj.*

cus´to·dy *n.* care and protection

cus´tom *adj.* made to order —*n.* common practice; tradition

cus´tom·ar·y *adj.* usual; according to custom —**cus´tom·ar´i·ly** *adv.*

cus´tom–built´ *adj.* made to order

cus´tom·er *n.* a patron

cus´tom·house *n.* a clearing house for imports and exports

cus´tom·ize *vt.* alter to suit

cus´tom–made *adj.* custom–built

cut *n.* incision; reduction; a sharp, derogatory comment —*vi.* use a sharp instrument; to disparage; move quickly —*vt.* to penetrate; reduce or trim; offend with a remark; pass across or through; discontinue or stop —**a cut above** significantly better —**cut and dried** a foregone conclusion; routine —**cut loose** act with abandon —**cut no ice** of no influence —**cut out for** suited to —**cut through** get to the point

cu·ta´ne·ous *adj.* relating to the skin

cut´back´ *n.* a reduction

cu´ti·cle *n.* outer layer of skin: the epidermis; skin around the nails

cut´ler·y *n.* utensils for cutting

cut´let *n.* a slice of meat from the rib or leg; a chopped meat patty

cut´off *adj.* of a limit —*n.* a shortcut; a device for shutting off flow

cut´–rate *adj.* reduced in price; of questionable quality

cut´throat *adj.* murderous; unmerciful; relentless —*n.* a murderer

cutting *adj.* sharp or piercing —*n.* the act of slicing; a thing cut off

cutting board a surface for cutting

cutting edge latest innovation

cut´up *n.* a joker

cu·vée´ *n.* a particular blend of wine

cy´cle *n.* time for a series of events; a bicycle or motorcycle —*vi.* occur by turns; pass through one occurrence; ride a bicycle, etc.

cy´clic, cy´cli·cal *adj.* occurring in cycles

cy´clist *n.* a bicycle, etc. rider

cy´clone´ *n.* a violent, rotating windstorm; a device that separates by whirling

cy´clo·tron´ *n.* a particle accelerator

cyn´ic *n.* one who denies the sincerity of others —**cyn´i·cal** *adj.*

cy·tol´o·gy *n.* study of cells

czar *n.* formerly, a male monarch; one having great power

d, D fourth letter of the alphabet; 500 in Roman numerals

dab *n.* a small quantity —*vi., vt.* pat lightly

dab´ble *vi.* engage in superficially

daf´fy *adj.* silly, ridiculous

daft *adj.* insane; foolish

dai´ly *adj.* each day —*adv.* every day

daily double a wager

dain´ty *adj.* delicate; fragile —**dain´ti·ly** *adv.* —**dain´ti·ness** *n.*

dair´y *n.* place for processing milk

dairy cattle cows cultivated for milk

daisy chain connected series

dal´li·ance *n.* flirtation

dal´ly *vi.* flirt or trifle; waste time

dam *n.* a barrier; an obstruction —*vt.* to hold back; to obstruct

dam´age *n.* breakage; injury causing loss of value —*vt.* to mar or injure

dam´ages *n.* compensation

dam´ask *n.* linen fabric; rose color —*adj.* of damask linen; rose colored

dame *n.* a matron

damp *adj.* slightly moist —*n.* humidity; moisture —*vt.* to moisten; slow a fire by reducing air supply; to check sound waves —**damp´ish** *adj.* —**damp´ly** *adv.*

damp´en *vt.* to moisten; check or deaden; to lessen enthusiasm —*vi.* become moist

damp´er *n.* a valve for controlling flow

dance *n.* graceful, rhythmic movement —*vi., vt.* move to music

danc´er·cise *n.* rhythmic exercise set to music

dan´der *n.* temper; anger

dan´di·fy *vt.* to dress like a dude

dan´dy *adj.* first–rate —*n.* a man overly attentive to appearance

dan´ger *n.* cause of injury or pain

dan´ger·ous *adj.* perilous; liable to injure or harm —**dan´ger·ous·ly** *adv.* —**dan´ger·ous·ness** *n.*

dan´gle *vi., vt.* to hang loosely

dank *adj.* disagreeably damp; clammy —**dank´ness** *n.*

dap´per *adj.* stylish; smartly dressed; alert, active

dare *n.* a challenge —*vi.* be bold —*vt.* to have courage; to challenge —**dar´ing** *adj.* —**dar´ing·ly** *adv.*

dare´dev·il *adj.* bold and adventurous —*n.* one who takes chances;—**dare´dev·il·ry, dare´dev·il·try** *n.*

dark *adj.* lacking light; dismal, gloomy; sinister; unenlightened —*n.* a lack of light; night —**dark´ish** *adj.*

dark´en *vi., vt.* to become or make dark; become obscure or confusing —**dark´en·er** *n.*

dark horse unexpectedly successful

dart *n.* a pointed missile; sudden movement —*vi., vt.* move suddenly and rapidly

dash *n.* a hasty move; mark (-) of punctuation; a small amount —*vi.* to rush; to smash —*vt.* to thrust or smash violently; act hastily

dash´board *n.* panel at the front an automobile

dash´ing *adj.* adventurous, gallant; jaunty; stylishly elegant —**dash´ing·ly** *adv.*

das´tard *n.* a malicious or cowardly person —**das´tard·ly** *adv.*

da´ta *n. pl., sing.* **dat´um** information; facts or figures

da´ta·base *n.* a collection of related data

data processing *n.* the manipulation of data, especially by a computer

date *n.* a point in time; an appointment; an escort; fruit of a palm —*vi.* exist from a particular time; become obsolete; to escort —*vt.* mark the date of; arrange a meeting with

date´book *n.* appointment book

dat´ed *adj.* marked with a date; from a previous time; out of style

daub *vi., vt.* apply crudely

daugh´ter *n.* female offspring

daugh´ter–in–law *n.* a son's wife

daunt *vt.* discourage

daunt´less *adj.* daring; heroic; not to be discouraged

dav´en·port *n.* (*Brit.*) a type of desk; (*US*) a sofa

daw´dle *vi., vt.* to waste time

dawn *n.* the start of day; a beginning —*vi.* to begin

day *n.* daylight hours, sunrise to sunset; a 24–hour span; an era

day´bed *n.* lounge used for a bed

day´book *n.* a daily journal

day´break *n.* dawn

day camp a camp that does not provide overnight accommodations

day care tending of children; a facility where children are tended

day´dream *n.* a fantasy —*vi.* to be lost in reverie

day´light *n.* sunlight

day nursery day care facility

day one the start of a venture

day room a recreation room

day shift the working hours from early morning until late afternoon

day´time *n.* sunrise to sunset

day´–to–day´ *adj.* regular; routine

daze *n.* a stupor; bewilderment —*vt.* to stun; bewilder —**daz´ed·ly** *adv.*

daz´zle *vi., vt.* blind temporarily; to amaze —**daz´zling·ly** *adv.*

dea´con, dea´con·ess *n.* a lay officer in a church; a minister's assistant

de·ac´ti·vate *vt.* make inoperable or ineffective; to release from service

dead *adj.* lacking life; lacking vitality or brilliance; dispassionate; numb; ancient or out of date; no longer useful; absolute: *dead on*; exhausted —**dead´ness** *n.*

dead´beat *adj.* an idler; one who doesn't repay debts

dead´bolt *n.* a latch

dead center at the exact center

dead´en *vt.* anesthetize; to reduce

dead end a road without an outlet; an unprofitable venture —**dead´–end´** *adj.* lacking means for continuation or advancement

dead´fall *n.* a snare; a fallen tree and the debris it carries

dead´head *n.* operating without cargo or passengers; dull or stupid person —*vi.* travel without cargo

dead heat a tie or stalemate

dead letter undeliverable mail

dead´line *n.* time established for completion

dead´lock *n.* a stalemate

dead´ly *adj.* apt to cause injury or death; lethal; extremely effective —**dead´li·ness** *n.*

dead´pan *adj., adv.* without expression —*n.* a blank look

dead reckoning estimating position based on experience

dead ringer a precise match

dead´wood *n.* something useless

deaf *adj.* unable to hear; unwilling to be persuaded —**deaf´ness** *n.*

deaf´en *vt.* make deaf; overwhelm with sound —**deaf´en·ing** *adj.*

deal *n.* an agreement; a business

transaction; distribution *—vi.* take action; do business *—vt.* to distribute **—deal´er** *n.*

deal´er·ship *n.* a business authorized to market a product

dean *n.* an officer in a school or college; one senior or preeminent

dear *adj.* cherished; expensive *—n.* a loved one *—adv.* with affection; at great cost **—dear´ly** *adv.*

dearth *n.* a lack or scarcity

death *n.* the termination of life

death benefit insurance payment on the death of a policyholder

death certificate the official record of a person's death

death´less *adj.* undying; enduring **—death´less·ly** *adv.*

death´like *adj.* gaunt; pale

death´ly *adj.* ghastly; deathlike *—adv.* to a deadly extent

death´trap *n.* an unsafe place

death´watch *n.* attendance at the bedside of a dying person

de·ba´cle *n.* the total dissolution of order; a rout

de·bar´ *vt.* to exclude; prohibit or restrict **—de·bar´ment** *n.*

de·bark´ *vi., vt.* leave a ship or aircraft; disembark

de·base´ *vt.* lower in worth or purity; adulterate **—de·base´ment** *n.*

de·bate´ *n.* an airing of opposing views; a formal argument *—vi., vt.* discuss openly; engage in formal argumentation; consider or contemplate **—de·bat´a·ble** *adj.*

de·bauch´ *vt.* to corrupt or debase **—de·bauch´er** *n.*

de·bauch´er·y *n.* revelry; intemperance; excessive indulgence

de·ben´ture *n.* a promissory note

de·bil´i·tate´ *vt.* to drain of strength or energy **—de·bil·i·ta´tion** *n.*

de·bil´i·ty *n.* weakness; infirmity

deb·o·naire´ *adj.* sophisticated, urbane; nonchalant, carefree

de·brief´ *vt.* to examine and instruct

dé·bris´ *n.* scattered remains; rubble

debt *n.* something owed; obligation

debt´or *n.* one who owes

de·bug´ *vt.* to correct errors or malfunctions

de·bunk´ *vt.* to expose; demystify

de·but´ *n.* a first public appearance; a beginning

deb´u·tante *n.* a young woman

dec´ade *n.* a group of ten; ten years

dec´a·dence *n.* deterioration or decline; a time of decline **—dec´a·dent** *adj.* **—dec´a·dent·ly** *adv.*

dec´a·gon *n.* a ten–sided form

dec·a·he´dron *n.* ten–sided solid

de´cal *n.* a decorative transfer

de·cal´ci·fy *vt.* remove calcium *—vi.* to lose calcium

de·cant´ *vt.* to pour off a liquid; pour from one container to another **—de·can´ta´tion** *n.* **—de·cant´er** *n.*

de·cap´i·tate *vt.* to behead **—de·cap·i·ta´tion** *n.*

de·cath´lon *n.* an athletic competition comprising ten events

de·cay´ *n.* decomposition of organic matter; slow deterioration *—vi., vt.* decompose; deteriorate slowly

de·cease´ *vi.* to die **—de·ceased´** *adj.*

de·ceit´ *n.* a misrepresentation; a dishonest action; trickery

de·ceit´ful *adj.* marked by deception; fraudulent **—de·ceit´ful·ly** *adv.* **—de·ceit´ful·ness** *n.*

de·ceive´ *vt.* mislead by lying or trickery *—vi.* practice deceit

de·cel´er·ate *vi., vt.* reduce speed **—de·cel·er·a´tion** *n.*

de´cent *adj.* proper; respectable; conforming to public standard; moderately good **—de´cen·cy** *n.*

de·cen´tral·ize *vt.* to disperse **—de·cen·tral·i·za´tion** *n.*

de·cep´tion *n.* deceit; being deceived; a misrepresentation

de·cep´tive *adj.* misleading; designed to misrepresent **—de·cep´tive·ly** *adv.* **—de·cep´tive·ness** *n.*

de·cer´ti·fy *vt.* revoke

de·cide´ *vt.* settle; bring to decision *—vi.* make a decision

de·cid´ed *adj.* certain, clear–cut; without reservation; determined, resolute **—de·cid´ed·ly** *adv.*

de·cid´u·ous *adj.* shed seasonally; temporary, ephemeral **—de·cid´u·ous·ly** *adv.*

dec´i·mal *adj.* of the number 10 **—decimal system** a number system in base 10

dec´i·mate *vt.* select and kill one in ten; to destroy or slaughter **—dec·i·ma´tion** *n.*

de·ci´pher *vt.* interpret the obscure **—de·ci´pher·a·ble** *adj.*

de·ci´sion *n.* a conclusion or judgment

de·ci´sive *adj.* conclusive; resolving uncertainty; determined, positive; extremely important

de·claim´ *vi., vt.* recite dramatically; proclaim; to speak out *—vi.* recite eloquently **—de·clam´a·to·ry** *adj.*

de·clar´a·tive *adj.* effecting to inform; making an assertion **—de·clar´a·tive·ly** *adv.*

de·clare´ *vt.* announce formally; state emphatically; reveal or name *—vi.* make a positive statement **—dec´la·ra´tion** *n.* **—de·clar´er** *n.*

de·clen´sion *n.* a declining; a slope; a deviation

dec·li·na´tion *n.* a slope or descent; deviation; a courteous refusal

de·cline´ *n.* a downward trend; deterioration *—vi.* to deteriorate; refuse politely; slope downward *—vt.* refuse to accept; cause to incline

de·cliv´i·ty *n.* a downward sloping **—de·cliv´i·tous** *adj.*

de·code´ *vt.* translate from code to plain text

de·com·mis´sion *vt.* to take out of service

de´com·pose´ *vt.* break down *—vi.* disintegrate or decay **—de·com´po·si´tion** *n.*

de·com·press´ *vt.* reduce pressure; permit expansion

decompression chamber a room with controlled air pressure

decompression sickness a painful, potentially fatal condition caused by nitrogen bubbles in the blood

de·con·tam´i·nate *vt.* free from harmful matter; to make safe

de·cor´ *n.* a style of decoration

dec´o·rate´ *vt.* to adorn; paint and refurnish; plan and direct refurbishing; to honor with a medal

dec´o·ra·tive *adj.* ornamental; artistic **—dec´o·ra·tive·ly** *adv.*

dec´o·rous *adj.* respectful; demure **—dec´o·rous·ly** *adv.*

de·cor´ti·cate *vt.* to peel; remove an outer layer **—de·cor·ti·ca´tion** *n.*

de·co´rum *n.* manners; propriety

de·cou·page´ *n.* decorative material mounted and varnished *—vt.*

de´coy *n.* a thing used to mislead or lure *—vi., vt.* to lure, as into a trap

de·crease´ *vi., vt.* become gradually less or smaller **—de´crease** *n.* the process or lessening; the amount of reduction **—de·creas´ing·ly** *adv.*

de·cree´ *n.* official proclamation *—vt.* order *—vi.* issue a decree

de·crep´it *adj.* worn out by age or use **—de·crep´i·tude´** *n.*

de·cry´ *vt.* denounce; criticize or condemn **—de·cri´al** *n.*

ded´i·cate *vt.* to set apart, devote to a cause, etc.; open with ceremony; pay homage **—ded·i·ca´tion** *n.*

ded´i·cat·ed *adj.* given over totally; for specific use

de·duce´ *vt.* conclude or infer by reasoning **—de·duc´i·ble** *adj.*

de·duct´ *vt.* to take away: subtract; conclude by reasoning: to deduce

de·duc´tion *n.* a subtraction; the process of reasoning; a determination **—de·duc´tive** *adj.*

deed *n.* an act; a notable achievement; document conveying interest in property *—vt.* to transfer by means of a legal document

deem *vi., vt.* to believe; to judge; to have as an opinion

de–em´pha·size *vt.* reduce in importance **—de–em´pha·sis** *n.*

deep *adj.* extending far; of a specific extent; penetrating; low in tone; abstract; earnest **—deep´ly** *adv.*

deep´en *vi., vt.* make deeper

deep´–fry *vt.* cook in hot grease

deep´–root·ed *adj.* having deep roots; firmly established

deep´–seat·ed *adj.* firmly established; difficult to overcome

deep space outer space

de·face´ *vt.* disfigure or mar; damage **—de·face´ment** *n.*

de fac´to *Latin* existing in fact

de·fame´ *vt.* slander or libel **—def´a·ma·tion** *n.* **—de·fam´a·to·ry** *adj.*

de·fault´ *n.* failure to fulfill an obligation; failure to appear *—vi., vt.* to fail in fulfilling

de·feat´ *vt.* overpower or conquer; to frustrate the efforts of another *—n.*

de·feat´ist *n.* one who expects or accepts defeat *—adj.* expecting misfortune

def´e·cate *vi.* eliminate waste from the body *—vt.* clear of impurities

de´fect, de·fect´ *n.* imperfection; deficiency **—de·fect´** *vi.* abandon a cause, etc.; join the opposition **—de·fec´tion** *n.* **—de·fec´tor** *n.*

de·fec´tive *adj.* imperfect or deficient **—de·fec´tive·ly** *adv.*

de·fence´ (*Brit.*) *n.* protection; means of protection; justification; in law, a defendant and solicitor or the arguments they present

de·fence´less (*Brit.*) *adj.* without protection; unable to defend; helpless

de·fend´ *vt.* protect; justify one's actions; to contest *—vi.* make a defense **—de·fend´a·ble** *adj.*

de·fend´ant *n.* in law, one against whom legal action is brought

de·fen·es·tra´tion *n.* the act of throwing out of a window

de·fense´ (*US*) *n.* protection; means of protection; justification; in law, a defendant and lawyer or the arguments they present

de·fense´less (*US*) *adj.* without protection; helpless **—de·fense´less·ly** *adv.*

de·fen´si·ble *adj.* able to be justified or defended **—de·fen´si·bly** *adv.*

de·fen´sive *adj.* resistant to criticism; recalcitrant; protective *—n.* prepared to resist **—de·fen´sive·ly** *adv.* **—de·fen´sive·ness** *n.*

de·fer´ *vi., vt.* to postpone; procrastinate; yield in deference to another **—de·fer´ra·ble** *adj.*

def´er·ence *n.* courteous regard

def´er·ent, def´er·en´tial *adj.* respectful; polite; obedient

de·fi´ance *n.* bold resistance; disposition to challenge **—de·fi´ant** *adj.*

de·fi´cience, de·fi´cien·cy *n.* a lack; something lacking

de·fi´cient *adj.* lacking; defective

def´i·cit *n.* a shortage

deficit financing borrowing to cover expenditures

deficit spending paying out in excess of income

de·file´ *vt.* corrupt or debase; profane **—de·file´ment** *n.*

de·fine´ *vt.* give precise value or meaning; describe; specify a limit **—de·fin´a·ble** *adj.*

def´i·nite *adj.* having exact limits; clear; positive **—def´i·nite·ly** *adv.*

def·i·ni´tion *n.* a statement of limits or meaning; clearly outlined

de·fin´i·tive *adj.* conclusive; precise; authoritative or accurate

de·flate´ *vi., vt.* collapse by release of gas; make smaller or less; to dishearten

de·flect´ *vi., vt.* turn aside **—de·flec´tion** *n.*

de·fo´li·ant *n.* chemical that causes a plant to shed **—de·fo´li·a´tion** *n.*

de·for´est *vt.* to clear of trees **—de·for·est·a´tion** *n.*

de·form´ *vt.* damage the appearance of; disfigure *—vi.* become disfigured **—de·for·ma´tion** *n.*

de·formed´ *adj.* misshapen or disfigured —**de·for´mi·ty** *n.*
de·fraud´ *vt.* take by deceit; swindle
de·fray´ *vt.* bear the expense of
de·frost´ *vt.* remove frost; to thaw
deft *adj.* skillful; dexterous —**deft´ly** *adv.* —**deft´ness** *n.*
de·funct´ *adj.* no longer existing; dead
de·fy´ *vt.* openly resist; baffle
de·gen´er·ate *adj.* morally depraved; deteriorated —*n.* one depraved or corrupted —*vi.* decline in quality
de·gen·er·a´tion *n.* worsening; progressive deterioration
de·grad´a·ble *adj.* that can be reduced chemically
de·grade´ *vt.* disgrace or debase; reduce; erode —*vi.* degenerate
de·grad´ed *adj.* reduced in rank, quality, etc.; corrupted or debased
de·grad´ing *adj.* debasing; humiliating —**de·grad´ing·ly** *adv.*
de·gree´ *n.* relative ranking; unit on a scale —**to a degree** somewhat
de·hu´man·ize *vt.* strip of human attributes; to make mechanical
de·hu·mid´i·fi·er *n.* a device that removes moisture from the air
de·hy´drate´ *vi.* lose water —*vt.* to remove or deprive of water
de·ice´ *vt., vi.* to remove ice; to prevent ice from forming
de´i·fy *vt.* to exalt, idealize; to worship —**de·i·fi·ca´tion** *n.*
de´ism *n.* belief in a supreme being not involved in the world
de´i·ty *n.* a god; a divinity
de·ject´ *vt.* to make unhappy; to depress—**de·jec´tion** *n.*
de·ject´ed *adj.* dispirited; depressed
de·lay´ *vt.* postpone; slow or detain —*vi.* to linger —*n.* that which causes lateness; a postponement
de´le *vt.* to take out: delete
de·lec´ta·ble *adj.* pleasing; delightful
de´lec·ta´tion *n.* delight; entertainment
del´e·gate´ *n.* one authorized to speak or act for others —*vt.* to authorize; send as a representative
de·lete´ *vt.* eliminate or erase
del´e·te´ri·ous *adj.* harmful; injurious
de·lib´er·ate *adj.* intentional; carefully planned; unhurried —*vi., vt.* consider carefully
de·lib´er·a´tion *n.* careful consideration
de·lib´er·a·tive *adj.* contemplative
del´i·ca·cy *n.* beauty or refinement; frailty; requiring sensitivity: *a matter of some delicacy*; a special food
del´i·cate *adj.* fine or dainty; fragile; subtle; requiring or displaying tact
del·i·ca·tes´sen *n.* ready–to–eat foods; store selling these foods
de·li´cious *adj.* pleasing to the senses —**de·li´cious·ly** *adv.*
de´light *n.* a quality that pleases: charm —*vi.* give or take pleasure —*vt.* please or gratify —**de·light´ful** *adj.* —**de·light´ful·ly** *adv.*
de·lin´e·ate *vt.* depict with drawings or words —**de·lin·e·a´tion** *n.*
de·lin´quen·cy *n.* failure to perform as required; a fault or misdeed
de·lin´quent *adj.* contrary to duty or law; overdue, as an obligation —*n.* one acting contrary to duty or law
de·lir´i·ous *adj.* marked by delirium; extremely excited
de·lir´i·um *n.* altered consciousness marked by anxiety, confusion, etc. —**de·lir´i·um tre´mens** delirium brought on by withdrawal or excessive ingestion of alcohol
de·liv´er *vt.* carry or give over to another; bring forth or produce a child; rescue —*vi.* fulfill a promise; perform as promised
de·liv´er·ance *n.* a freeing; a pardon; redemption
de·liv´er·y *n.* liberation; conveyance or transference of goods; childbirth; one's speaking style
dell *n.* a small grove; a shady retreat
de·louse´ *vt.* to free of lice
del´ta *n.* symbol (Δ) for the fourth letter of the Greek alphabet; thing shaped like a triangle; an alluvial deposit at the mouth of a river
del´toid *adj.* triangular —*n.* a triangular muscle
de·lude´ *vt.* to mislead or deceive
del´uge *n.* a great flood; heavy rainfall; a thing that overwhelms —*vt.* to flood; to overwhelm
de·lu´sion *n.* false or irrational belief —**de·lu´sion·al** *adj.*
de·luxe´ *adj.* luxurious; elegant
delve *vi.* search resolutely
de·mag´net·ize *vt.* to cancel or neutralize magnetic properties
dem´a·gogue *n.* a revolutionary; one who arouses by appeals to emotion or prejudice —**dem´a·gogu·er·y** *n.*
de·mand´ *n.* a bold request; a formal request: a claim; a need —*vt.* request boldly; claim as due; inquire formally; require —*vi.* make a demand
de·mand´ing *adj.* difficult, challenging; hard to please
de·mar·ca´tion *n.* a separation; a fixing of boundaries or limits
de·mean´ *vt.* debase or humble
de·mean´or *n.* one's behavior or appearance
de·ment´ed *adj.* mentally ill
de·men´tia *n.* impairment of mental faculties; mental illness
dem´i·god *n.* one who is godlike
de·mise´ *n.* death; transfer of rights or authority —*vt., vi.* transfer or be transferred by will or abdication
dem´i·tasse *n.* a small cup; strong black coffee
dem´o *n.* a demonstration
de·mo´bi·lize *vt.* to disband; discharge from military service
de·moc´ra·cy *n.* the principle of equality, opportunity, etc. for all; control shared by the populace
dem´o·crat´ *n.* an advocate of government by the people
de·moc´ra·tize *vt., vi.* to make or become democratic
dem·o·graph´ics *n.* classification by age, sex, etc.
de·mog´ra·phy *n.* study of vital and social statistics in a population
de·mol´ish *vt.* tear down; destroy completely; severely damage
dem´o·li´tion *n.* the process of tearing down or destroying —**dem´o·li´tions** *n.* explosives
de´mon *n.* an evil being; one showing great energy or enthusiasm —**de·mon´ic** *adj.*
de·mo´ni·ac, de´mo·ni´a·cal *adj.* demon–possessed; fiendish; furious; frenzied
de´mon·ism *n.* belief in demons
de·mon·ol´a·try *n.* demon worship
de·mon·ol´o·gy *n.* the study of demons and demonolatry
dem´on·strate´ *vt.* prove; show in operation; make evident —*vi.* act in protest —**de·mon´stra·ble** *adj.*
de·mon´stra·tive *adj.* able to be verified; open and outgoing; openly affectionate
de·mor´al·ize´ *vt.* dishearten; cause confusion
de·mote´ *vt.* lessen in status or rank
de·mur´ *n.* a delay; objection —*vi.* voice an objection; hesitate
de·mure´ *adj.* modest, reserved; affecting modesty
de·mur´rage *n.* compensation for delaying equipment
de·mys´ti·fy *vt.* expose, explain
de·my·thol´o·gize *vt.* to explain away that considered mythological
den *n.* an animal's lair; a gathering place; a study or retreat
de·na´ture *vt.* change through chemical action
de·ni´a·ble *adj.* possible to dispute; that can be withheld or disowned
de·ni´al *n.* a refusal; a disavowal; unwillingness to acknowledge
de·ni´er *n.* one who denies
de·nier´ *n.* a measure of fineness
den´i·grate *vt.* cast aspersions
den´im *n.* a stout cloth
den´i·zen *n.* an inhabitant; one who frequents a place
de·nom·i·na´tion *n.* a designation; a unit of value; a religious group
de·nom·i·na´tion·al·ism *n.* a system of separation by classification
de·nom´i·na·tor *n.* one that names; an attribute in common; a fractional part
de·note´ *vt.* signify or indicate; serve as a symbol
de·nounce´ *vt.* openly condemn
dense *adj.* compact; thick; opaque; slow to grasp —**dense´ly** *adv.*
den´si·ty *n.* relative mass
dent *n.* an indentation; partial accomplishment —*vi., vt.* to get or cause a dent
den´tal *adj.* of the teeth
den´tate *adj.* having teeth
den´ti·frice *n.* a product for cleaning the teeth
den´tist *n.* one who specializes in the care and treatment of the teeth —**den´tis·try** *n.*
den·ti´tion *n.* teething; the types and arrangement of the teeth
de´nu·date *adj.* naked; stripped of foliage —*vt.* to denude
de·nude´ *vt.* strip bare, as of foliage
de·nun´ci·ate *vt.* denounce
de·nun·ci·a´tion *n.* public condemnation —**de·nun´ci·a·tive** *adj.*
de·ny´ *vt.* refuse to acknowledge
de·o´dor·ant *adj.* able to mask odors —*n.* a substance that masks or destroys odors —**de·o´dor·ize´** *vt.*
de·ox·y·ri´bo·nu·cle·ic ac´id DNA, that carries genetic code in cells
de·part´ *vi., vt.* to leave —**depart from** deviate —**de·par´ture** *n.*
de·part´ment *n.* an operating division; a field of study; a section in a periodical —**de·part·men´tal** *adj.*
de·part·men´tal·ize *vt.* organize into separate operating units
department store a large retail establishment
de·par´ture *n.* setting out; divergence from a standard course
de·pend´ *vi.* rely on; place trust in; be contingent upon
de·pend´a·ble *adj.* reliable; trustworthy —**de·pend·a·bil´i·ty** *n.*
de·pen´dence, de·pen´dance *n.* reliance on another; faith or trust; an addiction
de·pend´ent *adj.* relying on another; contingent; subordinate; helpless —**de·pend´ent, de·pen´dant** *n.*
de·per´son·al·ize *vt.* consider objectively; cause loss of distinctiveness —**de·per´son·al·i·za´tion** *n.*
de·pict´ *vt.* to portray; represent or describe —**de·pic´tion** *n.*
dep´i·late *vt.* eliminate hair —**de·pil´a·to·ry** *adj., n.*
de·plete´ *vt.* use completely; lessen gradually —**de·ple´tion** *n.*
de·plor´a·ble *adj.* tragic; distressing; unfortunate —**de·plor´a·bly** *adv.*
de·plore´ *vt.* to condemn; regret
de·ploy´ *vt.* to position according to plan —**de·ploy´ment** *n.*
de·pop·u·la´tion *n.* a sharp reduction in inhabitants
de·port´ *vt.* expel from a country; to conduct oneself in a particular way
de´por·ta´tion *n.* banishment
de·port´ment *n.* one's behavior
de·pos´it *n.* a thing placed for safekeeping or security; a thing left behind, as silt by a flood —*vt.* to place —**de·pos´i·to´ry** *n.*
dep·o·si´tion *n.* removal from power; testimony taken outside court
de´pot *n.* a station; a storehouse
de·prave´ *vt.* to corrupt or pervert —**de·praved´** *adj.* —**de·prav´i·ty** *n.*
dep´re·cate *vt.* express disapproval; belittle —**dep·re·ca´tion** *n.*
dep´re·ca·tive, dep´re·ca·to·ry *adj.* tending to express disapproval
de·pre´ci·ate´ *vi.* fall in value —*vt.* to lessen in value; to consider of little value —**de·pre´ci·a·ble** *adj.*

de·press´ *vt.* lower one's spirit; lessen in value; press down —**de·press´ing** *adj.*
de·pres´sant *n.* an agent that slows vital functions; a sedative
de·pressed´ *adj.* pressed down; despondent; reduced in value
de·pres´sion *n.* despondency; economic stagnation; indent
de·pres´sive *adj.* tending to depress
de·prive´ *vt.* take from: dispossess; to keep from —**dep·ri·va´tion** *n.*
de·prived´ *adj.* lacking necessities or opportunity; underprivileged
dep´u·ty *n.* one acting for another; an aide or assistant; in some countries, a legislator —**dep·u·ta´tion** *n.* —**dep´u·tize** *vi., vt.*
de·rail´ *vi., vt.* cause to go off rails; cause to stop —**de·rail´ment** *n.*
de·range´ *vt.* to disorder or disturb; to make insane
de·range´ment *n.* mental illness
der´by *n.* a race; a type of felt hat
de·reg´u·late *vt.* free from government control —**de·reg·u·la´tion** *n.*
der´e·lict *adj.* abandoned; negligent or delinquent —*n.* a social outcast —**der·e·lic´tion** *n.*
de·ride´ *vt.* mock or ridicule
de·ri´sion *n.* ridicule; a display of scorn or contempt
de·ri´sive, de·ri´so·ry *adj.* marked by derision —**de·ri´sive·ly** *adv.*
der´i·va´tion *n.* something derived: a derivative; formation of a word
de·riv´a·tive *adj.* borrowed or learned —*n.* a thing produced from another source
de·rive´ *vt.* arrive at by reasoning; to trace to origin
der´ma *n.* the dermis —**der´mal** *adj.*
der·ma·ti´tis *n.* irritation of the skin
der·ma·tol´o·gy *n.* study of the skin, its diseases, and their treatment —**der·ma·tol´o·gist** *n.*
der´mis *n.* the layer of skin below the epidermis
de·rog´a·to´ry *adj.* disparaging; belittling
der´rick *n.* a machine for hoisting and moving heavy objects
der´rin·ger *n.* a small pistol
der´vish *n.* member of a Muslim sect
de·scend´ *vi., vt.* to progress downward; move from a higher level; derive from a source, as an ancestor
de·scend´ant, de·scend´ent *n.* one of particular lineage; that traced back to an earlier form
de·scend´er *n.* part of a typeset character below the baseline
de·scent´ *n.* a downward motion; an inclined surface; a lowering of status; a sudden onset
de·scribe´ *vt.* represent in speech or writing; draw or trace
de·scrip´tion *n.* an account that describes; a drawing or tracing
de·scrip´tive *adj.* serving to describe; illustrative —**de·scrip´tive·ly** *adv.*
de·scrip´tor *n.* identifying emblem
des´e·crate *vt.* violate that considered sacred; profane
de·sen´si·tize *vt.* benumb: make insensible by repeated exposure; protect from reaction to an antigen
des´ert *n.* a dry barren region
des·ert´ *vi., vt.* to abandon —**de·ser´tion** *n.*
de·serve´ *vi., vt.* be worthy of
de·served´ *adj.* honestly earned; justified or suitable
de·serv´ing *adj.* worthy of assistance, praise, etc.
des´ic·cate *vt.* dry thoroughly; preserve by drying —*vi.* to become dry
de·sign´ *n.* a detailed plan or schematic; an artistic rendering —*vt.* to invent or devise; make a representation; have as a purpose
des´ig·nate *vt.* specify or appoint; to set aside for a specific purpose —**des·ig·na´tion** *n.*
designated driver one who abstains in order to chauffer those drinking
designated hitter in baseball, one who hits in place of the pitcher
de·sign´ed·ly *adv.* intentionally; deliberately
designer drug a synthetic drug
de·sign´ing *adj.* scheming, crafty, or treacherous — *n.* the art or business of making designs or patterns
de·sir´a·ble *adj.* worth seeking or having; beneficial; pleasing or attractive —**de·sir·a·bil´i·ty** *n.*
de·sire´ *n.* a longing or craving; lust —*vt.* to want:; express a wish for —**de·sir´ous** *adj.*
de·sist´ *vi.* to cease; abstain from
desk *n.* a work station with drawers
desk´top *adj.* designed for use on a desk —*n.*
des´o·late *adj.* forsaken; dismal, dreary; forlorn —*vt.* lay waste; devastate —**des´o·la´tion** *n.*
de·spair´ *n.* loss of hope —*vi.* lose all hope —**de·spair´ing** *adj.*
des´per·ate *adj.* hopeless; dangerous; frantic —**des·per·a´tion** *n.*
des·pic´a·ble *adj.* detestable; deserving contempt; mean or vile
de·spise´ *vt.* regard with disdain; to look down on —**de·spis´al** *n.*
de·spite´ *n.* an insult; an act of spite —*prep.* notwithstanding
de·spond´ *vi.* lose hope; to become depressed or discouraged
de·spon´dent *adj.* suffering loss of hope; dejected —**de·spon´dence** *n.* —**de·spon´dent·ly** *adv.*
des´pot *n.* an absolute ruler; a tyrant —**des·pot´ic** *adj.*
des·sert´ *n.* final course of a meal
des´ti·na´tion *n.* place to which someone or something is going
des´tine *vt.* determined for a special goal or purpose
des´ti·ny *n.* inevitable course
des´ti·tute´ *adj.* completely lacking; without means of survival
de·stroy´ *vt.* ruin utterly; make useless; tear down or demolish
de·struc´ti·ble *adj.* capable of being destroyed; easily broken
de·struc´tion *n.* brought to ruin
de·struc´tive *adj.* producing destruction; tending to make ineffective —**de·struc´tive·ness** *n.*
des´ul·to·ry *adj.* lacking focus; random —**des´ul·to·ri·ness** *n.*
de·tach´ *vt.* disconnect; remove from attachment —**de·tach´a·ble** *adj.*
de·tached´ *adj.* aloof, impartial; separated
de·tach´ment *n.* separation; impartiality, indifference; a special unit
de´tail *n.* minute parts; a precise account; a detachment —*vt.* report precisely; dispatch for a purpose
de·tain´ *vt.* restrain or delay; hold in custody —**de·tain´ment** *n.*
de·tect´ *vt.* become aware of —**de·tect´a·ble, de·tect´i·ble** *adj.*
de·tec´tive *n.* one who investigates; one who painstakingly analyzes
de·tec´tor *n.* a device for discovering or disclosing
dé·tente´ *n.* a relaxing of tension
de·ten´tion *n.* custody; delay
de·ter´ *vt.* discourage by instilling doubt or fear
de·ter´gent *adj.* cleansing —*n.* a substance for cleansing
de·te´ri·o·rate´ *vi., vt.* become worse —**de·te·ri·o·ra´tion** *n.*
de·ter´min·a·ble *adj.* able to be ascertained or established
de·ter´mi·nant *n.* that fixes or limits
de·ter´mi·nate *adj.* exactly fixed or limited; conclusive
de·ter´mi·na·tive *adj.* tending to influence —*n.* that determines
de·ter´mine *vt.* set bounds; render a decision; conclude after study and consideration —**de·ter´min·er** *n.*
de·ter´mined *adj.* resolved; steadfast
de·ter´min·ism *n.* belief that all is predetermined by other events
de·ter´rent *adj.* tending to cause restraint —*n.* a thing that hinders; an obstacle —**de·ter´rence** *n.*
de·test´ *vt.* dislike intensely; despise; loathe —**de·tes·ta´tion** *n.*
de·test´a·ble *adj.* disgusting; abhorrent; despicable —**de·test·a·bil´i·ty** *n.* —**de·test´a·bly** *adv.*
de·throne *vt.* to remove from power —**de·throne·ment** *n.*
det´o·nate´ *vi., vt.* cause to explode —**det·o·na´tion** *n.*
de·tox´i·fy *vt.* counteract poisonous properties; rid of effects of poison; end dependence on alcohol or narcotics —**de·tox´i·fi·ca´tion** *n.*
de·tract´ *vt.* take away or withdraw —*vi.* undergo removal of a valued quality or part —**de·trac´tor** *n.*
det´ri·ment *n.* damage or loss; a thing causing damage —**det´ri·ment´al** *adj.*
de·tri´tus *n.* fragments of rock; disintegrated matter
de·val´u·ate, de·val´ue *vt.* reduce in value or significance
de·val´u·a´tion *n.* reduction in value
dev´as·tate *vt.* lay waste; overwhelm or stun —**dev·as·ta´tion** *n.*
de·vel´op *vt.* to realize potential or capability; expand or enlarge on; increase effectiveness —*vi.* grow or evolve: become revealed
de·vel´oped *adj.* technologically advanced; seen as highly evolved; of cleared land used profitably
de·vel´op·er *n.* a builder or contractor; one who finances construction; chemical used in the processing of photographic film
de·vel´op·ing *adj.* in the process of building industry and economy
de·vel´op·ment *n.* a community of dwellings; an occurrence
de´vi·ant *adj.* contrasting with the usual or normal —*n.* one who does not conform to accepted standards
de´vi·ate *vi.* depart from a normal or standard course —**de´vi·a´tion** *n.*
de·vice´ *n.* anything contrived; an ornamental embellishment
dev´il *n.* an evil spirit; a wicked person; one who is mischievous
dev´il·ment *n.* mischief
dev´il·ry, dev´il·try *n.* wickedness, sinfulness; mischief, impishness
devil's advocate one who explores the negative side of a proposition
de´vi·ous *adj.* deceptive; crafty; not direct —**de´vi·ous·ly** *adv.* —**de´vi·ous·ness** *n.*
de·vise´ *n.* a giving of real property by will; property given; a will that bequeaths real property —*vi., vt.* to create or contrive; to bequeath real property
de·vis´er *n.* one who contrives
dev·i´sor *n.* one who bequeaths
de·vi´tal·ize *vt.* to weaken or enfeeble; to deprive of life
de·void´ *adj.* lacking entirely; empty
de·volve´ *vt., vi.* to pass obligation to another
de·vote´ *vt.* to assign for a specific purpose; to give, as time or effort
de·vot´ed *adj.* dedicated; loving and faithful; thoughtful, solicitous
de·vo´tion *n.* affection or dedication; piety —**de·vo´tion·al** *adj.*
de·vour´ *vt.* eat or absorb completely
de·vout´ *adj.* religious; expressing devotion —**de·vout´ly** *adv.*
dew *n.* drops of moisture
dew point temperature at which moist air forms condensation
dew´y *adj.* moist; like dew; innocence —**dew´i·ness** *n.*
dew´y–eyed *adj.* innocenct
dex·ter´i·ty *n.* skill —**dex´ter·ous, dex´trous** *adj.*
dex´trose *n.* sugar from starch
di´a·bol´ic, di·a·bol´i·cal *adj.* satanic; fiendish, wicked —**di·a·bol´i·cal·ly** *adv.* —**di·a·bol´i·cal·ness** *n.*
di·ab´o·lism *n.* demon worship; fiendish or wicked deeds

di´a·crit´ic *n.* pronunciation mark over or under a letter (ñ, ç, é, ü)
di·a·crit´i·cal *adj.* distinguishing; marking difference
di´a·dem *n.* a crown
di´ag·nose *vi., vt.* make a critical analysis —**di·ag·nos´a·ble** *adj.*
di´ag·no´sis *n.* a critical analysis —**di·ag·nos´tic** *adj.*
di´a·gram *n.* a sketch or drawing that clarifies; a chart or graph
di´al *n.* face of a clock; a rotating disk or knob; a gauge or indicator
dialling code (*Brit.*) telephone number prefix that identifies locality
di´a·lect *n.* language variations; speech characteristic of a class, trade, etc.
di·a·lec´tic *n.* examination of ideas through argumentation or deduction —**di·a·lec´ti·cal** *adj.*
di´a·logue´ *n.* conversation; exchange of ideas; lines in a play; a conversational dissertation
di·al´y·sis *n.* means for removing impurities from the blood
di·am´e·ter *n.* distance across the center of a circle or sphere
di·a·met´ric, di·a·met´ri·cal *adj.* of a diameter; totally different or contrary —**di·a·met´ri·cal·ly** *adv.*
di´a·mond *n.* an extremely hard crystal of nearly pure carbon; a geometric form
di·aph´a·nous *adj.* extremely fine; transparent; thin and airy
di´a·phragm´ *n.* a membrane that serves to separate
di´a·ry *n.* a daily journal
di´a·tribe *n.* a harsh tirade; a denunciation
dice *n. pl., sing.* **die** small gaming cubes —*vt.* cut into small cubes
dic´ey *adj.* chancy; speculative
di·chot´o·my *n.* division into two; in biology, a forking
dick´er *vi.* barter; bargain
dic·tate´ *n.* a command; a guiding principle —*vi., vt.* to command; to speak for another to record
dic´ta´tor *n.* a ruler with unlimited power —**dic´ta·to´ri·al** *adj.*
dic·ta´tor·ship *n.* government by a dictator
dic´tion *n.* choice of words and clarity of enunciation in speech
dic´tion·ar´y *n.* an alphabetical list of words or references
dic´tum *n., pl.* **dic´tums, dic´ta** a pronouncement
di·dac´tic, di·dac´ti·cal *adj.* instructive; inclined to sermonizing
die *vi.* to stop living; to stop running, as a motor —*n.* a metal stamp
die´-hard *adj.* stubborn —*n.* one firmly committed to a concept, etc.
di´et *n.* food and drink; special food —*vi.* limit intake of food —**di´e·tar·y, di·e·tet´ic** *adj.*
di·e·tet´ics *n.* study of diet
dif´fer *vi.* disagree; to be different
dif´fer·ence *n.* a distinctive characteristic; that which differentiates; a variance in quantity, quality, etc.; a disagreement
dif´fer·ent *adj.* unlike; changed; diverse —**dif´fer·ent·ly** *adv.*
dif·fer·en´tial *adj.* of a difference; able to cause varied results —*n.* a difference; a gear that alters output
dif·fer·en´ti·ate *vi.* become different —*vt.* make different; recognize a difference; display a difference
dif´fi·cult´ *adj.* requiring considerable effort —**dif´fi·cul´ty** *n.*
dif´fi·dence *n.* lack of confidence
dif´fi·dent *adj.* lacking confidence; shy; insecure —**dif´fi·dent·ly** *adv.*
dif·fuse´ *adj.* widely spread; of rambling or wordy speech —*vi., vt.* to disperse widely
dif·fus´er, dif·fus´or *n.* that diffuses, as a baffle
dif·fus´i·ble *adj.* suitable for effecting diffusion; able to be diffused
dif·fu´sion *n.* the spread of soft light or sound
dig *vt.* make a hole; uncover by careful study —*n.* a sarcastic remark —**dig in** get to work —**digs** living quarters
di´gest *n.* condensation of a literary work; collection of works —**di·gest´** *vt.* to condense or summarize; convert food for absorption; study and absorb
di·gest´i·ble *adj.* able to be digested
di·ges´tive *adj.* pertaining to absorption of food —*n.* anything that aids digestion
digestive system organs that ingest and process food, discarding waste
dig´gings *pl. n.* material unearthed; a place where digging takes place
dig´it *n.* a finger or toe; unit of a numbering system
dig´i·tal *adj.* discrete, having specific value; expressed in units
dig´ni·fied *adj.* displaying dignity; courtly or reserved
dig´ni·fy´ *vt.* to honor; make seem more worthy
dig´ni·tar´y *n.* one of high position
dig´ni·ty *n.* a presence that commands respect; poise; stateliness
di·gress´ *vi.* to stray from the subject —**di·gres´sion** *n.*
di·gres´sive *adj.* marked by rambling or departure from the subject
dike *n.* a river embankment
di·lap´i·date *vi., vt.* fall into disrepair or ruin —**di·lap·i·da´tion** *n.*
di·lap´i·dat·ed *adj.* broken down; fallen into disrepair
di´late *vi., vt.* to make or become larger; expand
di´lat·ed *adj.* expanded or distended
di·la´tion *n.* a widening or expansion; the process of dilating
di·la´tor *n.* that causes dilation, as a muscle or surgical instrument
dil´a·to·ry *adj.* intended or inclined to delay
di·lem´ma *n.* choice between equally unpleasant options; a serious predicament
dil´et·tan·te *n.* one who dabbles for personal amusement; a lover of the arts —**dil´et·tan·tish** *adj.*
dil´i·gent *adj.* industious; showing painstaking effort —**dil´i·gence** *n.*
dill *n.* a flavoring herb
dil´ly·dal·ly *vi.* waste time
di·lute´ *adj.* thinned or weakened —*vt.* make thinner or weaker
dim *adj.* faint, murky; ill defined; indistinct; not encouraging —*vi., vt.* grow faint or indistinct
di·men´sion *n.* measure of a thing
di·min´ish *vt., vi.* to make or become reduced —**di·min´ish·a·ble** *adj.*
diminishing return less proportional increase as improvements or incentives are introduced
dim·i·nu´tion *n.* a lessening or reduction; something reduced
di·min´u·tive *adj.* very small; expressing small size —*n.* something small; a word form expessing small size
dim´mer *n.* a device for reducing the brightness of a lamp or light
dim´ple *n.* an indentation —*vt. vi.* mark with or form dimples
din *n.* a loud clamor
dine *vi.* to eat
din´er *n.* one eating; (*US*) a small informal restaurant
di·nette´ *n.* a small dining area; tables and chairs for a dining area
din´ghy *n.* a small boat
din´gy *adj.* drab or dirty; grimy
dink´y *adj.* diminutive; small
din´ner *n.* main meal of the day; a social event featuring a large meal
dinner jacket a jacket worn on formal occasions; tuxedo jacket
diph´thong´ *n.* a complex vowel sound
di·plo´ma *n.* document testifying to completion of a course of study
di·plo´ma·cy *n.* affairs between political entities; finesse and tact
dip´stick *n.* a rod for measuring liquid; a silly person
dire *adj.* serious; desperate; requiring immediate action
di·rect´ *adj.* straight; shortest course; uninterrupted; immediate; absolute; sincere —*vt.* control or manage; point out or guide; instruct; aim —**di·rect·ly** *adv.* —**di·rect´ness** *n.*
di·rec´tion *n.* instruction; supervision; a command; the point faced —**di·rec´tion·al** *adj.*
di·rec´tive *n.* an official order —*adj.* serving to rule or govern
direct marketing sale of goods or services by mail or telephone
di·rec´tor *n.* one who supervises
di·rec´to·rate *n.* a board of directors; the office of a company director —**di·rec·to´ri·al** *adj.*
di·rec´to·ry *n.* an alphabetical reference; a directorate
dirge *n.* a mournful musical work
dir´i·gi·ble *n.* an airship
dirk *n.* a dagger
dirt *adj.* surfaced with earth —*n.* soil or earth; anything unclean; gossip or scandal; pornography
dirt–cheap extremely inexpensive
dirt´y *adj.* soiled; vulgar, lewd; contaminated —*vi., vt.* soil or stain
dis·a´ble *vt.* make unfit; incapacitate —**dis·a·bil´i·ty** *n.*
dis·a´bled *adj.* inoperative; incapacitated —*n.* one impaired
dis·a·buse´ *vt.* rid of a false notion; to clarify
dis´ad·van´tage *n.* a handicap; unfavorable circumstances —*vt.* hinder —**dis´ad·van´taged** *adj.*
dis·af·fect´ *vt.* cause estrangement; to alienate —**dis·af·fec´tion** *n.*
dis´a·gree´ *vi.* differ; quarrel; produce discomfort, as certain foods —**dis·a·gree´ment** *n.*
dis·a·gree´a·ble *adj.* unpleasant; quarrelsome
dis·al·low´ *vt.* refuse to permit; reject
dis´ap·pear´ *vi.* pass from sight; become extinct
dis·ap·point´ *vt.* fail satisfy; prevent fulfillment of expectation
dis·ap·point´ed *adj.* frustrated
dis·ap·point´ing *adj.* not meeting expectation
dis·ap·prove´ *vi., vt.* frown upon; to condemn —**dis·ap·prov´al** *n.*
dis´arm´ *vt.* take weapons from; render powerless; charm —*vi.* relinquish arms —**dis´arm´ing** *adj.* —**dis´arm´ing·ly** *adv.*
dis´ar´ma·ment *n.* reduction of military forces
dis·ar·ray´ *n.* state of confusion or disorder —*vi.* throw into confusion
dis·as·sem´ble *vt.* to tear down or dismantle
dis·as·so´ci·ate *vt.* to separate; withdraw from an alliance or relationship —**dis·as·so·ci·a´tion** *n.*
dis·as´ter *n.* great harm or distress —**dis·as´trous** *adj.*
dis·a·vow´ *vt.* to deny knowledge or responsibility —**dis·a·vow´al** *adj.*
dis·band´ *vi.* cease to function as a group —*vt.* dissolve a group
dis·bar´ *vt.* withdraw a lawyer's right to practice —**dis·bar´ment** *n.*
dis´be·lieve´ *vi., vt.* refuse to believe; consider as false —**dis´be·lief´** *n.*
dis·burse´ *vt.* to pay out —**dis·burse´ment** *n.*
dis´card *n.* that cast off —**dis·card´** *vt.* throw away; cast aside or reject
dis·cern´ *vt.* to perceive; differentiate —*vi.* recognize a difference —**dis·cern´i·ble** *adj.* —**dis·cern´ment** *n.*
dis·cern´ing *adj.* having good judgment; discriminating
dis·charge´ *vt.* unload; release from duty; fulfill an obligation; fire a weapon —**dis·charge´**, **dis´charge** *n.* the act of unloading, dismissing, etc.; that which is discharged
dis·ci´ple *n.* an active follower
dis´ci·pline *n.* branch of learning; formal training; self–control; acceptance of authority; punishment —*vt.* to train or control; to punish

dis·ci·pli·nar´i·an *n.* one who maintains or upholds strict control
dis´ci·pli·nar·y *adj.* of a branch of learning; punitive
dis·claim´ *vt.* to give up or deny a claim or connection
dis·claim´er *n.* denial of responsibility; relinquishing of a right
dis·close´ *vt.* reveal or make known —**dis·clo´sure** *n.*
dis·col´or *vt.* alter by fading or soiling —*vi.* become faded — **dis·col·or·a´tion** *n.*
dis·com·bob´u·late *vt.* to embarrass; confuse
dis·com´fit *vt.* frustrate plans or aspirations; make uncomfortable
dis·com´fort *n.* physical or mental distress; uneasiness —*vt.* make uneasy —**dis·com´fort·a·ble** *adj.*
dis·com·mode´ *vt.* cause inconvenience —**dis·com·mo´di·ous** *adj.*
dis´con·cert´ *vt.* to confuse or embarrass
dis´con·cert´ed *adj.* characterized by confusion or embarrassment
dis·con·cert´ing *adj.* tending to cause confusion or embarrassment
dis´con·nect´ *vt.* to detach —**dis·con·nec´tion** *n.*
dis·con·nect´ed *adj.* separated; cut off; disjointed or incoherent
dis´con´so·late *adj.* dejected; inconsolable —**dis·con´so·late·ly** *adv.*
dis´con·tent´ *adj.* displeased — *n.* a lack of satisfaction —*vt.* to make displeased or dissatisfied
dis·con·tin´u·ance *n.* a temporary cessation; a suspension
dis´con·tin´ue *vi., vt.* stop or end
dis·con·tin´u·ous *adj.* disordered; disconnected; irrational
dis´cord´ *n.* disagreement; harsh sounds —**dis·cor´dance** *n.* — **dis´cord´ant** *adj.*
dis´count *n.* a reduction or rebate —**dis·count´** *vt.* sell at a reduction; reject as untrue or of little importance
dis·cour´age *vt.* advise against; to dishearten —**dis·cour´age·ment** *n.*
dis´course *n.* conversation; lengthly treatment in writing or speech —**dis·course´** *vi.* converse; write or speak at length
dis·cour´te·ous *adj.* impolite; rude —**dis·cour´te·ous·ly** *adv.*
dis·cour´te·sy *n.* bad manners
dis·cov´er *vt.* obtain knowledge; to detect or make known
dis·cov´er·y *n.* detection or disclosure; findings, a thing discovered
dis·cred´it *n.* damage to reputation —*vt.* cast doubt; damage a reputation —**dis·cred´it·a·ble** *adj.*
dis·creet´ *adj.* prudent; exercising caution —**dis·creet´ly** *adv.*
dis·crep´an·cy *n.* a variance or inconsistency
dis·crete´ *adj.* comprised of unconnected, distinct parts
dis·cre´tion *n.* quality of being discreet; freedom to make one's own decisions —**dis·cre´tion·ar·y** *adj.*
dis·crim´i·nate´ *vi., vt.* make distinction; differentiate —**dis·crim´i·na´tion** *n.*
dis·crim´i·nat·ing *adj.* discerning
dis·crim´i·na·to·ry *adj.* judgmental; discriminating
dis·cur´sive *adj.* rambling
dis·cuss´ *vt.* talk or write about
dis·dain´ *n.* a show of contempt —*vt.* treat with contempt; deem unsuited
dis·dain´ful *adj.* showing contempt
dis·ease´ *n.* illness; a harmful condition —**dis·eased´** *n.*
dis´em·bark´ *vi., vt.* leave a conveyance —**dis·em·bar·ka´tion** *n.*
dis·em·bod´y *vt.* to separate from physical existence
dis·en·chant´ *vt.* free from delusion —**dis·en·chant´ment** *n.*
dis·en·cum´ber *vt.* relieve of burden
dis·en·fran´chise *vt.* deprive of right or privilege; deprive of right to vote
dis·en·tan´gle *vt.* unsnarl; extricate; free of confusion
dis·fa´vor *n.* disapproval —*vt.* look upon with disapproval
dis·fig´ure *vt.* spoil the appearance of —**dis·fig´ure·ment** *n.*
dis·fran´chise *vt.* disenfranchise
dis·gorge´ *vi., vt.* discharge contents
dis·grace´ *n.* loss of honor; that brings dishonor —*vt.* bring dishonor upon; chastise publicly
dis·grun´tle *vt.* to make unhappy; to dissatisfy
dis·guise´ *n.* that used to conceal identity —*vt.* alter or conceal identity of; to misrepresent
dis·gust´ *n.* deep dislike; aversion —*vt.* to arouse dislike; to offend
dis·gust´ing *adj.* provoking disgust; distasteful, nauseating
dish *n.* a container for food; food prepared in a particular way — *vt.* to serve up
dis·ha·bille´ *n.* partial or incongruous dress
dis·har´mo·ny *n.* dissonance; discord
dis·heart´en *vt.* lessen courage, resolve, enthusiasm, etc. of
dis·heart´en·ing *adj.* causing loss of courage, enthusiasm, etc.
di·shev´eled, di·shev´elled *adj.* untidy; rumpled; disorderly — **di·shev´el** *vt.*
dis·hon´est *adj.* lacking honesty; deceitful; untrustworthy
dis·hon´or *n.* loss of respect, etc.; that causing loss of respect — *vt.* cause loss of honor; treat with disrespect; refuse to pay — **dis·hon´er·a·ble** *adj.*
dis´il·lu´sion *vt.* free from sentiment; to disappoint or disenchant —**dis·il·lu´sion·ment** *n.*
dis·in·clined´ *adj.* hesitant; reluctant
dis´in·fect´ *vt.* sanitize; sterilize
dis·in·fec´tant *adj.* serving to sanitize —*n.* substance used to sanitize
dis·in·fec´tive *adj.* disinfectant
dis´in·gen´u·ous *adj.* deceitful; insincere; crafty —**dis·in·gen´u·ous·ly** *adv.* —**dis·in·gen´u·ous·ness** *n.*
dis´in·her´it *vt.* deprive of a right or privilege —**dis·in·her´i·tance** *n.*
dis·in´te·grate *vi., vt.* to break into fragments —**dis´in·te·gra´tion** *n.*
dis·in·ter´ *vt.* to dig up from a grave —**dis·in·ter´ment** *n.*
dis·in´ter·est *n.* lack of concern
dis´in´ter·est·ed *adj.* free of bias; impartial; indifferent
dis·join´ *vt.* detach, separate — *vi.* become separated
dis·joint´ *vt.* dismember; cut or take apart; to separate
dis·joint´ed *adj.* disconnected; incoherent; rambling —**dis·joint´ed·ly** *adv.*
dis·junc´tive *adj.* separating; causing sharp divisions
disk *n.* a thin flat circular object
disk·ette´ *n.* a removable disk for computer data storage
dis·like´ *n.* distaste or aversion —*vt.* look upon with distaste
dis·lo´cate´ *vt.* to put out of proper place or position
dis·lodge´ *vt.* to force from a position
dis·loy´al *adj.* unfaithful —**dis·loy´al·ty** *n.*
dis´mal *adj.* dreary, bleak — **dis´mal·ly** *adv.*
dis·man´tle *vt.* take apart systematically
dis·may´ *n.* loss of resolve —*vt.* to cause loss of courage
dis·mem´ber *vt.* cut up; mutilate
dis·miss´ *vt.* send away; release from employment; put out of mind —**dis·mis´sal** *n.* —**dis·miss´i·ble** *adj.*
dis·mis´sive *adj.* lack of concern
dis´o·be´di·ent *adj.* defiant; insubordinate —**dis´o·be´di·ence** *n.*
dis´o·bey´ *vi., vt.* refuse to obey
dis·or´der *n.* confusion or disarray; public disturbance; illness —*vt.* to throw into confusion or disarray
dis·or´der·ly *adj.* untidy; lacking order; rowdy
dis·or´gan·ize *vt.* cause disorder
dis·o´ri·ent *vt.* confuse, bewilder
dis·own´ *vt.* refuse to acknowledge or accept; to disinherit
dis·par´age *vt.* to discredit; belittle —**dis·par´ag·ing** *adj.*
dis´pa·rate *adj.* dissimilar; diversified —**dis·par´ate·ly** *adv.*
dis·par´i·ty *n.* difference
dis·pas´sion *n.* a lack of emotional involvment; freedom from passion
dis·pas´sion·ate *adj.* free from emotional involvement; detached
dis·patch´ *n.* a sending; a message; promptness —*vt.* send out; act quickly; kill
dis·pel´ *vt.* drive away; eliminate
dis·pen´sa·ble *adj.* not essential; that can be distributed
dis·pen´sa·ry *n.* a place for obtaining medicines and medical aid
dis·pen·sa´tion *n.* distribution; thing distributed; release or exemption
dis·pense´ *vt.* distribute; give out; administer; absolve —**dispense with** do without —**dis·pens´er** *n.*
dis·perse´ *vt.* scatter widely; drive off; cause to dissipate, as mist; separate light into component colors —*vi.* be scattered; disappear —**dis·per´sal, dis·per´sion** *n.*
dis·place´ *vt.* to move; take the place of; remove from office — **dis·plac´a·ble** *adj.* —**dis·place´ment** *n.*
dis·play´ *n.* a public showing — *vt.* to show publicly
dis·please´ *vi., vt.* dissatisfy or annoy; to offend
dis·pos´a·ble *adj.* to be discarded after a single use
dis·pose´ *vt.* place in proper order; settle; adjust so as to be receptive
dis·po·si´tion *n.* one's temperament; a final settlement
dis·pos·sess´ *vt.* deprive of possession —**dis·pos·ses´sion** *n.*
dis´pro·por´tion *n.* lack of symmetry —*vt.* to make disproportionate
dis·pro·por´tion·ate *adj.* out of proportion; uneven
dis·prove´ *vt.* expose as false; refute
dis·pu´ta·ble *adj.* questionable; uncertain —**dis·put´a·bly** *adv.*
dis·pu´tant *n.* one who quarrels or disagrees —*adj.* involving dispute
dis´pu·ta´tion *n.* controversy; formal debate —**dis·pu·ta´tious** *adj.*
dis·pute´ *n.* a quarrel; disagreement —*vi., vt.* argue about; doubt the truth of
dis·qual´i·fy *vt.* to declare ineligible —**dis·qual·i·fi·ca´tion** *n.*
dis·qui´et *n.* anxiety —*vt.* to make anxious
dis·re·gard´ *n.* lack of respect — *vt.* to ignore or neglect
dis·re·pair´ *n.* in need of repair
dis·rep´u·ta·ble *adj.* lacking respectability
dis·re·pute´ *n.* loss of reputation
dis´re·spect´ *n.* discourtesy; insolence —*vt.* treat discourteously —**dis´re·spect´ful** *adj.*
dis·robe´ *vi., vt.* to undress
dis·rupt´ *vt.* to intrude; upset an orderly process —**dis·rup´tion** *n.*
dis·rup´tive *adj.* rebellious; unruly; intruding —**dis·rup´tive·ness** *n.*
dis·sat·is·fac´to·ry *adj.* not acceptable
dis·sat´is·fy *vt.* fail to please — **dis·sat´is·fied** *adj.*
dis·sect´ *vt.* separate into parts; examine closely —**dis·sec´tion** *n.*
dis·sem´ble *vt.* conceal; deceive —*vi.* conceal one's true nature
dis·sem´i·nate´ *vt.* scatter; spread widely —**dis·sem´i·na´tion** *n.*
dis·sen´sion *n.* a disagreeing; difference of opinion
dis·sent´ *n.* a difference of opinion —*vi.* express disagreement —**dis·sent´er** *n.* —**dis·sent´ing** *adj.*
dis·sen´tious *adj.* opposing; disagreeing —**dis·sen´tious·ly** *adv.*
dis´ser·tate *vi.* speak at length
dis´ser·ta´tion *n.* lengthly discourse
dis·serve *vt.* harm; treat badly

dis·serv´ice *n.* thoughtless deed
dis´si·dent *adj.* hostile; opposed; of those opposing —*n.* one who opposes —**dis´si·dence** *n.*
dis·sim´i·lar *adj.* different
dis·sim´i·lar´i·ty *n.* a difference; divergence or deviation
dis·sim´u·late *vi., vt.* conceal or disguise one's feelings —**dis·sim·u·la´tion** *n.* —**dis·sim´u·la·tive** *adj.*
dis´si·pate *vi.* waste in debauchery; vanish by dispersion —*vt.* scatter or disperse; use recklessly, waste —**dis´si·pa´tion** *n.*
dis´si·pat·ed *adj.* scattered; depleted; exhibiting effects of self–indulgence
dis·so´ci·ate *vi., vt.* to separate; sever ties —**dis·so·ci·a´tion** *n.*
dis·so´ci·a·tive *adj.* tending to produce separation
dis·sol´u·ble *adj.* able to dissolve
dis´so·lute *adj.* lacking restraint; immoral —**dis´so·lute·ly** *adv.*
dis´so·lu´tion *n.* a dissolving or termination, as of a business
dis·solve´ *vi., vt.* change into liquid; pass into solution; disintegrate or disappear; to end, as a marriage
dis´so·nance, dis´so·nan·cy *n.* disagreeable sound; lack of agreement —**dis´so·nant** *adj.*
dis·suad´a·ble *adj.* able to be persuaded against
dis·suade´ *vt.* to persuade from a course —**dis·sua´sion** *n.*
dis·sua´sive *adj.* intended to discourage or prevent
dis´tal *adj.* remote; far from origin or attachment
dis´tance *n.* time or space between; reserve, remoteness —*vt.* keep away; to act aloof
dis´tant *adj.* remote; far apart in time or space; reserved, aloof
dis·taste´ *n.* repugnance
dis·taste´ful *adj.* offensive; unpleasant —**dis·taste´ful·ly** *adv.*
dis·tem´per *n.* an affliction; an infectious disease of animals
dis·tend´ *vi., vt.* to inflate; to stretch —**dis·ten´si·ble** *adj.*
dis·til´, dis·till´ *vt.* to extract or concentrate by distillation
dis´til·late *n.* result of distillation
dis·til·la´tion *n.* refinement of liquid by heating, then cooling and collecting condensation; that produced by distilling —**dis·till´er·y** *n.*
dis·tinct´ *adj.* undeniably different; unmistakable; clearly perceptible —**dis·tinct´ly** *adv.*
dis·tinc´tion *n.* specific difference; distinguishing characteristic or quality; eminence or prestige
dis·tinc´tive *adj.* characteristic; having an uncommon quality
dis·tin´guish *vi., vt.* set apart; recognize clearly; bring prestige to
dis·tin´guish·a·ble *adj.* able to discern; perceptible; unique or different
dis·tin´guished *adj.* celebrated, well–known; refined; extraordinary
dis·tort´ *vt.* bend out of shape; misrepresent; alter —**dis·tor´tion** *n.*
dis·tor´tive *adj.* causing distortion
dis·tract´ *vt.* divert attention; create confusion —**dis·tract´ing** *adj.*
dis·tract´ed *adj.* diverted; confused;
dis·trac´tion *n.* that diverts one's attention; confusion or distress; a drawing away of one's attention
dis·traught´ *adj.* deeply troubled
dis·tress´ *n.* pain or anxiety; a condition requiring immediate help —*vt.* to inflict suffering
dis·tress´ful *adj.* causing worry or torment —**dis·tress´ful·ly** *adv.*
dis·trib´ute *vt.* disburse —**dis´tri·bu´tion** *n.*
dis·trib´u·tive *adj.* serving to disseminate or classify
dis·trib´u·tor *n.* one authorized to market a product; a merchant; a device that dispenses
dis´trict *n.* area specially defined
district attorney in the US, a prosecutor for the government
dis·trust´ *n.* lack of trust —*vt.* lack confidence in —**dis·trust´ful** *adj.*
dis·turb´ *vt.* upset serenity or order; interrupt; make uneasy
dis·tur´bance *n.* a commotion; disorder; deviation from the usual
dis·turbed´ *adj.* distressed, troubled; mentally or emotionally unstable
dis·u·nite´ *vi., vt.* divide, separate
dis·use´ *n.* state of neglect —*vt.* take out of service; abandon or discard
ditch *n.* a trench or channel —*vt.* get rid of; deliberately leave behind
di´the·ism *n.* belief in two supreme beings —**di·the·is´tic** *adj.*
dith´er *n.* nervous or excited state —*vi.* act nervous or excited; babble
dit´to *n.* same as previous; a repetition —*vt.* duplicate; make a copy; repeat —**ditto mark** a symbol (") to indicate a repeat of the above
dit´ty *n.* a simple song
ditty bag a small bag or pouch
di´u·ret´ic *adj.* tending to increase output of urine —*n.* a substance that increases output of urine
di·ur´nal *adj.* happening each day; in the daytime —**di·ur´nal·ly** *adv.*
di·van *n.* a davenport or sofa
dive *n.* a headlong leap; a sudden dropping; The descent of an airplane —*vi., vt.* to plunge or drop
di·verge´ *vi.* move in different directions —**di·ver´gence** *n.*
di´vers *adj.* several
div´ers *n. pl.* those who dive
di·verse´ *adj.* dissimilar; assorted —**di·verse´ly** *adv.* —**di·verse´ness** *n.*
di·ver´si·fied *adj.* disparate; dissimilar; sundry —**di·ver´si·ty** *n.*
di·ver´si·fy´ *vt.* add variety; branch into new fields —**di·ver´si·fi·ca´tion** *n.*
di·ver´sion *n.* a turning aside; a distraction —**di·ver´sion·ar·y** *adj.*
di·vert´ *vt.* to turn aside; to distract
di·vert´ing *adj.* engaging; pleasing; entertaining
di·ver´tisse·ment *n.* amusement or distraction
di·vest´ *vt.* get rid of; deprive of —**di·vest´i·ture, di·vest´ment** *n.*
di·vide´ *vt.* separate into parts or categories; distribute in portions; cause disagreement —*vi.* become separated; share
di·vid´ed *adj.* separated; in disagreement
divided highway (*US*) a road with separate lanes for opposing traffic
di·vid´er *n.* thing that serves to separate —**room divider** furniture or a screen that divides a room
div´i·dend *n.* a bonus; an unexpected benefit
div·i·na´tion *n.* art of prediction
di·vine´ *adj.* of the nature of a diety; godlike; pleasing —*vt.* predict
di·vin´er *n.* one who foretells; one who locates water underground
diving bell a device for exploring under water
diving board a springboard
divining rod a forked branch to locate water underground
di·vin´i·ty *n.* a divine nature; study of theology; type of candy
di·vis´i·ble *adj.* easily separated; capable of being evenly divided
di·vi´sion *n.* a partition; a portioning; a rift or disagreement
di·vi´sive *adj.* provoking disagreement —**di·vi´sive·ness** *n.*
di·vorce´ *n.* legal dissolution of a marriage; any radical separation —*vt.* dissolve a marriage; separate entities from association or influence
di·vulge´ *vt.* make known; reveal
di·vulse´ *vt.* to tear apart
diz´zy *adj.* light–headed; dazed; silly; flighty —**diz´zi·ness** *n.*
DNA *n.* deoxyribonucleic acid, that carries genetic code within cells
do *vi., vt.* perform; to cause; behave —**do in** to murder —**done in** tired; murdered —**do well** prosper
do´a·ble *adj.* able to be accomplished; profitable or expedient
do´cent *n.* a teacher or lecturer; (*US*) a tour guide —**do´cent·ship** *n.*
doc´ile *adj.* mild–mannered; submissive —**do·cil´i·ty** *n.*
dock *n.* a pier or wharf —*vt.* bring a ship into dock; cut short; deduct
dock´et *n.* a court calendar
doc´tor *n.* one licensed to practice medicine; highest degree awarded by a college or university —*vt.* treat illness or injury; repair in makeshift fashion; to alter
doc´tor·ate *n.* a doctor's degree
doc´tri·naire´ *adj.* theoretical —*n.* one favoring theory over fact
doc´trine *n.* principals or policy —**doc´tri·nal** *adj.*
doc´u·ment *n.* a written record —*vt.* furnish supporting information —**doc·u·men·ta´tion** *n.*
doc·u·ment´ary *adj.* of documents or a report; based on documents —*n.* a factual presentation
dod´der *vt.* to totter, as from age —**dod´der·ing** *adj.*
dodge *vt.* sidestep; avoid or evade by trickery —*vi.* move suddenly; employ trickery —*n.* a deception or ruse —**dodg´er** *n.*
do´er *n.* one who achieves
doff *vt.* to remove; to discard
dog *n.* animal related to the wolf
dog´–ear *vt.* to turn down a corner —*n.* folded corner of a page
dog´ged *adj.* persistent —**dog´ged·ly** *adv.* —**dog´ged·ness** *n.*
dog´ma *n.* statement of doctrine
dog·mat´ic, dog·mat´i·cal *adj.* adhering strictly; dictatorial
doi´ly *n.* a table mat or runner
dol´drums *n.* a depressed state
dole *n.* a charitable gift —*vt.* give charitably; portion out
dole´ful *adj.* mournful; full of sadness —**dole´ful·ly** *adv.*
do´lor *n.* sorrow; anguish —**dol´or·ous** *adj.* —**do´lo·rous·ly** *adv.*
dolt *n.* one who is slow–witted
do·main´ *n.* sphere of influence or control; territory controlled
do·mes´tic *adj.* of a household; caring for home or family; of a country; tamed —*n.* a servant
do·mes´ti·cate´ *vt.* bring under control; adapt to a new area
do·mes·tic´i·ty *n.* fondness for home and family
dom´i·cile *n.* residence; a home
dom´i·nate *vt.* control; have preeminence —**dom´i·nance** *n.* —**dom´i·nant** *adj.*
dom·i·neer´ *vi., vt.* tyrannize, bully
dom´i·neer´ing *adj.* assertive; overbearing
do·min´ion *n.* sovereignty
do´nate *vt.* contribute —**do·na´tion** *n.*
done *adj.* completed
do´nor *n.* a contributor
doom *n.* inevitable ruin; condemnation —*vt.* destine for ruination; to condemn
dooms´day *n.* final judgment
door *n.* an entryway
dope *n.* a drug; information
dor´mant *adj.* temporarily inactive —**dor´man·cy** *n.*
dor´mi·to´ry *n.* living quarters for students; room with sleeping accommodations for many people
dor´y *n.* a small rowboat
dose *n.* amount to be taken at one time —*vt.* give in measured amounts —**dos´age** *n.*
dos´si·er *n.* information relating to a particular matter or person
dot´age *n.* childish behavior in old age: senility; extravagant affection
do´tard *n.* a senile old person
dote *vi.* be excessively attentive —**dot´ing·ly** *adv.*
dou´ble *adj.* twofold; duplicated; paired; made for two —*n.* twice as much; look–alike —*vt.* make twice as much; to fold —*vi.* increase / twofold; reverse course; serve in extra capacity —**dou´bly** *adv.*
dou´ble–deal´ing *adj.* treacherous

dou´ble–deck´er *n.* a thing with two levels or layers

dou´ble–en·ten´dre *n.* word or phrase having two meanings

double helix coiled structure of DNA

double standard unevenly applied

dou´blet *n.* a pair; a short, close–fitting outer garment

double take a delayed reaction

doubt *n.* uncertainty; lack of trust; skepticism *—vi., vt.* be uncertain; skeptical **—doubt´ful** *adj.*

doubt´less *adj.* without question

dough´ty *adj.* valiant

dour *adj.* dreary; gloomy

douse *vt.* immerse; wet thoroughly

dove´tail´ *n.* a type of joint *—vi., vt.* to connect; fit closely

dow´a·ger *n.* a dignified elderly lady

dow´dy *adj.* shabby

dow´el *n.* round pin used to join

dow´er *n.* an endowment *—vt.* to furnish with an endowment

down *adv.* from higher to lower; from an earlier time; to a diminshed volume; to greater intensity *—adj.* toward a lower position; in a lower place; dejected *—vt.* subdue; swallow *—n.* a descent; reversal of fortune

down–and–out´ destitute

down´cast *adj.* dejected; despondent

down´fall *n.* a failure; disgrace

down´grade *vt.* reduce or lower

down´heart·ed *adj.* dejected; discouraged **—down´heart·ed·ly** *adv.*

down´pour *n.* a heavy rain

down´right *adj.* absolute; straightforward *—adv.* utterly

down´trod·den *adj.* oppressed

down´turn *n.* economic decline

down´ward *adj., adv.* toward a lower point **—down´wards** *adv.*

dow´ry *n.* property brought to a marriage by the bride

doze *n.* brief sleep *—vi.* sleep briefly

doz´en *n.* a set of twelve

drab *adj.* dull; colorless

draft (*US*) *adj.* drawn from a keg *—n.* a preliminary work; air current; order directing payment; selection for some purpose; depth of a vessel below water *—vt.* make a layout; sketch or write; select for service

drag *n.* act of pulling; a device normally pulled or that checks motion; an impedence; slow laborious movement; a tiresome thing; influence *—vi.* be pulled; lag behind; move slowly *—vt.* pull; draw slowly or with difficulty **—main drag** a main road

drag´on *n.* a legendary beast

dra·goon´ *n.* a cavalryman

drain *n.* a duct for waste water, etc.; that which draws off *—vi., vt.* draw off; depletion of energy, resources, etc. **—drain´age** *n.*

drake *n.* a male duck

dram *n.* a unit of weight; a small portion

dra´ma *n.* serious play or event; plays collectively **—dra·mat´ic** *adj.* **—dra·mat´i·cal·ly** *adv.*

dra´ma·tis per·so´nae *n.* a cast of characters

dra·mat´ics *n.* the art of staging drama; histrionics

dram´a·tize´ *vt.* adapt for a play; present in an exaggerated fashion **—dram·a·ti·za´tion** *n.*

drape *n.* a hanging cloth; the way cloth hangs *—vt.* cover with cloth; arrange cloth; hang loosely

dras´tic *adj.* extreme; strong and rapid **—dras´ti·cal·ly** *adv.*

draught (*Brit.*) *adj.* drawn from a keg *—n.* a preliminary work; air current; order directing payment; selection for purpose; depth of a vesscl below water *—vt.* make a layout; sketch or write; select

draughts *n.* (*Brit.*) a board game similar to checkers

draw *n.* that attracts or entices; a tie *—vi., vt.* pull or drag; suck; entice; compose or portray; to pull out **—draw the line** to set a limit

draw´back´ *n.* a disadvantage

draw´er *n.* one who draws; a sliding container in furniture

drawl *n.* a manner of speaking *—vi., vt.* speak slowly

dray *n.* a low, heavy cart

dray´age *n.* a fee for hauling

dread *n.* fearful anticipation *—vt.* anticipate with fear or reluctance

dread´ful *adj.* inspiring dread; unpleasant, distasteful

dread´nought *n.* a battleship

dream *n.* images during sleep; a vision; something pleasant *—vi.* experience in a dream; deem practical *—vt.* envision; waste time

dream´y *adj.* pleasant; soothing **—dream´i·ly** *adv.*

drear´y *adj.* bleak, dismal; dull **—drear´i·ly** *adv.* **—drear´i·ness** *n.*

dredge *n.* machine for clearing waterways *—vt., vi.* dig

dregs *pl. n.* residue; waste

drench *vt.* saturate; wet thoroughly

dress *vt.* clothe; trim or adorn *—vi.* don clothing *—n.* apparel **—dress up** improve appearance; don one's best clothing **—dress´mak·er** *n.*

dress´er *n.* a decorator; one attired well; (*US*) chest of drawers

dressing gown (*Brit.*) a loose, casual garment

drib´ble *n.* a small amount *—vi., vt.* trickle; flow a little at a time

drift *n.* something carried by wind or water; a gradual change; a trend *—vi.* carried by wind or water; wander aimlessly; to stray

drift´er *n.* a homeless person

drill *n.* practice exercises; a boring tool *—vt.* bore a hole; train

drink *n.* beverage *—vi., vt.* ingest a liquid **—drink´a·ble** *adj.*

drip *n.* a drop of liquid; the sound of a falling drop *—vi., vt.* fall in drops

drive *n.* operating a motor vehicle; an auto trip; path for an auto; a sharp blow to a ball; an organized effort; enthusiasm *—vi., vt.* operate or propel; hit a ball; press toward a goal

driv´el *n.* foolish talk *—vi., vt.* utter foolishly

drive´way *n.* private access road

driz´zle *n.* light rain *—vi., vt.* fall in small drops

droll *adj.* quaintly humorous

drone *n.* a loafer; dull humming sound *—vi.* to speak monotonously

droop *vi.* hang down; become dejected **—droop´y** *adj.*

drop *n.* a small amount; a sharp decline; distance between two levels; a location for depositing; material deposited *—vi., vt.* to fall or decline; to deposit

drop´let *n.* a small drop

drop´out´ *n.* one who abandons an undertaking

dross *n.* waste matter

drought *n.* a long period of dry weather; prolonged shortage

drove *n.* a large number moving together **—dro´ver** *n.*

drown *vi.* to die in liquid *—vt.* to kill in liquid; to overwhelm

drowse *vt., vi.* become sleepy

drow´sy *adj.* sleepy; sluggish

drub *vt.* beat with a stick; to vanquish *—n.* a heavy blow

drub´bing *n.* a one–sided defeat

drudge *n.* a menial worker *—vi.* to labor at a menial or dull task

drudg´er·y *n.* tiresome work

drug *n.* substance that alters a body function *—vt.* to medicate; add a narcotic to food or drink

dru´id *n.* a priest in ancient Gaul

drum *n.* a percussion instrument; a cylindrical receptacle; repetition *—vi., vt.* beat constantly **—drum out** expel **—drum up** summon or seek by persistence

drunk *adj.* affected by drink to the point of impairment; overcome by emotion *—n.* one legally or noticeable overcome by drink

dry *adj.* lacking moisture; of a non–liquid; plain, as of food or wine; boring; unproductive *—vi., vt.* become or make dry **—dry´ness** *n.*

dry´ad *n.* mythical wood nymph

dry cell *n.* a sealed battery

dry´dock *n.* a mooring for the repair of ships *—vi., vt.* to go into drydock

dry goods textile, fabrics

dry rot *n.* a fungal disease

dry run *n.* a rehearsal

dual *adj.* comprised of two parts

dual carriageway (*Brit.*) a road with separate lanes for opposing traffic

dub *vt.* bestow knighthood; confer with a title; to add music, subtitles, etc. to a film or recording

du·bi´e·ty *n.* doubt; uncertainty

du´bi·ous *adj.* questionable; suspect; causing doubt or uncertainty

du´bi·ta·ble *adj.* uncertain

du´cal *adj.* of a duke or duchy

duch´ess *n.* wife or widow of a duke

duch´y *n.* realm of a duke

duck *n.* a web–footed water bird *—vi., vt.* plunge into water; to evade

duck´ling *n.* a small or baby duck

duct *n.* a tubular channel

duc´tile *adj.* able to be hammered thin; easily led **—duc´til´i·ty** *n.*

dude *n.* a dandy

dud´geon *n.* sullen displeasure

due *adj.* scheduled or expected; fitting or deserved *—n.* anything owed or deserved

du´el *n.* formal combat *—vi., vt.* fight a duel

du·et´ *n.* a musical work for two

dug´out *n.* a canoe; an underground shelter

duke *n.* an English peer

duke´dom *n.* a duchy

dul´cet *adj.* pleasing to the ear; soothing **—dul´cet·ly** *adv.*

dul´ci·mer *n.* a stringed instrument

dull *adj.* mentally or physically slow; lacking spirit; boring; blunt; lacking brightness *—vt., vi.* make or become dull **—dull´ish** *adj.*

dul´lard *n.* a dull person

duly *adv.* in a proper manner

dumb *adj.* unable to speak; lacking intelligence

dumb´found, dum´found *vt.* astonish; make speechless from shock

dumb´struck *adj.* speechless

dum´my *n.* a stupid or foolish person; a representation; a silent player, as in bridge *—adj.* fake or counterfeit; representational

dump *vt., vi.* empty or unload; get rid of *—n.* a place for refuse; a distribution point

dump´ling *n.* a filled pastry; dough cooked in soup or stew

dump´ster *n.* (*US*) a trash container

dump´y *adj.* short and thick

dun *vt., vi.* press for payment

dunce *n.* an ignorant person

dune *n.* a hill or ridge of sand

dung *n.* animal excrement

dun·ga·ree´ *n.* a sturdy cotton cloth **—dun·ga·rees´** work clothes

dun´geon *n.* an underground cell

dunk *vi., vt.* to dip into liquid

du·o·de´num *n.* the part of the small intestine nearest the stomach

dupe *n.* one easily deceived *—vt.* to deceive

du´plex *adj.* double *—n.* (*US*) two connected housing units

du´pli·cate *adj.* copied *—n.* a copy *—vt.* make a copy; repeat

du·plic´i·ty *n.* deception **—du·plic´i·tous** *adj.* **—du·plic´i·tous·ly** *adv.*

du´ra·ble *adj.* able to withstand heavy use **—du´ra·bil´i·ty** *n.*

durable goods products having a relatively long life

du·ra´tion *n.* an interval of time

du·ress´ *n.* threat or coercion

dur´ing *prep.* throughout; in the course of

dusk *n.* early evening darkness

dust *n.* powder *—vt.* remove dust; sprinkle lightly **—dust´y** *adj.*

dust´er *n.* a protective garment

du´te·ous *adj.* obedient; attentive to duty **—du´te·ous·ly** *adv.*

du´ti·ful *adj.* having a sense of duty; obedient **—du´ti·ful·ly** *adv.*

duty *n.* that required; assigned task; a tax on imported goods

dwarf *n.* a thing notably smaller than most —*vt.* curb the growth of

dwell *vi.* reside; linger —**dwell´er** *n.*

dwin´dle *vi.* lessen gradually

dye *n.* coloring matter —*vt., vi.* to stain with liquid coloring

dy·nam´ic *adj.* relating to force; marked by change; forceful, intense —**dy·nam´i·cal·ly** *adv.*

dy·nam´ics *n.* the study of force; forces that make up a system

dy´na·mite *n.* an explosive —*vt.* destroy with an explosive

dy´na·mo´ *n.* a mechine for converting mechanical energy to electrical energy

dy´nas·ty *n.* succession of rulers

dyne *n.* a unit of force

dys´en·ter·y *n.* inflammation of the large intestine

dys·func´tion *n.* impaired function —**dys·func´tion·al** *adj.*

dys·lex´i·a *n.* a visual impairment —**dys·lex´ic** *adj.*

dys´pep´sia *n.* distressed digestion —**dys´pep´tic** *adj.*

dys·pha´gia *n.* difficulty in swallowing —**dys·phag´ic** *adj.*

dys·pha´sia *n.* difficulty with speech —**dys·pha´sic** *adj.*

dys´tro·phy *n.* a disorder caused by faulty nutrition

e, E fifth letter of the English alphabet

each *adj.* one of two or more —*adv.*

ea´ger *adj.* impatient or anxious

ea´gle–eyed *adj.* having keen sight

ear *n.* organ of hearing; heed

ear´ful *n.* gossip

ear´ly *adj.* near the beginning; before the usual or expected time

ear´mark *vt.* mark for identification; set aside —*n.* an owner's mark

earn *vt.* receive as payment; deserve for effort; to yield a profit

earnings *pl. n.* wages; profit

ear´nest *adj.* serious; intense; important —**earnest money** payment to seal a bargain

ear´shot *n.* hearing distance

earth *n.* dry land; a place of being as contrasted to the spirit world

earth´en *n.* made of earth or baked clay —**earth´en·ware** *n.*

earth´quake´ *n.* a surface tremor

earth´work *n.* a fortification

earth´y *adj.* crude, unrefined; natural —**earth´i·ness** *n.*

ease *n.* comfort; rest; freedom from difficulty —*vi., vt.* to lessen; move slowly and carefully —**ease´ful** *adj.*

ea´sel *n.* a stand for displaying

ease´ment *n.* relief; that providing relief; a right to use of property

east *n.* the direction from which the sun rises —**the East** an eastern region; Asia —**east´er·ly** *adj., adv.*

eas´y *adj.* without difficulty; unhurried, relaxing —**eas´i·ly** *adv.*

eas´y·go·ing *adj.* relaxed; unhurried

eat *vi., vt.* take in food; consume or destroy; annoy —**eat´a·ble** *adj.*

eat´er·y *n.* a restaurant

eaves *pl. n.* projecting edge of a roof

eaves´drop *vi.* to listen secretly

ebb *n.* a decline; receding tide (also **ebb tide**) —*vi.* decline; recede

eb´on·y *n.* hard wood, usually black —*adj.* made from ebony; black

e·bul´lient *adj.* exuberant; enthusiastic **e·bul´lience, e·bul´lien·cy** *n.*

ec·cen´tric *adj.* off center; having different centers; unconventional —*n.* device for transferring motion; an odd or unconventional person

ec·cle´si·as´tic *n.* a cleric —**ec·cle´si·as´tic, ec·cle·si·as´ti·cal** *adj.* pertaining to the church

ec·cle·si·ol´o·gy *n.* study of church function or ornamentation

ec·dys´i·ast *n.* a stripteaser

ech´e·lon *n.* a military formation; a level of responsibility or function

e·chid´na *n.* a spiny anteater

echo *n.* reflected sound —*vi.* to resound; be repeated —*vt.* to repeat

ech·o·lo´cate *vt.* to position by sound waves —**ech·o·lo·ca´tion** *n.*

é´clair, e·clair´ *n.* a filled pastry

e·clat´ *n.* a dazzling display; celebrity or renown

ec·lec´tic *adj.* from varied sources —*n.* one using various sources

e·clipse´ *n.* the obscuring of a celestial body; a dimming or diminishing —*vt.* to diminish; overshadow

e·clip´tic *n.* plane that intersects the sun and the earth's orbit

e·col´o·gy *n.* study of a changing environment —**ec·o·log´i·cal** *adj.*

e·co·nom´ic *adj.* of the production and management of wealth

e·co·nom´i·cal *adj.* done without waste; economic; of economics

e·co·nom´ics *n.* study of the production and management of wealth

e·con´o·my *n.* management of finances; care in use of resources; a system for managing resources

e·con´o·mize *vi.* to use carefully

ec´o·sys·tem *n.* a community of organisms and their environment

ec´ru *adj.* light brown

ec´sta·sy *n.* emotional rapture or delight —**ec·stat´ic** *adj.*

ec·u·men´ic, ec·u·men´i·cal *adj.* general or universal; promoting unity —**ec´u·me·nism** *n.*

ec´ze·ma *n.* a skin inflammation

e·da´cious *adj.* voracious

ed´dy *n.* a circling current —*vi., vi.* move in circles

e·de´ma *n.* morbid accumulation of fluid

e·den´tate *adj.* toothless

edge *n.* a border or margin; cutting part; a dividing line —*vt.* to border; sharpen; advance gradually

edg´y *adj.* irritable; nervous —**edg´i·ness** *n.*

ed´i·ble *adj.* fit to be eaten

e´dict *n.* formal decree; a strict order

ed´i·fice *n.* an imposing building

ed´i·fy *vt.* instruct, enlighten

ed´it *vt.* prepare for publication; to correct or alter —**ed´i·tor** *n.*

e·di´tion *n.* a published work; the number of copies issued

ed´i·to´ri·al *adj.* of an editor —*n.* an article expressing opinion

ed´u·cate *vt.* teach or train; inform

ed´u·cat·ed *adj.* well–schooled; cultivated in speech, manner, etc.

ed·u·ca´tion *n.* training the mind; knowledge; the art of teaching

ed´u·cat·ive *adj.* instructive

e·duce´ *vt.* draw out; formulate

ee´rie, ee´ry *adj.* weird; awesome; strange —**ee´ri·ness** *n.*

ef·face´ *vt.* obliterate; make oneself insignificant —**ef·face´ment** *n.*

ef·fect´ *n.* something brought about; power to influence —*vt.* produce or cause —**ef·fec´tive** *adj.*

ef·fec´tu·al *adj.* possessing power; in force —**ef·fec´tu·al·ly** *adv.*

ef·fec´tu·ate *vt.* bring about

ef·fem´i·nate *adj.* having female traits; marked by weakness and overrefinement —**ef·fem´i·na·cy** *n.*

ef·fer·ves´cent *adj.* emitting tiny bubbles; lively, vivacious —**ef·fer·vesce´** *vi.* —**ef·fer·ves´cence** *n.*

ef·fete´ *adj.* unproductive; self–indulgent —**ef·fete´ness** *n.*

ef´fi·ca´cious *adj.* producing desired effect —**ef´fi·ca·cy** *n.*

ef·fi´cient *adj.* produced with minimum effort, waste, etc.

ef´fi·gy *n.* a representative figure

ef·flo·resce´ *vi.* bear flowers

ef´flu·ence *n.* that flowing out

ef·flu´vi·um *n.* an emanation; noxious vapor —**ef·flu´vi·ous** *adj.*

ef´fort *n.* energy required to accomplish a task; an attempt

ef´fort·less *adj.* requiring little effort

ef·fron´ter·y *n.* boldness; insolence

ef·ful´gence *n.* a shining forth; radiance —**ef·ful´gent** *adj.*

ef·fuse´ *vt., vi.* pour forth

ef·fu´sive *adj.* overly demonstrative; gushing —**ef·fu´sive·ly** *adv.*

e·gal·i·tar´i·an *adj.* of political and social equality

egg *n.* a reproductive body; a female gamete —**egg on** incite

egg´head´ *n.* an intellectual

e´go *n.* the conscious self

e·go·cen´tric *adj.* self–centered

e´go·ism *n.* excessive concern with one's self; conceit; belief in self–interest as a primary goal —**e´go·ist** *n.* —**e´go·is´tic** *adj.*

e·go·ma´ni·a *n.* excessive concentration on one's self

e´go·tist *n.* one with an overblown sense of self–importance

e·gre´gious *adj.* exceptionally bad

e´gress *n.* a going out; an exit

ei´der *n.* a large sea duck

ei´ther *adj.* one of two

e·jac´u·late´ *vt.* utter or eject abruptly —**e·jac·u·la´tion** *n.*

e·ject´ *vt.* cast out —**e·jec´tion** *n.*

eke *vt.* to supplement; produce with difficulty

e·lab´o·rate *adj.* intricate —*vi., vt.* to work out in great detail —**e·lab´o·rate·ly** *adv.*

é·lan´ *n.* dash; vivacity

e·lapse´ *vi.* to pass by

e·las´tic *adj.* capable of quick recovery; easily adapting —*n.* a stretchable fabric —**e·las·tic´i·ty** *n.*

e·late´ *vt.* raise the spirits of —**e·lat´ed** *adj.*

e·la´tion *n.* exultation

el´bow *n.* joint at the bend of the arm; any angular joint or fitting

el´der *adj.* older; superior in rank —*n.* an older person

el´der·ly *adj.* somewhat old

el´dest *adj.* first–born

e·lect´ *adj.* chosen; singled out, exclusive —*n.* one chosen or singled out —*vt.* choose or vote for —**the elect** a favored group

e·lect´a·ble *adj.* able or likely to be elected

e·lec´tion *n.* the process of selecting

e·lec·tion·eer´ *vi.* canvass for votes

e·lec´tive *adj.* chosen by votes; open to choice: optional

e·lec´tor *n.* a voter; a member of the electoral college —**e·lec´tor·al** *adj.*

electoral college people chosen to formally elect the president and vice president of the U.S.

e·lec´tor·ate *n.* a body of voters

e·lec´tric, e·lec´tri·cal *adj.* of or operated by electricity; emotionally charged —**e·lec´tri·cal·ly** *adv.*

e·lec´tric´i·ty *n.* common source of energy; emotional excitement

e·lec´tri·fy *n.* equip for operation by electricity; to startle or thrill

e·lec·tro·car´di·o·gram *n.* a graph showing heart activity

e·lec´tro·car´di·o·graph´ *n.* instrument for recording heart activity

e·lec´trode *n.* a conducting element for an electric charge

e·lec·tro·dy·nam´ics *n.* interaction of electicity and magnetism

e·lec·tro·en·ceph´a·lo·gram *n.* a record of the brain's activity

e·lec·tro·mag´net *n.* a magnet produced by electricity

e·lec´tron *n.* a negatively charged atomic particle

e·lec´tron´ics *n.* the study of carriers of electric charge

el·ee·mos´y·nar·y *adj.* charity; nonprofit

el´e·gance *n.* a sense of propriety, grace, or beauty; tasteful luxury —**el´e·gant** *adj.* —**el´e·gant·ly** *adv.*

el´e·gy *n.* a classical poem —**el·e·gi´ac** *adj.* —**el´e·gize** *vt., vi.*

el´e·ment *n.* a basic component; one's natural environment —**el´e·men´tal, el´e·men´ta·ry** *adj.*

el´e·phant *n.* a huge mammal with a flexible trunk and tusks

el´e·vate *vt.* to raise or lift; improve one's moral or intellectual awareness; improve the spirits of

elf *n.* a mischievous sprite — **elf´in, elf´ish** *adj.*
e·lic´it *vt.* to draw out; bring out
e·lide´ *vt.* omit; ignore
el´i·gi·ble *adj.* qualified to participate
e·lim´i·nate *vt.* remove, reject
e·lite´ *n.* the aristocracy; a small powerful group —**e·lit´ist** *n.*
e·lix´ir *n.* a cure–all
elk *n.* a large deer with broad antlers
el·lipse´ *n.* an oval geometric form —**el·lip´tic, el·lip´ti·cal** *adj.*
el·lip´sis *n., pl.* **el·lip´ses** the omission of a word or phrase; marks that indicate omission as ... or ***
elo·cu´tion *n.* the art of public speaking —**el·o·cu´tion·ar·y** *adj.*
e·lon´gate *vt., vi.* make or grow longer —**e·lon´gate, e·lon´ga·ted** *adj.* made longer; slender
e·lope´ *vi.* run away to marry
el´o·quence *n.* expressive speech or writing —**el´o·quent** *adj.*
else *adj.* different or other; more
e·lu´ci·date *vt.* clarify; explain —**e·lu·ci·da´tion** *n.*
e·lude´ *vt.* evade or escape; slip from memory —**e·lu´sive, e·lu´so·ry** *adj.*
e·ma´ci·ate´ *vt.* make abnormally thin —**e·ma´ci·at·ed** *adj.*
em´a·nate´ *vi.* come forth
e·man´ci·pate´ *vt.* release from bondage —**e·man´ci·pa´tion** *n.*
e·mas´cu·late *vt.* to deprive of force —**e·mas·cu·la´tion** *n.*
em·balm´ *vt.* preserve a dead body; protect from change
em·bank´ment *n.* a protective mound —**em·bank´** *vt.*
em·bar´go *n.* restriction of trade —*vt.* place restriction on
em·bark´ *vi., vt.* go aboard —**em´bar·ka´tion** *n.* —**em·bark´ment** *n.*
em·bar´rass *vt.* make ill at ease; involve in financial difficulties —**em·bar´rass·ment** *n.*
em´bas·sy *n.* the post, trappings, staff, etc. of an ambassador
em·bat´tle *vt.* to equip for battle; to fortify —**em·bat´tled** *adj.*
em·bed´ *vt.* to set firmly
em·bel´lish *vt.* add detail or adornment —**em·bel´lish·ment** *n.*
em´ber *n.* a live coal —**embers** *n.* a dying fire
em·bez´zle *vt.* take illegally —**em·bez´zle·ment** *n.*
em·bit´ter *vt.* give rise to unhappiness
em·bla´zon *vt.* adorn or decorate
em´blem *n.* a symbol; a representation —**em´blem·at´ic** *adj.*
em·bod´y *vt.* collect into a whole; include or incorporate
em·bold´en *vt.* give courage to
em´bo·lism *n.* stoppage in a blood vessel
em´bo·lus *n.* an obstruction
em·bos´om *vt.* to take in; shelter
em·boss *vt.* to adorn with a raised design
em·brace´ *n.* a hug; acceptance —*vi.* join in a hug —*vt.* hug; accept; include —**em·brace´a·ble** *adj.*
em·broi´der·y *n.* ornamental needlework —**em·broi´der** *vt.*
em·broil´ *vt.* draw into a conflict
em´bry·o *n.* the early stage of an organism —**em´bry·on´ic** *adj.*
em·bry·ol´o·gy *n.* the study of embryos —**em·bry·ol´o·gist** *n.*
e·mend´, e´men·date *vt.* correct
em´er·ald *n.* a green precious stone
e·merge´ *vi.* come forth; come into view; form or evolve —**e·mer´gence** *n.* —**e·mer´gent** *adj.*
e·mer´gen·cy *n.* a situation requiring immediate action
e·mer´i·tus *adj.* retired, but retained in a honorary position
em´er·y *n.* a very hard mineral
e·met´ic *n.* medicine used to induce vomiting —*adj.* causing vomiting
em´i·grate´ *vi.* leave a country to settle in another —**é·mi·gré´** *n.*
em´i·nent *adj.* renowned, exalted; above others —**em´i·nence** *n.*
eminent domain right to take private property for public use
em´is·sar´y *n.* one on a mission
e·mis´sion *n.* something omitted
e·mit´ *vt.* give out; discharge
e·mol´u·ment *n.* compensation for office or employment
e·mote´ *vi.* act melodramatically
e·mo´tion *n.* strong feeling; mental agitation —**e·mo´tion·al** *adj.*
e·mo´tion·a·lize *vt.* make emotional
e·mo´tive *adj.* arousing emotion
em´pa·thy *n.* identification with the emotions, thoughts, etc. of another
em´per·or *n.* ruler of an empire
em´pha·sis *n.* forcefulness; special importance —**em´pha·size´** *vt.*
em·phat´ic *adj.* forceful; definite —**em·phat´i·cal·ly** *adv.*
em·phy·se´ma *n.* lung condition marked by shortness of breath
em´pire´ *n.* a vast organization
em·pir´ic, em·pir´i·cist *n.* a seeker of knowledge through experience —*adj.* empirical
em·pir´i·cal *adj.* based on experience —**em·pir´i·cal·ly** *adv.*
em·ploy´ *vt.* engage the services of; to use —**em·ploy´ment** *n.*
em·ploy´a·ble *adj.* capable of being put to use —**em·ploy´a·bil´i·ty** *n.*
em·po´ri·um *n.* a marketplace
em·pow´er *vt.* to enable or permit
emp´ty *adj.* having nothing within; insincere; frivolous —*vt., vi.* make or become empty; transfer contents —**emp´ti·ness** *n.*
e´mu *n.* a flightless bird
em´u·late *vt.* imitate; to strive to equal —**em´u·la´tion** *n.*
e·mul´sion *n.* solid particles suspended in liquid —**e·mul´sive** *adj.*
e·mul´si·fy *vt.* mix or whip —**e·mul·si·fi·ca´tion** *n.*
en·a´ble *vt.* make possible
en·act´ *vt.* make into law
en·am´el *n.* glossy coating —*vt.* surface with protective coating
en·am´or *vt.* to inspire love
en·cap´su·late *vt.* summarize
en·ceph·a·li´tis *n.* an inflammation of the brain —**en·ceph´a·lit´ic** *adj.*
en·ceph´a·lon *n.* the brain
en·chant´ *vt.* delight or charm —**en·chant´ing** *adj.* —**en·chant´ment** *n.*
en·ci´pher *vt.* translate into code
en·cir´cle *vt.* to surround
en´clave *n.* a distinct area enclosed within a larger one
en·close *vt.* surround or contain
en·co´mi·um *n.* a eulogy
en·com´pass *vt.* include; encircle or surround —**en·com´pass·ment** *n.*
en´core *n.* a repeat performance
en·coun´ter *n.* a meeting —*vi., vt.* to meet unexpectedly or in conflict
en·cour´age *vt.* support; inspire —**en·cour´age·ment** *n.*
en·croach´ *vi.* intrude —**en·croach´ment** *n.*
en·crust´ *vt.* cover with a hard coating; to decorate with jewels —**en·crus·ta´tion** *n.*
en·cum´ber *vi.* to weigh down —**en·cum´brance** *n.*
en·cy´clo·pae´di·a, en·cy´clo·pe´di·a *n.* authoritative reference
end *n.* a terminal point
en·dan´ger *vt.* imperil —**en·dan´ger·ment** *n.*
en·dear´ *vt.* make beloved —**en·dear´ing** *adj.*
en·dear´ment *n.* an expression of affection
en·deav´or *n.* sincere effort; an undertaking —*vi., vt.* make an effort
en·dem´ic *adj.* peculiar to a particular area or people
end´less *adj.* boundless; without end; forming a closed loop —**end´less·ly** *adv.* —**end´less·ness** *n.*
en·dorse´ *vt.* approve or support —**en·dorse´ment** *n.*
en·dow´ *vt.* provide income; equip —**en·dow´ment** *n.*
en·dure´ *vi., vt.* continue; bear up —**en·dur´a·ble** *adj.* —**en·dur´ance** *n.*
en´e·my *n.* one hostile to another
en·er·get´ic *adj.* displaying energy
en´er·gize *vt.* bring to action
en´er·gy *n.* power to act; power from natural sources —*adj.* pertaining or relating to power
en´er·vate *vt.* deprive of energy; weaken —**en·er·va´tion** *n.*
en·fee´ble *vt.* weaken; render helpless —**en·fee´ble·ment** *n.*
en·fold´ *vt.* embrace; to wrap
en·force´ *vt.* compel obedience —**en·force´a·ble** *adj.* —**en·forc´er** *n.*
en·fran´chise *vt.* endow with rights; free from bondage
en·gage´ *vi., vt.* hire; promise to marry; to occupy oneself with
en·gag´ing *adj.* charming
en·gen´der *vt.* bring about; produce
en´gine *n.* a machine that converts energy into force
en´gi·neer´ *n.* one who plans and manages —*vt.* to contrive; to plan and supervise
en´gi·neer´ing *n.* application of science to practical problems
en·grave´ *vt.* to carve or etch into a surface
en·gross´ *vt.* absorb entirely
en·gulf *vt.* swallow up; overwhelm
en·hance´ *vt.* embellish so as to improve —**en·hance´ment** *n.*
e·nig´ma *n.* something ambiguous or perplexing —**en´ig·mat´ic** *adj.*
en·join´ *vt.* forbid or prohibit
en·joy´ *vt.* pleasure in; have use of —**en·joy´a·ble** *adj.*
en·kin´dle *vt.* set on fire; excite
en·large´ *vt., vi.* make or become larger —**en·large·ment** *n.*
en·light´en *vt.* inform; impart knowledge —**en·light´en·ment** *n.*
en·liv´en *vt.* to stimulate
en·mesh´ *vt.* to entangle
en´mi·ty *n.* hostility
en·no´ble *vt.* confer nobility; honor or venerate
en´nui *n.* listlessness or indifference
e·nor´mous *adj.* of great size —**e·nor´mi·ty** *n.*
e·nough´ *adj.* adequate; sufficient —*adv.* sufficiently —*n.* an adequate supply —*interj.*
en·rage´ *vt.* make angry; infuriate
en·rap´ture *vt.* delight
en·rich´ *vt.* increase the wealth or quality of —**en·rich´ment** *n.*
en·rol, en·roll´ *vt.* register; place on record; enlist
en·sconce´ *vt.* settle snuggly
en·sem´ble *n.* a suitable or pleasing combination; group of performers
en·shrine´ *vt.* to hold sacred
en·shroud´ *vt.* to cover or conceal
en´sign *n.* a flag, banner, or symbol; a naval officer
en´si·lage *n.* stored fodder
en·slave´ *vt.* place in bondage; dominate
en·snare´ *vt.* to trap
en·sue´ *vi.* result; follow after
en·sure´ *vt.* to make safe or secure; make certain; guarantee
en·tail´ *vt.* impose as a consequence
en·tan´gle *vt.* complicate; involve in difficulties —**en·tan´gle·ment** *n.*
en·tente´ *n.* an understanding between nations
en´ter *vt.* gain admission; become a member; begin; record
en´ter·pris´ing *adj.* displaying initiative —**en´ter·prise´** *n.*
en´ter·tain´ *vt.* amuse; offer hospitality; consider —**en·ter·tain´ing** *adj.* —**en·ter·tain´ment** *n.*
en·thral´, en·thrall´ *vt.* to charm or fascinate
en·thu´si·asm *n.* great excitement or interest —**en´thu·si·as´tic** *adj.*
en·tice´ *vt.* attract with promises —**en·tice´ment** *n.* —**en·tic´ing** *adj.*
en·tire´ *adj.* complete; undivided
en·ti´tle *vt.* give right to; authorize
en´ti·ty *n.* any being; anything that exists
en·tomb´ *vt.* place for burial
en´to·mol´o·gy *n.* study of insects —**en·to·mo·log´i·cal** *adj.*
en·tou·rage´ *n.* companions; attendants
en´trance[1] *n.* act or means of entering —**en´trance·way** *n.*
en·trance´[2] *vt.* fill with delight —**en·tranc´ing** *adj.*

en´trant *n.* one taking part
en·trap´ *vt.* catch, ensnare; lure into danger or difficulty; lay a trap for —**en·trap´ment** *n.*
en·treat´ *vt., vi.* plead or implore
en·trench´ *vt.* fortify; establish firmly —**en·trench´ment** *n.*
en·tre·pre·neur´ *n.* one starting a business venture —**en·tre·pre·neur´i·al** *adj.*
en·trust´ *vt.* give for safekeeping
en´try *n.* means of access; act of entering; item entered; entrant
en·twine´ *vt., vi.* to twist together
e·nu´mer·ate *vt.* name one by one; to count —**e·nu´mer·a´tion** *n.*
e·nun´ci·ate *vt.* pronounce distinctly; state precisely; proclaim
en·vel´op *vt.* surround completely
en´ve·lope´ *n.* that which envelops; a wrapper for letters, etc.
en´vi·a·ble *adj.* provoking envy or admiration
en´vi·ous *adj.* experiencing or expressing envy —**en´vi·ous·ly** *adv.*
en·vi´ron·ment *n.* conditions affecting growth and development of an organism; one's surroundings
en·vi´ron·men´tal·ist *n.* advocate for environmental preservation
en·vi´rons *pl. n.* surrounding area; the environment
en·vis´age *vt.* visualize; form an image of
en·vi´sion *vt.* imagine; foresee
en´voy´ *n.* a diplomatic agent
en´vy *n.* resentment aroused by jealousy —*vt.* regard jealously
e´on *n.* an incalculable time
ep´au·let´ *n.* shoulder ornament
e·phem´er·al *adj.* short–lived; transitory —**e·phem´er·al·ly** *adv.*
ep´ic *n.* a work having a heroic theme —*adj.* grand; heroic
ep´i·cen·ter *n.* point above an earthquake source; a central point
ep´i·cure *n.* a discriminating person —**ep´i·cu´re·an** *adj., n.*
ep´i·dem´ic *n.* widespread condition —**ep´i·dem´ic** *adj.* affecting many at once
ep·i·de·mi·ol´o·gy *n.* study of epidemics —**ep·i·de·mi·ol´o·gist** *n.*
ep´i·der´mis *n.* outer layer of skin
ep´i·gram´ *n.* a thought–provoking saying
ep´i·lep·sy *n.* a nervous disorder
ep´i·logue *n.* concluding section
e·pis´co·pa·cy *n.* church government by bishops —**e·pis´co·pal** *adj.*
e·pis´co·pate *n.* office of a bishop
ep´i·sode´ *n.* one in a series of events; a notable incident
e·pis·te·mol´o·gy *n.* study of human knowledge —**e·pis·te·mol´o·gist** *n.*
e·pis´tle *n.* a letter of instruction
ep´i·taph´ *n.* inscription on a tomb
ep´i·thet´ *n.* word or phrase that characterizes a person or thing
e·pit´o·me *n.* a typical example; a brief summary
e·pit´o·mize *vt.* abridge; be typical of
ep´och *n.* period marked by extraordinary events —**ep´och·al** *adj.*
eq´ua·ble *adj.* of uniform condition; not easily disturbed
e´qual *adj.* of the same value; fair and impartial; balanced —*vt.* be equivalent —*n.* that which closely matches another —**e´qual·ly** *adv.*
e·qual´i·ty *n.* condition of being equal —**e´qual·ize** *vt.*
e´qua·nim´i·ty *n.* calmness; composure
e·quate´ *vt.* make equal; compare
e·qua´tion *n.* a complex array; a statement expressing equality
e·qua´tor *n.* a circle around the earth equidistant from the poles
e·ques´tri·an *adj.* of horses or horsemanship
e´qui·lat´er·al *adj.* having all sides equal —**e·qui·lat´er·al·ly** *adv.*
e·qui´li·brate *vi., vt.* balance; to be or bring to a state of equilibrium
e·qui·lib´ri·um *n.* a condition in which all are equal or balanced
e´quine *adj.* of horses —*n.* a horse
e´qui·nox *n.* time when day and night are of equal length
e·quip´ *vt.* to prepare, as by outfitting or training —**e·quip´ment** *n.*
eq´ui·ta·ble *adj.* fair; impartial —**eq´ui·ta·bly** *adv.*
eq´ui·ty *n.* fairness; impartiality; net assets
e·quiv´a·lent *adj.* equal or corresponding —*n.* that corresponds —**e·quiv´a·lence** *adj.*
e·quiv´o·cate´ *vi.* speak with intent to deceive —**e·quiv´o·ca´tion** *n.*
e´ra *n.* a period encompassing important dates, events, etc.
e·rad´i·cate´ *vt.* to destroy utterly —**e·rad·i·ca´tion** *n.*
e·rase´ *vt.* wipe out; remove
e·rect´ *adj.* upright; vertical; standing —*vt.* construct; set in an upright position —**e·rec´tion** *n.*
e·rec´tile *adj.* able to become erect; raised to an upright position
erg *n.* a unit of work or energy
er·go·nom´ics *n.* designing of equipment or workplace to minimize operator fatigue —**er·go·nom´ic** *adj.*
e·rode *vt., vi.* wear or become worn away —**e·ro´sion** *n.*
e·rog´e·nous *adj.* exciting sexually
e·rot´ic *adj.* arousing sexually
e·rot´i·ca *n.* erotic materials
err *vi.* make a mistake; to sin
er´rand *n.* short trip; a task
er´rant *adj.* wandering; straying from a proper course
er·rat´ic *adj.* deviating from the expected; lacking consistency
er·ro´ne·ous *adj.* inaccurate, incorrect —**er·ro´ne·ous·ly** *adv.*
er´ror *n.* wrongly done; inaccuracy
er´satz´ *adj.* being substitute
erst´while *adj.* former
er´u·dite *adj.* scholarly; learned
e·rupt´ *vi., vt.* burst forth —**e·rup´tion** *n.* —**e·rup´tive** *adj.*
es´ca·late´ *vi., vt.* increase; to ascend or carry up
es´ca·la·tor *n.* a moving staircase
es´ca·pade´ *n.* prank
es·cape´ *n.* breaking free; means to break free —*vi., vt.* to elude, avoid, or break free
es·ca´pism *n.* a turning from unpleasant reality
es·carp´ment *n.* a steep slope
es·cha·tol´o·gy *n.* theological study of the destiny of man
es·cheat´ *n.* reversion of property in the absence of heirs —*vi., vt.* cause to revert to the state
es·chew´ *vt.* shun or refrain from
es´cort *n.* one accompanying —**es·cort´** *vt.* to accompany
es´crow *n.* thing of value held until certain conditions are satisfied
es·cutch´eon *n.* a heraldic shield
e·soph´a·gus *n.* tube that connects mouth to the stomach
es·o·ter´ic *adj.* understood by a limited group; confidential
es·pe´cial *adj.* exceptional
es´pi·o·nage *n.* spying
es·pla·nade´ *n.* level public space
es·pouse´ *vt.* to give or take in marriage; to take up as a cause
es·pres´so *n.* coffee from darkly roasted, finely ground beans
es·py´ *vt.* to catch sight of
es·quire´ *n.* a title of courtesy; a candidate for knighthood
es´say *n.* a brief written work; a testing —*vt.* to test ore
es´sence *n.* basic nature or quality
es·sen´tial *adj.* fundamental; necessary —*n.* something required
es·tab´lish *vt.* create or install; authenticate —**es·tab´lish·ment** *n.*
es·tate´ *n.* one's entire wealth; landed property
es·teem´ *n.* respect; reverence —*vt.* to value; to regard as
es´ti·ma·ble *adj.* deserving of esteem
es´ti·mate´ *vt.* approximate; form an opinion —*n.* appraisal or evaluation; an opinion —**es´ti·ma´tion** *n.*
es·top´ *vt.* to prevent
estrange´ *vt.* alienate
es´tu·ar´y *n.* mouth of a river
etch *vi., vt.* engrave with acid; make a clear impression —**etch´ing** *n.*
e·ter´nal *adj.* without end; perpetual —**e·ter´nal·ly** *adv.* —**e·ter´ni·ty** *n.*
e·the´re·al *adj.* light, airy
eth´ic *n.* a set of principals
eth´i·cal *adj.* morally right
eth´ics *n.* accepted morality
eth´nic *adj.* of customs, food, etc. of a group or culture
eth´nol´o·gy *n.* study of cultures
e·ti·ol´o·gy *n.* study of origins
et´i·quette´ *n.* the rules for socially acceptable behavior
e´tude *n.* a musical exercise
et´y·mol´o·gy *n.* the origin and development of words
eu´gen´ics *n.* improvement by selective breeding
eu´lo·gy *n.* a tribute —**eu´lo·gize** *vt.*
eu´phe·mism *n.* substitute word or phrase —**eu´phe·mis´tic** *adj.*
eu·phon´ic, eu·pho´ni·ous *adj.* pleasant or agreeable sounding
eu·pho´ni·um *n.* a brass instrument
eu´pho·ny *n.* a pleasant sounding word combination
eu·pho´ri·a *n.* a feeling of well–being
eu·ryth´mics *pl. n.* musical interpretation through rhythmic body movements —**eu·ryth´mic** *adj.*
eu´tha·na´sia *n.* ending the life of a suffering person —**eu´tha·nize** *vt.*
e·vac´u·ate´ *vt.* to depart from; to withdraw —**e·vac´u·a´tion** *n.*
e·vade´ *vi., vt.* avoid by deceit
e·val´u·ate *vt.* determine the worth of; appraise —**e·val·u·a´tion** *n.*
ev´a·nesce´ *vt.* to vanish slowly
e´van·gel´ic, e´van·gel´i·cal *adj.* adhering closely to Christian scripture; marked by enthusiasm or ardor
e·van·gel·is´tic *adj.* of a crusading nature
e·van´gel·ize *vi., vt.* to preach
e·vap´o·rate *vi., vt.* convert liquid into vapor —**e·vap·o·ra´tion** *n.*
e·va´sive *adj.* deliberately vague; intended to avoid —**e·va´sion** *n.*
eve *n.* night before an event
e´ven *adj.* smooth, level; unchanging, constant; calm, tranquil; balanced —*vt., vi.* to make or become smooth, level, etc. —*adv.*
eve´ning *n.* close of the day
e·vent´ *n.* an important occasion; an incident; one of a series
e·vent´ful *adj.* momentous —**e·vent´ful·ly** *adv.* —**e·vent´ful·ness** *n.*
e·ven´tu·al *adj.* future, impending —**e·ven·tu·al´i·ty** *n.*
ev´er *adv.* at any time; in any way; always
e·vert´ *vt.* turn inside out
eve´ry *adj.* all, taken singly
e·vict´ *vt.* to turn out; dispossess
ev´i·dence *n.* that serves to make clear or prove —*vt.* make plain; attest —**ev·i·den´ti·ar·y** *adj.*
ev´i·dent *adj.* clear; obvious
e´vil *adj.* wicked, depraved; harmful —*n.* sinfulness; that which harms
e·vince´ *vt.* demonstrate clearly
e·vis´cer·ate *vt.* disembowel
e·voke´ *vt.* call forth or summon
ev·o·lu´tion *n.* process of evolving; gradual development or growth
ev·o·lu´tion·ism *n.* gradual biological change; a belief in biological evolution —**ev·o·lu´tion·ist** *n.*
e·volve´ *vi., vt.* develop gradually
ew´er *n.* a large pitcher
ex·ac´er·bate´ *vt.* make more intense
ex·act´ *adj.* very accurate; precise —*vt.* obtain by force or authority
ex·ac´tion *n.* extortion
ex·ag´ger·ate *vi., vt.* to overstate
ex·alt´ *vt.* to glorify or praise
ex·am´i·ne *vt.* inspect or test
ex·am´ple *n.* that which typifies
ex·as´per·ate *vt.* annoy or irritate
ex´ca·vate *vt.* make a hole; uncover by digging —**ex´ca·va´tion** *n.*

ex·ceed´ *vt.* to go beyond
ex·ceed´ing *adj.* surpassing
ex·cel´ *vi., vt.* to be better or superior; to surpass
ex´cel·lent *adj.* outstanding; of exceptional quality —**ex´cel·lence** *n.*
ex·cel´si·or *n.* packing material
ex·cept´ *vt.* to exclude —*vi.* to object —*prep.* with the exception of
ex·cep´tion *n.* that different or excluded; an objection
ex´cerpt *n.* an extract —**ex·cerpt´** *vt.* remove or extract; to quote
ex·cess´ *n.* amount greater than needed; amount greater than another; overindulgence —**ex´cess** *adj.* surplus —**ex·ces´sive** *adj.*
ex·change´ *vt.* to trade; reciprocate; replace —*vi.* make a trade —*n.* trading or reciprocating; a substitution; a place for trading
ex´cise *n.* an indirect tax or fee —**ex·cise´** *vt.* remove —**ex·ci´sion** *n.*
ex·cit´a·ble *adj.* high–strung; emotional; easily excited
ex·cite´ *vt.* stir the emotions; provoke —**ex·cit´ed** *adj.*
ex·cite´ment *n.* a state of high emotion; something that thrills
ex·cit´ing *adj.* exhilarating; intensely emotional
ex·claim´ *vi., vt.* cry out suddenly —**ex·clam´a·to·ry** *adj.*
ex·clude´ *vt.* put out; leave out; except —**ex·clu´sion** *n.*
ex·clu´sive *adj.* limited; regarded as incompatible; restricted
ex´com·mu´ni·cate´ *vt.* to expel —*adj.* expelled or excluded
ex·co´ri·ate *vt.* abrade the skin; to denounce
ex´cre·ment *n.* refuse matter; feces
ex·cre´ta *n.* the body's waste matter —**ex·cre´tion** *n.*
ex·cru´ci·at·ing *adj.* causing severe mental or physical pain; intense
ex´cul·pate´ *vt.* prove innocent
ex·cur´sion *n.* a short journey; a group tour
ex·cuse´ *vt.* to overlook; free from blame; offer a reason or apology; free from obligation —*n.* justification for offense; that which relieves obligation —**ex·cus´a·ble** *adj.*
ex´e·cra·ble *adj.* appallingly bad
ex´e·crate *vt.* denounce; loathe
ex´e·cute *vt.* to perform; put into effect; put to death
ex·ec´u·tive *n.* an official exercising control —*adj.* administrative; having ability to direct or control
ex·em´plar *n.* typical example
ex·em´pla·ry *adj.* worthy of imitation; commendable
ex·em´pli·fy *vt.* show by example
ex·empt´ *adj.* freed from obligation —*vt.* free from a duty or obligation
ex´er·cise *n.* activity to improve strength or endurance; practice to develop a skill; a ceremony —*vt.* to train; to make use of
ex·ert´ *vt.* put forth; bring to bear
ex·fo´li·ate *vt., vi.* to peel off; come off in flakes, layers, etc.
ex´hale´ *vi.* to breathe out
ex·haust´ *vt.* use up; drain of resources, energy, etc.
ex·haust´ed *adj.* used up; consumed; extremely tired
ex·haust´ing *adj.* tiring
ex·haus´tion *n.* extreme fatigue
ex·haus´tive *adj.* extensive; complete —**ex·haus´tive·ly** *adv.*
ex·hib´it *vt.* display; present for inspection —*vi.* place on display —*n.* a display; something displayed
ex·hi·bi´tion·ist *n.* one seeking attention; one driven to indecent exposure —**ex·hi·bi´tion·ism** *n.*
ex·hil´a·rate *vt.* to cheer; stimulate or enliven —**ex·hil´a·rat·ing** *adj.*
ex·hil·a·ra´tion *n.* elation; excitement
ex·hort´ *vt.* advise strongly; entreat
ex·hume´ *vt.* to disinter; disclose
ex·i´gen·cy *n.* an emergency; a pressing need —**ex´i·gent** *adj.*
ex·ig´u·ous *adj.* meager, sparse
ex´ile *n.* expulsion, banishment; one banished —*vt.* to expel or banish
ex·ist´ *vi.* have reality; be present; to continue to be —**ex·ist´ence** *n.*
ex·is·ten´tial·ism *n.* philosophy that stresses free will and personal responsibility —**ex·is·ten´tial·ist** *n.*
ex´it *n.* a going out; a way out
ex´o·dus *n.* departure or leaving
ex·og´a·my *n.* marrying outside one's social unit
ex·on´er·ate *vt.* clear of an accusation; prove blameless
ex·or´bi·tant *adj.* excessive
ex´or·cise´, ex´or·cize´ *vt.* drive out an evil spirit; free from evil influence —**ex´or·cism** *n.*
ex·ot´ic *adj.* foreign; strange or unusual; alluring
ex·pand´ *vi., vt.* to make or become greater; spread or extend
ex·panse´ *n.* unbroken space; wide extent —**ex·pan´sion** *n.*
ex·pan´sive *adj.* extensive; amiable or outgoing —**ex·pan´sive·ly** *adv.*
ex·pa´ti·ate *vi.* to speak at length and in great detail; to elaborate
ex·pect´ *vt.* to anticipate as likely or deserving —**ex·pect´ant** *adj.*
ex·pec·ta´tion *n.* something expected; hope for good
ex·pec´to·rant *n.* medication to clear mucus from the lungs
ex·pec´to·rate *vi., vt.* to spit
ex·pe´di·ent *adj.* appropriate; convenient; useful —*n.* thing suited to a pressing need
ex´pe·dite *vt.* hasten; to speed the progress of
ex·pe·di´tion *n.* a voyage; those who journey and their equipment
ex·pe·di´tious *adj.* rapid, speedy
ex·pel´ *vt.* to drive out by force; to eject by authority
ex·pend´ *vt.* spend or use up
ex·pend´i·ture *n.* an expense; a disbursement
ex·pense´ *n.* an outlay; a cost
ex·pen´sive *adj.* costly
ex·pe´ri·ence *n.* that learned from observation or involvement —*vt.* live through
ex·per´i·ment *n.* a test to learn or verify —*vi.* to try or test
ex·per´i·men´tal *adj.* in development —**ex·per´i·men´tal·ly** *adv.*
ex·per·i·men·ta´tion *n.* the process of testing and recording results
ex·pert´ *adj.* having great skill or knowledge —*n.* one knowledgeable or skilled —**ex´pert·ly** *adv.*
ex·per·tise´ *n.* the skill, knowledge, etc. of an expert
ex´pi·ate´ *vt.* make amends; to atone
ex·pire´ *vi.* to die; come to an end
ex·plain´ *vi., vt.* make clear or understandable —**ex´pla·na´tion** *n.*
ex´ple·tive *n.* an exclamation
ex´pli·ca·ble *adj.* explainable
ex´pli·cate *vt.* to explain
ex·plic´it *adj.* distinct; clearly stated or established —**ex·plic´it·ly** *adv.*
ex·plode´ *vi., vt.* blow up; burst
ex´ploit, ex·ploit´ *n.* a remarkable or daring feat —**ex·ploit´** *vt.* use to one's advantage; take unfair advantage of —**ex·ploit´a·ble** *adj.* —**ex·ploi·ta´tion** *n.*
ex·plore´ *vi., vt.* investigate or examine exhaustively
ex·plor´a·ble *adj.* able to be explored
ex·plo´sion *n.* a blowing up; a sudden outburst; a sudden increase
ex·plo´sive *adj.* pertaining to explosion; liable to cause violence or an outburst —*n.* a substance that can explode —**ex·plo´sive·ly** *adv.*
ex·po´nent *n.* one who promotes; a mathematic symbol
ex´port *n.* goods sent out of a country —**ex·port´** *vt.* send out
ex·po·sé´ *n.* description or airing
ex·pose´ *vt.* leave unprotected
ex·po·si´tion *n.* a public exhibition; detailed explanation
ex·po´sure *n.* revealing; condition of being open to the elements
ex·pos´tu·late´ *vi.* argue against
ex·press´ *vt.* convey in words; represent by symbols; to press or force out —*adj.* deliberate, definite; of a high speed or non–stop train —*adv.* by fast delivery —*n.* a system for transporting rapidly
ex·pres´sion *n.* a means of conveying; something conveyed; a saying
ex·pres´sive *adj.* demonstrative; meaningful —**ex·pres´sive·ly** *adv.*
ex·pul´sion *n.* being forced out or expelled —**ex·pul´sive** *adj.*
ex·punge´ *vt.* erase or delete
ex´qui·site *adj.* beautiful; delicately crafted —**ex·quis´ite·ly** *adv.*
ex´tant *adj.* still existing
ex·tem´po·ra´ne·ous, ex·tem´po·rar´y *adj.* improvised; speaking without notes
ex·tend´ *vi., vt.* enlarge; stretch out
ex·ten´sive *adj.* great in amount, extent, etc. —**ex·ten´sive·ly** *adv.*
ex·tent´ *n.* scope or range of a thing
ex·ten´u·ate *vt.* lessen seriousness by offering excuse
ex·te´ri·or *adj.* outermost; of the outside —*n.* the outside; an outer surface
ex·ter´mi·nate *vt.* destroy; eradicate completely —**ex·ter·mi·na´tion** *n.*
ex·ter´nal *adj.* on the outside
ex·tinct´ *adj.* no longer in existence
ex·tin´guish *vt.* quench; destroy
ex´tir·pate *vt.* uproot; destroy completely, exterminate
ex·tol´, ex·toll´ *vt.* praise; exalt
ex·tort´ *vt.* to obtain by violence or threats —**ex·tor´tion** *n.*
ex´tra *adj.* more than required; additional —*n.* something special or additional —*adv.* unusually
ex´tract *n.* a distillation; a quote —**ex·tract´** *vt.* draw out; quote
ex·tra·cur·ric´u·lar *adj.* outside the regular course of studies or work
ex´tra·dite *vt.* give an accused person to another jurisdiction
ex·tra´ne·ous *adj.* not belonging; unrelated —**ex·tra´ne·ous·ly** *adv.*
ex·tra·or´di·nar·y *adj.* unusual; out of the ordinary; exceptional
ex·trap´o·late *vt.* to project a value from available data
ex·tra·sen´so·ry *adj.* outside the range of normal senses
ex·trav´a·gance *n.* immoderation; excess spending —**ex·trav´a·gant** *adj.* —**ex·trav´a·gant·ly** *adv.*
ex´tra·vert, ex´tro·vert *n.* one active and agressive
ex·treme´ *adj.* most remote; utmost; to the greatest degree —*n.* limit; thing as far from another as possible —**ex·treme´ly** *adv.*
ex´tri·cate *vt.* release from difficulty; disentangle —**ex´tri·ca·ble** *adj.*
ex·u´ber·ant *adj.* spirited; enthusiastic —**ex·u´ber·ance** *n.*
ex·ult´ *vi.* to rejoice, celebrate
ex·ur´ban·ite *n.* one who lives in the suburbs of a city
f, F sixth letter of the alphabet
fa´ble *n.* story that teaches a lesson
fab´ric *n.* cloth; structure of a thing
fab´ri·cate´ *vt.* to manufacture or assemble; invent a story; to lie
fab´u·lous *adj.* imaginary, fictitious; incredible, astonishing
fac´et *n.* the small plane surface of a gem; any aspect of a thing
fa·ce´tious *adj.* amusing; whimsical
fac´ile *adj.* easily accomplished
fa·cil´i·tate´ *vt.* to make convenient or easier
fa·cil´i·ty *n.* absence of difficulty; skill; building or equipment
fac·sim´i·le *n.* a reproduction
fact *n.* the truth; reliable information; anything that happens
fac´tion *n.* an opposition group within an organization
fac´tious *adj.* tending to cause dissension —**fac´tious·ly** *adv.*
fac·ti´tious *adj.* forced or artificial; not genuine
fac´tor *n.* one acting as agent for another; a cause or condition

fac´to·ry *n.* place for the manufacture or assembling of goods
fac´ul·ty *n.* ability to act; mental or physical ability; a body of teachers
fade *vi.* to lose color or distinction; to diminish in some way
fail *vi., vt.* fall short of need; cease to function properly; be unsuccessful
faint *adj.* lacking strength; indistinct —*vi.* to swoon —**faint´ly** *adv.*
faith *n.* unflagging trust; belief without proof; belief in a supreme being: a religion; fidelity
fal´con *n.* a bird of prey
fall *vi.* descend; decline; collapse —*n.* act of falling; (*US*) autumn
fal´la·cy *n.* illogical reasoning —**fal·la´cious** *adj.*
fal´li·ble *adj.* questionable; liable to err —**fal·li·bil´i·ty** *n.*
false *adj.* deceitful; unfaithful; artificial —**false´ly** *adv.*
fal´si·fy *vt.* to misrepresent; alter with fraudulent intent
fa·mil´iar *adj.* intimate, informal; common; presumptuous
fam´i·ly *n.* members of a household; close relatives; a social unit; a related group of plants or animals
fam´ine *n.* a critical shortage of food
fam´ish *vi., vt.* be hungry; to starve or cause to starve
fa´mous *adj.* very well known; renowned —**fa´mous·ly** *adv.*
fa·nat´ic, fa·nat´i·cal *adj.* overly enthusiastic —*n.* one unreasonably zealous —**fa·nat´i·cism** *n.*
fan´cy *adj.* elaborate; intricate —*n.* a whim; a delusion —*vt.* to imagine; be fond of —**fan´ci·ful** *adj.*
fang *n.* a long, pointed tooth
fan·tas´tic *adj.* imaginary; strange, odd; fanciful
farce *n.* a broad comedy or satire; empty actions or ceremony
fare *n.* price for transport; a passenger; food —*vi.* prosper; to turn out
far´ther *adj.* more distant —*adv.* more remote in time or place
fas´ci·nate *vt.* to charm, bewitch; to captivate —**fas´ci·na´tion** *n.*
fash´ion *n.* a popular style of dress —*vt.* to make or adapt —**fash´ion·a·ble** *adj.* —**fash´ion·a·bly** *adv.*
fas´ten *vi.* to become attached —*vt.* to attach or secure —**fas´ten·er** *n.*
fas·tid´i·ous *adj.* particular; difficult to satisfy; oversensitive
fa´tal *adj.* deadly; decisive; fateful —**fa´tal·ist** *n.* —**fa·tal·is´tic** *adj.*
fate *n.* inescapable future; destiny —*vt.* to predestine —**fat´ed** *adj.*
fath´om *n.* a measure of depth, equal to 6 feet —*vt.* to comprehend
fa·tigue´ *n.* weariness, exhaustion —*vi., vt.* to make or grow exhausted
fat´u·ous *adj.* silly, foolish; dim–witted —**fat´u·ous·ly** *adv.*
fau´cet (*US*) *n.* a device for regulating flow of a liquid
fault *n.* a flaw; a mistake; a liability —**fault´i·ness** *n.* —**fault´y** *adj.*
faux pas´ *n.* a socially unacceptable error; a tactless deed
fa´vour (*Brit.*), **fa´vor** (*US*) *n.* approval; a generous act; preferential treatment; a small gift —*vt.* to approve; to assist —**fa´vour·a·ble, fa´vor·a·ble** *adj.* —**fa´vour·a·ble·ness, fa´vor·a·ble·ness** *n.* —**fa´vour·a·bly, fa´vor·a·bly** *adv.*
fa´vour·ite (*Brit.*), **fa´vor·ite** (*US*) *n.* thing regarded fondly; one granted privileges; one most likely to win —*adj.* especially liked; preferred
fawn *vi.* to dote on; to curry favor
faze *vt.* to disturb; confuse
fear *n.* anxiety or dread; uneasiness or concern —*vi.* be afraid —*vt.* dread; regard with awe —**fear´ful** *adj.* —**fear´ful·ly** *adv.*
fea´si·ble *adj.* within reason; possible —**fea·si·bil´i·ty** *n.*
feast *n.* a festivity; banquet —*vi.* to dine extravagantly —*vt.* entertain
feat *n.* an extraordinary deed
fea´ture *n.* a property or characteristic; a prominent written article
fe´ces *n. pl.* waste matter expelled by the body; excrement
fed´er·al *adj.* of a coalition of states
fed´er·ate *vi., vt.* unite under common authority —**fed·er·a´tion** *n.*
fee *n.* a charge
fee´ble *adj.* weak, infirm
feed *vi.* to eat; flow steadily —*vt.* furnish with food; supply with material —*n.* food for animals
feel *n.* sense of touch; emotional or intuitive perception —*vi., vt.* sense by touch; base on emotion or intuition —**feel´ing** *adj.*
feign *vi., vt.* to pretend
feint *n.* a deceptive move —*vi., vt.* make a deceptive move
feis´ty *adj.* lively or flamboyant; spirited —**feis´ti·ness** *n.*
fe·lic´i·tate *vt.* to congratulate; wish well; make happy
fe·lic´i·ty *n.* happiness; light–heartedness; a pleasing quality
fe´line *adj.* of or like a cat —*n.* a cat
fel´low *n.* an associate or colleague; a scholar
fel´on *n.* one guilty of crime
fel´o·ny *n.* a serious crime —**fe·lo´ni·ous** *adj.* —**fe·lo´ni·ous·ly** *adv.*
fe´male *adj.* of the sex that bears offspring; of a mechanical part —*n.* a female animal or plant
fem´i·nine *adj.* having qualities of a female —**fem·i·nin´i·ty** *n.*
fem´i·nist *n.* one who advocates equal rights for women
fence *n.* a barrier that divides or protects; a dealer in stolen goods —*vi.* be evasive; deal in stolen goods —*vt.* to restrict by a barrier; sell to a dealer in stolen goods
fenc´ing *n.* the art of combat with a foil, saber, etc.
fend *vi.* to provide for oneself —*vt.* to ward off; to defend
fend´er (*US*) *n.* a guard that protects from damage by contact
fer·ment´ *n.* substance that causes fermentation; state of agitation —*vt., vi.* cause or undergo fermentation; to agitate
fer·men·ta´tion *n.* chemical conversion by a ferment; agitation
fe·ro´cious *adj.* savage; unmericful; ravenous —**fe·ro´cious·ly** *adv.*
fer´ry *vt.* convey freight or passengers —*n.* vehicle for conveyance
fer´tile *adj.* productive; teeming; rich in resources —**fer·til´i·ty** *n.*
fer´vid *adj.* impassioned; zealous
fer´vour (*Brit.*), **fer´vor** (*US*) *n.* ardor; zeal; enthusiasm
fes´ter *vi., vt.* form pus; to rankle
fes´ti·val *n.* a celebration
fes´tive *adj.* joyous, lighthearted
fes·tiv´i·ty *n.* festival or celebration
fes·toon´ *n.* a hanging garland; a decorative molding —*vt.* to decorate with garlands
fete, fête *n.* a festival —*vt.* honor with a festival or celebration
fe´tish *n.* object having magical powers; an object of devotion
fet´id *adj.* having an offensive smell; stinking
fe·tol´o·gy *n.* discipline dealing with study and care of a fetus
fet´ter *n.* a shackle for the feet; a restraint —*vt.* to constrain; restrain
fe´tus *n.* an unborn young
feud *n.* a bitter, long–lasting quarrel —*vi.* sustain a quarrel
fe´ver *n.* a condition characterized by increased body temperature; a state of exceptional excitement
fi·an·cé´ *n.* a man engaged to marry
fi·an·cée´ *n.* a woman engaged to marry
fi·as´co *n.* a complete and utter failure; a debacle
fi´at *n.* a legal order; a decree
fi´ber (*US*), **fi´bre** (*Brit.*) *n.* a threadlike structure —**fi´brous** *adj.*
fick´le *adj.* flighty or unstable
fic´tion *n.* an imaginary story; a narrative portraying imaginary characters and events
fic·ti´tious *adj.* pretended; made up, imaginary —**fic·ti´tious·ly** *adv.*
fi·del´i·ty *n.* loyalty; devotion to duty; accuracy
fi·du´ci·ar´y *adj.* of one who holds in trust for another; of that held in trust —*n.* one who holds in trust
field *n.* open land; ground for crops or pasture; any unbroken expanse; an area of endeavor
fiend *n.* an evil spirit, a demon; one exceptionally cruel; one addicted
fierce *adj.* savagely cruel; violent; passionate or intense
fi´er·y *adj.* containing or like fire; impetuous or emotional
fight *vi., vt.* take part in conflict —*n.* conflict or struggle; boldness; readiness to struggle —**fight´er** *n.*
fig´ur·a·tive *adj.* symbolic; not taken literally —**fig´u·ra·tive·ly** *adv.*
fig´ure *n.* form or likeness; diagram; character representing a value —*vi., vt.* calculate; consider
fil´a·ment *n.* threadlike component
file *n.* a storage cabinet, folder, etc.; a collection of data; a line of people or things; a tool for smoothing —*vi.* march in line; formally petition to a court —*vt.* place and store documents, data, etc.; place on record; to smooth or scrape
fil´i·al *adj.* due of a son or daughter
fil´i·gree´ *n.* ornamental work
fill *n.* a thing used to take space or make full; built up land; a satisfactory amount —*vt.* bring to a desired level; make full; occupy; furnish that needed; satisfy hunger
fil´ly *n.* a young mare
film *n.* a thin layer or coating; sensitized material in photography; a motion picture —*vi., vt.* coat; make a motion picture
fil´ter *n.* a porous substance for separating materials —*vi., vt.* pass through a filter
filth *n.* dirt; grime; contamination; lewd material; obscenity
filth´y *adj.* dirty; obscene
fil´trate *vt.* strain or separate —*n.* a filtered substance —**fil·tra·tion** *n.*
fi´nal *adj.* at the end; conclusive —*n.* last of a series
fi´nance, fi·nance´ *n.* money management —*vt.* furnish money or credit —**fi·nan´cial** *adj.*
finances the resources of a person, company, etc.
fin·an·cier´ *n.* one specializing in financial operations
find *n.* amazing discovery —*vt.* to discover or perceive; experience
fine *adj.* of exceptional quality; small, thin, or keen —*n.* payment as penalty —*vt.* impose a fine
fin´ger *n.* a digit; thing resembling a finger —*vt.* to touch; point out
fin´ish *n.* an end; a completion; surface of an object; fineness of manner —*vt.* bring to an end; use up; apply a final coat
fi´nite *adj.* of a defined limit
fir *n.* cone–bearing evergreen tree
fire *n.* combustion; strong feeling, ardor; a discharge of firearms —*vt., vi.* set afire; bake in a kiln; excite, inspire; discharge a firearm; dismiss an employee
fire´proof *adj.* not easily burned —*vt.* make less combustible
firm *adj.* solid or dense; not yielding to pressure; secure, immovable; settled; determined —*n.* a business
fir´ma·ment *n.* the heavens
first *adj.* before all others —*n.* one above all; beginning —*adv.*
first aid emergency treatment
first´–class´, first´–rate´ *adj.* of the best quality —*adv.*
fis´cal *adj.* of taxation or public finances; of financial policy
fish *n.* an aquatic animal —*vi., vt.* try to catch fish —*adj.* pertaining to or made from fish
fis´sion *n.* a splitting —**nuclear fission** splitting of atoms for energy —**fis´sion·a·ble** *adj.*

fis´sure *n.* a long, narrow crack

fit *adj.* able, competent; appropriate, suitable; trim, healthy —*n.* being appropriate; a seizure —*vi.* to be suited —*vt.* be appropriate; alter to make suitable; insert in position

fit´ting *adj.* appropriate; suitable —*n.* process of testing or altering; a connector —**fit´ting·ly** *adv.*

fix *n.* an awkward situation —*vt.* to fasten firmly; establish with certainty; repair

fix·a´tion *n.* a preoccupation; obsession —**fix´ate** *vi., vt.*

fix´ture *n.* thing firmly fastened; that which seems permanent

flab´by *adj.* soft, weak; lacking good physical form —**flab´bi·ness** *n.*

flac´cid *adj.* weak, feeble, soft

flag *n.* a cloth banner —*vi.* to grow weak; tire —*vt.* signal by waving

flag´el·late *vt.* to whip

fla´grant *adj.* outragious; openly disgraceful —**fla´gran·cy** *n.*

flake *n.* a small, thin piece; one flightly or fickle —*vi., vt.* to form or chip off into flakes —**flak´y** *adj.*

flame *n.* light from a fire —*vi.* burn brightly; become excited; show the flush of excitement —**flam´ing** *adj.*

flange *n.* a projecting edge

flank *n.* side —*vt.* at the side of

flap *n.* a flat, broad piece; a slapping sound; a state of excitement —*vi., vt.* move back and forth; to flutter

flare *n.* a bright light; a sudden burst —*vi.* emit a sudden burst of light; spread out at one end

flash *adj.* happening suddenly —*n.* a brief gleam; that comes and goes quickly; ostentation —*vi.* emit a sudden light; pass swiftly —*vt.* display briefly —**flash´i·ness** *n.*

flash´back´ *n.* a memory or reminiscence; an interruption to portray an earlier event

flask *n.* a small bottle

flat[1] *adj.* even; with no variation; lying prone; bland; lacking finances —*n.* a level surface; a musical note —*adv.* —**flat´ten** *vi., vt.*

flat[2] *n.* (*Brit.*) living quarters

flat´ter *vt.* compliment excessively or disingenuously —**flat´ter·y** *n.*

flaunt *vi., vt.* make an ostentatious or impudent display

fla´vor (*US*) *n.* taste; a thing added to alter taste; a distinctive quality —*vt.* impart flavor to —**fla´vor·er** *n.*

fla´vor·ful (*US*) *adj.* full of flavor; delectable

fla´vor·ing (*US*) *n.* a substance that imparts flavor

fla´vor·less (*US*) *adj.* lacking flavor; flat or insipid

fla´vour (*Brit.*) *n.* taste; thing added to alter taste; distinctive quality —*vt.* impart flavor to —**fla´vour·er** *n.*

fla´vour·ful (*Brit.*) *adj.* full of flavor; delectable

fla´vour·ing (*Brit.*) *n.* a substance that imparts flavor

fla´vour·less (*Brit.*) *adj.* lacking flavor; flat or insipid

flaw *n.* a defect —*vt., vi.* to make or become defective

flay *vt.* to strip the skin from, as by whipping; criticize harshly

fleck *n.* a small particle —*vt.* to cover with specks

flee *vi., vt.* to run away or escape

fleece *n.* a coat of wool —*vt.* clip the wool from a sheep; defraud

fleet *adj.* swift; temporary —*vi.* proceed swiftly —**fleet´ness** *n.*

fleet *n.* ships, planes, etc., operating under a single authority

fleet´ing *adj.* passing quickly; transitory —**fleet´ing·ly** *adv.*

flesh *n.* meat of an animal; edible portion of fruits and vegetables; human body; human desires

flesh´ly *adj.* pertaining to the body; sensual; plump —**flesh´li·ness** *n.*

flex´i·ble *adj.* able to bend; amenable to change —**flex´i·bil´i·ty** *n.*

flex´time *n.* varied working hours

flight *n.* travel by air; fleeing, running away; a set of steps

flight´y *adj.* frivolous; whimsical

flim´sy *adj.* easily damaged; fragile; poorly fashioned —**flim´si·ness** *n.*

flinch *vi.* to wince or shrink back

fling *vt.* throw forcefully or violently; act spontaneously —*n.* a violent throw; a time of wild abandon

flint *n.* a very hard stone

flint´y *adj.* like flint; unyielding

flip´pant *adj.* frivolous; lacking reverence; impertinent

flirt *n.* a trifler; a coquette —*vi.* trifle with affection; consider briefly —**flir´ta´tion** *n.* —**flir·ta´tious** *adj.*

float *n.* that resting on the surface; a decorated platform —*vi.* rest on the surface; drift on the air

flock *n.* a group or congregation —*vi.* assemble in a group

flog *vt.* beat with a whip

flood *n.* covering of dry land with water; a deluge or glut —*vt.* to overflow, inundate, or glut

floor *n.* surface of a room; a bottom surface; level of a building; recognition to speak —*vt.* to build or refinish a surface; defeat or astound

flo´ra *n.* the plants of a region

flo´ral *adj.* of or like flowers

flor´id *adj.* gaudy, ornate; of a rosy complexion **flor´id·ness** *n.*

flor´ist *n.* one who sells flowers

flo·til´la *n.* a fleet of boats

floun´der *n.* a flatfish —*vi.* have difficulty; struggle

flour *n.* a fine meal —*vt.* to make into flour; to sprinkle with flour

flour´ish *n.* anything showy; a sweeping motion; an elaborate fanfare —*vi.* prosper —*vt.* decorate ornately; wave with a sweep of the arm

flout *vi., vt.* to mock; regard contemptuously —*n.* a mocking insult

flow *n.* emanation; rate of discharge; course of a river, etc.; a continuous stream —*vi.* move in a stream; progress smoothly

flow´er *n.* bloom; plant cultivated for blossoms; the best part —*vi.* to bloom; attain the best level

fluc´tu·ate´ *vi.* to vary continuously; to waver —*vt.* to cause to waver

flue *n.* an exhaust for smoke, etc.

flu´ent *adj.* smooth flowing; able to speak or write well —**flu´en·cy** *n.*

flu´id *adj.* flowing; graceful in movement; readily changed —*n.* a substance that flows

fluke *n.* happening by chance

flunk *vi., vt.* to fail in school

flunk´y *n.* a servant; one engaged for menial tasks

flush *adj.* well supplied; even —*n.* a rapid flow; a warm glow; sudden exhilaration —*vi., vt.* flow rapidly; clean with flowing liquid; to blush

flus´ter *vi., vt.* to make or become nervous or confused

flut´ter *n.* rapid waving or fluctuation; a commotion —*vi., vt.* wave or fluctuate rapidly; move restlessly

flux *n.* flowing; constant change

fly *n.* a flap over an opening; an insect —*vi., vt.* to travel by air; to operate an aircraft; to flee

fo´cus *n.* a point of convergence or concentration —*vi., vt.* to adjust to produce a clear image —**fo´cal** *adj.*

foe *n.* an adversary, enemy

fog *n.* a dense mist —*vt.* obscure —**fog´gi·ness** *n.* —**fog´gy** *adj.*

foi´ble *n.* a minor weakness

foil *n.* a thin sheet of metal; a fencing sword —*vt.* to frustrate

foist *vt.* to pass off by trickery

fold *n.* a doubling; a pen for sheep —*vi.* close a business —*vt.* to double; to envelop

fo´li·age *n.* plant leaves

folk *adj.* of the common people —*n.* people generally; tribe, family, nation, etc. —**folks·y** *adj.*

folk´lore´ *n.* traditions of a culture

fol´low *vi., vt.* come next; conform; happen as a result; trail or pursue —**follow through** to complete

fol´low·ing *adj.* ensuing —*n.* supporters; a calling

fol´ly *n.* foolishness; a frivolous act or undertaking

fo·ment´ *vt.* advocate; incite

fond *adj.* cherished; doting or indulgent —**fond´ly** *adv.* —**fond´ness** *n.*

fon´dle *vt.* caress or stroke

font *n.* size and style of type; a water basin or fountain; a place of origin

food *n.* a substance that nourishes; something that stimulates the senses

fool *n.* one lacking sense; a silly person —*vi.* act silly —*vt.* mislead or cheat —**fool´ish** *adj.*

fop *n.* one overly devoted to personal appearance

for´age *n.* food for animals, fodder —*vi., vt.* search for food or supplies

for´ay *n.* a raid or venture —*vt.* raid

for·bear´ *vi., vt.* abstain; restrain oneself —**for·bear´ance** *n.*

for·bid´ *vt.* prohibit; order against; to prevent —**for·bid´den** *adj.*

for·bid´ding *adj.* frightening; unpleasant —**for·bid´ding·ly** *adv.*

force *n.* potency, might; power to compel; an organized group —*vt.* overpower; compel by might

fore´bear *n.* an ancestor

fore·bode´ *vi., vt.* predict; anticipate

fore´cast *n.* a prediction —*vi., vt.* to anticipate

fore·close´ *vi., vt.* take away the right to property —**fore·clo´sure** *n.*

fore´fa·ther *n.* an ancestor

for´eign *adj.* from another country; unfamiliar; exotic

fore´man *n.* one in charge

fo·ren´sic *adj.* pertaining to legal or formal argumentation

fore´run´ner *n.* one coming before; ancestor; a sign or omen

fore·see´ *vt.* to predict; foretell

fore´sight´ *n.* ability to anticipate

for´est *n.* extensive growth of trees

fore·tell´ *vi., vt.* predict

for·ev´er *adv.* for all time

for´feit *n.* that lost by neglect, etc. —*vt.* to give up —**for´fei·ture** *n.*

fore·warn´ *vt.* warn beforehand

forge *n.* a furnace for heating metal —*vi., vt.* to form laboriously, as metal; to falsify in order to deceive

for´ger·y *n.* an illegal making or altering; an imitation or fake

for·get´ *vi., vt.* to lose from memory; to overlook or neglect

for·get´ful *adj.* losing ability to remember; careless, neglectful

for·give´ *vt.* to pardon; overlook

fork *n.* a device with prongs; a dividing —*vi., vt.* split into branches

for·lorn´ *adj.* abandoned; wretched, without hope

form *n.* configuration; a mold; type; convention; method —*vi., vt.* mold or shape; conceive in the mind

for´mal *adj.* according to custom; correct or suitable; precise; stodgy

for·mal´ity *n.* careful adherence to custom; an official act

for·ma´tion *n.* a thing formed; arrangement or configuration

for´mer *adj.* coming before; preceding; the first of two

for´mi·da·ble *adj.* awesome; threatening; overwhelming

for´mu·la *n.* a representation using symbols; a precise specification

for´mu·late *vt.* to conceive or develop; express as a formula

for·ni·ca´tion *n.* sexual intercourse between unmarried persons

for·sake´ *vt.* forgo; leave or abandon

forte *n.* one's special ability

for´ti·fy *vt.* make stronger

for´ti·tude *n.* strength of character; determination

fort´night *n.* two weeks time

for·tu´i·tous *adj.* occurring by chance; fortunate —**for·tu´i·ty** *n.*

for´tu·nate *adj.* lucky; auspicious

for´tune *n.* luck; fate; riches

fo´rum *n.* meeting for discussion

fos´sil *n.* preserved remains
fos´ter *vt.* to promote; to nurture
foul *adj.* offensive; profane; underhanded; entangled; unpleasant —*vi., vt.* soil; entangle
found *adj.* discovered —*vt.* to bring into being; to cast metal
foun·da´tion *n.* a fundamental principle; a charitable endowment
foun´dry *n.* the process of casting metal; a place where metal is cast
foun´tain *n.* a natural or artificial spring; a reservoir
fox´y *adj.* crafty, cunning; attractive, seductive —**fox´i·ness** *n.*
fra´cas *n.* a brawl
frac´tion *n.* a small part; value expressed as parts of a whole
frac´tious *adj.* unruly; difficult to manage; irritable or testy
frac´ture *n.* a crack or break —*vi., vt.* to crack or break
frag´ile *adj.* easily damaged; delicate
frag´ment *n.* a part or piece
fra´grance *n.* a pleasant odor
frail *adj.* easily damaged; delicate; feeble, weak —**frail´ty** *n.*
frame *n.* skeletal structure; general form; field of view —*vt.* shape or form; provide a border
frame of reference aspect from which something is viewed
fran´chise´ *n.* a right or privilege
fran´gi·ble *adj.* fragile; brittle
frank *adj.* open and honest
frantic *adj.* distraught; highly emotional —**fran´ti·cal·ly** *adv.*
fra·ter´nal *adj.* brotherly
frat´er·nize *vi.* have friendly relations with —**frat·er·ni·za´tion** *n.*
fraud *n.* deception; swindler, faker
fraud´u·lent *adj.* deceitful; marked by fraud —**fraud´u·lence** *n.*
fray *n.* a brawl —*vi., vt.* become worn
freak *adj.* abnormal; bizarre —*n.* an abnormality —**freak´ish** *adj.*
free *adj.* not busy; independent; unrestrained; without obligation; without cost —*vt.* release, make available —**free´ly** *adv.*
fren´zy *n.* a sudden burst of agitation or activity —**fren´zied** *adj.*
fre´quent *adj.* happening often —**fre·quent´** *vt.* to stop by often
fres´co *n.* painting on wet plaster
fresh *adj.* newly made; natural; uninitiated; impertinent, impudent
fret *vt., vi.* be irritated or annoyed —**fret´ful** *adj.* —**fret´ful·ly** *adv.*
fri´a·ble *adj.* easily crumbled
fric´tion *n.* rubbing or abrasion; discord caused by differences
friend *n.* an ally or supporter
fright *n.* sudden alarm or terror; a startling sight
fright´en *vt.* to cause alarm or terror
frill *n.* gathered edging; an unnecessary adjunct —**frill´y** *adj.*
fringe *adj.* at the edge; minor or peripheral —*n.* edging; an outer edge —*vt.* decorate with a fringe
fringe benefit indirect compensation
frisky *adj.* energetic; playful
frit´ter *n.* deep–fried food coated with batter —*vt.* to waste bit by bit
friv´o·lous *adj.* trivial; not serious or sensible —**fri·vol´i·ty** *n.*
frol´ic *n.* merriment, play —*vi.* play
front *n.* the forward part; appearance or demeanor; an area of activity —**fron´tal** *adj.*
fron·tier´ *n.* the border of a country; an unexplored area
frost *n.* ice crystals; coldness —*vt.* to coat with frosting —**frost´i·ness** *n.*
froth *n.* foam; something trivial —*vi., vt.* to foam
frown *n.* a stern look —*vi., vt.* scowl; show disapproval
frugal *adj.* thrifty; inexpensive
fruit *n.* edible portion of a plant; a consequence —**fruit´ful** *adj.*
fru·i´tion *n.* results; fulfillment
frus´trate´ *vt.* nullify the efforts of another —**frus·tra´tion** *n.*
fu´el *n.* anything consumed to produce energy
fu´gi·tive *n.* one who flees; something elusive
ful´crum *n.* support for a lever
ful·fill´ *vt.* perform or accomplish
full *adj.* containing all possible; of the highest degree; puffed out
ful´mi·nate´ *n.* an explosive salt —*vi., vt.* to denounce loudly; explode
ful´some *adj.* obsequious or fawning; abundant
fum´ble *vi., vt.* to grope awkwardly; blunder
fume *n.* a vapor —*vi.* give off vapor; show anger
fu´mi·gate´ *vt.* disinfect
func´tion *n.* normal use; an event —*vi.* perform as designed
fund *n.* an institution that manages designated assets —*vt.* to finance
fun´da·men´tal *adj.* essential; basic —*n.* a principle; an essential part
fu´ner·al *n.* ceremony concerned with burial of the dead
fu·ne´re·al *adj.* solemn
fur´bish *vt.* restore; to polish
fu´ri·ous *adj.* enraged; frenzied
fur´nace (*US*) *n.* an appliance for producing heat
fur´nish *vt.* supply; to provide
fur´nish·ings *pl. n.* household goods; clothing and accessories
fur´ni·ture *n.* equipment that makes a room fit for habitation
fu´ror *n.* a state of excitement
fur´row *n.* a rut; a deep wrinkle —*vt., vt.* make a rut or wrinkle
fur´ther *adj.* additional; more distant —*adv.* farther; to a greater extent; moreover —*vt.* to aid or promote —**fur´ther·more** *adv.*
fur´tive *adj.* stealthy, sneaky
fu´ry *n.* violent anger; violence
fuse *n.* device for setting off an explosive; device that prevents overloading an electrical circuit —*vi., vt.* to unite or blend
fu´sion *n.* a melting or joining by heat; a nuclear reaction
fuss *n.* a quarrel; a commotion; needless concern —*vi.* complain; bother over trifles —*vt.* worry needlessly
fu´tile *adj.* hopeless; trivial
fu´ture *adj.* to come; expected —*n.* a time or event to come; outlook
fuzz´y *adj.* indistinct
g, G seventh letter of the alphabet; slang term for 1000 dollars
gab *n.* idle talk —*vi.* to gossip
gabble *n.* meaningless chatter —*vi., vt.* to jabber or chatter
gadg´et *n.* any implement; a device of limited utility
gag *n.* a joke; a thing placed over the mouth; restriction of free speech —*vi.* choke or retch —*vt.* to silence
gai´e·ty *n.* mirth; festivity; gaudiness
gain *n.* an increase; an advantage —*vi., vt.* to acquire; reach
gala *adj.* joyful —*n.* a celebration
gal´ax·y *n.* star system; gathering of distinctive persons or things
gale *n.* a strong wind
gall *n.* bile; impertinence
gal´lant *adj.* chivalrous; dashing —**gal·lant´** *n.* a lover; one who is chivalrous —**gal´lant·ly** *adv.*
gal´lon *n.* a liquid measure equal to four quarts
gam´bit *n.* a strategy designed to gain an advantage
gam´ble *n.* a risk —*vi., vt.* take a risk
gam´bol *vi.* jump about; frolic
gan´der *n.* a male goose
gang *n.* a group
gang´ster *n.* a criminal
gaol (*Brit.*), **jail** (*US*) *n.* a place of confinement —*vt.* to confine —**gaol´er** (*Brit.*), **jail´er** (*US*) *n.*
gape *n.* a large opening; an open–mouthed stare —*vi.* yawn; stare in amazement; to open wide
ga·rage´ *n.* a building for storing or repairing an automobile
garb *n.* clothing —*vt.* to clothe
gar´ble *vt.* confuse or distort
gar´bage (*US*) *n.* waste, trash
gar´den *n.* plot of cultivated land —*vi., vt.* cultivate a plot of land
gar´gle *n.* a solution for medicating or cleansing the throat —*vi., vt.* to cleanse or medicate the throat
gar´ish *adj.* overly ornate, gaudy
gar´ment *n.* an article of clothing
gar´ner *vt.* collect and store; acquire
gar´nish *n.* a decoration —*vt.* to decorate
gar´ret *n.* an attic room
gar´ru·lous *adj.* chattering; wordy
gas *n.* vapor; a mixture used for anesthesia, fuel, etc.; something enjoyable; (*US*) gasoline
gash *n.* deep cut —*vt.* make a cut
gasket *n.* a washer; a seal
gas·o·line´ *n.* a liquid fuel
gasp *n.* a catching of the breath —*vi.* inhale sharply or with difficulty
gas´tric *adj.* relating to the stomach
gath´er *vi., vt.* convene or assemble; accumulate; draw together; to infer or conclude
gaud´y *adj.* garish; vulgar
gauge *n.* a standard measure; a measuring device —*vt.* measure or estimate
gaunt *adj.* thin and bony; drawn; dreary, barren
gay *adj.* lively, merry; bright
gaze *n.* a steady look —*vi.* to look intently; to stare
gaz´et·teer´ *n.* a geographical dictionary or index
gear *n.* personal property; equipment; a device that transmits energy
gem *n.* a precious stone; anything prized for its value
gene *n.* unit that transmits hereditary characteristics
gen´e·al´o·gy *n.* a record of one's lineage; the study of lineage
gen´er·al *adj.* extensive and diversified; non–exclusive; imprecise
gen´er·ate´ *vt.* to originate or bring into being; produce
gen´er·a´tion *n.* process of producing; a stage of development
ge·ner´ic *adj.* of a class or group
gen´er·ous *adj.* gracious, unselfish; ample —**gen·er·os´i·ty** *n.*
gen´e·sis *n.* origin
ge·net´ic, ge·net´i·cal *adj.* of origin or ancestry —**ge·net´i·cal·ly** *adv.*
ge·net´ics *n.* study of ancestry
gen´ial *adj.* pleasant; amiable
gen´ius *n.* exceptional natural ability or mental capacity
gen´o·cide´ *n.* the systematic extermination of a people
gen´tle *adj.* kindly; temperate; courtly; tame
gen´u·ine *adj.* authentic; sincere and honest
ge·og´ra·phy *n.* study of the earth and its inhabitants; physical nature of an area
ge·ol´o·gy *n.* study of the earth's structure and development
germ *n.* basic form; a microorganism; a basic concept
ger´mi·nate´ *vi., vt.* sprout; begin growth —**ger·mi·na´tion** *n.*
ges·tic´u·late´ *vi., vt.* gesture
ges´ture *n.* a move that emphasizes; something done for effect
get *vt.* to acquire; to understand
ghast´ly *adj.* shocking; terrifying; ghostlike; offensive
ghet´to *n.* an isolated community
ghost *n.* a disembodied spirit; a faint suggestion
gi´ant *adj.* of great size —*n.* anything of exceptional size
gibe *n.* a taunting remark —*vi., vt.* to taunt or ridicule
gift *n.* something freely given; a natural ability
gi·gan´tic *adj.* enormous
gig´gle *n.* a silly nervous laugh —*vi.* to laugh nervously
gild *vt.* to coat with gold; to make seem attractive
gilt *adj.* gilded —*n.* gilding
gim´mick *n.* a thing designed to deceive; device to gain attention
gird *vt.* encircle with a belt or band
gird´er *n.* large supporting beam
gist *n.* the primary concept
give *vi., vt.* to contribute; impart; to yield to pressure
glad *adj.* happy; pleased —**glad´den** *vt.* —**glad´ly** *adv.*
glade *n.* open space in a woods
glance *n.* a brief look; a deflecting —*vi.* to fly off at an angle; look briefly
glare *n.* intense light; fixed stare —*vi.* shine intensely; stare
glaze *n.* a glassy finish —*vt.* give a glassy finish; fit with glass

gleam *n.* a flash of light; a faint display *—vi.* to appear briefly
glean *vt.* collect grain left by reapers; obtain piecemeal —**glean´ings** *n.*
glee *n.* gaiety, merriment
glib *adj.* fluency —**glib´ly** *adv.*
glide *n.* a smooth, flowing movement *—vi.* move smoothly
glim´mer *n.* a faint light; a trace *—vi.* to appear faintly
glimpse *n.* a quick view *—vi.* to glance *—vt.* view briefly
glis´ten *vi.* to sparkle or shine
glit´ter *n.* sparkling light; bits of decorative material *—vi.* sparkle; be brilliant —**glit´ter·y** *adj.*
gloat *vi.* to view with malicious pleasure
glob´al *adj.* world–wide; comprehensive
globe *n.* a sphere; the earth
glob´ule *n.* a tiny globe; a drop
gloom *n.* dimness or darkness; despondency —**gloom´y** *adj.*
glo´ri·ous *adj.* splendid; pleasant; famed —**glo´ri·ous·ly** *adv.*
glo´ry *n.* splendor; fame; a state of well–being *—vi.* be proud of; rejoice in —**glo´ri·fy´** *vt.* —**glo´ri·ous** *adj.*
gloss *n.* shine or luster; a superficial image *—vt.* make shiny; pass over or cover up —**gloss´i·ness** *n.*
glos´sa·ry *n.* list of definitions
glow *n.* soft light; a feeling of warmth *—vi.* give off light; be flushed
glow´er *n.* a scowl *—vi.* to scowl
glue *n.* an adhesive *—vt.* to affix
glum *adj.* sullen, dejected
glut *n.* an oversupply *—vt.* to oversupply; to overburden
glut´ton *n.* an overeater
gnaw *vi., vt.* wear away with the teeth; to worry
goad *vt.* to prod or urge; provoke
goal *n.* an objective
gob´ble·dy·gook *n.* wordy, ambiguous language
gob´let *n.* a stemmed drinking glass
gob´lin *n.* a mischievous elf
gone *adj.* departed; used up
gon´er *n.* one beyond help
gore *n.* blood from a wound *—vt.* wound with a horn
gorge *n.* a ravine *—vi., vt.* devour
gor´geous *adj.* exceptionally beautiful; delightful
gos´sip *n.* idle chatter; one who gossips *—vi.* engage in idle chatter
gouge *n.* type of chisel; an overcharging *—vt.* cut into; cheat
gour·mand´ *n.* one fond of good food
gour·met´ *n.* a good judge of fine food and drink
gov´ern *vi., vt.* to control or influence; to regulate or restrain
gov´ern·ment *n.* a system of administration and its agencies
gown *n.* a long flowing garment
grab *vt.* seize roughly; take by deceit; attract one's attention; to impress
grace *n.* a pleasing quality; good will; a temporary extension; a blessing *—vt.* adorn; dignify
grace´ful *adj.* having elegance
gra´cious *adj.* courteous, affable; compassionate; comfortable or luxurious —**gra´cious·ly** *adv.*
gra·da´tion *n.* a gradual progression
grade *n.* a level in a progression; a rating; degree of slope *—vt.* to rate or classify; change the slope of
gradient *adj.* sloping *—n.* a slope
grad´u·al *adj.* progressing in slow or regular steps —**grad´u·al·ly** *adv.*
grad´u·ate´ *n.* one completing a course of study; a container for measuring *—vi.* complete a course of study *—vt.* award a diploma; mark a container for measuring
graf·fi´to *n., pl.* **graf·fi´ti** a crudely–drawn inscription
graft *n.* joining of tissue; tissue so joined; profit by extortion *—vi., vt.* to join tissue; obtain by extortion
gram´mar *n.* the structure of a language; rules for use of a language
grand *adj.* high in rank; imposing; luxurious; noble —**grandeur** *n.*
gran´dil´o·quent *adj.* spoken pretentiously
gran´di·ose *adj.* pompous
grant *n.* something given *—vt.* to give
gran´u·lar *adj.* grainy
gran´ule *n.* a small particle
graph´ic, graph´i·cal *adj.* explicit; described clearly; regarding anything written or pictorial
grap´ple *vi.* struggle *—vt.* to seize
grasp *n.* a firm hold; comprehension *—vt.* to take hold; comprehend
grasp´ing *adj.* greedy
grate *n.* a framework of metal bars *—vt., vi.* make a harsh sound; irritate; to shred
grate´ful *adj.* appreciative
grat´i·fy´ *vt.* to afford pleasure; to indulge —**grat´i·fi·ca´tion** *n.*
grat´i·tude´ *n.* appreciation
gra·tu´i·tous *adj.* given freely; without cause —**gra·tu´i·tous·ly** *adv.*
gra·tu´i·ty *n.* gift for services
grave *adj.* serious; somber *—n.* a place for burial
grav´el *n.* crushed rock
grav´i·tate´ *vi.* to be inclined or attracted towards —**grav·i·ta´tion** *n.*
grav´i·ty *n.* seriousness; attraction between celestial bodies
graze *vi., vt.* to feed on; touch lightly
grease *n.* melted animal fat; a lubricant *—vt.* to lubricate
great *adj.* large; extensive; important; skillful
greed *n.* excessive desire
greet *vt.* welcome; acknowledge
gre·gar´i·ous *adj.* sociable; tending to associate in groups
grid *n.* network of horizontal and vertical parallel lines, bars, etc.
grid´dle *n.* a flat iron pan
grief *n.* sadness, sorrow; a difficulty
griev´ance *n.* a wrong; a complaint
grieve *vt., vi.* to express grief
grim *adj.* stern; forbidding
grime *n.* dirt; filth —**grim´y** *adj.*
grin *n.* a broad smile *—vi.* to smile
grind *vt.* to crush; shape by rubbing
grip *n.* hold; device for grasping; small suitcase *—vi., vt.* hold
gripe *n.* complaint *—vi.* complain
gris´ly *adj.* horrible, ghastly
grit *n.* small, hard particles; determination or pluck *—vt.* to clench or grind the teeth —**grit´ty** *adj.*
groan *n.* a sound of distress; a moan *—vi.* make a low moaning sound
grog´gy *adj.* sluggish or dazed
grom´met *n.* reinforcement for a hole in cloth, etc.
groom *n.* a bridegroom; one who tends horses *—vt.* to make attractive; train for a purpose
groove *n.* a channel; a settled pattern *—vt.* cut a channel
grope *vi.* to feel around or search uncertainly *—vt.* to fondle
gross *adj.* coarse, unrefined; offensive; flagrant; total *—n.* a total; twelve dozen *—vi., vt.* earn in total
gro·tesque´ *adj.* bizarre; distorted; hideous —**gro·tesque´ly** *adv.*
grot´to *n.* a cavern
grouch *n.* one prone to complain; a discontented person *—vi.* to grumble or complain; to sulk
ground *n.* a surface; soil; an area set aside for a special use; a basis or foundation *—vt.* place on the surface; provide a basis
grounds *pl. n.* land around an estate
ground´less *adj.* without cause
group *n.* a number of persons or things *—vi., vt.* arrange together
group´ie *n.* an avid fan
grouse *n.* a game bird *—vi.* complain
grove *n.* a stand of trees
grov´el *vi.* to cower; to fawn over; to humble oneself
grow *vi.* come to be; to increase *—vt.* cultivate —**growth** *n.*
grown *adj.* mature; cultivated
grub´by *adj.* filthy; wretched
grudge *n.* ongoing resentment
gru´el·ing *adj.* extremely demanding; exhausting
grue´some *adj.* frightful; hideous; grotesque
gruff *adj.* brusque; surly
grum´ble *vi.* complain; rumble
grump´y *adj.* grouchy
grun´gy *adj.* filthy; shabby
guar´an·tee´ *n.* assurance; surety *—vt* assure —**guar´an·tor** *n.*
guard *n.* protection *—vt.* keep watch; to protect
guard´ed *adj.* protected; cautious
gu´ber·na·to´ri·al *adj.* relating to the office of governor
guess *n.* an estimate *—vi., vt.* to estimate; presume
guest *n.* a visitor; a visiting artist
guide *vt.* lead, direct —**guid´ance** *n.*
guild *n.* an association
guile *n.* craftiness, cunning
guilt *n.* liability —**guilt´y** *adj.*
guise *n.* appearance; pretense
gulch *n.* a ravine
gulf *n.* large inlet; a wide expanse
gul´li·ble *adj.* easily deceived —**gul·li·bil´i·ty** *n.* —**gul´li·bly** *adv.*
gul´ly *n.* a small ravine
gump´tion *n.* initiative; nerve
gu´ru *n.* a spiritual advisor
gush *n.* a strong flow *—vi.* to surge; be overly enthused —**gush´y** *adj.*
gust *n.* sudden burst or rush
gus´ta·to´ry *adj.* pertaining to the sense of taste
gus´to *n.* enthusiasm, ardor
gut´tur·al *adj.* harsh or throaty
guz´zle *vi., vt.* drink greedily
gyp *n.* a swindle or swindler *—vi., vt.* to swindle or cheat
gy´rate´ *vi.* revolve in a circle
h, H eighth letter of the alphabet
hab´er·dash·er *n.* (*Brit.*) seller of sewing needs; one who sells men's clothing —**hab´er·dash·er·y** *n.*
hab´it *n.* customary behavior; addiction; a manner of dress
hab´i·tat *n.* native environment
hab·i·ta´tion *n.* a dwelling
ha·bit´u·é *n.* a habitual visitor
hack´neyed *adj.* commonplace; trite
hag *n.* ugly old woman; a witch
hag´gard *adj.* drawn or gaunt
hag´gle *vi.* bargain
hail *n.* frozen rain; a greeting; a barrage *—vi.* fall as frozen rain *—vt.* greet with cheers; call out
hair grip (*Brit.*) a metal hair pin
hair slide (*Brit.*) a small appliance for keeping hair in place
hal´cy·on *adj.* tranquil
hale *adj.* healthy
half *adj.* partial *—adv.* partly *—n.* one of two equal parts
half´heart´ed *adj.* lacking enthusiasm —**half´heart´ed·ly** *adv.*
hal´i·to´sis *n.* stale breath
hall *n.* a large room; passageway
hall´mark *n.* a mark of quality; a distinctive feature
hal´low *vt.* regard as holy
hal·lu´ci·nate *vi., vt.* see that which is not real; fantasize —**hal·lu´ci·na·to·ry** *adj.*
hal·lu´ci·no·gen *n.* a substance that causes one to hallucinate
halt *n.* a stop *—vi.* stop; hesitate or be uncertain *—vt.* cause to stop
halve *vt.* divide; to reduce by half
ham´let *n.* a small village
ham´per *n.* a large basket *—vt.* prevent from moving freely
hand *n.* part of the body at the end of the arm *—vt.* provide
hand´book *n.* a manual
hand´ful *n.* a small amount; that difficult to manage
hand´i·cap´ *n.* a hindrance *—vt* to hinder
hand´i·work´ *n.* that done by one's own efforts
han´dle *n.* part designed for gripping *—vt.* to touch, hold, etc.; manage or deal with; to trade in
hand´out *n.* a gift; a promotional flyer
hand´pick´ *vt.* choose with care
hand´some *adj* attractive; impressive
hand–to–mouth *adj.* barely subsisting
hand´y *adj.* easily accessible; useful; skillful —**hand´i·ly** *adv.*
hang *vi., vt.* suspend
hang´ing *adj.* suspended *—n.* a decorative device
hang–up *n.* difficulty or inhibition

hap´haz´ard *adj.* random —*adv.* by chance
hap´less *adj.* unlucky
hap´pen *vi.* occur
hap´pen·ing *n.* important event
hap´py *adj.* fortunate; pleased
ha·rangue´ *n.* a bombastic lecture —*vi., vt.* to lecture harshly
har´ass *vt.* to pester or worry
har´bin·ger *n.* precursor —*vt.* herald
har´bor *n.* a refuge —*vt.* provide shelter; entertain or cling to
hard *adj.* inflexible; intense; unyielding; difficult —*adv.* with difficulty; diligently; with force
hard–bitten *adj.* tough
hard´en *vi., vt.* make tougher
hard´head´ed *adj.* practical; obstinate
hard´ly *adv.* barely; probably not
hard´–nosed´ *adj.* stubborn; practical
hard´ship *n.* difficulty
har´dy *adj.* strong; resolute
harm *n.* damage —*vt.* cause damage
harm´less *adj.* unlikely to cause damage or distress
har´mo·ny *n.* agreement; a pleasing combination —**har´mo´ni·ous** *adj.*
har´row·ing *adj.* distressing
har´ry *vt.* to raid or harass
harsh *adj.* disagreeably coarse or rough; stern —**harsh´ly** *adv.*
har´vest *n.* a season's crop; gathering a crop; time for gathering; outcome of an action —*vi., vt.* get as the result of effort
has´–been *n.* one no longer famous, productive, etc.
has´sle *n.* a quarrel; difficulty —*vi.* to quarrel —*vt.* to annoy
haste *n.* quickness; fast action
has´ten *vi.* be quick; accelerate
hast´y *adj.* overly quick; done in a hurry; impetuous —**hast´i·ly** *adv.*
hate *n.* intense dislike —*vi., vt.* dislike intensely —**ha´tred** *n.*
haugh´ty *adj.* proud, arrogant; contemptuous of others
haul *n.* pulling or carrying; that carried; distance traveled —*vi., vt.* to pull or carry
haunt *n.* place often visited —*vt.* visit often; pervade
have *vt.* possess; gain; control
ha´ven *n.* a shelter; a refuge
hav´oc *n.* chaos; destruction
haz´ard *n.* uncertainty, danger —*vt.* endanger; venture
haze *n.* light mist; vagueness —**haz´i·ness** *n.* —**haz´y** *adj.*
head *n.* body part with organs for sight, smell, taste, hearing, and feeding; intellect; foremost part; a leader —*vt.* lead or direct
head´ing *n.* forming a head; direction of motion
head´long *adj.* uncontrollable; reckless —*adv.* recklessly
head´–on´ *adj.* direct —*adv.* directly
heal *vi., vt.* make healthy
health *n.* soundness of body or mind
heap *n.* an accumulation; a mound; large amount —*vt.* to amass; give in large amounts
hear *vi., vt.* sense sound; be informed; heed; consider formally
hear´say *n.* rumor
heart *n.* body organ that pumps blood; essence or core
heart´en *vt.* encourage
heart´felt *adj.* sincere
heart´less *adj.* insensitive
heart´rend·ing *adj.* distressing
heart´y *adj.* enthusiastic; robust; unreserved —**heart´i·ness** *n.*
heat *n.* warmth; warming —*vi., vt.* become hot; become aroused
heat´ed *adj.* intense
heav´y *adj.* weighty; over–weight; serious or intense; greater than normal —**heav´i·ness** *n.*
heav´y–hand´ed *adj.* tactless
heav´y–heart´ed *adj.* sad
heck´le *vt.* to taunt —**heck´ler** *n.*
hec´tic *adj.* frenzied
hedge *n.* a boundary of bushes —*vi.* be evasive; make compensating investments to lessen risk —*vt.* set a border of bushes; to surround with restrictions; lessen a risk
heed *n.* close attention —*vi., vt.* to pay attention
heft´y *adj.* large; weighty
height *n.* an extreme; elevation; distance from bottom to top
height´en *vi., vt.* to become or make higher or more intense
hein´ous *adj.* atrocious
help *n.* aid; a remedy; employees —*vi., vt.* assist; remedy or improve —**help´ful** *adj.* —**help´ful·ly** *adv.*
help´less *adj.* powerless; incapable of aiding —**help´less·ly** *adv.*
hence *adv.* from now; therefore
hence´forth´ *adv.* from now on
her´ald *n.* a harbinger —*vt.* to foretell or publicize
her´biv·ore *n.* an animal that feeds on plants —**her·biv´o·rous** *adj.*
herd *n.* a large group —*vi., vt.* gather or move; tend a group of animals
he·red´i·tar·y *adj.* inherited
he·red´i·ty *n.* inherited
her´e·sy *n.* rejection of an accepted concept or belief
her´e·tic *n.* one who rejects an established belief —**he·ret´i·cal** *adj.*
her´it·age *n.* that inherited; culture, tradition, etc. that is handed down
her´mit *n.* a recluse
he´ro *n.* one noted for courage, greatness, etc.; central figure in a story —**he·ro´ic**, **he·ro´i·cal** *adj.*
hes´i·tant *adj.* uncertain, doubtful
hes´i·tate´ *vi.* to pause or waver; be uncertain —**hes´i·ta´tion** *n.*
hes´si·an *n.* (*Brit.*) a coarse cloth
hew *vt.* to chop or hack
hex (*US*) *n.* spell —*vt.* cast a spell
hi·a´tus *n.* a break in continuity; an interruption
hic´cup, **hic´cough** *n.* an involuntary closing of the respiratory tract
hid´den *adj.* concealed; secret
hide *vi., vt.* to conceal
hide´bound *adj.* opinionated
hid´e·ous *adj.* repulsive; terrifying
high *adj.* elevated; prominent; greater than normal
high´er–up *n.* one superior
high´hand·ed *adj.* haughty
high´–spir·it·ed *adj.* lively
high´–strung´ *adj.* nervous
high´way (*US*) *n.* a main road
hi´jack *vt.* take by force
hike *n.* long walk; a rise in prices —*vi.* to walk —*vt.* raise; pull up
hi·lar´i·ous *adj.* very funny
hill *n.* high ground; a pile or mound
hill´ock *n.* a small hill
hin´der *vi., vt.* delay or obstruct
hin´drance *n.* an obstacle
hinge *n.* a flexible joint —*vi. vt.* make contingent on something else
hint *n.* a slight indication —*vi., vt.* to intimate
hire *vt.* to employ for payment
hir´sute *adj.* hairy
his·tor´ic, **his·tor´i·cal** *adj.* relating to the past; notable
his´to·ry *n.* account of the past
hit *n.* a blow; a success —*vi., vt.* to strike; to discover
hoard *n.* a hidden supply —*vt.* obtain and store in reserve
hoarse *adj.* harsh sounding
hoar´y *adj.* grayish–white; old
hoax *n.* a deception
hob´by *n.* a favored pastime
hob´nob *vi.* to socialize
ho´bo (*US*) *n.* a vagrant
hod *n.* a V–shaped trough for hauling bricks or mortar; a coal scuttle
hoist *n.* act of lifting; device for raising loads —*vt.* lift or pull up
ho´kum *n.* nonsense
hold *n.* act of grasping; an influence or controlling force —*vi., vt.* to grasp; to sustain; contain
hole *n.* an opening; a hollow; a crude or squalid shelter
hol´i·day´ *adj.* festive —*n.* a day of rest, commemoration, etc.
hol´ler *n.* a yell —*vi., vt.* call out
hol´low *adj.* empty inside; sunken or indented —*n.* a recess —*vi., vt.* become or make hollow
hol´o·caust´ *n.* great destruction
hom´age *n.* a profession of fealty or loyalty; worship
home *n.* where one lives; one's native state, country, or land —*adj.* relating to residence or origin —*adv.* at or in the direction of home
home´ly *adj.* plain; unpretentious
home´stead´ *n.* buildings and land that constitute a home
home´y *adj.* simple; comfortable
hom´i·cide *n.* killing; one who kills —**hom´i·ci´dal** *adj.*
hom·i·let´ics *n.* art of sermonizing
hom´i·ly *n.* a sermon or lecture
hom´i·ny *n.* hulled and dried corn
ho·mo·ge´ne·ous *adj.* of a similar kind or type; uniform throughout
ho·mog´e·nize *vt.* make homogeneous; to disperse evenly throughout
ho·mol´o·gous *adj.* corresponding or similar in many aspects
hom´o·nym *n.* word that sounds like another but differs in meaning
Ho´mo sa´pi·ens *n.* human race
ho´mo·sex´u·al *n.* one attracted to persons of the same sex
hone *vt.* to sharpen —*n.* a stone for sharpening
hon´est *adj.* free of deceit; marked by integrity; respectable; trustworthy; fair —**hon´es·ty** *n.*
hon´ey *n.* a thick, sweet liquid —*vt.* to sweeten with honey
hon´ey·comb *n.* network of cells —*vt.* permeate with small holes
hon´ey·moon *n.* a wedding trip; a brief period of accord
honk *n.* the call of a wild goose; any similar sound —*vi., vt.*
hon´or *n.* great respect; special recognition; reputation; exalted rank —*vt.* esteem or respect; afford special recognition; to recognize as a due debt —**hon´or·a·ble** *adj.*
hon·o·rar´i·um *n.* fee paid a speaker
hon´or·ar·y *adj.* conferred without duties or pay
hon·or·if´ic *adj.* that which shows respect —*n.* an honorary title
hon´our (*Brit.*) *n.* great respect; special recognition; reputation; an exalted rank —*vt.* esteem or respect; afford special recognition; recognize as a due debt
hood *n.* a covering; a hoodlum —*vt.* cover with a hood
hood´lum *n.* a rowdy; a gangster
hood´wink *vt.* to deceive
hoof *n.* horny covering of the feet of certain mammals —*vi., vt.* to walk or dance
hoof´er *n.* one who dances
hook *n.* a connector; a fishhook; means to attract or snare —*vt.* catch, connect, suspend; steal
hoo´li·gan *n.* a hoodlum
hoop *n.* a band of metal or wood; anything similar —*vt.* secure with a band
hoot´e·nan´y *n.* an informal gathering of folk musicians
hop *vi.* jump on one foot; move quickly —*n.* a short distance; a quick trip
hope *vi.* to desire or anticipate —*n.* confident expectation
hop´per *n.* a container emptied through the bottom; one that hops
horde *n.* a great crowd; a throng
ho·ri´zon *n.* convergence of earth and sky; extent of one's interest
hor´i·zon´tal *adj.* level with or parallel to the horizon
hor´mone *n.* a substance produced in the body to regulate activity
horn *n.* projection from the head of an animal; the coating of an animal horn; something the shape of a horn; a brass wind instrument
hor´net *n.* a type of wasp
ho·rol´o·gy *n.* the study of time; the art of creating timepieces
hor´o·scope *n.* aspect of heavens used to foretell the future
hor·ren´dous *adj.* dreadful
hor´ri·ble *adj.* inspiring horror; dreadful
hor´rid *adj.* hideous; shocking
hor´ri·fy´ *vt.* overwhelm with terror
hor´ror *n.* great revulsion or fear
hors d´oeu·vre *pl. n.* appetizers
horse *n.* hoofed mammal; a carpenter's frame; cavalry —*adj.* of a horse —*vt.* provide with a horse

horse´play *n.* rough boisterous play
horse´pow·er *n.* a unit of power
hor´ta·to·ry *adj.* expressing encouragement
hor´ti·cul´ture *n.* the science of cultivating plants
hose *n.* socks or stockings; a flexible pipe —*vt.* wet with a hose; deceive
ho´sier·y *n.* socks and stockings
hos´pice *n.* a lodging or shelter
hos´pi·ta·ble *adj.* cordial, helpful, or generous; suitable for habitation
hos´pi·tal *n.* location for care of the sick and injured
host *n.* one who receives guests; a master of ceremonies; a throng; an organism on which another lives
hos´tage *n.* one held as security
hos´tel *n.* lodging for hikers
host´ess *n.* a female host; a greeter at a restaurant or club
hos´tile *adj.* feeling ill will; threatening; antagonistic; detrimental to health or well–being —*n.* an enemy
hot *adj.* of high temperature; burning to taste or touch; marked by passion; angry —*adv.* in a hot manner —**hot´ly** *adv.*
hot´–blood´ed *adj.* passionate
hot´dog´ *n.* a frankfurter served on a roll; a daredevil or showoff
ho·tel´ *n.* an establishment offering lodging and meals
hot´house *n.* a greenhouse with controlled heat and humidity
hot´line *n.* a direct channel of communication
hot´–rod´ *n.* a car modified to increase acceleration or speed
hound *n.* a dog used in hunting; one diligent in pursuit —*vt.* to badger
hour *n.* sixty minutes; set time for an activity; a significant time —**hour´ly** *adv.*
house *n.* a dwelling or shelter; family or lineage; a business establishment; branch of the legislature —*vt.* provide living space; to shelter
house´hold *n.* all those sharing a dwelling —*adj.* pertaining to or used in a dwelling; commonplace
hov´el *n.* a wretched dwelling
hov´er *vi.* to remain over, in, or near
how *adv.* in what manner; by what means; to what extent
how·ev´er *adv.* by whatever means
howl *n.* a plaintive wail; something funny —*vi., vt.* utter a wail
hoy´den *n.* boisterous woman
hub *n.* center of a wheel; a center of interest or activity
hub´bub´ *n.* uproar, bustle
hub´cap´ *n.* covering for a hub
huck´ster *n.* a pitchman; one who promotes with overblown claims
hud´dle *vi., vt.* to crowd together; to crouch —*n.* a dense crowd; a quick, informal meeting
hue *n.* a gradation of color; a tint
huff *vi.* be indignant or offended —*n.* a feeling of anger or annoyance
huff´y *adj.* easily offended
hug *vt.* embrace; keep close to; hold fast —*n.* an embrace
huge *adj.* exceedingly large; of great extent
hulk *n.* old unwieldy or unseaworthy ship; abondoned hull; anything bulky or unwieldy
hull *n.* a husk: the outer covering of a seed or fruit; body of a ship —*vt.* remove the husk from
hum *vi., vt.* make a low, droning sound; sing without words —*n.* a low, droning sound
hu´man *adj.* having form or characteristics of a human being; of human attributes —*n.* a human being —**hu´man·ly** *adv.*
hu·mane´ *adj.* marked by compassion; pertaining to human values
hu·man´i·tar´i·an *n.* one concerned with the welfare of others
hu·man´i·ty *n.* the human race; the quality of being human or humane
hu´man·ize *vt., vi.* to make or become human or humane
hum´ble *adj.* meek; submissive; unpretentious —*vt.* to humiliate; to abase
hu´mid *adj.* moist or damp
hu·mid´i·fi·er *n.* a device for adding moisture to the air
hu·mid´i·ty *n.* dampness; a measure of moisture in the air
hu´mi·dor *n.* a tobacco container
hu·mil´i·ate´ *vt.* embarrass or shame —**hu·mil·i·a´tion** *n.*
hu·mil´i·ty *n.* humbleness; modesty
hum´ming·bird´ *n.* a tiny bird noted for the ability to hover and dart
hu´mor (*US*) *n.* an amusing quality; that intended to incite laughter; one's disposition —*vt.* to indulge
hu´mor·ist *n.* one who specializes in relating amusing stories
hu´mor·ous *adj.* expressing humor; amusing —**hu´mor·ous·ly** *adv.*
hu´mour (*Brit.*) *n.* an amusing quality; that intended to incite laughter; one's disposition —*vt.* indulge
hu´mus *n.* organic matter in soil
hun´ger *n.* desire or craving —*vi.* a strong desire —**hun´gry** *adj.*
hunk *n.* a large piece
hunt *vi., vt.* seek or search —*n.* the seeking of wild game; a hunting expedition; a diligent search
hur´dle *n.* a barrier or obstacle —*vt., vi.* surmount an obstacle
hurl *vt.* throw violently; utter vehemently; to vomit
hur´ri·cane *n.* a violent storm
hur´ry *vi., vt.* move with haste —*n.* haste
hurt *vt.* to injure; impair or lessen —*n.* something that causes suffering —**hurt´ful** *adj.* —**hurt´ful·ly** *adv.*
hur´tle *vt., vi.* throw; move violently
hus´band *n.* a married man —*vt.* to conserve or use economically
hus´band·ry *n.* study of agriculture or livestock breeding; careful management
husk *n.* outer covering of seeds, fruits, or vegetables —*vt.* remove the covering from
husk´y *adj.* voice with a hoarse or rough quality; sturdily built
hus´sy *n.* a saucy female
hus´tle *vi., vt.* move energetically; convince by dubious means
hut *n.* a crude dwelling
hy´brid *n.* a combination of dissimilar species or elements —*adj.* pertaining to a hybrid
hy´dra *n.* a freshwater polyp; persistent evil
hy´drant *n.* outlet from a water main
hy´drate *n.* a compound of water and other molecules or atoms —*vt.*
hy´drau´lic *adj.* operated by fluid
hy´drau´lics *n.* science of the dynamics of fluid in motion
hy´dro·e·lec´tric *adj.* of electricity generated by water power
hy´dro·foil *n.* structure that holds a boat out of water when in motion; a boat equipped with hydrofoils
hy´dro·gen *n.* a flammable gas, lightest of all the elements
hydrogen bomb a powerful explosive device
hy·drom´e·ter *n.* a device to measure the specific gravity of a liquid
hy´dro·plane *n.* seaplane; a boat that skims the surface; a hydrofoil —*vt.* skim atop water
hy·dro·pon´ics *n.* the cultivation of plants without soil
hy·e´na *n.* a scavenging carnivorous mammal of Africa and Asia
hy´giene *n.* practice that serves to promote health
hymn *n.* a song of praise
hym´nal *n.* a book of hymns
hy·per´bo·la *n.* a geometric curve
hy·per´bo·le *n.* a figure of speech using exaggeration for emphasis
hy·per·bol´ic *adj.* shaped like a hyperbola; containing hyperbole
hy·per·crit´i·cal *adj.* exacting
hy·per·sen´si·tive *adj.* excessively tense or delicate
hy´per·son´ic *adj.* capable of moving at several times the speed of sound
hy´per·ten´sion *n.* high blood pressure
hy·per·thy´roid·ism *n.* a disorder caused by an overly active thyroid
hy´phen *n* punctuation mark (-)
hyp·no´sis *n.* a sleep–like state
hyp·not´ic *adj.* of hypnosis; spellbinding
hyp´no·tism *n.* the act of inducing hypnosis —**hyp´no·tize´** *vt.*
hy·po·chon´dri·a *n.* excessive anxiety about one's health
hy·poc´ri·sy *n.* pretending to a belief —**hyp´o·crite** *n.*
hy´po·der´mic *adj.* of tissue or injection beneath the skin —*n.* an injection, needle, or syringe
hy´po·ten´sion *n.* low blood pressure
hy·pot´e·nuse´ *n.* side opposite the right angle of a right triangle
hy´poth´e·sis *n., pl.* **hy´poth´e·ses** a theory put forth for testing
hys·ter·ec´to·my *n.* surgical excision of the uterus
hys·te´ri·a *n.* uncontrollable emotion; neurosis marked by physical ailment without apparent cause
hys·ter´ic, hys·ter´ic·al *adj.* characterized by hysteria
hys·ter´ics *n.* attack of hysteria
i, I ninth letter of the alphabet; Roman symbol for one
ice *n.* frozen water; a dessert of shaved ice and flavoring —*vt.* to cool with ice; decorate a cake
ice´berg´ *n.* mound of floating ice
ice´box *n.* a refrigerator; an insulated cabinet to cool food
ice´cap *n.* ice covering a tract of land
ice sheet *n.* a continental glacier
ich·thy·ol´o·gy *n.* study of fishes
i´ci·cle *n.* a hanging taper of ice
i´ci·ly *adv.* in a cold or haughty manner
ic´ing *n.* mixture to decorate a cake
i´con *n.* an image; a sacred picture; one revered; computer image representing a command
i´con´o·clast *n.* a destroyer of sacred images or traditional institutions
i´cy *adj.* covered with ice; cold or slippery; cold and unfriendly
id *n.* the subconscious concerned with primitive impulses
i·de´a *n.* a mental image; a scheme; concept or opinion
i·de´al *adj.* perfect or excellent; typical; existing in theory —*n.* a model for perfection —**i·de´al·ly** *adv.*
i·de´al·ism *n.* seeking the best in everything; belief that all is good
i·de´al·ist *n.* a visionary; one inspired by that which is ideal
i·de´al·ize´ *vt.* envision as ideal
i·den´ti·cal *adj.* alike in every way
i·den´ti·fi·ca´tion *n.* recognition or classification; credentials
i·den´ti·fy *vt.* establish identity —*vi.* establish unity with certain others
i·den´ti·ty *n.* that by which a person or thing is recognized or defined
id´e·ol´o·gy *n.* set of beliefs or doctrines —**i·de·ol´o·gist** *n.*
id´i·o·cy *n.* folly; mental retardation
id´i·om *n.* usage peculiar to a language or region
id·i·o·syn´cra·sy *n.* characteristic peculiar to a person or group
id´i·ot *n.* one foolish or stupid
id·i·ot´ic *adj.* foolish or stupid
i´dle *adj.* not busy or in use —*vt.* waste time —**i´dly** *adv.*
i´dol *n.* an image; an object of worship; one revered or adored
i´dol´a·try *n.* the worship of idols; excessive devotion —**i·dol´a·ter** *n.*
i´dol·ize´ *vt.* subject to devotion
i´dyl, i´dyll *n.* a short work depicting the pastoral or romantic
if *conj.* on condition that; whether or not —*n.* a supposition or condition
ig´ne·ous *adj.* pertaining to fire; formed by fire
ig´nite´ *vt.* to set afire; to arouse passion —*vi.* to burn

ig·ni´tion *n.* setting or being set on fire; a system for igniting the fuel in an internal–combustion engine
ig·no´ble *adj.* base; vulgar; of low birth
ig´no·min·y *n.* disgrace; shame
ig´no·ra´mus *n.* ignorant person
ig´no·rance *n.* lack of knowledge; being uninformed
ig´no·rant *adj.* lacking knowledge; uninformed
ig·nore´ *vt.* to disregard
ilk *n.* type or kind
ill *adj.* sick; harmful; hostile —*n.* harmful; a cause of suffering
ill–ad·vised´ *adj.* unwise; evidencing lack of careful thought
ill´–bred´ *adj.* crude; impolite
il·le´gal *adj.* prohibited by law —*n.* one who enters the country illegally —**il´le·gal´i·ty** *n.*
il·leg´i·ble *adj.* impossible to decipher; unreadable
il·le·git´i·mate *adj.* contrary to law; illegal; born out of wedlock
ill´–fat´ed *adj.* likely to end badly
ill´–got´ten *adj.* obtained dishonestly
il·lib´er·al *adj.* selfish; bigoted; vulgar, ill–bred
il·lic´it *adj.* unlawful; prohibited
il·lit´er·a·cy *n.* the state of being unable to read or write
il·lit´er·ate *adj.* lacking education; lacking comprehension —*n.* one unable to read and write
ill´ness *n.* sickness or disease
il·log´i·cal *adj.* contrary to reason; unreasonable
ill´–tem´pered *adj.* querulous; irritable —**ill´–tem´pered·ly** *adv.*
il·lum´i·nate, il·lu´mine *vi., vt.* light or make brighter; to clarify; to decorate a printed page
il·lu·mi·na´tion *n.* lighting; clarification or instruction
il·lu´sion *n.* an erroneous or deceptive impression
il·lu´so·ry *adj.* based on illusion; deceptive; not real
il´lus·trate *vt.* to clarify or explain; decorate with pictures
il·lus·tra´tion *n.* an example or explanation; a picture
il·lus´tra·tive *adj.* serving to illustrate or explain; symbolic
il·lus´tri·ous *adj.* distinguished; eminent
ill will malevolence; hostility
im´age *n.* likeness; thing closely resembling another; a concept
im´a·ge·ry *n.* a mental image; imaginative language
im·ag´i·na·ble *adj.* that can be imagined; conceivable; plausible
im·ag´i·na·ry *adj.* fanciful; theoretical; nonexistent
im·ag´i·na´tion *n.* creativity; the formation of mental images
im·ag´i·na·tive *adj.* inventive; creative —**im·ag´i·na·tive·ly** *adv.*
im·ag´ine *vi., vt.* picture in the mind
im·bal´ance *n.* unevenness
im·be·cil´ic *adj.* silly; foolish
im´be·cile *n.* foolish person; one lacking intellect —**im´be·cil´i·ty** *n.*
im·bibe´ *vt.* to drink
im·bro´glio *n.* an entanglement; confusion
im·bue´ *vt.* to permeate
im´i·tate *vt.* to copy in appearance or style; to mimic
im·i·ta´tion *n.* copy or likeness; a substitute of lesser quality
im´i·ta·tive *adj.* involving imitation; not original or genuine; deceptive
im·mac´u·late *adj.* absolutely pure or clean; without blemish
im´ma·nent *adj.* existing within; deep–seated —**im´ma·nence** *n.*
im·ma·te´ri·al *adj.* lacking importance or substance; insignificant
im·ma·ture´ *adj.* not ripe; not fully grown; childish: wanting of adult qualities
im·meas´ur·a·ble *adj.* boundless; incapable of being measured
im·me´diate *adj.* at this instant; near the present time; near at hand —**im·me´di·a·cy** *n.*
im·me·mo´ri·al *adj.* before memory or recorded history
im·mense´ *adj.* extremely large
im·merse´ *vt.* to submerge; become deeply involved; baptize by submersing in water
im´mi·grant *n.* one newly–arrived with intent to settle
im´mi·grate *vi.* enter a country with intent to settle
im·mi·gra´tion *n.* settlement in a new land
im´mi·nent *adj.* impending; about to occur
im·mo·bil´i·ty *n.* the state of being motionless or unable to move
im·mod´er·ate *adj.* excessive
im·mod´est *adj.* bold; egotistical; lacking modesty
im´mo·late *vt.* to sacrifice
im·mor´al *adj.* lacking virtue; counter to accepted morality
im·mo·ral´i·ty *n.* a lack of virtue; an immoral act
im·mor´tal *adj.* that cannot die; everlasting; enduring —*n.* a god; person worth remembering
im·mor·tal´i·ty *n.* living or being remembered forever
im·mov´a·ble *adj.* fixed in place; unable to be moved
im·mune´ *adj.* not affected; exempt
im·mu´ni·ty *n.* exemption from restriction; protection from disease
im´mu·nize *vt.* protect from disease
im·mu·nol´o·gy *n.* science dealing with the immune system
im·mure´ *vt.* to confine within a wall; to protect or imprison
im·mu´ta·ble *adj.* not subject to change
imp *n.* a small demon; a michievous child
im´pact *n.* a collision; force of collision; an effect —**im·pact´** *vt.* to strike with force; to pack firmly; to have effect on —**im·pact´ed** *adj.*
im·pair´ *vt.* cause to diminish, as in quantity or value
im·pale´ *vt.* thrust a sharp stake through; render helpless
im·pal´pa·ble *adj.* not perceived by touch; not easily grasped
im·pan´el *vt.* prepare a list for duty
im·part´ *vt.* to give or confer; convey knowledge
im·par´tial *adj.* not biased; without prejudice —**im·par´tial·ly** *adv.*
im·par´ti·al´i·ty *n.* objectivity; not partial or biased
im·pass´a·ble *adj.* unable to be travelled over or through
im´passe *n.* lacking room for compromise; a stalemate
im·pas´si·ble *adj.* apathetic; not easily aroused
im·pas´sioned *adj.* ardent; designed to arouse passion
im·pas´sive *adj.* insensible to pain; showing no emotion
im·pa´tience *n.* restlessness; intolerance
im·pa´tient *adj.* unable to wait; restless; anxious; intolerant
im·peach´ *vt.* charge with misconduct in office; attempt to discredit
im·pec´ca·ble *adj.* nattily attired; without flaw or imperfection
im·pe·cu´ni·ous *adj.* lacking means; penniless
im·pede´ *vt.* to slow the progress of; to obstruct
im·ped´i·ment *n.* an obstruction; that which prevents clear articulation; in law, an obstacle that bars the making of a legal contract
im·pel´ *vt.* to drive or urge forward; to spur to action
im·pend´ *vi.* about to happen; to approach and threaten
im·pen´e·tra·ble *adj.* unable to be penetrated; incomprehensible
im·pen´i·tent *adj.* without regret or remorse —**im·pen´i·tence** *n.*
im·per´a·tive *adj.* pressing; obligatory —*n.* an order or obligation
im·per·cep´ti·ble *adj.* that cannot be perceived —**im·per·cep´ti·bly** *adv.*
im·per´fect *adj.* deficient; flawed
im·per·fec´tion *n.* a flaw
im·pe´ri·al *adj.* of a ruler or empire; majestic; of great size
im·pe´ri·al·ism *n.* extending an empire by acquiring territory or establishing dominance
im·per´il *vt.* to endanger
im·pe´ri·ous *adj.* arrogant; overbearing —**im·pe´ri·ous·ly** *adv.*
im·per´ma·nent *adj.* not lasting; transient —**im·per´ma·nence** *n.*
im·per´me·a·ble *adj.* not subject to penetration by moisture
im·per´son·al *adj.* cold or indifferent
im·per´son·ate´ *vt.* to pretend to be another; to mimic for the purpose of entertaining
im·per´ti·nent *adj.* disrespectful, insolent —**im·per´ti·nence** *n.*
im·per·turb´a·ble *adj.* calm; not disposed to becoming agitated
im·per´vi·ous *adj.* impenetrable; not influenced by emotion
im·pet´u·ous *adj.* marked by sudden impulse or passion; spontaneous
im´pe·tus *n.* a stimulus; action caused by a stimulus; momentum
im·pinge´ *vi., vt.* to touch or encroach upon
im´pi·ous *adj.* lacking piety; blasphemous —**im´pi·ous·ly** *adv.*
im·pla´ca·ble *adj.* unable to be placated; unbending
im·plant´ *vt.* to establish or instill; to plant surgically —*n.* a thing inserted by surgery
im·plau´si·ble *adj.* not believable
im´ple·ment *n.* a tool or device —*vt.* to use or put into force
im´pli·cate´ *vt.* to incriminate; imply; to entangle or involve
im´pli·ca´tion *n.* something implied
im·plic´it *adj.* understood or implied; absolute —**im·plic´it·ly** *adv.*
im·plode´ *vt., vi.* to burst inward
im·plore´ *vt.* to beg or plead
im·ply´ *vt.* infer; signify indirectly
im·po·lite´ *adj.* rude; discourteous
im·pol´i·tic *adj.* imprudent; unwise
im·pon´der·a·ble *adj.* impossible to evaluate —**im·pon·der·a·bil´i·ty** *n.*
im·port´ *vt.* bring from another country; to transfer computer data —*vi.* be of significance —**im´port** *n.* a thing brought in; meaning or significance —**im´por·ta´tion** *n.*
im·port´ed *adj.* foreign; brought from elsewhere
im·por´tance *n.* significance; personal distinction or standing
im·por´tant *adj.* significant
im·por´tu·nate *adj.* persistently pleading; urgently requesting
im´por·tune´ *vi., vt.* to plead
im·pose´ *vt.* apply with authority; force on others; lay out a publication for printing —*vi.* to take advantage of
im·pos´ing *adj.* impressive by virtue of size or power
im´po·si´tion *n.* something burdensome or forced upon; advantage taken; layout of a publication
im·pos´si·bil´i·ty *n.* that which is unattainable or likely to end in failure
im·pos´si·ble *adj.* unattainable; not believable of existing; difficult to cope with —**im·pos·si·bil´i·ty** *n.*
im·pos´tor *n.* one who assumes a false identity
im·pos´ture *n.* deception using an assumed identity
im´po·tence *n.* weakness; inability to have sexual intercourse
im´po·tent *adj.* lacking strength or power; ineffective; unable to have sexual intercourse
im·pound´ *vt.* legally seize and hold
im·pov´er·ish *vt.* deprive of wealth
im·pov´er·ished *n.* devoid of wealth or resources; poverty–stricken
im·prac´ti·cal *adj.* not effective, prudent, or economical; unable to function efficiently
im´pre·cate´ *vt.* to call evil down upon; to curse —**im´pre·ca´tion** *n.*
im·preg´na·ble *adj.* impossible to take by assault; impossible to contest or challenge
im·preg´nate´ *vt.* to saturate; make pregnant

im·pre·sa´ri·o *n.* an organizer or manager of musical entertainment
im·press´ *vt.* find favor; attract notice; plant in the mind; to mark by pressure; to force into service
im·pres´sion *n.* an image in the mind; a vague notion; a mark made by pressure; a printed image; all of the copies of a publication printed at one time
im·pres´sion·a·ble *adj.* receptive to outside influence
im·pres´sion·ism *n.* a school of art that focuses on a hasty concept
im·pres´sive *adj.* stirring; tending to impress
im·pri·ma´tur *n.* approval; sanction
im´print *n.* a distinguishing mark —**im·print´** *vt.* to produce a mark on
im·pris´on *vt.* to confine
im·prob´a·ble *adj.* unlikely or doubtful —**im·prob·a·bil´i·ty** *n.*
im·promp´tu *adj.* spontaneous; unrehearsed —*adv.* extemporaneously
im·prop´er *adj.* unsuitable or inappropriate; not in compliance with common decency
im·prove´ *vt., vi.* make more useful
im·prove´ment *n.* an enhancement or addition; an enhanced condition
im·prov´i·dent *adj.* without due caution; rash
im´pro·vise´ *vt.* to perform without advance preparation; create from materials at hand
im·pru´dent *adj.* unwise
im´pu·dent *adj.* marked by audacity; impertinent; bold
im·pugn´ *vt.* challenge as false
im´pulse´ *n.* surge; sudden urge that leads to action; a stimulus
im·pul´sive *adj.* acting on a whim; characterized by rash action
im·pun´i·ty *n.* immunity or deliverance from punishment or loss
im·pure´ *adj.* contaminated; adulterated; lewd or obscene
im´pu·ta´tion *n.* an insinuation
im·pute´ *vt.* assign a quality
in´a·bil´i·ty *n.* lack of capability
in·ac·ces´si·ble *adj.* not approachable; remote; unattainable
in·ac´cu·ra·cy *n.* an error
in·ac´cu·rate *adj.* incorrect; not exact; misleading
in·ac´tion *n.* immobility or idleness
in·ac´tive *adj.* immobile or idle; not currently in use; retired from service —**in´ac·tiv´i·ty** *n.*
in·ad´e·qua·cy *n.* a weakness; ineptitude
in·ad´e·quate *adj.* not sufficient
in·ad·mis´si·ble *adj.* not allowed
in´ad·vert´ent *adj.* careless or thoughtless; not intentional
in·al´ien·a·ble *adj.* not allowing of change or transfer
in·am·o·ra´ta *n.* a woman one loves
in·ane´ *adj.* pointless; lacking substance; empty of meaning
in·an´i·mate *adj.* lacking spirit or energy
in·ap·pro´pri·ate *adj.* unsuitable
in·apt´ *adj.* inept; inappropriate
in·ar·tic´u·late *adj.* unable to express in words; unable to speak distinctly; incomprehensible
in·at·ten´tive *adj.* indifferent, preoccupied —**in·at·ten´tive·ly** *adv.*
in·au´gu·rate´ *vt.* bring into use with ceremony; cause to begin
in·au´gu·ra´tion *n.* a ceremony of installation or induction
in·aus·pi´cious *adj.* unfavorable
in´born *adj.* present at birth; innate
in´bred *adj.* inborn
in·cal´cu·la·ble *adj.* that cannot be calculated; unpredictable
in·can·des´cent *adj.* glowing from being heated; shining brilliantly
in·can·ta´tion *n.* chant to invoke magic; a ritual supplication
in·ca´pa·ble *adj.* lacking qualification or competence
in·ca·pac´i·tate´ *vt.* deprive of potential; to invalidate or disqualify
in·ca·pac´i·ty *n.* a lack of ability; something that disqualifies
in·car´cer·ate´ *vt.* to imprison; to confine —**in·car´cer·a´tion** *n.*
in·car´nate *adj.* manifest in human form; personified —*vt.* to manifest or personify —**in´car·na´tion** *n.*
in·cen´di·ar´y *adj.* causing fire; inclined to inflame emotions —*n.* that causing fire; one who sets fire; one who incites rebellion
in´cense *n.* substance that creates a pleasing aroma —**in·cense´** *vt.* excite to anger
in·cen´tive *n.* something that encourages or inspires; the prospect of penalty or reward
in·cep´tion *n.* a beginning
in·ces´sant *adj.* continuous; without interruption —**in·ces´sant·ly** *adv.*
in´cest *n.* sexual intercourse between closely related persons
in´ci·dence *n.* the act of occurring; rate of occurrence
in´ci·dent *n.* a single event; a relatively minor occurrence
in·ci·den´tal *adj.* accidental, unplanned —*n.* minor expense
in·cin´er·ate´ *vi., vt.* to burn entirely
in·cip´i·ent *adj.* starting to come into being —**in·cip´i·ence** *n.*
in·cise´ *vt.* cut into; engrave
in·ci´sion *n.* a cut; surgical scar
in·ci´sive *adj.* keen or sharp
in·ci´sor *n.* a front cutting tooth
in·cite´ *vt.* provoke to action; to instigate
in·clem´ent *adj.* stormy; cruel or merciless
in·cli·na´tion *n.* a disposition or preference; an inclined surface
in·cline´ *vi.* slope or lean; tend toward; show a preference; deviate —*n.* a slope
in·clined´ *adj.* sloping or leaning; tending toward as a preference
in·clude´ *vt.* take in, embrace, or contain —**in·clu´sion** *n.*
in·clu´sive *adj.* incorporating most or all; including all in the range specified —**in·clu´sive·ness** *n.*
in·cog·ni´to *adj., adv.* with identity hidden or obscured
in·co·her´ence *n.* lack of order; the inability to communicate clearly
in·co·her´ent *adj.* lacking order or agreement; disjointed; unable to communicate in a distinct or organized manner; inarticulate
in´come *n.* a thing received in exchange for labor; earnings
in´com·ing *adj.* coming in; about to come in
in·com·men´su·ra·ble *adj.* not to be measured or compared
in·com·men´su·rate *adj.* disproportionate; inadequate
in·com·mo´dious *adj.* inconvenient or uncomfortable
in·com´pa·ra·ble *adj.* exceptional; beyond comparing
in·com·pat´i·bil´i·ty *n.* the inability to exist harmoniously
in·com·pat´i·ble *adj.* unsuited; contradictory; mutually exclusive; irreconcilable; mutually repelling; incongruous
in·com´pe·tence *n.* lack of ability
in·com´pe·tent *adj.* inadequate or unsuited; not mentally qualified —*n.* one unable to function in certain circumstances
in·com·plete´ *adj.* not finished; missing a part; failure to complete requirements of a course of study
in·com·pre·hen´si·ble *adj.* difficult to understand or accept
in·con·ceiv´a·ble *adj.* impossible to grasp or accept; highly improbable
in·con·gru´i·ty *n.* inconsistency; something inconsistent
in·con´gru·ous *adj.* inappropriate or incompatible; inconsistent
in·con·se·quen´tial *adj.* of little importance
in·con·sid´er·a·ble *adj.* trivial
in·con·sid´er·ate *adj.* thoughtless of others; insensitive; lacking consideration —**in·con·sid´er·ate·ly** *adv.*
in·con·sist´en·cy *n.* discrepancy
in·con·sis´tent *adj.* lacking agreement; not logical; erratic; unpredictable —**in·con·sis´tent·ly** *adv.*
in·con·spic´u·ous *adj.* not easily seen; hardly noticeable
in·con´stant *adj.* fickle —**in·con´stan·cy** *n.* —**in·con´stant·ly** *adv.*
in·con·test´a·ble *adj.* unquestionable —**in·con·test´a·bly** *adv.*
in·con´ti·nent *adj.* lacking self–control —**in·con´ti·nence** *n.*
in·con·tro·vert´i·ble *adj.* not subject to question; unable to deny or disprove —**in·con·tro·vert´i·bly** *adv.*
in·con·ven´ience *n.* not convenient; a source of bother —*vt.* to cause difficulty or annoyance
in·con·ven´ient *adj.* unsuited to comfort or needs; difficult to use; poorly timed
in·cor´po·rate *vi., vt.* become united or combined; (*US*) form a legal corporation
in·cor·po·ra´tion *n.* thing added; (*US*) legally incorporating
in·cor·po´re·al *adj.* lacking physical form; spiritual
in·cor·rect´ *adj.* inaccurate; unsuitable or improper
in·cor´ri·gi·ble *adj.* incapable of reform; difficult to control or restrain —*n.* one who cannot be changed or reformed
in·crease´ *vt., vi.* become more or larger —**in´crease** *n.* amount or rate of augmentation
in·cred´i·ble *adj.* so unlikely as to cause disbelief; amazing; startling
in·cred´u·lous *adj.* not inclined to believe; showing disbelief
in´cre·ment *n.* steady growth; an addition; slight increase; one of a series —**in·cre·men´tal** *adj.*
in·crim´i·nate *vt.* accuse of involvement; implicate by inference
in´cu·bate *vt.* provide environment for growth and development; hatch —*vi.* develop and hatch —**in·cu·ba´tion** *n.*
in´cu·ba·tor *n.* a controlled environment, as for life support
in´cu·bus *n.* a nightmare; a male demon
in·cul´cate *vt.* teach by repeated instruction —**in´cul·ca´tion** *n.*
in·cul´pate *vt.* incriminate —**in´cul·pa´tion** *n.*
in·cum´bent *adj.* obligatory; resting on something else; in office —*n.* one who holds office
in·cur´ *vt.* become liable for
in·cur´a·ble *adj.* incapable of being remedied —**in·cur´a·bly** *adv.*
in·cur´sion *n.* entering into another's territory; an invasion
in·debt´ed *adj.* obligated
in·dec´ent *adj.* contrary to good taste —**in·dec´ent·ly** *adv.*
in·de´cen·cy *n.* immodesty, lewdness
in·de·ci´sion *n.* inability to decide
in·de·ci´sive *adj.* prone to doubt; inconclusive
in·de·fat´i·ga·ble *adj.* tireless
in·de·fen´si·ble *adj.* unable to be defended —**in·de·fen·si·bil´i·ty** *n.*
in·def´i·nite *adj.* lacking precise limits; uncertain; vague
in·del´i·ble *adj.* impossible to remove; unable to forget
in·dem´ni·fy *vt.* compensate
in·dem´ni·ty *n.* protection from loss or injury
in·den´ture *n.* a contract; a legal binding of servant to master
in·de·pend´ence *n.* autonomy; freedom
in·de·pend´ent *adj.* free from control; self–supporting
in–depth´ *adj.* detailed
in·de·struct´i·ble *adj.* permanent; unable to be destroyed
in·de·ter´mi·nate *adj.* not precisely fixed; indefinite
in´dex *n., pl.* **in´dex·es, in´di·ces** a list of contents; an indicator that characterizes data —*vt.* provide an index; to list, catalog, or otherwise arrange
in´di·cate *vt.* point out or signify; to comment briefly
in·di·ca´tion *n.* a hint or suggestion; something suggested as practical for treatment of an illness

in·dic´a·tive *adj.* serving to designate; characteristic
in´di·ca·tor *n.* that which serves to measure or quantify a value; (*Brit.*) a turn signal on a car
in·dict´ *vt.* charge with wrongdoing
in·dict´ment *n.* a formal accusation
in·dif´fer·ence *n.* unconcern or detachment; coldness, aloofness
in·dif´fer·ent *adj.* not involved; neutral or unconcerned; of little consequence or quality
in·dig´e·nous *adj.* native; natural; inherent —**in·dig´e·nous·ly** *adv.*
in´di·gence *n.* poverty
in´di·gent *adj.* impoverished —*n.* one poor or needy
in·di·gest´i·ble *adj.* impossible or difficult to digest
in·di·ges´tion *n.* discomfort caused by difficulty in digesting
in·dig´nant *adj.* angry over a wrong or injustice —**in·dig´nant·ly** *adv.*
in·dig·na´tion *n.* righteous anger
in·dig´ni·ty *n.* an affront; humiliation
in´di·go´ *n.* a blue dye
in·di·rect´ *adj.* roundabout; devious
in·dis·creet´ *adj.* tactless; imprudent; thoughtless
in·dis·crete´ *adj.* undivided; tightly bound; that can not be divided
in·dis·cre´tion *n.* tactlessness
in·dis·crim´i·nate *adj.* random; without order
in·dis·pen´sa·ble *adj.* essential; definitely needed
in·dis·posed´ *adj.* reluctant or unwilling to honor; ill or ailing
in·dis·put´a·ble *adj.* not to be denied; incontestable
in·dis·sol´u·ble *adj.* that cannot be destroyed; perpetually binding
in·dis·tinct´ *adj.* not clear; dim or faded; not easily understood
in·di·vid´u·al *adj.* of one only; by or for one; distinctive —*n.* a thing considered apart from its group; one marked by a special quality
in·di·vid·u·al´i·ty *n.* qualities that make one distinctive; uniqueness
in·doc´tri·nate *vt.* instruct in a doctrine or ideology; acquaint with new rules or policies
in·doc·tri·na´tion *n.* instruction or training
in´do·lent *adj.* habitually lazy; idle —**in´do·lence** *n.*
in·dom´i·ta·ble *adj.* unable to be subdued; unconquerable
in·du´bi·ta·ble *adj.* undeniable; too obvious to be doubted
in·duce´ *vt.* to persuade to action; to cause or bring about
in·duce´ment *n.* an incentive; something that persuades
in·duct´ *vt.* formally place in office; acquaint or instruct in
in·duc´tion *n.* entrance into office; reasoning that draws broad conclusions from specific facts
in·duc´tive *adj.* relating to logical induction —**in·duc´tive·ly** *adv.*
in·dulge´ *vt.* yield to desires —*vi.* gratify one's desires; take part
in·dul´gence *n.* an act of gratification; intemperance
in·dus´tri·al *adj.* of or relating to manufacturing and trade
in·dus´tri·al·ize *vt.* convert to economy based on industry; make into an industry
in·dus´tri·ous *adj.* dedicated to a task —**in·dus´tri·ous·ly** *adv.*
in´dus·try *n.* manufacture and trade in commercial goods; active dedication to a task
in·e´bri·ate *vt.* intoxicate; exhilarate —**in·e´bri·ate, in·e´bri·a·ted** *adj.* intoxicated; drunken
in·ef´fa·ble *adj.* indescribable; taboo —**in·ef´fa·bly** *adv.*
in·ef·fec´tive *adj.* not as intended effect; inadequate
in·ef·fec´tu·al *adj.* fruitless
in·ef·fi´cient *adj.* wasteful; incompetent —**in·ef·fi´cien·cy** *n.*
in·el´i·gi·ble *adj.* precluded by restrictions or lack of ability
in·ept´ *adj.* lacking ability; incompetent; clumsy —**in·ept´i·tude** *n.*
in·e·qual´i·ty *n.* a difference or disparity
in·eq´ui·ta·ble *adj.* unfair —**in·eq´ui·ta·bly** *adv.*
in·eq´ui·ty *n.* an injustice
in·ert´ *adj.* motionless; inactive; unable to move; lethargic
in·er´tia *n.* resistance to change; reluctance to move or act
in·ev´i·ta·ble *adj.* impossible to prevent; unavoidable; inescapable
in·ex´o·ra·ble *adj.* unyielding; implacable; not to be persuaded
in·ex·pe´ri·ence *n.* a lack of skill
in·ex·pe´ri·enced *adj.* lacking skill or knowledge
in·ex´pert *adj.* unskilled
in·ex´pi·a·ble *adj.* that may not be atoned for
in·ex´pli·ca·ble *adj.* impossible to explain or understand
in·ex·press´i·ble *adj.* that cannot be described —**in·ex·press´i·bly** *adv.*
in·ex´tri·ca·ble *adj.* that cannot be disentangled; impossible to resolve
in·fal´li·ble *adj.* incapable of failure or error —**in·fal´li·bil´i·ty** *n.*
in´fa·mous *adj.* having a very bad reputation; deserving of low regard
in´fa·my *n.* disgrace
in´fan·cy *n.* childhood; the early stages of development
in´fant *n.* a young child; a minor —*adj.* of a young or early state
in´fan·tile *adj.* relating to infancy; childlike
in´fan·try *n.* soldiers trained to fight on foot
in·fat´u·ate *vt.* provoke unreasoning affection; incite foolish behavior
in·fect´ *vt.* contaminate, corrupt
in·fec´tion *n.* invasion of the body by disease; an infectious disease
in·fec´tious *adj.* caused by infection; tending to spread
in·fer´ *vt.* presume from available evidence; insinuate or hint
in´fer·ence *n.* reaching a conclusion from information available
in·fe´ri·or *adj.* of a lesser quality or value; subordinate —*n.* one who is lower in rank or station
in·fe·ri·or´i·ty *n.* a state of low rank
in·fer´nal *adj.* fiendish
in·fer´no *n.* place of fiery heat
in·fest´ *vt.* to inhabit in overwhelming numbers
in·fi·del´i·ty *n.* sexual unfaithfulness; a lack of loyalty
in´fight·ing *n.* dissension between rivals in an organization
in´fil·trate *vt.* secretly enter; to permeate by a liquid
in´fi·nite *adj.* without limit
in´fin·i·tes´i·mal *adj.* minuscule; immeasureably small
in·fin´i·ty *n.* a limitless expanse, time, or quantity
in·firm´ *adj.* feeble or weak from old age or disease; irresolute
in·fir´ma·ry *n.* a small clinic or dispensary
in·fir´mi·ty *n.* ailment or weakness
in·flame´ *vi., vt.* become excited or aroused; to redden and swell; set on fire
in·flam´ma·ble *adj.* combustible; easily excited
in´flam·ma´tion *n.* redness or swelling from irritation or infection
in·flam´ma·to·ry *adj.* intended to arouse passion, violence, etc.; causing inflammation
in·flate´ *vt.* fill with air; to enlarge or expand —*vi.* to become enlarged or swelled —**in·fla´tion** *n.*
in·flect´ *vt.* modify in tone or pitch
in·flex´i·bil´i·ty *n.* unwillingness or inability to change
in·flex´i·ble *adj.* not easily bent or changed; inelastic; rigid
in·flict´ *vt.* to impose punishment or hardship
in´flu·ence *n.* power that effects; an effect shaped by control or persuasion —*vt.* effect by persuasion
in·flu·en´tial *adj.* having the power to influence
in·flu·en´za *n.* a contagious viral disease
in´flux *n.* a flowing in
in·form´ *vi., vt.* make known; provide information; reveal
in·for´mal *adj.* casual; unofficial
in´for·mal´ity *n.* casualness; the absence of ceremony or formality
in·form´ant *n.* one who testifies
in·for·ma´tion *n.* a body of knowledge or data
in·for´ma·tive *adj.* providing information; revealing
in·frac´tion *n.* a violation of rules
in·fran´gi·ble *adj.* incapable of being smashed
in·fra·red´ *adj.* pertaining to radiation between red and microwave
in´fra·struc·ture *n.* elements of a structure, system, etc.
in·fre´quent *adj.* at large intervals of time or space —**in·fre´quen·cy** *n.*
in·fringe´ *vi., vt.* to intrude upon; to transgress —**in·fringe´ment** *n.*
in·fu´ri·ate´ *vt.* to enrage
in·fuse´ *vt.* introduce into; to inspire; to steep in order to extract
in·gen´ious *adj.* resourceful, clever
in·ge·nu´i·ty *n.* resourcefulness
in·gen´u·ous *adj.* innocent; straightforward; lacking sophistication
in·gest´ *vt.* take into the body; to eat
in·glo´ri·ous *adj.* marked by failure or disgrace —**in·glo´ri·ous·ly** *adv.*
in´got *n.* a lump of cast metal
in·grain´ *vt.* to fix in the mind
in´grate *n.* one who is ungrateful
in·gra´ti·ate *vt.* to curry favor
in·gre´di·ent *n.* part of a mixture
in·hab´it *vt.* to occupy or reside in; to fill —**in·hab´it·ant** *n.*
in·hal´ant *n.* medicine inhaled as a vapor —**in´ha·la·tor** *n.*
in·hale´ *vt.* draw into the lungs; take in quickly —*vi.* breathe in
in·her´ent *adj.* inherited; intrinsic
in·her´it *vt.* to receive, acquire, or take over from another
in·hib´it *vt.* hold back or restrain
in·hi·bi´tion *n.* a restraint; something that inhibits
in·hos·pi´ta·ble *adj.* unfriendly; barren: offering little to promote life or growth
in·hu´man, in·hu·mane´ *adj.* lacking human qualities
in·im´i·cal *adj.* unfriendly
in·im´i·ta·ble *adj.* that cannot be imitated
in·iq´ui·ty *n.* wickedness; evil; a wicked or evil act
in·i´tial *adj.* first instance; beginning —*n.* first letter of a proper name —*vt.* to approve with initials
in·i´ti·ate *vt.* introduce; start; induct into a club —*n.* one newly allowed membership; an inductee
in·i·ti·a´tion *n.* a ceremony for induction; bringing into being
in·i´ti·a·tive *n.* motivation that drives one to begin; a first move; the power to originate
in·ject´ *vt.* to insert or introduce into
in·ju·di´cious *adj.* unwise; lacking judgement —**in·ju·di´cious·ly** *adv.*
in·junc´tion *n.* a command or directive; a legal order that prohibits
in´jure *vt.* cause harm to; wound
in·jur´i·ous *adj.* harmful
in´ju·ry *n.* damage or harm; a basis for legal redress
in·jus´tice *n.* instance of wrongdoing; a violation of rights
ink *n.* colored liquid used for writing or printing —*vt.* to mark with ink
ink´ling *n.* a hint, suggestion, or notion
in´lay *vt.* to set decorative material into —*n.* —**in´laid** *adj.*
in´let *n.* coastal recess; an access from the sea to inland waters
in´mate *n.* one confined
in´most *adj.* furthest from the exterior; secret or intimate
inn *n.* lodging for travelers; a tavern or restaurant
in·nate´ *adj.* inborn
in´ner *adj.* further inside; private or secret

in´ner·most *adj.* most intimate
inn´keep·er *n.* one who operates a public hostelry
in´no·cence *n.* freedom from guilt; a lack of cunning or guile
in´no·cent *adj.* uncorrupted; blameless; unsophisticated; harmless —*n.* an unsophisticated person
in·noc´u·ous *adj.* inoffensive; unlikely to stimulate; having no harmful qualities
in´no·vate *vi., vt.* to introduce or change
in·no·va´tion *n.* something new; introduction of something new
in·nu·en´do *n.* an insinuation
in·nu´mer·a·ble *adj.* incalculable; too many to count
in·oc´u·late *vt.* to immunize by vaccination —**in·oc´u·la´tion** *n.*
in·of·fen´sive *adj.* harmless; without fault
in·op´er·a·ble *adj.* unable to function; inappropriate for surgery
in·op´er·a·tive *adj.* not working; no longer in force
in·op·por·tune´ *adj.* ill–timed
in·or´di·nate *adj.* excessive; exceeding reasonable bounds
in´put *n.* that directed into; data entered in a computer
in´quest *n.* an investigation or inquiry
in·qui´e·tude *n.* a state of unrest
in·quire´ *vi., vt.* to investigate or ask about
in´quir·y *n.* investigation; a question
in·qui·si´tion *n.* an investigation
in·quis´i·tive *adj.* overly curious; eager to learn
in·quis´i·tor *n.* an examiner
in´road *n.* an encroachment or invasion
in·sane´ *adj.* psychotic; marked by immoderate or foolish action
in·san´i·ty *n.* mental disorder; an extremely foolish action
in·sa´ti·a·ble, in·sa´ti·ate *adj.* unable to be satisfied
in·scribe´ *vt.* write or carve; engrave; dedicate, as a book
in·scrip´tion *n.* words written or engraved; a dedication
in·scru´ta·ble *adj.* incomprehensible
in´sect *n.* a small animal with segmented body and six legs
in·sec´ti·cide *n.* a chemical used to kill insects
in·se·cure´ *adj.* uncertain; lacking stability —**in·se·cur´i·ty** *n.*
in·sem´i·nate *vt.* impregnate
in·sen´sate *adj.* inanimate: lacking reason; incapable of sensation; hard–hearted
in·sen´si·ble *adj.* unconscious; indifferent
in·sen´si·tive *adj.* numb; incapable of feeling; unconcerned —**in·sen·si·tiv´i·ty** *n.*
in·sen´ti·ent *adj.* inanimate: totally lacking in life or consciousness
in·sep´a·ra·ble *adj.* indivisible; closely associated
in·sert´ *vt.* to place into or among —**in´sert** *n.* an enclosure in a publication
in·ser´tion *n.* something added; the act of adding or inserting
in·side´ *adj.* inner; select or confidential —*adv.* into —*n.* an interior surface or part —**in·sid´er** *n.*
in·sid´i·ous *adj.* harmful and subtly conveyed or accumulated
in´sight *n.* ability to recognize the true nature of a situation
in·sig´ni·a *n.* a badge or emblem
in·sig·nif´i·cance *n.* unimportance
in·sig·nif´i·cant *adj.* unimportant; having little force or value; of small size or quantity
in·sin·cere´ *adj.* pretentious; deceitful or hypocritical
in´sin·cer´i·ty *n.* deceit; hypocrasy
in·sin´u·ate *vt.* convey a notion or opinion in a subtle manner
in·sin·u·a´tion *n.* a subtle hint
in·sip´id *adj.* uninteresting; dull; lacking flavor —**in·sip´id·ly** *adv.*
in·sist´ *vi.* be firm or persistent —*vt.* demand firmly or persistently
in´so·lent *adj.* rude or disrespectful; insulting —**in´so·lence** *n.*
in·sol´u·ble *adj.* not to be dissolved; insolvable
in·solv´a·ble *adj.* impossible to solve or explain
in·sol´vent *adj.* unable to pay debts —*n.* one who is bankrupt
in·som´ni·a *n.* inability to sleep
in·spect´ *vt.* to examine carefully or critically
in·spec´tion *n.* examination
in·spec´tor *n.* one who examines; a police officer
in·spi·ra´tion *n.* stimulation to creativity; a sudden creative idea
in·spire´ *vt.* to invigorate or encourage
in·spir´it *vt.* to exhilarate; instill with courage
in·stall´ *vt.* to set up or build into; admit into office
in·stal·la´tion *n.* the placement of fixtures or equipment; something installed
in·stall´ment *n.* one of a series
in´stance *n.* an occurrence; an example or illustration
in´stant *adj.* immediate; designed for quick preparation —*n.* a point in time —**in·stan·ta´ne·ous** *adj.*
in´stant·ly *adv.* immediately
in·stead´ *adv.* alternatively
in´sti·gate *vt.* initiate, incite, or urge —**in·sti·ga´tion** *n.*
in·still´ *vt.* to implant or infuse; to teach or indoctrinate
in´stinct *n.* inborn or natural behavior
in·stinc´tive *adj.* intuitive; natural
in´sti·tute *n.* established organization; buildings and land of an organization —*vt.* enact or establish
in·sti·tu´tion *n.* a founding or establishing; custom or tradition; an organization or its buildings and land —**in·sti·tu´tion·al** *adj.*
in·struct´ *vt.* educate or edify; order or direct —*vi.* discharge the duties of an instructor
in·struc´tion *n.* guidance; imparting of knowledge; a direct order
in·struc´tor *n.* a teacher; one who passes on knowledge
in´stru·ment *n.* an implement or tool; device for producing musical sounds; a legal contract
in·stru·men´tal *adj.* serving as agency for; responsible; of music without words
in·stru·men·tal´i·ty *n.* agency
in·sub·or´di·nate *adj.* rebellious; hesitant or unwilling to obey
in´sub·or´di·na´tion *n.* rebellion against authority
in·suf´fer·a·ble *adj.* intolerable; difficult to endure
in·suf·fi´cient *adj.* not enough; lacking —**in·suf·fi´cient·ly** *adv.*
in´su·lar *adj.* detached; isolated
in´su·late *vt.* separate or protect with a barrier
in·su·la´tion *n.* protective covering; protection from external influence
in·sult´ *vi., vt.* to offend; treat offensively —**in´sult** *n.* an offensive act or utterance
in·su´per·a·ble *adj.* impossible to be overcome —**in·su´per·a·bly** *adv.*
in·sup·port´a·ble *adj.* intolerable; that cannot be justified
in·sur´ance *n.* protection from loss
in·sure´ *vt.* make certain; protect against loss —**in·sur·ed´** *adj.*
in·sur´gent *n.* one rebeling against authority —*adj.* rebellious
in·sur·mount´a·ble *adj.* that cannot be overcome
in·sur·rec´tion *n.* open rebellion
in·sus·cep´ti·ble *adj.* not vulnerable
in·tact´ *adj.* complete; not damaged or diminished in any way
in·tan´gi·ble *adj.* indefinable by the senses
in´te·ger *n.* a whole number
in´te·gral *adj.* necessary; essential
in´te·grate *vt.* bring together; unify
in·te·gra´tion *n.* a unifying or blending
in·teg´ri·ty *n.* compliance to a standard; being whole or sound
in´tel·lect *n.* the capacity for reason or understanding
in·tel·lec´tu·al *adj.* appealing to the intellect; intelligent —*n.* one given to intellectual pursuits
in·tel´li·gence *n.* capacity for knowledge; information or news
in·tel´li·gent *adj.* having knowledge; able to acquire knowledge
in·tel·li·gent´si·a *n.* intellectual elite
in·tel´li·gi·ble *adj.* understandable
in·tem´per·ance *n.* excessive indulgence
in·tend´ *vt.* to have in mind
in·tend´ed *adj.* intentional
in·tense´ *adj.* extreme in force or magnitude; emotional
in·ten´si·fy *vi., vt.* grow stronger
in·ten´sive *adj.* marked by vigor or concentration
in·tent´ *adj.* firmly fixed in the mind —*n.* something intended
in·ten´tion *n.* aim; purpose
in·ten´tion·al *adj.* deliberate; planned —**in·ten´tion·al·ly** *adv.*
in·ter´ *vt.* to bury or entomb
in·ter·act´ *vi.* relate or act mutually
in·ter·cede´ *vt.* to plead on behalf of another
in·ter·cept´ *vt.* interrupt the progress of —**in·ter·cep´tion** *n.*
in·ter·ces´sion *n.* a plea for another; mediation
in·ter·change´ *vi., vt.* to change successively —**in´ter·change** *n.* a system of highway access ramps
in´ter·course *n.* communication between persons; sexual relations
in·ter·de·pen´dence, in·ter·de·pend´en·cy *n.* mutually dependent
in·ter·dict´ *vt.* prohibit by law or order of the church
in·ter·dic´tion *n.* a legal prohibition; censure by the church
in´ter·est *n.* curiosity; right to a share; fee for the loan of money —*vt.* hold one's attention
in´ter·est·ed *adj.* connected or affected in some way
in´ter·est·ing *adj.* inviting attention
in·ter·fere´ *vt.* to invene
in·ter·fer´ence *n.* an obstruction; an act of interrupting or obstructing
in·ter·ga·lac´tic *adj.* existing between galaxies
in´ter·im *n.* a time between events —*adj.* effective for a time
in·te´ri·or *adj.* inside; away from the coast —*n.* the internal part; the internal affairs of a political entity
in·ter·ject´ *vt.* insert between other components —**in·ter·jec´tion** *n.*
in·ter·lace´ *vt.* weave or entwine
in´ter·leaf *n.* a blank sheet between pages in a book
in´ter·lock *vt., vi.* join together; link
in´ter·lop·er *n.* one who meddles
in´ter·lude *n.* a lull; intervening time
in·ter·me´di·ar·y *n.* an agent or mediator
in·ter·me´di·ate *adj.* occurring between
in·ter´ment *n.* burial
in·ter´mi·na·ble *adj.* without terminus; endless; tiresome
in·ter·min´gle *vt., vi.* combine or become mingled together
in·ter·mis´sion (*US*) *n.* a pause between events, as the acts of a play
in·ter·mit´tent *adj.* not continuous
in·ter·mix´ *vt., vi.* to mix together
in´tern *n.* an apprentice —**in·tern´** *vt.* to confine —*vi.* serve as apprentice
in·ter´nal *adj.* of the area within borders —**in·ter´nal·ly** *adv.*
in·ter·na´tion·al *adj.* worldwide; between nations
in·ter·nec´ine *adj.* of an internal struggle; mutually destructive
in·tern´ment *n.* confinement
in·ter´nist *n.* a physician
in·ter·per´son·al *adj.* between persons
in´ter·play *n.* interaction
in·ter´po·late *vt.* to derive data from that which precedes and follows it

in·ter·pose´ *vt.* to inject into or between elements

in·ter´pret *vt.* to translate, explain, or illuminate

in·ter·pre·ta´tion *n.* explanation; presentation marked by a particular style or point of view

in·ter´pret·er *n.* one who translates or explains

in·ter·re·late´ *vt., vi.* to come into interdependent association

in·ter´ro·gate *vt.* cross–examine

in·ter·ro·ga´tion *n.* a formal questioning

in·ter·rupt´ *vt.* break in or interfere

in·ter·rup´tion *n.* delay or intrusion

in·ter·sect´ *vt., vi.* to cross or abut; form an intersection

in·ter·sec´tion *n.* a point where lines, streets, etc. abut or cross

in·ter·sperse´ *vt.* place at regular intervals

in´ter·twine *vt., vi.* to unite by interlacing

in´ter·val *n.* space or time between

in·ter·vene´ *vi.* to come between; to interfere

in·ter·ven´tion *n.* interference in the affairs of another

interview *n.* meeting to elicit or exchange information

in·tes´tine *n.* the passage between stomach and anus that plays a major role in digestion

in´ti·ma·cy *n.* closeness

in´ti·mate *adj.* marked by innermost thoughts, feelings, etc.; closely associated; of informality and privacy —*n.* a close associate —*vt.* hint

in·ti·ma´tion *n.* information communicated subtly and indirectly; a hint

in·tim´i·date *vt.* to frighten; to pressure by threatening

in·tol´er·a·ble *adj.* unbearable; grossly offensive

in·tol´er·ant *adj.* bigoted or prejudiced; unwilling to accept: *intolerant of evil*

in·to·na´tion *n.* voice modulation

in·tone´ *vt., vi.* to recite or chant in a monotone

in·tox´i·cant *n.* agent of intoxication

in·tox´i·cate *vt.* to inebriate or befuddle by strong drink; to stimulate, as by good news, beauty, etc.

in·tox·i·ca´tion *n.* drunkenness; stimulation

in·trac´ta·ble *adj.* obstinate or undisciplined; difficult to control

in·tran´si·gence *n.* refusal to compromise; obstinacy; stubborness

in·tran´si·gent *adj.* intolerant and inflexible; obstinate

in·tra·ve´nous *adj.* injected into or situated within a vein

in·trep´id *adj.* fearless —**in·trep´id·ly** *adv.*

in´tri·ca·cy *n.* something extremely complex

in´tri·cate *adj.* complex or involved

in·trigue´ *n.* a secret scheme —*vi.* to plot secretly —*vt.* arouse interest

in·trin´sic *adj.* of an inborn quality

in·tro·duce´ *vt.* present for consideration; acquaint one with another

in·tro·duc´tion *n.* presentation of a person, idea, etc.; a time or ceremony of presentation

in·tro·duc´to·ry *adj.* of presentation of something new

in·tro·spec´tion *n.* contemplation and self–examination

in´tro·vert *n.* one whose interests are directed inward

in·trude´ *vi., vt.* to intervene where one is not wanted

in·trud´er *n.* one who meddles or enters improperly

in·tru´sion *n.* an interruption; meddling —**in·tru´sive** *adj.*

in·tu·i´tion *n.* an instinctive feeling

in·tu´i·tive *adj.* instinctive; perceived or determined without reason —**in·tu´i·tive·ness** *n.*

in´un·date *vt.* to overwhelm

in·un·da´tion *n.* a flooding or overflowing

in·ure´ *vt.* acclimate or accustom to something unpleasant

in·vade´ *vt.* to attack; to enter and remain —**in·vad´er** *n.*

in·val´id *adj.* not legal; not legally binding; faulty —**in´va·lid** *n.* one who is disabled by illness or injury

in·val´i·date *vt.* revoke or nullify

in·val´u·a·ble *adj.* priceless

in·var´i·a·ble *adj.* unchanging

in·va´sion *n.* attack; infestation

in·va´sive *adj.* tending to invade or intrude

in·vec´tive *adj.* marked by abusive language —*n.* abusive language; denunciation

in·veigh´ *vt.* to protest vigorously

in·vei´gle *vt.* to entice or trick by coaxing or flattery

in·vent´ *vt.* create something new; to misrepresent, as by way of excuse

in·ven´tion *n.* something newly created

in·ven´tive *adj.* clever; creative; resourceful —**in·ven´tive·ly** *adv.*

in´ven·to·ry *n.* goods in stock; an accounting —*vt.* to count and record goods on hand

in·verse´ *adj.* reversed

in·vert´ *vt.* to reverse position

in·ver´te·brate *adj.* lacking a backbone —*n.* an animal that has no backbone

in·vest´ *vt.* buy in anticipation of profit; to charge with authority; to formally install in office

in·ves´ti·gate *vi., vt.* to make careful inquiry

in·ves·ti·ga´tion *n.* detailed inquiry

in·vest´ment *n.* the placing of resources in the hope of profit

in·vet´er·ate *adj.* well–established; persisting

in·vid´i·ous *adj.* expressing ill–will; malicious —**in·vid´i·ous·ly** *adv.*

in·vig´o·rate *vt.* enliven; energize —**in·vig·o·ra´tion** *n.*

in·vig´o·rat·ing *adj.* tending to energize; refreshing or stimulating

in·vin´ci·ble *adj.* unconquerable —**in·vin·ci·bil´i·ty** *n.*

in·vi´o·la·ble *adj.* that cannot be profaned; invincible

in·vi´o·late *adj.* not violated; pure

in·vis´i·ble *adj.* unseen; not open to view —**in·vis´i·bly** *adv.*

in·vi·ta´tion *n.* a formal request; an allurement or temptation

in·vi·ta´tion·al *n.* an event limited to those invited —*adj.* restricted to invited participants

in·vite´ *vt.* formally request; tempt

in·vit´ing *adj.* attractive; enticing

in·vo·ca´tion *n.* appeal; a prayer

in´voice *n.* a statement of charges —*vt.* to tender a bill

invoke´ *vt.* to call up, as a spirit; to beseech or appeal earnestly

in·vol´un·tar·y *adj.* unintentional; instinctive

in·vo·lu´tion *n.* involvement; complexity

in·volve´ *vt.* include or connect to; implicate or incriminate; become engrossed in; complicate

in·volved´ *adj.* complicated; engrossed; emotionally committed

in·volve´ment *n.* participation; entanglement

in·vul´ner·a·ble *adj.* invincible; impossible to harm or damage

in´ward *adj.* related to the inside —*adv.* toward the inside

i·o´ta *n.* a small amount

i·ras´ci·ble *adj.* irritable; quick to anger; marked by anger

i´rate, i·rate´ *adj.* incensed; marked by anger

ire *n.* anger

irk *vt.* vex or annoy

irk´some *adj.* annoying; disturbing

i´ron *n.* a metallic element; something made from iron; a symbol of strength —*vt., vi.* smooth clothing —*adj.* made of or containing iron; strong and unyielding

i·ron´ic, i·ron´i·cal *adj.* paradoxical; mocking —**i·ron´i·cal·ly** *adv.*

i´ro·ny *n.* a paradox; a literary syle that mocks or satirizes convention

ir·ra´di·ate *vt.* to clarify or illuminate; to expose to radiation

ir·rad´i·ca·ble *adj.* impossible to destroy

ir·ra´tion·al *adj.* not subject to reason; illogical; silly

ir·rec·on·cil´a·ble *adj.* that cannot be justified

ir·re·deem´a·ble *adj.* that cannot be redeemed; impossible to recover or reform

ir·re·fut´a·ble *adj.* indisputable; not subject to argument or dispute

ir·reg´u·lar *adj.* contrary to the normal or conventional; not symmetrical or uniform

ir·reg·u·lar´i·ty *n.* an abnormality or oddity

ir·rel´e·vance, ir·rel´e·van·cy *n.* the quality of being trivial or not pertinent

ir·rel´e·vant *adj.* not pertinent

ir·re·li´gious *adj.* not religious: hostile to religion

ir·re·mis´si·ble *adj.* incurable; unpardonable

ir·rep´a·ra·ble *adj.* hopeless; impossible to mend or correct

ir·re·place´a·ble *adj.* priceless; that cannot be replaced

ir·re·press´i·ble *adj.* that cannot be controlled; overly enthusiastic

ir·re·proach´a·ble *adj.* blameless

ir·re·sist´i·ble *adj.* overwhelming; compelling —**ir·re·sist´i·bly** *adv.*

ir·res´o·lute *adj.* lacking in purpose or resolution; wavering —**ir·res´o·lute·ly** *adv.* —**ir·res·o·lu´tion** *n.*

ir·re·spec´tive *adj.* regardless

ir·re·spon´si·ble *adj.* lacking a sense of duty; thoughtless; unpredictable

ir·rev´er·ence *n.* a lack of respect

ir·rev´er·ent *adj.* disrespectful of that considered proper

ir·rev´o·ca·ble *adj.* that cannot be retracted or changed

ir´ri·gate *vt.* furnish water for growing plants; to cleanse with liquid

ir·ri·ga´tion *n.* system or process of providing water for plants or liquid for cleansing

ir´ri·ta·ble *adj.* ill–tempered; easily provoked or offended

ir´ri·tant *n.* something that annoys

ir´ri·tate *vt.* provoke to anger; chafe or abrade —**ir´ri·tat·ing·ly** *adv.*

ir´ri·tat·ed *adj.* troubled or disturbed

ir´ri·ta´tion *n.* something that troubles or vexes; an irritant

is´land *n.* land surrounded by water; an isolated structure or area

i´so·late *vt.* set apart

i·so·la´tion *n.* separation; seclusion

i·so·la´tion·ist *n.* one opposed to involvement in the affairs of others

is´sue *n.* a flowing out; something published or distributed; an edition —*vi., vt.* to flow out; orginate from a source; to distribute

itch *n.* skin irritation; a desire —*vi.* sense an irritation or desire

i´tem *n.* a single element that is part of a whole

i´tem·ize *vt., vi.* to enumerate, one by one —**i´tem·i·za´tion** *n.*

it´er·ance, it·er·a´tion *n.* repetition

it´er·ate *vt.* to repeat

i·tin´er·ant *adj.* roving —*n.* a wanderer —**i·tin´er·ant·ly** *adv.*

i·tin´er·ar·y *n.* a travel plan

i´vied *adj.* coated with ivy

i´vy *n.* climbing or trailing plant

j, J tenth letter of the alphabet

jab *n.* a quick poke or punch —*vi., vt.* to poke or punch sharply

jab´ber *vi., vt.* speak rapidly or nonsensically —*n.* senseless talk

ja·bot´ *n.* ornamental ruffles

jack *n.* a device for raising heavy objects; type of food fish; (*US*) a plug for electronic devices —*vt.* raise with a jack; raise prices

jack´al *n.* a wild dog

jack´ass *n.* the male ass; a stupid person

jack´boot *n.* a heavy boot reaching above the knee

jack´daw *n.* a small black bird related to the crow

jack´et *n.* a short coat; an outer covering or container —*vt.* to cover —**jack´et·ed** *adj.*

jack´knife *n.* a pocket knife
jack´pot *n.* a prize or pool of money; winnings; a bonanza or reward
jack´rab·bit *n.* a large American hare
jade *vt., vi.* wear out by overindulgence —*n.* shrewish woman; a gemstone, usually pale green
jad´ed *adj.* world–weary; pretentiously indifferent
jag´ged *adj.* characterized by an irregular edge —**jag´ged·ness** *n.*
jag´uar *n.* a large spotted cat
jail (*US*), **gaol** (*Brit.*) *n.* a place of confinement —*vt.* confine in a jail
jail´er (*US*), **gaol´er** (*Brit.*) *n.* one charged with the upkeep of a jail
ja·la·pe´ño *n.* a pungent tropical pepper having red or green fruit
ja·lop´y *n.* old, broken–down car
jal´ou·sie *n.* a door or window covering with adjustable slats
jam *n.* a preserve of sugar and fruit; a crush of people; a difficult situation —*vt., vi.* cram in a tight space
jamb *n.* side panel of a door or window
jam·ba·lay´a *n.* spicy Creole dish
jam´bo·ree´ *n.* a large gathering; a festive celebration
jam session an unrehearsed gathering or meeting
jan´gle *n.* discordant metallic sound —*vi., vt.*
jan´i·tor (*US*) *n.* one charged with the maintenance of a building
ja·pan´ *n.* a hard glossy coating; an item coated in the Japanese manner —*vt.* coat with japan
jape *n.* a jest or prank —*vi.* to joke or jest —**jap´er** *n.* —**jap´er·y** *n.*
jar *n.* a small cylindrical container; a jolt or bump —*vi., vt.* to shake or cause to shake; to irritate or shock
jar´di·niere´ *n.* an ornamental pot or stand for flowers
jar´gon *n.* a patois or dialect; the terms of a profession or trade
jas´mine *n.* a species of flowering shrubs used in fragrances and tea; a fragrance or tea of jasmine
jas´per *n.* a type of yellow, red, or brown quartz
jaun´dice *n.* abnormal yellowing of the skin, eyeballs, etc.; hostility —*vt.* to affect with jaundice; influenced by envy or distrust
jaunt *n.* an excursion; a short pleasure trip —*vi.* to make a short trip
jaun´ty *adj.* in a free and easy manner; buoyant; self–confident
jav´e·lin *n.* a short light spear
jaw *n.* bony structures that frame the mouth; anything that grips like a jaw —*vi., vt.* talk or scold
jaw´bone *n.* a bone of the jaw —*vt., vi.* urge or argue vigorously
jazz *n.* an American musical form —*adj.* pertaining to jazz
jeal´ous *adj.* envious; fearful of competition; protective
jeal´ous·sy *n.* possessive envy
jeer *n.* an abusive or mocking remark —*vi., vt.* to mock or ridicule
je·june´ *adj.* dull or lifeless; childlike
jell *vi., vt.* become firm; take shape
jel´ly *n.* a gelatinous food
jeop´ar·dize *vt.* expose to danger
jeop´ar·dy *n.* risk of loss; danger
jerk *n.* a sudden action; a silly or foolish person —*vt., vi.* make a lurching or quivering move
jer´kin *n.* a short jacket
jerk´y *adj.* marked by short, abrupt movement
jer´ky *n.* cured meat
jer·o·bo´am *n.* 3 liter wine bottle
jer´ry–built *adj.* shoddily constructed; improvised
jer´sey *n.* knitted fabric; a pullover shirt or sweater
jest *n.* a joke or prank —*vi.* to tease or mock; speak in fun
jest´er *n.* a professional comedian; one given to light banter
jet *n.* a flow of fluid at high pressure; a device creating such a flow; a vehicle propelled by this flow; a dense, black color —*vi.* travel in a jet–propelled aircraft
jet engine *n.* an engine that develops thrust from exhaust
jet´sam *n.* material jettisoned by a ship in distress
jet´ti·son *vt.* to throw overboard, as from a ship; to discard
jet´ty *n.* a structure protecting a harbor or shoreline
jew´el *n.* a precious stone; an ornament set with precious stones; something highly prized
jew´el·ler·y (*Brit.*) **jew´el·ry** (*US*) *n.* ornaments made of precious metals and set with precious stones
jif´fy *n.* a brief span of time
jig *n.* a lively dance; a device for holding or guiding —*vi.* dance a jig
jig´ger *n.* a $1^1/2$ ounce measure
jig´gle *vi.* to bounce lightly up and down or from side to side
ji·had´ *n.* holy war or pious quest
jilt *vi.* to reject suddenly
jim´my *n.* a short crowbar —*vt.* to force with a crowbar
jin´gle *n.* a short rhyme or song; a light metallic sound —*vi., vt.* to make a metallic sound
jin´go *n.* one who aggressively supports his or her nation
jin´go·ism *n.* extreme nationalism
jinx *n.* a hex or spell; thing bringing bad luck —*vt.* to bring bad luck
jit´ney *n.* a small passenger vehicle; a delapidated vehicle
jive *n.* the jargon of jazz; nonsensical talk —*vt., vi.* talk nonsensically
job *n.* work for pay; the work one does; a task or duty; something worked on or at
job´ber *n.* one who buys in large quantities and sells to retailers
job´less *adj.* out of work
jock´ey *n.* a professional rider; one associated with a particular vehicle, profession, etc. —*vi., vt.* ride a horse; manuever
jo·cose´ *adj.* given to humor —**jo·cose´ly** *adv.*
joc´u·lar *adj.* given to joking
joc´und *adj.* lighthearted —**jo·cun´di·ty** *n.* —**joc´und·ly** *adv.*
jodh´purs *n.* riding pants
jog *n.* a slow, steady trot; a slight jostling or nudge —*vi., vt.* to move at a slow run; to jostle or nudge
jog´gle *vt., vi.* to shake lightly
join *vt., vi.* to bring together; connect
join´er *n.* a carpenter; a tool designed to fashion joints
joint *n.* a place where pieces come together; a seedy establishment; a marijuana cigarette —*adj.* shared
joist *n.* a horizontal beam
joke *n.* an amusing story or act —*vi.* speak or act in fun
jok´er *n.* a jester or prankster
jol´li·ty *n.* merriment
jol´ly *adj.* cheerful; exhibiting good humor —**jol´li·ly** *adv.*
jolt *n.* a jarring bump; a shock or surprise —*vt.* to jar with a sharp blow; to shock
josh *vi.* to joke; to tease playfully
jos´tle *vt.* to push or bump while passing
jot *n.* a small amount —*vt.* to write hastily
jot´ted *adj.* written hastily
jot´ting *n.* a short note
jounce *n.* a jolting movement —*vi., vt.* to move with a jolt
jour´nal *n.* an account of finances or activities; newspaper or periodical —**jour´nal·ize** *vt.*
jour´nal·ism *n.* the writing and editing of news items
jour´nal·ist *n.* one who writes for a newspaper or periodical
jour´ney *n.* the act of traveling; distance traveled —*vi., vt.* to travel
jour´ney·man *n.* one who has completed an apprenticeship
joust *n.* medieval combat; a competition; a confrontation —*vi.* to compete; engage in a battle of words or wits
jo´vi·al *adj.* extremely cordial and sociable —**jo´vi·al·ly** *adv.*
jowl *n.* flesh of the cheek or jaw
jowl´y *adj.* having loose hanging flesh about the cheeks and jaws
joy *n.* intense happiness or pleasure; that which causes such pleasure
joy´ful *adj.* expressing or feeling joy
joy´less *adj.* lacking joy; sad
joy´ous *adj.* causing or expressing joy —**joy´ous·ly** *adv.*
joy´stick *n.* a cursor control
ju´bi·lant *adj.* extremely happy; rapturous —**ju´bi·lance** *n.*
ju´bi·late *vi.* to rejoice
ju·bi·la´tion *n.* rapture; a manifestation of joy
ju´bi·lee *n.* a celebration; an occasion for rejoicing
judge *n.* an officer of the court; one appointed to arbitrate or decide —*vt.* decide after argument; to form an opinion based on careful study
judg·mat´ic, judg·mat´i·cal *adj.* judicious —**judg·mat´i·cal·ly** *adv.*
judge´ship *n.* the office and authority of a judge
judge´ment, judg´ment *n.* ability to discern; opinion based on observation and consideration
judg·men´tal *adj.* tending to judge; relating to judgment
ju·di´cial *adj.* relating to a court of law; pronouncing judgment
ju·di´ciar·y *n.* the court system; those who administer justice
ju·di´cious *adj.* marked by prudence; careful; discreet; sensible
ju´do *n.* a form of combat
jug *n.* a large, rounded container with a small mouth and a handle
jug´ger·naut *n.* overwhelming force
jug´gle *vt.* keep in the air by alternately tossing and catching; to have difficulty moving between activities; to alter so as to deceive
jug´u·lar *adj.* about the neck or throat
juice *n.* liquid derived from plant or animal tissue
juic´y *adj.* full of juice; mouth-watering; having special meaning
juke´box *n.* a coin–operated phonograph
ju·li·enne´ *n.* a broth containing strips of vegetable —*adj.* cut into long, thin strips
jum´ble *n.* a confusing mixture —*vt., vi.* to mix in a haphazard fashion
jum´bo *adj.* large in size
jump *n.* leap; span of a leap —*vi., vt.* move or change suddenly
jump´er *n.* one who jumps; a shunt for an electrical circuit; (*Brit.*) a sweater; (*US*) a sleeveless dress
jump´i·ness *n.* nervousness
jump´suit *n.* one–piece garment
jump´y *adj.* nervous
junc´tion *n.* place where two things meet —**junc´tion·al** *adj.*
junc´ture *n.* a junction; place where two things are joined
jun´gle *n.* tangled undergrowth; a jumbled or confusing accumulation; intense rivalry
jun´ior *adj.* younger; lower in rank —*n.* younger of two; one lower in rank; a third year student
junk *n.* objects cast off; something of poor quality —*vt.* discard —*adj.* worthless
junk bond a high yield corporate bond entailing high risk
junk´er *n.* an old, beat–up car
jun´ket *n.* an outing; trip at public expense —**jun´ke·teer´** *n.*
junk food snack food
jun´ta *n.* a group of rulers
ju´ral *adj.* relating to the law
ju´rat *n.* certification on an affidavit
ju·rid´ic, ju·rid´i·cal *adj.* relating to administration of the law
ju·ris·dic´tion *n.* the range or extent of one's authority
ju·ris·dic´tion·al *adj.* relating to the limits of one's rights or authority
ju·ris·pru´dence *n.* the science of law —**ju·ris·pru´dent** *adj., n.*
ju´rist *n.* one experienced in the law
ju·ris´tic *adj.* relating to a jurist or matters of the law
ju´ror *n.* one serving on a jury
ju´ry *n.* a group sworn to hear an issue and to pass judgment
ju´ry–rig *vt.* rig for emergency use; improvise

just *adj.* fair and fitting; conforming to what is right; impartial —*adv.* precisely; barely —**just´ly** *adv.*
jus´tice *n.* adhering to what is right or just
jus´ti·fi·a·ble *adj.* proved correct; warranted —**jus´ti·fi·a·bly** *adv.*
jus·ti·fi·ca´tion *n.* defense; explanation
jus´ti·fy *vt.* prove correct; absolve of blame
jut *vi., vt.* to extend or profect outward
ju´ve·nile *adj.* young; relating to the young; marked by immature behavior
jux´ta·pose *vt.* place side by side for comparison —**jux·ta·po·si´tion** *n.*
k, K eleventh letter of the alphabet
ka·lei´do·scope *n.* an optical device that produces changing colored patterns; something constantly changing —**ka·lei·do·scop´ic** *adj.*
kan´ga·roo´ *n.* an Australian marsupial
kan´ji *n.* Japanese picture writing
ka´pok *n.* a cottonlike fiber
ka·put´ *adj.* not working; used up or gone bad
ka·ra´te *n.* a system of self–defense
kar´ma *n.* one's destiny
katz´en·jam·mer *n.* a hangover; a bewildered state
kay´ak *n.* an enclosed canoe propelled with a double–ended paddle
ka·zoo´ *n.* an instrument with a vibrating membrane that produces a humming sound
ke·bob´ *n.* bits of food broiled on a skewer; a shish kebob
kedge *n.* a light anchor
keel *n.* the lowest point along the length of a vessel —*vi.* roll over
keen *adj.* sharp; intelligent and perceptive; sensitive; eager for
keep *vt.* retain; tend or care for; continue without change; restrain or prevent —*vi.* continue; remain unchanged —*n.* care or support; a stronghold, as in a castle
keep´er *n.* an overseer
keep´sake *n.* a memento
ke·fir´ *n.* a drink made from fermented cow's milk
keg *n.* a small barrel; a 100 pound measure for nails
keg´ler *n.* one who bowls
kelp *n.* a type of seaweed
kempt *adj.* neat; orderly
ken´nel *n.* an animal shelter; the boarding or breeding of dogs
ker´a·tin *n.* a tough protein that forms nails, horns, etc.
ker´chief *n.* large handkerchief; a bandanna
kerf *n.* a cut made by an axe or saw
ker´nel *n.* a grain or seed; the most significant or central part
ker´o·sene (*US*) *n.* a fuel distilled from petroleum
ketch *n.* a two–masted vessel
ket´tle *n.* a metal pot, often with a handle and a lid; a teakettle
key *n.* a notched device for unlocking, winding, etc.; a critical element; pitch of a musical tone
key´board *n.* a set of keys as on a typewriter, piano, etc.
key´board·ist *n.* one who plays a piano, synthesizer, etc.
keycard *n.* a rigid card that unlocks with a coded electronic strip
key club a private club
keynote address an opening speech
key´pad *n.* device for inputting data
key´stone *n.* the topmost stone in an arch; a fundamental element
khak´i *n.* a tannish brown color; a cloth of this color
kib´itz *vi.* chat informally; intrude; offer unwanted advice
kick *n.* a blow with the foot; a thrust of the foot; vigor or stimulation —*vi., vt.* to strike out with the foot
kick´back *n.* payback: a bribe; a violent reaction; a backlash
kick´er *n.* one who kicks; an important contingency
kick´off *n.* traditional beginning
kid *n.* young of certain animals; the meat or hide of a young goat; a young person —*vi., vt.* to engage in good–natured banter —**kid´der** *n.*
kid´nap *vt.* to abduct or hold illegally
kid´ney *n.* one of a pair of organs that filter body fluids
kid´skin *n.* leather from the skin of a young goat
kill *vt.* put to death; to destroy, extinguish, or end; to overwhelm —*n.* an act of killing; that killed
kill´joy *n.* one who undermines the pleasure of others
kiln *n.* an oven for baking or drying
kil´o·byte *n.* a computer unit equal to 1,024 bytes
kil´o·cal·o·rie *n.* a unit of potential energy in food; a nutritionist's calorie, a large calorie
kil´o·cy·cle *n.* one thousand cycles
ki·lom´e·ter *n.* one thousand meters
ki·mo´no *n.* a robe–like outer garment indigenous to Japan
kin *adj.* of the same ancestry —*n.* those to whom one is related
kind *adj.* benevolent, compassionate, and humane —*n.* a class unified by common traits; something similar
kin´der·gar·ten *n.* school for young children
kind´heart·ed *adj.* having a kind and sympathetic nature
kin´dle *vt., vi.* set on fire; stimulate emotion —**kin´dling** *n.*
kind´ly *adj.* of a kind disposition —*adv.* pleasantly or politely
kind´ness *n.* being kind; acting in a kind manner; a courtesy; an act of charity
kin´dred *adj.* of common origins or nature
ki·net´ic *adj.* producing motion
kinetic energy the energy of a body attributable to its motion
ki·net´ics *n.* the study of the dynamics of material bodies
king *n.* a male sovereign; one superior in a field —*adj.* preeminent
king´dom *n.* domain of a king; a broad domain: *the animal kingdom*
king´ly *adj.* regal; in the manner of a king —*adv.* —**king´li·ness** *n.*
king´pin *n.* a leader; the most important person
kink *n.* a tight curl; a cramp; a quirk or impediment
kink´y *adj.* tightly curled; strange or quirky —**kink´i·ness** *n.*
kin´ship *n.* relationship by blood
ki´osk *n.* a small, free–standing structure, such as a gazebo
kip´per *n.* a fish cured by salting and smoking —*vt.* to cure
kir *n.* dry white wine flavored with crème de cassis
kirk *n.* a Scottish church
kirsch *n.* a clear cherry brandy
kiss *n.* a touching of the lips; a light, fleeting touch —*vi., vt.* touch with the lips; touch lightly
kit *n.* collection of articles or a container for holding such a collection
kitch´en *n.* an area for food preparation; a staff or implements for preparing food
kitch·en·ette´ *n.* a small kitchen
kitch´en·ware *n.* implements used in the preparation of food
kite *n.* a hawk; a paper–covered frame flown in the wind; a counterfeit negotiable instrument —*vt., vi.* obtain money by counterfeiting
kit´ty *n.* money pooled for a purpose
klep·to·ma´ni·ac *n.* one with an obsessive urge to steal
klutz *n.* one clumsy or lacking in social grace —**klutz´y** *adj.*
knack *n.* a special talent or skill
knap´sack *n.* a sturdy bag with shoulder straps
knave *n.* one of humble birth; a rascal or rogue —**knav´ish** *adj.*
knav´er·y *n.* deceitful or underhanded transactions
knead *vt.* to fold and press with the hands; to massage
knee *n.* a joint of the leg; part of a garment that covers the knee —*vt.* to strike with the knee
knee´–jerk *adj.* involuntary, as a reaction; unthinking acceptance
kneel *vi.* rest on one or both knees
knell *n.* slow, solemn tolling of a bell
knick´er·bock·ers (*US*) *n.* full trousers that are cut off and tied just below the knee
knick´knack *n.* a small curio or ornamental piece
knife *n.* a tool consisting of a thin blade attached to a handle
knight *n.* a medieval mounted soldier; one who champions a cause
knight–er´rant *n.* a knight seeking adventure; an adventure-seeker
knight´hood *n.* a rank conferred by a sovereign for outstanding service
knish *n.* a savory filled pastry that is baked or fried
knit *vt., vi.* intertwine strands of yarn; to join tightly; to draw together in wrinkles
knit´ting, knit´wear *n.* garments made by knitting
knob *n.* a stubby projection; a rounded handle —**knobbed** *adj.*
knob´by *adj.* have the appearance of a knob, as *knobby knees*
knock *vi., vt.* strike solidly; to collide; to criticize —*n.* a sharp blow
knock´off *adj.* a cheap imitation
knoll *n.* a low, rounded hill; a hillock
knot *n.* fastener or decoration made by tying; a tight group of people; a tight feeling; joint of a tree; one nautical mile; a speed of one nautical mile per hour —*vt., vi.* form into a knot; become entangled
knot´ty *adj.* snarled; having many knots; difficult to resolve
know *vt., vi.* to possess information and understanding; comprehend
know´–how *n.* expertise
know´ing *adj.* knowledgeable; shrewd; secretly aware; deliberate or intentional —**know´ing·ly** *adv.*
knowl´edge *n.* awareness or information from study or experience
knowl´edge·a·ble *adj.* possessing learning or experience
knuck´le *n.* bulge of bones in a joint
knurl *n.* a protuberance; small ridges that aid in gripping
ko·a´la *n.* an Australian arborial marsupial
ko´an *n.* a Zen riddle in the form of a paradox
kook *n.* an unconventional person —**kook´y** *adj.*
ko´sher *adj.* conforming to Jewish dietary laws; valid or legitimate
ko´to *n.* a Japanese stringed instrument
kraut *n.* sauerkraut
kris *n.* a Malaysian dagger
kryp´ton *n.* an inert gas
ku´chen *n.* yeast dough coffee cake
ku´dos *n.* aclaim for achievement
küm´mel *n.* caraway seed liqueur
kum´quat *n.* a small, orange–like fruit
kung fu *n.* Chinese martial art similar to karate
l, L twelfth letter of the alphabet
lab *n.* laboratory
la´bel *n.* a tag or stamp; a distinguishing appellation —*vt.* attach or ascribe with a label
la´bor (*US*) *n.* physical effort; workers collectively; the exertion of childbirth —*vi.* expend energy; toil conscientiously; move with difficulty; experience childbirth
lab´o·ra·to·ry *n.* a place of research or learning
la´bored (*US*) *adj.* accomplished with great effort
la´bor–inten´sive *adj.* requiring an excessive amount of physical labor
la·bo´ri·ous *adj.* difficult or exhausting —**la·bo´ri·ous·ly** *adv.*
la´bour (*Brit.*) *n.* physical effort; workers collectively; the exertion of childbirth —*vi.* expend

energy; toil conscientiously; move with difficulty; experience childbirth
la´boured (*Brit.*) *adj.* accomplished with great effort
lab´y·rinth *n.* a maze; something intricate —**lab·y·rin´thi·an** *adj.*
lace *n.* a cord used to fasten; a delicate fabric —*vt.* place by threading or intertwining; spread throughout —**lace into** to assail verbally
lac´er·ate *vt.* to cut or tear, as flesh —*adj.* torn
lac·er·a´tion *n.* a jagged wound
lach´ry·mose *adj.* tearful; causing tears —**lach´ry·mal** *adj.*
lack *n.* a deficiency in substance or quality —*vi., vt.* have little; need
lack·a·dai´si·cal *adj.* languid; lacking spirit
lack´ey *n.* a menial; a fawning attendant
lack´lus·ter *adj.* wanting in vitality
la·con´ic, la·con´i·cal *adj.* not wordy; disinclined to converse
lac´quer *n.* a clear, protective coating —*vt.* coat with lacquer
la·crosse´ *n.* type of field hockey
lac´tate *vi.* produce milk
lac·ta´tion *n.* production of milk in mammary glands; period of such production —**lac·ta´tion·al** *adj.*
lac´te·al *adj.* relating to milk
lac´tic *adj.* relating to or derived from milk
lac´y *adj.* resembling lace; flimsy —**lac´i·ness** *n.*
lad *n.* a young man
lad´der *n.* parallel sides joined by rungs for climbing; analogous means of ascent or descent
lade *vt.* load with cargo; dip or ladle
lad´en *adj.* weighed down; oppressed
la´dle *n.* a deep–bowled serving spoon —*vt.* serve or apportion
la´dy *n.* a well–mannered woman; the female head of a household
la´dy·like *adj.* having the manners or bearing of a lady
lag *vi.* to fall behind; falter
la´ger *n.* a type of beer
lag´gard *n.* one who falls behind; a straggler —*adj.* slow
la·goon´ *n.* a shallow body of water
la´ic, la´i·cal *adj.* secular —*n.* a layperson
laid´–back´ *adj.* serene or casual
lair *n.* an animal's den; one's habitat or domain
lais´sez–faire *n.* a policy of noninterference
la´i·ty *n.* those not of the clergy
lake *n.* a large inland body of water
lam·baste´ *vt.* to rebuke sharply; to reprimand
lame *adj.* disabled; halting; weak or ineffective —*vt.* to disable
la·mé´ *n.* fabric of metallic thread
la·ment´ *n.* an expression of sorrow —*vi., vt.* express grief, sorrow, or remorse —**lam´en·ta·ble** *adj.*
lam·en·ta´tion *n.* a lament
lam´i·nate *n.* a thin covering material —*vt.* to cover with a thin material; to form from thin layers
lam´i·nat·ed *adj.* coated with or formed from thin layers
lam·i·na´tion *n.* a coating or joining; material formed from such process
lamp *n.* a device that provides light or heat
lamp´black *n.* fine carbon used as a pigment
lam·poon´ *n.* a satirical work that ridicules —*vt.* to satirize
la·nai´ *n.* a roofed porch or patio
lance *n.* a long shaft with a pointed end —*vt.* to pierce with a pointed weapon or instrument —**lanc´er** *n.*
lan´cet *n.* a surgical knife
land *n.* real estate; a nation or country —*vi., vt.* to come to a place
land bridge dry ground that joins two land masses
land´ed *adj.* possessing property
land´fill *n.* land created by depositing waste between layers of soil
land grant property deeded by a government
land´hold·er *n.* a property owner
land´ing *n.* termination of a voyage; a place for transferring cargo; the termination of a staircase
land´locked *adj.* without access to the sea
land´mark *n.* a boundary marker; a prominent feature; a building or area preserved for posterity
land´scape *n.* a scenic view —*vt., vi.* beautify by contouring, planting, etc.; beautify land as a vocation
lane *n.* a narrow byway; a defined channel
lan´guage *n.* a system of sounds, symbols, gestures, etc. for communicating
lan´guid *adj.* lacking vitality or force; sluggish —**lan´guid·ness** *n.*
lan´guish *vi.* be or become weak or neglected
lan´guor *n.* lack of energy; a lethargic condition —**lan´guor·ous** *adj.*
lank *adj.* lean and gaunt
lank´y *adj.* tall and thin; awkward
lan´tern *n.* a lamp with a protective case
lan´yard *n.* a short rope; a decorative cord
lap *n.* the surface formed when one is seated; amount by which one piece lies over another; act or sound of taking in liquid with the tongue —*vi., vt.* to lie over: overlap; to take in or the make sounds of taking in with the tongue
la·pel´ *n.* an extended collar that folds back against a garment
lap´i·dar·y *n.* one who finishes or deals in gems
lapse *n.* a temporary fault or break; a deterioration; termination of a right —*vi.* deteriorate or deviate from accepted course; lose a right
lap´top *n.* a small portable computer
lar´ce·nous *adj.* given to larceny
lar´ce·ny *n.* unlawful taking of property
lard *n.* rendered fat —*vt.* to prepare meat by injecting with strips of fat
lar´der *n.* store of food; a pantry
large *adj.* of greater than average size or scope; extensive; important; significant —**large´ly** *adv.*
lar·gess´ *n.* generosity; generous gift
lark *n.* a songbird; a spontaneous escapade —**lark´er** *n.*
las·civ´i·ous *adj.* lewd; arousing sexual desire
lash *n.* a whip; a sudden blow; a stinging attack of words; an eyelash —*vi., vt.* strike suddenly; attack with words
las´si·tude *n.* lethargy; a feeling of apathy or fatigue
las´so *n.* a noose used mainly to control livestock —*vt.* to catch with a noose
last *n.* the end or one at the end —*adj., adv.* final; the only one left; most recent but one —*vi., vt.* to continue; to endure or persist
last´ing *adj.* permanent; enduring
last name (*US*) a surname; a family name
last word final say; latest or most modern
latch *n.* a catch or lock as for a door or window —*vi., vt.* close or lock
latchkey child a child of working parents left at home unsupervised
late *adj.* after the usual or expected time; well on in time; recent; former or deceased —*adv.* after the usual or expected time; recently
late´ly *adv.* recently
lat´en *vi., vt.* to become late
la´tent *adj.* potential; undeveloped
lat´er·al *adj.* to the side; sideways
lat´est *n.* newest; most recent
lath *n.* a thin wood strip
lathe *n.* a machine for cutting and shaping wood or metal
lath´er *n.* foam —*vt., vi.* to coat with lather
lat´i·tude *n.* an angular distance from the equator or a celestial body; a range in which to function
la·trine´ *n.* a communal toilet
lat´ter *adj.* the second of two; nearer the end
lat´tice *n.* a panel of criss–crossed slats
laud *vt.* to praise —**laud·a·bil´i·ty** *n.*
laud´a·ble *adj.* worthy of praise —**laud´a·bly** *adv.*
lau´da·to·ry *adj.* bestowing praise
laugh *vi.* express amusement by an impromptu, inarticulate sound; mock with such sounds
laugh´a·ble *adj.* disdainful
laugh´ing *adj.* expressing amusement
laugh´ter *n.* the sound of merriment or derision
launch *vt.* set in motion —*vi.* begin
launch pad a platform and scaffold for launching a spacecraft
laun´der *vt.* to wash; to conceal or obscure the origin of
laun´dry *n.* clothes to be washed; a place for washing clothes
lau´re·ate *adj.* decked with laurel; distinguished —*n.* one deserving of special honor for achievement
la´va *n.* molten rock from a volcano; cooled and hardened volcanic rock
lav´a·to·ry *n.* a public bathroom; a washbasin; a toilet
lave *vt.* to bathe
lav´ish *adj.* extravagant; profuse —*vt.* to furnish in abundance
law *n.* a code or system of conduct
law´–a·bid´ing *adj.* faithful to law
law´ful *adj.* sanctioned by law —**law´ful·ly** *adv.*
law´less *adj.* not founded in law; without sanction; disregarding legal constraints
law´mak·er *n.* a legislator
lawn *n.* a tended tract of grass
law´suit *n.* a court action
law´yer *n.* one who gives counsel and support in legal matters
lax *adj.* slack, indifferent; not exacting or demanding —**lax´i·ty** *n.*
lay *vt.* place or arrange —*adj.* of the laity; not of a particular profession
lay´a·bout *n.* a loafer
lay´er *n.* a single thickness; a hen kept for egg production —*vi., vt.* to form in layers
lay´off *n.* suspension from jpb for lack of work; period of inactivity
laze *vi., vt.* to loaf
la´zy *adj.* inclined to inactivity; inviting idleness —**la´zi·ness** *n.*
lea *n.* a meadow
lead *vt., vi.* guide or direct; go first —*n.* first position; amount by which one is ahead; a clue or suggestion
lead´en *adj.* heavy; dull or listless
lead´er *n.* a guide; one in command; a person of influence or importance; that which precedes or joins
lead´er (*Brit.*) *n.* a written work expressing editorial opinion
lead´er·ship *n.* guidance; capacity to guide or command
lead´–in *n.* an introduction
lead´ing *adj.* most prominent; at the front; designed to elicit a response; directing or guiding
leaf *n.* an appendage issuing from the stem of a plant; a thin sheet of material; a page of a book —*vi., vt.* browse through
leaf´let *n.* a pamphlet or flier
leaf´y *adj* having leaves; producing leaves
league *n.* an association —*vi., vt.* to come or bring together in association
leak *n.* an opening that allows escape; substance that has escaped —*vi., vt.* allow escape; disclose through unauthorized channels
leak´y *adj.* inclined to leak
lean *adj.* having little fat; thin or spare; without excess or waste —*vi., vt.* to incline
lean´ing *n.* a tendency or preference
lean´–to *n.* a makeshift shelter; a structure with a long scoping roof
leap *vi., vt.* to jump or act abruptly

learn *vi., vt.* to acquire knowledge or understanding; to memorize —**learn´er** *n.*

learn´ed *adj.* scholarly

learn´ing *n.* knowledge or understanding acquired by study

learning curve time needed to acquire a skill

lease *n.* a contract for the use of property —*vt.* to grant use by contract —**leas´a·ble** *adj.*

lease´hold *n.* property controlled by a lease

leash *n.* a restraint —*vt.* to restrain

least *adj.* lowest in rank, importance, or magnitude —*adv.*

leath´er *n.* dressed hide of an animal

leath´er·work *n.* things made from leather; decorative work on leather

leath´er·y *adj.* having the texture or consistency of leather; tough

leave *n.* consent; a departure —*vt.* to depart; to abandon or overlook

leav´en, leav´en·ing *n.* a substance that causes fermentation

leav´ings *n.* remains or residue

lech´er·y *n.* preoccupation with sex; lust —**lech´er·ous** *adj.*

lec´tern *n.* a speaker's stand

lec´ture *n.* an address intended to enlighten; a reprimand —*vi., vt.* to expound; deliver a talk; admonish

lec´tur·er (*Brit.*) *n.* an educator; instructor at a college or university

ledge *n.* horizontal projection

ledg´er *n.* a book for recording financial transactions

leech *n.* a worm that feeds on blood; a parasite —*vi., vt.* to draw off resources

leer *n.* a sly look of lust —*vi.* to view with lust or maliciousness

leer´y *adj.* wary; distrustful

lee´way *n.* a margin; latitude

left´ist *n.* a radical —*adj.* liberal or radical

leg *n.* a limb that supports or propels; part of clothing covering the leg; a segment, as of a journey or a contest

leg´a·cy *n.* something passed on from an ancestor or predecessor

le´gal *adj.* based on, established by, or in conformity with law

le·gal·ese´ *n.* jargon of the legal profession

le´gal·ism *n.* overly strict interpretation of the law

le´gal·ize *vt.* make legal; sanction by law —**le·gal·i·za´tion** *n.*

legal pad a writing tablet of ruled sheets, $8^1/_2$ x 14 inches

legal tender currency that must be accepted for the payment of debts

leg´end *n.* a heroic fable; a famed person or deed; an inscription

leg´end·ar·y *adj.* of the nature of a legend; celebrated

leg´er·de·main´ *n.* sleight of hand; trickery

leg´i·ble *adj.* clear; able to be read

le´gion *n.* large number; a multitude

leg´is·late *vi., vt.* to write or enact laws —**leg´is·la·tor** *n.*

leg·is·la´tion *n.* law or set of laws

leg´is·la·tive *adj.* of a governing body; referring to the making of law

leg´is·la·ture *n.* a governing body charged with the making of laws

le·git´i·mate *adj.* complying with the law or standards; reasonable or logical —**le·git´i·ma·cy** *n.*

leg´ume *n.* a pod that splits to reveal edible seeds —**le·gu´mi·nous** *adj.*

lei *n.* crown or wreath of flowers

lei´sure *n.* free time

lei´sure·ly *adj.* marked by an unhurried pace—*adv.* in an unhurried way

lemon law law requiring repair or replacement of a defective product

lend *vt.* permit temporary use of; offer or impart

length *n.* measure of distance or duration —**go to great length** make significant effort; do all that is necessary

length´en *vi., vt.* make longer

length´y *adj.* somewhat long; longer than seems necessary

le´ni·ent *adj.* indulgent; not strict —**le´ni·ence, le´ni·en·cy** *n.*

lens *n.* transparent material shaped to bend light rays

le´o·tard *n.* close-fitting garment

lep´er *n.* one afflicted with leprosy; one shunned —**lep´rous** *adj.*

lep´re·chaun *n.* a fairy cobbler of Irish folklore

lep´ro·sy *n.* a tropical disease that can cause paralysis, numbness, and deformity

les´bi·an *n.* homosexual woman

le´sion *n.* a wound or abrasion

less, less´er *adj.* smaller or not as important

les·see´ *n.* one who leases

less´en *vt., vi.* make or become less

les´son *n.* something learned; a part of a course of instruction

les´sor *n.* one who leases to another

let *vt.,vi.* permit or allow; rent or lease

let´down *n.* disappointment

le´thal *adj.* harmful; able to cause death

le·thar´gic, le·thar´gi·cal *adj.* sluggish; listless; apathetic

leth´ar·gy *n.* dullness; apathy

let´ter *n.* a written symbol; written communication

let´tered *adj.* learned; inscribed with letters

let´up *n.* a pause or lull

leu·ke´mi·a *n.* a disease of the blood

lev´ee *n.* an embankment to hold back water

lev´el *n.* relative ranking; a flat surface; device for determining deviation from the horizontal —*adj.* having the same ranking; horizontal —*vt.* make horizontal or flat; measure deviation from the horizontal —**on the level** honest; fair

lev´el·head´ed *adj.* having common sense

lev´er *n.* a simple machine composed of a rigid rod pivoting on a fulcrum; a protruding handle

lev´er·age *n.* an advantage, as provided by a lever; political or financial power

leveraged buyout use of a company's own assets to finance its acquisition

le·vi´a·than *n.* a monster; an exceptionally large specimen

lev´i·tate *vi., vt.* float in the air with no visible means of support —**lev·i·ta´tion** *n.*

lev´i·ty *n.* frivolity; flippancy

lev´y *vt.* assess and collect, as taxes —*n.* monies collected

lewd *adj.* obscene; depraved

lex·i·cog´ra·phy *n.* the work of compiling a dictionary

lex´i·con *n.* a dictionary; a collection of terms peculiar to a discipline

li·a·bil´i·ty *n.* a debt or obligation

li´a·ble *adj.* legally responsible; at risk; extremely likely

li´ai·son *n.* a connection or link; one who serves as a link; a clandestine affair

li´ar *n.* one who deceives by lying

li·ba´tion *n.* a beverage

li´bel *n.* a malicious falsehood that defames —*vt.* —**li´bel·ous, li´bel·lous** *adj.* —**li´bel·ous·ly, li´bel·lous·ly** *adv.*

lib´er·al *adj.* open to new ideas and concepts; not strict; lavish in gift–giving

lib´er·al·ize *vi., vt.* become or make more liberal

lib´er·ate *vt.* set free, as from bondage or onerous convention

lib·er·a´tion *n.* the act of freeing or being set free

lib·er·tar´i·an *n.* a believer in freedom from government intervention

lib´er·tine *n.* one lacking moral restraint; a reprobate

lib´er·ty *n.* freedom from restraint or restriction; rights granted

li·bid´i·nous *adj.* displaying lust; salacious —**li·bid´i·nous·ly** *adv.*

li·bi´do *n.* energy associated with biological impulses; sexual appetite

li´brar·y *n.* a collection of printed matter, recordings, etc.; the place where a collection is kept

li·bret´to *n.* words set to music

li´cence (*Brit.*) *n.* legal authorization; lack of restraint or adherence to common practice

li´cense (*US*) *n.* legal authorization; lack of restraint or adherence to common practice —*vt.* grant authorization; formally permit

li·cen´tious *adj.* lacking restraint or regard for accepted morality

lic´it *adj.* legal

lick *n.* a stroking or touching with the tongue; a small amount; a blow —*vt.* stroke with the tongue; overcome; to punish by striking

lick´ing *n.* spanking; a hard loss

lid *n.* cover for a container

lie *n.* something meant to deceive; the manner in which a thing is positioned —*vi.* pass on false information or create a false impression; recline; be in a certain place

lien *n.* the right to property as security for a debt

lieu·ten´ant *n.* officer in a military or quasi–military organization; a deputy or assistant

life *n.* the condition of a functioning creature; the time between birth and death; a group of living things; a segment of one's existence

life´–and–death´ *adj.* critical

life cycle the stages of development of a living creature

life´less *adj.* dead; inanimate; lacking spirit

life´like *adj.* precisely imitating life

life style a mode of living

lift *vi.* rise; disperse —*vt.* raise; give a ride to; steal —*n.* an instance of rising; a ride offered; a rise in condition or attitude

lift (*Brit.*) *n.* a conveyance between floors of a building: an elevator

lig´a·ment *n.* connective tissue of the body

lig´a·ture *n.* a cord, bandage, etc. that binds; a symbol created from two or more characters, such as æ

light *n.* illumination, or its source; clarification; source of fire —*vi., vt.* give off illumination; start to burn; dismount from a vehicle —*adj.* illuminated; of color that is less dark; relatively little in weight, quantity, force, etc.; insubstantial

light´en *vi., vt.* to make brighter; to make less heavy or oppressive

light´–fin·gered *adj.* inclined to steal; adept at petty theft

light´heart·ed *adj.* free of care

light´ing *n.* style or fixtures for artificial illumination; an amount of light provided

light´ly *adv.* with little exertion; delicately; in a free and easy way

light´ning *n.* a natural electric discharge —*adj.* quick or abrupt

light show a display of laser light

light´weight *n.* a weight class in sports; one lacking in knowledge, ability, etc. —*adj.* relatively light in substance or weight

light´–year *n.* distance traveled by light in one year

like *vt.* enjoy or be inclined toward —*vi.* show preference for —*n.* a preference —*adj.* similar —*prep.* in the same or a similar manner —**lik´a·ble, like´a·ble** *adj.*

like´li·hood *n.* probability

like´ly *adj.* possible; believable

like´–mind´ed *adj.* in agreement

lik´en *vt.* to compare

like·ness *n.* a representation

like´wise *adj.* also

lik´ing *n.* fondness; preference

lilt *n.* a light, cheerful style; a jaunty walk —*vi., vt.* to speak or sing in a light, cheerful style

limb *n.* an appendage

lim´ber *adj.* flexible; supple

limber up to flex; make flexible

lime´light *n.* a center of attention

lim´er·ick *n.* a light verse of five lines

lim´it *n.* a boundary; restriction or condition; amount not to be exceeded —*vt.* confine within a boundary; firmly establish

lim·i·ta´tion *n.* a restriction; a deficiency
lim´it·ed *adj.* restricted or deficient; cramped or confined —*n.* a train making only express stops
limited edition a work produced in specified numbers
lim´it·ing *adj.* serving to limit
lim´it·less *adj.* unbounded; without limit; infinite
lim´o, lim´ou·sine *n.* a large, elegant automobile
limp *n.* a hesitant or hobbling gait —*vi.* move haltingly; hobble —*adj.* lacking rigidity; lacking strength or vigor
lim´pid *adj.* of a clear, serene liquid; logical and lucid
line *n.* a real or imaginary stripe: *firing line*; things in a row or series; a sequence; a connection: *phone line*; a transportation system; field of competence or employment; a row of words or symbols; a brief note; a concept or notion —*vt.* cover the interior of
lin´e·age *n.* ancestry
lin´e·al *adj.* directly descended; relating to lineage
lin´e·ar *adj.* in a line; one–dimensional —**lin´e·ar·ly** *adv.*
lin´en *n.* cloth made from flax thread —*adj.* made of or resembling linen
linen closet a storage area for bedding, tablecloths, etc.
lin´er *n.* material covering the inside; a large passenger ship or airplane
lines´man *n.* a sports official who judges from the sideline
line´up *n.* persons assembled for identification; a group of people identified with a common purpose
lin´ger *vi.* remain longer than anticipated; be slow to act
lin·ge·rie´ *n.* women's underclothing
lin´guist *n.* one who studies language —**lin·guis´tic** *adj.*
lin·guis´tics *n.* the study of human speech
lin´i·ment *n.* a liquid applied to relieve pain or tension
lin´ing *n.* backing material
link *n.* one of a series; a connector —*vi., vt.* to connect
linked *adj.* connected
li·no´le·um *n.* a floor covering
lint *n.* bits of shed fiber; downy fibers from linen, used as dressing
lin´tel *n.* the brace at the top of a window or door frame
li´on *n.* a large carniverous feline; a distinguished person
li´on·heart·ed *adj.* extremely brave
li´on·ize *vt.* treat as a celebrity
lip *n.* fleshy structure surrounding the mouth; impertinent speech
lip service insincere agreement
liq´ue·fy *vi., vt.* to make liquid
li·queur´ *n.* a sweet beverage, often flavored with fruit, herbs, or spices
liq´uid *adj.* capable of flowing; of assets readily convertible
liq´ui·date *vt.* discharge an obligation; convert into cash; destroy —*vi.* close out a business by disposing of assets —**liq´ui·da·tor** *n.*
li´quor (*US*) *n.* distilled beverage; liquid obtained from cooking
lisle *n.* a fine cotton fabric
lisp *n.* a speech defect —*vi., vt.* to speak with a lisp
list *n.* a catalog of items, as for shopping, etc.; a tilting —*vt.,vi.* itemize; cause to tilt
lis´ten *n.* be attentive; heed
lis´ten·a·ble *adj.* pleasing to the ear
list´less *adj.* lacking vitality or spirit; apathetic, indifferent
list price recommended selling price
lit´a·ny *n.* responsive prayer; something often repeated
li´ter (*US*) *n.* a unit of volume
lit´er·a·cy *n.* education, as the ability to read and write
lit´er·al *adj.* precise interpretation; verbatim
lit´er·al·ly *adv.* precisely; word for word
lit´er·ar·y *adj.* relating to or fond of literature
lit´er·ate *adj.* educated; well–informed —**lit´er·ate·ness** *n.*
lit·e·ra´ti *n. pl.* cultivated or well–educated persons
lit´er·a·ture *n.* printed matter; a collection of writings
lithe, lithe´some *adj.* supple or graceful
lith´o·graph *n.* a print made by lithography —*vt.* —**lith´o·graph´ic** *adj.*
li·thog´ra·phy *n.* a process for printing fine reproductions
lit´i·gant *n.* one involved in a lawsuit —*adj.* engaged in a lawsuit
lit´i·gate *vi., vt.* take part in legal action —**lit·i·ga´tion** *n.*
li·ti´gious *adj.* tending to be involved in legal action
litmus test a chemical test to determine acidity; use of a single determinant to test
li´tre (*Brit.*) *n.* a unit of volume equal to approximately 33.8 US ounces
lit´ter *n.* discarded trash; young from a single birth; material lining a cage; a framework for transporting —*vi., vt.* scatter trash
lit´tle *n.* a small amount —*adj.* modest in size or amount; unimportant —*adv.* slightly; not at all
lit´ur·gy *n.* a set form for worship or ritual —**li·tur´gi·cal** *adj.*
liv´a·ble, live´a·ble *adj.* fit for habitation; acceptable or tolerable
live *vi.* possess life; exist —*adj.* having life; useable, having potential: *live wire*; physically present
live´li·hood *n.* means of support
live´ly *adj.* marked by energy and spirit; active —*adv.*
liv´en *vi., vt.* to become lively
liv´er·ied *adj.* uniformed
liv´er·y *n.* a uniform; care and boarding of horses; a service that rents vehicles
live´stock *n.* domestic animals
live wire *n.* wire attached to a power source; an extremely dynamic person
liv´id *adj.* extremely angry
liv´ing *adj.* having life; pertaining to existence —*n.* being alive; a means to support life
living wage earnings sufficient to provide necessities
living will *n.* a stipulation for treatment if the maker is alive but unable to respond
load *n.* that which is carried, supported, etc.; burden of work or responsibility —*vi., vt.* put or place
load´ed *adj.* carrying a full load; of a troublesome or hidden meaning
loaf *n.* an oblong mass
loaf´er *n.* one frequently inactive or unemployed —**loaf** *vi.*
loan *n.* something given or received for temporary use
loan shark one who lends money at high interest
loath *adj.* hesitant or reluctant
loathe *vt.* despise
loath´ing *n.* aversion
loath´some *adj.* arousing intense dislike
lob´by (*US*) *n.* an entryway; persons attempting to influence —*vi., vt.* attempt to influence legislators —**lob´by·ist** *n.*
lo´cal *adj.* of a relatively small area or political subdivision; not widespread —*n.* a regional chapter; a train that stops at every station
lo·cale´ *n.* a site or setting
lo·cal´i·ty *n.* a specific place
lo´cal·ize *vt.* restrict to a particular area
lo´cate *vi.* situate —*vt.* learn the position of; assign to a place
lo·ca´tion *n.* a place or position; a place designated
lock *n.* device for securing; closed section of a channel for raising or lowering water level; a bit of hair —*vi., vt.* make secure; immobilize; link together
lock´er *n.* a storage compartment
lock´et *n.* a small hinged case
lock´out *n.* closing of a workplace to striking employees
lo·co·mo´tion *n.* act of moving
lo·co·mo´tive *adj.* able to move —*n.* a self–propelled engine
lode *n.* a mineral deposit; an abundant source
lodge *n.* a rustic dwelling; a meeting hall —*vi., vt.* to provide temporary living space; to place or plant
lodg´ing *n.* place to live —**lodg´er** *n.*
loft *n.* an open area directly under a building's roof; a gallery or alcove
loft´y *adj.* tall or towering; arrogant or haughty
log *n.* a cut tree; a record, as of performance —*vt.* set down in writing; accumulate, as time or distance
log´book *n.* book for recording official data
loge *n.* front rows of the mezzanine or box in a theater
log´ic *n.* fundamentals of reasoning; sound reasoning; comparable functions in a computer program
log´i·cal *adj.* capable of analytical thought; reasonable
lo·gis´tics *n.* planning and managing of an operation
lo´go, log´o·type *n.* symbol or trademark of a business
lo´gy *adj.* lethargic; muddled
loi´ter *vi.* loll or linger about; waste time
loll *vi.* to move or lie about
lone *adj.* without anyone or anything else; lacking companionship
lone´ly *adj.* saddened by being alone; deserted —**lone´li·ness** *n.*
lon´er *n.* one who works alone or shuns company of others
lone´some *adj.* lonely
long *vi.* have a craving or desire —*adj.* relatively lengthy; of specific length or duration
lon·gev´i·ty *n.* long life or duration
long´hair *n.* one with refined taste in art —**long´hair, long´haired** *adj.*
long´hand *n.* cursive writing
long´ing *n.* craving or desire
lon´gi·tude *n.* angular distance from the prime meridian or a celestial body
lon·gi·tu´di·nal *adj.* of longitude; running lengthwise
long´shore·man *n.* a dock worker
long shot a venture with little prospect of success
long´–suf´fer·ing *adj.* uncomplaining; patiently enduring
long´–wind·ed *adj.* wordy or tiresome
loo´fa, loo´fah *n.* dried sponge-like part of a tropical fruit, used for cleansing the skin
look *n.* a gaze, stare, glance, etc.; appearance or fashion —*vi., vt.* use sight; occupy one's attention; seek out or search; appear to be
loom *vi.* hover over; menace
loop *n.* a circular pattern; a circle —*vi., vt.* form or fasten into a circle; move in a circular pattern
loop´hole *n.* an oversight that provides escape
loose *adj.* not attached or confined; poorly attached or fitted; lacking discipline; vague —*vi., vt.* become or make less restrained; release
loose end unresolved detail
loos´en *vi., vt.* make loose or looser
loot *n.* stolen goods —*vi., vt.* to plunder —**loot´er** *n.*
lop *vt.* cut off or eliminate
lope *n.* a leisurely gait —*vi.*
lop´sid·ed *adj.* tipped to one side
lo·qua´cious *adj.* talkative —**lo·quac´i·ty** *n.*
lord *n.* one of high rank; a god —*vi.* to domineer
lord´ly *adj.* majestic or noble; pretentious; domineering
lore *n.* collected traditions or wisdom; knowledge
lor·gnette´ *n.* corrective lenses on a short handle
lose *vt.* be deprived of; unable to keep; rid oneself of —*vi.* endure loss —**los´er** *n.*
loss *n.* deprivation; something taken, misplaced, etc.
lost *adj.* no longer in one's possession or in evidence
lot *n.* group of associated things; large amount; token selected at random; one's fate; plot of land

lo´tion *n.* a liquid applied as medication or cosmetic
lot´ter·y *n.* selection made by lot
loud *adj.* of high amplification; bright in color; glaringly bad design
loud´mouth *n.* one who speaks loudly or thoughtlessly
lounge *n.* a waiting room; a tavern or café; a type of couch —*vi., vt.* recline; pass time leisurely
louse *n.* a parasitic insect; disreputable person
lous´y *adj.* infested; of poor quality; unpleasant
lout *n.* one regarded as ill–mannered or tiresome —**lout´ish** *adj.*
lou´ver *n.* angled slats that provide ventilation
lov´a·ble, love´a·ble *adj.* having qualities that invite affection
love *n.* strong attraction; an object of affection or desire; sexual intercourse —*vt.* have affection or desire for; engage in sexual intercourse
love affair an intimate relationship; a strong attraction
love feast a symbolic meal to promote friendship
love´–in *n.* a gathering intended to promote love and understanding
love´lorn *adj.* deprived of love or a lover
love´ly *adj.* beautiful and charming; attractive or appealing —*adv.*
lov´er *n.* one devoted to a person, activity, etc.; a sexual partner
love´sick *adj.* distracted by love
lov´ing *adj.* affectionate
loving cup decorative urn; award
low *adj.* less than usual or acceptable in height, quality, etc. —*adv.*
low´born *adj.* of humble birth
low´boy *n.* a chest of drawers
low´bred *adj.* unrefined
low´brow *n.* one of unrefined tastes —*adj.* suited to the unrefined
low comedy burlesque or slapstick comedy
low´down *n.* gossip; the latest information
low´–down *adj.* base; contemptible
low´er *adj.* less in price, position, etc. —*n.* a menacing look —*vi., vt.* to become less; to look menacing
low´–key´ *adj.* restrained; subdued
low´life *n.* a disreputable person
low´ly *adj.* unpretentious; humble —*adv.*
low´–pres·sure *adj.* relaxed; easy-going
low´–pro´file *adj.* acting so as to avoid undue attention
low–tech *adj.* of that which does not employ or require modern technology
lox *n.* smoked salmon
loy´al *adj.* marked by allegiance; faithful —**loy´al·ty** *n.*
loz´enge *n.* a medicated candy
lu´au *n.* a traditional Hawaiian feast
lu´bri·cate *vt.* apply a substance to reduce friction —**lu´bri·cant** *n.*
lu´cent *adj.* clear or transparent; luminous —**lu´cen·cy** *n.*
lu´cid *adj.* clear; easily understood; sane or rational —**lu·cid´i·ty** *n.*
luck *n.* chance events
luck´i·ly *adv.* by good fortune
luck´y *adj.* having or bringing good fortune
lu´cra·tive *adj.* profitable
lu´cre *n.* money
lu´di·crous *adj.* incongruous; laughable
lug *vi., vt.* pull or carry with difficulty
luge *n.* a racing sled
lug´gage *n.* travelling bags; effects carried by a traveler
luke´warm *adj.* slightly warm; lacking enthusiasm
lull *n.* relative quiet or calm —*vt.* to calm or quiet, as fears
lull´a·by *n.* song that soothes
lum´ber *n.* (*Brit.*) unwanted items; (*US*) wood used in construction —*vi.* to move clumsily; to plod
lu´mi·nar·y *n.* a distinguished person; a model for others
lu·mi·nes´cence *n.* light accompanied by little heat
lu´mi·nous *adj.* emitting light; easily understood
lump *n.* a bulge or swelling; a clump; a total amount —*adj.* complete: *lump sum* —*vt.* consider as a whole —**lump´y** *adj.*
lu´na·cy *n.* madness; foolishness or silliness
lu´nar *adj.* involving the moon
lunar month time of a moon's orbit
lunch, lunch´eon *n.* midday meal —*vi.* eat a midday meal
lunge *n.* sudden thrust —*vi., vt.* thrust forward suddenly
lurch *n.* a jerking movement; an unsteady gait —*vi.* move jerkily; walk unsteadily
lure *n.* an enticement —*vt.* attract or entice, especially with inducement
lu´rid *adj.* gruesome or ghastly; pale or sallow
lurk *vi.* to prowl stealthily; to lie in wait
lus´cious *adj.* sweet and juicy; beautiful or sensuous
lush *adj.* marked by abundance; luxurious
lust *n.* intense craving —*vi.* have an intense desire
lus´ter (*US*), **lus´tre** (*Brit.*) *n.* radiance; brilliance; gloss on pottery achieved by glazing —*vt.* apply a glaze —*vi.* become glossy —**lus´trous** *adj.*
lust´y *adj.* robust; boisterous
lux·u´ri·ant *adj.* marked by abundant growth; lavish
lux·u´ri·ate *vi.* revel in luxury
lux·u´ri·ous *adj.* marked by extravagance or indulgence
lux´u·ry *n.* that contributing to comfort and enjoyment
lyr´ic *adj.* of musical verse
lyr´i·cal *adj.* melodious
lyr´i·cist, lyr´ist *n.* one who writes song lyrics
m, M thirteenth letter of the alphabet; 1000 in Roman characters
ma·ca´bre *adj.* gruesome; horrible
mac´er·ate *vi., vt.* make soft by soaking
mach´i·nate *vt.* to plot
ma·chine´ *n.* a device to modify and transfer energy; any contrivance that aids; one who performs in a predictable manner —*adj.* of or like a mechanical device —*vi., vt.* fashion with a mechanical device —**ma·chin´er·y** *n.*
ma·chis´mo *n.* an inflated notion of masculinity
ma´cho *adj.* marked by show of masculinity —*n.* one overly impressed with masculinity or virility
mac·ro·bi·ot´ics *n.* promotion of health and well–being by regulation of diet
mac´ro·cosm *n.* the universe; a, multifaceted aggregate
mac´ro·scop´ic *adj.* that can be seen with the naked eye
mad *adj.* angry; insane; lacking judgment
mad´am *n.* a polite form for addressing a woman
mad´cap *adj.* wild and reckless; uninhibited
mad´den *vi., vt.* make angry
mad´den·ing *adj.* tending to cause anger
made *adj.* fashioned or produced
made´–to–or´der *adj.* fashioned according to instructions; well–suited
made´–up´ *adj.* fictitious; complete
mad´ly *adj.* in a foolish or frenzied manner
mad´ness *n.* insanity; excessive enthusiasm
mad´ri·gal *n.* a vocal composition for several voices
mael´strom *n.* a large whirlpool; a turbulent situation
mae´stro *n.* a master
mag´a·zine´ *n.* a printed periodical; storage compartment
mag´got *n.* insect larva; a grub
mag´ic *n.* supernatural power; sorcery; sleight of hand, misdirection, illusion, etc.; a mystifying quality —*adj.* relating to the supernatural; mystical —**mag´i·cal** *adj.*
mag´is·trate *n.* a local official such as justice of the peace
mag´is·tra·cy *n.* office or jurisdiction of a magistrate
mag´ma *n.* molten rock that forms part of Earth's core
mag·na·nim´i·ty *n.* generosity
mag·nan´i·mous *adj.* generous; inclined to forgive
mag´nate *n.* a prominent industrialist
mag´net *n.* anything that attracts
mag·net´ic *adj.* having power to attract
mag´net·ism *n.* energy of a magnet; power to attract
mag´net·ize *vt.* to make magnetic; to fascinate or attract
mag·ni·fi·ca´tion *n.* enlargement of an image
mag·nif´i·cence *n.* grandeur; splender
mag·nif´i·cent *adj.* majestic or noble; exceptionally good
mag´ni·fy *vt.* make or appear larger
mag´ni·tude *n.* size or extent; importance
magnum opus a masterpiece
maid´en *n.* an unmarried woman —*adj.* unmarried; original or beginning
mail (*US*) *n.* material delivered by the postal system —*vi., vt.* send by post
mail order buying or selling by mail
maim *vt.* mutilate or disable
main *adj.* most significant —*n.* the dominant part; a large pipe or conduit; open sea
main´frame *n.* a large computer serving many users
main´land *n.* large body of land; a continent
main´ly *adv.* largely; predominantly
main´stream *n.* dominant or accepted views —*adj.* conventional or traditional
main·tain´ *vt.* uphold; preserve in a desired state
main´te·nance *n.* care required to preserve
maî´tre d'hô·tel´ *n.* a headwaiter
ma·jes´tic *adj.* stately or dignified; magnificent
maj´es·ty *n.* grandeur and nobility of a sovereign; elegance or splendor
ma´jor *n.* a military rank —*adj.* among the most important; of exceptional scope, size, etc.
ma·jor–do´mo *n.* chief steward of a household; a butler
ma·jor´i·ty *n.* more than half; group that controls the most votes; legally of age
make *vi., vt.* assemble or fashion; create or produce; to cause
make´–be·lieve *n.* a flight of fancy —*adj.* fanciful
make´–do, make´shift *n.* a convenient substitute —*adj.* temporary; provisional
make´up *n.* manner of arrangement; cosmetics; compensation for missing or unsatisfactory work
mal´ad·just´ed *adj.* poorly fitted to the stresses of life
mal´a·droit´ *adj.* inept; unskilled
mal´a·dy *n.* ailment or affliction
mal·aise´ *n.* a feeling of uneasiness or despondency
mal´a·prop·ism *n.* substitution of a word for one that sounds similar
ma·lar´ia *n.* infectious disease marked by chills and fever
mal´con·tent *n.* one habitually disgruntled; an agitator —*adj.* disgruntled
male *adj.* of the sex that fertilizes eggs of the female; masculine; of a coupling device —*n.*
mal·e·dic´tion *n.* a curse
mal´e·fac·tor *n.* a criminal
ma·lef´i·cent *adj.* harmful or hurtful; wicked
ma·lev´o·lence *n.* malicious or spiteful behavior
ma·lev´o·lent *adj.* malicious, spiteful; giving rise to evil
mal·fea´sance *n.* impropriety by a public official
mal´for·ma´tion *n.* deformity
mal·func´tion *n.* a breakdown —*vi.* perform poorly
mal´ice *n.* a desire to harm; spite —**ma·li´cious** *adj.*
ma·lign´ *vt.* speak ill of; slander
ma·lig´nant *adj.* extremely harmful; malevolent

ma·lin´ger *vi.* avoid duty by feigning illness
mall (*US*) *n.* a shaded walk; an enclosed shopping complex; a park–like public area
mal´le·a·ble *adj.* flexible or adaptable; able to be molded
mal´let *n.* a type of hammer
mal·nour´ished *adj.* lacking proper food
mal·o´dor·ous *adj.* foul smelling
mal·prac´tice *n.* improper treatment or conduct by a professional
malt *n.* grain that has germinated and dried; a beverage brewed or flavored with malt
mal´treat´ *vt.* to abuse
mam´mal *n.* any of a class of warm–blooded vertebrates that suckle their young —**mam·ma´li·an** *adj.*
mam·mal´o·gy *n.* the study of mammals
mam´mon *n.* wealth deemed to exert a harmful influence
mam´moth *n.* a large extinct elephant; anything very large —*adj.* huge; enormous
man *n.* an adult male human; humans generally; a male underling —*vt.* to assign or take a position; hire a staff
man´a·cle *n.* a restraint —*vt.* to constrain
man´age *vi., vt.* direct or control; administer; bring about; have control of —**man´a·ge´ri·al** *adj.*
man´age·a·ble *adj.* compliant; submissive
man´age·ment *n.* those who guide or direct a business
man´date *n.* a declaration; an assignment; a charge —*vt.* assign or require
man´da·to·ry *adj.* required; compulsory
mane *n.* long hair growing about the neck
ma·neu´ver (*US*) *n.* a change in speed, direction, etc.; a move or series of moves —*vi., vt.* change course; influence people or events
mange *n.* skin disease of animals
man´ger *n.* a feeding trough
man´gle *vt.* disfigure; ruin through ineptness
man´han·dle *vt.* treat roughly
ma´nia *n.* an obsession; irrational behavior
ma´ni·ac *n.* an insane person; one who acts in an irrational or capricious manner
man´i·cure *n.* cosmetic care of fingernails —*vt.* care for fingernails; crop closely and evenly
man´i·fest *adj.* evident; obvious —*n.* list of cargo, passengers, etc. —*vt.* become evident
man·i·fes·ta´tion *n.* evidence or proof; embodiment of a spirit
ma·nip´u·late *vt.* control or shape; persuade deviously —**ma·nip·u·la´tion** *n.*
man´kind´ *n.* humanity; the human race
man´ly *adj.* masculine
man´–made´ *adj.* manufactured; artificial
man´ne·quin *n.* a model used to display clothing
man´ner *n.* a style or mode
man´ner·ism *n.* a distinctive trait; affectation; artistic style
man´ner·ly *adj.* having excellent manners —*adv.* politely
ma·noeu´vre (*Brit.*) *n.* a change in speed, direction, etc.; a move or series of moves —*vi., vt.* change course; influence
man´or *n.* a landed estate; main house on an estate —**ma·no´ri·al** *adj.*
man´sard *n.* roof with a double pitch
manse *n.* a clergyman's house
man´sion *n.* a large house
man´slaugh·ter *n.* murder by accident
man·teau´ *n.* a cloak
man´tel, man´tel·piece *n.* shelf over a fireplace
man´tle *n.* a cloak; thing that covers or conceals —*vt., vi.* cover or conceal
man´tra *n.* a chant that aids in meditation
man´u·al *adj.* relating to the hands —*n.* reference or instruction book
manual training training in practical arts
man·u·fac´ture *vi., vt.* fashion, fabricate, or assemble; create a false report —*n.* production of goods
man·u·mit´ *vt.* to liberate
ma·nure´ *n.* dung or decaying matter —*vt.* to fertilize
man´u·script *n.* text lettered by hand; unpublished text
man·y *n., pron.* a large number —*adj.* numerous
man´y·fold *adv.* a large number
map *n.* depiction of an area —*vt.* to survey and depict graphically; set out in detail
mar *vt.* damage or deface
mar´a·thon *n.* competition requiring endurance
ma·raud´ *vi., vt.* attack and plunder
mar´ble *n.* a multicolored stone —**mar´ble, mar´ble·ize** *vt.* streak with color —**mar´bled** *adj.*
marble cake a cake streaked with colored batters
mar´bling *n.* streaking resembling marble
march *n.* orderly forward movement; a gathering to protest or champion a cause —*vi., vt.* move forward in an orderly, methodical manner
mar´ga·rine *n.* a butter substitute
mar´gin *n.* a limit; an allowance for variation
mar´gin·al *adj.* barely acceptable
ma·ri´na *n.* a docking area
mar´i·nade´ *n.* seasoned liquid
mar´i·nate *vi., vt.* to soak in a marinade —**mar·i·na´tion** *n.*
ma·rine´ *adj.* relating to the sea or seamen
mar´i·o·nette´ *n.* a puppet
mar´i·tal *adj.* relating to marriage
mar´i·time *adj.* at or near the sea; of the sea or seamen
mark *n.* a random impression; a representative symbol; a rating; an objective —*vi., vt.* imprint; scratch or blotch; identify by symbol; label; notice —**make one's mark** be successful or notable —**mark time** wait for a propitious time —**wide of the mark** a failure
marked *adj.* noticeable; prominent
mark´er *n.* thing that identifies; writing implement
mar´ket *n.* the business of buying and selling; a place where goods are traded; trade in a commodity —*vi., vt.* buy or sell
mar´ket·place *n.* site where goods are traded; a distinct domain: *literary marketplace*
market research accumulation and analysis of consumer–related data
mark´ing *n.* a characteristic feature or pattern
mar´ma·lade *n.* fruit preserve
mar´riage *n.* legal union of two people; joining of two elements
mar´riage·a·ble *adj.* suited or able to be married
mar´ry *vt.* join; combine or closely unite —*vi.* take as a life partner —**mar´ried** *adj.*
marsh *n.* land that is wet and muddy —**marsh´land** *n.*
mar´shal *n.* an officer of the law —*vt.* gather or arrange: *marshal forces*
marsh´mal·low *n.* a soft, spongy confection
marsh·y *adj.* wet and muddy
mar·su´pi·al *n.* mammal that bears its young in an external pouch
mart *n.* a market
mar´tial *adj.* referring to war or warriors —**mar´tial·ist** *n.*
mar´ti·net´ *n.* a strict disciplinarian
mar´tyr *n.* one who suffers for a belief; one who suffers without complaint; one who exaggerates discomfort for sympathy —*vt.* persecute for devotion to a belief or cause —**mar´tyr·dom** *n.*
mar´vel *n.* a thing of awe or wonder —*vi., vt.* wonder at; be amazed
mar´vel·ous *adj.* wonderous; impressive
mas´cot *n.* a symbol believed to bring good fortune
mas´cu·line *n.* characteristic of a male; attributes associated with a male —**mas·cu·lin´i·ty** *n.*
mash *n.* a pulpy mass —*vt.* reduce to a pulpy mass
mask *n.* concealment or protection for the face; a representational wall ornament —*vi., vt.* to conceal or cover
mas´och·ist *n.* one who derives pleasure from abuse
ma´son *n.* one who works with stone
mas´quer·ade´ *n.* a costume party; a deception —*vi.* assume a disguise
mass *n.* a clump; physical bulk; undetermined amount —*vi., vt.* assemble into a mass —*adj.* large in number or scale
mas´sa·cre *n.* indiscriminate slaughter —*vt.* to slaughter
mas·sage´ *n.* a rubdown —*vt.* relax muscles by rubbing or kneading; manipulate data
mas·seur´, mas·seuse´ *n.* one trained in the art of massage
mas´sive *adj.* large or bulky; imposing; cumbersome
mass´–pro·duce´ *vt.* manufacture in large quantities
mass transit local transportation systems that regularly carry large numbers
mas´ter *adj.* primary or controlling; proficient or knowledgeable —*n.* one who owns or controls; a teacher; one proficient in a craft; one who possesses exception knowledge or ability —*vt.* control; acquire knowledge or ability
mas´ter·ful *adj.* domineering; exhibiting skill
mas´ter·mind *n.* one with ability to conceive or direct a complex operation —*vt.* plan and direct
master of ceremonies one who presides over a formal gathering
mas´ter·piece *n.* outstanding work
mas´ter·stroke *n.* a notable action or achievement
mast´head *n.* name of a publication as it appears on a cover or leading page; the listing in a publication of its ownership, staff, etc.
mas´ti·cate *vi., vt.* chew food; reduce to a pulp
mas´to·don *n.* an extinct elephant–like animal
mas·tur·ba´tion *n.* sexual stimulation without intercourse
mat *n.* material for a bed, covering, protection, etc.; border for a picture —*vi., vt.* to press or tangle
mat´a·dor *n.* a bullfighter
match *n.* a small strip used to produce fire; a thing nearly like another; thing compatible or harmonious; a sporting contest —*vt.* to give or to get something identical, comparable, or compatible
match´less *adj.* without equal
match´mak·er *n.* one who arranges marriages
mate *n.* one of a pair; a close friend or ally —*vi., vt.* to pair
ma·te´ri·al *adj.* relevent; tangible —*n.* unprocessed matter, information, etc.
ma·te´ri·al·ism *n.* excessive concern for possessions
ma·te´ri·al·ize *vi.* appear suddenly —*vt.* come forth
ma·ter´nal *adj.* of a mother or motherhood
ma·ter´ni·ty *n.* emotions associated with motherhood —*adj.* relating to pregnancy or childbirth
math, math·e·mat´ics *n.* the science of numbers
math·e·mat´i·cal *adj.* pertaining to numbers
mat´i·nee´ *n.* afternoon performance
ma´tri·arch *n.* woman who heads a family; a respected woman
ma´tri·ar·chy *n.* society that traces lineage through women
ma·tric´u·late *vt., vi.* be permitted into a course of study
ma·tri·lin´e·age *n.* maternal lineage
mat´ri·mo·ny *n.* union of two persons; being married
ma´trix *n.* a mold or pattern
ma´tron *n.* a mature woman; a female supervisor
matte *n.* a soft or dull finish —*adj.* having a dull finish

mat´ter *n.* substance; something of interest —*vi.* be important
mat´ter–of–fact´ *adj.* objective; unimaginative
mat´ting *n.* a rough fabric, as for floor covering
mat´tress *n.* pad for sleeping
mat´u·rate *vi.* mature or ripen
ma·ture´ *adj.* fully developed; ripe —*vi., vt.* ripen; become due —**ma·tur´i·ty** *n.*
maud´lin *adj.* tearful; nauseatingly sentimental
maul *n.* a heavy hammer —*vt.* beat or batter; mangle
mau·so·le´um *n.* a tomb; a tomb–like room or building
ma´ven *n.* an expert
mav´er·ick *adj.* independent; radical —*n.* a nonconformist; one acting independently
mawk´ish *adj.* overly sentimental
max´im *n.* an adage or motto
max´i·mize *vt.* increase or emphasize to the utmost
max´i·mum *adj.* of the largest possible —*n.* largest amount or extent
may´be *adv.* possibly —*n.* a possibility
may´hem *n.* deliberate injury; reckless damage or destruction; a state of turmoil
may´o, may´on·naise *n.* a thick, rich sauce or dressing
may´or *n.* a municipal administrator
maze *n.* a complex pattern of paths; a network of complicated or confusing elements
mead´ow *n.* an expanse of pasture or grassland
mea´ger (*US*), **mea´gre** (*Brit.*) *adj.* scant; lacking
meal *n.* edible grain; food eaten at a sitting
mean *adj.* cruel or malicious; low in quality or amount; selfish or miserly —*n.* midway between extremes —*vt.* indicate or intend
me·an´der *vi.* wander aimlessly —*n.* a winding course
mean´ing *adj.* having purpose —*n.* significance or purpose; that understood
mean´ing·less *adj.* without purpose; insignificant
mean´ly *adv.* in a shabby way
mean´ness *n.* cruelty or malice; a lack; selfishness
mean´–spir´it·ed *adj.* characterized by pettiness
mea´sur·a·ble *adj.* that can be quantified; finite; significant
mea´sure *n.* a standard unit of size, weight, etc.; a device calibrated to a standard; an unspecified amount; an unspecified action —*vi., vt.* express or gauge in terms of a standard unit —**beyond measure** incalculable
mea´sured *adj.* steady and deliberate
mea´sure·ment *n.* determination of size, capacity, etc.
meat *n.* edible flesh; a main idea
meat´y *adj.* containing meat; important or significant
me·chan´ic *n.* one who repairs machines
me·chan´i·cal *adj.* relating to mechanical action; perfunctorily
mechanical advantage ratio of output to input energy
me·chan´ics *n.* the study of force; study of machinery
mech´a·nism *n.* the parts, action, or operation of a mechanical device
mech´a·nize *vt.* to equip with machines; automate
med´al *n.* an ornament recognizing a person, event, etc.
me·dal´lion *n.* medal or emblem that serves as ornament, identification, etc.; food cut or formed in circles
med´dle *vi.* interfere in the affairs of another
med´dle·some *adj.* tending to interfere
med´e·vac *n.* medical *evac*uation: transporting of injured by air to a medical facility
me´dia *n.* mass communication collectively, as newpapers, television, etc.
me´di·al *adj.* median
me´di·an *adj.* relating to the middle —*n.* a middle part
me´di·ate *vt.* resolve a dispute —*vi.* act as an agent of reconciliation —**me·di·a´tion** *n.*
med´i·cal *adj.* of the science of healing
me·dic´a·ment *n.* a medicine
med´i·cate *vt.* treat with medicine —**med·i·ca´tion** *n.*
med´i·cine *n.* science of healing; something to treat illness —**me·dic´i·nal** *adj.*
me·di·e´val *adj.* of the Middle Ages; antiquated; barbaric
me·di·e´val·ism *n.* study of life in the Middle Ages
me´di·o´cre *adj.* unexceptional; barely acceptable; inferior
med´i·tate *vi., vt.* deliberate or consider; emgage in quiet contemplation —**med·i·ta´tion** *n.*
med´i·ta·tive *adj.* thoughtful or reflective; marked by quiet contemplation
me´di·um *adj.* between extremes —*n.* a thing midway between; means by which something is attained
medium of exchange accepted currency
med´ley *n.* an assortment; a conglomeration
meek *adj.* subdued or submissive; humble
meet *vt.* come upon or confront; make acquaintance of; gather; satisfy —*vi.* come together; assemble; be introduced —*n.* a gathering
meet´ing *n.* encounter or confrontation; a gathering; an intersecting
meg´a·hertz *n.* one million cycles per second
meg´a·lith *n.* a large stone monument
meg·a·lo·ma´ni·a *n.* obsession with wealth or power
meg·a·lop´o·lis *n.* an area of closely joined cities
meg´a·phone *n.* a device that amplifies
mel´an·cho´lia *n.* mental disorder marked by depression
mel´an·choly *adj.* sadly quiet and contemplative —*n.* a condition marked by gloom and quiet attitude
me·lange´ *n.* collection or jumble
mel·a·no´ma *n.* dark growth on the skin, often malignant
meld *n.* a blending together —*vi., vt.* to become mingled
me´lee *n.* a violent clash
mel´io·rate *vi., vt.* to improve
mel´low *adj.* soft and rich, as of sound; pleasant and unhurried —*vi., vt.*
me·lod´ic *adj.* tuneful
me·lo´di·ous *adj.* pleasing to the ear; harmonious
mel´o·dra·ma *n.* theatre marked by overdrawn characterizations and exaggerated emotion
mel´o·dy *n.* a musical strain; theme of a musical composition
melt *vi., vt.* transform from solid to liquid; to soften, dissolve, or disappear
mem´ber *n.* one who belongs; part of an organism; a distinct part
mem´ber·ship *n.* affiliation; collectively, those affiliated
mem´brane *n.* thin tissue that serves as cover or lining
me·men´to *n.* a keepsake
mem´o, mem·o·ran´dum *n.* a written communication
mem´oir *n.* an autobiography
mem·o·ra·bil´ia *pl. n.* souvenirs or mementos
mem´o·ra·ble *adj.* worth remembering; unusual
me·mo´ri·al *adj.* commemorative —*n.* a monument or ceremony
me·mo´ri·al·ize *vt.* to commemorate
mem´o·rize *vt.* to commit to memory
mem´o·ry *n.* ability to remember and recall; thing remembered
men´ace *n.* a threat —*vt.* to threaten
me·nag´er·ie *n.* an assortment of animals; a place where animals are confined; a collection
mend *vi., vt.* make better; to correct, repair, or heal
men·da´cious *adj.* lying or deceitful —**men·dac´i·ty** *n.*
men´di·cant *adj.* of a beggar; depending on alms —*n.* a beggar —**men·dic´i·ty** *n.*
me´ni·al *adj.* servile or humble; befitting a servant —*n.* a servant
men´tal *adj.* relating to the mind —**men´tal·ly** *adv.*
men´tal·ism *n.* concept of mental phenomena beyond explanation; parapsychological incident, as telepathy
men·tal´i·ty *n.* intellectual capacity; manner of thinking
men´tion *n.* casual reference; a tribute —*vt.* refer to
men´tor *n.* advisor or teacher
men´u *n.* a list of food items; any list of options
mer´can·tile *adj.* relating to marketing; commercial
mer´ce·nar·y *n.* one in the pay of a foreign government; one motivated by personal gain —*adj.* desire for gain
mer´chan·dise *n.* goods bought and sold —*vi., vt.* to sell; promote the sale of
mer´chant *adj.* pertaining to trade —*n.* one who sells for profit
mer´ci·ful *adj.* showing mercy
mer´ci·less *adj.* showing no mercy; lacking compassion
mer·cu´ri·al *adj.* volatile; fluctuating; prone to abrupt change
mer´cy *n.* compassion; an act of foregiveness or compassion
mere *adj.* insignificant; inconsequential —**mere´ly** *adv.*
mer·e·tri´cious *adj.* gaudy; insincere
merge *vt., vi.* combine
merg´er *n.* a combining
me·ringue´ *n.* stiffened egg whites baked as a topping
mer´it *n.* a worthwhile quality —*vt.* be worthy of; deserve
mer·i·toc´ra·cy *n.* hierarchy based on ability
mer·i·to´ri·ous *adj.* praiseworthy; commendable
mer´ri·ment *n.* lively fun; gaiety
mer´ry *adj.* joyous; happy; marked by mirth
me´sa *n.* a broad plateau
mesh *n.* a loose, open fabrication of thread, wire, etc. —*vi., vt.* fit together
mes´mer·ize *vt.* fascinate; hypnotize
mess *n.* disordered clutter; a jumble; a large quantity —*vi., vt.* clutter; make untidy
mes´sage *n.* communication; an underlying lesson or guidance
mess´y *adj.* disorderly; unpleasant
met´a·bol´ic *adj.* relating to metabolism
me·tab´o·lism *n.* process of converting food, synthesizing needed substances, manufacturing tissue, etc.
met´al *n.* elements that are usually shiny, good conductors, and ductile —**me·tal´lic** *adj.*
met´al·lur·gy *n.* the extraction or combining of metals
met·a·mor´pho·sis *n.* transformation, esp. one that seems miraculous
met´a·phor *n.* a figure of speech using one thing to designate another
met´a·phys´ics *n.* branch of philosophy dealing with the nature of reality
mete *vt.* measure and distribute
me´te·or *n.* bright streak in the sky as a meteoroid enters the earth's atmosphere
me·te·or´ic *adj.* of atmospheric phenomenon; swift
me´te·or·ite *n.* object from space fallen into the earth's atmosphere
me´te·or·oid *n.* matter moving through space
me·te·o·rol´o·gy *n.* the study of atmospheric phenomenon
me´ter *n.* (*Brit. & US*) a measuring device; (*US*) a rhythmic pattern, as in poetry; unit of length in the metric system —*vt.* to measure
meth´od *n.* systematic procedure; orderliness
me·thod´i·cal *adj.* in a systematic or orderly fashion
meth·od·ol´o·gy *n.* systematic procedures for study or investigation
me·tic´u·lous *adj.* precise; attentive to detail
me´tre (*Brit.*) *n.* a rhythmic pattern, as in poetry; unit of

length in the metric system —*vt.* measure with a meter; give in measured amounts
metric system *n.* a decimal system of weight and measure
me·trop´o·lis *n.* a major urban area —**met´ro·pol´i·tan** *adj.*
met´tle *n.* courage; strength of character
mez´za·nine´ *n.* a balcony; a landing between floors
mi·as´ma *n.* foul air; corrupting influence
mi´crobe *n.* a microorganism
mi´cro·bi·ol´o·gy *n.* study of microorganisms —**mi´cro·bi·ol´o·gist** *n.*
mi ´cro·cosm *n.* small representation of a larger system
mi·cro·or´ga·nism *n.* a microscopic creature
mi´cro·scope *n.* device for viewing that which cannot be seen with the naked eye
mi´cro·wave *n.* electromagnetic energy wave; microwave oven —*vt.* cook in a microwave oven
mid´dle *adj.* positioned midway between —*n.* a center or midpoint
mid´dle·man *n.* a go–between
mid´land *n.* central part of a country
mid´riff *n.* the part of the body between chest and abdomen
midst *n.* positioned in or among; located at or near the midpoint
mid´way *n.* carnival sideshows, games, etc.; halfway
mid´wife *n.* one trained to assist in childbirth
mien *n.* appearance or demeanor
miff *vi., vt.* be offended or annoyed
might *n.* strength or power
might´y *adj.* strong or powerful; imposing; impressive
mi´graine *n.* a severe headache
mi´grant *adj.* migratory —*n.* one who moves regularly
mi´grate *vi.* move regularly from one place to another
mi·gra´tion *n.* a moving together
mi´gra·to·ry *adj.* tending to move with the seasons
mild *adj.* gentle or moderate
mil´dew *n.* a type of fungus; a coating caused by fungus
mile *n.* a measure of distance
mile´age *n.* distance traveled; an amount allowed for travel
mile´post, mile´stone *n.* a distance marker beside a road; a mark of progress
mi·lieu´ *n.* environment; surroundings
mil´i·tant *adj.* belligerent or aggressive —**mil´i·tance** *n.*
mil´i·ta·rism *n.* emphasis on military preparedness; belief in military spirit or values —**mil´i·ta·ris´tic** *adj.*
mil´i·tar·y *adj.* of the armed forces or war
mi·li´tia *n.* a citizen army
milk *n.* fluid from mammals to feed their young; similar fluid from a plant —*vt.* to extract milk from; take advantage of —**milk´y** *adj.*
mill *n.* place for grinding grain; a factory; device that transforms by grinding, etc.; thing that functions methodically —*vt.* transform by a machine —*vi.* move about in a disorderly fashion
mil´li·ner *n.* one who makes or sells women's hats
mi´lion·aire´ *n.* a wealthy person
mill´stone *n.* a stone used in milling grain; a burden
milque´toast *n.* timid person
mime *n.* silent performer; a pantomime —*vi., vt.* communicate with gestures
mim´ic *n.* one who portrays another —*vt.* imitate closely
min´a·ret´ *n.* tower on a mosque
mince *vi.* walk or speak in an affected manner —*vt.* chop; lessen or cushion to be polite: *mince words*
mince´meat *n.* a thick, spicy concoction of fruit and meat
mind *n.* awareness of being; intellect; ability to think —*vi., vt.* behave; give heed to; be concerned
mind´ful *adj.* careful, attentive
mind´less *adj.* without reason or purpose; lacking care or caution; indifferent
mind·set, **mind´–set** *n.* a fixed attitude or response; a predilection
mind's eye imagination
mine *n.* a hole or tunnel; a source; an explosive device —*vi., vt.* dig a tunnel; extract minerals; set an explosive
mine´field *n.* area seeded with explosive devices; something potentially dangerous or unpleasant
min´er·al *n.* naturally occurring inorganic matter —*adj.* of inorganic matter
min·er·al´o·gy *n.* the study of minerals
min´gle *vi., vt.* to combine or mix together
min´i·a·ture *adj.* small for its type —*n.* something small; a copy or model
min´i·a·tur·ize *vt.* make smaller; make a model
min´i·bus *n.* a small bus; a public conveyance
min´i·mal *adj.* the smallest possible; barely adequate
min´i·mal·ism *n.* an art form characterized by simplicity of form, color, etc.
min´i·mize *vt.* to downplay
min´i·mum *n.* the least possible or allowable —*adj.*
min´ion *n.* subordinate; a toady
min´i·se·ries *n.* a program aired in several episodes
min´is·ter *n.* a clergyman; a government official —*vi.* care for others —**min´is·te´ri·al** *adj.*
min·is·tra´tion *n.* the act of caring for another
min´is·try *n.* office and duties of a minister; department of government; care of others
min´now *n.* a small fish
mi´nor *adj.* of less significance —*n.* less by comparison; one not of legal age
mi·nor´i·ty *n.* a smaller group; time before legal age
min´strel *n.* wandering singer and poet
mint *adj.* new in appearance —*n.* place where coins are struck; plentiful amount —*vt.* make or strike coins
min´us·cule *adj.* tiny
min´ute *n.* a short time; part of an hour —**mi·nute´** *adj.* very small; detailed or exacting
mi·nu´ti·a *n., pl.* **mi·nu´ti·ae** a small insignificant detail
minx *n.* a flirtatious or defiant woman —**minx´ish** *adj.*
mir´a·cle *n.* unexplainable event; a supernatural occurrence
mi·rac´u·lous *adj.* of the nature of a miracle
mi·rage´ *n.* an illusion; something flimsy or fanciful
mire *n.* wet, muddy ground; a swamp; a difficult situation —*vi., vt.* become stuck
mir´ror *n.* a surface that reflects; something thought of as representing an image
mirror image a reverse
mirth *n.* lighthearted merriment —**mirth´ful** *adj.*
mirth´less *adj.* lacking gaiety; somber —**mirth´less·ly** *adv.*
mis·ad·ven´ture *n.* misfortune
mis´an·thrope *n.* one who dislikes or distrusts people; a recluse
mis·an´thro·py *n.* hatred or distrust of people
mis´ap·pre·hend´ *vt.* misunderstand
mis·ap·pro´pri·ate *vt.* take or use improperly or illegally
mis·be·have´ *vt.* conduct oneself badly or improperly —*vi.* behave badly
mis·car´riage *n.* premature birth of a nonviable fetus; a spontaneous abortion; a failure or malfunction
mis·cel·la´ne·a *pl. n.* a collection of written works
mis·cel·la´ne·ous *adj.* comprising a variety
mis·chance´ *n.* misfortune
mis´chief *n.* a deliberate act causing damage or distress
mis´chie·vous *adj.* inclined to be playful or bothersome
mis·con·cep´tion *n.* a misunderstanding
mis´con·strue´ *vt.* misinterpret
mis´cre·ant *n.* a villain; a criminal —*adj.* villainous
mis·deed´ *n.* a violation
mis´de·mean´or *n.* a minor crime
mis·di·rect´ *vt.* improperly instruct; draw attention away from —**mis·di·rec´tion** *n.*
mi´ser *n.* one who hoards
mis´er·a·ble *adj.* wretched; unpleasant
mi´ser·ly *adj.* stingy
mis´er·y *n.* suffering, distress; thing that causes suffering
mis´fit´ *n.* a nonconformist; a maladjusted person
mis·for´tune *n.* bad luck; adversity
mis·giv´ing *n.* doubt or uncertainty
mis·guid´ed *adj.* improperly directed; based on bad information —**mis·guide´** *vt.* —**mis·guid´ance** *n.*
mis·han´dle *vt.* mismanage; treat roughly or clumsily
mis´hap *n.* an accident
mis·in·form´ *vt.* advise inadequately or inaccurately; mislead
mis·in·ter´pret *vt.* misunderstand; explain incorrectly
mis·judge´ *vt.* form a wrong or unfair opinion
mis·lay´ *vt.* place and forget
mis·lead´ *vt.* direct wrongly or improperly; lead astray
mis·lead´ing *adj.* deceptive
mis·no´mer *n.* an inappropriate name or designation
mis·og´a·mist *n.* one who hates marriage
mis·og´y·nist *n.* one who hates women
mis·pri´sion *n.* concealment of crime
mis·rep·re·sen·ta´tion *n.* a false or misleading depiction
miss *n.* a failing; form of address for an unmarried woman —*vi., vt.* fail to make contact; to exclude or allow to pass; endure loss of
mis´sal *n.* a prayer book
mis´sile *n.* a projectile
miss´ing *adj.* absent or lacking; gone
mis´sion *n.* an organization established for a purpose; function or task of a group
mis´sive *n.* a letter or memo
mis·step´ *n.* a slip or stumbling; a mistake or blunder
mist *n.* droplets forming a haze; thing that obscures —*vt., vi.* make dim; rain in fine droplets —**mist´y** *adj.*
mis·take´ *n.* error; misunderstanding —*vi.* make a mistake —*vt.* misinterpret; to wrongly identify
mis·tak´en *adj.* misinformed or misguided; wrong
mis´ter *n.* form of address for a man
mis·treat´ *vt.* handle roughly or clumsily
mis´tress *n.* a woman in authority, who owns or controls; a teacher; one of exception knowledge or ability; a companion supported by a man not her husband
mis·tri´al *n.* a trial without verdict or declared invalid
mis·trust´ *n.* uncertainty, doubt, or suspicion —*vi., vt.* doubt or suspect
mist´y–eyed *adj.* sentimental; tearful
mi´ter *n.* ornamental headdress worn by a bishop; one of the bevels of a miter joint —*vt.* raise to the rank of bishop; join with a miter
miter joint a coupling of two angled pieces, as at a corner
mit´i·gate *vi., vt.* to become or make less intense or severe
mitt *n.* a glove
mit´ten *n.* a mitt with a pocket for the thumb
mix *n.* a combination of ingredients —*vi., vt.* to become combined; to blend in; confuse —**mix´a·ble** *adj.*
mixed *adj.* combined; consisting of differing elements
mixed´–up´ *adj.* confused or befuddled
mix´er *n.* a device that combines or blends; non–alcoholic beverage in a cocktail; a type of gathering; one who meets easily with others
mix´ture *n.* a mix; that which results from combining;

mix´–up *n.* a state of turmoil or confusion
mne·mon´ics *n.* a technique used as a memory aid
moan *n.* a low, doleful sound
moat *n.* a protective ditch
mob *n.* a large crowd; a group of criminals —*vt.* crowd; overwhelm
mo´bile *adj.* movable; easily moved —*n.* hanging art made of freely moving pieces
mo·bil´i·ty *n.* movement; the ability to move easily
mo´bi·lize *vt.* make moveable; organize and deploy
mob´ster *n.* a criminal
moc´ca·sin *n.* footwear
mo´cha *n.* rich coffee; flavoring of coffee and chocolate
mock *adj.* imitation; false —*vi., vt.* to ridicule or imitate derisively —**mock´ery** *n.*
mock´–up *n.* a scale model; layout for a printed page
mode *n.* a particular manner or fashion —**mod´al** *adj.*
mod´el *n.* a copy or prototype; one who poses, displays clothing, etc.; an ideal —*vi., vt.* make a model; pose; to display by wearing
mod´er·ate *adj.* not extreme or excessive —*n.* one not inclined to extreme views —*vi., vt.* make less extreme; to preside
mod´er·a·tor *n.* one who mediates or officiates
mod´ern *adj.* of recent time or development
mod´ern·ize *vi., vt.* make contemporary
mod´est *adj.* unpretentious; diffident; conforming to convention; not extreme —**mod´es·ty** *n.*
mod´i·cum *n.* a small amount; a pinch
mod·i·fi·ca´tion *n.* change or alteration —**mod´i·fy** *vt.*
mod´ish *adj.* smart or trendy; in the current style
mod´ule *n.* a separate component, as part of a sound or computer system —**mod´u·lar** *adj.*
mo´dus ope·ran´di *n.* a manner of operating
mo´gul *n.* one rich or powerful
moi´e·ty *n.* a half; a portion
moist *adj.* slightly wet; damp
moist´en *vi., vt.* to become or make slightly wet
mois´ture *n.* slight wetness
mois´tur·ize *vt.* make wet
mo´lar *n.* a large tooth
mo·las´ses *n.* thick, sweet syrup
mold[1] *(US) n.* a form for casting —*vi.* shaped in a form —*vt.* form or shape
mold[2] *(US) n.* a fungal growth
mold´er *(US) vi.* gradually decay
mold´ing *n. decorative trim, as around a door or window*
mold´y *(US) adj.* spoiled by a fungal growth; having a musty odor
mol´e·cule *n.* the smallest particle with distinct chemical and physical properties
mo·lest´ *vt.* disturb or annoy; accost improperly
mol´li·fy *vt.* soothe or pacify
mol´lusk *n.* marine invertebrate with soft body and protective shell
molt *(US) vi., vt.* to shed
mol´ten *adj.* extremely hot and melted or liquified
mo´ment *n.* a brief interval; importance
mo´men·tary *adj.* existing briefly
mo·men´tous *adj.* of great importance
mo·men´tum *n.* force of a body in motion; energy generated by ideas or events
mon´arch *n.* an absolute ruler
mon´as·ter·y *n.* religious community
mon´e·tary *adj.* regarding money or finance
mon´ey *n.* legal tender; currency, etc. issued by a government; an expression of wealth
mon´eyed *adj.* wealthy
mon´ger *n.* a tradesman; a promoter or advocate
mon´grel *adj.* of mixed breed —*n.* an interbred plant or animal
mon´i·tor *n.* device that controls or oversees; an adviser or assistant; an overseer —*vt.* oversee or regulate
mon´i·to·ry *adj.* admonishing; cautionary
monk *n.* member of a religious order
monk´ish *adj.* characteristic of a monk or a monastic life; austere or disciplined
mo·nog´a·my *n.* having one mate at a time; taking one spouse or mate for a lifetime
mon´o·gram *n.* letters designed as a distinguishing emblem —*vt.* adorn with a monogram
mon´o·graph *n.* a scholarly dissertation
mon´o·lith *n.* a large stone column or monument
mon´o·log, mon´o·logue *n.* discourse by one person
mon·o·pho´bi·a *n.* fear of being alone
mo·nop´o·lize *vt.* dominate; to solely control
mo·nop´o·ly *n.* absolute control of a market
mon´o·rail *n.* a train suspended from a single rail
mon´o·syl·lab´ic *adj.* of one syllable
mon´o·the·ism *n.* belief in a single god
mon´o·tone —*n.* single tone; listless or boring delivery
mo·not´o·nous *adj.* tedious or tiresome
mon´ster *n.* a frightening creature; one abnormally cruel; a deformed organism
mon´strous *adj.* frightening; abnormally cruel; deformed; huge
mon·tage´ *n.* art made up of a number of elements
month *n.* a period of approximately one cycle of the moon; one of twelve parts of a year
month´ly *adj.* occurring every month —*n.* a periodical that is published every month
mon´u·ment *n.* a memorial; an anchored structure: *a boundry marker*
mon·u·men´tal *adj.* impressive in size or significance
mooch *vi., vt.* freeload or get by begging —**mooch´er** *n.*
mood *n.* state of mind or attitude
mood´y *adj.* sullen; susceptible to depression; temperamental
moon *n.* a satellite —*vi.* to languish about —*vt.* bare the buttocks playfully
moon´light *n.* light reflected from the moon —*vi* work a second job
moon´shine *n.* illegal whiskey
moon´struck *adj.* beguiled by romantic notions
moor *vi., vt.* secure or anchor
moor´age, moor´ing *n.* place for securing a vessel; charge for use
moot *adj.* that can be disputed; of no significance
mop *n.* soft material used for cleaning; a soft clump or mass —*vi., vt.* wash by rubbing; make clean
mope *vi.* act dejected; sulk
mop´pet *n.* a child
mo·raine´ *n.* debris deposited by a glacier
mor´al *adj.* conforming to what is right or just —*n.* a truth or principle; a lesson
mo·rale´ *n.* attitude, enthusiasm, resolve, or confidence
mor´al·ist *n.* overly concerned with morals; one inclined to impose values on others
mo·ral´i·ty *n.* a sense of what is right or just
mor´al·ize *vi., vt.* pronounce judgement or lecture
mo·rass´ *n.* a wetland; a marsh or bog; something that impedes
mor·a·to´ri·um *n.* a suspension or delay
mor´bid *adj.* diseased; gruesome; abnormally preoccupied by the gruesome
mor´dant *adj.* sharp or incisive; caustic
more *adj.* greater in number or degree; enhanced or extended —*n.* additional amount —*adv.*
mo´res *n.* accepted standards, as in customs, morals, etc.
morgue *n.* a place where dead await burial; a library or reference file
mor´i·bund *adj.* nearing death; outdated
morn´ing *n.* that part of the day from midnight to noon or from sunrise to noon
mo·rose´ *adj.* surly or gloomy
mor·phol´o·gy *n.* scientific study of form and structure
mor´sel *n.* a bit of food; a small amount
mor´tal *adj.* of the physical person; susceptible to death; deadly —*n.* a human being
mor´tar *n.* bonding material; type of cannon; a container in which material is ground with a pestle
mort´gage *n.* pledge of property as security —*vt.* to pledge property
mor·ti´cian *n.* one who prepares dead for burial
mor·ti·fi·ca´tion *n.* humiliation or shame; discipline or penance
mor´ti·fy *vi.* undergo self–denial —*vt.* to humiliate or shame; discipline oneself by self–denial
mor´tise *n.* a slot designed for a tenon to form a joint
mor´tu·ary *n.* a place where bodies are kept for burial
mo·sa´ic *n.* a design of joined colored pieces, such as tiles
mosque *n.* Muslim house of worship
most *adj.* of the greatest number or amount —*n.* the larger part; the greatest amount —*adv.* to the greatest degree, extent, etc.
mot *n.* a witty remark
mote *n.* a speck
mo·tel´ *n.* lodging for travelers
moth´er *adj.* being derived from —*n.* a female parent; one who gives birth —*vt.* give birth; rear
moth´er·ly *adj.* nurturing; having qualities of a mother
mo·tif´ *n.* a recurring theme
mo´tile *adj.* able to move
mo·tion *n.* a movement; act of moving; a proposal put before a group —*vi., vt.* gesture or guide
mo´ti·vate *vt.* rouse to action
mo·ti·va´tion *n.* an inducement —**mo·ti·va´tion·al** *adj.*
mo·tive *n.* that which induces
mot´ley *adj.* varied; marked by variety or incongruity; multicolored —*n.* an incongruous mixture
mo´tor *adj.* of motion —*n.* device that produces mechanical energy —*vi., vt.* travel by motor vehicle
mot´tled *adj.* spotted
mould[1] *(Brit.) n.* a form for casting —*vi.* shaped in a form —*vt.* to form or shape
mould[2] *(Brit.) n.* a fungal growth
mould´er *(Brit.) vi.* gradually decay
mould´y *(Brit.) adj.* spoiled by fungal growth; having a musty odor
moult *(Brit.) vi., vt.* to shed
mound *n.* a pile or heap; a knoll or small hill —*vt.* make into a heap
mount *n.* a riding horse; a device that holds —*vi., vt.* to ascend; get onto; fix in place; increase, as cost
mount, moun´tain *n.* elevated land of substantial height and mass; a large amount —**moun´tain·ous** *adj.*
moun´te·bank *n.* a charlatan; a fast–talking salesman
mourn *vi., vt.* express grief or sorrow —**mourn´ful** *adj.*
mourn´ing *n.* a grieving for the dead; signs of grieving
mouse *n.* small rodent; timid person; a computer device
mousse *n.* food bound by whipped cream and gelatin, served cold; a preparation used to style the hair
mous´tache *n.* hair on the upper lip
mouth *n.* a body opening for feeding; opening of a river or cave —*vi., vt.* to speak; form words without sound
mouth´y *adj.* given to excessive or offensive speech; talkative
move *vi., vt.* advance from one place to another; alter position; act or be active; be emotionally aroused; propose, as in formal meeting
move´ment *n.* a steady or gradual change
mov´ing *adj.* in motion; of the transfer of goods; arousing emotional response

much *adj.* considerable in quantity or extent —*n.* considerable amount —*adv.* to a great degree; approximately
muck *n.* a wet sticky mixture; filth; something offensive —*vt.* soil; botch —**muck´y** *adj.*
mud *n.* mix of soil and water; plaster or mortar
mud´dle *n.* confusion or disorder; a predicament —*vi., vt.* to confuse; mismanage
mud´dy *adj.* stained; murky or hazy
muf´fle *vt.* suppress or deaden; maintain secrecy
muf´fler *n.* heavy scarf; (*US*) device for deadening sound of an engine
mug *n.* a heavy cup; one's face or expression; a gangster —*vi.* contort the face for effect —*vt.* assault
mulch *n.* ground cover around plants —*vt.*
mul´ish *adj.* obstinate
mull *vi., vt.* to ponder
mul´ti·far´i·ous *adj.* having great variety; diverse
mul´ti·ple *adj.* relating to several
mul·ti·pli·ca´tion *n.* increasing a number by adding to itself; organic reproduction —**mul´ti·ply** *vi., vt.*
mul·ti·plic´i·ty *n.* a large or varied collection
mul´ti·tude *n.* a large number; the general public
mum´ble *n.* indistinct articulation —*vi., vt.* speak indistinctly —**mum´bler** *n.*
mum·mi·fi·ca´tion *n.* preparation for burial in the manner of ancient Egyptians; natural drying and preservation —**mum´mi·fy** *vi., vt.*
mun·dane´ *adj.* common or ordinary; not exceptional
mu·nic´i·pal *adj.* relating to a local government
mu·nic·i·pal´i·ty *n.* a local governmental unit
mu·nif´i·cent *adj.* generous
mu´ral *n.* art applied directly to a wall or ceiling
mur´der *n.* unlawful killing; something arduous or unpleasant —*vt.* kill or destroy; corrupt —**mur´der·ous** *adj.*
murk´y *adj.* dark or hazy
mur´mur *n.* a low–pitched, indistinct sound —*vi., vt.* complain or utter in a low tone
mus´cle *n.* fibrous tissue that serves to achieve movement; strength or force —*vi.* crowd or intrude
mus´cu·lar *adj.* relating to muscles; inferring power
muse *n.* a spiritual or intellectual guide —*vi.* to ponder or meditate
mu·se´um *n.* a place for preservation of art or history
mush *n.* porridge; a pasty mass; exaggerated affection
mush´room *n.* a type of fungus; the shape of a mushroom —*vi.* grow rapidly —*adj.* relating to or like a mushroom
mu´sic *n.* sound that is pleasant to the ear; a musical score —**mu´si·cal** *adj.*
mu·si´cian *n.* one who composes or performs music
mu·si·col´o·gy *n.* study of music
mus´lin *n.* a coarse fabric
mus´sel *n.* a type of marine or freshwater mollusk
must *n.* something required —*aux. verb* a requirement; a command: *you must do this*; a likelihood: *they must know*; a certainty: *this must end*; intention: *I must go*
mus´ter *n.* a gathering —*vi.* assemble —*vt.* call together; summon or marshal
must´y *adj.* stale, as of a smell; old or out of date
mu´ta·ble *adj.* changeable
mu·ta´tion *n.* a modification; process of changing; thing created by change —**mu´tant** *n.*
mute *adj.* unable or unwilling to speak —*n.* one who cannot speak
mut´ed *adj.* subdued
mu´ti·late *vt.* maim or cripple; disfigure
mu´tiny *n.* open rebellion; revolt —**mu´ti·nous** *adj.*
mu´tu·al *adj.* reciprocal or common
muz´zle *n.* snout of an animal; device to cover a snout; that prevents free speech —*vt.* restrain; prevent from speaking
my·o´pia *n.* nearsightedness
myr´i·ad *adj.* innumerable —*n.* a large number
mys´ter·y *n.* that not easily understood; a work of fiction —**mys·te´ri·ous** *adj.*
mys´tic, mys´ti·cal *adj.* of mysticism; mysterious; incomprehensible —**mys´ti·cism** *n.*
mys´ti·fy *vt.* puzzle or perplex
mys·tique´ *n.* mysterious quality
myth *n.* a legend or folk tale; something untrue —**myth´ic, myth´i·cal** *adj.*
my·thol´o·gy *n.* a collection of myths; the study of myth —**myth·o·log´i·cal** *adj.*
n, N fourteenth letter of the alphabet; symbol for an inexact number
nab *vt.* snatch or seize; arrest
na´dir *n.* the lowest point
na·ive´ *adj.* unsophisticated; guileless; gullible
na·ive·té´ *n.* inexperience; ingenuousness
na´ked *adj.* uncovered or unprotected —**na´ked·ness** *n.*
name *n.* word by which a thing is known; designation or title; a disparaging epithet —*vt.* give a designation; appoint or assign, as to a rank
nap *n.* brief sleep; soft raised surface as on a carpet —*vi.* sleep briefly
nape *n.* back of the neck
na´per·y *pl. n.* household linens
nar´cis·sism *n.* excessive devotion to one's self —**nar·cis·sis´tic** *adj.*
nar´rate *vi., vt.* recite, describe; give an account; provide commentary
nar·ra´tion *n.* a recounting of events; that which is related
nar´ra·tive *n.* a vocal account —*adj.* marked by narration
nar´row *adj.* small in width; confined or limited; extremely close —*n.* confined passage —*vi., vt.* make confined or restricted
nas´cent *adj.* beginning; emerging
nas´ty *adj.* offensive; unpleasant
na´tal *adj.* of birth
na´tion *n.* people bound by common government, heritage, etc.
na´tive *adj.* associated with a particular place; connected by birth; natural or inherited —*n.* one connected by birth
na·tiv´i·ty *n.* birth
nat´u·ral *adj.* occurring in nature; usual, typical, or characteristic; simple and unrehearsed —*n.* one well-suited —**nat´u·ral·ness** *n.*
nat´u·ral·ist *n.* one who studies natural history; one in harmony with nature
nat·u·ral·i·za´tion *n.* the process of becoming accepted or acclimated
natural law principles that derive from nature
na´ture *n.* realm of the living; processes and power that control the living; a personal quality
nau´sea *n.* illness marked by a queasy stomach; revulsion —**nau´se·ate** *vi., vt.* —**nau´seous** *adj.*
nau´ti·cal *adj.* of ships or shipping
nave *n.* central aisle of a church
na´vel *n.* process on a mammal left by an umbilical cord
nav´i·gate *vi., vt.* plot or direct a course; travel by ship —**nav·i·ga´tion** *n.* —**nav´i·ga·tor** *n.*
near *adj., adv.* approaching or close to; almost —*vi., vt.* come or draw near —**near´ly** *adv.* —**near´ness** *n.*
neat *adj.* orderly or tidy; clever or adroit; undiluted
neat´en *vt.* put in order; make tidy
neb´u·lous *adj.* hazy or indistinct; vague or confused
nec´es·sar·y *adj.* essential; required
ne·ces´si·tate *vt.* require; make compulsory
ne·ces´si·ty *n.* something essential or required
neck *n.* a narrow body part that joins; a narrow section —*vi., vt.* to kiss and caress
neck´wear *n.* clothing or jewelry worn about the neck
nec´ro·man·cy *n.* communication with the dead; black magic
nec·ro·phil´i·a *n.* obsession with death and dead bodies
nec·ro·pho´bi·a *n.* abnormal fear of death
ne·crop´o·lis *n.* place of burial, esp. near an ancient city
need *n.* lack; a thing required or desired; necessity; state of poverty —*vt.* have want of; require —*vi.* be in want; be obliged or compelled —**need´ful** *adj.*
needless *adj.* unnecessary; useless
need´y *adj.* poor; overly dependent on others
ne·far´i·ous *adj.* very wicked
ne·gate´ *vt.* nullify or retract
neg´a·tive *adj.* expressing opposition or denial; lacking any affirmative quality —**neg·a·tiv´i·ty** *n.*
ne·glect *n.* indifference or carelessness —*vt.* disregard; be indifferent; be careless or irresponsible —**ne·glect´ful, neg´li·gent** *adj.*
neg´li·gi·ble *adj.* insignificant; inconsequential
ne·go´ti·ate *vi.* confer in attempt to reach agreement —*vt.* compromise or agree; transfer ownership —**ne·go´ti·a·ble** *adj.*
neigh´bor (*US*), **neigh´bour** (*Brit.*) *n.* one who lives near; that near or adjacent —*vi., vt.* live or be situated near —*adj.* near to; adjacent —**neigh´bor·ly, neigh´bour·ly** *adj.*
nei´ther *adj.* not either; not one or the other
nem´e·sis *n.* an enemy; one seeking retribution or revenge; something harmful
ne·o·clas´sic, ne´o·clas´si·cal *adj.* of the revival of earlier forms in music or literature
ne´o·phyte *n.* a novice; a recent convert
nep´o·tism *n.* favoritism to a relation
nerd *n.* one engrossed in scholarly pursuits —**nerd´y** *adj.*
nerve *n.* fiber that transmits signals throughout the body; courage; impudence
ner´vous *adj.* of the nerves; high–strung or excitable; agitated, apprehensive
ne´science *n.* ignorance; lack of knowledge or awareness
nest *n.* a cozy shelter; a refuge; objects that fit together —*vi., vt.* fit together snugly
nes´tle *vi., vt.* to lie or place snugly or comfortably
net *adj.* remaining after deductions—*n.* amount remaining; mesh —*vt.* produce profit; to catch
net´tle·some *adj.* irritating
net´work *n.* system or structure with interconnecting bonds
neu´ral *adj.* regarding the nerves or nervous system
neu·ri´tis *n.* inflammation of a nerve —**neu·rit´ic** *adj.*
neu·rol´o·gy *n.* study of the nervous system
neu´ron *n.* a nerve cell
neu·ro´sis *n.* a mental or emotional disorder
neu´tral *adj.* not supporting either side; unbiased or disinterested; drab or colorless —**neu´tral·ize** *vt.*
nev´er *adv.* not ever
new *adj.* recently formed or discovered; previously unused; different; inexperienced —**new´ ly** *adv.*
next *adj.* following immediately in sequence—*n.* that which comes immediately after —*adv.*
nib´ble *n.* a small bite —*vi.* , *vt.* take or eat in small bites —**nib´bler** *n.*
nice *adj.* pleasing; courteous, considerate; delicate, subtle
ni´ce·ty *n.* a precise, subtle, or refined quality
niche *n.* a recess or alcove; a special area of interest
nig´gard·ly *adj.* closefisted; reluctant to give or spend
nig´gle *vi.* to nag or complain over trifles —**nig´gling** *adj.*

nigh *adj., adv.* near; nearly
night *n.* period between sunset and sunrise; evening before midnight
night´ly *adj.* every night; during the night *—adv.* by night; every night
ni´hi·lism *n.* philosophy that denies all existence; rejection of religion and morality
nim´ble *adj.* quick and agile; sharp witted **—nim´bly** *adv.*
nim´bus *n.* a halo or disk of light
nip *n.* a sip; a small bite or particle; a sharp or stinging quality *—vt.* sip; bite or pinch off; sting **—nip´py** *adj.*
nir·va´na *n.* an ideal state
nit´pick *vi.* quarrel over trifles
no´ble *adj.* pertaining to or having qualities attributable to nobility **—no·bil´i·ty** *n.*
no´cent *adj.* harmful
noc·tur´nal *adj.* occurring in the night
noc´turne *n.* night scene; gentle, dreamy musical composition
noc´u·ous *adj.* harmful or detrimental
nod *n.* assent or agreement *—vi., vt.* move the head in assent or acknowledgement; to briefly drift off to sleep
nod´ule *n.* a small lump
noise *n.* a loud or unpleasant sound; complaint; interference; unwanted or meaningless data *—vt.* spread gossip **—nois´y** *adj.*
noi´some *adj.* disgusting, esp. of an odor; dangerous or deadly, as fumes
no´mad *n.* a wanderer; one lacking a permanent home **—no·mad´ic** *adj.*
no´men·cla·ture *n.* a name or designation; a system of names
nom´i·nal *adj.* of a name or designation; of a token amount; existing in name only **—nom´i·nal·ly** *adv.*
nom´i·nate *vt.* name as a candidate; appoint to office
non´age *n.* legally underage
non´cha·lant´ *adj.* seemingly casual or indifferent
non·com·mit´tal *adj.* guarded about feelings or opinions
non´de·script *adj.* lacking distinctive characteristics
none *adv.* not at all *—pron.* no one
non·en´ti·ty *n.* thing of no importance
non·fea´sance *n.* failure to discharge an obligation
non´pa·reil´ *adj.* without equal
non·par´ti·san *adj.* neutral; unaligned *—n.*
non´plus´ *vt.* bewilder; put at a loss for words
non´sense *n.* lacking meaning; of no value; foolishness **—non·sen´si·cal** *adj.*
noon *n.* midday; time when the sun is at or near its highest point
nor´mal *adj.* typical, usual, or standard; sane
north *n.* to the left of sunrise, perpendicular to the sun's path
nose *n.* the organ for detecting odors; sense of smell; aroma, as of wine; ability to find as if by smell; the front
nos·tal´gia *n.* sentimental longing for the past
nos´tril *n.* the opening of the nose
nos´trum *n.* an untested medicine or remedy
not *adv.* in no way
no´ta·ble *adj.* distinctive or remarkable; deserving notice
no´ta·ry, no´ta·ry pub´lic *n.* one certified for certain legal duties **—no´ta·rize** *vt.*
no·ta´tion *n.* a note or comment; a system of symbols
note *n.* a short, informal letter; an annotation, reminder, etc.; currency or convertible to currency *—vt.* make a written record of; take notice of
not´ed *adj.* distinguished; famous
note´wor·thy *adj.* deserving notice
noth´ing *adj.* meaningless *—n.* thing of no value *—pron.* not anything
no´tice *n.* announcement or warning; observation or attention *—vt.* observe; become aware of
no´ti·fy *vt.* serve notice; to inform or make known
no´tion *n.* idea or opinion; theory; disposition toward
no·to·ri´e·ty *n.* fame; reputation
no·to´ri·ous *adj.* infamous; well–known
not·with·stand´ing *prep.* in spite of *—adv.*
noun *n.* a word that names a person, place, thing, etc.
nour´ish *vt.* promote development of; provide with food or other necessities
nou·velle´ cui·sine´ a style of cooking that stresses fresh ingredients and light sauces
nov´el *adj.* new and unusual *—n.* a book–length, fictional story **—nov´el·ist** *n.*
nov´el·ette´ *n.* a short novel
nov´el·ty *n.* being original or fresh; something unique; a fad; a trinket
nov´ice *n.* one new to a trade or activity; an apprentice
now *adj.* at this time *—adv.* immediately; promptly
nox´ious *adj.* harmful
noz´zle *n.* a spout or outlet for controlling flow
nu´ance *n.* subtlety; slight variation
nu´bile *adj.* of marriageable age; sexually mature
nu´cle·ar *adj.* of a nucleus; atomic
nuclear reactor a device for harnessing nuclear energy
nu´cle·us *n.* center or essence
nude *adj.* unclothed or uncovered *—n.* a naked body **—nu´di·ty** *n.*
nudge *n.* a light push *—vt.* touch or push gently
nui´sance *n.* bother or annoyance; interference with rights of others
null *adj.* nonexistent or insignificant; invalid **—nul´li·fy** *vt.*
numb *adj.* lacking feeling *—vt., vi.* make numb
num´ber *n.* an integer; one in a progression; numerals representing something *—vt.* assign a position; count or total
nu´mer·al *n.* a symbol representing a number **—nu·mer´ic, nu·mer´i·cal** *adj.*
nu·mer·ol´o·gy *n.* belief in a secret meaning associated with numbers
nu´mer·ous *adj.* many; a large number
nu·mis·mat´ics *n.* the study or collection of coinage
nup´tial *adj.* of marriage or a marriage ceremony
nurse *n.* one who ministers to the sick; one in charge of young children *—vt.* tend or care for another; sustain or conserve **—nurs·er** *n.*
nurs´ing *n.* the profession of a nurse; the care of a nurse
nur´ture *vt.* care for; aid to grow and improve
nut *n.* a seed within a hard shell; an eccentric; a fanatic
nu´tri·ent *adj.* nourishing *—n.* a source of nourishment
nu´tri·ment *n.* food; anything that promotes growth and development
nu·tri´tion *n.* study of nourishment; process by which food is used in the body
nu·tri´tious *adj.* nourishing
nuz´zle *vi.* , *vt.* nestle; push gently with the nose
o, O fifteenth letter of the alphabet
oaf *n.* one slow–witted or clumsy
oa´sis *n., pl.* **oa´ses** a haven of greenery in a wasteland; a place of refuge
oath *n.* solemn promise; irreverent or blasphemous utterance
ob´du·rate *n.* hardhearted; stubborn
o·be´di·ent *adj.* deferential to authority; submissive
o·bese´ *adj.* overweight
o·bey´ *vi., vt.* accept or comply
ob´fus´cate *vt.* make confused
o·bit´u·ar·y *n.* published account of a death
ob´ject *n.* thing perceived by the senses; goal or objective; a recipient **—ob·ject´** *vi., vt.* oppose or dissent
ob·jec´tion *n.* opposition; a reason for opposing
ob·jec´tion·a·ble *adj.* offensive
ob·jec´tive *adj.* fair and unbiased *—n.* a tangible goal
ob´li·gate *adj.* essential *—vt.* bind or compel by indebtedness, etc. **—ob·li·ga´tion** *n.*
o·blig´a·to·ry *adj.* required; morally or legally binding
o·blige´ *vt.* require; accommodate or assist
o·blique´ *adj.* inclined or slanting; angled; indirect: *oblique reference*
ob·lit´er·ate *vt.* remove completely **—ob·lit·er·a´tion** *n.*
ob·liv´i·on *n.* obscurity; nonexistence
ob·liv´i·ous *adj.* preoccupied; lacking awareness
ob´long *adj.* elongated
ob·nox´ious *adj.* offensive or objectionable; impolite
ob·scene´ *adj.* contrary to accepted morality or propriety **—ob·scen´i·ty** *n.*
ob·scure´ *adj.* not clearly perceived; indistinct *—vt.* conceal or make indistinct
ob·scu´ri·ty *n.* being unknown or indistinct
ob·se´qui·ous *adj.* groveling or subservient; fawning
ob·serv´a·ble *adj.* noticeable; perceived by eye
ob·serv´ance *n.* traditional rite or celebration; an act of compliance **—ob·serv´ant** *adj.* **—ob·ser·va´tion** *n.*
ob·serve´ *vt.* notice; watch carefully; celebrate a tradition; abide by custom or law; mention *—vi.* make a casual remark; take notice
ob·ses´sion *n.* unnatural or irrational fascination
ob·ses´sive *adj.* compulsive
ob´so·lete´ *adj.* no longer useful or in use; out–of–date **—ob·so·les´cence** *n.*
ob´sta·cle *n.* a hindrance; a barrier or obstruction
ob·stet´rics *n.* care during and directly following pregnancy **—ob·ste·tri´cian** *n.*
ob´sti·nate *adj.* stubborn; defying control or treatment
ob·strep´er·ous *adj.* unruly; defiant
ob·struct´ *vt.* interfere or hinder; block view of **—ob·struc´tive** *adj.* **—ob·struc´tion** *n.*
ob·tain´ *vt.* gain possession of
ob·tru´sive *adj.* interfering; overly conspicuous **—ob·tru´sive·ness** *n.*
ob·tuse´ *adj.* dull or ignorant; lacking understanding
ob´vi·ate *vt.* make unnecessary; render unnecessary
ob´vi·ous *adj.* clearly seen or understood
oc·ca´sion *n.* an event or opportunity *—vt.* to cause
oc·ca´sion·al *adj.* occurring infrequently
oc·cult´ *adj.* obscured or hidden; mysterious; relating to the supernatural **—oc·cult´ism** *n.*
oc´cu·pan·cy *n.* possession of an office, home, etc.
oc´cu·pant *n.* one who fills a position or inhabits a place
oc·cu·pa´tion *n.* activity, esp. for livlihood; occupancy
oc´cu·py *vt.* fill time or space; hold one's attention; control after conquest
oc·cur´ *vi.* happen; present itself, as an idea **—oc·cur´rence** *n.*
o´cean *n.* large body of salt water; large amount **—o·ce·an´ic** *adj.*
o·cean·og´ra·phy *n.* study of the ocean and its phenomena **—o·cea·nog´ra·pher** *n.*
oc´ta·gon *n.* an eight–sided polygon **—oc·tag´o·nal** *adj.*
oc·tet´ *n.* a group of eight
oc´u·lar *adj.* of eyes or sight
oc´u·list *n.* a physician who treats the eyes; an optomotrist or opthalmologist
odd *adj.* strange or different; unusual or unexpected; an uneven amount
odds *n. pl.* probability
ode *n.* lyric poem **—od´ic** *adj.*
o´di·ous *adj.* offensive; engendering aversion
o´di·um *n.* hatred or aversion
o·dom´e·ter *n.* a device for measuring distance traveled
o´dor (*US*) *n.* something perceived by smell; an aroma

o·dor·if´er·ous *adj.* having an aroma

o´dor·ous *adj.* having a distinctive aroma

o´dour (*Brit.*) *n.* thing perceived by smell; an aroma

off *adj., adv., prep.* away from; at a distance; removed

of´fal *n.* waste

of·fence´ (*Brit.*) *n.* a violation; that arousing disapproval

of·fend´ *vi., vt.* arouse disapproval —**of·fend´er** *n.*

of·fense´ (*US*) *n.* a violation; that arousing disapproval

of·fen´sive *adj.* disagreeable; vulgar or insulting

of´fer *n.* something for consideration —*vt.* present or submit

of´fer·ing *n.* a gift

of´fi·cer *n.* one in authority

of·fi´cial *adj.* relating to an office or position; authorized —*n.* one in authority

of·fi´ci·ate *vt.* preside; perform the duties of office

of·fi´cious *adj.* overly eager

of´ten *adv.* frequently

o´gle *vi., vt.* stare rudely

o´gre *n.* a mythical monster

oint´ment *n.* a salve

old *adj.* aged or elderly; of a specific age; showing signs of age or wear; seasoned or matured

o´le·o·mar´ga·rine *n.* margarine, a substitute for butter

ol·fac´to·ry *adj.* of the sense of smell

ol´i·gar·chy *n.* government controlled by a small group

ol·i·gop´o·ly *n.* market dominated by few suppliers

ol·i·gop´so·ny *n.* market dominated by few buyers

o´li·o *n.* a stew; mixture or collection

om´buds·man *n.* an investigator and mediator

o´men *n.* a sign or indication

om´i·nous *adj.* threatening; inauspicious

o·mis´sion *n.* something omitted; failure to perform

omit´ *vt.* leave out

om´ni·bus *adj.* including many —*n.* a large passenger vehicle

om·nip´o·tent *adj.* having unlimited power

om·nis´cient *adj.* having unlimited knowledge

om·niv´o·rous *adj.* subsisting on either plants or animals —**om´ni·vore** *n.*

on´er·ous *adj.* difficult or troublesome

o´nus *n.* responsibility; burden

ooze *n.* that leaks out; slimy mud —*vi., vt.* flow or leak out slowly; give off

o·paque´ *adj.* not transparent; impervious to light; ambiguous, obscure —**o·pac´i·ty** *n.*

o´pen *adj.* accessible; unobstructed; candid and straightforward; lacking prejudice —*vi., vt.* become accessible; to begin —**o´pen·ing** *n.*

op´er·a *n.* a musical drama

op´er·ate *vi.* function; perform surgery —*vt.* control, cause to function; manage —**op´er·a·ble** *adj.* —**op´er·a·tor** *n.*

op·er·a´tion *n.* a condition of functioning; a procedure or method; surgery

op´er·a·tive *adj.* functioning

op·er·et´ta *n.* a light opera

oph·thal·mol´o·gy *n.* study of the eye, its diseases, and treatment —**oph·thal·mol´o·gist** *n.*

o´pi·ate *n.* a sedative; anything that dulls the senses

o·pin´ion *n.* belief or judgment

o·pin´ion·at·ed *adj.* having strong beliefs

o´pi·um *n.* a narcotic derived from the opium poppy

op·po´nent *adj.* acting in opposition —*n.* one opposing

op´por·tune´ *adj.* timely or suitable

op·por·tun´ist *n.* one who takes advantage

op·por·tu´ni·ty *n.* an advantageous occasion or time

op·pos´a·ble *adj.* able to be reversed; that can be confronted or countered

op·pose´ *vt.* act in conflict; place across from —**op´po·site** *adj.*

op·po·si´tion *n.* conflict; those disagreeing

op·press´ *vt.* suppress by maltreatment or abuse; overburden —**op·pres´sor** *n.* —**op·pres´sive** *adj.*

op·pro´bri·ous *adj.* contemptuous, reproachful; shameful —**op·pro´bri·um** *n.*

op´ti·cal *adj.* relating to vision

op´tics *pl. n.* the branch of science dealing with vision and light —**op·ti´cian** *n.*

op´ti·mal *adj.* most favorable

op´ti·mism *n.* expectation of a favorable outcome

op´ti·mize *vt.* maximize effectiveness

op´ti·mum *adj.* favorable

op´tion *n.* a choice; a right to choose —**op´tion·al** *adj.*

op·tom´e·try *n.* examination, diagnosis, and treatment for problems of the eyes —**op·tom´e·trist** *n.*

op´u·lent *adj.* marked by wealth or abundance

o´pus *n.* a creative literary or musical composition

or´a·cle *n.* a prophet; a visionary; one having great wisdom —**o·rac´u·lar** *adj.*

o´ral *adj.* spoken; relating to speech or the mouth

o·rate´ *vi.* speak formally

or·a·tor´i·cal *adj.* pertaining to an orator or oratory

or´a·to·ry *n.* public speaking

orb *n.* a sphere

or´bit *n.* the path of one body around another; a sphere of influence —*vi.* travel an orbit —*vt.* place in orbit

or·dain´ *vt.* charge with holy orders; decree or dictate

or´deal *n.* a trying experience

or´der *n.* logical arrangement; a command; group or organization —*vt.* arrange; instruct or direct

or´der·ly *adj.* neat; systematic; peaceful and law–abiding —*n.* an attendant

or´di·nance *n.* a local law

or´di·nary *adj.* common; unexceptional

ore *n.* mineral rock

or´gan *n.* a musical instrument; a body part; a publication

or·gan´ic *adj.* of or relating to living tissue

or´ga·nism *n.* a life form

or·ga·ni·za´tion *n.* a bringing together; persons united for a common purpose

or´ga·nize *vt.* make orderly or functional; bring together —**or´ga·nized** *adj.*

or´gasm *n.* sexual climax

or´gy *n.* revelry; uncontrolled indulgence

o´ri·ent *vt.* position to points of the compass; familiarize

or´i·fice *n.* an opening

or´i·gin *n.* beginning; a source

o·rig´i·nal *adj.* first or new; different or imaginative —*n.* that from which others derive; a prototype —**o·rig·i·nal´i·ty** *n.* —**o·rig´i·nal·ly** *adv.* —**o·rig´i·nate** *vi., vt.*

or´na·ment *n.* decoration or embellishment —*vt.*

or´na·men´tal *adj.* decorative

or·nate´ *adj.* elaborately styled or decorated

or·ni·thol´o·gy *n.* study of birds

or´phic *adj.* mystical

ort *n.* a scrap, esp. of food

or·tho·don´tia, or·tho·don´tics *n.* prevention and correction of dental irregularities —**or·tho·don´tist** *n.*

or´tho·dox *adj.* adhering to traditional or established ways —**or´tho·dox·y** *n.*

or·tho·pe´dics *n.* medical treatment for ailments of the skeletal system

os´cil·late *vi.* move back and forth; to vibrate

os´cu·late *vi.* come together —*vt.* to kiss —**os·cu·la´tion** *n.*

os·mo´sis *n.* passage of fluids through a membrane; gradual process of absorbing or learning —**os·mot´ic** *adj.*

os·si·fi·ca´tion *n.* process of forming bone or hardening

os·ten´si·ble *adj.* appearing as; professed or pretended

os·ten·ta´tion *n.* pretentious display

os´tra·cize *vt.* isolate; banish

oth´er *adj.* distinct from

o´ti·ose *adj.* idle, indolent

oust *vt.* eject; force out

out *adj., adv.* exterior; away or apart from; distinct from the usual or accepted

out´er *adj.* external or exterior

out´fit *vt.* furnish with clothing or equipment

out´growth *n.* a result

out´lay *n.* an expenditure

out´rage *n.* an offensive act; anger —*vt.* make violently angry —**out·ra´geous** *adj.*

out·side´ *adj.* of an outer limit —*n.* an outer surface or limit

out´spo·ken *adj.* candid

out´wit´ *vt.* trick or deceive

o´val *adj.* elliptical; egg–shaped —*n.*

o·va´tion *n.* spirited applause

o´ver *adj.* extreme; extra —*adv.* above; across; as far as; completed or done —*prep.*

o´ver·age *n.* an excess

o´ver·alls *n.* (*Brit.*) garment worn over street clothes; (*US*) loose trousers with a bib front

o·ver·bear´ing *adj.* domineering or arrogant

o´ver·flow *n.* excess; a device that allows excess to escape —*vi., vt.* spill over; abound

o´ver·joyed *adj.* delighted

o´ver·look *n.* a vantage point —**o´ver·look´** *vt.* watch over, supervise; disregard or omit

o·ver·pow´er *vt.* to overwhelm

o·ver·shad´ow *vt.* dominate

o´ver·sight *n.* supervision; an unintentional error

o·vert´ *adj.* open and public; sanctioned —**o·vert´ly** *adv.*

o´ver·ture *n.* musical introduction; an approach signaling readiness to negotiate

o´vine *adj.* pertaining to sheep; sheeplike

o´void *adj.* shaped like an egg

owe *vi., vt.* be indebted

ow´ing *adj.* unpaid

own *adj.* of one's possession —*vt.* possess or control —*vi., vt.* admit or acknowledge

ox·i·da´tion *n.* a combining with oxygen —**ox´i·dize** *vt.*

ox´y·gen *n.* a nonmetallic element necessary for plant and animal respiration

ox·y·mo´ron *n.* a contradictory phrase: *sweet sadness*

p, P sixteenth letter of the alphabet

pace *n.* manner of walking; speed of a walk, action, event, etc.; a stride —*vt., vi.* walk; measure by paces

pa·cif´ic *adj.* peaceful, tranquil —**pac·i·fi·ca´tion** *n.*

pac´i·fy *vt.* ease anger or conflict —**pac´i·fist** *n.*

pack *n.* a small package; set of items; bag with straps; a group functioning as a unit —*vt., vi.* to place in a container; to compress

pack´age *n.* a container; a group of elements taken together —*vt.* offer as a unit

pact *n.* agreement; contract

pad *n.* a cushion; joined sheets of paper —*vt.* cushion; increase deceitfully

pa´gan *adj.* without religion —*n.* a nonreligious person

page *n.* one side of a sheet of paper —*vt.* to summon

pag´eant *n.* an elaborate procession or celebration

pa·go´da *n.* an ornate multi–storied Buddhist shrine

pail *n.* a cylindrical container with a handle

pain *n.* a disagreeable sensation; suffering —*vi., vt.* cause pain

pains´tak·ing *adj.* requiring great care; careful

pair *n.* two persons or things —*vi., vt.* bring two together

pal *n.* a friend

pal´ace *n.* a grand and sumptuous residence

pal´at·a·ble *adj.* edible; acceptable —**pal´ate** *n.*

pal´ette *n.* a flat for mixing colors; an artist's colors

pal´in·drome *n.* a word or phrase that reads backward or forward

pal·i·sade´ *n.* a steep cliff

pall *n.* gloom; dark cover

pal´li·ate *vt.* relieve or ease

pal´li·a·tive *adj.* serving to relieve

pal´lid *adj.* pale; ashen

pal´pa·ble *adj.* obvious; tangible

pal´pi·tate *vi.* tremble or quiver

pal´try *adj.* trivial; insignificant; of little worth
pam´per *vt.* cater to; indulge
pan *n.* a container, as for cooking; harsh critcism —*vi., vt.* separate by rinsing; criticize
pan·a·ce´a *adj.* a cure–all
pan·dem´ic *adj.* general; universal
pan·de·mo´ni·um *n.* noisy confusion
pan´der *vi.* procure for sexual affairs —*n.* procurer or pimp
pane *n.* a panel of glass; a flat piece or surface
pan´el *n.* a flat or decorative section; a group formed to judge, discuss, etc. —*vt.* provide with panels
pang *n.* a sudden sharp pain
pan´han·dle (*US*) *vi.* to beg
pan´ic *n.* sudden fear; general hysteria —*vi., vt.* —**pan´icked, pan´ick·ing, pan´ic–strick·en** *adj.*
pan´o·ply *n.* an extensive or impressive display
pan·o·ram´a *n.* extensive view
pant *vi.* take short rapid breaths
pan´to·mime *n.* communication by gestures —*vt., vi.* perform without speech
pan´try *n.* an area where foods are stored or prepared
par *adj.* normal —*n.* an established standard; face value
par´a·ble *n.* story with a moral
pa·rade´ *n.* a procession
par´a·digm *n.* example or model
par´a·dise *n.* a perfect place of peace and beauty
par´a·dox *n.* a seeming contradiction; an enigma
par´al·lax *n.* optical displacement from change in position —**par·al·lac´tic** *adj.*
par´al·lel *adj.* of equal distance at all points; being in concert —*n.* a resemblance —*vt.*
par´a·lyse (*Brit.*) *vt.* render unable to move or function
pa·ral´y·sis *n.* loss of ability to move or function
par´a·lyze (*US*) *vt.* render unable to move or function
par·a·med´ic *n.* one providing emergency treatment or assisting a doctor
pa·ram´e·ter *n.* a boundry
par´a·mount *adj.* of primary importance; dominant
par´amour *n.* a lover
par·a·noi´a *n.* irrational fear
par·a·nor´mal *adj.* outside the realm of normal knowledge
par´a·pher·na´lia *n.* implements; equipment
para·ple´gia *n.* paralysis of the lower body
par´a·psy·chol´o·gy *n.* the study of paranormal activity
par´a·site *n.* an organism supported by another; one who relies on others
par´cel *n.* a package; a section of land —*vt.* portion out
parch *vt., vi.* to dry or shrivel; make or become thirsty
par´don *n.* foregiveness —*vt.* deliver from punishment; forgive
pare *vt.* to trim
par´ent *n.* an ancestor; a mother or father: a source
par´ent·age *n.* one's lineage
pa·ri´ah *n.* an outcast
par´ish *n.* a church congregation; civil district similar to a township or county
par´i·ty *n.* equality
park *n.* a recreation area; a designated area: *industrial park* —*vt.* place and leave temporarily
par´lance *n.* style of speech; jargon
par´lia·ment *n.* a legislative body
par´lor *n.* a formal room
pa·ro´chi·al *adj.* of a local parish; local or conservative; provincial
par´o·dy *n.* a comic work that ridicules; something so bad as to be a mockery —*vt.* to ridicule; make a travesty of
par´ox·ysm *n.* a sudden outburst; sudden attack of a disease —**par´ox·ys´mal** *adj.*
par·quet´ *n.* a floor of inlaid wood
par´ri·cide *n.* murder of a relative, esp. of parents
parry *n.* evasion —*vi., vt.* ward off or avoid
parse *vt.* to break down and examine
par·si·mo´ni·ous *adj.* frugal
par·take´ *vt., vi.* receive a share in —**par·tak´er** *n.*
par´tial *adj.* incomplete; prejudiced or biased
par·tial´i·ty *n.* fondness or preference; bias
par·tic´i·pate *vi.* engage or share in
par´ti·cle *n.* tiny piece; least possible amount
par·tic´u·lar *adj.* fussy, attentive to detail; of a specific thing; noteworthy —*n.* a detail or specific
par´ti·san *adj.* biased —*n.* an ardent supporter
par·ti´tion *n.* a separation —*vt.* divide or separate
part´ner *n.* one allied with another; an associate
par´ty *adj.* of a group; of a social gathering —*n.* a group or gathering; a participant: *party to the action* —*vi.* carouse —**par´ty·er** *n.*
pass *n.* a passageway; ticket or permit; a throw; sexual overture —*vi., vt.* move by; transfer; be satisfactory
pass´a·ble *adj.* navigable; acceptable; adequate
pas´sage *n.* a journey; path or road; movement, transition, or progress; an excerpt; enactment, as of a law
pas·sé´ *adj.* no longer fashionable
pas´sen·ger *n.* a rider
pas´sion *n.* intense emotion
pas´sive *adj.* without reaction; complacent
past *adj.* former or prior; gone by —*n.* a former time or event —*prep.* beyond
paste *n.* a thick smooth adhesive —*vt.* fasten with paste
pas·tel´ *n.* a pale color; a chalk–like artist's medium
pas´teur·ize *vt.* process food so as to retard spoilage
pas´time *n.* amusement or diversion
pas´to·ral *adj.* of the country; rustic —*n.* an artistic work emulating country life, in music called a *pas·to·rale´*
pas´ture *n.* vegetation for grazing animals —*vt.* put an animal out to graze
pat *adj.* to the point —*n.* light tap or caress; a small bit of food —*vt.* lightly tap or caress; flatten or compress
patch *n.* a small piece or part —*vt.* mend or decorate
pat´ent *adj.* obvious, apparent —*n.* right granted to protect work for a time —*vt.* apply for or grant a patent
pa·ter´nal *adj.* of fatherhood —**pa·ter´nal·ism, pa·ter´ni·ty** *n.*
path *n.* a route for travel
pa·thet´ic *adj.* deserving of pity; inspiring contempt
path·o·log´i·cal *adj.* of habitual or obsessive behavior
pa·thol´o·gy *n.* study of diseases
pa´thos *n.* sympathy, sorrow
pa´tience *n.* ability to accept without complaint
pa´tient *adj.* accepting delay or difficulty; tolerant —*n.* one under care
pat´i·na, pat·i´na *n.* change or color by age and exposure
pat´io *n.* outdoor living space adjacent to a dwelling
pa´tois *n.* a provincial dialect
pa´tri·arch *n.* man heading a family or group; an elder
pa´tri·archy *n.* tracing of lineage through men
pa·tri´cian *n.* an aristocrat; one of refined manners and taste —*adj.*
pa´tri·ot *n.* supporter of one's country —**pa´tri·ot´ic** *adj.*
pa´tron *n.* a customer; one who supports a cause —**pa´tron·ize** *vt.*
pat´tern *n.* a model or drawing used as a guide; a reoccurring characteristic —*vt.* make according to a model
pau´ci·ty *n.* a lack or scarcity
pau´per *n.* impoverished person
pause *n.* temporary halt; hesitation for effect —*vi.*
pave´ment (*US*) *n.* durable covering for a path or road
pa·vil´ion *n.* an open shelter
pawn *n.* security; one held hostage —*vt.* use or give as security —**pawn´shop** *n.*
pay *vt.* give value for goods or services; reward or punish; render, as a compliment —*vi.* make payment; be profitable —*n.* compensation
peace *n.* freedom from hostility; serenity —**peace´ful** *adj.*
peak *adj.* at an upper limit —*n.* a pointed top; height of development —*vi.* bring to a climax
peaked *adj.* pointed
peak´ed *adj.* appearing sickly
peal *n.* a ringing —*vi., vt.*
peas´ant *n.* a rustic
peb´ble *n.* small stone
pec´ca·ble *adj.* likely to sin
pec´u·late *vt.* wrongfully appropriate; embezzle
pe·cu´liar *adj.* odd or unusual; unique; characteristic to a person, group, etc.
ped·a·gog´ics, ped´a·go·gy *n.* the teaching profession
ped´a·gogue *n.* an instructor; a narrow-minded teacher
ped´al *adj.* relating to the foot —*n.* pad for the foot —*vt., vi.* to operate with a pedal
pe·dan´tic *adj.* overly concerned with scholarship and formality
ped´dle *vi., vt.* to sell or offer for sale; promote, as an idea
ped´es·tal *n.* foundation; base
pe·des´tri·an *adj.* of travel by foot; ordinary or trite —*n.* one moving on foot
pe·di·a·tri´cian *n.* doctor who treats infants
ped´i·gree *n.* a list of ancestors; lineage
pe·do·phile, pe·do·phil´i·ac *n.* an adult sexually attracted to children
peek *n.* momentary view —*vi.* view quickly; emerge gently
peel *n.* an outer covering —*vi., vt.* to strip off
peer *vi.* stare —*n.* an equal; one of noble birth
pe·jo´ra·tive *adj.* disparaging or derisive —*n.* a derisive word or phrase
pelt *n.* an animal skin —*vt.* to strike repeatedly
pen *n.* writing instrument; an enclosure —*vt.* write; confine
pe´nal *adj.* relating to punishment —**pe´nal·ize** *vt.*
pen´al·ty *n.* consequences
pen´ance *n.* an act of remorse
penchant *n.* an inclination or tendency; a predisposition
pen´cil *n.* a writing instrument —*vt.* to write
pen´dant *n.* a hanging ornament
pen´dent *adj.* hanging or projecting
pend´ing *adj.* awaiting settlement —*prep.*
pen´du·lum *n.* a hanging weight —**pen´du·lous** *adj.*
pen´e·trate *vt.* gain entrance; pierce; affect profoundly —**pen´e·tra·ble** *adj.*
pe·nin´su·la *n.* a point of land that projects into water
pen´i·tent *adj.* sorrowful or atoning for guilt —*n.* — **pen´i·tence** *n.*
pen·i·ten´tia·ry (*US*) *n.* a prison
pen´nant *n.* a streamer
pe·nol´o·gy *n.* the study of prisons and rehabilitation
pen´sion *n.* money paid during retirement —*vt.*
pen´sive *adj.* inclined to thought —**pen´sive·ness** *n.*
pent´house *n.* a residence at or near the top of a building
pe·nu´ri·ous *adj.* frugal, miserly; unproductive, barren
pen´u·ry *n.* poverty
peo´ple *n.* humans in general —*vt.* to populate
per·ceive´ *vt., vi.* understand; become aware
per·cep´ti·ble *adj.* able to be discerned —**per·cep´tion** *n.*
per·cep´tive *adj.* observant
per´co·late *vi., vt.* to filter —*n.* a filtered liquid
pe·ren´ni·al *adj.* long–lasting or enduring; recurring often
per´fect *adj.* complete; free of fault; well–suited; capable —**per·fect´** *vt.* further develop or complete; make flawless
per·fid´i·ous *adj.* unfaithful or treacherous —**per´fid·y** *n.*
per´fo·rate *vt.* pierce; mark with holes for separating
per·form´ *vt., vi.* act on; function; to entertain

per´fume *n.* an aromatic substance; a pleasant aroma
per·func´to·ry *adj.* indifferent; act mechanically, casually, or carelessly
per·haps´ *adv.* possibly
per´il *n.* exposure to danger
pe·rim´e·ter *n.* boundary
pe´ri·od *n.* span of time; (*US*) punctuation mark that ends a sentence
pe´ri·od´ic *adj.* cyclical; recurring at regular intervals —**pe·ri·od´i·cal** *n.*
per·i·pa·tet´ic *adj.* roaming about; itinerant —*n.* one given to roaming
pe·riph´er·al *adj.* outer; minor
pe·riph´ery *n.* outermost part
per´ish *vi.* die; pass from existence —**per´ish·a·ble** *adj.*
per´jure *vt.* testify falsely; violate an oath —**per´jury** *n.*
per´ma·nent *adj.* durable; enduring; unchanging
per´me·ate *vt., vi.* spread throughout
per·mis´si·ble *adj.* allowed
per·mis´sion *n.* approval or authorization
per·mis´sive *adj.* lenient
per·mit´ *vt.* allow or authorize —**per´mit** *n.* a document that grants permission
per·ni´cious *adj.* harmful
per´o·rate *vi.* speak at length
per·pen·dic´u·lar *adj.* at right angles to the horizon
per´pe·trate *vt.* commit, as a crime — **per´pe·tra·tor** *n.*
per·pet´u·al *adj.* continuing indefinitely; recurrent
per·pet´u·ate *vt.* endure
per·plex´ *vt.* to confound or confuse —**per·plexed´** *adj.*
per´qui·site *n.* benefit associated with a position
per´se·cute *vt.* oppress or abuse —**per·se·cu´tion** *n.*
per·se·ver´ance *n.* patience and persistence; determination —**per´se·vere´** *vi.*
per´si·flage *n.* banter
per·sist´ *vi.* persevere; endure
per´son *n.* an individual; a living human body
per´son·a·ble *adj.* pleasant
per´son·al *adj.* relating to a particular person; intimate
per·son·al´i·ty *n.* qualities of a person; distinctive attributes; a famous person
per·son´i·fy *vt.* endow with human qualities
per´son·nel´ *n.* employees
per·spec´tive *n.* viewpoint; a panorama; a flat rendering of three dimensions
per·spi·ca´cious *adj.* demonstrating unusual insight —**per·spi·cac´i·ty** *n.*
per·suade´ *vt.* convince
per·sua´sion *n.* power to convince —**per·sua´sive** *adj.*
pert *adj.* vivacious; saucy
per·tain´ *vi.* to relate to
per´ti·nent *adj.* relevant
per·turb´ *vt.* disquiet or worry
pe·ruse´ *vt.* study thoroughly; scrutinize —**pe·rus´al** *n.*
per·vade´ *vt.* penetrate or permeate —**per·va´sive** *adj.*
per·verse´ *adj.* evil or wicked; obstinate —**per·ver´sion** *n.*
per·vert´ *vt.* use improperly; distort meaning; corrupt
per´vi·ous *adj.* permeable
pest *n.* a nuisance; something harmful, as a virus
pes´ter *vt.* harass or annoy
pes´ti·lence *n.* an epidemic; a dangerous or harmful agent
pes´tle *n.* a device for crushing or blending in a mortar
pet *n.* one treated affectionately —*adj.* regarded as a favorite —*vt.* indulge; caress
pe·tite´ *n.* small
pe·ti´tion *n.* an appeal —*vi., vt.* make an appeal
pet´ri·fy *vt.* fossilize; paralyze with fright
pet´rol (*Brit.*) *n.* fuel for a motor vehicle
pe·tro´le·um (*US*) *n.* crude oil
pet´tish *adj.* irritable; peevish
pet´ty *adj.* trivial, unimportant; mean or miserly
pet´u·lant *adj.* ill–tempered; irritable
phan´tasm *n.* an apparition
phan´tom *adj.* illusory; imaginary —*n.* an apparition
phar·ma·ceu´tics *pl. n.* preparation of medicinal compounds —**phar·ma·ceu´ti·cal** *adj.* —**phar´ma·cist** *n.*
phar·ma·col´o·gy *n.* study of drugs and their uses
phe·nom´e·nal *adj.* extraordinary or remarkable
phi·lan´thro·py *n.* charity; humanitarian endeavor
phi·lat´e·ly *n.* stamp collecting —**phi·lat´e·list** *n.*
phi·lol´o·gy *n.* classical studies —**phi·lol´o·gist** *n.*
phi·los´o·phy *n.* study of knowledge; a fundamental principle; a system of beliefs
pho´bia *n.* an irrational fear or aversion —**pho´bic** *adj.*
pho·net´ics *n.* the sounds of speech —**pho·net´ic** *adj.*
pho´ny *adj.* artificial; fake —*n.* an imitation; a fake
pho·to·syn´the·sis *n.* deriving nourishment using light as an energy source
phys´i·cal *adj.* of the body or tangible matter
phy·si´cian *n.* doctor of medicine; one devoted to healing
phys´ics *n.* study of matter and energy —**phys´i·cist** *n.*
phys·i·ol´o·gy *n.* the study of living organisms
phy·sique´ *n.* the structure and appearance of the body
pick *vt.* select or separate; to gather or pluck —**pick´er** *n.*
pic´nic *n.* an outdoor meal; something easy or enjoyable
pic´ture *n.* a visual or oral depiction; a mental image —*vt.* visualize; describe vividly
piece *n.* part or portion; thing of a type —*vt.* join together
pierce *vt.* penetrate
pi´e·ty *n.* devotion, reverence
pig´ment *n.* a dye or coloring
pile *n.* an accumulation —*vt., vi.* to make or form a heap
pil´fer *vt., vi.* to steal
pil´grim *n.* a traveler, esp. on a sacred journey
pil´lage *vt.* plunder
pil´lar *n.* supporting column
pi´lot *n.* one who or that which operates or guides
pinch *n.* a sprinkling; a predicament —*vt.* squeeze so as to cause discomfort; arrest; steal —*vi.* squeeze; be stingy; become constricted
pin´na·cle *n.* crest or summit
pi´o·neer´ *adj.* early, experimental; adventurous —*n.* explorer of new territory —*vt., vi.* lead; prepare the way
pi´ous *adj.* devout, reverent
pipe *n.* a hollow tube; a smoking implement —*vt.* convey through a pipe
pi´quant *adj.* spicy; interesting or charming
pique *n.* indignation or ire —*vt.* irritate; excite or arouse
pit *n.* hole in the ground; a small indentation; recessed area —*vt., vi.* mark with indentations; place in conflict
pit´e·ous *adj.* pitiful; deserving pity —**pit´e·ous·ly** *adv.*
pith *n.* core or essence
pith´y *adj.* meaningful; brief
pit´i·ful *adj.* arousing pity or contempt; pathetic
pit´tance *n.* a trifling sum
pit´y *n.* compassion
pix´i·lat·ed *adj.* frivolous or whimsical —**pix·i·la´tion** *n.*
plac´a·ble *adj.* inclined to tolerance or acceptance
pla´cate *vt.* appease or pacify
place *n.* a position, space, or locality; one's status, job, etc. —*vt.* situate; appoint; find a home or job for
pla·ce´bo *n.* a fake or phony medication; a sugar pill
plac´id *adj.* peaceful or calm
pla´gia·rism *n.* misappropriation of the works of another
plague *n.* sudden spread of disease; a sudden outbreak —*vt.* annoy; afflict
plain *adj.* unadorned; simple; open or obvious; ordinary
plain´tive *adj.* mournful; lamenting
plan *n.* strategy; a diagram —*vt.* work out means for doing; have as an intention
plan´et *n.* heavenly body revolving around a star
plan·ta´tion *n.* land under cultivation; an estate
plat *n.* a plot of land; a map of building lots, streets, etc. —*vt.* make a map
plate *n.* a flat piece; food service for one —*vt.* to overlay or coat —**plat´ed** *adj.*
pla·teau´ *n.* a flat–topped hill
plat´form *n.* a raised landing; statement of beliefs or goals
plat´i·tude *n.* a trite expression; a cliché
pla·ton´ic *adj.* spiritual; ideal
plau´si·ble *adj.* probable; convincing
play *vi., vt.* act out; perform; participate in a game —*n.* a dramatic performance; looseness of a machine part
plaz´a *n.* a public square
plea *n.* a request or appeal
plead *vi., vt.* beseech; offer an excuse or justification
pleas´ant *adj.* providing pleasure —**pleas´ant·ly** *adv.*
pleas´ant·ry *n.* a polite or humorous remark
please *vi., vt.* give pleasure
plea´sure *n.* delight; that brings happiness or enjoyment; a preference —**plea´sur·a·ble** *adj.*
pledge *n.* a binding promise; security for payment —*vt.*
plen´ty *n.* adequate amount; abundance —**plen´ti·ful** *adj.*
pleth´o·ra *n.* an excess
pli´a·ble *adj.* flexible
pli´ant *adj.* yielding; docile
plight *n.* predicament or difficulty; a condition or state; a promise —*vt.* a pledge
plod *vi., vt.* move or work steadily and painstakingly
plot *n.* parcel of land; story line; plan or conspiracy —*vt.* locate on a map; take part in conspiracy —*vi.* conspire
plug *n.* material that closes or obstructs; electrical connector; mention of a product —*vt., vi.* stop up or close off; advertise a product
plumb *adj.* precisely vertical —*adv.* squarely —*n.* line to establish a precise vertical —*vt.* make vertical
plum´met *vi.* fall rapidly
plump *adj.* full and rounded —*vt., vi.* become plump
plun´der *n.* stolen property —*vt. vi.* take by force
plunge *vi., vt.* to fall or thrust
plu´ral *adj.* more than one
plush *adj.* sumptuous; opulent —**plush´i·ness** *n.*
ply *n.* a thin layer —*vt.* to regularly practice, as a trade
po·di´a·try *n.* branch of medicine dealing with the feet
po´di·um *n.* a speaker's platform
po´em *n.* a work in verse
po´et·ry *n.* poetic works; the traits of a poem
poi´gnant *adj.* mentally intense; distressing or moving
point *n.* sharp end; a projection; a dot; a distinct element, quality, or condition —*vi., vt.* direct attention to
poise *n.* grace, dignity, and composure —*vt., vi.* to balance or hover
po´lar·ize *vt.* consolidate around differing views
po·lem´ics *n.* the art of debate
po·lice´ *n.* persons charged with law enforcement —*vt.*
pol´i·cy *n.* a plan or procedure; a contract
pol´ish *n.* luster or sheen; refinement —*vt.* make smooth and bright; make refined
po·lite´ *adj.* considerate, tactful; courteous
pol´i·tics *n.* science of government; tactics for gaining power —**po·lit´i·cal** *adj.*
pol·lute´ *vt.* contaminate —**pol·lu´tion** *n.*
pol´ter·geist *n.* a supernatural being creating disorder
pomp *n.* pageantry
pomp´ous *adj.* pretentious; boastful and arrogant
pond *n.* a small body of water
pon´der *vt.* consider carefully
pon´der·ous *adj.* weighty; dull or lifeless
pon·tif´i·cate *vi.* speak dogmatically
pool *n.* accumulation of liquid; small body of water; an assemblage —*vi., vt.*

poor *adj.* lacking wealth; lacking basic needs; inferior
pop´u·lar *adj.* generally accepted; well-liked —**pop·u·lar´i·ty** *n.* —**pop´u·lar·ize** *vt.*
pop´u·late *vt.* to inhabit; furnish with inhabitants
pop·u·la´tion *n.* people of an area; a particular grouping
po´rous *adj.* having pores; absorbent; penetrable
por´ta·ble *adj.* easily carried or moved —**por·ta·bil´i·ty** *n.*
por´tal *n.* an entryway
por·tend´ *vt.* predict or foretell
por´tent *n.* a sign or omen
por·ten´tous *adj.* ominous or foreboding
port·fo´li·o *n.* a folder; a collection of documents
por´tion *n.* part or share; amount for one person —*vt.* separate; distribute
port´ly *adj.* stout
por·tray´ *vt.* to represent
pose *n.* a feigned attitude; an affectation —*vi.* assume a position; feign an attitude; misrepresent —*vt.* cause to sit for a portrait; put forth, as a question —**pos´er** *n.*
posh *adj.* comfortable
po·si´tion *n.* a specific place; a viewpoint; social or professional status —*vt.* to place
pos´i·tive *adj.* certain, absolutely sure; decisive; direct
pos·sess´ *vt.* have; dominate
pos·ses´sion *n.* thing owned or in one's custody
pos´si·ble *adj.* likely or able to be —**pos´si·bly** *adv.*
post *n.* a shaft or rod to support or connect; mail —*vt.* appoint or assign; (*Brit.*) send via the postal system
pos·te´ri·or *adj.* situated behind —*n.* buttocks
pos·ter´i·ty *n.* succeeding generations
post´hu·mous *adj.* after death
post·pone´ *vt.* to put off
pos´tu·late *n.* supposition —*vt.* presume without proof
pos´ture *n.* characteristic bearing, manner, or attitude —*vi.* affect an attitude
po´ta·ble *adj.* suitable for drinking —*n.* a beverage
po´tent *adj.* strong; powerful
po·ten´tial *adj.* possible —*n.* unrealized capacity
po·tion *n.* a medicine or drug
pot´pour·ri´ *n.* mixture or medley; a conglomeration
pot´sherd *n.* fragment of pottery
pouch *n.* a bag or recepticle
pounce *vi.* attack or seize suddenly
pound *n.* unit of weight or currency; place of confinement —*vt.* strike repeatedly; tread heavily; confine
pour *vi., vt.* flow in a steady stream; rain profusely
pov´er·ty *n.* a state of want
pow´der *n.* fine particles —*vi., vt.* make granular; pulverize
pow´er *n.* strength, energy; authority —*vt.* provide with means of propulsion —*adj.* operated by motor or electricity —**pow´er·ful** *adj.*
prac´ti·cal *adj.* useful or usable; workable or sensible
prac´ti·cal·ly *adv.* almost
prac´tice *n.* repetition to improve; mode or manner of functioning; a profession —**prac´tice** (*US*), **prac´tise** (*Brit.*) *vt., vi.* repeat an action to acquire skill; perform according to custom; work at a profession
prag·mat´ic *adj.* practical; concerning facts and logic
praise *n.* expression of approval —*vt.* express approval; honor or glorify
prank *n.* a practical joke
prate *n.* idle chatter —*vi., vt.* talk idly and frivolously
prayer *n.* an earnest appeal or supplication —**pray** *vi., vt.*
pre´am·ble *n.* a preface
pre·car´i·ous *adj.* uncertain or unstable
pre·cau´tion *n.* care taken
pre·cede´ *vt., vi.* come before
pre´cious *adj.* valuable; cherished; overly refined —*adv.*
pre·cip´i·tate *adj.* hasty or rash —*vi., vt.* fall, as rain; hasten occurrence
pre·cip·i·ta´tion *n.* haste or rashness; falling moisture
pre·cip´i·tous *adj.* steep
pré·cis´ *n.* a summary
pre·cise´ *adj.* exact; well–defined —**pre·ci´sion** *n., adj.*
pre·clude´ *vt.* exclude or prohibit —**pre·clu´sion** *n.*
pre·co´cious *adj.* exhibiting early maturity
pre·cog·ni´tion *n.* foresight; prescience
pred´a·tor *n.* one preying on others —**pred´a·to·ry** *adj.*
pre·dic´a·ment *n.* difficult situation
pre·dict´ *vt.* assert —*vi.* foretell or prophesy —**pre·dict´a·ble** *adj.* —**pre·dic´tion** *n.*
preen *vt., vi.* groom or primp; to gloat
pref´ace *n.* an introduction —*vt.* furnish an opening message; serve as introduction
pre·fer´ *vt.* favor over another; like better —**pref´er·ence** *n.*
pref´er·a·ble *adj.* more desirable —**pref´er·a·bly** *adv.*
pref·er·en´tial *adj.* favored; granting assistance
preg´na·ble *adj.* pervious; vulnerable
preg´nant *adj.* carrying a developing offspring; significant or meaningful
pre·hen´sile *adj.* adapted for grasping, as a monkey's tail
pre·his·tor´ic *adj.* of time before recorded history
prej´u·dice *n.* prejudgment; opinion founded on bias —*vt.* influence to prejudge; wrong by opinion or action
pre·lim´i·nar·y *adj.* introductory —*n.* an introduction; that which precedes
pre·mier´ *adj.* foremost —*n.* a chief administrative officer
pre·miere´ *n.* an introductory performance —*vt., vi.* present the first time
prem´ise *n.* an assumption that is the basis for debate
pre´mi·um *adj.* excellent; superior; —*n.* reward or bonus; excess over value
pre·mo·ni´tion *n.* foreboding; a sign or omen
pre·oc´cu·pied *adj.* distracted; troubled
prep·a·ra´tion *n.* readiness; organization; a mixture
pre·par´a·to·ry *adj.* introductory or preliminary —*adv.* in making ready for
pre·pare´ *vt.* arrange in advance; provide needs; make complete
pre·pon´der·ant *adj.* superior; dominant
pre·pos´ter·ous *adj.* absurd; irrational
pre·rog´a·tive *n.* a right or privilege, as by rank or birth
pre´sci·ence *n.* foreknowledge
pre·scribe´ *vt.* direct or order
pre·scrip´tion *n.* directions or instructions; a formula
pres´ence *n.* attendance, proximity, or influence; appearance or bearing
pres´ent[1] *adj.* at this moment; current; existing; here; near at hand —*n.* now
pres´ent[2] *n.* a gift —**pre·sent´** *vt.* offer or give, as a gift
pre·sent´a·ble *adj.* suitable for offering or giving
pres´ent·ly *adv.* soon
pre·serv´a·tive *n.* a substance that prevents spoiling —*adj.*
pre·serve´ *n.* area kept in a natural state —*vt.* protect; save in a natural state; prepare so as to prevent spoilage —**pres·er·va´tion** *n.*
pre·side´ *vi.* officiate
pres´i·dent *n.* chief officer or executive; one who presides
press *n.* journalism or journalists; machine for printing; device to apply pressure; urgency —*vt., vi.* apply pressure
pres´sure *n.* constant application of force —*vt.* persuade
pres·tige´ *n.* distinction or renown; esteem
pre·sume´ *vt.* take for granted; undertake without authorization —*vi.* make excessive demands on
pre·tend´ *vt., vi.* feign or mimic; make believe; be deceitful; attempt to deceive —**pre·tence´** (*Brit.*), **pre·tense´** (*US*) *n.*
pre·ten´tious *adj.* presumptuous or arrogant; pompous or showy —**pre·ten´sion** *n.*
pre´text *n.* subterfuge
pret´ty *adj.* attractive; considerable; insubstantial —*adv.* quite; somewhat
pre·vail´ *vi.* overcome; influence or effect
prev´a·lent *adj.* common or widespread
pre·var´i·cate *vi.* to lie
pre·vent´ *vt.* keep from happening; prohibit or hamper
pre·ven´tive *adj.* hindering; precautionary —*n.* a thing that prevents, as from disease —**pre·ven´tive·ly** *adv.*
pre´vi·ous *adj.* former; having occurred earlier
prey *n.* one hunted; a victim —*vi.* to hunt; to victimize
price *n.* cost —*vt.* set value
pride *n.* self–esteem; haughtiness, disdain
pri´mal *adj.* primitive; original; primary
pri´mary *adj.* first; earliest; fundamental; principal
prime *adj.* of the finest quality; original —*n.* age of full perfection or vigor; best of anything —*vt.* prepare or make ready
pri·me´val *adj.* ancient; primitive
prim´i·tive *adj.* simple; ancient; uncivilized
primp *vt., vi.* groom with care
prin´ci·pal *adj.* first or leading —*n.* a person of importance
prin´ci·ple *n.* a fundamental rule or concept; an ideal
pri´or *adj.* preceding
pris´tine *adj.* unspoiled
pri´vate *adj.* not open to the public; not public; secluded
pri·va´tion *n.* abject poverty
priv´i·lege *n.* a special right
prize *n.* award; a thing desired —*adj.* valued —*vt.* to value highly
prob´a·ble *adj.* likely; worth believing —**prob·a·bil´i·ty** *n.*
pro´bi·ty *n.* honesty; integrity
prob´lem *adj.* difficult to manage —*n.* something to be considered; a puzzle or dilemma
pro·ce´dure *n.* manner or system of doing
pro·ceed´ *vi.* move forward
proc´ess *n.* a system
pro·ces´sion *n.* an orderly progression; a parade
pro·claim´ *vt.* announce; praise
proc·la·ma´tion *n.* a formal announcement or edict
pro·cliv´i·ty *n.* an inherent inclination or tendency
pro·cras´ti·nate *vi.* to put off —*vt.* postpone or delay
pro·cure´ *vt.* acquire
prod *vt.* goad or provoke —*n.* that incites to action
prod´i·gal *adj.* wasteful
pro·di´gious *adj.* extraordinary or impressive
prod´i·gy *n.* one with exceptional talent; a genius
prod´uce *n.* farm products —**pro·duce´** *vt.* make or manufacture; create
pro·duc´tive *adj.* fruitful or prolific; effective
pro·fane´ *adj.* sacrilegious or irreverent; vulgar or base —*vt.* desecrate or debase
pro·fan´i·ty *n.* irreverence; abusive or vulgar language
pro·fess´ *vt.* claim or declare; pretend or feign
pro·fes´sion *n.* an occupation; a declaration of faith
pro·fes´sion·al *adj.* skillful —*n.* one specially trained
pro·fes´sor *n.* (*Brit.*) a distinguished college or university teacher; (*US*) an educator, esp. at a college or university —**pro·fes·so´ri·al** *adj.*
prof´fer *vt.* to offer
pro·fi´cient *adj.* competent
pro´file *n.* summary; a side view
prof´it *n.* gain from a business —*vt., vi.* realize gain or benefit; be of benefit to
prof´li·gate *adj.* extravagant or wasteful
pro·found´ *adj.* deep or penetrating; scholarly
pro·fuse´ *adj.* abundant
pro·fu´sion *n.* an abundance
prog´e·ny *n.* offspring
prog·nos´ti·cate *vt.* to predict
pro´gram (*US*) *n.* schedule, agenda; radio or television

show; computer instructions —*vt.* prepare a schedule or agenda; to write computer instructions
pro´gramme (*Brit.*) *n.* a schedule or agenda; radio or television show —*vt.* prepare a schedule or agenda
prog´ress *n.* advancement, development, or improvement —**pro·gress´** *vi.* move forward; grow or improve
pro·gres´sive *adj.* receptive to fresh ideas or concepts
pro·hib´it *vt.* forbid or ban
pro·hib´i·tive *adj.* forbidding
proj´ect *n.* a plan; a serious undertaking —**pro·ject´** *vt.* extend or thrust forward
pro·jec´tion *n.* a bulge; an extended part; a forecast
pro·lif´er·ate *vi., vt.* increase rapidly —**pro·lif·er·a´tion** *n.*
pro·lif´ic *adj.* abundant
pro·lix´ *adj.* excessively wordy
pro´logue *n.* introductory text
pro·long´ *vt.* extend or lengthen
prom´i·nent *adj.* clearly discernable; well–known, celebrated —**prom´i·nence** *n.*
pro·mis´cu·ous *adj.* tending to casual relationships; indiscriminate; random
prom´ise *n.* a pledge or vow —*vt.* —**prom´is·so·ry** *adj.*
prom´on·to·ry *n.* high point of land extending into water
pro·mote´ *vt.* advance to a higher level; attempt to make popular or prominent
prompt *adj.* punctual; timely —*vt.* arouse or provoke; remind —**prompt´ly** *adv.*
prom´ul·gate *vt.* announce publicly or officially
prone *adj.* lying face downward; disposed to, likely
prong *n.* pointed extension; (*US*) contact points for a connection
pro´noun *n.* designation that substitutes for a noun
pro·nounce´ *vt., vi.* speak clearly; announce officially
pro·nun·ci·a´tion *n.* accepted sound of a spoken word
proof *n.* evidence; demonstration of authenticity
prop·a·gan´da *n.* information to promote a point of view
prop´a·gate *vt.* breed or multiply; to spread or extend
pro·pel´ *vt.* drive forward
pro·pen´si·ty *n.* an inclination or tendency
prop´er *adj.* appropriate; fitting; conventional
prop´er·ty *n.* belongings or possessions; section of land; a characteristic or quality
proph´e·cy *n.* a prediction
proph´e·sy *vt.* to predict
proph´et *n.* one who pronounces or interprets by divine inspiration
pro·pi´ti·ate *vt.* appease
pro·pi´tious *adj.* promising or favorable; kindly disposed
pro·po´nent *n.* an advocate or defender; a supporter
pro·por´tion *n.* a share; relative magnitude; symmetry
pro·pos´al *n.* an offer; a plan
pro·pose´ *vt.* recommend; put forth for consideration; intend —*vi.* make an offer
pro·pri´e·tor *n.* an owner; one having exclusive right to —**pro·pri´e·tar·y** *adj.*
pro·pri´e·ty *n.* good breeding; conformity to society
pro·sa´ic *adj.* commonplace; mundane, humdrum, or dull
pro·scribe´ *vt.* to condemn or forbid —**pro·scrip´tion** *n.*
prose *n.* style of ordinary speech
pros´pect *n.* expectation —*vt., vi.* to search or explore
pros´per *vi.* to thrive —**pros´per·ous** *adj.*
pros·per´i·ty *n.* affluence or well–being
pros´trate *adj.* prone; submissive; overcome —*vt.* bow down or lie flat; be overcome
pro·tag´o·nist *n.* the principal character in a story
pro·tect´ *vt.* safeguard
pro´té·gé *n.* one endorsed by a person of influence
pro´test *n.* declaration or display of disapproval —**pro·test´** *vt.* object strongly
pro´to·col *n.* code of conduct; proper etiquette; ceremony
pro´to·type *n.* a model
pro·tract´ *vt.* prolong
pro·trude´ *vt., vi.* jut or thrust outward —**pro·tru´sion** *n.*
proud *adj.* full of self–esteem; vain or arrogant; dignified
prove *vt.* establish by argument or evidence —**prov´en** *adj.*
prov´en·der *n.* supplies; provisions
prov´erb *n.* a saying or adage —**pro·ver´bi·al** *adj.*
pro·vide´ *vt.* to supply or furnish; stipulate
prov´i·dence *n.* advance preparation; divine guidance
prov´ince *n.* an outlying area
pro·vin´cial *adj.* crude or unsophisticated
pro·vi´sion *n.* supplies; a requirement —*vt.* to supply
pro·vi´sion·al *adj.* temporary
pro·vi´so *n.* a stipulation
pro·voke´ *vt.* induce, as to action or anger —**prov·o·ca´tion** *n.* —**pro·voc´a·tive** *adj.*
prow´ess *n.* skill or daring
prowl *vt., vi.* move stealthily
prox·im´i·ty *n.* nearness
prox´y *n.* an agent; authority to act as agent
pru´dence *n.* caution in the conduct of one's business
pru´ri·ent *adj.* overly interested in sexual matters
pry *vi.* snoop —*vt.* force open *n.* a lever or bar for prying
pseu´do·nym *n.* an alias
psy´che *n.* subconscious mind; the soul
psych·e·del´ic *adj.* marked by hallucination —*n.* a substance that alters awareness
psy·chi´a·try *n.* diagnosis and treatment of mental disorders —**psy·chi´a·trist** *n.*
psy´chic *adj.* mental; of exceptional mental processes —*n.* a spiritualist
psy·cho·log´i·cal *adj.* of the mind or emotions
psy·cho·path´ic *adj.* antisocial, agressive, or perverted
psy·cho·ther´a·py *n.* treatment for a mental or emotional disorder
pub *n.* a public house; a tavern
pub´lic *adj.* common or shared; of a community
pub·li·ca´tion *n.* printed material; communication
public house (*Brit.*) a tavern
pub·lic´i·ty *n.* information of a promotional nature
pu´er·ile *adj.* childish or juvenile
puff´er·y *n.* exaggerated praise; promotion
pu´gi·lism *n.* the sport of boxing —**pu´gi·list** *n.*
pug·na´cious *adj.* belligerent
pul´chri·tude *n.* great beauty
pule *vi.* to whine or whimper
pull *n.* allure; influence —*vt.* draw toward; tug; attract —*vi.* use force in hauling
pul´ley *n.* a simple machine
pul´sate *vi.* vibrate rhythmically —**pul·sa´tion** *n.*
pulse *n.* a rhythmic beating
pul´ver·ize *vt.* crush; reduce to powder
pump *n.* a device for moving liquid —*vi., vt.* move with a pump; move up and down
pun *n.* a play on words —*vi.*
punch *n.* a piercing tool; a fruit beverage —*vt.* strike
punc·til´i·ous *adj.* attentive to detail; precise
punc´tu·al *adj.* on time; prompt —**punc·tu·al´i·ty** *n.*
punc·tu·a´tion *n.* written marks to indicate pauses, separations, etc.
punc´ture *vt.* pierce —*n.* a hole
pun´dit *n.* a critic or scholar
pun´gent *adj.* sharp or biting
pun´ish *vt.* penalize
pup´pet *n.* a figure moved by strings, hands, etc.; one controlled by another
pur´chase *n.* a thing bought —*vt.* to buy —**pur´chas·er** *n.*
pure *adj.* free of pollutants; without fault —**pu´ri·ty** *n.*
pu·rée´ *n.* a smooth paste —*vt.* reduce to a smooth paste
pur´ga·tive *adj.* tending to cleanse —*n.* a medication for purging bowels: a laxative —**pur·ga´tion** *n.*
purge *vt.* cleanse or purify; rid of impurities —*n.* act of purification; action to rid of undesirable elements
pu·ri·fi·ca´tion *n.* an act of cleansing
pu´ri·fy *vt.* free of impurities or defilement —**pu´ri·fi·er** *n.*
pur·loin´ *vi., vt.* steal
pur·port´ *vt.* claim or have intention —**pur·port´ed** *adj.*
pur´pose *n.* aim; an intention
pur´pose·ful *adj.* having intent —**pur´pose·ful·ly** *adv.*
purse *n.* (*Brit.*) small tote used for currency, etc.; (*US*) woman's handbag; an award of money —*vt.* gather in small folds
pur·sue´ *vt.* chase or hunt; aspire or strive for —**pur·suit´** *n.*
pur´view *n.* extent of ability, authority, etc.; range of understanding
push *vt., vi.* apply force; to press —*n.* energy; drive
put *vt.* to place; cause to be placed —*vi.* to proceed
pu´ta·tive *adj.* supposed
pu·tre·fac´tion *n.* decomposed organic matter
pu´trid *adj.* decaying; corrupt; vile or offensive
put´ter *n.* a golf club —*vt.* poke about —*vi.* waste time
puz´zle *n.* a mystery —*vt.* baffle or bewilder
pyre *n.* a formation of material for burning a dead body
q, Q seventeenth letter of the alphabet
quad´ran·gle *n.* a plane figure with four sides; an area enclosed by buildings
quad´rant *n.* a 90° arc; one fourth of a circle
quaff *vt., vi.* to drink
quag´mire *n.* a slough or swamp; a difficult situation
quaint *adj.* curious or uncommon; picturesque
quake *n.* an earthquake —*vi.* to tremble or shake
qual´i·fied *adj.* capable; limited: *a qualified success*
qual´i·fy *vi., vt.* be eligible; describe; limit
qual´i·ty *n.* a characteristic or trait; excellence
qualm *n.* uncertainty
quan´da·ry *n.* dilemma
quan´ti·ty *n.* an amount; a considerable volume
quar´an·tine *n.* isolation, esp. to prevent spread of disease —*vt.* place in isolation
quar´rel *n.* disagreement; an argument —*vt.*
quar´ry *n.* something pursued; an excavation —*vt.* to dig up stone
quar´ter *n.* one–fourth —*vt.* divide into four; furnish lodging
quash *vt.* to suppress
qua´ver *vi.* to tremble
quea´sy *adj.* nauseated; uneasy or troubled
queer *adj.* strange, unusual; unconventional
quell *vt.* suppress; ease, calm
quench *vt.* extinguish; drench
quer´u·lous *adj.* complaining; peevish; disgruntled
que´ry *n.* a question or inquiry —*vt.* to question
quest *n.* search; journey of exploration —*vi.*
ques´tion *n.* inquiry; that open to discussion —*vi., vt.* interrogate; doubt; challenge
queue *n.* a waiting line
quib´ble *n.* a petty argument —*vi.* fret over trivial matters
quick *adj.* swift and abrupt; alert, intelligent —**quick´en** *vt., vi.*
qui·es´cent *adj.* still; inactive
qui´et *adj.* silent; calm; tranquil —*vi., vt.* to make or become still; make serene
quin·tes´sence *n.* essential quality
quip *n.* witty remark
quirk *n.* an idiosyncrasy
quit *vi., vt.* resign or relinquish; discontinue; to leave
quite *adv.* totally; absolutely; to a great extent: *quite nice*
quiv´er *n.* vibration —*vi.* shudder or tremble
quix·ot´ic *adj.* idealistic
quiz *n.* a short test —*vt.* to question —**quiz´zi·cal** *adj.*
quote *vt.* repeat another's words; cite; state a price
quo·tid´i·an *adj.* commonplace; daily

r, R eighteenth letter of the alphabet
rab´bi *n.* a Jewish scholar
rab´ble *n.* unruly mob; riffraff
rab´id *adj.* fanatical; frenzied
race[1] *n.* people linked by appearance, location, etc.
race[2] *n.* a contest of speed; a rivalry —*vi.* take part in a race; proceed at great speed
rack *n.* framework for holding, etc.; an instrument of torture; a cut of meat —*vt.* cause severe distress
rac´on·teur *n.* a storyteller
rac´y *adj.* spirited; risqué or suggestive; lewd
ra´di·ant *adj.* emitting heat or light; bright, glowing
ra´di·ate *vi., vt.* extend from a central point; emit
rad´i·cal *adj.* deviating; extreme —*n.* an advocate of extreme change
ra·di·ol´o·gy *n.* use of radioactive materials to diagnose and treat disease
raf´ter *n.* a supporting beam
rage *n.* violent anger; passion —*vi.* to speak or act violently
rag´ged *adj.* tattered; worn or frayed; rough or uneven
rag´time *n.* American music form
raid *n.* an unexpected assault —*vi., vt.* invade —**raid´er** *n.*
rai´ment *n.* clothing
raise *vt.* move or make higher; increase; build —**rais´er** *n.*
ral´ly *n.* an assemblage —*vi.* assemble; recover
ram´ble *n.* leisurely stroll —*vi.* wander aimlessly
ram·i·fi·ca´tion *n.* a consequence
ramp *n.* a sloping surface
ram´pant *adj.* uncontrolled; without restraint
ran´cid *adj.* stale or tainted
ran´cor *n.* harsh resentment; animosity —**ran´cor·ous** *adj.*
ran´dom *adj.* lacking order; haphazard
rand´y *adj.* lascivious
range *n.* reach or scope; area or extent; a limit —*vi.* wander; vary within limits
rank *adj.* of an offensive odor; utter or complete: *rank amateur* —*n.* station or position —*vt.* arrange in position
ran´kle *vt.* to irritate
ran´sack *vt.* to search or seek aggressively
rant *vi., vt.* speak wildly or incoherently —**rant´er** *n.*
ra·pa´cious *adj.* avaricious or greedy; ravenous
rap´id *adj.* swift; occurring with unusual speed —**ra·pid´i·ty** *n.*
rap·port´ *n.* understanding
rapt *adj.* enthralled or engrossed; spellbound
rap´ture *n.* joy, ecstasy —**rap´tur·ous** *adj.*
rare *adj.* uncommon, unusual; excellent, incomparable —**rar´i·ty** *n.*
rash *adj.* impulsive or impetuous; reckless
rasp *n.* a coarse file; a harsh sound —*vt., vt.* abrade; speak in a hoarse voice
rate *n.* relative value; charge per unit —*vt.* set a value on
rath´er *adv.* preferably; to some extent; more accurately
rat´i·fy *vt.* approve; sanction
ra´tio *n.* a proportion
ra´tion *n.* an assigned measure —*vt.* allot or distribute
ra´tio·nal *adj.* sane; able to reason —**ra´tio·nal·ize** *vt.*
ra´tio·nale´ *n.* grounds for reasoning; interpretation
rau´cous *adj.* loud and rowdy; boisterous
rav´age *vi., vt.* destroy
rave *vi., vt.* babble incoherently; to praise
rav´en·ous *adj.* hungry; insatiable; greedy
raw *adj.* not processed; inexperienced; exposed
reach *n.* extent or range—*vi., vt.* extend to; arrive
re·act´ *vi.* to respond or reply
re·ac´tion·ar·y *adj.* in opposition to progress
read *vi., vt.* study and understand —**read´a·ble** *adj.*
read´y *adj.* prepared and available; eager
re´al *adj.* genuine; not imaginary
re´al·is´tic *adj.* practical; truly representative
re´al·ize *vt.* recognize as true; make true
re´al·ly *adv.* truly; exceptionally
realm *n.* one's domain
re´al·ty *n.* real estate
reap *vi., vt.* harvest; to gain
rea´son *n.* explanation; intellect; a cause to believe —*vi., vt.* consider logically; persuade by logic
rea´son·a·ble *adj.* able to reason; governed by reason
re´as·sure´ *vt.* encourage; restore confidence
reb´el *n.* one who defies authority —**re·bel´** *vt.* to resist authority
re·bel´lion *n.* show of defiance
re·buke´ *n.* a reprimand —*vt.*
re·cal´ci·trant *adj.* stubbornly defiant —**re·cal´ci·trance** *n.*
re·cant´ *vt.* retract or disavow
re·ca·pit´u·late *vt.* summarize
re·cede´ *vi.* move back
re·ceiv´a·ble *adj.* unpaid —*n.* an outstanding account
re·ceive´ *vt.* get, take possession of; experience or undergo; make welcome
re´cent *adj.* at a time just earlier than now
re·cep´ta·cle *n.* a container
re·cep´tion *n.* a greeting; a social gathering; acceptance
re·cep´tive *adj.* able or willing to receive; open–minded
re´cess *n.* a hollow; intermission —*vi.* take a break
re·ces´sion *n.* a receding; an economic downturn
re·cid´i·vism *n.* reversion to earlier conduct
re·cip´i·ent *n.* receiver
re·cip´ro·cal *adj.* complementary; interdependent
re·cip´ro·cate *vi., vt.* give or take in return; move back and forth
re·cit´al *n.* a public performance; a detailed chronicling
re·cite´ *vt.* repeat a memorized text; recount in detail
reck´less *adj.* rash; heedless of consequences
reck´on *vt.* calculate, consider
rec´luse *n.* one in seclusion
rec´og·nize *vt.* distinguish; identify; acknowledge
re·coil´ *vi.* draw back
rec·ol·lect´ *vi., vt.* remember
rec·om·mend´ *vt.* endorse
rec´om·pense *n.* compensation —*vt.* to repay
rec´on·cile *vt.* resolve differences —**rec´on·cil·a·ble** *adj.*
rec´ord *n.* document, registry, etc.; information —**re·cord´** *vt.* set down information
re·coup´ *vt.* regain
re·cov´er *vt.* regain; return to a former state
rec·re·a´tion *n.* diversion or amusement
re·crim·i·na´tion *n.* countering one charge with another
rec´ti·fy *vt.* to correct
rec´ti·tude *n.* righteousness
re·cum´bent *adj.* reclining
re·cu´per·ate *vt., vi.* recover from illness or adversity
re·cuse´ *vt.* seek disqualification
red´o·lent *adj.* suggesting or reminiscent —**red´o·lence** *n.*
re·doubt´a·ble *adj.* formidable; awe–inspiring
re·duce´ *vt.* diminish or decrease —**re·duc´tion** *n.*
re·dun´dant *adj.* superfluous; unnecessary
reel *n.* device for flexible material, as tape or rope; (*Brit.*) a device to hold cotton or thread; a lively dance —*vt.* wind —*vi.* lurch or stagger
re·fer´ *vt.* direct to; assign or attribute to —*vi.* mention; make reference
ref·er·en´dum *n.* submission to popular vote
re·fine´ *vt., vi.* make or become pure; rid of unsuitable elements; make or become more elegant or polished
re·flect´ *vt.* mirror; cast an image —*vi.* ponder
re·flec´tive *adj.* given to deep thought
re´flex *adj.* instinctive —*n.* involuntary response
re·form´ *adj.* advocating change —*n.* correction or improvement —*vt.* correct or improve —**re·form´er** *n.*
re·frain´ *vi.* abstain; hold back from
re·fresh´ *vt.* revive or restore
ref´uge *n.* place of safety or shelter
re·ful´gent *adj.* radiant; glorious —**re·ful´gence** *n.*
re·fur´bish *vt.* restore or renovate
re·fuse´ *vt. vi.* decline or deny —**ref´use** *n.* trash, waste
re·fute´ *vt.* disprove; contradict —**ref·u·ta´tion** *n.*
re´gal *adj.* befitting royalty; stately; splendid
re·gale´ *vt.* entertain lavishly
re·ga´lia *n.* trappings of royalty; impressive array
re·gard´ *n.* respect or admiration; heed —*vt.* admire; observe carefully; deem to be —*vi.* heed; gaze
re·gime´ *n.* a government, management, order, etc.
reg·is·tra´tion *n.* official recording —**reg´is·try** *n.*
re·gress´ *vi.* move backward; degenerate —**re·gres´sion** *n.*
re·gret´ *n.* sorrow or remorse —*vt.* feel remorse
reg´u·lar *adj.* normal or usual; methodical; periodic; conforming to expectations
reg´u·late *vt.* control, or direct; adjust
re·ha·bil´i·tate *vt.* restore health
re·hearse´ *vt.* to practice
re·im·burse´ *vt.* pay back
re·it´er·ate *vt.* repeat
re´ject *n.* that discarded —**re·ject´** *vt.* refuse; discard
re·join´der *n.* a response
re·ju´ve·nate *vt.* refresh and revitalize
re·late´ *vt.* recount or describe; connect or associate
rel´a·tive *adj.* connected or affiliated; comparable —*n.* a family member
re·lax´ *vi., vt.* ease tension; make less intense
re´lay, re·lay´ *vt.* transmit; send forward
re·lease´ *n.* liberation; a catch —*vt.* set free; publish
rel´e·gate *vt.* assign, as a task or position
re·lent´ *vi.* surrender; soften
rel´e·vant *adj.* pertinent to the matter at hand
re·li´a·ble *adj.* dependable
re·li´ance *n.* confidence or trust —**re·li´ant** *adj.*
rel´ic *n.* an artifact; a thing of historical value
re·lief´ *n.* aid or assistance; alleviation from distress, etc.
re·li´gion *n.* a system of belief; order of worship
re·lin´quish *vt.* give up
re·luc´tant *adj.* hesitant or unwilling —**re·luc´tance** *n.*
re·ly´ *vi.* trust completely; depend on for help or support
re·main´ *vi.* continue unchanged; to stay
re·mark´ *n.* a comment —*vt.* comment briefly; to notice
re·mark´a·ble *adj.* noteworthy; striking or exceptional
re·me´di·al *adj.* intended to correct
rem´e·dy *n.* something that corrects —*vt.* make right
re·mem´ber *vi.* keep in the mind; retain —*vt.* recall
rem·i·nisce´ *vi.* dwell on the past —**rem·i·nis´cent** *adj.*
re·miss´ *adj.* negligent, careless
re·mis´sion *n.* a lessening
re·mit´ *vt.* transfer for deposit or payment
rem´nant *n.* a scrap; a trace or indication
re·mon´strate *vi.* protest —*vt.* argue against
re·morse´ *n.* repentance; sorrow for misconduct
re·mote´ *adj.* distant; secluded
re·move´ *vt.* take away —*vi.* relocate —**re·mov´a·ble** *adj.*
re·mu´ner·ate *vt.* compensate
ren´ais·sance´ *n.* revival, rebirth
rend *vt.* tear apart
ren´der *vt.* provide for payment or approval; depict by drawing; express by performing —**ren´der·ing** *n.*
ren´dez·vous *n.* meeting —*vi., vt.* meet at specific place and time
ren·di´tion *n.* performance or interpretation, as of music
ren´e·gade *n.* rebel; traitor, defector
re·nege´ *vi.* fail to honor a commitment —**re·neg´er** *n.*

re·new´ *vt.* restore; make new; reaffirm or extend
re·nounce´ *vt.* repudiate or deny; forsake, as a right
re·nowned´ *adj.* celebrated; distinguished —**re·nown´** *n.*
rent *n.* payment for occupancy or use —*vi.* hire out —*vt.* gain use for payment —**rent´al** *n.*
re·pair´ *vt.* restore to useable condition; rectify, make up for —*n.* an assessment of condition: *in good repair*
rep·a·ra´tion *n.* compensation for loss; atonement
re·pay´ *vt.* reimburse, pay back; refund
re·peal´ *vt.* revoke, as a law
re·peat´ *vt., vi.* say or do again
re·pel´ *vt.* repulse or ward off; disgust or offend
re·pent´ *vi., vt.* feel remorse or regret; to change
re·per·cus´sion *n.* backlash; unexpected consequence
rep´er·toire *n.* works adopted by a performer or performers
rep·e·ti´tion *n.* reiteration; process of repeating
re·place´ *vt.* put back; substitute or supplant; return or restore
re·plete´ *adj.* abundant; lavish
rep´li·ca *n.* a copy
rep´li·cate *vt.* duplicate, as an experiment; make copies
re·ply´ *n.* a response —*vi.* give an answer; respond
re·port´ *n.* account; a rumor —*vt.* inform; present an account of
re·pose´ *n.* sleep; calm; peacefulness —*vi.* lie prone
re·pos´i·to·ry *n.* place for safekeeping; a container
re·pos·sess´ *vt.* reclaim
rep·re·hen´si·ble *adj.* deserving blame; wicked
rep·re·sent´ *vt.* present a likeness of; stand in place of
rep·re·sent´a·tive *adj.* typical; characteristic —*n.* an example; an agent or delegate
re·press´ *vt.* restrain, control; quell, curb
re·prieve´ *n.* relief; deferment or repeal of punishment —*vt.* to suspend temporarily
rep´ri·mand *n.* censure; condemnation —*vt.* admonish or censure
re·pri´sal *n.* retaliation
re·proach´ *n.* condemnation; disgrace —*vt.* criticize or rebuke —**re·proach´ful** *adj.*
rep´ro·bate *adj.* perverted —*n.* an immoral person
re´pro·duce´ *vt.* copy or duplicate; propagate
re·proof´ *n.* disapproval
re·prove´ *vt.* criticize; admonish —**re·prov´al** *n.*
re·pub´lic *n.* government controlled by citizens or their representatives
re·pu´di·ate *vt.* reject or disavow; disown
re·pug´nant *adj.* offensive; revolting —**re·pug´nance** *n.*
re·pulse´ *vt.* fend off or repel; spurn by insolence or indifference —**re·pul´sive** *adj.*
rep·u·ta´tion *n.* one's standing; the way in which one is regarded by others; prominence or notoriety
re·quest´ *n.* entreaty; something desired —*vt.* express desire
re·quire´ *vt.* need; demand or request —**re·quire´ment** *n.*
req´ui·site *adj.* required —*n.* that necessary or obligatory
re·quite´ *vt.* compensate; repay; return in kind
re·scind´ *vt.* repeal; nullify
res´cue *vt.* liberate; set free
re·search´ *n.* scientific examination; deliberate study
re·sem´blance *n.* similarity
re·sent´ *vt.* take offense, as at insult or slight
re·serve´ *n.* restraint; caution; a thing set aside —*vt.* set aside —**re·serv´ed** *adj.*
res´er·voir *n.* a reserve supply
re·side´ *vi.* inhabit; live in
res´i·dence *n.* one's home
res´i·due *n.* remainder
re·sign´ *vt.* renounce, give up; accept as unavoidable
re·sign´ed *adj.* complacent; submissive
re·sil´ience, re·sil´ien·cy *n.* flexibility —**re·sil´ient** *adj.*
re·sist´ *vt.* defy or oppose; withstand
re·sist´ance *n.* force that hinders or opposes; capacity to ward off harm
res´o·lute *adj.* determined
res·o·lu´tion *n.* determination; outcome; a formal pronouncement; visual clarity
re·solve´ *n.* sense of purpose; determination —*vt.* decide; solve; end successfully
res´o·nant *adj.* vibrant; loud
re·sort´ *n.* a vacation retreat; a resource —*vt.* fall back on
re·sound´ *vi.* echo; reverberate
re´source *n.* that available for use, as equipment or property
re·source´ful *adj.* clever or imaginitive
re·spect´ *n.* esteem or admiration; consideration; a feature or detail —*vt.* admire
re·spect´a·ble *adj.* worthy of esteem; conventional
re·spec´tive *adj.* specific, distinct
res·pi·ra´tion *n.* breathing
res´pite *n.* a short rest
re·splen´dent *adj.* brilliant, sparkling
re·spond´ *vi.* answer; react
re·sponse´ *n.* reply or reaction
re·spon´si·ble *adj.* accountable; capable of acting alone
re·spon´sive *adj.* tending to respond or react
rest *n.* relaxation; pause; remainder —*vi., vt.* relax; lie against or on —**rest´ful** *adj.*
res´tau·rant *n.* a public eating place —**res´tau·ra·teur´** *n.*
res·ti·tu´tion *n.* restoration; compensation
res´tive *adj.* impatient
rest´less *adj.* uneasy; impatient —**rest´less·ness** *n.*
re·stor´a·tive *adj.* having power to restore; corrective —*n.* medication for health or well–being
re·store´ *vt.* return to former condition, position, etc.; make amends
re·strain´ *vt.* check, hold back; confine
re·strict´ *vt.* limit —**re·stric´tive** *adj.*
re·sult´ *n.* an effect —*vi.* follow as an outcome
re·sume´ *vt.* begin again
ré´su·mé *n.* (*Brit.*) a summing up; (*US*) description of one's qualifications for employment
re·sur´gence *n.* renewal or reawakening
res·ur·rect´ *vt.* restore or revive
re·sus´ci·tate *vt., vi.* revive
re·tain´ *vt.* keep possession; remember; hire for a fee
re·tain´er *n.* a fee paid to engage or reserve services; a servant
re·tal´i·ate *vi., vt.* repay in kind; avenge
re·tard´ *n.* a slowing —*vt.* impede the course of
re·ten´tion *n.* memory; ability to keep and hold
ret´i·cent *adj.* restrained or reserved; hesitant
ret´i·nue *n.* followers
re·tire´ *vi., vt.* withdraw or be removed, as from an occupation; go to bed
re·tir´ing *adj.* withdrawn
re·tort´ *n.* a sharp reply —*vt., vi.* to respond
re·tract´ *vt., vi.* take back, as a claim —**re·trac´tion** *n.*
ret·ri·bu´tion *n.* compensation; reward or punishment
re·trieve´ *vt.* regain
ret·ro·ac´tive *adj.* applying to a prior period
ret´ro·grade *adj.* opposite; regressing to a prior state
ret´ro·gress *vi.* revert to an earlier state
ret´ro·spect *n.* reflection of things past; a look back
re·turn´ *adj.* of a coming back —*n.* that brought or sent back; a profit —*vi., vt.* go or send back; yield, as profit; revert to a former owner
re·un´ion *n.* a gathering of former members
re·vamp´ *vt.* reorganize, renovate
re·veal´ *vt.* expose; disclose
rev´el *vi.* delight in; carouse —*n.* celebration
rev·e·la´tion *n.* a thing revealed; sudden inspiration
re·venge´ *n.* reprisal or retribution —*vt.* retaliate
rev´e·nue *n.* income; receipts
re·ver´ber·ate *vt.* resound or echo repeatedly
re·vere´ *vt.* regard with awe; venerate —**rev´er·ence** *n.*
rev´er·ie *n.* idle contemplation; daydreaming
re·verse´ *adj.* backward; opposite —*n.* an opposite side, condition, etc.; misfortune —*vt.* change to the opposite
re·vert´ *vi.* return to previous condition —**re·ver´sion** *n.*
re·view´ *n.* reexamination; critique, criticism —*vt.* reconsider, restudy
re·vile´ *vt.* berate
re·vise´ *vt.* change or modify
re·vive´ *vt., vi.* restore consciousness; bring back into use
re·voke´ *vt.* nullify or repeal
re·volt´ *n.* rebellion —*vi.* oppose; rebel; disgust
rev·o·lu´tion *n.* rotation; radical change
re·volve´ *vi.* rotate; turn on an axis
re·vue´ *n.* musical comedy show
re·vul´sion *n.* sudden aversion or abhorrence
re·ward´ *n.* compensation —*vt.* recompense
rhap´so·dy *n.* state of ecstasy; excessive enthusiasm; an elegant literary or musical work
rhet´o·ric *n.* effective speaking or writing; pretentious, vacuous speech
rhyme *n.* verse with lines ending in similar sounds
rhythm *n.* regular cadence or accent; harmonious pattern
rib´ald *adj.* of vulgar humor
rib´bon *n.* a thin strip for tying, decoration, etc.
rich *adj.* wealthy; plentiful; elegant or lavish —**rich´es** *n.*
rick´et·y *adj.* wobbly
rid *vt.* release or free from
rid´dle *n.* a puzzle —*vt.* perforate
ride *vi.* be conveyed; transported: *riding on a cloud* —**rid´er** *n.*
rid´i·cule *n.* that intended to mock; derision —*vt.* make fun of —**ri·dic´u·lous** *adj.*
rife *adj.* abundant
ri´fle *n.* a firearm —*vt.* search through; plunder
rift *n.* a fracture or tear
right *adj.* fitting and proper; equitable; accurate; lawful —*adv.* exactly; quite —*n.* that which is proper; privilege —*vt.* correct
right´eous *adj.* moral; virtuous —**righ´teous·ness** *n.*
rig´id *adj.* stiff; inflexible
rig´or (*US*), **rig´our** (*Brit.*) *n.* harshness; hardship
rile *vt.* anger; irritate or vex
rim *n.* border or edge
ring *n.* a circular object, area, shape, etc.; a group or gang
rinse *n.* liquid used in washing, etc. —*vt.* to wash lightly
ri´ot *n.* public disturbance by a large group; an eruption, as of revelry —*vi.*
ripe *adj.* mature; fully developed —**rip´en** *vt., vi.*
rip´ple *n.* a small wave or wave–like motion —*vi.*
rise *vi.* move upward; increase, as in price; get up, as from a chair; emerge or originate
risk *n.* possible hazard; probability for loss —**risk´y** *adj.*
ris·qué´ *adj.* lewd; suggestive
rite *n.* a formal ritual or solemn ceremony
rit´u·al *n.* observance; formality; an orderly procedure —*adj.* —**rit´u·al·is´tic** *adj.*
ri´val *n.* one in competition —*vt.* equal or exceed *adj.* competing
riv´er *n.* a large body of naturally flowing water; abundant flow
riv´et *n.* a metal fastener —*vt.* join with a rivet; fasten firmly; attract and hold attention —**riv´et·er** *n.*
roam *vt., vi.* wander or move about
roar *n.* a deep, prolonged cry; a burst of laughter —*vi., vt.*
roast *vt.* cook with dry heat; subject to excessive heat; deride —*n.* (*US*) a cut of meat; derision —*adj.*
robe *n.* a loose flowing garment; a dressing gown
ro´bot *n.* a device programmed to perform tasks; one who functions mechanically —**ro·bot´ic** *adj.*

ro·bot´ics *n.* the study or creation of robots
ro·bust´ *adj.* strong and healthy
rock *n.* a hard formation; firm support *—vi., vt.* wobble or sway **—rock´y** *adj.*
ro·co´co *n.* an ornate style
rod *n.* a thin straight shaft
rogue *n.* a scoundrel; a mischievous person; an abnormal plant or animal
roil *vt.* to disturb or stir up
role *n.* part for an actor; expected behavior
roll *n.* a cylinder; small baked bread; a registry; rocking motion *—vi., vt.* move by turning; suggest movement
rol´lick·ing *adj.* playful; boisterous
ro·mance´ *n.* passionate fondness; fascination; fantasy or fictional account
ro·man´tic *adj.* marked by infatuation, idealism, etc.; visionary; impractical *—n.*
romp *vi.* frolic or play *—n.* noisy frolic; an easy victory
room *n.* adequate space; an area within a structure *—vi.* to lodge **—room´y** *adj.*
root *n.* base of a plant; a base, source, or core; mental or emotional attachment
ros´ter *n.* a list
ros´trum *n.* speaker's platform
rot *n.* decomposition; silliness *—vi.* decay or disintegrate
ro´tate *vt., vi.* revolve; proceed by turns **—ro·ta´tion** *n.*
rote *n.* learning by repetition
rough *adj.* coarse or irregular; crude or impolite; difficult; disorderly **—rough´en** *vt.*
round *adj.* curved; of a curved shape; full–toned; approximate
rouse *vi. vt.* awaken; excite to action
rout *n.* defeat; disorderly flight *—vt.* defeat or put to flight
route *n.* road or course; an itinerary *—vt.* direct by a certain course
rou·tine´ *adj.* usual or customary *—n.* a regular procedure.
row *n.* a continuous line; a disturbance *—vt.*
row´dy *adj.* clamorous; disorderly *—n.* a ruffian
rub *vi., vt.* stroke *—n.* a pitfall
rub´bish *n.* trash; nonense
rub´ble *n.* stone fragments
rub´down *n.* a massage
rude *adj.* ill–mannered; unrefined; crude, primitive
ru´di·ment *n.* a basic component **—ru·di·men´ta·ry** *adj.*
ruf´fle *n.* frilled trim *—vi.* rumple or wrinkle; irritate or annoy
rug´ged *adj.* sturdy; strong; tempestuous
ru´in *n.* total destruction *—vt.* destroy utterly
rule *n.* governing authority; regulation; generally accepted condition or course of action *—vi., vt.* direct and control; judge or decree
rum´ble *n.* a deep undulating sound *—vi.* **—rum´bly** *adj.*
ru´mi·nate *vi., vt.* ponder; consider intently
ru´mor *n.* gossip; unconfirmed news
rum´ple *vt.* wrinkle
run *n.* indefinite period: *run of a play —vi.* move swiftly; operate; flow, as liquid from a container; extend **—run´ning** *adj., n.*
rup´ture *n.* break *—vt., vi.* break apart
ru´ral *adj.* of the country
ruse *n.* a ploy or stratagem
rush *n.* abrupt motion; haste; a swell of emotion *—vi.* move quickly
rus´tic *adj.* rural; unsophisticated
rut *n.* a groove worn into a path or roadway
ruth´less *adj.* lacking pity or compassion
s, S nineteenth letter of the alphabet
sab·bat´i·cal *n.* leave of absence
sa·bot´ *n.* a wooden shoe
sab´o·tage *n.* action to obstruct or defeat an enemy *—vi., vt.* **—sab´o·teur´** *n.*
sa·chet´ *n.* a perfumed parcel
sack *n.* a bag; dismissal from a job *—vt.* plunder; dismiss
sac´ra·ment *n.* a religious rite
sa´cred *adj.* deserving of reverence or respect
sac´ri·fice *n.* an offering *—vt.* give up something of value
sac´ri·lege *n.* desecration or disrespect of that considered sacred **—sac·ri·le´gious** *adj.*
sac´ro·sanct *adj.* sacred or hallowed
sad *adj.* unhappy; sorrowful; somber; dire, unfortunate
sa·fa´ri *n.* a journey
safe *adj.* free from risk or danger *—n.* a repository
sag *vi.* droop or slump
sa·ga´cious *adj.* discerning; wise **—sa·gac´i·ty** *n.*
sage *adj.* wise and discerning
sake *n.* reason or purpose; advantage or self–interest
sa·la´cious *adj.* arousing desire; lascivious
sal´a·ry *n.* fixed wages
sale *n.* exchange of goods or services for money
sa´li·ent *adj.* important or conspicuous; protruding
sa´line *adj.* consisting or or characteristic of salt; salty
sal´low *adj.* of a sickly or pasty complexion
sal´ly *n.* sudden assault; excursion; witty remark *—vi.* rush out suddenly or energetically
sa·lon´ *n.* a large room or gallery; a fashionable gathering
sa·lu´bri·ous *adj.* healthy or wholesome
sal´u·tar·y *adj.* beneficial
sal·u·ta´tion *n.* a greeting
sa·lute´ *n.* a greeting; a gesture of welcome or honor *—vt.* greet
sal´vage *n.* property saved from destruction *—vt.* retrieve for future use
salve *n.* ointment *—vt.* alleviate or remedy
same *adj.* identical
sam´ple *n.* a representative part; an example *—vt.* test
san·a·tar´i·um, san·a·to´ri·um *n.* a hospital or retreat
sanc·ti·mo´ni·ous *adj.* pretentiously pious
sanc´tion *n.* authorization; penalty for nonconformity *—vt.* approve; punish for violation
sanc´tu·ar·y *n.* a sacred place; an asylum
sane *adj.* of sound mind
san´guine *adj.* optimistic; confident; red or ruddy
san´i·tar´i·um *n.* sanatorium
san´i·tar·y *adj.* uncontaminated; free of germs
san·i·ta´tion *n.* sanitary conditions; a local agency responsible for trash removal
san´i·ty *n.* soundness of mind
sap´i·ent *adj.* wise
sar´casm *n.* a caustic rejoinder **—sar·cas´tic** *adj.*
sar·coph´a·gus *n.* stone coffin
sar·don´ic *adj.* sarcastic
sar·to´ri·al *adj.* of a clothier or clothing
sash *n.* cloth band; window frame
sas´sy *adj.* insolent, disrespectful; spirited, jaunty
sa·tan´ic *adj.* wicked; diabolic
sate *vt.* satiate
sat´el·lite *n.* an orbiting body; a dependency
sa´ti·ate *vt.* satisfy completely
sat´ire *n.* literary work using mockery or ridicule
sat·is·fac´tion *n.* gratification; fulfillment of obligation
sat´is·fy *vt.* fulfill a desire or promise; convince or persuade; pacify *—vi.* be sufficient **—sat´is·fied** *adj.*
sa´trap *n.* a petty official
sat´u·rate *vt.* soak or fill completely **—sat·u·ra´tion** *n.*
sa´tyr *n.* a mythical creature, part man and part goat
sauce *n.* a seasoned liquid or condiment
sau´cy *adj.* impudent; pert
saun´ter *vi.* stroll leisurely
sav´age *adj.* uncivilized; vicious, ferocious *—n.* a rude or unruly person *—vt.* attack
save *vt.* rescue from danger or destruction; set aside for the future; conserve
sa´vor *n.* characteristic flavor or quality *—vt.* season; taste; relish, enjoy
say *vt.* speak; express in words; allege *—vi.* to speak
scab´rous *adj.* roughened; difficult to handle; salacious
scaf´fold *n.* a raised platform; a temporary structure
scal´a·wag *n.* a worthless person; a rascal
scald *vt., vi.* to burn; clean with hot liquid or steam *—n.*
scale *vt., vi.* ascend; climb
scal´lop *n.* a hinged–shell mollusk; ornamental edging
scalp *n.* skin of the head *—vt.* resell tickets for profit
scal´pel *n.* a surgical knife
scamp *n.* rogue or rascal; scalawag; an impish child
scam´per *vi.* run quickly
scan *vt.* examine closely; glance
scan´dal *n.* injury to one's reputation; malicious gossip
scan´dal·ize *vt.* shock; outrage morally
scant *adj.* meager; less than
scant´y *adj.* insufficient; less than necessary
scar *n.* mark left after healing
scarce *adj.* rare, unusual; insufficient **—scar´ci·ty** *n.*
scare *vt.* frighten **—scar´y** *adj.*
scarp *n.* a steep slope
scathe *vt.* criticize severely; denounce **—scath´ing** *adj.*
scat´ter *vt.* throw about; disperse *—vi.* separate
scav´enge *vt.* forage; scrounge
scene *n.* a locality or area; setting for a drama
sce´nic *adj.* of a beautiful natural vista
scent *n.* an odor or aroma; a fragrance **—scent´ed** *adj.*
scep´ter *n.* a staff of authority
sched´ule *n.* (*US*) timetable; (*Brit.*) a list of appointments, social activities, etc.; a detailed plan *—vt.* plan for a specified time
sche·mat´ic *n.* a diagram
scheme *n.* a plan or program; a plot *—vt., vi.* plan or plot
schism *n.* division
schol´ar *n.* a learned person; an authority
schol´ar·ship *n.* learning; aid to a student
school *n.* an educational institution; a congregation of fish *—vi.* come together in a school **—scho·las´tic** *adj.*
school´ing *n.* formal education; classroom instruction
sci´ence *n.* knowledge from observation and experiment
scin·til´la *n.* a trace
scin´til·late *vi.* be witty
sci´on *n.* a descendant
scoff *vi.* to address scornfully or derisively
scold *vt., vi.* find fault; nag
sconce *n.* ornamental bracket
scope *n.* range of view
scorch *vt.* burn slightly *—n.* the mark of a burn
score *n.* points in a game or test; written music; a group of 20
scorn *n.* contempt *—vt.* treat with contempt
scoun´drel *n.* unscrupulous person; a villain
scour *vt.* clean thoroughly; brighten by rubbing
scourge *n.* a whip; severe punishment; a cause of suffering *—vt.* flog; punish
scout *n.* one sent ahead for information *—vt.* spy on
scowl *n.* a gloomy aspect *—vi.* wrinkle the brow; look threatening or angry
scrag´gly *adj.* uneven
scram´ble *vi.* move in a disorderly manner *—vt.* mix hurriedly or haphazardly *—n.* a struggle
scrap *n.* a fragment; a quarrel *—vt.* discard *—vi.* quarrel *—adj.* waste; fragmentary
scrape *vt.* rub so as to abrade; gather with effort *—n.* act, effect, or noise of scraping; a difficult situation; a fight
scratch *vt.* to mark; scrape lightly; write hurriedly; cancel or withdraw, as an entry *—vi.* manage with difficulty *—n.* a mark or sound of scraping *—adj.* hasty or haphazard **—scratch´y** *adj.*
scrawl *n.* irregular or illegible writing *—vt., vi.* to write hastily or illegibly
scrawn´y *adj.* lean and bony
scream *n.* a piercing cry *—vt., vi.* to cry out **—scream´er** *n.*
screech *n.* a shrill sound
screed *n.* prolonged tirade; harangue

screen *n.* a light partition; fine mesh; that conceals or protects; a panel for projecting images —*vt.* conceal; sift; classify
scrib´ble *vt.* write hastily —*n.*
scribe *n.* a clerk; public writer
scrim *n.* a lightweight fabric
scrip *n.* writing; an instrument of entitlement
script *n.* cursive writing; text of a play —**script´er** *n.*
scrip´ture *n.* sacred writings
scriv´en·er *n.* scribe or notary
scroll *n.* a parchment roll
scrounge *vt., vi.* scavenge
scrub *vt., vi.* rub vigorously
scruff *n.* nape of the neck
scruff´y *adj.* shabby, seedy
scrump´tious *adj.* delicious; elegant
scru´ple *n.* reluctance fostered by disapproval
scru´ti·nize *vt.* examine carefully; observe
sculp´ture *n.* three–dimensional art —*vt.* to fashion
scur´ril·ous *adj.* grossly offensive; abusive
scur´ry *vi.* move hurriedly
scut´tle *n.* a covered opening —*vt.* wreck or destroy
sea *n.* great body of salt water; the ocean; anything vast
seal *n.* impression attesting to authenticity; decorative stamp —*vt.* close securely or permanently —**seal´able** *adj.*
seam *n.* a visible joint
seam´y *adj.* unpleasant; depraved or base; squalid
sear *vt.* dry up or wither; to scorch —*adj.* withered
search *vt.* look for thoroughly; seek out —*n.* —**search´er** *n.*
sea´son *n.* a part of the year; time of special activity —*vt.* add spices, etc. to food; improve by aging
sea´son·a·ble *adj.* usual for the time; practical for the season —**sea´son·a·bly** *adv.*
seat *n.* a place to sit —*vt.* place in a sitting position; accommodate: *seat 30 people*; set firmly in a place
se·cede´ *vt.* formally withdraw
se·clude´ *vt.* set apart; isolate
sec´ond *n.* a unit of time; an angular measure; a formal attendant; thing of inferior quality —*adj.* of a brief time; next in order; of lesser value —*vt.* formally support
se´cret *adj.* kept hidden; esoteric; not revealed; mysterious —*n.* a mystery; that known to only a few
sec´re·tary *n.* an office worker; an official responsible for record keeping; head of a government department; writing desk
se·crete´ *vt.* conceal; hide away; to form and release a substance —**se·cre´tion** *n.*
sec´tion *n.* a part —*vt.* divide into parts
sec´u·lar *adj.* worldly; temporal; not religious
se·cure´ *adj.* unlikely to be threatened; confident —*vt.* protect; make certain; obtain
se·cur´i·ty *n.* being secure; those responsible for protection; measures providing protection; a pledge
se·date´ *adj.* composed; dignified —*vt.* to calm
sed´a·tive *n.* medicine that serves to calm
sed´en·tary *adj.* inactive
sed´i·ment *n.* matter that settles in a liquid; material deposited by water, ice, etc.
se·di´tion *n.* resistance or action against lawful authority
se·duce´ *vt.* lead astray; tempt or entice into a wrong —
sed´u·lous *adj.* industrious
see *vt.* view with the eyes; perceive in the mind; encounter; be certain: *see that you go* —*vi.* exercise power of sight; comprehend; be attentive
seed *n.* ovule that produces a plant; origin; a small granular fruit —*vt.* plant; scatter; remove seeds from
seek *vt.* search or strive for
seem *vi.* appear to be
seem´ly *adj.* proper; decorous
seep *vi.* gradually diffuse; penetrate through
se´er *n.* a prophet
seethe *vi.* boil; be agitated
seg´ment *n.* a distinct part —*vt., vi.* cut or separate
seg´re·gate *vt.* isolate; separate —*adj.* set apart
se´gue *vi.* move smoothly from one element to another
seis·mol´o·gy *n.* study of earthquakes and related phenomena —**seis´mic** *adj.* —**seis·mol´o·gist** *n.*
seize *vt.* grasp suddenly and forcefully; take possession; take immediate advantage
sel´dom *adv.* infrequently —*adj.* infrequent or rare
se·lect´ *vt., vi.* choose —*adj.* superior; careful in choosing
self *n.* distinct identity and individuality
self´ish *adj.* motivated by personal gain
sell *vt.* transfer property for a consideration —*vi.*
se·man´tics *pl. n.* study of structure, meaning, shift, etc. of speech forms; deliberate distortion of meaning
sem´blance *n.* likeness or resemblance; the barest trace
sem´i– *prefix* partly; exactly half; occurring twice in a period
sen´ate *n.* a legislative body
send *vt.* transmit; cause or enable to go; drive or impel
se´nile *adj.* of old age
sen´ior *adj.* older in years, time of service, etc. —*n.* an elderly person; one advanced in rank, dignity, etc.
sen´sate *adj.* having physical sensation; perceived by the senses
sen·sa´tion *n.* stimulation; response to stimulation
sen·sa´tion·al *adj.* causing excitement
sense *n.* faculty to respond to stimuli; special capacity to appreciate; vague perception; power to reason —*vt.* perceive; become aware
sen´si·ble *adj.* having mental perception; perceptible —**sen·si·bil´i·ty** *n.*
sen´si·tive *adj.* acutely responsive to sensation or to others; appreciative of aesthetic or intellectual qualities; easily offended
sen´su·al *adj.* indulgent to the appetites or senses
sen´su·ous *adj.* appealing to the senses
sen´tence *n.* determination or judgement; a penalty; words that express a thought
sen´tient *adj.* possessing powers of perception
sen´ti·ment *n.* delicate sensibility; a complex of feelings
sen´ti·nel, sen´try *n.* a guard
sep´a·rate *vt.* set apart or divide —*vi.* become divided; draw apart —*adj.* distinct; detached —**sep·a·ra´tion** *n.*
sep´ul·cher *n.* a burial place
se´quel *n.* an ongoing narrative; a consequence
se´quence *n.* following in order —**se·quen´tial** *adj.*
se·ques´ter *vt.* place apart or seclude; property held in custody pending a claim
ser´e·nade´ *n.* a love song —*vi., vt.* sing, especially to one's love
se·rene´ *adj.* untroubled; tranquil —**se·ren´i·ty** *n.*
se´ries *n.* an arrangement of related things —**se´ri·al** *adj.*
se´ri·ous *adj.* thoughtful, sober; involving much work; of grave importance
ser´mon *n.* a lecture; a serious talk; a discourse
ser´pent *n.* a snake
ser´pen·tine *adj.* winding
ser´rate, ser´rat·ed *adj.* of a saw-like edge or structure
se´rum *n.* fluid constituent of blood; a fluid that confers immunity
ser´vant *n.* one employed to assist in domestic matters
serve *vi., vt.* work as a servant; be of service; satisfy a requirement; perform duties of an office
serv´ice *n.* an act or manner of serving; maintenance and repair; public worship —*vt.* maintain or repair —*adj.* of the act of serving; designated for those who serve
serv´ice·a·ble *adj.* useful; beneficial; durable
ser´vile *adj.* submissive; abject —**ser·vil´i·ty** *n.*
ses´sion *n.* a meeting
set *vt.* place; fix in place; bring to a specified condition; establish; mount a gem —*vi.* wane; solidify; begin —*n.* an allied group; things belonging together
set´tle *vt.* put in order; set to rights; establish in place; calm; sink; determine finally; pay a debt —*vi.* come to rest; sink gradually; become established; pay a bill
set´tle·ment *n.* area newly colonized; agreement or adjustment
sev´er *vt.* separate; break off —*vi.* break or come apart
sev´er·al *adj.* a few; individually different, diverse
se·vere´ *adj.* harsh; extremely strict; austere; plain and simple —**se·ver´i·ty** *n.*
sew *vt., vi.* make, mend, or fasten with thread
sex *n.* division of organisms for reproductive functions; activity concerned with reproduction —**sex´u·al** *adj.*
sex´ism *n.* discrimination against the opposite sex
sex´ton *n.* a church officer
shab´by *adj.* threadbare
shack *n.* a crude dwelling
shade *vt.* to screen; represent by gradation of color —*n.* relative darkness; darkened color; a minute variation; a screen that partly obscures
shad´ow *n.* image produced by interruption of light; a trace —*vt.* cast a shadow; follow —**shad´ow·y** *adj.*
shad´y *adj.* dark; sheltered; morally or legally suspect
shake *vt., vi.* vibrate; agitate or rouse —**shak´y** *adj.*
shal´low *adj.* lacking depth or extent; superficial
sham *adj.* false; pretended —*n.* a hoax; a counterfeit; artificiality or pretension
sham´ble *vi.* walk with a shuffling or unsteady gait
shame *n.* guilt; disgrace or humiliation; disappointment —*vt.* humiliate; dishonor
shame´ful *adj.* disgraceful; scandalous; indecent
shame´less *adj.* brazen; immodest; done without shame
shan´ty *n.* a shack
shape *n.* outward form; final form —*vt.* give form to; adapt or modify; put in final form —*vi.* develop
shard *n.* a pottery fragment
share *n.* a portion; stock in a company —*vt., vi.* participate in; divide into parts
sharp *adj.* having a keen edge; capable of cutting or piercing; abrupt; well–defined; quick to perceive; shrewd; intense —**sharp´en** *vt., vi.*
shat´ter *vt.* damage or demolish —*vi.* burst
shave *vt.* remove hair; trim closely; slice thinly —*n.* a cutting; a thin slice
shawl *n.* a cloth wrap
shed *vt.* pour forth; radiate; repel; cast off; get rid of —*vi.* cast off by natural process —*n.* a small storage building
sheen *vi.* glisten —*n.* luster
sheep´ish *adj.* embarrassed; meek or timid
shelf *n.* a platform or ledge
shell *n.* hard outer covering; framework; a hollow pastry; an explosive projectile —*vt.* remove an outer covering; bombard
shel´ter *n.* that which protects —*vt.* provide cover
shift *vt., vi.* change position —*n.* a change in attitude, loyalty, etc.; an unbelted dress
shift´y *adj.* marked by deceit or trickery; resourceful
shim´mer *vi.* shine faintly; glimmer —*n.* a gleaming
shine *vi.* emit light; glow; excel —*vt.* brighten by rubbing —*n.* radiance; sheen
ship *n.* a deep–water vessel; an aircraft —*vt.* transport
ship´ment *n.* goods transported
shirk *vt., vi.* avoid obligation
shiv´er *vi.* tremble with cold or fear —**shiv´er·y** *adj.*

shock *n.* a violent blow; trauma associated with injury —*vt.* horrify or disgust
shod´dy *adj.* poorly made
shoot *vt.* wound; fire a weapon; send forth; pass over swiftly; photograph —*vi.* discharge; move swiftly; put forth buds —*n.* the act of shooting; early growth
shop *n.* place where goods are sold, manufactured, or repaired —*vi.* inspect and purchase goods —**shop assistant** (*Brit.*) one who works in a retail store —**shop´per** *n.*
shore *n.* land adjoining water
short *adj.* less than usual extent; of brief duration; of a limited distance; less than required —**short´en** *vt., vi.*
short´ly *adv.* soon
shove *vt., vi.* push; press forcibly against —**shov´er** *n.*
show *vt.* present to view; explain or prove; lead —*vi.* become visible —*n.* a movie or stage production; exhibition; a competition; ostentation
show´er *n.* a brief rain; a sudden outpouring; a party; a cleansing with a fine spray of water —*vt., vi.* honor; make wet; bathe
show´y *adj.* flamboyant; ostentatious —**show´i·ness** *n.*
shred *n.* a fragment —*vt.* cut or tear into fragments
shrewd *adj.* having keen insight; calculating
shriek *n.* a shrill cry —*vi.*
shrill *adj.* high–pitched and piercing —*vi., vt.*
shrine *n.* sacred place; site or structure respected for importance; a memorial
shrink *vi., vt.* contract; diminish; recoil, as in disgust
shriv´el *vt., vi.* contract into wrinkles; become helpless
shroud *n.* cloth to wrap a corpse; that which conceals —*vt.* cover or conceal
shud´der *vi.* tremble
shuf´fle *vt., vi.* move with a dragging gait; mix; move, change, or rearrange —*n.* a trick or deception
shunt *vt., vi.* turn aside; divert —*n.* a connector that diverts
shut *vt.* close, as a door; collapse, as an umbrella
shut´–in *n.* an invalid; one unable to leave —*adj.*
shy *adj.* uneasy with others; timid; easily startled; expressing reserve —*vt.* draw back: *shy away*
shy´ster *n.* an unscrupulous businessman
sib´i·lant *adj.* hissing; of the consonants *s, z, sh,* and *zh*
sib´ling *n.* a brother or sister
sick *adj.* ill; diseased; weak; nauseated; emotionally upset —**sick´ly** *adj., adv.*
side *n.* boundry; lateral half of a surface; aspect, point of view; a group competing together
si·de´re·al *adj.* of the stars
si´dle *vi.* move sideways —*n.* sideways movement
siege *n.* surrounding so as to sieze; a prolonged bout —*vt.* besiege or assault
sift *vt.* examine carefully; filter: *sift fact from fiction*; separate out
sigh *n.* deep audible breath —*vi.* express sorrow, weariness, etc.
sight *n.* vision; an image; mental perception; device for aiming; observation with a telescope —*vt.* catch a view of; observe —*vi.* take aim; make an observation —*adj.*
sign *n.* telltale indication; action used to communicate; a symbol; a device for advertising —*vt., vi.* write a signature; indicate or signal
sig´nal *n.* a sign to convey information —*adj.* notable —*vt.* communicate by a sign
sig´na·to·ry *n.* bound by a signed document —*adj.* being a signer
sig´na·ture *n.* a person's name written by himself; a part of a book; symbols that show time and key for music
sig·nif´i·cant *adj.* rich in meaning; important
sig´ni·fy *vt.* represent; make known —*vi.* have meaning or importance
si´lent *adj.* soundless; taciturn, disinclined to talk; not audible; free from disturbance; absence of comment —**si´lence** *n.*
sil·hou·ette´ *n.* a profile
sil´ly *adj.* foolish; frivolous
sim´i·lar *adj.* having resemblance or like characteristics
sim´i·le *n.* a figure of speech expressing likeness
si·mil´i·tude *n.* similarity
si´mo·ny *n.* buying or selling of that which is sacred
sim´per *vi.* smirk —*vt.* utter with a smirk —*n.* a silly, self–conscious smile
sim´ple *adj.* easy; plain, unadorned; free from affectation; silly or foolish; ordinary
sim´pli·fy *vt.* make easy
sim´u·late *vt.* make pretense of; assume appearance of
si·mul·ta´ne·ous *adj.* occurring at the same time
sin *n.* transgression against moral or religious law —*vi.* do wrong
since *adv.* from past to present; at a time before the present —*prep.* from a time in the past —*conj.* inasmuch as
sin·cere´ *adj.* genuine; free from hypocrisy or deceit
sin´e·cure *n.* a profitable position requiring little effort
sing *vi.* produce music with the voice —*vt.* perform vocally; chant
singe *vt.* burn slightly —*n.* a superficial burn
sin´gle *adj.* consisting of one; solitary; unmarried
sin´gu·lar *adj.* unique; remarkable; uncommon
sin´is·ter *adj.* of the left; evil; ominous; threatening misfortune
sink *vi., vt.* descend; slope gradually; approach death; lessen; defeat —*n.* wash basin; a depression; device that absorbs or dissipates energy
sin´u·ous *adj.* winding or undulating; devious
sip *vt., vi.* drink in small quantities —*n.* a small drink
si´phon *n.* a device for transferring liquid —*vt.* draw off
sir *n.* respectful address to a man; a title
sire *n.* male parent
si´ren *n.* enticing woman; device that warns —*adj.* seductive
sis´sy *n.* a weakling
sis´ter *n.* a female sibling
sit *vi.* rest on the buttocks; perch or roost; pose; hold a session; be situated or located —*vt.* seat oneself
site *n.* a specific location
sit´u·ate *vt.* to place or locate
sit·u·a´tion *n.* way in which a thing rests; condition as modified or determined by circumstance; a salaried post; a state of affairs
size *n.* dimensions; one of a set of standard measures
skel´e·ton *n.* supporting framework of a structure; a sketch or outline
skep´ti·cal *adj.* doubtful, suspicious —**skep´ti·cism** *n.*
sketch *n.* a rough drawing; a preliminary study; a brief description; a short play
sketch´y *adj.* lacking detail; superficial
skiff *n.* a light boat
skill *n.* proficiency; craft or trade
skim *vt., vi.* remove from a surface; move lightly over; cover with a thin film; read hastily —*n.* a thin coating
skimp *vi., vt.* do poorly or carelessly; provide too little
skin *n.* outer covering; container made from the animal hide
skir´mish *n.* a minor encounter —*vi.* battle
skirt *n.* a garment that hangs from the waist; border of an area —*vt., vi.* form or pass along a border; avoid
skit *n.* a short play
skit´tish *adj.* easily frightened; playful
skulk *vi.* move about furtively
sky *n.* heaven; upper atmosphere
slab *n.* a thick, flat slice
slack *adj.* hanging loosely; listless; careless
slake *vt.* to quench
slam *vt.* shut violently; dash; criticize —*vi.* shut with force —*n.* severe criticism
slan´der *vt., vi.* utter falsely; defame —*n.* false statement —**slan´der·ous** *adj.*
slang *n.* unconventional use of standard vocabulary
slant *vt.* to slope; promote a biased view —*adj.* sloping —*n.* an incline; an opinion
slap *vt.* strike with the open hand; insult —*n.* a blow; an insult
slash *vt.* cut violently; strike with a whip; reduce sharply —*vi.* make a long sweeping stroke —*n.* a cut or gash; an ornamental slit; a forest clearing covered with debris
slat *n.* a thin strip of wood
slaugh´ter *vt.* kill for food; murder savagely —*n.* savage killing
slave *n.* one owned by another; one controlled by another, a habit, or influence —*vi.* toil ceaselessly
slay *vt.* kill violently
slea´zy *adj.* shoddy or shabby; vulgar or tawdry
sleek *adj.* smooth and glossy; well–groomed; slick
sleep *n.* period of complete rest —*vt., vi.* rest; fall asleep
sleep´er *n.* one sleeping; a railway car; something that unexpectedly excels; (*Brit.*) a section that separates and supports railway tracks
sleet *n.* frozen rain —*vi.* fall as frozen rain —**sleet´y** *adj.*
sleeve *n.* part that covers the arm; a covering or wrapper
sleigh *n.* a horse–drawn vehicle with runners for travel over snow or ice
slen´der *adj.* long and thin; attractively slim
sleuth *n.* a detective
slice *n.* a thin piece; a portion —*vt., vi.* cut divide into parts
slick *adj.* smooth, sleek; deceptively clever —*n.* a film
slight *adj.* of small importance; slender; frail —*vt.* do carelessly or thoughtlessly; treat as trivial —*n.* an act of disrespect
slim *adj.* lacking girth; meager —*vt., vi.* make or become slimmer
sling *n.* a strap for hurling; a device to support or lift —*vt.* throw or fling
slink *vi.* move furtively
slink´y *adj.* stealthy; graceful, serpentine —**slink´i·ness** *n.*
slip *vt.* put on or off easily; convey slyly; pass unobserved —*vi.* to slide; fall into error; escape; move stealthily; overlook —*n.* a sudden slide; error; a woman's undergarment; a pillowcase; undesired motion
slit *n.* a long, narrow opening —*vt.* cut lengthwise
slith´er *vi.* glide like a snake —*n.* a sinuous gliding
slob *n.* an ill–kempt person
slog *vt., vi.* to plod
slo´gan *n.* a motto
sloop *n.* a small sailboat
slop *vi., vt.* cause to splash or spill —*n.* waste food; swill
slope *vi.* slant —*n.* a slanting surface; degree of inclination
slosh *vi.* to splash; flounder
slot *n.* a narrow groove or opening: *coin slot*; a narrow cut to receive a corresponding part; an opening, as for a job —*vt.* cut a slot; assign
sloth *n.* a slow–moving mammal; laziness
slouch *n.* drooping appearance; an incompetent person —*vi.* sit or move in an ungraceful, drooping manner
slough *n.* a stagnant swamp or backwater
slov´en·ly *adj.* untidy and careless —*adv.*
slow *adj.* taking time; dull; tedious; not brisk —*vt., vi.* make slow or slower; delay —*adv.* at less than normal speed
slug´gard *n.* a slow or lazy person; an idler
slug´gish *adj.* inactive; habitually slow and lazy
sluice *n.* a channel for water; a device for controlling flow
slum *n.* a squalid living area
slum´ber *vi.* sleep lightly —*n.* quiet sleep —**slum´ber·ous** *adj.*

slur *vt.* slight or disparage; to pronounce indistinctly *—n.* a disparaging remark
sly *adj.* stealthy; roguish
smack *n.* a quick, sharp sound; a noisy kiss; a slap
small *adj.* unimportant; having little body or volume; mean–spirited *—n.* a petite or slender part
smart *n.* a stinging sensation *— vi., vt.* feel a stinging pain; feel remorse or anguish *—adj.* intelligent; clever or shrewd; impertinent; brisk: *a smart pace*; fashionable
smash *vt.* break into pieces; crush; strike *—n.* an outstanding success
smat´ter·ing *n.* a little bit; superficial knowledge
smear *vt.* soil; apply thickly; slander
smell *vt.* perceive, examine, or discover by odor *—n.* an unpleasant odor
smirk *n.* a sarcastic or derisive grin *—vi.* to grin
smock *n.* a loose garment
smog *n.* a noxious mist
smoke *n.* vaporous byproduct of combustion; a tobacco product *—vi.* give off smoke; use tobacco products *— vt.* flavor by treating with smoke; force out
smol´der *vi.* burn slowly; have suppressed emotions
smooth *adj.* even; without lumps; sauve and flattering *—vt., vi.* make even; free of lumps
smoth´er *vt.* prevent breathing; suffocate; stifle or overwhelm
smudge *vt., vi.* smear or become smeared *—n.* a stain; heavy smoke
smug *adj.* self–satisfied; complacent
smug´gle *vt.* take in or out of a country illegally
smut *n.* blackening from soot; something obscene; a fungal disease of plants
snag *n.* a jagged bulge; an obstacle or difficulty *—vt.* to catch on a protrusion
snap *n.* a sharp sound; a quick, sharp closing of jaws; sudden breaking or release; a fastener; brisk energy; an easy task *— adj.* done suddenly *—vi., vt.* grasp suddenly; speak sharply; move quickly and smartly
snare *n.* a trap; something that misleads *—vt.* trap; entrap by trickery
snatch *vt.* seize suddenly or eagerly; obtain as opportunity allows
sneak *vi., vt.* move stealthily *—n.* a stealthy movement; a dishonest person *—adj.* stealthy *—* **sneak´y** *adj.*
sneak´er (*US*) *n.* a flexible sports shoe
sneer *n.* scornful grimace *—vi.* show or express contempt
snif´ter *n.* a brandy goblet
snip *vt., vi.* cut with short, quick strokes *—n.* small cut
snip´py *adj.* abrupt; insolent
snitch *vt.* steal *—vi.* inform on
sniv´el *vi.* whine tearfully *—n.*
snob *n.* one preoccupied with wealth and station
snoop *vi.* to pry *—n.*
snub *vt.* treat with disdain *— n.* a deliberate slight
snug *adj.* cozy; close–fitting
snug´gle *vt., vi.* nestle, cuddle
soak *vt.* saturate; drench
soap *n.* a cleansing agent
soar *vi.* float aloft; glide through air
sob *vi., vt.* weep audibly
so´ber *adj.* unaffected by drugs or alcohol; temperate, rational; solemn or serious *—vt., vi.* make or become sober *—***so·bri´e·ty** *n.*
so´bri·quet *n.* a nickname
so´cia·ble *adj.* prefering company; friendly
so´cial *adj.* of society or its mores; friendly; pertaining to public welfare; existing in communities *—n.* informal gathering
so´cial·ite *n.* one prominent in fashionable society
so·ci´e·ty *n.* persons sharing certain attributes as language or customs; fashionable members of a community; association based on common purpose, shared interest, etc.
so·ci·ol´o·gy *n.* study of the evolution of society *—***so·ci·ol´o·gist** *n.*
so´ci·o·path *n.* one who is antisocial
sodden *adj.* saturated; drenched; dull from drink
soft *adj.* yielding; easily worked; smooth and delicate; expressing sympathy
soi·rée´ *n.* an evening reception
so´journ *vi.* stay temporarily *—n.* a short stay
sol´ace *vt.* comfort; alleviate, soothe *—n.* that which furnishes comfort
so´lar *adj.* of the sun
sol´e·cism *n.* grammatical error; an incongruity
sol´emn *adj.* sacred; marked by ceremony or majesty
so·lem´ni·ty *n.* a solemn rite
so·lic´it *vt.* ask earnestly; entice to an immoral act
so·lic´i·tous *adj.* concerned
sol´id *adj.* having shape and volume; resistant to pressure; filling space; of the same substance throughout; well–built; financially sound; reliable *—n.* a three–dimensional object
so·lil´o·quy *n.* a speech by a lone actor
sol´ip·sism *n.* concept that self knowledge is the only reality
sol´i·tar·y *adj.* alone; remote or excluded
sol´i·tude *n.* seclusion; loneliness
sol´stice *n.* semiannual event when the sun is farthest from the celestial equator
sol´u·ble *adj.* able to be solved; able to be dissolved
so·lu´tion *n.* a mixture; answer to a problem
solve *vt.* work out a solution or answer *—***solv´a·ble** *adj.*
sol´vent *adj.* financially sound; able to be dissolved *—n.* substance capable of dissolving other substances
som´ber *adj.* dark, gloomy; melancholy
some *adj.* of an indeterminate number *—pron.* an undetermined number *—adv.*
son´ic *adj.* relating to sound
son´net *n.* a poem of 14 lines
so·no´rous *adj.* of a deep rich sound; lofty sounding
soon *adv.* in the near future;
soothe *vt.* calm; relieve, as pain *—vi.* afford relief
sooth´say·er *n.* one who claims to foretell the future
soph´ism *n.* a misleading argument; a fallacy
so·phis´ti·cate *n.* one presumed to be worldly–wise
soph´o·more (*US*) *n.* a second–year student *—adj.* of the second year of school
soph·o·mor´ic (*US*) *adj.* of a sophomore; shallow, pretentious; immature
sop·o·rif´ic *adj.* sleepy
so·pra´no *n.* music of the highest range
sor´cer·er *n.* a wizard
sor´cer·y *n.* magic; witchcraft
sor´did *adj.* degrading; vile; squalid *—***sor´did·ness** *n.*
sore *n.* a bruise, inflammation, etc.; thing causing pain or trouble *—adj.* tender; pained, distressed
sor´row *n.* pain or sadness of loss; event that causes distress; expression of grief
sor´ry *adj.* feeling regret or remorse; affected by sorrow; paltry or worthless
sort *vt.* arrange *—n.* a particular kind
soul *n.* moral or spiritual part of man; emotional or spiritual depth or vitality; essence; the disembodied spirit of one who has died
sound *n.* that perceptible by hearing; noise of a particular quality; significance: *a sinister sound —vi., vt.* give forth a noise *—adj.* healthy; free from flaw, decay, etc.; correct or logical; financially solvent; thorough
soup·çon´ *n.* small quantity; a taste
source *n.* origin or derivation
souse *vt., vi.* steep in liquid; pickle *—n.* pickled meat; a drunkard
south *n.* direction to the right of sunrise *—adj.* in a southerly direction
sou·ve·nir´ *n.* a memento
space *n.* expanse of the universe; a specific distance or area; area designed for particular use *— adj.*
spa´cious *adj.* roomy
span *vt.* measure; extend across or over *—n.* distance between two points; a part that extends over
spare *vt.* treat mercifully; relieve; use frugally *—adj.* held in reserve; lean; scanty *—n.* thing saved for future use
sparse *adj.* scattered; not dense *—***spar´si·ty** *n.*
spasm *n.* sudden, involuntary muscular contraction; sudden action or effort
spas·mod´ic, spas·mod´i·cal *adj.* temporary; transitory
spas´tic *adj.* marked by spasms *—***spas´ti·cal·ly** *adv.*
spate *n.* overflow; sudden outpouring, as of words
spa´tial *adj.* relating to space
speak *vi.* utter; express or convey; deliver an address; converse *—vt.* make known; utter; be able to converse, esp. in a foreign language
spe´cial *adj.* out of the ordinary; designed for specific purpose; notable *—n.* thing designated *—* **spe´cial·ist** *n.*
spe´ci·al·ize *vi.* to focus on an activity, branch of learning, etc. *—vt.* adapt for particular use or purpose
spe´cie *n.* coined money
spe´cies *n.* a category of animals or plants
spe·cif´ic *adj.* distinct; explicit *— n.* medicine; a particular item or detail
spec·i·fi·ca´tion *n.* a detailed description
spec´i·fy *vt.* state in full and explicit detail
spec´i·men *n.* that regarded as representative; a sample for laboratory anyalysis
spe´cious *adj.* plausible, but without merit
spec´ta·cle *n.* a grand display; a deplorable exhibition
spec·tac´u·lar *adj.* wonderfully exciting; lavish
spec´ter *n.* an apparition
spec´u·late *vi.* ponder, theorize; involve in endeavor or investment entailing risk
speech *n.* power to speak; that spoken; a public address or lecture
speed *n.* rapid motion; rate of movement *—vi.* move or go rapidly *—vt.* promote forward progress
spell´bind *vt.* to enthrall
spe·lunk´er *n.* one who explores and studies caves
spend *vt.* pay out; use up; use wastefully or squander
spew *vi.* come or issue forth *—vt.* eject or send forth
sphere *n.* a perfectly round body; field of activity, influence, etc. *—***spher´i·cal** *adj.*
sphinx *n.* a mythical monster; a mysterious person
spice *n.* aromatic flavoring; that which gives zest or adds interest *—vi.*
spill *vi., vt.* to run over or cause to run over *—n.* something spilled
spin *vt.* twist fiber into thread, yarn, etc.; produce a web; tell a story*—vi.* make thread or yarn; whirl rapidly *—n.* a pleasure jaunt; uncontrolled spiral descent of an airplane
spin´et *n.* a small harpsichord or upright piano
spin´ster *n.* a woman who has never married
spi´ral *n.* a winding curve *—vi., vt.* take or cause to take a spiral form or course
spir´it *n.* animating element; a supernatural being; mood or disposition; vivacity or energy; unspecified intent *—vt.* carry off mysteriously *—adj.* of ghosts
spir´it·ed *adj.* lively, animated; of a characteristic
spir´i·tu·al *adj.* of moral or intellectual qualities; sacred or religious; supernatural

spite *n.* malicious bitterness or resentment —*vt.* vex maliciously
splen´did *adj.* magnificent, imposing; conspicuously illustrious —**splen´dor** *n.*
split *vt.* separate into parts; divide and distribute —*vi.* divide lengthwise; share with others —*n.* separation into factions; a share —*adj.* divided or separated
spoil *vt.* damage or destory; overindulge another —*vi.* become tainted or decayed
spoils *n.* plunder; jobs for faithful supporters
spo´ken *adj.* uttered aloud
sponge *n.* a plantlike marine animal; absorbent substance; leavened dough —*vt.* wipe with a sponge; impose on others
spon´sor *n.* one acting as surety; a person or group that establishes or finances —*vt.* act as sponsor
spon·ta´ne·ous *adj.* arising naturally; produced without human involvement
spoof *vt., vi.* deceive; satirize —*n.* a hoax; a playful parody
spoor *n.* footprints or other traces of a wild animal
spo·rad´ic *adj.* infrequent; not widely diffused
spore *n.* reproductive body in plants; a minute organism
sport *n.* a diversion; spirit of raillery; a laughingstock —*vi.* jest —*adj.* pertaining to sports; of casual wear
spouse *n.* partner in marriage
spout *vi., vt.* pour out under pressure; utter angrily
sprawl *vi.* sit or lie ungracefully; to spread out
spread *vt.* open or unfold; force apart; disperse widely —*vi.* be extended or expanded; be dispersed
spree *n.* a period of heavy drinking; boisterous fun
sprig *n.* a shoot or sprout
spring *vi.* jump; occur suddenly; proceed from a source —*vt.* cause to move or occur suddenly —*n.* a device that yields under stress and recovers; a flow of water; season preceding summer
spring´y *adj.* elastic; resiliant
sprint *n.* short race —*vi.* run fast
sprite *n.* a fairy; an elflike person
sprout *vi.* put forth shoots; develop or grow rapidly —*n.* a new shoot on a plant
spruce *adj.* smart and neat in appearance —*n.* a type of pine tree
spry *adj.* quick; agile
spume *n.* froth or foam —*vi.* foam
spur *n.* a thing that incites or urges; a lateral mountain ridge; a railroad branch —*vt.* urge, as with a spur
spu´ri·ous *adj.* not genuine or authenticated
spurn *vt., vi.* reject
spurt *n.* a sudden gush —*vi.* gush forth; make a sudden, forceful effort
squab´ble *vi.* quarrel —*n.* a petty argument
squal´id *adj.* dirty, neglected, or poverty-stricken
squall *n.* screaming outcry; brief commotion; burst of wind and rain or snow
squan´der *vt.* spend wastefully —*n.* wastefulness
square *n.* a plane figure of four equal sides; a device to lay out a right angle; a park bordered by intersecting streets —*adj.* perfectly adjusted; honest, fair —*vt.* make square; test for squareness —*vi.* be at right angles; conform, harmonize
squash *vt.* crush; suppress —*vi.* be crushed —*n.* crush; sound made walking through muck; an indoor game played with rackets and ball; edible gourd
squat *vi.* crouch or cower; settle on land illegally; settle on government land according to regulation —*adj.* short and thick —*n.* a crouch
squeam´ish *adj.* easily shocked; overly scrupulous
squeeze *vt.* extract by pressure; embrace —*vi.* apply pressure; yield to pressure —*n.* pressure; an embrace; time of difficulty
squelch *vt.* squash; silence with a retort —*n.* a crushing reply —**squelch´er** *n.*
squire *n.* (*Brit.*) prominent landowner; (*US*) a lawyer or justice of the peace; an escort or suitor
squirt *vi., vt.* come forth or eject in a thin stream —*n.* a jet of liquid
stab *vt., vi.* thrust with a pointed weapon —*n.* a wound; sharp pain; an effort
sta´ble *adj.* standing firm; having permanence; resistant to change —*n.* lodging for livestock; performers, writers, etc. under the same agency —**sta´bly** *adv.*
sta´di·um *n.* a large structure for sporting events
staff *n.* a stick or rod; a cudgel; emblem of authority; pole that supports; group of assistants or advisors
stage *n.* a platform; step or level in a process; portion of a journey —*vt.* exhibit on stage; plan and carry out; simulate —**the stage** any activity associated with theater or drama
stag´ger *vi., vt.* move unsteadily; overwhelm; place alternately —*n.* an unsteady walk
stag´nant *adj.* not flowing; foul from standing; sluggish
staid *adj.* sedate; serious
stake *n.* sharpened stick; something wagered; share in an enterprise —*vt.* mark a boundary; wager; back with money, equipment, etc.
stale *adj.* no longer fresh; deteriorated; lacking effectiveness, spontaneity, etc.
stale´mate *n.* a deadlock —*vt.* bring to a standstill
stalk *n.* a supporting part, a plant stem —*vi., vt.* approach stealthily
stal´wart *adj.* strong and robust; determined; courageous —*n.* an uncompromising partisan
stam´i·na *n.* endurance
stam·pede´ *n.* a sudden, impulsive rush; a spontaneous trend —*vt., vi.*
stance *n.* a mode of standing; a point of view
stanch *vt.* stop or check; end
stand *vi.* take or have position; assume an attitude —*vt.* place upright; endure —*n.* a designated place; an opinion or attitude; structure similar to a stage; a stall where merchandise is traded; a growth of trees
stan´dard *n.* flag or banner; an emblem or symbol; a model; an established reference —*adj.* of recognized excellence, popularity, etc.; not special; typical —**stan´dard·ise** (*Brit.*), **stan´dard·ize** (*US*) *vt.*
stare *vi., vt.* gaze fixidly —*n.* a steady, fixed gaze
stark *adj.* barren, bleak; severe; lacking ornamentation; grim, pitiless —*adv.* utterly
start *vi., vt.* make a quick, involuntary movement; begin; set in motion; establish —*n.* a quick movement; beginning or commencement
star´tle *vt., vi.* arouse or be aroused; excite suddenly
starve *vi.* perish from lack of food; suffer extreme hunger; suffer lack —*vt.* cause to die of hunger; to deprive
state *n.* a condition; status; a grand, ceremonious, or luxurious style; a sovereign political unit —*adj.* of government; intended for ceremonial use —*vt.* set forth in speech or writing
state´ly *adj.* dignified; majestic —*adv.* loftily
stat´ic *adj.* of bodies at rest or forces in equilibrium; at rest; not active —*n.* electrical noise
sta´tion *n.* assigned place; headquarters; stop for conveyance; social rank or standing —*vt.* assign a place; set in position
sta´tion·ar·y *adj.* remaining in one place; fixed
sta´tion·er·y *n.* office supplies
sta·tis´tic *n.* a value based on sampling
stat´ue *n.* a three-dimensional representation
stat´ure *n.* natural height; status or reputation
sta´tus *n.* state or condition; relative position or rank
stat´ute *n.* an established law or regulation
stay *vi.* stop, halt; remain —*vt.* bring to a halt; hinder; postpone —*n.* suspension
stead *n.* in place of another
stead´fast *adj.* firmly fixed
stead´y *adj.* stable; unfaltering, constant; regular —*vt., vi.* to make or become steady
steal *vt.* take unlawfully; obtain subtly —*vi.* move stealthily; commit theft —*n.* a bargain
steep[1] *adj.* sloping sharply; precipitous; costly
steep[2] *vt.* soak in liquid
stee´ple *n.* the lofty structure above the roof of a church
steer *vt., vi.* direct the course
stench *n.* an offensive odor
sten´cil *n.* an openwork pattern for copying a design
stere *n.* a cubic meter
ster´ile *adj.* having no reproductive power; free of microorganisms; lacking vigor
stern *adj.* severe or harsh; austere; resolute
stick´ler *n.* one with exacting standards; a baffling issue
stiff *adj.* rigid; resistant; unnatural; strong and steady: *stiff breeze*; thick, viscous; harsh; stubborn, unyielding; difficult, arduous —*n.* an awkward or unresponsive person —**stiff´ness** *n.*
sti´fle *vt.* kill by suffocating; suppress, as tears —*vi.* die of suffocation
stig´ma *n.* mark of disgrace; spot or scar on the skin
still *adj.* motionless; free of disturbance; silent; soft, subdued —*adv.* up to now; in spite of; in increasing degree —*conj.* nevertheless —*vt.* silence; allay —*vi.* become still —**still´ness** *n.*
stim´u·late *vt.* rouse to activity; affect by intoxicants —*vi.* act as stimulus or stimulant
stim´u·lus *n.* anything that rouses to activity
sting *vt., vi.* prick painfully; suffer sharp, smarting pain
stin´gy *adj.* miserly; meager or scanty
stink *n.* a foul odor —*vi., vt.* give forth a foul odor
stint *vt.* limit —*vi.* be frugal or sparing —*n.* a restriction or limit; specified task or time
sti´pend *n.* a regular fixed allowance
stip´u·late *vt.* specify —*vi.* demand as a requirement *n.*
sto·chas´tic *adj.* characterized by conjecture; involving probability
stock *n.* goods on hand; original from which others are descended; main stem of a plant; shares in a corporation; raw material; broth —*vt.* supply; keep on hand to sell; put aside for future use —*adj.* commonplace, ordinary
stodg´y *adj.* dull, boring; heavy or indigestible
sto´ic *n.* one unaffected by emotion —**sto´ic**, **sto´i·cal** *adj.* impassive or indifferent
stol´id *adj.* without feeling; impassive —**stol´id·ly** *adv.*
stomp *vt., vi.* to tread heavily upon —*n.* a jazz dance
stone *n.* a small rock; shaped rock; something small and hard; pit of a fruit —*adj.* made of stone —*vt.* hurl stones at; remove pits from
stooge *n.* a dupe
stool *n.* a seat; a low bench
stoop *vi.* lean forward and down; lower or degrade oneself —*vt.* bend forward —*n.* habitual inclination of head and shoulders; a small porch
stop *vt.* bring to a halt; prevent completion; cease doing; check or stanch; close, as with a cork —*vi.* come to a halt —*n.* an obstruction
stor´age *n.* placing for safekeeping; charge for storing
store *vt.* put away for future use —*n.* a business that sells merchandise
sto´rey (*Brit.*) *n.* level of a building
sto´ried *adj.* having a notable history

storm *n.* heavy prolonged winds and precipitation; a violent outburst; political or social disturbance —*vi.* blow or rage —*vt.* attack
sto´ry *n.* narrative; anecdote; plot of a fictional account; falsehood; (*US*) level of a building
stout *adj.* thick–set; courageous —*n.* strong dark beer
stow *vt.* pack; store
stow´age *n.* space or charge for storing; goods stored
strad´dle *vt.* stand or sit with legs on either side; favor both sides of an issue
strag´gle *vi.* stray or wander; fall behind
straight *adj.* without curve or bend; erect; fair and honest; correctly arranged; accepted as normal or conventional —*adv.* in a direct course; at once; without qualification
strain *vt.* exert; injure by overexertion; remove with a filter —*vi.* make an effort; become wrenched or twisted; filter —*n.* taxing demand on resources; a violent effort; injury from excessive effort
strait *n.* narrow passage of water
strange *adj.* unfamiliar; peculiar, out of the ordinary; out of place
stran´ger *n.* one unfamiliar; one ignorant of
stran´gle *vt.* choke to death; suppress
stra·te´gic *adj.* vital, essential
strat´e·gy *n.* a broad–based plan; the use of artifice
strat´i·fy *vt., vi.* form in layers
stray *vi.* wander; to deviate from right or goodness —*adj.* wandering; out of place —*n.* a domestic animal that has wandered —**stray´er** *n.*
stream *n.* a flow of water; an uninterrupted flow —*vi.* pour forth or issue; proceed without interruption
strength *n.* ability to apply or withstand force; intensity
stren´u·ous *adj.* marked by effort or exertion
stress *n.* physical or emotional tension; emphasis; pressure —*vt.* subject to stress; give emphasis to
stretch *vt.* draw out; strain to the utmost; adapt to circumstances —*vi.* extend; —*n.* continuous space or time —*adj.* able to be distended
stri´ate *vt.* mark with grooves, stripes, etc. —**stri·a´tion** *n.*
strick´en *adj.* affected by injury, disease, sorrow, etc.
strict *adj.* harsh, stern, exacting; absolute
stric´ture *n.* that which restricts; narrowing or closure
stri´dent *adj.* loud and harsh
strife *n.* angry contention
strike *vt.* hit; affect suddenly; cease work in protest; make a bargain —*vi.* come into violent contact; cease work —*n.* blow; sudden success; work stoppage
strin´gent *adj.* rigid or severe; convincing —**strin´gen·cy** *n.*
strip *n.* a narrow piece; set of cartoon drawings —*vt.* lay bare; deprive; damage gears or threads —*vi.* undress
stripe *n.* a contrasting band; a distinctive quality; blow struck with a whip or rod —*vt.* mark with a band
strip´ling *n.* a lad
strive *vi.* make an effort; fight
stroll *vi.* walk casually —*n.* a leisurely walk —**stroll´er** *n.*
strong *adj.* physically powerful; healthy, robust; especially competent or able; firm, tenacious —*adv.* in a firm manner
struc´ture *n.* a fabrication; founded on a plan —*vt.* build; conceive as a whole
strug´gle *n.* arduous effort; a war —*vt.* contend; strive
strut *n.* pompous walk; a supporting member —*vi.* walk pompously —*vt.* support or separate with a brace
stub´born *adj.* inflexible; not easily overcome
stu´dent *n.* one engaged in a course of study
stu´dio *n.* working area for an artist, photographer, etc.
stud´y *n.* the process of acquiring knowledge; a branch of knowledge; a room for reading or studying —*vt.* acquire knowledge; examine thoroughly —*vi.* apply the mind to learning
stuff *vt.* fill completely; plug or stop up —*n.* fundamental element; personal possessions; unspecified matter; a miscellaneous collection
stuff´y *adj.* poorly ventilated; impeding respiration; strait-laced, stodgy
stum´ble *vi.* miss one's step; speak in a halting manner; happen upon by chance; do wrong
stump *n.* portion left when a part is cut off; a place for political speech —*adj.* of political campaigning —*vt.* make a political speech
stun *vt.* render incapable of action; astound, overwhelm
stu·pen´dous *adj.* astonishing; immense
stu´por *n.* abnormal lethargy; intellectual dullness
stur´dy *adj.* robust and powerful; firm and resolute
style *n.* fashionable appearance; distinctive fashion, manner, etc. —*vt.* give a name or title; alter
suave *adj.* pleasant and courteous
sub·con´scious *adj.* not attended by full awareness
sub·due´ *vt.* gain dominion over; repress —**sub·du´er** *n.*
sub´ject *adj.* under power of; having a tendency —*n.* one under power of another; a theme or topic; a branch of learning —**sub·ject´** *vt.* bring under control; make liable
sub·jec´tive *adj.* of personal feeling or opinion; influenced by emotion or prejudice —**sub·jec·tiv´i·ty** *n.*
sub´ju·gate *vt.* conquer; make subservient
sub´li·mate *vt.* convert a urge to that which is socially acceptable
sub·lime´ *adj.* characterized by grandeur
sub·lim´in·al *adj.* below the threshold of consciousness; too slight to be perceived
sub·merge´ *vt.* place under water —*vi.* sink beneath the surface
sub·merse´ *vt.* submerge
sub·mers´i·ble *adj.* that may be submerged —*n.* craft for operation on the surface or under water; underwater craft used for observation, rescue, etc.
sub·mis´sion *n.* yielding; presenting for consideration; something submitted, as a manuscript
sub·mis´sive *adj.* inclined to submit
sub·mit´ *vt.* to yield; present for consideration —*vi.* surrender; obey
sub·or´di·nate *adj.* lower in rank; secondary —*n.* one of lower rank; a helper or assistant —*vt.* assign a lower rank; make subservient
sub·orn´ *vt.* bribe to commit perjury; incite to an unlawful act
sub·poe´na *n.* writ requiring a court appearance
sub´ro·gate *vt.* substitute one for another, esp. a creditor
sub·scribe´ *vt.* sign one's name to express assent; promise to pay; give approval; agree; pay in advance, as for a periodical
sub´se·quent *adj.* following in time, order, etc. —**sub´se·quent·ly** *adv.*
sub·ser´vi·ent *adj.* servile, obsequious —**sub·ser´vi·ence** *n.*
sub·side´ *vi.* lower; calm
sub·sid´i·ar·y *adj.* supplementary or auxiliary —*n.* a business with over half its assets owned by another
sub´si·dize *vt.* aid
sub´si·dy *n.* a financial grant
sub·sist´ *vi.* continue to exist; to maintain life
sub·sist´ence *n.* that by which one exists, as food or earnings
sub´stance *n.* material of which a thing is made; essential component; wealth or property; the quality of being constant or solid
sub·stan´tial *adj.* firm and solid; tangible; of significant worth or importance —**sub·stan´tial·ly** *adv.*
sub·stan´ti·ate *vt.* prove
sub´stan·tive *n.* a noun or pronoun, or a verbal form replacing a noun —*adj.* that can be used as a noun; denoting existence; having substance —**sub´stan·tive·ly** *adv.*
sub´sti·tute *vt.* put in place of; take the place of —*vi.* act as substitute —*n.* an alternate or replacement —*adj.* alternative; temporary
sub·sti·tu´tion *n.* replacing; being a replacement; a substitute
sub´ter·fuge *n.* deception
sub·ter·ra´ne·an *adj.* below the surface of the earth
sub´tle *adj.* not easily detected; not obvious; skillful or ingenious
sub´tle·ty *n.* the quality of being subtle; a small differentiation
sub·tract´ *vt., vi.* take away or deduct —**sub·trac´tive** *adj.*
sub´urb *n.* an area adjacent to a city; an outlying district
sub·ur´ban·ite *n.* resident of a suburb
sub·ur´bi·a *n.* the suburbs or suburbanites collectively; the cultural world of those living in the suburbs
sub·ver´sive *n.* one trying to weaken or overthrow —*adj.* tending to undermine or weaken
sub·vert´ *vt.* corrupt; destroy utterly
sub´way *n.* an underpass; an underground railway
suc·ceed´ *vi.* accomplish or turn out as intended; come next in order —*vt.* to come after in time or order
suc·cess´ *n.* a favorable termination; gaining of fame, wealth, etc.; the scale or level of gain
suc·cess´ful *adj.* ending in success
suc·ces´sion *n.* following in order; right to office, possessions, etc.
suc·ces´sive *adj.* following in order
suc·cinct´ *adj.* clear and concise; marked by brevity
suc´cu·lent *adj.* juicy; having thick fleshy leaves; interesting —*n.* a succulent plant —**suc´cu·lence** *n.*
suc·cumb´ *vi.* to yield; to die
such *adj.* being the same or similar: *times such as these*; extreme: *such an uproar* —*pron.* the same as implied or indicated —*adv.* especially: *in such good spirits*
suck *vt.* draw in by partial vacuum; to pull or draw in: *the lure of profit sucked him in* —*vi.* draw in by suction; suckle
suc´tion *n.* partial vacuum —*adj.* created or operated by suction
sud´den *adj.* happening quickly without warning; hasty, rash
suds *pl. n.* froth, foam —**suds·y** *adj.*
sue *vt.* take legal action to redress a wrong; prosecute —*vi.* start legal proceedings; seek to persuade by entreaty: *sue for peace*
suede *n.* hide or fabric having a napped surface
suf´fer *vi.* feel pain or distress; sustain loss or injury; undergo punishment —*vt.* have inflicted on one; endure; allow
suf´fer·ance *n.* permission granted or implied; capacity for suffering
suf·fice´ *vi.* be sufficient or adequate
suf·fi´cient *adj.* all that is needed; enough —**suf·fi´cient·ly** *adv.*
suf´fix *n.* addition to a word that modifies —*vt.* to add
suf´fo·cate *vt., vi.* distress or kill by depriving of oxygen; to stifle: *suffocate with affection*; smother, as a fire
suf´frage *n.* voting; a vote
suf·fuse´ *vt.* spread through or over: *suffuse with light* —**suf·fu´sion** *n.*
sug·gest´ *vt.* present for consideration; associate: *gold suggests wealth*; imply
sug·gest´i·ble *adj.* that can be recommended; easily lead

sug·ges´tion *n.* something offered for consideration; small amount, a trace

sug·ges´tive *adj.* stimulating reflection or thought; hinting of something improper

su´i·cide *n.* taking of one's own life; ruin brought on by one's own actions —**su´i·ci´dal** *adj.*

suit *n.* a garment or set of garments; a grouping of compatible things: *bedroom suit*; a court proceeding; the courting of a woman —*vt.* meet requirements; satisfy; adapt; furnish with clothes —*vi.* prove satisfactory —**suit´a·ble** *adj.*

suite *n.* things intended for use together, as connecting rooms; a set of matched furniture

sulk *vi.* be sullen and withdrawn —*n.* a sullen mood

sulk´y *n.* a light, horse–drawn vehicle —*adj.* sullen and withdrawn

sul´len *adj.* ill–humored; glum; depressing; slow or sluggish

sul´ly *vt.* soil; shame or defile

sul´try *adj.* hot and humid; arousing passion; sensual —**sul´tri·ness** *n.*

sum *n.* entire amount; summary

sum´ma·rize *vt.* present a summary

sum´ma·ry *n.* a brief account —*adj.* containing essential details; performed without ceremony or delay

sum·ma´tion *n.* adding numbers; a final review of main points

sum´mit *n.* the highest point or part; the highest level or office

sum´mon *vt.* send for; call together; rouse to action —**sum´mon·er** *n.*

sum´mons *n.* a notice to appear in court

sump´tu·ous *adj.* lavish; luxurious

sunk´en *adj.* at the bottom; lower than the surrounding area

sun *n.* a star, as at the center of the solar system —*vt.* expose to the sun —*vi.* bask in the sun

sun´ny *adj.* filled with sunlight; bright, cheerful —**sun´ni·ly** *adv.*

sun´set *n.* time at which sun falls below the horizon; final period

su´per *adj.* surpassing others of its kind; outstanding —*n.* a superintendent

su´per·a·ble *adj.* that can be overcome

su·perb´ *adj.* extraordinarily good

su·per·cil´i·ous *adj.* haughtily disdainful; arrogant

su·per·fi´cial *adj.* on or near the surface; trivial, not profound; hasty; apparent: *superficial resemblance* —**su·per·fi´cial·ly** *adv.*

su·per´flu·ous *adj.* surplus; exceeding what is needed; unnecessary or irrelevant

su·per·in·tend´ *vt.* direct or supervise —**su·per·in·tend´ence** *n.*

su·per·in·tend´ent *n.* one in charge; one responsible for maintenance and repair

su·pe´ri·or *adj.* higher in rank, quality, etc.; affecting an attitude of indifference or disdain —*n.* one who is higher in rank

su·per´la·tive *adj.* of the highest degree; most excellent; exaggerated —*n.* thing of the highest grade

su·per·nat´u·ral *adj.* existing outside of nature; miraculous or divine; of ghosts, demons, etc. —*n.* unnatural phenomena

su·per·sede´ *vt.* replace with something newer or better; take the place of —**su·per·sed´er** *n.*

su·per·son´ic *adj.* moving faster than the speed of sound

su·per·sti´tion *n.* an irrational belief; any practice inspired by such belief

su·per·sti´tious *adj.* influenced by superstition; based on superstition

su´per·vise *vt.* have charge of; oversee or manage —**su´per·vi·sor** *n.*

su·pine´ *adj.* lying face up

sup´per *n.* the evening meal; last meal of the day

sup·plant´ *vt.* displace, as something outdated; displace by treachery

sup´ple *adj.* flexible; agile or graceful; yielding readily, compliant; adaptable —*vt., vi.* make supple

sup´ple·ment *n.* that added to correct or augment —*vt.* make an addition to —**sup·ple·men´tal** *adj.*

sup´pli·cate *vt., vi.* ask humbly or by earnest prayer —**sup·pli·ca´tion** *n.*

sup·ply´ *vt.* make available; furnish —*vi.* take the place of temporarily —*n.* quantity on hand or available

sup·port´ *vt.* bear the weight of; hold in position; provide with necessities; substantiate; provide with means to endure —*n.* person or thing that supports

sup·port´er *n.* one who provides with necessities; a brace

sup·port´ive *adj.* contributing significantly —**sup·port´ive·ness** *n.*

sup·pose´ *vt.* believe to be possible; expect; imply —**sup·pos´a·bly** *adv.*

sup·posed´ *adj.* accepted as genuine; imagined —**sup·pos·ed´ly** *adv.*

sup·po·si´tion *n.* conjecture or assumption —**sup´po·si´tion·al** *adj.*

sup·press´ *vt.* end or stop; hold back or repress; check

sup·pres´sion *n.* instance of suppressing; exclusion of unpleasant memories, etc. from consciousness

su·prem´a·cy *n.* supreme power or authority

su·preme´ *adj.* dominant; highest in degree, etc.; ultimate

sur·cease´ *n.* a cessation —*vt., vi.* to end

sure *adj.* without doubt; positive

sur´e·ty *n.* security against loss

surf *n.* sea breaking on the shore —*vi.* ride a surfboard

sur´face *n.* exterior; a superficial aspect —*vt.* apply or improve an exterior; cause to rise —*vi.* rise; come to public notice

sur´feit *vt.* supply to excess —*vi.* overindulge in food or drink —*n.* an excessive amount

surge *vi.* move with a swelling motion; increase suddenly —*n.* a great swelling or rolling; a sudden increase

sur´ger·y *n.* medical treatment by operative means; branch of medicine concerned with treatment by surgery; an operating room

sur´ly *adj.* ill–humored; gruff or insolent —**sur´li·ness** *n.*

sur·mise´ *vt., vi.* infer on slight evidence —*n.* a supposition

sur·mount´ *vt.* overcome; pass over, as an obstacle; place above —**sur·mount´a·ble** *adj.*

sur´name *n.* a family name; a cognomen or nickname —*vt.* furnish with a nickname

sur·pass´ *vt.* to go beyond or past

sur´plus *n.* that over what is required —*adj.* excess

sur·prise´ *vt.* feel wonder or astonishment; take unawares —*n.* astonishment; that causing astonishment —**sur·pris´ing** *adj.*

sur·re´al *adj.* having a dreamlike quality —**sur·re´al·ly** *adv.*

sur·re´al·ism *n.* art characterized by use of dreamlike elements

sur·ren´der *vt.* yield; give up in favor of another; give oneself over to —*vi.* to give oneself up —*n.* the act of surrendering

sur·rep·ti´tious *adj.* accomplished by secret means; acting with stealth —**sur·rep·ti´tious·ly** *adv.*

sur´ro·gate *n.* one acting in place of another; probate court judge —*vt.* deputize or substitute

sur·round´ *vt.* encircle

sur·round´ings *n.* one's environment

sur·veil´lance *n.* discreet observation of someone or something

sur·vey´, sur´vey *vt.* look at carefully; scrutinize; determine accurately the area, boundaries, etc. of land —*n.* surveying land; systematic collection and analysis of data; a general or overall view

sur·viv´a·ble *adj.* that can be survived

sur·vive´ *vi.* remain in existence; live past the death of another —*vt.* outlast; go on living in spite of

sus·cep´ti·ble *adj.* readily affected; vulnerable; able to be influenced

sus·pect´ *vt.* think guilty without proof; distrust or doubt —*vi.* have suspicions —**sus·pect´, sus´pect** *adj.* inspiring suspicion —**sus´pect** *n.* one who may be guilty

sus·pend´ *vt.* bar, cease, or interrupt for a time; defer action; move freely while hanging from a support

sus·pense´ *n.* anxiety caused by uncertainty —**sus·pense´ful** *adj.*

sus·pen´sion *n.* temporary removal, withholding of privilege, etc.; cessation or deferment; hanging freely; dispersion in liquid or gas

sus·pi´cion *n.* uncertain belief in another's guilt; a slight amount

sus·pi´cious *adj.* questionable; disposed to doubt

sus·tain´ *vt.* keep up or maintain; provide with necessities; endure or withstand; suffer or undergo; uphold or prove as being true or just

sus´te·nance *n.* maintenance of life or health; that which sustains

svelte *adj.* slender; smart or chic

swab *n.* a soft, absorbent substance on a short stick for applying medication, etc.; specimen for medical examination; a mop for cleaning —*vt.* clean or apply with a swab

swad´dle *vt.* wrap in strips of cloth —*n.* bands or cloth for swaddling

swag *n.* a decorative hanging, as a gathered drape at the top of a window; a similar carved motif; stolen property; (*Austral.*) a bundle of personal belongings

swag´ger *vi.* walk with an air of self–confidence; behave in a self–satisfied manner —*n.* a self–confident gait —*adj.* showy

swal´low *vt.* cause to pass from the mouth into the stomach; take in or engulf; submit to, as insults; suppress: *swallow one's pride* —*n.* amount taken in at one time; mouthful; small bird

swamp *n.* low land saturated with water —*vt.* drench with water; overwhelm —*vi.* sink in water

swank *n.* ostentatious display; stylishness —*adj.* stylish or smart

swank´y *adj.* ostentatiously fashionable

swap *vt., vi.* exchange or trade —*n.* something traded

swarm *n.* a large crowd or mass —*vi.* come together or move in great numbers; be overrun

swarth´y *adj.* dark complected

swat *vt.* to strike with a quick blow

swath *n.* a strip or row, as cut grain

swathe *vt.* bind or wrap, as with bandages —*n.* a bandage

sway *vi.* swing from side to side; incline in opinion, sympathies, etc.; to control —*vt.* cause to swing or lean; influence —*n.* power or influence; a turning from side to side

swear *vi.* make a solemn affirmation; make a vow; use profanity —*vt.* assert solemnly; vow; declare emphatically

sweat *vi.* exude salty moisture from pores; condense moisture on a surface; work hard; suffer from anxiety —*vt.* join metal with solder; subject to rigorous interrogation —*n.* —**sweat´y** *adj.*

sweep *vt.* clear or clean; pass over swiftly; win overwhelmingly —*vi.* clean a surface with a broom, etc.; move quickly; extend: *the road sweeps along the lake* —*n.* a long stroke or movement; the act of clearing; an unbroken stretch; an overwhelming victory; one who cleans chimneys, streets, etc.; a flowing contour

sweet *adj.* flavored like sugar; pleasing to the senses —*n.* something pleasing

sweet´en *vt.* make agreeable or pleasing —**sweet´en·er** *n.*
swell *vi.* increase in size or volume, as by inflation or absorption; to increase in amount, etc.; arise in waves; bulge —*vt.* cause to increase; cause to bulge; puff with pride —*n.* expansion; a rise or undulation; a bulge; a long continuous wave —*adj.* fashionable, elegant — **swell´ing** *n., adj.*
swel´ter *vi., vt.* suffer oppressive heat —*n.* oppressive heat
swerve *vi., vt.* turn or cause to turn aside —*n.* sudden turning
swift *adj.* capable of moving with great speed; happening without delay —**swift´ly** *adv.*
swill *vt., vi.* drink greedily —*n.* semiliquid food for animals; unappetizing food; garbage
swim *vi.* move through water with the limbs; move with a flowing motion; to be flooded —*vt.* traverse by swimming; cause to swim —*n.* swimming; the distance swum
swin´dle *vt.* cheat or defraud; obtain by fraud —*vi.* practice fraud —*n.* the act of defrauding
swing *vi., vt.* move to and fro rhythmically; pivot; be suspended; be contemporary and sophisticated; conclude successfully: *swing a deal* —*n.* a free swaying motion; a hanging seat; a trip or tour: *a swing through the low country*; a type of jazz
swirl *vi., vt.* to move or cause to move with a whirling motion — *n.*
switch *n.* a flexible rod or whip; a mechanism for shifting or changing —*vt.* whip or lash; turn aside or divert; exchange —*vi.* turn aside; change — **switch´er** *n.*
swiv´el *n.* pivot permiting independent rotation; thing turning on a pivot —*vt., vi.* to turn
swoon *vi.* faint —*n.* fainting spell
swoop *vi.* descend suddenly; pounce —*vt.* seize suddenly —*n.* a sudden violent descent
sword *n.* long blade fixed in a hilt
syc´o·phant *n.* a servile flatterer
syl·lab´ic *adj.* pertaining to syllables; having every syllable distinctly pronounced
syl·lab´i·cate, syl·lab´i·fy *vt.* divide into syllables
syl´la·ble *n.* a word or part of a word uttered in a single vocal impulse
syl´la·bus *n.* concise description
syl´lo·gism *n.* a conclusion derived from commonality of two premises
syl´van *adj.* of a wooded area; of a creature living in woods
sym·bi´o·sis *n.* a mutually advantageous relationship between dissimilar organisms
sym´bol *n.* a mark, emblem, etc. representing something
sym´bol·ism *n.* investing with symbolic meaning; system of symbolic representation
sym´bol·ize *vt.* represent symbolically; to use symbols
sym´me·try *n.* balancing of elements; beauty and harmony resulting from balance
sym·pa·thet´ic *adj.* having compassion for others; in accord or harmony; of sounds produced by responsive vibrations
sym´pa·thize *vi.* understand sentiments of another; feel or express compassion; be in harmony or agreement
sym´pa·thy *n.* agreement of feeling; compassion for another; agreement, accord; support or approval
sym·pho´ni·ous *adj.* in accord; harmonious
sym´pho·ny *n.* agreeable mingling of sounds, color, etc.; composition for orchestra — **sym·phon´ic** *adj.*
sym·po´si·um *n.* to meeting for to discussion of a particular subject; to writing on a particular subject
symp´tom *n.* condition indicating presence of disease; an indication: *a symptom of civil unrest*
syn´a·gogue *n.* a place of meeting for Jewish worship and religious instruction; a Jewish congregation
syn´apse *n.* junction of two neurons across which nerve impulses pass
syn·chron´ic *adj.* of the events of a particular time
syn´chro·nism *n.* concurrence; grouping of historic persons or events by date
syn´chro·nize *vi.* occur at the same time; operate in unison — *vt.* cause to operate together; assign the same date or period
syn´chro·nous *adj.* occurring at the same time
syn·co·pa´tion *n.* suppression of an expected rhythmic accent in music
syn´di·cate *n.* association united to engage in an enterprise —*vt.* combine into a syndicate
syn´drome *n.* combined symptoms characteristic of a disease; traits regarded as characteristic of a condition, etc. — **syn´drom·ic** *adj.*
syn´er·gism *n.* reinforcing action of separate organs, agents, etc.
syn´er·gy *n.* synergism
syn´od *n.* ecclesiastical council
syn´o·nym *n.* a word having almost the same meaning as another
syn·on´y·mous *adj.* equivalent or similar in meaning
syn·op´sis *n.* condensation of a story, book, etc.; a summary
syn·op´tic *adj.* giving a general view; offering a similar point of view
syn´tax *n.* arrangement of words in grammatical construction
syn´the·sis *n., pl.* **syn´the·ses** the assembly of subordinate parts into a new form; the resulting complex form created
syn´the·size *vt.* to produce by synthesis
syn´the·siz·er *n.* an electronic device used to create musical tones
syn·thet´ic *adj.* produced artificially, as by chemical synthesis; artificial
sy·ringe´ *n.* a device to remove or inject fluids
sys´tem *n.* an arrangement of parts, facts, etc. that interact with each other; a group of logically related facts, beliefs, etc.; a method of classication, arrangement, etc.
sys´tem·a·tize *vt.* organize methodically
sys·tem´ic *adj.* of a system; affecting the entire body: *systemic poison*
t, T *n.* 20th letter of the alphabet —**to a T** perfectly, precisely
tab *n.* a flap, projection, etc. as on a garment or file card —*vt.* provide with a tab
tab´er·na·cle *n.* a house of worship; recepticle for the eucharistic elements; portable sanctuary of the Israelites
ta´ble *n.* an article of furniture with a flat top and legs; surface for serving food; food served; elements arranged in rows and columns for easy reference; a listing: *table of contents*; a tablet or slab —*vt.* to postpone discussion
tab´leau *n., pl.* **tab´leaux** or **tab´leaus** a picturesque representation
table d'hôte a complete meal served at a fixed price
ta´ble·spoon *n.* measure equal to three teaspoons; tablespoonful
ta´ble·spoon·ful *n.* amount a tablespoon will hold
tab´let *n.* a pill; a pad of paper; a flat surface intended for an inscription or design
ta´ble·ware *n.* dishes and implements for dining
tab´loid *n.* a newspaper in which news is presented concisely and often sensationally
ta·boo´, ta·bu´ *n.* ban based on religious belief, custom, etc. — *adj.* restricted or prohibited — *vt.* place under taboo
tab´u·lar *adj.* arranged in a table or list
tab´u·late *vt.* arrange in a table or list —**tab·u·la´tion** *n.*
ta·chom´e·ter *n.* a device indicating speed of rotation, as for an engine
tach´y·car´di·a *n.* abnormally rapid heartbeat
tac´it *adj.* not spoken; inferred or implied —**tac´it·ly** *adv.*
tac´i·turn *adj.* habitually reserved
tack *n.* small nail with a broad flat head; policy or course of action; a temporary fastening —*vt.* fasten with a tack; secure temporarily —*vi.* change one's course of action
tack´le *n.* combination of ropes and pulleys for hoisting; rigging of a ship; sport or work gear — *vt.* undertake: *tackle a problem*; seize suddenly and forcefully
tack´y *adj.* slightly sticky; in poor taste —**tack´i·ness** *n.*
tact *n.* ability to say or do the proper thing —**tact´ful** *adj.*
tac´ti·cal *adj.* pertaining to tactics; adept at planning and maneuvering —**tac·ti´cian** *n.*
tac´tics *n.* strategy; the art of maneuvering to gain an end
tac´tile *adj.* of the sense of touch; that may be perceived by touch
tact´less *adj.* lacking tact
taf´fe·ta *n.* a fine, stiff fabric — *adj.* made of taffeta
taf´fy *n.* a chewy confection
tag *n.* an attachment that identifies, prices, etc.; a children's game —*vt.* fit with a tag; follow closely; touch
ta·hi´ni *n.* sesame seed butter
tail *n.* flexible appendage of an animal; an extension: *tail of a comet*; hind or back portion — *vt.* be at the end of; follow stealthily —*vi.* follow closely; diminish gradually —*adj.* rearmost; coming from behind
tail´gate *n.* hinged gate on a motor vehicle —*vt., vi.* follow too closely
tai´lor *n.* one who makes or repairs garments —*vi.* do a tailor's work —*vt.* fit with garments; adapt to meet a need — **tai´lor·ing** *n.*
tai´lored *adj.* custom–made; severe or tight–fitting
tai´lor–made´ *adj.* made by a tailor; perfectly suited to a need
taint *vt., vi.* affect by contamination or corruption —*n.* a cause or result of contamination
take *vt.* lay hold or gain possession of; choose; steal; undergo or submit to; accept; charm or captivate; perform: *take action*; to feel —*vi.* acquire; be captivated: *taken with her beauty*; require; enter upon: *take a job*; assume: *take blame*; have intended effect —*n.* something taken or received; amount received —**tak´er** *n.*
tale *n.* story; narrative of events; idle or malicious gossip; a lie
tale´bear·er *n.* one who gossips or spreads rumors
tal´ent *n.* natural ability; aptitude; those with special ability
tal´is·man *n.* object to ward off evil or bring good luck; thing with seeming magical power
talk *vi.* express audibly; convey a message: *money talks*; make sounds suggesting speech —*vt.* express in words —*n.* conversation or speech; conference or discussion; sounds suggesting speech
talk´a·tive *adj.* given to much talk
talk´y *adj.* talkative; given overly to talk: *a talky movie* —**talk´i·ness** *n.*
tall *adj.* of more than average height; of a specified height; exaggerated; extensive: *a tall order* —*adv.* proudly: *walk tall*
tal´low *n.* rendered animal fat
tal´ly *n.* score or mark; a reckoning; mark indicating a number —*vt.* to score; reckon; to make correspond —*vi.* keep score; agree precisely
tal´on *n.* claw of an animal
ta·ma´le *n.* seasoned meat rolled in corn meal, then wrapped in leaves and steamed
tame *adj.* domesticated; docile, subdued; lacking spirit, uninteresting —*vt.* domesticate; tone down
tamp *vt.* pack down
tam´per *vi.* meddle or interfere with; make potentially harmful changes; use improper measures

tan *vt.* convert into leather; darken by exposure to sunlight —*vi.* become darkened —*n.* a yellow–brown color; dark skin coloring
tan´dem *adv.* one behind the other —*n.* team of horses harnessed one behind the other: the carriage they pull; a bicycle with two or more seats —*adj.*
tang *n.* a sharp, penetrating taste or odor —**tang´y** *adj.*
tan´gent *adj.* touching without intersecting —**tan´gen·cy** *n.*
tan·gen´tial *adj.* touching lightly
tan´ger·ine´ *n.* variety of orange
tan´gi·ble *adj.* perceptible by touch; real or concrete —*n.* assets having value that can be appraised
tan´gle *vt.* twist into a mass; ensnare or enmesh; involve so as to confuse —*vi.* become tangled —*n.* confused intertwining
tan´go *n.* Latin American dance; music for such a dance —*vi.*
tank *n.* a large receptacle; an armored combat vehicle —*vt.* store in a tank
tan´kard *n.* a large, handled drinking cup, often with a cover
tan´ner·y *n.* place for curing leather
tan´ta·lize *vt.* torment by withholding —**tan´ta·liz·ing·ly** *adv.*
tan´ta·mount *adj.* equivalent to
tan´trum *n.* a fit of temper
tap *n.* act or sound of striking gently; spout for drawing liquid; plug or stopper —*vt.* touch or strike gently; open or provide with a spigot; draw upon
tape *n.* a narrow strip for measuring or binding —*vt.* secure with tape
ta´per *n.* a slender candle; wick for lighting candles; a cone —*vt., vi.* make or become thin toward one end; lessen gradually —*adj.*
tap´es·try *n.* a heavy woven textile with a pictorial design
tape´worm *n.* a parasitic worm
tap·i·o´ca *n.* a starchy food obtained from cassava
tar·an·tel´la *n.* a lively dance
ta·ran´tu·la *n.* large hairy spider
tar´dy *adj.* not happening as anticipated; moving ahead slowly
tar´get *n.* object of an action —*vt.* establish as a goal
tar´iff *n.* duties imposed on imports and exports; a price schedule —*vt.* fix a price on
tarn *n.* a small mountain lake
tar´nish *vt.* dim the luster of; sully or debase —*vi.* become tarnished
ta´ro *n.* tropical plant having a starchy edible rootstock
ta´rot *n.* cards used mainly for fortunetelling
tar·pau´lin *n.* waterproof material used as protective covering
tar´pon *n.* a large game fish
tar´ra·gon *n.* a European plant with leaves used for seasoning
tar´ry *vi.* put off going; linger; remain temporarily
tar´sal *adj.* pertaining to the ankle
tar´sus *n.* the ankle
tart *n.* a small filled pastry —*adj.* having a sharp sour taste; caustic, as a remark —**tart´ly** *adv.*
tar´tan *n.* woolen fabric, esp. one distinctive to a Scottish clan
task *n.* a designated job; a difficult assignment —*vi.* assign a task; overburden
task´mas·ter *n.* one who assigns tasks, esp. burdensome ones
tas´sel *n.* an ornamental tuft of loose hanging cords —*vt.* adorn with tassels —*vi.* put forth tassels, as on corn
taste *vt., vi.* perceive flavor; consume a small amount; experience: *taste victory*; have a specific flavor —*n.* stimulation of the taste buds; a small quantity; special fondness: *taste for music*; respect for propriety and refinement
taste buds flavor receptors on the tongue
taste´ful *adj.* conforming to good taste —**taste´ful·ly** *adv.*
taste´less *adj.* without flavor; lacking tact or decorum
tast´y *adj.* having a fine flavor
tat´ter *n.* a torn shred — *vt., vi.* make or become ragged —**tat´ters** ragged clothing
tat·ter·de·ma´lion *n.* one wearing ragged clothing; ragamuffin
tat´ter·sall *n.* a pattern of intersecting dark lines on a light background; cloth of this design —*adj.*
tat´tle *vi., vt.* gossip —*n.* idle chatter
tat´tle·tale *n.* an informer —*adj.* revealing: *tattletale signs*
tat·too´ *vt.* mark skin with patterns —*n.* pattern or design on the skin; a drumbeat; sounding of drum or bugle to signal return to quarters
tat´ty *adj.* worn or shabby
taunt *n.* a sarcastic remark; a jibe —*vt.* provoke with derision or insults
taupe *n.* a brownish gray color
taut *adj.* stretched tight; tidy
tau·tol´o·gy *n.* needless repetition in speaking —**tau·to·log´i·cal** *adj.*
tav´ern *n.* an inn; place licensed to sell alcoholic beverages
taw´dry *adj.* cheap and showy; lacking taste or quality
tawn´y *adj.* tan–colored —*n.* tan
tax *n.* charge levied for support of government; heavy demand —*vt.* levy a tax; impose a burden on —**tax shelter** a financial manipulation designed to reduce tax liability
tax·a´tion *n.* process of taxing; amount levied; revenue raised
tax´i *n.* a taxicab —*vi.* ride in a taxicab; move along the surface
tax´i·cab *n.* a vehicle for hire
tax´i·der·my *n.* the art of stuffing and mounting animals
tax´ing *adj.* difficult, trying
tax·on´o·my *n.* principles for classification of plant and animal life
T cell *n.* a type of white blood cell essential to the immune system
tea *n.* leaves of an Asian plant used to prepare a beverage; a beverage; a social gathering
teach *vt.* provide instruction; instruct in: *teach French*; train —**teach´er** *n.*
teaching machine a computer that presents material for learning and provides corrective feedback
teak *n.* an extremely durable wood
team *n.* a group working together as a unit —*vi.* work as a unit —**team player** one who works cooperatively —**team´work** harmony of action among members of a group
team´ster *n.* one driving a team of horses or a motor vehicle
tear *n.* fluid from the eye; a break or rip; a violent outburst —*vt.* pull apart; wound or lacerate; distress or disrupt —*vi.* to become torn; to move with haste or energy
tear´ful *adj.* causing tears; accompanied by tears —**tear´ful·ly** *adv.*
tear´ing *adj.* with great haste
tear´jerk·er *n.* a book, play, etc. designed to evoke tears
tear´y *adj.* filled or wet with tears; sentimental; overemotional
tease *vt.* annoy or vex; coax or beg; comb —*vi.* annoy in a petty way —*n.* one who teases —**teas´er** *n.*
tea´spoon *n.* a small spoon
tea´spoon, tea´spoon·ful *n.* the amount a teaspoon will hold
tech´ni·cal *adj.* relating to a particular art, trade, etc.; exhibiting technique; according to accepted rules —**tech´ni·cal·ly** *adv.*
tech·ni·cal´i·ty *n.* method peculiar to an art, trade, etc.; a petty detail
tech·ni´cian *n.* one skilled in a particular field
tech´nics *n.* the study or principles of an art, trade, etc.
tech·nique´ *n.* a way of working; degree of skill exhibited; a method of accomplishing
tech·noc´ra·cy *n.* government dominated by technicians
tech·nol´o·gy *n.* technical means for meeting needs of a society; technical terms
tec·ton´ics *n.* the art of construction; study of the movements of the earth's crust —**tec·ton´ic** *adj.*
te´di·ous *adj.* boring or repetitious
te´di·um *n.* the quality of being boring, monotonous, etc.
teem *vi.* be full or overflowing
teen´age, teen´–age, teen´aged, teen´–aged *adj.* of the ages from 13 to 19 —**teen, teen´ager, teen´–ag´er** *n.*
tee´ter *vi.* walk unsteadily; vacillate or waver
teethe *vi.* develop teeth
tee·to´tal *adj.* advocating abstention from alchoholic beverages
tel´e·cast *vt., vi.* broadcast by television —*n.*
tel·e·com·mu·ni·ca´tion *n.* communicating by radio, television, telephone, etc.
tel´e·com·mut·ing *n.* working from home through a computer link
tel´e·con´fer·ence *n.* a meeting conducted by telephone or closed circuit television —*vi.* participate in a teleconference
tel´e·graph *n.* system for transmitting messages by wire over distance
tel·e·ki·ne´sis *n.* unexplained movement of objects, as by occult power
tel´e·mar·ket·ing *n.* selling by telephone or television
te·lem´e·try *n.* automatic measurement and transmission of data
tel·e·ol´o·gy *n.* study of final causes; explanation of natural phenomenon in terms of design and purpose —**tel·e·ol´o·gist** *n.*
te·lep´a·thy *n.* extrasensory communication —**tel·e·path´ic** *adj.*
tel´e·phone *n.* a device for transmitting speech —*vt., vi.* communicate by telephone
te·leph´o·ny *n.* the technology of telephone communication
tel´e·pho´to *adj.* of a lens which produces a near view of far objects
tel·e·pho·tog´ra·phy *n.* technique for producing magnified photographs of distant objects
tel´e·scope *n.* an instrument for viewing distant objects
tel´e·thon *n.* a television show intended to raise funds
tel·e·van´ge·lism *n.* the broadcasting of religious shows
tel´e·vise *vt., vi.* transmit a television signal
tel´e·vi·sion *n.* a system for transmission and reception of visual images and sound
tell *vt.* narrate or relate in detail; express in words; ascertain or distinguish: *tell who is taller* —*vi.* give an account; serve as an indication: *their rags tell of their poverty*
tell´er *n.* one who narrates; (*US*) a bank employee
tell´ing *adj.* producing a marked effect —**tell´ing·ly** *adv.*
tell´tale *adj.* revealing —*n.* tattler; outward sign or indication
tem·er·ar´i·ous *adj.* daring or reckless —**tem·er·ar´i·ous·ly** *adv.*
te·mer´i·ty *n.* disregard for danger
tem´peh *n.* a high–protein food made from fermented soybeans
tem´per *n.* a fit of anger; a tendency to anger; temperament; hardness of a metal —*vt.* moderate, as by adding; toughen, as by hardship —*vi.* be or become tempered
tem´per·a *n.* a type of paint
tem´per·a·ment *n.* nature or disposition; a moody disposition
tem´per·a·men´tal *adj.* overly excitable, capricious, etc.; unpredictable —**tem´per·a·men´tal·ly** *adv.*
tem´per·ance *n.* moderation, self–control —*adj.* restraint
tem´per·ate *adj.* marked by moderation; not extreme; calm, restrained
tem´per·a·ture *n.* relative heat or cold; excess of heat in a body
tem´pered *adj.* of a particular temperament: *quick–tempered*; modified: *discipline tempered with love*
tem´pest *n.* a violent wind; violent disturbance

tem·pes´tu·ous *adj.* stormy, turbulent —**tem·pes´tu·ous·ly** *adv.*

tem´plate *n.* a pattern

tem´ple *n.* a place of worship; a structure dedicated to a special purpose: *a temple of learning*

tem´po *n.* relative speed and rhythm

tem´po·ral *adj.* worldly; material as contrasted to spiritual; transitory; of time —**tem´po·ral·ness** *n.*

tem´po·rar·y *adj.* lasting for a time only; not permanent —*n.* a seasonal or substitute employee

tem´po·rize *vi.* act evasively to gain time or defer commitment; give in to a situation, circumstances, etc.; compromise

tempt *vt.* try to persuade; risk provoking: *tempt fate*; influence: *tempted by profit*

temp·ta´tion *n.* that which tempts; the state of being tempted

tempt´ing *adj.* attractive; seductive

tem´pu·ra *n.* vegetables or seafood fried in a light batter

ten´a·ble *adj.* capable of being maintained or defended

te·na´cious *adj.* obstinate or persistent; strongly retentive —**te·nac´i·ty** *n.*

ten´an·cy *n.* the holding of property; the period of possession

ten´ant *n.* one who rents or has title to property belonging to another; an occupant —*vt., vi.*

tend *vi.* have an aptitude or inclination; attend, serve; give attention or care —*vt.* care for; watch over

tend´en·cy *n.* inclination; movement toward an end or result

ten·den´tious, ten·den´cious *adj.* disposed to a particular view

ten´der[1] *adj.* delicate, fragile; youthful: *a tender age*; marked by gentleness and consideration; expressing affection; sensitive

tend´er[2] *vt.* present for acceptance —*n.* an offer; that offered, esp. of money; boat that ferries passengers or supplies; railway car that carries fuel and water; person who tends or ministers

ten´der·foot *n.* a newcomer or beginner —*adj.* inexperienced

ten´der·heart·ed *adj.* responsive to another's troubles; compassionate; sympathetic

ten´der·loin *n.* cut of meat; a district known for crime and corruption

ten·di·ni´tis, ten·do·ni´tis *n.* inflammation of a tendon

ten´don *n.* tough, fibrous tissue that attaches muscle to bone

ten´dril *n.* a delicate, curling extension by which certain plants attach themselves

ten´e·ment *n.* rented rooms; a low–rent run–down building; property held by a renter

ten´et *n.* a principle or doctrine

ten´on *n.* projection for insertion into a mortise to form a joint

ten´or *n.* character or nature; a general course or tendency; male voice higher than a baritone —*adj.* of a voice, singing part, or musical instrument in the upper range

tense *adj.* stretched tight; under mental stress; providing suspense —*vt., vi.* make or become tense —*n.* quality of a verb that denotes time or state of being

ten´sile *adj.* of tension; capable of being stretched

tensile strength resistance of material to force that tends to rupture

ten´sion *n.* a stretching or being stretched; mental strain, anxiety; device on a machine that regulates stress —**ten´sion·al** *adj.*

ten´sor *n.* a muscle that tenses or stretches —**ten·so´ri·al** *adj.*

tent *n.* a portable shelter —*vi.* pitch a tent; camp

ten´ta·cle *n.* a long, flexible appendage for touching, grasping, etc.

ten´ta·tive *adj.* not finalized, subject to change; somewhat uncertain

ten´ter *n.* drying frame for cloth

ten´ter·hook *n.* a pin for holding cloth on a tenter —**be on tenterhooks** be in a state of anxiety

ten´u·ous *adj.* weak, lacking substance, as of evidence; thin: lacking density

ten´ure *n.* right or condition, etc. of holding property, office, etc.

tep´id *adj.* moderately warm; unenthusiastic —**tep´id·ly** *adv.*

te·qui´la *n.* an alcoholic beverage of Mexican origin

te·rat´o·gen *n.* agent that causes malformation in a developing fetus —**te·rat·o·gen´ic** *adj.*

ter´i·ya´ki *n.* a Japanese dish of broiled marinated fish or meat

term *n.* word or expression to name, convey a concept, etc.; conditions of an agreement; a fixed period; a prescribed period —*vt.* to designate

term insurance life insurance active for a specific period

ter´ma·gant *n.* a scolding woman — *adj.* abusive or quarrelsome

ter´mi·na·ble *adj.* that may be terminated —**ter´mi·na·bly** *adv.*

ter´mi·nal *adj.* of an end to action, life, etc.; at or forming an end or limit —*n.* an intermediate or terminating point; an electrical junction; a computer work station

ter´mi·nate *vt., vi.* end; bound or limit —**ter´mi·na·tive** *adj.*

ter·mi·na´tion *n.* ending, outcome, or conclusion; being terminated; a bound or limit

ter´mi·na·tor *n.* one who or that which terminates

ter·mi·nol´o·gy *n.* terms relating to a discipline, such as art, science, etc.

ter´mi·nus *n.* final point or end; a terminal

ter·mi·tar´i·um *n.* a termite nest

ter´mite *n.* an insect resembling the ant, noted for boring into wood

terp´si·cho·re´an *adj.* of dancing

ter´race *n.* a raised level area; a raised street fronting row houses; paved area connected to a house —*vt.* provide with a terrace —**terrace house** (*Brit.*) one of a row of dwellings that share common walls with those adjoining

ter´ra cot´ta clay pottery; a reddish–brown color —**ter´ra–cot´ta** *adj.*

ter´ra fir´ma solid ground

ter·rain´ *n.* land area described by a particular characteristic

ter·rane´ *n.* a series of similar rock formations

ter´ra·pin *n.* a type of tortoise

ter·rar´i·um *n.* a glass enclosure for growing small plants

ter·raz´zo *n.* flooring of stone chips set in mortar

ter·res´tri·al *adj.* belonging to the planet Earth; pertaining to earth; of land as distinct from water

ter´ri·ble *adj.* causing fear or dread; severe or extreme: *a terrible headache*; dreadful: *a terrible meal*

ter´ri·er *n.* a breed of small dogs

ter·rif´ic *adj.* arousing fear or terror; unusually good

ter´ri·fy *vt.* fill with terror

ter·rine´ *n.* a dish for cooking and serving food

ter·ri·to´ri·al *adj.* of a territory; restricted to a particular territory

territorial waters coastal waters under government jurisdiction

ter·ri·to´ri·al·ize *vt.* create or extend a territory

ter´ri·to·ry *n.* a governed domain; a distinctive area: *sales territory*; a region self–governed but lacking the status of a state or province

ter´ror *n.* great fear; that which causes fear; a difficult child

ter´ror·ism *n.* violence to achieve political end —**ter´ror·ist** *n.*

ter´ror·ize *vt.* terrify or intimidate, esp. by acts of violence

ter´ry, ter´ry·cloth *n.* an absorbent pile fabric

terse *adj.* short and to the point

ter´ti·ar·y *adj.* third in importance

test *vt.* subject to examination —*vi.* undergo examination —*n.* an examination; a criterion or standard

tes´ta·ment *n.* a will; statement testifying to some belief; proof

tes´tate *adj.* having a will

tes´ter *n.* one who administers tests; a canopy, as over a bed

tes´ti·cle *n.* one of the two sex glands of the male

tes´ti·fy *vi.* make a solemn declaration; bear witness; serve as evidence

tes·ti·mo´ni·al *n.* an endorsement of character, value, etc.; public acknowledgment

tes´ti·mo·ny *n.* a statement under oath; public acknowledgment; evidence or proof

tes´ty *adj.* irritable —**tes´ti·ness** *n.*

tet´a·nus *n.* an often fatal bacterial disease marked by spasmodic muscular contractions

tête´–à–tête´ *adj.* confidential —*n.* a private conversation

teth´er *n.* line for restraining an animal; limit of power, etc.

te·tral´o·gy *n.* a series of four novels, plays, etc.

text *n.* words of an author or speaker; main body of matter in a book; words of a song, opera, etc.

text´book *n.* a book used as a standard or basis of instruction

tex´tile *n.* a fabric —*adj.* of weaving or woven fabric

tex´tu·al *adj.* of or relating to text

tex´tu·al·ism *n.* strict religious interpretation of a text

tex´ture *n.* characteristic appearance, tactile qualities: *texture of bread*; structure, form, etc. of a work: *tightly–knit texture of his prose*; basic nature

thal´a·mus *n.* matter at the base of the brain involved in sensory transmission

than·a·tol´o·gy *n.* the study of death and dying —**than·a·tol´o·gist** *n.*

thane *n.* in Anglo–Saxon England, one granted land for military service; chief of a Scottish clan

thank *vt.* express gratitude

thank´ful *adj.* feeling or expressing gratitude

thank´less *adj.* unlikely to elicit approval; unappreciated

thanks´giv´ing *n.* giving of thanks; a means of expressing thanks

that *adj.* of something previously mentioned, understood, or pointed out; denoting something remote —*pron.* a thing mentioned, understood, etc.; the thing more remote —*adv.* to the extent required: *I can't see that far* —*conj.*

thatch *n.* a covering of leaves, reeds, etc. made to shed water; material used for such covering —*vt.* cover with a thatch —**thatch´er** *n.*

thaw *vi.* melt; rise in temperature; become less aloof —*vt.* cause to thaw —*n.* warmth of temperature; progression toward sociability

the´a·ter *n.* structure or area for presentation of entertainment, lectures, etc.; legitimate stage; area of action: *theater of war*

the·at´ric, the·at´ri·cal *adj.* pertaining to any aspect of the theater; dramatically compelling; pretentious —**the·at·ri·cal´i·ty** *n.*

the·at´rics *n.* undue dramatization

theft *n.* stealing; that which is stolen

the´ism *n.* belief in a god or gods

theme *n.* main subject or topic of art, speech, etc.; a short essay

the·oc´ra·cy *n.* government by religious authority

the·od´o·lite *n.* a surveying instrument

the·og´o·ny *n.* chronicle of the geneology of gods —**the·o·gon´ic** *adj.*

the·o·lo´gi·an *n.* one trained or engaged in study of religious belief

the·o·log´ic, the·o·log´i·cal *adj.* relating to religious matters

the·ol´o·gy *n.* the study of religion and religious doctrine

the´o·rem *n.* a proposition demonstrably true or considered to be so

the·o·ret´ic, the·o·ret´i·cal *adj.* relating to theory; existing in theory only; disposed to speculation
the´o·rize *vi.* speculate; put forth as a theory —**the´o·rist** *n.*
the´o·ry *n.* conjecture speculation; fundamental or abstract principles; a proposed explanation
the·os´o·phy *n.* religious philosophy based on mystical insight
ther´a·peu´tic *adj.* having curative powers —**ther´a·peu´ti·cal·ly** *adv.*
ther·a·peu´tics *n.* the study of treatment for illness and disease
ther´a·py *n.* treatment of illness and disease; a type of treatment: *physical therapy* —**ther´a·pist** *n.*
there *adv.* in or at that place; yonder; in that respect —*n.* position away from the speaker
there´a·bout, there´a·bouts *adv.* approximately
there´af´ter *adv.* from that time on
there´by´ *adv.* through agency of
there´fore´ *adv., conj.* for that reason; consequently
there·in´ *adv.* in that respect
there·in·af´ter *adv.* in a subsequent part
ther´e·min *n.* an electronic instrument for producing music
there´upon´ *adv.* following or in consequence of
there·with´ *adv.* thereupon
ther´mal, ther´mic *adj.* relating to or caused by heat; warm — *n.* a rising current of warm air
ther·mo·dy·nam´ics *n.* the relationship between heat and other energy sources
ther´mo·gram *n.* the record made by a thermograph
ther´mo·graph *n.* device that records temperature as it is registered
ther·mog´ra·phy *n.* use of heat to produce raised letters on paper; the recording of temperature with a thermograph
ther·mom´e·ter *n.* device for measuring temperature
ther´mo·nu´cle·ar *adj.* fusion of atomic particles by heat
ther·mo·plas´tic *adj.* soft when heated —*n.* a thermoplastic resin
ther´mo·stat *n.* a device to control temperature indoors
ther·mo·trop´ic *adj.* tending to grow toward or move toward heat
the·sau´rus *n.* collection of words with their synonyms; words relating to a specific subject
the´sis *n., pl.* **the´ses** a proposition advanced and defended by argumentation; an unproved premise; a formal treatise
thes´pi·an *adj.* relating to drama —*n.* an actor or actress
they *pron.* persons or things previously mentioned; people in general
thi·am´in, thi·am´ine *n.* vitamin B_1
thick *adj.* relatively large in depth or extent; being a specified dimension; closely packed; viscous; dense; noticeable: *thick accent* —*n.* most dense or intense part: *the thick of battle* —*adv.*
thick´en *vt., vi.* make or become thick or thicker
thick´et *n.* a dense growth
thick´set´ *adj.* short and stocky; closely planted
thick´–skinned´ *adj.* slow to anger; indifferent to insults
thief *n.* one who takes without permission
thieve *vt.* steal —*vi.* be a thief
thiev´er·y *n.* stealing
thigh *n.* part of the leg between the hip and knee
thin *adj.* of little depth or width; lean and slender; lacking density: *thin sauce* —*vt., vi.* make or become thin —*adv.*
thing *n.* a separate entity; circumstance: *things are changed*; an act: *the right thing to do*; an idea or notion: *don't put things in her head*; an unexplainable or mysterious quality or attraction
think *vt.* conceive mentally; determine by reasoning; believe to be true; remember or recall; intend —*vi.* engage in thought; weigh in the mind; have an opinion, feeling, etc.; recall
think´a·ble *adj.* possible; worth considering —**think´a·bly** *adv.*
think´ing *adj.* intellectually active —*n.* result of thought; one's opinion or bias
think tank *n.* a group of scientists, executives, etc., joined to study a particular problem
thin´–skinned´ *adj.* easily offended
third *adj., adv.* next in order after the second; being one of three parts —*n.*
third´–rate´ *adj.* of poor quality
third world underdeveloped nations
thirst *n.* a need for water; any craving: *thirst for glory* —*vi.* have a desire or craving
thirst´y *adj.* lacking moisture; parched; eagerly desirous
this *adj.* that near or present, understood, or just mentioned —*pron.* a person or thing near or present, etc. —*adv.*
thong *n.* a narrow strip, as for fastening; a lash of a whip; type of sandal; type of beach wear
tho·rac´ic *adj.* relating to the thorax
tho´rax *n.* the body between the neck and abdomen, enclosed by ribs; middle segment of an insect
thorn *n.* a sharp outgrowth; a source of discomfort
thorn´y *adj.* full of thorns; difficult or perplexing —**thorn´i·ness** *n.*
thor´ough *adj.* attentive to detail; complete, exhaustive —**thor´ough·ness** *n.*
thor´ough·bred *adj.* bred from pure stock; possessing excellence —*n.* horse bred for racing
thor´ough·fare (*US*) *n.* main road
thor´ough·go·ing *adj.* characterized by thoroughness
though *conj.* notwithstanding; even if; and yet —*adv.*
thought *n.* process or product of thinking; concepts identified with a time, place, discipline, etc.: *modern political thought*; consideration or attention; preoccupation
thought´ful *adj.* contemplative, reflective; attentive or considerate; preoccupied —**thought´ful·ness** *n.*
thought´less *adj.* marked by lack of care or regard; inconsiderate; flighty —**thought´less·ness** *n.*
thrall *n.* one held in bondage
thrash *vt.* to thresh grain; beat; defeat utterly —*vi.* move about violently
thread *n.* slender cord or line; filament; that runs through: *the thread of a plot* —*vt., vi.*
thread´bare *adj.* worn; commonplace
threat *n.* declaration of intent to harm; danger
threat´en *vt., vi.* utter threats; appear menacing —**threat´en·ing** *adj.*
thresh *vt.* beat to separate grain from husks —*vi.* thrash about
thresh´old *n.* a doorsill; an entering point or beginning
thrift *n.* care in the management of resources —**thrift´y** *adj.*
thrift´shop shop for used goods
thrill *vi., vt.* feel excitement —*n.* a feeling of excitement
thrill´er *n.* an exciting story
thrive *vi.* be succesful; prosper; flourish —**thriv´ing·ly** *adv.*
throat *n.* front part of the neck; passage at the back of the mouth; any narrow passage
throat´y *adj.* guttural or husky
throb *vi.* pulsate rhythmically; show emotion by trembling —*n.* pulsation —**throb´bing·ly** *adv.*
throe *n.* violent pain, as in death or childbirth
throm·bo´sis *n.* formation of a blood clot, as in the heart or an artery
throm´bus *n.* a clot
throne *n.* authority of a ruler; a seat symbolizing authority
throng *n.* a closely packed group —*vi., vt.* gather or crowd together
throt´tle *n* a valve controlled flow —*vt.* choke or strangle; silence or suppress; change speed by means of a throttle
through *prep.* from end to end, side to side, etc.; permeating; by way of —*adv.*
through·out´ *adv.* in every part —*prep.* all through
throw *vt.* hurl; place carelessly; direct or project —*vi.* cast or fling —*n.* casting or flinging; distance flung; a scarf or light covering
thrust *vt.* push or shove with force; pierce —*vi.* make a sudden push; force oneself through —*n.* sudden forceful push; vigorous attack; force that drives or propels; a salient force: *the thrust of his remarks*
thud *n.* a dull, heavy sound; a blow or fall —*vi.*
thug *n.* hoodlum or ruffian; formerly, a professional assassin
thumb *n.* a digit of the human hand; similar part on animals
thumb index indentations along the edge of a book to indicate sections
thumb´screw *n.* a screw turned with the fingers; instrument of torture
thumb´tack *n.* a broad–headed tack
thump *n.* a blow with a blunt object; the sound of a blow —*vt., vi.* beat or strike
thun´der *n.* sound accompanying lightning; a similar noise —*vi., vt.* make a noise like thunder
thun´der·bolt *n.* lightning attended by thunder; a forceful person
thun´der·clap *n.* the sound of thunder
thun´der·cloud *n.* a large, dark cloud
thun´der·ous *adj.* of a loud sound
thun´der·show·er *n.* rain accompanied by thunder and lightning
thun´der·storm *n.* heavy blowing rain accompanied by thunder
thun´der·strick·en, thun´der·struck *adj.* astonished
thwart *vt.* frustrate or foil; extend across —*n.* seat or brace extending across a small boat or canoe —*adj.* extending or passing across
thyme *n.* plant of the mint family; leaves of the plant, used for seasoning
thy´mus *n.* a ductless glandlike structure at the base of the neck
thy´roid *n.* cartilage of the larynx which form the Adam's apple; a large, ductless gland located near the larynx —*adj.*
ti·ar´a *n.* jeweled head ornament
tib´ia *n.* larger of two leg bones extending below the knee; the shinbone —**tib´i·al** *adj.*
tic *n.* involuntary muscular spasm
tick´et *n.* thing showing entitlement to transportation, a show, etc.; a tag or label; candidates on a ballot; a court summons —*vt.* attach a label; furnish with a ticket
tick´le *vt.* cause to laugh by touching; amuse or entertain —*vi.* have or cause a tingling sensation —*n.*
tick´ler *n.* a file, note, etc. that serves as reminder
tick´lish *adj.* responsive to tickling; easily offended; requiring tact
tid´al *adj.* pertaining to or influenced by tides; dependent on tides
tidal wave a great incoming rise of water; a surge, as of public opinion
tid´bit *n.* a delicacy
tide *n.* periodic rise and fall of the ocean's water
tide´land *n.* land periodically covered by a rising tide
tide´wa·ter *n.* water near a coast affected by the tides
ti´dings *n.* news
ti´dy *adj.* neat and orderly —*vt., vi.* put in order —**ti´di·ness** *n.*
tie *vt.* make a knot; fasten or join; equal another —*vi.* make a connection; make the same score —*n.* fastener; a bond or connection; (*US*) timber that supports tracks

tier *n.* one arranged above another
tiff *n.* a spat; a small argument —*vi.* take part in a spat
ti´ger *n.* a large striped carnivorous feline; a fiercely determined person
ti´ger–eye *n.* yellow and brown semiprecious stone
tight *adj.* firmly fixed or secure; fully stretched; difficult or demanding; closely fitted; scarce; stingy; intoxicated —*adv.* securely
tight´en *vt., vi.* to make tight or tighter
tight´–fist´ed *adj.* stingy
tight´–lipped *adj.* uncommunicative; secretive
tights *n.* close–fitting garment, worn by dancers, gymnasts, etc.
tight´wad *n.* a miser
til´de *n.* diacritical mark (~) used to indicate a change in pronunciation
tile *n.* a thin ornamental piece for covering roofs, floors, walls, etc. —*vt.* cover with tiles
till *vt., vi.* work soil for cultivation —*n.* a money drawer; available cash
till´age *n.* cultivation of land
tilt *vi., vt.* incline at an angle
tim´bal *n.* a kettledrum
tim´bale *n.* baked custard with cheese, fish, etc.
tim´ber *n.* (*Brit.*) wood dressed for use in construction; standing trees
tim´ber·land *n.* land covered with trees
tim´ber·line *n.* an imaginary line beyond which trees do not grow, as on a mountainside
tim´bre *n.* quality of a sound
time *n.* the concept of continuous existence; a moment or period; system for measuring duration; musical tempo —*adj.* relating to time; payable in the future —*vt.* record speed or duration; mark rhythm
time´–hon´ored *adj.* accepted as customary or traditional
time´less *adj.* eternal; not limited to a specific time —**time´less·ness** *n.*
time´ly *adj.* occurring at a proper or convenient time —**time´li·ness** *n.*
time´ous *adj.* timely
time´–shar·ing *n.* access to a central computer; use of vacation property by several owners
time´ta·ble *n.* schedule; plan for completion of parts of a project
time´worn *adj.* ineffective by time or overuse, as a motto or maxim
tim´id *adj.* fearful; lacking self–confidence —**ti·mid´i·ty** *n.*
tim´ing *n.* regulating occurance to insure maximum effect
tim´o·rous *adj.* fearul; anxious
tim´o·thy *n.* a perennial grass
tim´pa·ni *n.* kettledrums
tin *n.* metallic element used as a coating or making alloys
tinc´ture *n.* a medicinal solution; coloring substance; slight trace
tin´der *n.* dry substance that ignites easily —**tin´der·y** *adj.*
tin´der·box *n.* container of material for starting a fire; highly flammable material; an excitable person
tine *n.* a prong, as on a fork
tinge *n.* a faint trace, as of color —*vt.* to tint or color lightly
tin´gle *vi., vt.* experience a prickly, stinging sensation —*n.* a stinging sensation —**tin´gly** *adv.*
tin´kle *vi., vt.* produce light metallic sounds, as of a bell
tin·ni´tus *n.* a ringing or buzzing in the ears
tin´ny *adj.* of or containing tin; flimsy; of a flat sound
tin´sel *n.* thin glittering bits of ornamentation; something showy, but of little value —*adj.* decorated with tinsel; gaudy or showy —*vt.* hang with tinsel —**tin´sel·ry** *n.*
tin´smith *n.* one who works with tin
tint *n.* a pale color; shading or gradation of color —*vt.* apply color
tin·tin·nab·u·la´tion *n.* ringing of bells
ti´ny *adj.* very small
tip *n.* a light tap; gift of money for service; a helpful hint; confidential information; an extremity; an end or cap —*vt.* lean; overturn; strike lightly; adorn the tip of —*vi.* become tilted; overturn
tip´off *n.* a warning
tip´ple *vt., vi.* drink frequently and habitually
tip´sy *adj.* unsteady; intoxicated
ti·rade´ *n.* a prolonged denunciation
tire *vt.* reduce the strength of by exertion; make weary or impatient —*vi.* become weary; lose patience —*n.* (*US*) covering for a wheel
tired *adj.* weary; fatigued
tire´less *adj.* not easily fatigued; energetic
tire´some *adj.* tedious or boring; mundane
tis´sue *n.* an aggregate of organic cells and associated matter; a light fabric; light disposable paper
tissue culture tissue kept alive and growing in a culture medium
tissue paper thin wrapping paper
ti´tan *n.* a giant
tithe *n.* one tenth; contribution for support of the clergy and church; a tax or levy —*vt.* pay a tithe
tit´il·late *vt.* cause a tickling sensation; stimulate or excite erotically
ti´tle *n.* a descriptive name; name of a book, song, etc.; a designation of rank, profession, etc.; legal right to property —*vt.* give a name or designation; entitle to
ti´tled *adj.* having a title
tit´ter *n.* a suppressed laugh
tit´tle *n.* the tiniest amount
tit´u·lar *adj.* existing in name only
tiz´zy *n.* a bewildered state of mind
toad *n.* a jumping amphibian resembling a frog; a loathsome person
toad´y *adj.* an obsequious flatterer; one acting without scruples to gain favor —*vt., vi.* to flatter or serve without question —**toad´y·ism** *n.*
toast *vt., vi.* make warm or browned; drink to one's health —*n.* a tribute followed by a drink; one well–known and greatly admired
toast´mas·ter *n.* host at a public banquet
toast´y *adj.* comfortably warm
to·bog´gan *n.* a sledlike vehicle for traveling over snow or ice —*vi.* ride on a toboggan
tod´dle *vi.* walk unsteadily —*n.* a shaky walk
tod´dy *n.* spirits mixed with hot water, spices, and sugar
toe *n.* a digit of the foot
to´fu *n.* a cheese–like food made from soybeans
to´ga *n.* a loose flowing robe
to·geth´er *adv.* in the company of others; collectively, as one unit
tog´ger·y *n.* clothing
toil *n.* strenuous labor —*vi.* work hard —*vt.* accomplish with great effort —**toil´er** *n.*
toi´let *n.* a bathroom fixture; the process of grooming —*adj.* used in grooming: *toilet articles*
toi´let·ry *n.* soap, cologne, etc. for personal grooming
toil´some *adj.* involving hard work; difficult
to´ken *n.* tangible evidence of affection, authority, etc.; a metal piece issued in place of currency —*adj.* nominal or minimal; partial
to´ken·ism *n.* attempting to fulfill an obligation with a symbolic gesture
tol´er·a·ble *adj.* endurable; barely satisfactory —**tol´er·a·bly** *adv.*
tol´er·ance *n.* freedom from prejudice; ability to bear hardship; allowance for variation
tol´er·ant *adj.* long–suffering; indulgent
tol´er·ate *vt.* allow or concede; bear
toll *n.* charge for passage; sound of a bell rung slowly and regularly —*vi., vt.* take or exact a charge; to sound, as a bell
tomb *n.* a burial place —*vt.* entomb or bury
tomb´stone *n.* marker on a grave
tome *n.* a large heavy book
tom·fool´er·y *adj.* nonsensical behavior; foolishness
to·mor´row *n.* the day after today
to´nal *adj.* pertaining to tone or tonality —**to´nal·ly** *adv.*
to·nal´i·ty *n.* a system or scheme of tones, as in music or art
tone *n.* musical sound or its quality; characteristic tendency or quality: mode of writing or speech; style or elegance; effect of light and color —*vt.* impart a desired sound or color
tongue *n.* muscular organ of the mouth; manner of speaking; language or dialect; anything resembling a tongue
ton´ic *n.* that promoting health or well–being; quinine water —*adj.* of tone; stimulating or refreshing
ton´sil *n.* either of two lymphoid masses located in the opening between the mouth and larynx
ton·sil·lec´to·my *n.* surgical removal of the tonsils
ton·sil·li´tis *n.* inflammation of the tonsils
ton·so´ri·al *adj.* of a barber or barbering
ton´sure *n.* shaving of the head —*vt.*
ton´tine *n.* agreement by which an investment held in trust reverts to a survivor
too *adv.* also; excessive; extremely
tool *n.* an implement used to accomplish: *books are tools of learning*; one used for the designs of another —*vt.* form or shape with a tool; to scribe a motif or design
tool´mak·er *n.* a machinist who makes or repairs tools
tooth *n.* hard structure for seizing and chewing food; small projection on a saw, gear, etc.; rough surface; appetite or taste
tooth´ache *n.* pain in a tooth
tooth´less *adj.* lacking teeth; lacking effectiveness —**tooth´less·ly** *adv.*
tooth´some *adj.* pleasant tasting
top *n.* uppermost part; upper surface; a lid; highest degree; the best —*adj.* relating to the top; most important, best —*vt.* remove the uppermost part; provide a top; surmount or surpass
top´coat *n.* a light overcoat
top´–heavy *adj.* unstable due to excess weight at the top; of an organization with an overly large executive staff
to´pi·ar·y *n.* bushes or trees formed in decorative shapes —*adj.* pertaining to the art of topiary
top´ic *n.* subject matter, as for a speech
top´i·cal *adj.* relating to matters of local or current interest; pertaining to a topic
top´knot *n.* a tuft, knot of hair, etc.; an ornament worn as a headdress
top´less *adj.* lacking a top; nude above the waist
top´–lev´el *adj.* of the highest rank or importance
to·pog´ra·phy *n.* physical features of a region; topographic surveying
top´o·nym *n.* a place name —**top·o·nym´ic** *adj.*
to·pon´y·my *n.* study of place names
top´ple *vi.* to fall —*vt.* cause to fall; to overthrow
top´soil *n.* surface soil of land
top´sy–tur´vy *adj., adv.* upside down; in utter disarray —*n.* a state of disorder
tor *n.* a rocky peak
torch *n.* a flaming stick or rod; anything that brightens; a device producing an intense flame
torch´bear·er *n.* one who carries a torch; one who conveys truth or knowledge; leader of a cause
to´re·a·dor *n.* a bullfighter
tor´ment *n.* intense pain or anguish, or its source —**tor·ment´** *vt.* torture; harass

tor·na´do *n.* a whirling wind of exceptional force
tor´pid *adj.* dormant; sluggish; apathetic —**tor´pid·ness** *n.*
tor´por *n.* loss of sensibility or power of motion; apathy, listlessness
torque *n.* turning or twisting force; measure of tendency to rotation
tor´rent *n.* rapid, turbulent stream; a violent flow: *torrent of abuse*
tor´rid *adj.* intensely hot and dry; extremely passionate — **tor´rid·ness** *n.*
tor´so *n.* the trunk of the human body
tort *n.* a civil wrong not involving breach of contract —**tor´tious** *adj.*
tor´te *n.* a rich cake
tor·tel·li´ni *n.* ring-shaped pasta stuffed with cheese, spinach, etc.
tor·ti´lla *n.* a small, flat bread made of corn meal and baked on a skillet
tor´toise *n.* a land turtle
tor´tu·ous *adj.* twisting, as a road; devious: *tortuous logic*
tor´ture *n.* intense suffering; something that causes pain — *vi.* to inflict pain upon; cause to suffer
tor´tur·ous *adj.* pertaining to torture
toss *vt.* throw or cast; pitch or fling about; interject casually; turn over and mix —*vi.* be thrown about; roll about restlessly, as in sleep —*n.* a throw; a quick movement
toss´pot *n.* a drunkard
to´tal *n.* entire amount —*adj.* complete —*vt.* ascertain the amount
to·tal´i·tar´i·an *adj.* of an oppressive government with absolute power
to·tal´i·ty *n.* total amount; the state of being whole
tote *vt.* to carry —*n.* something carried —**tot´a·ble** *adj.*
to´tem *n.* an object or representation that serves as emblem for a group, tribe, etc.
tot´ter *vi.* tremble or waver; seem near to collapse; to walk unsteadily —*n.* an unsteady or wobbly walk
tou´can *n.* a tropical bird with colorful plumage and a large beak
touch *vt.* perceive by feel; be or come into contact with; to affect; impress emotionally —*vi.* come into contact —*n.* contact; sensation conveyed by contact; a distinctive manner or style: *master's touch*; a trace —**touch on** concern or relate to —**touch up** correct or correction
touched *adj.* effected emotionally; mentally unbalanced; peculiar or eccentric
touch´ing *adj.* appealing to emotion —*prep.* with regard to; concerning
touch´y *adj.* apt to take offense; liable to cause offense or contention
tough *adj.* able to bear stress or strain; difficult to chew; requiring intense effort; severe or harsh; unyielding —*n.* a rowdy
tough´en *vt., vi.* make or become tough or tougher —**tough´en·er** *n.*
tough´-mind´ed *adj.* facing difficulty with resolve; unsentimental
tou·pee´ *n.* a small wig
tour *n.* a journey or excursion; fixed period of service —*vt., vt.* to go on a trip; take a show on the road
tour´ist *n.* one traveling for pleasure —*adj.* suitable for recreational travelers —**tour´ist·y** *adj.*
tour´na·ment *n.* a series of competitive events
tour´ni·quet *n.* a tight bandage used to control severe external bleeding
tou´sle *vt.* to dishevel —*n.* mussed hair
tout *vt.* solicit; praise highly; sell information —*vi.* solicit customers, patronage, etc.; sell information —*n.* one who sells information
tow *vt.* pull or drag —*n.* something towed —**in tow** drawn or brought along
to´ward *prep.* in the direction of; for the purpose of; near, approaching
tow´el *n.* material for wiping or polishing
tow´el·ing *n.* material for making towels
tow´er *n.* a tall structure; a place of security —*vi.* to extend to great height
tow´er·ing *adj.* very tall; very great
town (*US*) *n.* an incorporated area larger than a village and smaller than a city; a city; inhabitants or government of a town —*adj.* of a town or its population
town house (*US*) a house sharing a common wall with those adjoining
tow´path *n.* a road along a waterway, used by men, animals, or machines towing boats
tox·e´mi·a *n.* the presence of toxins in the blood
tox´ic *adj.* tending to be poisonous; caused by poison or a toxin —**tox·ic´i·ty** *n.*
tox´i·cant *n.* a poison —*adj.* poisonous
tox·i·col´o·gy *n.* the study of poisons —**tox·i·col´o·gist** *n.*
tox´in *n.* a poisonous substance
toy *n.* that serving as a plaything; something trifling or ineffectual —*vi.* consider: *toy with an idea*; use for one's amusement —*adj.* designed as or resembling a toy
trace *n.* a vestige or mark; a barely detectable quality, characteristic, etc. —*vt.* find by investigation; copy onto an overlay —*vi.* follow a track, course of development, etc.
trac´er·y *n.* delicate ornamentation
tra´chea *n.* the windpipe; an air passage —**tra´che·al** *adj.*
tra·che·ot´o·my, **tra·che·os´to·my** *n.* surgical incision of the trachea
tra·cho´ma *n.* a contagious viral disease of the eye
track *n.* mark left by passage; a path beaten down by use; a trail or roadway; a following or tracing; a continuous belt on which some vehicles ride; metal rails —*vt.* follow the course of; trail; make tracks —*vi.* leave tracks; be in agreement: *on the same track*
track record a history of achievement
tract *n.* an extended area; a short discourse or pamphlet
trac´ta·ble *adj.* easily led; malleable
trac´tion *n.* the act of pulling; pulling power; rolling friction, as of tires on the road
trac´tor *n.* a farm machine; a motor vehicle used to haul a trailer of freight
trade *n.* a business or craft; those engaged in a particular business; buying, selling, or exchange; customers —*vt.* give in exchange; barter —*vi.* engage in commerce
trade´mark *n.* that used to distinguish a product; a distinctive mark or feature —*vt.* to legally protect
tra·di´tion *n.* a body of knowledge transmitted through generations
tra·di´tion·al·ism *n.* strict adherence to tradition —**tra·di´tion·al·ist** *n.*
tra·duce´ *vt.* to willfully harm through misrepresentation; to defame or slander —**tra·duc´er** *n.*
traf´fic *n.* passage of people, messages, etc.; those moving; business of buying and selling; transit
tra·ge´di·an *n.* a dramatic actor or writer
trag´e·dy *n.* a drama which ends unhappily; a calamitous incident
trag´ic *adj.* of the nature of a tragedy; causing suffering
trag·i·com´e·dy *n.* a drama having characteristics of both comedy and tragedy; an incident of this nature
trail *vt.* draw lightly over a surface; follow the track of; follow behind —*vi.* to hang or extend loosely; grow along the ground; lag behind —*n.* traces left by passage; something that follows; (*US*) a worn path, as through a wilderness area
trail´blaz·er *n.* one who breaks a new trail; an innovator or pioneer
trail´er (*US*) *n.* drawn vehicle
train *n.* a series of rail cars; a thing drawn along or following behind; a connected set —*vt.* make skillful or proficient; teach; to point —*vi.* undergo a course of instruction
train´er *n.* one who coaches; a device to improve physical fitness or skill; (*Brit.*) a flexible sports shoe
train´ing *n.* systematic instruction
traipse *vi.* walk or wander about
trait *n.* distinguishing quality
trai´tor *n.* one who betrays a trust; a person found guilty of treason
trai´tor·ous *adj.* constituting treason; characteristic of a traitor
tra·jec´to·ry *n.* the path described by a body moving through space
tramp *vi., vt.* to wander; walk heavily —*n.* one who lives by odd jobs or charity; a long walk; a heavy tread
tram´ple *vi., vt.* tread heavily; injure or crush by treading
trance *n.* a dreamlike state as induced by hypnosis, etc.; profound concentration — **trance´like** *adj.*
tran´quil *adj.* calm; peaceful — **tran´quil´ness** *n.*
tran´quil·ize *vt., vi.* to make tranquil
tran´quil·iz·er *n.* a drug that calms without impairing consciousness
tran·quil´li·ty *n.* the state of being tranquil
trans·act´ *vt.* to accomplish —*vi.* to conduct business —**trans·ac´tion** *n.*
tran·scend´ *vt.* go beyond limits; rise above —*vi.* excel
tran·scen·den´tal *adj.* beyond ordinary limits; supernatural; pertaining to transcendentalism
tran·scen·den´tal·ism *n.* belief that one can attain knowledge that surpasses sensory phenomena
tran·scribe´ *vt.* copy or record
tran´script *n.* a copy; a thing recorded, as from notes
tran·sect´ *vt.* to divide by cutting across —**tran·sec´tion** *n.*
trans´fer, **trans·fer´** *vt.* convey from one person or place to another —**trans´fer** *n.* that conveyed; assignment of title or property
trans·fig·u·ra´tion *n.* a change in appearance
trans·fig´ure *vt.* change appearance of; make splendid
trans·fix´ *vt.* pierce through; impale; render motionless
trans·form´ *vt.* change form or appearance of; change the nature or character of
trans·fuse´ *vt.* cause to flow from one to another; pass into, permeate —**trans·fu´sion** *n.*
trans·gress´ *vt.* to overstep the bounds of propriety or good taste —*vi.* break a law; sin — **trans·gres´sion** *n.*
tran´sient *adj.* not permanent; transitory; residing temporarily —*n.* a temporary resident; a visitor; a vagrant or tramp — **tran´sience** *n.*
tran´sit *n.* passing over or through; a change; carrying across; transportation; a surveying instrument
tran·si´tion *n.* passage from one place, condition, etc. to another
tran´si·to·ry *adj.* existing briefly; ephemeral
trans·late´ *vt.* convert to another language; explain in other words
trans·lu´cent *adj.* allowing the passage of light, but not transparent
trans·mi´grate *vi.* to move from one place to another; to pass

into another body, as of the soul at death
trans·mis´si·ble *adj.* able to be transmitted
trans·mit´ *vt.* to send or pass from one to another; serve as a medium of passage —**trans·mis´sion** *n.*
trans·mog´ri·fy *vt.* to transform radically; make into something different
tran´som *n.* a horizontal piece over an opening: a lintel; a small window over a door
trans·par´en·cy *n.* the quality of being transparent; a section of photographic film
trans·par´ent *adj.* that can be seen through; easy to understand; obvious —**trans·par´ent·ness** *n.*
trans·plant´ *vt.* uproot and replant; move for resettlement; implant living tissue —*n.* that which is relocated —**trans·plant·ta´tion** *n.*
trans·port´ *vt.* to carry or convey; to seize by emotion —**trans´port** *n.* a means or system of conveyance; a state of emotional bliss
trans·por·ta´tion *n.* a means of transport or travel; conveyance of passengers or freight
trans·pose´ *vt.* reverse
trans·sex´u·al *n.* one identifying with the opposite sex
tran·sub·stan´ti·ate *vt.* to transform from one substance into another
trans·verse´ *adj.* lying across —*n.* a thing that lies across, from side to side, as a beam
trans·ves´tite *n.* a person who wears the clothing of the opposite sex
trap *n.* a device for catching; a plan for catching one unawares; a device that prevents a return flow —*vt.* to catch —*vi.* to set traps for game
tra·peze´ *n.* a suspended bar for exercise or acrobatics
trap´e·zoid *n.* a four–sided plane figure with only two parallel sides
trap´pings *n.* adornment or ornamentation; goods or privilege: *the trappings of wealth*
trash *n.* (*US*) waste material; foolish talk; anything that is worthless
trat·to·ri´a *n.* an Italian restaurant
trau´ma *n.* a physical or emotional injury; a shock —**trau·mat´ic** *adj.*
travail´ *n.* pain or anguish; labor associated with childbirth —*vi.* to suffer the pangs of childbirth; to toil
trav´el *vi.* to make a journey; proceed; to go from place to place —*vt.* to move or journey across or through —*n.* passage to or over a certain place; a distance moved
trav´eled *adj.* having made many journeys; frequented by travelers
trav´el·og, trav´el·ogue *n.* a film or illustrated lecture on travel
tra·verse´ *vt.* to pass over, across, or through —*vi.* to move across; to move back and forth —**trav´erse** *n.* a crosspiece; a screen or barrier—*adj.* lying across
trav´es·ty *n.* an absurd rendering, as if in mockery —*vt.* to parody
trawl *n.* a large fishing net; an anchored line from which many lines are strung —*vi.* to fish with a trawl —*vt.* drag to catch fish —**trawl´er** *n.*
treach´er·ous *adj.* likely to betray; potentially dangerous or unreliable
treach´er·y *n.* violation of confidence; treason
trea´cle *n.* molasses; overly sentimental speech —**trea´cly** *adj.*
tread *vt.* to step or walk; trample; to oppress —*vi.* to walk; press beneath the feet —*n.* the act or sound of treading or trampling; the part of a wheel that contacts the surface; an impression made by a tire, foot, etc.; a step
trea´dle *n.* a foot–operated lever —*vi.*
tread´mill *n.* mechanism rotated by a walking animal; a monotonous routine
trea´son *n.* betrayal; a breech of faith —**trea´son·ous** *adj.*
trea´son·a·ble *adj.* involving betrayal
trea´sure *n.* accumulated riches; something precious —*vt.* set a high value on
trea´sur·er *n.* one responible for funds of an organization
trea´sure–trove *n.* a hidden treasure; a rich or rewarding discovery
trea´sur·y *n.* a department of finance; place where funds are received and disbursed
treat *vt., vi.* look upon or regard; to provide medical attention; deal with; to buy for another —**treat´er** *n.*
treat´a·ble *adj.* responsive to treatment
trea´tise *n.* a formal critique
treat´ment *n.* an act, manner, or process; measures designed to heal or alleviate
trea´ty *n.* a formal agreement
treb´u·chet *n.* a medieval catapult
tree *n.* a woody perennial; something resembling a tree —*vt.* force to take refuge; to corner or trap
trek *vi.* move along slowly or with effort; to journey —*n.* an arduous journey
trel´lis *n.* a lattice used to support plants, etc.
trem´ble *vi.* shake involuntarily; to vibrate —*n.* a perceptible shaking
tre·men´dous *adj.* extraordinarily large; awe–inspiring; marvelous
trem´or *n.* a sudden shaking or vibration; agitation or excitement
trem´u·lous *adj.* characterized by trembling; showing timidity
trench *n.* long, narrow ditch; a deep section, as on the ocean floor —*vt., vi.* dig a ditch
tren´chant *adj.* clear and effective; cutting or caustic
trench´er·man *n.* a hearty eater
trend *n.* prevailing tendency; a probable course; popular preference —*vi.* follow a general course; exhibit a tendency
trend´y *adj.* of the latest style; fashionable; inclined to current fashion
trep´id *adj.* timid; timorous; trembling —**trep´id·ly** *adv.*
trep·i·da´tion *n.* agitation from fear or apprehension
tres´pass *vt.* violate the rights of another; go beyond the bounds of what is right or proper —*n.* transgression of law or moral duty; an intrusion —**tres´pass·er** *n.*
tress *n.* a lock of hair
tres´tle *n.* the framework for a table, platform, etc.; a framework bridge
tri´ad *n.* a group of three
tri·age´ *n.* allocation of a scarce commodity; selection for medical treatment based on immediacy and prospect for survival
tri´al *n.* examination in a court; the process of testing; hardship —*adj.*
tri´an·gle *n.* a three–sided figure; something involving three persons, positions, etc.
tri·an·gu·la´tion *n.* a method of positioning using trigonometry
tri·ath´lon *n.* an ahtletic contest comprising three events
tribe *n.* people united by common ancestry, language, or culture —**trib´al** *adj.*
trib·u·la´tion *n.* distress or suffering; cause for distress
tri·bu´nal *n.* a judicial body; a seat for magistrates, etc.
trib´u·tar·y *adj.* flowing into a larger body; owing tribute
trib´ute *n.* that paid for peace or protection; any obligatory payment
tri·chi´na *n.* a roundworm which carries trichinosis
trich·i·no´sis *n.* an affliction caused by eating undercooked meat
trick *n.* a deception or practical joke; a malicious act; a peculiar trait or skill —*vt., vi.* to practice deceit
trick´le *vi., vt.* flow or cause to flow in a thin stream —*n.* a thin stream
trick´y *adj.* deceitful; requiring dexterity or skill
tri´dent *n.* a three–pronged spear
tried *adj.* tested; freed of impurities
tri·en´nial *adj.* every third year; lasting three years
tri´fle *vi.* treat as of no value or importance; toy with —*vt.* spend idly and purposelessly —*n.* a thing of little value or importance; a small amount
tri´fling *adj.* frivolous; insignificant
tri·fo´li·ate *adj.* having three leaves
tri·fur´cate, tri·fur´cat·ed *adj.* having three forks or branches
trig·o·nom´e·try *n.* science of the relationships between the sides and angles of a triangle
tri·lat´er·al *adj.* having three sides
trill *vt.* sing or play in a quavering tone —*n.* successive quavering tones; a warble
tril´o·gy *n.* a dramatic or literary work in three parts
trim *vt.* to remove by cutting; to ornament; to smooth or make neat —*n.* good physical condition; molding or ornamentation
tri·mes´ter *n.* a three–month period
trin´ket *n.* a small ornament; a trifle
tri´o *n.* a group of three
trip *n.* a journey; a misstep; a nimble step; a blunder —*vi., vt.* stumble or cause to stumble; move quickly and lightly; make an error
tri´ple *vt., vi.* make or become three times as many or as large
trip´let *n.* any of three children from one birth
trip´li·cate *n.* one of three —*vt.* make a set of three
tri´pod *n.* three–legged stand
trip´tych *n.* a work of art on three adjacent panels
tri´reme *n.* ancient warship with three banks of oars
tri·sect´ *vt.* divide into three parts
trite *adj.* commonplace or hackneyed —**trite´ness** *n.*
trit´u·rate *vt.* reduce to a powder; to pulverize —*n.* a powdered pharmaceutical —**trit·u·ra´tion** *n.*
tri´umph *vi.* win a victory; be successful —*n.* an important success
tri·um´phant *adj.* victorious; exultant in victory
tri·um´vi·rate *n.* a coalition of three
triv´et *n.* a three–legged stand for holding a cooking vessel
triv´ia *n.* insignificant matters
triv´i·al *adj.* of little importance; insignificant
triv´i·al·ize *vt.* regard as unimportant; make trivial
tro´che *n.* a medicated lozenge
trog´lo·dyte *n.* a prehistoric man; a person considered to be primitive
troop *n.* a gathering; a flock or herd; a unit of cavalry —*vi.* move as a group
trope *n.* a figure of speech
tro´phy *n.* proof of victory
trot *n.* a slow running gait —*vi., vt.* go at a slow run
trou´ba·dour *n.* a wandering minstrel
trou´ble *n.* distress or worry; that which causes difficulty, a difficult situation; disease or ailment; effort; general unrest —*vt.* distress or worry; to inconvenience or annoy; to cause physical pain or discomfort —*vi.* take pains
trou´ble·mak·er *n.* one who habitually causes distress
trou´ble·shoot·er *n.* one assigned to resolve problems, mediate disputes, etc.
trou´ble·some *adj.* difficult or trying; of a source of difficulty
trough *n.* a food or water container for animals; a long, narrow depression, as between waves
trounce *vt.* to beat or thrash severely
troupe *n.* a company of performers —*vi.* a group of traveling performers

trous´seau *n.* clothing and linens assembled by a bride
trove *n.* a collection of valuable items
trow´el *n.* an implement for digging, applying, smoothing, etc. —*vt.* to dig or smooth with a trowel
tru´ant *n.* one absent without permission; one who shirks a responsibility —*adj.* a juvenile offender; a loafer —*vi.* to shirk responsibility
truce *n.* agreement to suspend hostilities; a respite
truck *n.* (*US*) a vehicle for transporting heavy loads —*vi.* carry goods; drive a truck
truck´ing (*US*) *n.* the business of operating trucks
truck´le *vi., vt.* yield or submit weakly; to move or cause to move on rollers or casters —*n.* a small wheel
truc´u·lent *adj.* savage; inclined to ferocity —**truc´u·lence** *n.*
trudge *vi.* to walk wearily or laboriously —*n.* tiresome or difficult walk
true *adj.* real or genuine; faithful or dependable to friends, promises, etc. —*vt.* to bring into conformity with a standard —*adv.* in truth, truly; within tolerance
truf´fle *n.* an edible fungus, similar to a mushroom; a chocolate confection
tru´ly *adv.* conforming to fact; with accuracy; with loyalty
trump *n.* a card or suit of the highest rank; a hidden advantage —*vt.* take with a trump card; to surpass or beat; to outdo or outmaneuver —*vi.* play a trump —**trump up** invent for fraudulent purposes
trump´er·y *n.* worthless finery; nonsense
trum´pet *n.* brass wind instrument; resembling the flaring bell of a trumpet; a loud penetrating sound —*vt.* sound or publish abroad —*vi.* play a trumpet; sound forth
trun´cate *vt.* to cut the top from —*adj.* ending abruptly
trun´cheon *n.* a short, thick stick or club; a mark of office or authority; (*Brit.*) a policeman's nightstick —*vt.* beat; cudgel
trunk *n.* the main stem of a tree; the central part of the body; a passage for blood, transportation, communication, etc.; a large container
truss *n.* supporting framework, as for a roof or bridge —*vt.* to support or brace; bind
trust *n.* reliance on the integrity of another; that committed to one's care; confident expectation; an affiliation to control output, prices, etc. —*vt.* rely on; to commit to the care of another; expect or believe —*vi.* to place confidence in —*adj.* held in trust
trust·ee´ *n.* a person entrusted with the property or affairs of another
trust´ful *adj.* inclined to believe; showing trust
trust fund assets held in trust
trust´ing *adj.* showing trust —**trust´ing·ly** *adv.*
trust´wor·thy *adj.* deserving of confidence; reliable
trust´y *adj.* faithful to duty
truth *n.* conformity to fact; that which is true
truth´ful *adj.* conforming to fact; telling the truth
try *vt.* attempt; experiment with; subject to a test; subject to stress; extract by rendering —*vi.* make an attempt; put forth effort; make a test —*n.* an attempt; a test
try´ing *adj.* difficult to endure
tryst *n.* an appointment; a meeting
tsu·nam´i *n.* an immense wave generated by the aftershock of an earthquake
tub *n.* a large flat–bottomed container; (*US*) a bathtub
tub´by *adj.* round and fat; resembling a tub
tube *n.* a long, hollow cylinder
tu´ber *n.* short, thickened portion of a root; a tubercle
tu´ber·cle *n.* a small rounded eminence
tu·ber´cu·lar *adj.* affected with tubercles; tuberculosis
tu·ber·cu·lo´sis *n.* a disease marked by tubercles in the lungs
tu´ber·ous *adj.* bearing projections or prominences
tu´bu·lar *adj.* having the form of a tube; consisting of tubes
tuft *n.* a clump of hair, feathers, etc. —*vt.* to provide with tightly drawn buttons, as on upholstery; to cover or adorn with tufts — *vi.* to form or grow in tufts —**tuft´ed** *adj.* —**tuft´er** *n.*
tug *vt., vi.* to pull with effort —*n.* a violent pull; a strenuous effort
tu·i´tion *n.* payment for instruction
tum´ble *vi.* to toss about; to perform acrobatics —*vt.* to cause to fall
tum´bler *n.* a drinking glass; an acrobat; a revolving cage or cylinder as on a clothes dryer
tum´brel *n.* a rude cart
tu´me·fy *vi., vt.* to swell
tu·mes´cent *adj.* swelling; timid
tu´mor *n.* a growth or swelling on or in the body —**tu´mor·ous** *adj.*
tu´mult *n.* commotion or disturbance; agitation
tu·mul´tu·ous *adj.* greatly disturbed; stormy, tempestuous
tun *n.* a large cask
tu´na *n.* a large food fish
tun´dra *n.* a rolling treeless plain
tune *n.* a coherent succession of musical tones; correct pitch; harmony; a fine adjustment —*vt.* to adjust
tune´ful *adj.* melodic
tu´nic *n.* a loose outer garment gathered at the waist; a short coat
tun´nel *n.* underground passageway —*vt.* dig; make a passageway under
tun´ny *n.* tuna
tur´ban *n.* a head covering; a traditional Moslem headdress
tur´bid *adj.* muddy; dense or opaque; confused
tur´bine *n.* a rotary engine
tur´bot *n.* a large European flatfish
tur´bu·lent *adj.* violently disturbed or agitated; tending to disturb
tu·reen´ *n.* a covered serving bowl
turf *n.* a section of grass; an area regarded possessively —*vt.* cover with sod
tur·ges´cent *adj.* swollen; pompous
tur´gid *adj.* unnaturally distended; swollen
tur´key *n.* a large North American bird; something lacking quality; a disappointment
tur´moil *n.* disturbance; tumult; extreme confusion
turn *vi., vt.* to revolve or cause to revolve; to change direction; give finished form; to bend, curve, twist, etc.; to transform —*n.* a change of direction
turn´ing *n.* the art of shaping on a lathe
turn´pike *n.* a toll road
tur´pi·tude *n.* depravity
tur´ret *n.* a small projecting tower
tur´tle *n.* a four–limbed reptile with a soft body encased in a shell
tusk *n.* a long projecting tooth —*vt.* to gore, root, etc. with a tusk
tus´sle *vt., vi.* scuffle or struggle —*n.* a scuffle
tu´te·lage *n.* being under care of a tutor or guardian; the office of a guardian; the performance of tutoring
tu´tor *n.* a private teacher —*vt., vi.* to act as a tutor —**tu·to´ri·al** *adj.*
tu´tu *n.* a ballet skirt
tux·e´do *n.* formal attire
twad´dle *n.* pretentious, silly talk
twang *vt., vi.* make a sharp, vibrant sound; speak with a nasal sound —*n.* a vibrating or nasal sound
tweak *vt.* pinch or twist sharply; fine–tune —*n.* a pinch
tweed *n.* a woolen fabric
tweez´ers *n.* small pincers
twig *n.* a small shoot or branch as from a tree
twi´light *n.* the period after sunset and before sunrise; any faint light; waning glory
twin *n.* either of two young from the same birth; one greatly similar
twine *vt.* twist together; coil —*vi.* interlace; proceed on a winding course —*n.* string; act of entwining
twinge *n.* a sudden sharp pain; a mental pang —*vi., vt.* to feel or cause to feel sudden pain
twinkle *vi.* to shine intermittently; to sparkle; to move lightly and rapidly —*vt.* cause to flicker —*n.* quick movement of the eyelids; a glimmer
twin´kling *n.* an instant, a moment; a wink; the act of blinking
twirl *vt., vi.* whirl or rotate rapidly; twist or curl —*n.* a whirling motion; a curl or twist
twist *vt.* wind around; form by winding; deform or distort —*vi.* become wound; move in a winding course; squirm or writhe —*n.* a curve or bend; strain of a joint; unnatural inclination; unexpected turn or development
twist´er *n.* one or that which twists; a tornado or cyclone
twit *vt.* taunt —*n.* a reproach or taunt; a foolish person
twitch *vt., vi.* move with a quick spasmodic jerk —*n.* a sudden involuntary muscle contraction
two´–faced *adj.* double–dealing; insincere
tycoon´ *n.* a wealthy, powerful businessman or financier
tyke *n.* a small child
type´ *n.* traits in common; a standard; raised characters used for printing —*vt.* represent; typify; classify
typhoid fever an infectious disease contracted from contaminated water or food
ty·phoon´ *n.* a violent tropical windstorm
ty´phus *n.* a contagious disease spread by fleas or lice
typ´i·cal *adj.* characteristic of a group or type —**typ´i·cal·ly** *adv.*
typ´i·fy *vt.* serve as example
ty´po *n.* an error in typing or printing
ty·pog´ra·pher *n.* one who sets material into type suitable for printing
ty·po·graph´ic, ty·po·graph´i·cal *adj.* relating to typesetting or printing —**ty·pog´ra·phy** *n.*
ty·ran´nic, ty·ran´ni·cal *adj.* of or like a tyrant; despotic or arbitrary
tyr´an·nize *vi.* exercise power cruelly; rule as a tyrant — *vt.* treat cruelly; domineer
tyr´an·nous *adj.* despotic; cruel
ty´rant *n.* one ruling oppressively or cruelly; one exercising power or authority in a harsh, cruel manner
tyre (*Brit.*) *n.* covering for a wheel
ty´ro *n.* a novice or beginner
u, U twenty–first letter of the alphabet
u·biq´ui·tous *adj.* seeming everywhere at once; omnipresent
ug´ly *adj.* distasteful; repulsive; morally revolting
ul´cer *n.* an open sore; a corrupt condition —**ul´cer·ous** *adj.*
ul´na *n.* the larger bone of the forearm
ul´ster *n.* a long, loose overcoat
ul·te´ri·or *adj.* intentionally unrevealed; secondary in importance
ul´ti·ma *n.* the last syllable of a word
ul´ti·mate *adj.* last or final; beyond all others; fundamental —*n.* the best, latest, most fundamental, etc. —**ul´ti·mate·ly** *adv.*
ul·ti·ma´tum *n.* a statement of final terms
ul´tra *adj.* extreme
ul´tra·light *n.* a lightweight airplane
ul·tra·mod´ern *adj.* extremely fresh and new
ul·tra·son´ic *adj.* of inaudible sound
ul·tra·sound´ *n.* the use of ultrasonic waves for medical diagnosis
ul·tra·vi´o·let *adj.* of a wavelength between visible violet and X–rays
ul´u·late *vi.* to howl or wail

um´ber *n.* brown iron oxide; coloring made from umber —*adj.* pertaining to umber or its brown color
um·bil´i·cal *adj.* of or situated near the naval —*n.* a tube that links an astronaut or aquanaut to a craft
um·bil´i·cus *n.* the naval
um´brage *n.* anger or resentment; shade or shadow
um·brel´la *n.* a portable canopy to protect from sun or rain; something serving as a cover or shield
um´laut *n.* an altered vowel sound; two dots over a vowel, as ä, ë, etc., used to mark a change in sound
um´pire *n.* one who settles disagreements or disputes; one who enforces rules of certain games
un·a·bat´ed *adj.* maintaining original force or intensity
un·a·bridged´ *adj.* containing all; complete
un·a·dorned´ *adj.* plain; lacking embellishment
un·a·dul´ter·at·ed *adj.* pure; not dilute; complete, utter
un·af·fect´ed *adj.* natural or sincere; not influenced or changed
u·nan´i·mous *adj.* in full agreement; without dissent —**u·na·nim´i·ty** *n.*
un·a·vail´ing *adj.* ineffective; futile
un·a·wares´ *adv.* unexpectedly; without premeditation
un·be·liev´a·ble *adj.* incredible; too astonishing to be believed
un·bend´ing *adj.* resolute; firm; not relaxed or able to relax
un·bi´ased *adj.* impartial; not prejudiced
un·bid´den *adj.* spontaneous, without asking; not ordered or invited
un·blink´ing *adj.* without emotion; fearless
un·break´a·ble *adj.* impossible or difficult to break
un·bri´dled *adj.* unrestrained; uncontrolled
un·bro´ken *adj.* uninterrupted; continuous
un·bur´den *vt.* relieve from cares or worries; confess
un·can´ny *adj.* unnatural; weird; seeming to be supernatural
un·car´ing *adj.* lacking concern or sympathy
un·ceas´ing *adj.* continuous; without stopping; eternal
un·cen´sored *adj.* not examined for inappropriate material; complete
un·cer·e·mo´ni·ous *adj.* casual, informal; without preamble; rude or discourteous
un·char·ac·ter·is´tic *adj.* unusual; strange or exceptional: *uncharacteristic generosity*
un·chart´ed *adj.* unknown; unexplored
un·civ´il·ized *adj.* barbarous; rude and uncouth; remote
un·com´mon *adj.* remarkable; strange
un·con´scion·a·ble *adj.* unscrupulous; unbelievably bad or wrong
un·couth´ *adj.* boorish or unrefined
unc´tion *n.* an anointing; a substance for anointing; something that soothes; excessive or affected sincerity
unc´tu·ous *adj.* greasy to the touch; marked by excessive or affected sincerity; overly smooth or suave
un´der *prep.* beneath; covered by; lower than; less in value, amount, etc.; inferior to; subordinate to; being subject to; by virtue of; having regard to —*adv.* underneath; in an inferior position; less in amount, value, etc. —*adj.*
un´der·brush *n.* small trees, shrubs, etc. growing beneath forest trees
un´der·cur·rent *n.* air or water flowing beneath another layer; concealed or secret force or tendency
un´der·growth *n.* underbrush; growth beneath forest trees
un´der·hand·ed *adj., adv.* in a sly or treacherous manner
un·der·stand´ *vt., vi.* come to know the meaning or import of; to perceive the nature or character of; to comprehend; suppose or believe; to accept as a condition; to have sympathy or tolerance for —**un·der·stand´a·ble** *adj.*
un·der·stand´ing *n.* comprehension; capacity to think; an agreement; a viewpoint or opinion; sympathy or tolerance for others —*adj.* marked by comprehension, sympathy, tolerance, etc.
un·der·stat´ed *adj.* marked by restraint; showing good taste
un´der·take *vt.* agree to attempt; to contract to do
un´der·write *vt.* to sign; to assume liability; guarantee —*vi.* act as a guarantor
un·doubt´ed *adj.* assured or certain; unsuspected
un·du´ly *adv.* excessively; improperly or unjustly
un·earth´ *vt.* dig up; discover
un·earth´ly *adj.* seemingly not of this world; supernatural; terrifying
un·eas´y *adj.* disturbed; disquieted; causing discomfort; not stable or secure
un·ex·pect´ed *adj.* without warning; not foreseen
un·feigned´ *adj.* sincere
un·flap´pa·ble *adj.* impassive; imperturbable
un·for´tu·nate *adj.* unlucky; resulting from misfortune; regrettable —*n.* a victim
un·gain´ly *adj.* awkward; clumsy; poorly proportioned
un´guent *n.* an ointment or salve
un´gu·late *adj.* having hoofs —*n.* a hoofed animal
u·ni·cel´lu·lar *adj.* consisting of a single cell
u´ni·corn *n.* a mythical horned creature resembling a horse
u´ni·fy *vt.* to bring together or unite; to make alike —**u·ni·fi·ca´tion** *n.*
u·ni·lat´er·al *adj.* affecting one only; having only one side; recognizing only one aspect
un·im·peach´a·ble *adj.* beyond question; blameless
un´ion *n.* a joining; that formed by joining or combining; a device for joining mechanical parts —*adj.* pertaining to a union
u·nique´ *adj.* being the only one of its kind; without equal; very unusual or remarkable
u´ni·son *n.* perfect agreement; speaking or singing together
u´nit *n.* a standard of comparison; a measure of requirements for a scholastic degree; a quantity required for a desired effect; persons or things considered as constituent parts of a whole —*adj.* being a distinct part —**u´ni·tar·y** *adj.*
u·nite´ *vt., vi.* to join; bring into close connection; to possess in combination; to combine —**u´ni·ty** *n.*
u·ni·ver´sal *adj.* common everywhere; including all, without exception; adapted to a variety of uses —*n.* a general notion or idea; a trait common to all
u´ni·verse *n.* aggregate of all existing things; a field of thought or activity
u·ni·ver´si·ty *n.* an institute of higher learning including buildings, faculty, etc.
un·just´ *adj.* not fair; wrongful
un·kempt´ *adj.* not neat or tidy
un·less´ *conj.* except that —*prep.* excepting
un·men´tion·a·ble *adj.* not fit for discussion; embarrassing
un·nerve´ *vt.* deprive of resolve, courage, etc.; make nervous
un·or´tho·dox *adj.* contrary to convention or tradition
un·plumbed´ *adj.* not fully measured or explored
un·prec´e·dent·ed *adj.* without precedent; new or novel
un·read *adj.* uninformed; unlearned; not yet examined
un·re·gen´er·ate *adj.* not changed; sinful; stubbornly recalcitrant
un·ru´ly *adj.* tending to resist regulation; difficult to control
un·scathed´ *adj.* not injured
un·ten´a·ble *adj.* impossible to defend, preserve, etc.
un·til´ *prep.* up to the time of —*conj.* to the time when; to the place or degree that
un·u´su·al *adj.* odd, rare, or extraordinary
un·writ´ten *adj.* based on tradition; understood
up *adv.* toward a higher place; in or on a higher place; to or at that deemed higher —*adj.* moving or directed upward; at or to a high level, condition, etc. —*prep.* toward or at a point higher or farther above or along —*n.* an ascent; a state or condition of prosperity
up´beat *n.* an unaccented beat in music —*adj.* optimistic; confident
up´braid´ *vt.* reproach
up·hol´ster *vt.* fit with covering, cushions, etc.
up·hol´ster·y *n.* cover or repair of furniture; material for covering
up´keep *n.* the act, state, or cost of maintaining in good and usable condition
up´per *adj.* higher in position, rank, etc. —*n.* something above another
up´per·most *adj.* highest in rank, authority, etc.; foremost —*adv.*
up´right *adj.* erect; righteous —*n.* being erect; something erect —*adv.* in an upright or vertical position
up·stand´ing *adj.* honest, straightforward; upright; placed erect
up´start *n.* one who attains sudden power or importance
up´tight´ *adj.* anxious or nervous; angry; conventional, conservative
up´ward *adv.* toward a higher place; in the upper parts; toward a better condition —*adj.* directed toward or located in a higher place
ur´ban *adj.* pertaining to a city or city life; living or located in a city
ur·bane´ *adj.* refined; suave
ur´ban·ism *n.* life in a city; the study of city life
ur·ban·ol´o·gy *n.* the study of cities and city problems —**ur·ban·ol´o·gist** *n.*
urban renewal revitalization of cities by restoring or rebuilding
urban sprawl spread of population, shopping centers, etc. into rural or undeveloped areas
u·re´mi·a *n.* a toxic condition caused by failure of the kidneys to filter waste products from the blood
urge *vt.* to drive or force forward; to entreat earnestly —*vi.* to present arguments, claims, etc. —*n.* a strong impulse; the act of urging
ur´gent *adj.* requiring prompt action; insistent —**ur´gen·cy** *n.*
urn *n.* a footed receptacle
u·rol´o·gy *n.* study of the urinary system —**urol´o·gist** *n.*
us´a·ble, use´a·ble *adj.* that can be used; that may be useful
us´age *n.* an act or manner of using; customary or habitual practice; the accepted manner of using words
use *vt.* to put into service; take advantage of —*n.* the act of using or state of being used; function; advantage or usefulness; the purpose for which something is employed
use´ful *adj.* serviceable; helpful
use´less *adj.* having no use; serving no function
ush´er *n.* one who escorts patrons to their seats; an official doorkeeper; male attendant in a wedding party —*vi., vt.* to serve as an usher
u´su·al *adj.* customary or common
u·su´ri·ous *adj.* practicing usury; of or pertaining to usury
u·surp´ *vt.* to seize without authority; to take possession by force
u´su·ry *n.* the lending of money at excessive or unlawful interest rates; excessive or unlawful interest
uten´sil *n.* an implement that serves a useful purpose
u´tile *adj.* useful
u·til´i·ty *n.* fitness, suitability
u´ti·lize *vt.* make use of

ut´most *adj.* of the highest or greatest degree; at the furthest limit; extreme —*n.* the most or best possible
ut´ter *vt.* say, express, give out, or send forth; put in circulation —*adj.* complete; unqualified
ut´ter·ance *n.* a manner of speaking; a thing uttered
v, V twenty–second letter of the alphabet; in Roman characters, the symbol for five
va´cant *adj.* containing nothing; empty; not being used; having no incumbent, officer —**va´can·cy** *n.*
va´cate *vt.* to make vacant; to set aside, as a ruling —*vi.* to leave
va·ca´tion (*US*) *n.* time for recreation or rest; a holiday —*vi.* take a holiday
vac´ci·nate *vt.* innoculate as a preventive measure
vac·cine´ *n.* a preparation used to provide immunity
vac´il·late *vi.* waver; be irresolute
va·cu´i·ty *n.* emptiness; vacant space; lack of intelligence; something inane or stupid
vac´u·ous *adj.* empty; lacking intelligence; lacking substance; devoid of meaning or expression
vac´u·um *n.* space nearly devoid of matter; reduction of pressure below that of surroundings
vag´a·bond *n.* a wanderer without visible means of support; shiftless, irresponsible person —*adj.* wandering; aimless; irresponsible
va´gar·y *n.* a wild fancy or extravagant notion
va´grant *n.* one without a home or job; a tramp —*adj.* wandering aimlessly; wayward
vague *n.* lacking definition; indistinct; not clearly stated
vain *adj.* excessively proud; unproductive or useless —**in vain** to no purpose
vain´glo·ry *n.* excessive vanity; ostentation —**vain·glo´ri·ous** *adj.*
val´ance (*US*) *n.* decorative drapery edging a canopy or the top of a window; a decorative panel that covers fixtures above a window
val·e·dic´tion *n.* a farewell
val·e·dic·to´ri·an *n.* student who delivers the farewell address at a graduation ceremony, customarily, the student with the highest grade point average
val´e·dic´to·ry *adj.* of a leave–taking —*n.* parting address
va´lence *n.* the capacity of an atom or radical to combine with another
val´et *n.* a personal servant; one who performs personal services for guests at a hotel, inn, etc. —*vt. vi.* to serve as valet
val·e·tu·di·nar´i·an *n.* a chronic invalid —*adj.* infirm or ailing; overly concerned about one's health
val´iant *adj.* strong and courageous; performed with valor
val´id *adj.* based on facts or evidence; well–founded; effective; legally binding —**va·lid´i·ty** *n.*
val´i·date *vt.* to confirm as true; to declare to be legally binding; to mark or stamp; to give sanction to or make official —**val·i·da´tion** *n.*
va·lise´ *n.* a traveling bag
val´ley *n.* area drained by a river; low land; a hollow
val´or *n.* remarkable courage; bravery —**val´or·ous** *adj.*
val´u·a·ble *adj.* having significant worth or value; costly —**val´u·a·bles** *n.* expensive or treasured articles
val·u·a´tion *n.* an estimate of worth; an estimated value
val´ue *n.* worth; that regarded as desirable or worthy; a market price; a bargain; a number represented by a symbol; the relative lightness or darkness of a color — *vt.* to assess or appraise; to regard highly; to consider relatively important
val´ued *adj.* hightly esteemed: *a valued friend*; of specific worth
val´ue·less *adj.* worthless
valve *n.* a device that controls movement or flow
vam´pire *n.* in folklore, a reanimated corpse that feeds on human blood; one who preys on those of the opposite sex; a bat that feeds on the blood of mammals
van *n.* a large, enclosed wagon or truck; (*Brit.*) a railroad car for freight or baggage; (*Brit.*) a caravan; (*US*) a passenger vehicle somewhat like a small bus
van´dal·ism *n.* willful defacement of property
van´dal·ize *vt.* willfully deface or destroy property
vane *n.* a thin plate on a pivot to indicate wind direction; an arm or plate of a windmill, propeller, etc.
van´guard *n.* forward part of an advancing army; foremost position; leaders of a movement, trend, etc.
va·nil´la *n.* an orchid of tropical America; a flavoring extract; vanilla flavoring made synthetically
van´ish *vi.* disappear; pass out of existence
van´i·ty *n.* excessive pride in one's talents, etc.; something worthless or futile; a dressing table —**vanity case** a case for cosmetics
van´quish *vt.* defeat in battle; suppress, or overcome, as fear
van´tage *n.* superiority or advantage; a position or condition that offers advantage; an overall view
vap´id *adj.* flat or dull; lacking flavor or attraction
va´por *n.* moisture in the air; cloudy substance; something insubstantial and fleeting —*vt.* to vaporize —*vi.* to emit or pass off in vapor
va´por·ize *vt., vi.* convert or be converted into vapor
va´por·ous *adj.* misty; emitting or forming vapor; whimsical
var´i·a·ble *adj.* having capacity to change; likely to change; of no fixed size, amount, etc. —*n.* that liable or able to change
var´i·ance *n.* a discrepancy or difference; permission or license or to do that contrary to local ordinance
var´i·ant *adj.* differing from a standard or type —*n.* an alternative, as in spelling or pronunciation
var·i·a´tion *n.* a difference or modification; the extent of difference; that which differs from others of the same type
var´ied *adj.* diverse; modified or altered —**var´ied·ly** *adv.*
var´i·e·gat·ed *adj.* varied in color
va·ri´e·tal *adj.* describing a variety —*n.* a wine named for a grape variety
va·ri´e·ty *n.* diversity, difference; a sort or kind; a collection or assortment
var´i·ous *adj.* different from one another; several; separate; multifaceted
var´nish *n.* a finish for wood; outward show —*vt.* to coat with varnish; to hide or gloss over: *varnish the truth*
var´y *vt.* to change or modify; diversify —*vi.* to deviate; become changed
vas´cu·lar *adj.* pertaining to body vessels or ducts
vast *adj.* immense; great in quantity, importance, etc.; extensive
vat *n.* a large open vessel or tub
vaude´ville *n.* a theatrical entertainment of short sketches, songs, dances, etc.; a variety show
vault *n.* an arched roof or ceiling; a room or compartment for storage or safekeeping; a burial chamber —*vi., vt.* to leap
vault´ing *n.* construction that forms a vault
vaunt *vi., vt.* to speak boastfully or brag about
veer *vi.* turn; to shift from an opinion, belief, etc. —*vt.* to change direction of
veg´an *n.* a vegetarian whose diet is limited to food derived from plants
veg´e·ta·ble *n.* a plant cultivated for food; the edible part of a plant —*adj.* relating to or derived from plants; made from edible plants
veg´e·tal *adj.* of plants or vegetables
veg·e·tar´i·an *n.* one who does not eat meat; one who advocates a diet that excludes meat and sometimes seafood or animal products as well —*adj.* of vegetarians or vegetarianism; consisting only of vegetables, grains, fruit, nuts, and seeds
veg´e·tate *vi.* grow, as a plant; exist in a monotonous, passive state
veg·e·ta´tion *n.* plant life
ve´he·ment *adj.* marked by strong feeling or passion; acting with great force
ve´hi·cle *n.* any conveyance for passengers or freight —**ve·hic´u·lar** *adj.*
veil *n.* a thin fabric for covering; anything that conceals or covers —*vt.* to cover, conceal, disguise, etc.
veil´ing *n.* a covering; material for making a veil
vein *n.* a tubular vessel that conveys blood; a branching structure such as ribs in a leaf or the wings of an insect; a colored streak in wood, stone, etc.; a distinctive tendency or disposition —*vt.* to extend or mark throughout like veins
veld, veldt *n.* a South African plain
vel´lum *n.* fine parchment
ve·loc´i·ty *n.* speed; quickness of motion
ve·lour´ *n.* a soft fabric having a short, thick pile
vel´vet *n.* a fabric with short, smooth pile on one side and a smooth underside —*adj.* made of velvet; smooth and soft to the touch
ve´nal *adj.* characterized by corruption or bribery
vend *vt.* to sell —*vi.* be employed in selling
ven·det´ta *n.* private feud in which relatives of a wronged person seek revenge; any bitter quarrel
ve·neer´ *n.* thin layer; surface or show: *veneer of civility* —*vt.* cover with veneer; to conceal something
ven´er·a·ble *adj.* worthy of respect because of dignity, age, etc.
ven´er·ate *vt.* to regard with respect or awe —**ven·er·a´tion** *n.*
ve·ne´re·al *adj.* of or proceeding from sexual intercourse
ve·ne·re·ol´o·gy *n.* the study of sexually transmitted disease
ven´geance *n.* a deserved penalty; retribution
venge´ful *adj.* seeking revenge; unforgiving
ve´ni·al *adj.* slight or trivial, as a fault —**ve·ni·al´i·ty** *n.*
ven´i·son *n.* flesh of a wild animal used for food
ven´om *n.* poison secreted by certain reptiles, insects, etc.; ill will or bitterness
ve´nous *adj.* pertaining to or carried by veins; of blood returning to the heart and lungs; having veins
vent *n.* an outlet or opening; a slit in a garment —*vt.* give expression to; permit escape, as of a gas; make a vent in
ven·ti·la´tion *n.* free circulation of air; exposure to examination and discussion; oxygenation blood
ven´tral *adj.* toward, at, or near the abdomen
ven´tri·cle *n.* small cavity in the body —**ven·tric´u·lar** *adj.*
ven´ture *vt.* expose to risk —*vi.* take risk —*n.* an undertaking marked by risk
venture capital investment in an untried business
ven´ture·some *adj.* bold or daring; involving risk
ven´tur·ous *adj.* adventurous; risky
ven´ue *n.* place or setting of action or event; in law, location of a crime or cause of action, or where a trial must be held
ve·ra´cious *adj.* truthful; accurate
ve·rac´i·ty *n.* honesty; accuracy
ve·ran´da *n.* an open porch
verb *n.* a word that expresses action, existence, or occurence

ver´bal *adj.* referring to words: *verbal image*; of words rather than ideas: literal —*n.* in grammar, a noun derived from a verb
ver´bal·ize *vt.* express in words —*vi.* speak or write in a wordy fashion
ver·ba´tim *adj., adv.* exactly, word for word
ver´bi·age *n.* use of too many words; manner of expression
ver·bose´ *adj.* overly wordy; repetitive, redundant; containing unnecessary words
ver´dant *adj.* covered with vegetation; inexperienced
ver´dict *n.* decision of a jury; conclusion or opinion
ver´dure *n.* fresh greenness of growing vegetation; lush vegetation
verge *n.* extreme edge; a boundary —*vi.* be contiguous or adjacent; approach or come close to
ver·i·fi·ca´tion *n.* proof, confirmation
ver´i·fi·a·ble *adj.* that can be confirmed or proven
ver´i·fy *vt.* prove; test the accuracy or truth of
ver·i·si·mil´i·tude *n.* the appearance of truth or reality; that which has the appearance of truth or reality
ver´i·ta·ble *adj.* genuine or real; actual
ver´i·ty *n.* truth; the quality of being true or real
ver´mi·form *adj.* shaped like a worm
ver´min *n.* destructive animals or insects; a repulsive person
ver·mouth´ *n.* a fortified wine
ver·nac´u·lar *n.* language peculiar to a locality; common daily speech; specialized vocabulary of a trade or profession —*adj.* of a particular language or argot; relating to a locality
ver´nal *adj.* appropriate to spring; fresh or youthful —**ver´nal·ly** *adv.*
ver´sa·tile *adj.* having many talents; having many uses
verse *n.* poetry; a line or group of lines of poetry, scripture, etc.
versed *adj.* skilled; trained; knowledgeable
ver´si·fy *vt.* to convert into poetry —*vi.* write poetry
ver´sion *n.* translation or rendition; an adaptation: *film version of a novel*; a personal account
ver´so *n.* a left–handed page; the reverse of a coin or medallion
ver´sus *prep.* against; alternative of
ver´te·bra *n., pl.* **ver´te·brae** a bone of the spinal column
ver´te·brate *adj.* having a backbone
ver´ti·cal *adj.* upright or erect; directly overhead; at right angles to the horizon —*n.* something upright
ver·tig´i·nous *adj.* affected by vertigo; spinning
ver´ti·go *n.* dizziness; disorientation; a disorder in which a person or surroundings seem to whirl about
verve *n.* energy; enthusiasm
ver´y *adv.* to a high degree; exactly —*adj.* suitable; identical; a thing itself: *the very thing I wanted*
ves´i·cle *n.* a small cavity or cyst; a blister —**ve·sic´u·lar** *adj.*
ves´pers *n.* evening worship
ves´sel *n.* an open container; a physical process for fluid: *blood vessel*; a ship or aircraft
vest *n.* (*Brit.*) a garment worn under a shirt; (*US*) a short, sleeveless outer garment —*vt.* to confer, as authority
vest´ed *adj.* inalienable or absolute; clothed, esp. as an ecclesiastic
ves´ti·bule *n.* an entryway or antechamber; enclosed passageway between cars of a passenger train
ves´tige *n.* a discernible trace; a remnant —**ves·tig´ial** *adj.*
vest´ment *n.* an article of clothing; a ritual garment
ves´try *n.* a church room for storing vestments, conducting meetings, etc.; church's administrative body
vet´er·an *n.* one experienced
vet´er·i·nar·y *adj.* of prevention and treatment of diseases and injuries of animals —**vet·er·i·nar´i·an** *n.*
ve´to *vt.* refuse, as approval or consent —*n.* right to cancel, prohibit, or postpone; exercising such right
vex *vt.* annoy; trouble or afflict; baffle or confuse —**vex·a´tion** *n.*
vexed *adj.* annoyed or disturbed; baffled
vex·a´tious *adj.* annoying; disturbing
vi´a *prep.* by way of; by means of
vi´a·ble *adj.* capable of living and developing normally; workable —**vi·a·bil´i·ty** *n.*
vi´a·duct *n.* a bridgelike structure of arched masonry
vi´al *n.* a small bottle
vi´brant *adj.* vigorous, enthusiastic; energetic, powerful
vi´brate *vi., vt.* move back and forth rapidly —**vi·bra´tion** *n.*
vi·bra´to *n.* cyclical variation in the pitch of a tone
vic´ar *n.* one authorized to act in the stead of another; a church representative
vi·car´i·ous *adj.* suffered or done in place of another; identifying with experience of another; delegated
vice *n.* moral depravity; an immoral action, trait, etc.; habitual failing or shortcoming; (*Brit.*) a clamping device, as for woodworking
vice´roy *n.* one who rules by authority of a sovereign
vi·chys·soise´ *n.* a cream soup of potato and leeks, usually served cold
vi·cin´i·ty *n.* nearness; proximity; a nearby area, region, etc.
vi´cious *adj.* dangerous; marked by evil intent: *vicious rumor*, depraved or immoral; forceful or intense
vi·cis´si·tude *n.* change or alteration —**vi·cis´si·tudes** *pl. n.* irregular changes of conditions, fortune, etc.
vic´tim *n.* one harmed, as by injury, disease, fraud, trickery, etc.
vic´tim·ize *vt.* cause to suffer; cheat or dupe
vic´tor *n.* one who wins —**vic·to´ri·ous** *adj.*
vie *vi.* put forth effort; compete; contend for superiority
view *n.* range of vision; something seen; an opinion or belief —*vt.* look at; examine; consider; regard in a certain way
vig´il *n.* time of keeping watch
vig´i·lant *adj.* alert to danger; wary
vig·i·lan´te *n.* an advocate for preempting the law
vi·gnette´ *n.* a picture shading off into the background; a brief literary sketch; a decorative design
vig´or *n.* energy; vital or natural growth; intensity —**vig´or·ous** *adj.*
vile *adj.* morally base; corrupt; loathsome; very bad: *vile tasting*
vil´i·fy *vt.* speak of abusively; defame —**vil·i·fi·ca´tion** *n.*
vil´lage *n.* (US) a residential area smaller than a town but larger than a hamlet; the inhabitants of a village collectively —**vil´lag·er** *n.*
vil´lain *n.* a scoundrel
vil´lain·ous *adj.* wicked; evil
vin´ci·ble *adj.* easily overcome; that can be conquered
vin´di·cate *vt.* to clear of suspicion; maintain a right or claim; to justify
vin·dic´tive *adj.* having a vengeful spirit
vine *n.* a climbing plant
vin´e·gar *n.* a variously flavored condiment and preservative; ascerbity, as of speech
vine´yard *n.* an area devoted to the cultivation of grapes
vin´i·cul·ture *n.* cultivation of wine grapes
vin´i·fy *vt.* convert into wine
vi´nous *adj.* pertaining to or characteristic of wine
vin´tage *n.* yield of grapes or wine for a season; region and year in which a wine is produced —*adj.* of a fine wine; of a good year for wine
vint´ner *n.* wine maker or merchant
vi´nyl *n.* a type of plastic
vi·o´la *n.* a musical instrument similar to a violin
vi´ol·a·ble *adj.* that can be or is likely to be violated
vi´o·late *vt.* break a law, agreement, etc.; ravish or rape; offend
vi´o·lence *n.* physical force used to injure, damage, or destroy; intensity, severity; injury or damage
vi´o·lent *adj.* marked by physical force or intense emotional excitement; characterized by intensity
vi´o·let *n.* a bluish–purple color; a plant bearing violet–colored flowers
vi·o·lin´ *n.* a stringed instrument of the highest register; a violinist
vi·o·lin´ist *n.* one who plays violin
vi´ol·ist *n.* one who plays viola
vi·o·lon·cel´lo *n.* a cello
vi´per *n.* kind of snake; a treacherous or spiteful person —**vi´per·ish** *adj.*
vi´per·ous *adj.* pertaining to vipers or snakes; treacherous or spiteful
vi·ra´go *n.* an ill–tempered woman; a shrew
vi´ral *adj.* pertaining to or caused by a virus —**vi´ral·ly** *adv.*
vi·res´cent *adj.* greenish
vir´gin *n.* one who has never had sexual intercourse; an unmarried woman —*adj.* being a virgin; pertaining or suited to a virgin; uncorrupted, pure; not hitherto used or processed: *virgin wool*
vir´gule *n.* a diagonal mark (/)
vir·i·des´cent *adj.* greenish; turning green
vir´ile *adj.* having vigor or strength of manhood; able to procreate
vi·rol´o·gy *n.* the study of viruses
vir´tu·al *adj.* existing in essence or effect, but not in actual form
vir´tue *n.* moral excellence; an admirable quality
vir·tu·os´i·ty *n.* technical mastery
vir·tu·o´so *n.* a master of technique, esp. in the arts —*adj.* capable of or displaying extraordinary skill
vir´tu·ous *adj.* righteous; pure and chaste —**vir´tu·ous·ly** *adv.*
vir´u·lent *adj.* extremely harmful; infectious; full of hatred
vi´rus *n.* a parasite able to reproduce only in living cells; disease caused by a parasite; an evil influence
vi´sa *n.* endorsement on a passport that permits entrance to a country
vis´age *n.* appearance; aspect
vis´cer·a *n.* internal organs
vis´cer·al *adj.* pertaining to the viscera; instinctive or emotional
vis·cos´i·ty *n.* property by which fluids resist flow or change
vis´cous *adj.* relatively resistant to flow; of high viscosity —**vis´cous·ness** *n.*
vise (*US*) *n.* a clamping tool, as for woodworking —*vt.* to hold or squeeze
vis´i·ble *adj.* capable of being seen; that which can be perceived
vi´sion *n.* sight; that seen; something beautiful; a mental image; foresight; imagination
vi´sion·ar·y *adj.* existing in imagination; speculative; impractical —*n.* one who has visions; a person whose plans or projects are impractical or unrealistic
vis´it *vt.* call on; go or come to a place; be a guest of; inflict upon —*vi.* pay a call; stay with temporarily —*n.* a social call; a short stay
vis·it·a´tion *n.* a visit; official inspection or examination
vi´sor *n.* a projection to shield the eyes
vis´ta *n.* a view; mental image
vi´su·al *adj.* pertaining to sight; perceptible by sight —*n.* pictures, charts, etc. that enhance

a presentation —**vis´u·al·ly** *adv.*
vis´u·al·ize *vt., vi.* form a mental image; picture in the mind
vi´tal *adj.* pertaining to life; essential to or supporting life; of utmost importance; dynamic, full of life
vi·tal´i·ty *n.* the power to live and develop; physical or mental energy
vi´tal·ize *vt.* endow with life or energy; to make spirited or energetic
vi´ta·min *n.* a naturally occurring substance essential to health
vi´ti·ate *vt.* impair use or value; render weak or ineffective; make legally invalid —**vi·ti·a´tion** *n.*
vit´i·cul·ture *n.* the cultivation of grapes
vit´re·ous *adj.* glassy; obtained from glass; regarding the vitreous humor
vitreous humor the clear jelly–like substance that fills the eyeball
vit´ri·fy *vt., vi.* change into glass or a glass–like substance
vit´ri·ol *n.* a sulfate of metal; sulfuric acid; harshness or bitterness of thought or expression; reproach
vit·ri·ol´ic *adj.* acrimonious; harsh or bitter
vi·tu´per·ate *vt.* fault abusively; berate or scold
vi·tu·per·a´tion *n.* harsh or abusive language; use of such language
vi·va´cious *adj.* full of life and spirit
viv´id *adj.* strong or intense, as of color; suggesting lifelike images; producing a sharp impression
viv´i·fy *vt.* give life to; animate; make more vivid or striking
vi·vip´a·rous *adj.* bringing forth live young grown in the mother's body
viv·i·sec´tion *n.* cutting or dissection on a living animal
vix´en *n.* female fox; quarrelsome or malevolent woman
vo·cab´u·lar·y *n.* words of a language; the words one understands
vo´cal *adj.* of the voice; able to speak or utter sounds; speaking freely —**vo´cal·ise** (*Brit.*), **vo´cal·ize** (*US*) *vt., vi.*
vo´cal·ist *n.* a singer; one who sings as a profession
vo·ca´tion *n.* a regular job or profession; a career
vo·ca´tion·al *adj.* pertaining to a job or profession; of training designed to provide specific useful skills
vo·cif´er·ate *vt., vi.* to cry out; to protest boisterously —**vo·cif´er·ous** *adj.*
vogue *n.* fashion or style; popularity
voice *n.* sound produced by vocal organs; quality of sound; the right to expression; an agency for expressing, as a newspaper —*vt.* put into speech; give expression to
void *adj.* containing nothing; completely lacking; having no legal force; useless
voile *n.* a fine, sheer fabric
vol´a·tile *adj.* evaporating rapidly; prone to change suddenly and sharply; fleeting —**vol·a·til´i·ty** *n.*
vol´a·til·ize *vi., vt.* pass off as vapor; become or make volatile
vol·can´ic *adj.* of, produced by, or like a volcano; explosive or violent
vol·ca´no *n.* an opening in the earth where hot matter is ejected; a mound formed by ejected material
vol·can·ol´o·gy *n.* the study of volcanoes
vo·li´tion *n.* exercise of the will; willpower; the power to make a choice
volt *n.* a unit of electric and electromotive potential
volt´age *n.* electromotive force expressed in volts
vol´u·ble *adj.* fluent; talkative
vol´ume *n.* a book, esp. one of a set; bound periodicals; an amount; capacity; space occupied —**vo·lu´mi·nous** *adj.*
vol´un·ta·rism *n.* the use of volunteer labor; willing participation; belief that free will is fundamental to individual action or experience
vol´un·tar·y *adj.* of one's own free will; acting without constraint; intentional; able to choose or elect: optional; supported by charitable donations —**vol´un·tar´i·ly** *adv.*
vol·un·teer´ *n.* an unpaid worker; one who performs of his own free will —*adj.* pertaining to or composed of volunteers —*vt.* offer or give voluntarily —*vi.* enter into service without pay
vo·lup´tu·ar·y *n.* one inclined to luxury and indulgence —*adj.* of luxury and extravagance
vo·lup´tu·ous *adj.* pertaining to sensual gratification; suggesting the satisfaction of sensual desire
voo´doo *n.* a religion marked by belief in sorcery, use of charms, etc.; a charm or spell —*vt.* to bewitch —*adj.*
vo·ra´cious *n.* eager, insatiable; eating greedily
vo´ta·ry *n.* one bound by vows; one intensely devoted
vor´tex *n., pl.* **vor´tex·es, vor´ti·ces** a mass of rotating or whirling fluid; something resembling a vortex
vote *n.* a means for expressing choice; ballots cast; right to choose —*vt., vi.* determine by vote; cast one's vote
vo´tive *adj.* performed in fulfillment of a vow
vouch *vi.* give assurance or guarantee; support or justify —*vt.* bear witness; declare; provide support or justification —**vouch´er** *n.*
vouch·safe´ *vt.* permit; grant —*vi.* condescend or deign
vow *n.* solemn promise; emphatic affirmation —*vt.* make a solemn promise or threat —*vi.* make a vow
voy´age *n.* a long journey —*vi.* take a journey
vo·yeur´ *n.* one gratified by observing objects or acts; one obsessed with viewing sensational or sordid events —**voy·eur·is´tic** *adj.*
vul´can·ize *vt., vi.* process in order to increase strength and elasticity
vul´gar *adj.* lacking manners, taste, etc.; offensive or obscene; pertaining to the common people; of a common language or dialect
vul´gar·ism *n.* word or expression in poor taste
vul´gar·ize *vt.* make common or coarse; popularize
vul´ner·a·ble *adj.* open to attack or injury; susceptible to temptation
vul´ture *n.* a large bird that feeds on carrion; one who preys in others
vy´ing *adj.* that vies or competes
w, W twenty–third letter of the alphabet
wad *n.* a small, compact mass; a large amount: *a wad of cash* —*vt.* to press, roll, fold, etc. into a mass
wad´dle *n.* a clumsy, rocking walk —*vi.* move awkwardly
wade *vi.* to walk through something that offers resistance, as water or brush; to proceed slowly or laboriously: *wade through paperwork* —*vt.* walk through; to cross by walking on the bottom
wader, wading bird a long–legged bird that feeds in shallow water
wa´fer *n.* thin, crisp cookie, cracker, etc.; a disk of material for sealing or attaching
waf´fle *n.* a crisp batter cake —*vi.* be evasive
waft *vt.* bear gently through air or over water —*vi.* to float on the wind; blow gently, as a breeze —*n.* lightly passing air, sound, or aroma
wag *vi., vt.* move or cause to move rapidly —*n.* a wagging motion; a droll person; a wit
wage *n.* payment for service; reward or consequence: *wages of sin* —*vt.* engage in: *wage war*
wa´ger *vt., vi.* gamble —*n.* a bet; amount at stake
wag´gish *adj.* humorous; said or done as a joke
waif *n.* a homeless child
wail *vi.* make a mournful, crying sound —*vt.* mourn or lament; cry out in sorrow
wain´scot, wain´scot·ing *n.* paneling for inside walls
wain´wright *n.* one who fashions wagons
waist *n.* middle of the body; middle of a thing
waist´coat (*Brit.*) *n.* a short, sleeveless garment worn over a shirt; (*US*) a vest
wait *vi., vt.* anticipate: *wait to be called*; pause; delay or postpone; remain expectant or in readiness; serve as waiter or waitress —*n.* (*Brit.*) musicians employed to play at a public function; street carolers —**wait´ing** *n.*
waive *vt.* relinquish or forego a claim; put off temporarily
waiv´er *n.* voluntary relinquishment; an instrument which evidences relinquishment
wake[1] *vi.* emerge from sleep; become aware or alert —*vt.* rouse from sleep; make aware —*n.* a watch or vigil over the deceased; (*Brit.*) an annual parish festival; (*Brit.*) an annual vacation
wake[2] *n.* trail left by a vessel moving through water; turbulence left by anything that has passed
wake´ful *adj.* not sleepy; watchful, alert; restless —**wake´ful·ness** *n.*
wak´en *vt.* rouse from sleep; stir up: *waken patriotic fervor* —*vi.* cease sleeping; wake up; become active or animated —**wak´en·er** *n.*
wak´ing *adj.* characterized by consciousness or awareness
wale *n.* a ridge or rib on cloth —*vt.* raise welts by striking; manufacture cloth with ridges
walk *vi.* to move or progress on foot; to behave a certain way: *walk in peace*; to leave abruptly —*vt.* to pass through at a walk; to force or help to walk: *walk a bicycle uphill*; to accompany or escort on a walk; to move: *walk a refrigerator away from a wall* —*n.* the act of walking; a distinctive manner of walking; a place for walking; status or position: *people of all walks* —**walk all over** to mistreat or use badly —**walk off with** steal —**walk on air** to feel exhilarated or euphoric —**walk out on** to abandon
walk´out *n.* a labor strike
walk´–up *n.* dwelling above the first floor in a building with no elevator
wall *n.* a structure that encloses or divides; something similar to a wall: *wall of water, wall of silence* —*vt.* to provide a wall; to enclose or separate with a wall —*adj.* attached to or built into a wall —**drive up a wall** to frustrate or distress —**off the wall** descriptive of that which is unconventional or eccentric
wal´la·by *n.* a small kangaroo
wall´eye *n.* an eye with a light–colored iris; a condition in which the eyes diverge; a type of fish
wall´flow·er *n.* one who is shy or unpopular
wal´lop *vt.* beat soundly; strike a blow —*n.* a hard blow
wal´lop·ing *adj.* very large —*n.* beating; a crushing defeat
wal´low *vi.* roll about in mud, snow, etc.; enjoy: *wallow in profits*; indulge oneself: *wallow in self–pity* —*n.* the act of wallowing; a depression or hollow
waltz *n.* a ballroom dance —*vi.* dance; move quickly
wan *adj.* pale from illness; faint or feeble —**wan´ly** *adv.*
wand *n.* the rod of a conjurer; a staff of authority; a musician's baton
wan´der *vi.* roam; go casually or indirectly; twist, meander; stray —*vt.* to meander across or through

wan´der·lust *n.* an impulse to travel; restlessness
wane *vi.* diminish; decline or decrease gradually —*n.* a decreasing; a period of decline
wan´gle *vt.* obtain indirectly or dishonestly —*vi.* resort to indirect or irregular methods
want *vt.* desire; lack or be deficient in; request —*vi.* have need; be destitute —*n.* a lack, scarcity, or shortage; poverty or destitution
want´ing *adj.* missing or lacking; not up to standard, need, or expectation
wan´ton *adj.* licentious, lewd; heartless, malicious; unrestrained; capricious, unprovoked —*vi.* to act in a wanton manner —*vt.* to waste or squander —*n.* a lewd or licentious person
wap´i·ti *n.* the American elk
war *n.* armed strife; any conflict or struggle; warfare —*vi.* wage war; fight or take part in war; be in opposition or contention —*adj.* pertaining to war or its aftermath
war´ble *vi., vt.* sing with trills, tremulo, etc. —*n.* the act or sound of warbling
war chest a special fund, as for a political campaign
ward *n.* section of a hospital; administrative division of a city; one in the care of a guardian; the act of guarding or being guarded —*vt.* repel or turn aside
war´den *n.* supervisor or custodian; (*Brit.*) an executive or administrator, as a crown officer, college official, or church trustee; (*US*) chief administrative officer of a prison
ward´er *n.* one who guards or protects; (*Brit.*) a prison guard
ward´robe *n.* a cabinet or closet for wearing apparel; costumes belonging to a theater group; collectively, all of one's garments or those suited to a season
ware *n.* articles of a type; dishes or pottery; merchandise displayed for sale
ware´house *n.* storage for goods awaiting sale or use; (*Brit.*) a large cut–rate or retail store —*vt.* to place or keep in a warehouse
war´fare *n.* waging of war; struggle or strife
war horse a veteran of many struggles, as a politician
war´like *adj.* fond of war; threatening war
war´lock *n.* a male witch; a sorcerer
war´lord *n.* a military commander who governs; a militaristic head of state
warm *adj.* moderately hot; imparting or preserving warmth; heated from exertion; cordial, friendly; recently made: *warm from the oven*; suggesting warmth, as of a color —*vt., vi.* make or become heated, interested, excited: *warmed to the idea*; become friendly; feel pleasure: *warm the heart* —**warm´ly** *adv.*
warm´–blood´ed *adj.* having nearly constant, warm body temperature; ardent or passionate
warmed´–o´ver *adj.* reheated; ineffectual from overuse
warm´–heart·ed *adj.* kind; sympathetic; generous
warmth *n.* a feeling of comfort; ardor or excitement; friendliness
warn *vt.* alert; advise; give notice —*vi.* give warning
warn´ing *n.* an act of giving notice or being alerted; a sign or signal —*adj.* serving as notice: *warning bell*
warp *vt.* twist; corrupt or pervert; divert; arrange strands for weaving —*vi.* become twisted or distorted; turn aside from a proper course; go astray —*n.* a distortion; an abnormality; mental or moral aberration; woven strands running the length of a fabric
war´rant *n.* legal authorization for arrest, search, etc.; a guarantee or warrantee; sanction or justification —*vt.* assure or guarantee quality or condition; guarantee against loss; give legal authority; guarantee clear title to property
war´rant·ee´ *n.* recipient of a warrant or warranty
war´ran·tor, **war´rant·er** *n.* one who issues a warrant or warrnty
war´ran·ty *n.* guarantee by a seller; official authorization or warrant; justification for action
war´ren *n.* an enclosure for small animals; overcrowded living space
war´ri·or *n.* one engaged or experienced in warfare
wart *n.* a small, hard growth on the skin; natural growth on plants and animals
war´y *adj.* watchful; marked by caution; shrewd or wily
wash *vt.* cleanse or remove; cover with liquid; soak or rinse; flow against or over; coat with a thin layer of pigment —*vi.* bathe or launder; be removed or drawn off by liquid —*n.* a wetting or cleaning; clothes to be laundered; a surge of water; removal or deposit of topsoil by water; a preparation for cleaning or coating; a thin coating of pigment: a tint
washed´–out´ *adj.* lacking intensity: faded; exhausted
washed´–up´ *adj.* finished; no longer capable or needed
wash´out *n.* erosion by the action of water; a failure
wash´room *n.* a lavatory
wash´stand *n.* cabinet for a pitcher, washbowl, etc.; a bathroom sink
wasp *n.* a flying insect with a slender segmented body
wasp´ish *adj.* slender; irritable or bad–tempered
was´sail *n.* an ancient toast; a spiced drink of ale and wine; a celebration —*vi.* revel or carouse
waste *vt.* use thoughtlessly; squander; make weak or feeble; fail to use or take advantage of; devastate —*vi.* lose vigor, bulk, etc.; diminish; pass gradually —*n.* unnecessary consumption; failure to benefit; a desolate place; gradual wearing away; something discarded
wast´ed *adj.* squandered; useless, excessive: *wasted effort*; frail or feeble from illness; inebriated or under influence of a narcotic
waste´ful *adj.* prone to or causing waste; extravagant
waste´land *n.* barren or desolate countryside
was´trel *n.* a spendthrift; an idler
watch *vi.* observe closely; be alert; wait expectantly; work as a guard; keep a religious vigil —*vt.* look at attentively; keep informed; be alert for; guard —*n.* careful observation; attitude of alertness; a time of guard duty; a small timepiece; a religious vigil
watch´dog *n.*; one who oversees waste, unlawful or prohibited acts, etc.
watch´ful *adj.* vigilant; alert
watch´word *n.* a password; a slogan
wa´ter *n.* colorless liquid essential to all organisms; a supply of water; preparation holding a substance in solution —*vt.* provide with water; dilute with water —*vi.* secrete or discharge water —**keep one's head above water** stay out of difficulty —**water down** reduce or dilute —**water under the bridge** a bygone event
wa´ter·bed *n.* bed with a water–filled mattress
wa´ter·borne *adj.* floating on water; transported by ship
water clock a timepiece operated by water
water closet (*Brit.*) a toilet
wa´ter·col·or *n.* a water–soluble pigment; a painting rendered in watercolors —*adj.* painted with watercolor pigments —**wa´ter·col·or·ist** *n.*
wa´ter·course *n.* a flow of water, as a river, etc.; a channel for water
wa´ter·front *n.* a property close to or overlooking a body of water; an area of docks, warehouses, etc.
water gap a deep ravine permitting passage of a river or stream
wa´ter·glass *n.* a drinking vessel; a gauge for indicating water level; a bucket–like device with glass bottom, used to see under water
watering hole a pond or pool frequented by wildlife; a tavern or pub
wa´ter·logged *adj.* soaked with water; so saturated as to be unmanageable and barely able to float
water main conduit for water
wa´ter·mark *n.* a waterline; a design impressed into paper —*vt.* impress on paper
water mill a mill operated by water
water nymph a mythical being that dwells in a stream, lake, etc.
water pipe conduit for water; a tobacco pipe in which the smoke is filtered by water
wa´ter·pow·er *n.* energy derived from flowing water
wa´ter·shed *n.* an area draining into a river; a decisive turning point
wa´ter·spout *n.* a moving, whirling column of water; a pipe for discharging water
water table the upper level of saturated subterranean rock
wa´ter·tight *adj.* so closely made as not to leak; that cannot be misunderstood, found illegal, or in error
water tower a reservoir used to maintain water pressure
water vapor moisture mixed in air in fine droplets
wa´ter·way *n.* a river, channel, etc.
water wheel a wheel turned by flowing water
wa´ter·works *n.* a system of pumps, pipes, etc. for supplying water
wa´ter·worn *adj.* worn smooth or eroded by running or falling water
wa´ter·y *adj.* like water; diluted; insipid
watt *n.* a unit of electrical power
watt´age *n.* a measure of electrical power
wat´tle *n.* woven framework of poles and twigs; a fold of skin hanging from the throat of a bird or lizard
wave *vi.* to move or flap in the wind; to greet or signal with the hand; to become curved or curled —*vt.* to move freely; flourish; to signal by waving; to form into curves or curls —*n.* a ridge or undulation; a motion of the hand; a series of curves: *a hair wave*; an upsurge: *a wave of nausea*; a prolonged condition: *heat wave*; a pattern formed by energy: *a sound wave*
wave´form *n.* the curve produced by the movement of a wave of energy
wave´length *n.* the distance between crests or troughs in cycles of an energy wave
wa´ver *vi.* to move back and forth; be uncertain; falter —*n.* a wavering
wav´y *adj.* full of curves: *wavy hair*; undulating
wax *n.* a pliable substance insoluble in water and that burns in the air; a waxlike product, as paraffin or furniture polish —*adj.* made with or from wax —*vt.* to coat or polish with wax —*vi.* to gradually increase; a way to express oneself: *wax poetic*
wax´en *adj.* consisting of or covered with wax; pale or pallid; malleable or pliant
wax museum a place that exhibits life–size wax figures
wax paper paper coated with wax, used in food preparation
wax´works *n.* an exhibit of wax sculptures
wax´y *adj.* resembling or abounding in wax; appear pale or pallid
way *n.* a direction; course or

passage; space: *make way*; process or means: *a way to succeed*; customary manner: *the way we live*; condition: *in a bad way* —**in a way** to some extent —*adv.*
way´bill *n.* a document that accompanies a shipment
way´far·er *n.* one who travels, usually aimlessly
way´lay *vt.* lie in ambush; meet on the way
ways and means methods for defraying costs
way´ward *adj.* willful, headstrong; not predictable
weak *adj.* lacking strength, vigor, etc.; not effective or forceful; lacking skill or experience; deficient
weak´en *vt., vi.* make or become weak or weaker
weak´ling *n.* a feeble person or animal
weak´ly *adj.* sick or feeble —*adv.* in a weak manner
weak´ness *n.* the quality of being fragile or delicate; a slight failing or fault; a strong liking
weal *n.* a welt, as from a blow
wealth *n.* riches; the state of being rich; great abundance
wealth´y *adj.* possessing riches; characterized by abundance
wean *vt.* to end dependence on mother's milk; to withdraw from a detrimental habit or association
weap´on *n.* anything for use against an adversary —**weap´on·ry** *n.*
wear *vt.* have on, as a garment or ornament; display; damage by use; exhaust —*vi.* be gradually diminished by use; withstand the effects of use, time, etc.; have a tiring effect —*n.* act of wearing or being worn; articles of dress; destruction from use or time; durability
wear´a·ble *adj.* suitable for wear
wear·a·bil´i·ty *n.* ability to withstand use or time
wear´ing *adj.* tiresome; exhausting
wea´ry *adj.* tired; fatigued; discontented or bored; indicating fatigue —*vt., vi.* make or become weary
wea´ri·some *adj.* causing fatigue; tiresome
wea´sel *n.* a small, slender carnivorous animal; a sly or treacherous person —*vi.* renege on a promise: *weasel out of a deal*; equivocate
weath´er *n.* general atmospheric conditions; unpleasant conditions — *vt.* to expose to the elements; to show effects of exposure; to pass through and survive —*vi.* undergo change from exposure; to resist the action of weather —*adj.* facing the wind
weath´er–beat·en *adj.* showing effects of exposure
weath´ered *adj.* worn or damaged; visibly improved by or intended to emulate exposure: *weathered brick*
weath´er·ing *n.* the process by which exposure causes change; alteration by exposure, esp. for effect
weath´er·proof *adj.* capable of withstanding harsh weather —*vt.* make weatherproof
weath´er·strip·ping *n.* material in or over crevices to exclude drafts, rain, etc. —*vt.* attach or apply weatherstripping
weave *vt.* interlace; make by interlacing thread, cane, reeds, etc.; produce by linking parts: *weave a tale*; move from side to side —*vi.* make by weaving; become interlaced; make one's way by weaving
web *n.* network spun by a spider; an artfully contrived trap; entanglement: *web of deceit*; a complex network: *world–wide web*; membrane — *vt.* create a web; trap
webbed *adj.* of or pertaining to a web: *webbed feet*
wed *vt., vi.* to marry
wed´ding *n.* the rite of marriage; anniversary of a marriage
wedge *n.* a taper of metal, wood, etc. used to split a log, tighten a joint, etc.; something that facilitates entry, intrusion, etc. —*vt.* force apart or fix in place with a wedge; crowd or squeeze —*vi.* force oneself in
wed´lock *n.* marriage
wee *adj.* very small
weed *n.* an unwanted or unsightly plant —*vt., vi.* remove unwanted growth; remove that considered undesirable: *weed out useless data*
week *n.* seven calendar days; period described by an event: *Christmas week*; portion of a week dedicated to business: *a five–day week*
week´ly *adj., adv.* occurring every week; once a week; pertaining to a week —*n.* periodical issued once a week
weep *vt.* shed tears; form liquid on, as by condensation —*vt.* weep for; shed liquid —*n.* the act of weeping; an exhudation of liquid, as from a sore
weep´y *adj.* weeping or inclined to weep
wee´vil *n.* a small destructive beetle
weigh *vt.* to determine the weight of; to measure by weight; to consider carefully —*vi.* to have a specified weight; have importance: *weigh heavy on the mind*; to be burdensome: *weigh down with guilt*
weight *n.* heaviness; a measure of heaviness; a piece used as a standard in weighing; a unit of heaviness; burden or pressure: *weight of responsibility*; importance or consequence; a heavy object used in competition or for exercise; an object used to hold down: *paperweight* —*vt.* to make heavy; to oppress or burden
weight´ed *adj.* having weight; adjusted to reflect the importance of elements: *weighted average*
weight´y *adj.* of great importance; effectual: *a weighty argument*; oppressive; heavy
weir *n.* a dam to raise or divert the water; a fence in a stream, used to catch or hold back fish
weird *adj.* odd or bizarre; of the supernatural or a supernatural occurrence —**weird´ness** *n.*
wel´come *vt.* greet pleasantly or hospitably; receive with pleasure —*n.* a warm reception —*adj.* received cordially; producing satisfaction or pleasure; free to use or enjoy
weld *vt.* unite, as metal by the application of heat; bring into close association —*n.* a joining; a joint
wel´fare *n.* well–being; prosperity; assistance to those in need
welfare state a system by which a government assumes responsibility for health care, retirement, etc.
well *n.* a shaft sunk into the earth; a source of continued supply; a depression to hold or collect water; a vertical opening through a building for light, ventilation, stairs, etc. —*vi.* rise to the surface —*vt.* gush or pour forth —*adv.* satisfactorily; in a correct manner; to a considerable extent; quite, positively —*adj.* suitable or proper; fortunate; in good health; prosperous
well´–ad·just·ed *adj.* mentally sound
well´–be´ing *n.* health, happiness, or prosperity
well´born *adj.* of good family; titled; aristocratic
well´–nigh´ *adv.* almost
well´spring *n.* a source
well´–timed´ *adj.* happening at a propitious time
well´–wish·er *n.* a supporter
welt *n.* a raised mark on the skin from a blow; material used to cover or strengthen a seam —*vt.* decorate with a welt; to whip or flog
wen *n.* a cyst
wend *vt.* go on; proceed
west *n.* the general direction in which the sun sets —*adj.*
west´er·ly *adj., adv.* in, toward, or of the west
west´ern *adj.* of, in, directed toward, or facing the west; from the west
west´ern·ize *vt.* adapt to customs of a western nation; adopt trappings of the American west
wet *adj.* moistened or covered with liquid; marked by rainfall; not yet dry, as paint —*n.* moisture; rainy weather —*vt., vi.* make or become wet —**all wet** completely wrong —**wet behind the ears** inexperienced
wet´land *n.* land area saturated or partly under water
whack *vt., vi.* strike sharply —*n.* a resounding blow
whale *n.* a large marine mammal; a thing very good, large, or impressive: *whale of a party*
wharf *n., pl.* **wharfs**, **wharves** a place for docking and loading or unloading ships; a pier or dock
what *pron.* which specific thing, amount, circumstance, etc.; that which; whatever situation or contingency: *take what comes* —*adj.* which one; —*adv.* how much: *what does it matter?*
what´not *n.* shelving designed to hold and display small objects; a small decorative object
wheal *n.* a small pimple on the skin
wheat *n.* a cereal grass
wheat germ the nutricious embryo of the wheat kernel
whee´dle *vt.* persuade or obtain by flattery, cajolery, or coaxing —*vi.* use flattery or cajolery
wheel *n.* a disk or rim on a central axis; a turning or rotating movement; a person of influence —*vt.* move or convey on wheels; cause to turn; provide with wheels —*vi.* turn, as on an axis; change one's course; move on wheels
wheel´bar·row *n.* one–wheeled vehicle with opposing handles —*vt.* convey in a wheelbarrow
wheel´chair *n.* a wheeled seat for the use of one unable to walk
wheel´er–deal´er *n.* one who acts freely, aggressively, and often unscrupulously
wheel´wright *n.* a man whose business is making or repairing wheels
wheeze *vt., vi.* to breathe with a husky, whistling sound —*n.* the sound of wheezing —**wheez´y** *adj.*
whelp *n.* the young of a dog, wolf, etc.; a worthless young fellow —*vt., vi.* to give birth
when *adv.* at what or which time; at an earlier time; under what circumstances —*conj.*
whence *adv.* from what place or source —*conj.*
where *adv.* at or in what place or situation; to or from what place
where´with·al *n.* necessary means or resources
whet *vt.* sharpen, as a knife; excite or stimulate: *whet the appetite*
whet´stone *n.* a fine stone for sharpening knives, etc.
whey *n.* clear liquid produced from curdled milk
which *pron.* what thing; that previously indicated —*adj.* what specific one
whiff *n.* a gust of air; an aroma; a puff
while *vt.* pass time pleasantly —*n.* a span of time —*conj.* during the time that; at the same time; whereas
whim *n.* a sudden, capricious idea or notion
whim´per *vi., vt.* to cry or utter a plaintive sound
whim´si·cal *adj.* capricious; marked by erratic or unpredictable conduct; odd or quaint
whim´sy *n.* whim or caprice; odd or quaint humor
whine *vi.* utter a high, plaintive, nasal sound; complain in a fretful or childish way; make a steady high–pitched sound, as of a machine —*vt.* utter with a whine —*n.*
whip *vt.* strike with a lash, rod, etc.; buffet; beat to a froth; seize, jerk, throw, etc. with a sudden motion —*vi.* move or turn suddenly; thrash about —*n.* a lash; a whipping or thrashing motion; a legislator appointed to enforce discipline,

attendance, etc.; a dessert containing whipped cream or beaten egg whites
whip´lash *n.* end of a whip; neck injury caused by a sudden snap of the head
whipping boy one who receives undeserved blame or punishment
whir *vt., vi.* fly or move with a buzzing sound —*n.* a whizzing sound; confusion or bustle
whirl *vi., vt.* turn or cause to turn or revolve rapidly; move or go swiftly; feel a spinning sensation —*n.* swift rotating motion; state of confusion; round of activities: *social whirl*
whirl´pool *n.* an eddy or vortex of rapidly whirling water
whirl´wind *n.* a rapidly spinning column of air; a destructive force —*adj.* extremely swift or impetuous: *a whirlwind tour*
whisk *vt.* brush or sweep lightly; beat with quick movements —*vi.* move quickly and lightly —*n.* light sweeping motion; a kitchen untensil for whipping or blending
whisk´er *n.* the hair of a beard; long bristly face hair on an animal
whis´key, **whis´ky** *n.* an alcoholic beverage —*adj.* pertaining to or made with whiskey
whis´per *n.* hushed speech; a secret communication; low, rustling noise —*vi.* speak in hushed tones; speak furtively; make a low, rustling sound —*vt.* utter in a low tone
whist *n.* a card game similar to bridge
whis´tle *vi.* make a sharp, shrill sound; sound a whistle —*vt.* produce a sound by whistling —*n.* a sharp, shrill sound; device for making such a sound
whis´tle–blow´er *n.* one who exposes wrongdoing
whistle stop town along the course of a railway where a train stops only when signaled; a small town, one of little importance; a brief stop by a political candidate
whit *n.* the smallest bit
white *n.* color produced by reflection of all visible colors of the spectrum; the condition of being white; anything white or nearly white; the white part of something, as an egg; light–colored pieces, as of chess men —*adj.* lacking hue; relatively light in color; relatively unmarked or clean; harmless or innocuous
white blood cell blood cells that help stave off infection and disease
white´–col´lar *adj.* designating salaried or office workers
white dwarf a small, faint, extremely dense star
white elephant a burden; expensive to maintain; of uncertain value
whit´en *vt., vi.* make or become white, as by bleaching
white paper an authoritative report on an important topic
white´wash *n.* a thin mixture of lime, water, sizing, etc. for coating walls, fences, etc.; a suppressing or concealing of faults or failure —*vt.* coat with whitewash; suppress or gloss over wrongdoing
whit´tle *vt.* make or shape by cutting; reduce or wear away a little at a time: *whittle away an inheritance* —*vi.* to cut or shape wood
whiz *vi., vt.* make or cause a hissing, humming sound —*n.* a whizzing sound; one of extraordinary ability
whiz kid a relatively young person who is extremely clever, talented, or successful
who·dun´it *n.* a mystery story
whole *adj.* complete or entire; not broken or defective; being the full amount —*n.* all the parts or elements that make up a thing
whole´heart·ed *adj.* complete and unreserved enthusiasm, energy, dedication, etc.
whole´sale *n.* sale of goods in bulk, usually for resale —*adj.* of the buying or selling of goods in bulk; made or done on a large scale —*adv.* in bulk or quantity; extensively or indiscriminately
whole´some *adj.* tending to promote health; advocating mental or moral righteousness
whol´ly *adv.* completely, totally; exclusively, only
whoop *vi.* utter loud cries —*vt.* call or chase with loud cries —*n.* shout of excitement, joy, derision, etc.
whop´per *n.* something large or remarkable; an outrageous lie —**whop´ping** *adj.*
why *adv.* for what cause, purpose, or reason —*n.* a cause or reason
wick *n.* a cord or strand conveying fuel to a flame —*vt., vi.* to convey or be conveyed by capillary action
wick´ed *adj.* delibegrately evil; mischievous or roguish; mean or troublesome
wide *adj.* broad or spacious; off a desired point: *wide of the mark*; having great scope —*adv.* extensively —**wide´ly** *adv.*
wid´en *vt., vi.* to make or become wide or wider —**wid´en·er** *n.*
wide´spread´ *adj.* extending over a large area; extensive
wid´ow *n.* a woman whose husband has died
wid´ow·er *n.* a man whose wife has died
width *n.* dimension of an object from side to side
wield *vt.* to use, as a weapon or tool; to exercise authority, power, influence, etc. —**wield´a·ble** *adj.*
wield´y *adj.* easily handled or managed
wie´ner, wie´ner·wurst *n.* a kind of smoked sausage
wife *n.* a woman joined in marriage —**wife´ly** *adj.*
wig *n.* a head covering that replaces or augments hair —*vt.* furnish with a wig
wig´gle *vi., vt.* move from side to side —*n.* —**wig´gly** *adj.*
wild *adj.* in a natural state; uncivilized; undisciplined; reckless, imprudent; extremely odd, strange, or bizarre; disorderly or disarranged; off the mark: *a wild throw* —*n.* an uninhabited or uncultivated place —*adv.* in a wild manner —**wild´ly** *adv.* —**wild´ness** *n.*
wild´cat *n.* a feral cat, as the lynx, cougar, etc.; an aggressive, quick–tempered person; a tricky or unsound business venture —*adj.* unsound or risky; unofficial or unauthorized —*vt., vi.* drill for oil
wildcat strike an unauthorized walkout or labor stoppage
wil´der·ness *n.* an uncultivated or uninhabited area
wild´fire *n.* a raging fire
wild´fowl *n.* a wild game bird
wild–goose chase pursuit of the unknown or unattainable
wild´life *n.* wild animals collectively
wild rice an aquatic grass of North America or its edible grain
wild´wood *n.* natural forest land
wile *n.* a trick or artifice —*vt.* lure, beguile, or mislead
will *n.* power to choose; a specific purpose, choice, etc.; strong determination; self–control —*vt.* to choose; resolve as an action or course; to decree —*vi.* to wish or desire
will´ful *adj.* deliberate, intentional; stubborn or headstrong
will´ing *adj.* favorably disposed; readily acting, responding, giving, etc.
wil´low *n.* a tree or shrub with flexible shoots often used in basketry —*adj.* made of willow wood
wil´low·y *adj.* tall and graceful; lithe or flexible; supple; abounding in willow trees
will´pow·er *n.* control of one's actions or desires; firm determination
wilt *vi., vt.* lose or cause to lose freshness, energy, etc.; droop
wil´y *adj.* sly or cunning
wimp *n.* one regarded as a weakling; one who whimpers
win *vi.* be victorious — *vt.* be successful in; gain victory; influence —*n.* a victory
wince *vi.* shrink back; be startled; recoil, as in pain —*n.* a startled motion
wind *n.* movement of air; breath; idle chatter —*vt.* exhaust the breath of
wind *vt., vi.* coil or twine
wind´break *n.* that protecting from the wind
wind´ed *adj.* out of breath
wind´fall *n.* something, such as ripened fruit, brought down by the wind; an incident of unexpected good fortune
wind´ing *adj.* turning about an axis or core; having bends or turns
wind´jam·mer *n.* a sailing vessel
wind´lass *n.* a device for hoisting or hauling
win´dow *n.* an opening to admit light or air
window dressing arrangement in a store window; means for making something seem more attractive
win´dow·sill *n.* ledge beneath a window opening
wind´shear *n.* a strong rapid change in wind direction
wind´swept *adj.* exposed to or brushed by wind
wind tunnel a device that artificially produces wind for the study of effects on design, materials, etc.
wind´up *n.* a conclusion
wind´ward *adj.* toward the wind; on the side exposed to the wind —*n.* direction facing the wind —*adv.* against the wind
wind´y *adj.* stormy; tempestuous; boastful or talkative
wine *n.* fermented fruit juice; color of red wine —*vt.* entertain or treat with wine
wine cellar a storage area for wines
wine´press *n.* an apparatus for extracting juice; place where juice is extracted
win´er·y *n.* an establishment where wine is made
wing *n.* the organ of flight; anything resembling or suggesting a bird's wing; an attachment or extension, as of a building or stage —*vt.* to pass over in flight; to accomplish by flying; to disable by wounding —*vi.* fly —**winged** *adj.*
wink *vi., vt.* blink or cause to blink; signal by closing the lid of one eye; twinkle —*n.* fleeting time; twinkle; a hint conveyed by winking —**forty winks** a short nap
win´ner *n.* one who prevails; a victor; one likely to succeed
win´ning *adj.* successful; charming
win´now *vt.* separate, as grain from chaff; eliminate that which is bad —*vi.* separate grain from chaff —*n.* a device to separate grain
win´some *adj.* charming; attractive
win´ter *n.* the coldest season, between autumn and spring; a year: *a man of ninety winters* —*vi.* pass the winter —*vt.* protect during the winter —*adj.* suitable for or characteristic of winter
win´ter·green *n.* a small evergreen plant or flavoring oil extracted from its leaves
win´ter·y, win´try *adj.* of or like winter: cold, stormy, bleak, etc.
win´y *adj.* having the taste, color, etc. of wine
wipe *vt.* to rub —*n.* —**wipe out** destroy utterly
wire *n.* a slender strand of metal; something made of wire; telegram —*vt.* fasten with wire; equip with wire, as for providing electricity; send a telegram
wired *adj.* fitted out for electricity, telephones, etc.; keyed up; excited
wire´less *adj.* not requiring wires —*n.* device operating without wires; (*Brit.*) a radio
wire´tap *n.* a device for listening in on a telephone conversation —*vt.* connect or listen with a wiretap —*vi.* to use a wiretap
wir´ing *n.* wires installed in a building, etc. to provide electricity, telephone service, etc.; the process of connecting or

installing wires
wir´y *adj.* lean; tough and sinewy; stiff or bristly
wis´dom *n.* the ability to make sound judgements; insight or intuition; extensive knowledge; an accumulated body of knowledge
wise *adj.* having insight, common sense, or knowledge; shrewd and calculating —**wise´ly** *adv.*
wise´crack *n.* an insolent or supercilious remark
wish *n.* desire or longing; something desired —*vt.* have a desire or longing for; request or entreat —*vi.* feel a desire; express a desire
wish´ful *adj.* having or indicating a desire
wishful thinking believing that what one wants to be true is going to be true
wish´y–wash´y *adj.* lacking in purpose; indecisive or ineffective
wisp *n.* a small bunch of straw, hair, etc.; an indication: *wisp of perfume*; slight, delicate thing: *wisp of a child* —**wisp´y** *adj.*
wist´ful *adj.* wishful, yearning; musing, pensive —**wist´ful·ly** *adv.*
wit *n.* intelligence; mental acuity; guile: *live by one's wits*; a clever or amusing person
witch *n.* woman who practices sorcery; an ugly or cruel old woman; a fascinating woman —*vt.* work a spell upon; fascinate or charm
witch´craft *n.* black magic, sorcery; extraordinary influence or charm
witch hunt investigation or harassment of dissenters
with·draw´ *vt.* to take away or remove; to take back or rescind; to prevent from using, selling, etc. —*vi.* retreat; to remove oneself
with·draw´al *n.* a taking back, removing, retreating, etc.; process or effects of overcoming an addiction
with·drawn´ *adj.* not responsive; introverted; isolated
with´er *vi.* become limp or dry; to waste, as flesh —*vt.* cause to become limp or dry; disconcert or humble, as by a scornful glance
with·hold´ *vt.* hold back; refuse to grant, permit, etc. —*vi.* to refrain from
with·stand´ *vt., vi.* resist, oppose, or endure
wit´less *adj.* lacking intelligence; silly or foolish
wit´ness *n.* one competent to testify by virtue of having seen or learned something; a person who attests to authenticity —*vt.* to see or know personally; to give testimony; to subscribe to the authenticity of a document, signature, etc. —*vi.* to testify
wit´ti·cism *n.* a clever or humorous remark
wit´ty *adj.* clever or humorous —**wit´ti·ness** *n.*
wiz´ard *n.* a sorcerer; one exceptionally skillful or clever —*adj.* (*Brit.*) extraordinary: *a wizard pianist*
wiz´ard·ry *n.* practice or methods of a wizard
wiz´ened *adj.* shriveled; dried up
wob´ble *vi.* to sway unsteadily; show indecision —*vt.* cause to wobble —*n.* unsteadiness; instability
woe *n.* overwhelming sorrow; suffering
woe´be·gone *adj.* mournful; sorrowful
woe´ful *adj.* causing sorrow; paltry —**woe´ful·ly** *adv.*
wolf *n.* a wild, carnivorous mammal related to the dog; a cruel or rapacious person; a man who flirts
wom´an *n.* an adult human female; a female attendant or servant —*adj.* of a woman or women; female
wom´an·ly *adj.* having qualities suited to a woman
womb *n.* a place where a thing is engendered or brought into life; a sheltering space or area
wom´bat *n.* a burrowing marsupial of Australia
won´der *n.* feeling of mingled surprise, admiration, and astonishment; that causing wonder —*vt.* have curiosity or doubt —*vi.* to marvel; be curious or doubtful —*adj.* spectacularly successful
won´der·ful *adj.* astonishing; very good —**won´der·ful·ly** *adv.*
won´der·ment *n.* astonishment or awe; something marvelous; puzzlement
won´drous *adj.* wonderful; marvelous; extraordinary —*adv.* surprisingly
wont *adj.* accustomed
wont´ed *adj.* commonly used or done; accustomed
woo *vt.* seek affection or approval; entreat earnestly —*vi.* pay court
wood *n.* hard fibrous material that constitutes the bulk of a tree; a forest —*adj.* pertaining to or using wood
wood´craft *n.* survival in the wild; the art of fashioning wooden articles
wood´cut *n.* engraved block or prints from the block
wood´ed *adj.* abounding with trees
wood´en *adj.* made of wood; stiff or awkward
wood´land *n.* land covered with trees; timberland —*adj.* belonging to or dwelling in the woods
wood nymph a forest sprite
wood´wind *n.* a musical instrument that uses a wood or wood-like reed
wood´work *n.* things made of wood; interior trim, as door and window frames
wood´y *adj.* made of or containing wood; resembling wood; wooded
wool *n.* a soft, durable fiber from the fleece of animals; yarn, fabric, etc. made from animal fibers —**wool, wool´en** *adj.*
wool´ly, wool´y *adj.* resembling wool; not clear
word *n.* smallest meaningful unit of a language; speech; a brief remark, message, comment, etc.; a promise
word´ing *n.* style or arrangement of words; phraseology
word´play *n.* clever repartee
word´y *adj.* in too many words —**word´i·ness** *n.*
work *n.* physical or mental exertion; employment; one's profession or trade; place of employment —*vi.* perform work; be employed; prove effective —*vt.* cause or bring about; make or shape by toil or skill; cause to be productive; achieve by effort
work´a·ble *adj.* capable of being worked or developed; practicable
work´ing *adj.* employed; occupied by work; functional; sufficient for use or action: *working agreement*
working capital finances available for operation of a business
working class those who work for wages
work´man·like *adj.* like or befitting a skilled workman; skillfully done
work´man·ship *n.* art or skill of a workman; quality of work; work accomplished
work of art a thing of beauty; fine art; anything done with great skill
work´out *n.* activity to improve skill, physical fitness, etc.; strenuous or intense activity
work sheet record of an employee's work times; preliminary notes or calculations; a spreadsheet
work´shop *n.* an area set aside for projects, a hobby, etc.; a seminar for training or discussion
world *n.* the earth; the universe; a celestial body; part of the earth: *Third World*; division of time, etc.: *ancient world, animal world*; large amount: *world of knowledge*
world´ly *adj.* of a world; devoted to secular, earthly things; sophisticated —**world´li·ness** *n.*
world´ly–wise *adj.* schooled in the ways of the world; sophisticated
world´–wea·ry *adj.* discontented with life
worm *n.* an elongated, limbless, soft–bodied creature; despicable person —*vt.* proceed like a worm; draw forth by artful means: *worm information*; rid of intestinal worms —*vi.* progress slowly and stealthily
worn *adj.* damaged by wear; showing effects of anxiety, etc.; hackneyed
worn–out *adj.* having lost value or effectiveness; tired, exhausted
wor´ri·some *adj.* causing concern or anxiety
wor´ry *vi.* be uneasy; feel anxiety —*vt.* cause to feel uneasy; bother or pester; bite, pull, or shake with the teeth —*n.* anxiety or uneasiness; something causing such a state
worse *adj.* bad or ill to a greater degree; less favorable —*adv.* in a less favorable manner; with greater intensity, severity, etc.
wors´en *vt., vi.* make or become less favorable
wor´ship *n.* adoration, homage; rituals, prayers, etc. in tribute to a diety; excessive or ardent admiration —*vt.* venerate; have intense admiration or love for —*vi.* perform acts of veneration
wor´ship·ful *adj.* feeling or showing love, reverence, etc.
worst *adj.* extremely bad or ill; least favorable —*adv.* to the extreme degree of inferiority, badness, etc. —*vt.* to defeat, vanquish
wor´sted *n.* a woolen yarn, or fabric made from such yarn —*adj.* made from worsted
worth *n.* value; a quality that makes estimable or desirable; amount obtainable for a sum: *two dollars worth*; wealth —*adj.* equal in value to; deserving of
worth´less *adj.* having no value —**worth´less·ness** *n.*
worth´while´ *adj.* sufficiently important to occupy; of sufficient value to repay effort
wor´thy *adj.* having valuable or useful qualitites; deserving —*n.* a person of eminent worth
would´–be *adj.* desiring, professing, or intending
wound *n.* an injury; a cause of pain or grief —*vt., vi.* to inflict a wound; to injure the feelings or pride of
wraith *n.* an apparition seen shortly before or after death; a specter
wran´gle *vi.* argue noisily and angrily —*vt.* argue, debate; get by arguing stubbornly; herd livestock —*n.* an angry dispute —**wran´gler** *n.*
wrap *vt.* surround and cover; to fold or wind about something —*n.* an outer garment
wrap´per *n.* material for enclosing; a dressing gown; one who covers or encloses
wrap´ping *n.* a covering
wrath *n.* violent rage or fury
wrath´ful *adj.* full of wrath; extremely angry; expressing or resulting from rage
wreak *vt.* to inflict or exact, as vengeance; to give free expression to
wreath *n.* a circular band of flowers, leaves, etc.; curling or spiral band
wreathe *vt.* form into a wreath, as by twisting or twining; adorn or encircle —*vi.* take the form of a wreath; twist, turn, or coil
wreck *vt.* cause destruction of; bring ruin upon —*vi.* suffer destruction; engage in destroying —*n.* the act of destroying; that ruined or destroyed; remnants, remains
wreck´age *n.* a broken remnant; fragments from a wreck
wreck´er *n.* one causing destruction; one employed in tearing down and removing structures; person or machine that clears disabled or damaged automobiles
wrench *n.* a violent twist; a sprain, twist, or pull of a part of the body; (*US*) a tool for turning, twisting, etc. —*vt.* twist violently; twist forcibly so as to injure —*vi.* give a twist

wrest *vt.* to pull away by violent twisting; seize forcibly; gain by great effort

wres´tle *vi.* engage in wrestling; struggle or contend —*vt.* contend in wrestling —*n.* a difficult struggle

wres´tling *n.* a sport in which unarmed contestants endeavor to force each other to the ground

wretch *n.* a vile person; miserable or unhappy person

wretch´ed *adj.* profoundly unhappy; marked by misery or poverty; despicable or contemptible

wrig´gle *vi.* twist in a sinuous manner; make one's way by evasive or indirect means —*vt.* cause to wriggle; advance by evasive or sly means —*n.* the motion of one who or that wriggles —**wrig´gly** *adj.*

wrig´gler *n.* something that wriggles; a mosquito larva

wring *vt.* to squeeze or compress by twisting; to force out by twisting; acquire forcibly; to distress —*n.* a twisting or forcing —**wring´er** *n.*

wrin´kle *n.* a small fold or crease; modification: *a new wrinkle* —*vt., vi.* make or become creased

wrist *n.* the arm between forearm and hand; part of a garment covering the wrist

write *vt.* inscribe on a surface; communicate by letter; be author or composer of; leave evidence of —*vi.* to inscribe; communicate in writing; work as an author

writhe *vi.* twist or distort the body in pain; suffer from embarrassment, sorrow, etc. —*vt.* cause to be twisted or distorted —**writh´er** *n.*

wrong *adj.* mistaken; inappropriate; not moral or legal; not working properly; unintentional —*adv.* incorrectly or improperly; erroneously —*n.* an injury or injustice; a violation of rights —*vt.* to violate the rights of; to impute evil unjustly; to treat dishonorably

wrong´do·er *n.* one who does wrong; one who acts unlawfully

wrong´ful *adj.* characterized by wrong or injustice; unlawful, illegal

wroth *adj.* angry

wrought *adj.* hammered into shape; formed delicately or elaborately

wrought up disturbed, excited

wry *adj.* bent to one side; contorted or askew; somewhat perverse or ironic: *wry humor* —**wry´ly** *adv.*

wurst *n.* sausage

x, X twenty–fourth letter of the alphabet

xan´thous *adj.* yellow

X chromosome a sex chromosome paired in the female and coupled with a Y chromosome in the male

xen·o·pho´bi·a *n.* fear of strangers or foreigners —**xen·o·pho´bic** *adj.*

x ray, x–ray *n.* a wavelength shorter than ultraviolet and longer than a gamma ray; an image made with x-rays —*adj.* of, made by, or producing x–rays —*vt.* to examine or treat with x–rays

xy´lo·phone *n.* a percussion instrument of graduated bars, played by striking with small mallets

y, Y twenty–fifth letter of the alphabet

yacht *n.* a relatively small ship for pleasure or racing

ya´hoo *n.* a crude or awkward person; a bumpkin

yak *n.* a large, shaggy wild ox; idle chatter —*vi.* to talk a great deal

ya´ku·za *n.* a Japanese gangster

yam *n.* a fleshy, edible tuberous root; a variety of sweet potato

yam´mer *vi.* to whine or complain —*vt.* to utter in a peevish manner

yank *vt., vi.* jerk or pull suddenly —*n.* a sudden sharp jerk

yap *vi.* talk or jabber; to yelp, as a dog —*n.* a yelp; worthless talk; the mouth

yard *n.* a plot of ground enclosed or set apart; (*Brit.*) paved area adjacent to a building; (*US*) grounds adjacent to a building; a slender spar set across a ship's mast; (*US*) a unit of length equal to three feet

yard´age *n.* length in yards; something dispensed in yards, as cloth

yard´stick *n.* a measuring stick one yard in length; a standard for measuring

yarn *n.* spun fiber for use in weaving, knitting, etc.; tale of adventure

yaw *vi.* move erratically, as a ship in heavy seas —*vt.* cause to yaw

yawl *n.* a small sailboat

yawn *vi.* open the mouth wide with a full inhalation from boredom, drowsiness, etc.; stand wide open —*vt.* express with a yawn —*n.* a wide opening —**yawn´er** *n.*

yaws *n. pl.* a contagious tropical disease marked by skin lesions

yea *adv.* yes —*n.* an affirmative vote; one casting an affirmative vote

year *n.* the time Earth takes for one revolution around the sun; a period of 12 months; time any planet takes to revolve around its sun; a distinct period: *the school year*

year´book *n.* a book documenting events of the previous year

year´ly *adj.* of a year; occurring once a year; continuing for a year —*adv.* once a year; annually

yearn *vi.* desire earnestly

yearn´ing *n.* a strong emotional longing or desire

yeast *n.* a preparation used to leaven bread, make alcoholic beverages, etc.; froth or spume —*vi.* to foam

yeast·y *adj.* of or resembling yeast; causing fermentation; covered with froth or foam

yell *vt., vi.* shout, scream, or cheer —*n.* a sharp cry of terror, pain, etc.; a rhythmic cheer

yel´low *adj.* colored by age, illness, etc.; of a light brown or yellowish complexion; offensively sensational: *yellow journalism*; cowardly —*n.* between green and orange in the color spectrum; the color of ripe lemons; yolk of an egg —*vt., vi.* to become colored with age

yelp *vi.* utter a sharp or shrill cry —*vt.* express with a yelp

yen *n.* basic monetary unit of Japan; an ardent longing or desire —*vi.* yearn

yen´ta *n.* a gossip or meddler

yeo´man *n.* a petty officer in the U.S. Navy or Coast Guard; a yeoman of the guard; an attendant to noblility or royalty; a diligent worker

yeo´man·ly *adj.* of the attributes of a yeoman; brave or rugged —*adv.* like a yeoman; bravely

yes *n.* an affirmative response —*vt.* give an affirmative response —*adv.* as you say; truly

yes man one who invariably agrees with his superiors

yes´ter·day *n.* the day before today; the near past —*adv.*

yes´ter·year *n.* last year; time past: *songs of yesteryear* —*adv.*

yield *vt.* produce by natural process or by cultivation; give in return as profit; surrender or relinquish —*vi.* provide a return; give up, surrender; give way; comply —*n.* amount produced; result of cultivation, investment, etc. —**yield´er** *n.*

yield´ing *adj.* productive; flexible or pliant; obedient

yip *n.* a yelp, as from a dog —*vi.* to yelp

yo´del *vt., vi.* sing by alternating between low notes and falsetto

yo´ga *n.* a Hindu discipline directed to spiritual illumination; exercises based on yoga techniques

yo´gi *n.* one who practices yoga

yo´gurt *n.* a soft food of milk curdled with bacteria cultures

yoke *n.* a curved frame for coupling draft animals; a similar contrivance; animals joined by a yoke; a thing that binds or connects; servitude —*vt.* attach with a yoke; join, as with a yoke —*vi.* be joined or linked

yo´kel *n.* a country bumpkin

yon´der *adj.* at a distance —*adv.* in that place; there

yore *n.* time long past

young *adj.* of or in an early stage of life or growth; newly formed; fresh and vigorous; immature —*n.* young people as a group; offspring of animals —**young´ster** *n.*

youth *n.* the condition of being young; period when one is young; early period of being or development; young people as a group

youth´ful *adj.* fresh or vigorous; having youth

yowl *vi.* howl —*n.* prolonged wailing

z, Z twenty–sixth letter of the alphabet

za´ny *adj.* absurdly funny; ludicrous

zap *vt.* strike; kill; confront suddenly and forcefully

zeal *n.* ardor or enthusiasm

zeal´ot *n.* a fanatic

zeal´ous *adj.* filled with determination; showing exceptional enthusiasm

ze´bra *n.* a striped African mammal allied to the horse

ze´nith *n.* point of the celestial sphere exactly overhead; highest or culminating point

zeph´yr *n.* gentle wind; light woolen or worsted yarn

ze´ro *n.* the numeral or symbol *0*; nothing; lowest or starting point —*vt.* adjust to an arbitrary zero point

zero gravity a condition of apparent weightlessness achieved in outer space

zero hour a critical time

zero population growth a condition in which deaths and births in a population are closely matched

zero–sum a situation in which gains and losses are offset

zest *n.* agreeable excitement; keen enjoyment; a quality that imparts emotion; a piquant flavoring

zig´zag *n.* a path or pattern marked by sharp turns or angles — *vt., vi.* to move in zigzags —*adj., adv.*

zilch *n.* nothing; zero

zil´lion *n.* a large, indeterminate number

zing *n.* a sharp buzzing or humming sound; energy, vitality; a verbal attack —*vi.* make a shrill humming sound —*vt.* to criticize sharply

zip *n.* a sharp, hissing sound; energy, vitality —*vt.* close with a zipper; give speed and energy —*vi.* to move with speed and energy

zip´py *adj.* brisk, energetic

zith´er *n.* a multi–stringed instrument played by plucking

zi´ti *n.* a tubular pasta

zo´di·ac *n.* an imaginary belt of twelve parts, encircling the heavens

zom´bie *n.* a snake diety in voodoo cults; a reanimated corpse; one who behaves mechanically

zone *n.* region or area set off by a special characteristic —*vt.* divide into zones, esp. of a municipality where activity is restricted by zone

zoo *n.* a place where wild animals are exhibited; a chaotic place or situation

zo·o·ge·og´ra·phy *n.* study of the distribution of animals and their environment —**zo·o·ge·og´ra·pher** *n.*

zo·og´ra·phy *n.* the branch of zoology dealing with descriptions of animals —**zo·og´ra·pher** *n.*

zo·ol´o·gy *n.* the study of animals and their structure, development, etc.; the animal life of an area

zo´o·phyte *n.* an invertebrate animal resembling a plant

zy·mol´o·gy *n.* the science of fermentation

zy´mur·gy *n.* the chemistry of fermentation as applied to brewing, making yeast, and making wine

NOTES

NOTES

NOTES

NOTES

NOTES

NOTES